Honoring Richard Ruiz and his Work on Language Planning and Bilingual Education

FSC
www.fsc.org
MIX
Paper from
responsible sources
FSC® C013604

BILINGUAL EDUCATION & BILINGUALISM

Series Editors: Nancy H. Hornberger, *University of Pennsylvania, USA* and Wayne E. Wright, *Purdue University, USA*

Bilingual Education and Bilingualism is an international, multidisciplinary series publishing research on the philosophy, politics, policy, provision and practice of language planning, Indigenous and minority language education, multilingualism, multiculturalism, biliteracy, bilingualism and bilingual education. The series aims to mirror current debates and discussions. New proposals for single-authored, multiple-authored, or edited books in the series are warmly welcomed, in any of the following categories or others authors may propose: overview or introductory texts; course readers or general reference texts; focus books on particular multilingual education program types; school-based case studies; national case studies; collected cases with a clear programmatic or conceptual theme; and professional education manuals.

Full details of all the books in this series and of all our other publications can be found on http://www.multilingual-matters.com, or by writing to Multilingual Matters, St Nicholas House, 31–34 High Street, Bristol BS1 2AW, UK.

BILINGUAL EDUCATION & BILINGUALISM: 105

Honoring Richard Ruiz and his Work on Language Planning and Bilingual Education

Edited by
Nancy H. Hornberger

MULTILINGUAL MATTERS
Bristol • Blue Ridge Summit

Library of Congress Cataloging in Publication Data
Names: Hornberger, Nancy H., editor. | Ruiz, Richard, honouree.
Title: Honoring Richard Ruiz and his Work on Language Planning and Bilingual Education/Edited by Nancy H. Hornberger.
Description: Bristol: Multilingual Matters, [2016] | Series: Bilingual Education & Bilingualism: 105 | Includes bibliographical references and index.
Identifiers: LCCN 2016030412| ISBN 9781783096695 (hbk : alk. paper) | ISBN 9781783096688 (pbk : alk. paper) | ISBN 9781783096725 (kindle)
Subjects: LCSH: Bilingualism—Study and teaching. | Language and languages—Study and teaching—Bilingual method. | Language planning. | Education, Bilingual.
Classification: LCC P115.2 .H67 2016 | DDC 306.44—dc23 LC record available at https://lccn.loc.gov/2016030412

British Library Cataloguing in Publication Data
A catalogue entry for this book is available from the British Library.

ISBN-13: 978-1-78309-669-5 (hbk)
ISBN-13: 978-1-78309-668-8 (pbk)

Multilingual Matters
UK: St Nicholas House, 31–34 High Street, Bristol BS1 2AW, UK.
USA: NBN, Blue Ridge Summit, PA, USA.

Website: www.multilingual-matters.com
Twitter: Multi_Ling_Mat
Facebook: https://www.facebook.com/multilingualmatters
Blog: www.channelviewpublications.wordpress.com

The policy of Multilingual Matters/Channel View Publications is to use papers that are natural, renewable and recyclable products, made from wood grown in sustainable forests. In the manufacturing process of our books, and to further support our policy, preference is given to printers that have FSC and PEFC Chain of Custody certification. The FSC and/or PEFC logos will appear on those books where full certification has been granted to the printer concerned.

Typeset by Nova Techset Private Limited, Bengaluru & Chennai, India.
Printed and bound in the UK by the CPI Books Group Ltd.
Printed and bound in the US by Edwards Brothers Malloy, Inc.

Contents

To Marie Ruiz, Richard's loving life partner,
and to my own, Stephan H. Hornberger

Richard by a Palo Verde tree, University of Arizona, Tucson, AZ, 2014
Courtesy of Marie Ruiz.

Introduction: Richard Ruiz and His Legacy

Nancy H. Hornberger

Introduction

Richard Ruiz – inspiring mentor, brilliant thinker, gentle spirit and tireless advocate for social justice; his thinking, writing and teaching on language policy and planning and on bilingual and language minority education have had an enormous impact in shaping those fields. It has been my honor and inspiration to follow his career almost from its beginnings, since January 1980 when I was assigned to be his advisee upon my entry for PhD studies at University of Wisconsin–Madison. Young and newly minted scholar though he was, I could not have hoped for a more knowledgeable and supportive mentor, then and in all the ensuing years until his untimely and unexpected death a year ago as I write this. An impressive intellect and knowledgeable scholar whom I admired and held in awe from day one, it is only in very recent years that I began to feel comfortable addressing my mentor as Richard, as I will refer to him in this Introduction.

Born in Mesa, Arizona on New Year's Eve in 1948 as one of eight children of agricultural workers Prudencio and Guadalupe Ruiz, Richard's life path took him to Harvard for undergraduate studies in French Literature (AB *cum laude*), Stanford for graduate studies in Anthropology (MA) and Philosophy of Education (PhD), the University of Wisconsin–Madison for his first faculty position (Educational Policy Studies) and back to Arizona, where for the final three decades of his life he was professor and department head at the University of Arizona in Tucson (Language, Reading and Culture; Teaching, Learning and Sociocultural Studies; Mexican American Studies). Generous and wise as scholar and colleague, Richard was a member – often chair or executive committee member – of numerous university-wide interdisciplinary programs and faculty committees, including Second Language Acquisition and Teaching, Comparative Cultural and Literary Studies, the Diversity Coalition and the College of Humanities Promotion and Tenure Committee. Perhaps most memorably, he was regularly called on to serve

Richard and Nancy at University of Wisconsin–Madison Commencement, May 1985
Courtesy of Nancy H. Hornberger.

Richard at the home of Professor Simin Karimi, Head of the Linguistics Department, University of Arizona, Tucson, AZ, December 17, 2011
Courtesy of Olga Bever.

multi-year stints as the go-to problem-solving head of various departments – and did so with skill and humor.

Among many distinctions, Ruiz was recently appointed University of Arizona Honors Professor and recognized with a Lifetime Achievement Award by the University's Hispanic Alumni Association. Other distinctions include the Maria Urquides Laureate Award for outstanding service to bilingual children, a Distinguished Visiting Professorship at the Mexican Academy of Science, and selection to serve on the Clinton–Gore Transition Team on Education. He contributed editorial service to the *Bilingual Research Journal, Urban Education, Teaching Education, Journal of Teacher Education, Critical Multilingualism Studies* and *Anthropology and Education Quarterly*. He also served in multiple and meaningful leadership roles in the American Educational Research Association (AERA) – on the editorial board of the *Review of Educational Research,* as a member of numerous Presidential task forces, e.g. on governance and on the role and future of minorities, and as the inaugural Director of Social Justice. AERA Division G recognized him with their Distinguished Contributions to Social Contexts in Education Research – Lifetime Achievement Award in April 2016 (posthumously). Professor Ruiz was also active in national and international academic and policy consulting on bilingual education, language planning, teacher education and adult literacy – in various US states as well as Aruba, Guatemala and Mexico.

These accomplishments and distinctions only touch on the depth and reach of Richard's intellectual and leadership contributions over a lifetime of dedication to issues at the core of social justice and education in the world. I will say more about this below.

For those who knew him, though, the impact of Richard's life came equally or perhaps even more powerfully through the person he was. I had hoped this introduction would include some of Richard's own reflections on his life in an interview with me, but time robbed us of that opportunity. I know only the barest bones of his personal life and must leave it to others to tell pieces of it beyond my experience – as his University of Arizona colleagues and students do in their contributions to the present volume.

Of his family, I know only that his lovely lifetime partner Marie and their beloved sons Zachary and Daniel were at the very center of his being – unerringly and unshakably so. Of his colleagues, I know that they are both heartbroken and simultaneously overwhelmingly grateful to have had Richard in their midst for the years they shared. Of his students – the hundreds who have benefited from his wisdom and generous mentoring across decades of teaching at UW-Madison and the University of Arizona, I have no doubt that their experiences, like mine, have had deep and enduring impact. I hope Richard had at least an inkling of how very much his colleagues and mentees esteemed him.

Among my vivid memories of Richard as my professor and advisor at University of Wisconsin–Madison over three decades ago are: exploratory conversations in his office about what became his seminal conceptual contribution on language planning orientations; the year-long dissertation writing fellowship he applied for on my behalf, unbeknownst to me while I was still in the field in Peru; and our co-authored, never-published article on Quechua language planning in Peru, about which we joked for years afterwards. As for the dissertation writing itself, I still have my original manuscript with Richard's thoughtful comments on it, in his beautiful penmanship. At my defense, Richard (I think quite purposefully) posed a question that enabled me to shine because I had plenty to say – about my researcher positionality and the many roles I inhabited as ethnographer in the highland Quechua-speaking communities where I did my fieldwork; being able to answer that question gave me confidence in tackling other questions from my committee members that were not so easy for me. As further illustration of his constant encouragement, Richard had, the night before my defense, called to invite me out to lunch afterwards, asking me who else I'd like to invite. I distinctly remember the huge sense of relief I felt upon receiving that call and realizing that he must think I was going to pass if he was planning a celebratory lunch afterwards.

Most important of all, Richard always treated me – and my work – with respect, as his equal. I never once experienced anything less. Perhaps this was because we early on discovered we were very close in age and had graduated from Harvard within just a few years of each other, but I rather think not. My observation of Richard over the years since then is that he treated everyone with that same fundamental sense of equality. Indeed, his egalitarian and supportive mentoring is a model I have taken with me and sought to emulate in my own mentoring over the years since.

Our paths continued to cross over the decades: for one thing, we were among few US academics who regularly taught a language policy seminar; later we worked together as editors of the *Anthropology and Education Quarterly*, an enterprise to which he brought his trademark good humor and penetrating insight. In our editorial meetings via Skype, as in any phone call or email I ever got from Richard over the years, it was as if we were starting right where we had left off last time – even if months or years had gone by in between. He had a remarkable memory and sense of continuity – we always seemed to start our conversations seamlessly *in medias res*.

Honoring Richard Ruiz and His Work on Language Planning and Bilingual Education

All the more bittersweet, then, that this volume of Richard's writings, begun collaboratively with him, was interrupted *in medias res*. Over the last few years, he and I made headway on a table of contents for a volume of his published and unpublished writings (Parts 1–4 in the present volume), but we had not yet started to assemble the pieces. I am indebted to Marie Ruiz and to Richard's Arizona colleagues and students for helping to bring the volume to fruition *in memoriam*. Luis Moll and D. Lane Santa Cruz found the missing pieces on Richard's computer. I am also deeply grateful to Luis, and to Norma González, Perry Gilmore, Teresa McCarty and Mary Carol Combs, who offered invaluable advice and encouragement along the way and not only contributed their own introductory reflections on Richard and his work, but recruited co-authorship and contributions from Richard's students. Without these collaborations, the volume would not be nearly the full and rich testament to Richard's legacy that it is.

As I have often remarked to my students, Richard was a scholar whose publications are more about quality than quantity – a model of scholarship increasingly rare in our time. I never read anything of his that I did not enjoy, learn from and remember. His writing was – and is – a delight to read and his thinking was, over and over again, ahead of his time. This is reflected in the themes and writings included in the present volume.

Perhaps not so coincidentally, I have found in putting this volume together that the four thematic parts Richard chose and the two I later added run remarkably parallel to his ideas as I encountered them across the years – on language planning orientations, bilingual education and language and education planning, language and voice, language threat and endangerment, Indigenous education and interculturality. In what follows, I intertwine an overview of the volume's contents with accounts of my personal encounters with these themes in Richard's work.

Part 1, *Language Planning*, introduced by Teresa McCarty, begins with Ruiz's brilliant formulation of the language-as-problem/right/resource orientations underlying educational policy and practice for minoritized language groups in the USA and around the world. This was an idea ahead of its time, foreshadowing important and influential work on language ideology emerging about a decade later (Woolard & Schieffelin, 1994).

I have a very strong memory of sitting with Richard in his office on Bascom Hill in the early 1980s, as he told me he could detect at least three ways language planners and policy makers tended to think about language and language diversity in relation to education and society – as problem, as right, and as resource.[1] He went on to ask me what I thought about that idea. I was immediately struck by how on target his analysis was and shortly thereafter incorporated it in my own dissertation and my later writings, teaching and mentoring up to the present day. The idea has not worn out with time, but has only become more powerful – indeed, a paradigm in the field of language education policy. I consider it a huge privilege to have been one of the first to hear and learn about it from its author and originator; and I have always felt a special responsibility to represent the idea accurately and credit its author explicitly in my own work, encouraging my students to do the same.

Part 1 continues with his writings on official languages and language planning, language planning in Indigenous communities, threat inversion and language policy in the United States, and English language planning and transethnification in the USA.

Part 2, *Bilingual Education*, introduced by Norma González and Eric Johnson, offers a set of critical definitional pieces: a comprehensive report prepared for the National Institute of Education on language teaching in American education, a dictionary definition of bilingual education, an encyclopedia entry on the paradox of bilingualism, and an encyclopedia review on the knowledge base of bilingual education.

In April 1984, Richard and the LEPs, aka the Language and Education Planning group he organized while at University of Wisconsin–Madison, hosted a day-long on-campus symposium on *Language, Society and Education: National and International Dimensions*, in which various of his students presented case studies on language policy and bilingual education based on our research in Gambia (Dianne Bowcock), the Philippines (Maria Dalupan), the Andes (Nancy Hornberger), and Hmong refugees in the US (Joan Strouse). Another student provided a conceptual introduction (Julia Richards), colleagues spoke on language planning processes (Magdalene Hauner), language and ethnicity (Michael Olneck), and the case of Black English (Gail Dreyfuss), while Richard provided an overview on language policy and bilingual education in the US, using frameworks and charts I have kept to this day and use in my own teaching. These handouts, like so much of his work including the essays here in Part 2, are testimony to Ruiz' ability to synthesize, analyze, and interpret across broad phenomena and a wide interdisciplinary literature.

Part 3, *Language Fun*, introduced by Perry Gilmore, Brendan O'Connor and Lauren Zentz, provides a glimpse into the poetic and prophetic genius so treasured by those who knew him. Richard was intent on including these unpublished pieces under the rubric of fun: *The Parable of the Pigs*, dating from the 1990s and commenting on US bilingual education policy; *Jesus was Bilingual*, offering international perspectives on heritage language education partly provoked by Arizona's passage of Proposition 203 ending bilingual education; and *The Ontological Status of Burritos*, a meditation on language, ethnicity and education inspired by a Massachusetts judge's 2006 ruling that a burrito was not a sandwich, in the case of *Panera v. Qdoba*.

Richard loved words and word play and used these expertly as a way to entertain, to teach and, more seriously, to reflect on life's paradoxes and problems. He was always teasing me about 'unpeeling the onion,' eventually putting it in writing: 'I had always peeled onions (as well as potatoes, bananas, and oranges), so I wondered whether un-peeling was the opposite, i.e. putting them back together' (Ruiz, 2011: 177, referring to Ricento & Hornberger, 1996). Another running joke was our unpublished article on 'Quechua language planning in Peru' which I think he kept on his CV partly as a joke and partly in honor of our early collaboration. This was a piece I had originally submitted as a graduate student to a new (and ultimately short-lived) journal titled something like *Language Planning and Education*. Upon receiving the response that the journal did not accept submissions from non-PhD'd authors, Richard graciously agreed to co-author it with me; we exchanged the manuscript through long-distance mail from Puno, Peru to Madison to finalize it (no email in those days), whereupon the editor eventually suggested he would like to include it in a book he was editing for Fishman's Contributions to the Sociology of Language series. Over the next years, we received at one point a disastrously copy-edited version, to which we replied, and various other communications, until eventually we heard nothing more and sadly, were not sure what had happened to the book and more importantly, the editor. The book never did appear, but Richard 'checked in with me' about it periodically, in his gently humorous way, reminding us both perhaps of the vagaries and ephemerality of publishing and life.

Part 4, *Language Minority Education*, introduced by Luis Moll and D. Lane Santa Cruz, explores issues of ethnic minority group interest, empowerment, voice and sovereignty in four essays spanning three decades, including one previously unpublished.

In May 1990, Ruiz was one of three speakers in a symposium on *Spanish Literacy in the United States: Implications for Educational Achievement* I was invited to organize on the occasion of the University of Pennsylvania's 250th anniversary. It was there, according to my notes, that I first heard Richard articulate the memorably compelling phrase I have since quoted many times, as have my students and many others, citing the all-too-frequent and painfully paradoxical instances where: *'inclusion of the language of a group has coincided with the exclusion of their voice'* (Ruiz, 1991, reprinted here; Hornberger, 2006).

Part 4 includes not only the above essay on the empowerment of language minority students, but also: one on ethnic group interests, law and language in education, first presented at the symposium on *Ethnicity, Law, and the Social Good* organized by the University of Wisconsin American

Ethnic Studies Coordinating Committee; Ruiz's unpublished essay on the representation of the ethnic in public discourse, originally presented at an invitational symposium on the *Public Representation of Youth Violence* held at meetings of the American Educational Research Association in 2000; and a co-authored essay with Luis Moll on the educational sovereignty of Latino/a students in the USA.

Part 5, *Perspectives on Language Planning Orientations and Language Threat Inversion*, moves us on to essays contributed by Richard's students in his memory, exploring language ideologies, language policies and bilingual education, through Ruizian lenses in the cases of Florida's Coral Way school (Erin Mackinney), Indigenous languages in Guatemala (Julia Richards and Janelle Johnson), and the linguistic landscape of Ukraine (Olga Bever). In the last essay of Part 5, Kevin Carroll and Joyce Pereira take up the concepts of language threat and threat inversion introduced in Ruiz's heretofore unpublished 2006 paper (in Part 1).

At a March 2006 Georgetown University Roundtable colloquium on *Language Threat and Endangerment* organized by Richard, I heard him present his language threat typology followed by case study presentations by his students Kevin Carroll on Puerto Rico, Stephen Nover on deaf education in the US, and Lydia Emerencia on language planning in Aruba. The panel raised questions like (inverted question marks in the original): ¿What does it mean for a language to be threatened? ¿Are all threatened languages also endangered? ¿what evidence can be produced that demonstrates threat or endangerment, and what are the sources of these? ¿Is there an 'objective' standard for what constitutes a threat to a language? ¿Are some threats manufactured for political, economic, or other reasons? ¿Is 'endangerment' always about language death, or are there other types of endangerment that should also concern us? Juxtaposing his typology with well-known classifications of endangerment and vitality (e.g. Fishman, 1991; Krauss, 1992), Ruiz found a wide range of perceived threats to language, including to very powerful languages of wider communication (LWCs) that themselves have been accused of linguicism (cf. Trudgill's 1991 characterization of English as a 'killer language'), and concluded with a broader reflection on war and 'the other', arguing that war is not possible without 'the other' and that this 'other' is created from promotion of threat, both external and internal. He asked, poignantly, 'How can we reconceptualize education so that future generations feel less threatened by, perhaps even start to value, the differences they see around them?'

In an email to my language policy seminar students at the time, I summarized Ruiz's talk as follows, with the quoted parts taken verbatim from the PowerPoint he sent me: The basic argument as I understand it so far is that there are different types and degrees of real and perceived threat to languages both small and great (including LWCs) – and that 'threat-inversion' refers to policy/societal/individual responses to those real/perceived threats – responses which can take the form of exclusion, violence, separation, demonization, disenfranchizement, categorization, language-as-problem discourses. Indeed, 'threat-inversion dominates public policy in the US (especially education) and results in reduced civil liberties, calls for "accountability," deskilling of teachers, and greater not less social fragmentation.' Calling it 'threat-inversion' is meant to convey that the threat posed BY a big powerful language gets inverted into a threat TO that language (in policy, discourse, etc.), however 'unfounded, irrational, or stupid' that might be.

As I look back now on this paper partly inspired by the unprecedented events of 9/11 (see his last paragraph) and reflect on recent growing attention to sociolinguistics and security (e.g. Charalambous et al., 2015; Rampton et al., 2015), I am struck once again by how far ahead of his time Ruiz was. Ruiz's paper, and the Puerto Rican and Aruban case studies that were part of the colloquium, are published in this volume for the first time.

Part 6, *Communities as Linguistic Resources Across the Americas*, brings together a symposium of essays by Ruiz's students revisiting his foundational thinking on language as resource, voice and empowerment in the light of his teaching/mentoring and as they have taken up these concepts in their own work.

In August 2015, this Symposium Honoring the Legacy of Richard Ruiz was presented, bilingually, at the *VI Simposio Internacional de Bilingüismo y Educación Bilingüe en América Latina-Bilinglatam VI/6th International Symposium on Bilingualism and Bilingual Education in Latin America-Bilinglatam VI* in Lima, Peru. The audience including me were treated to an introduction by Mary Carol Combs and Sheilah Nicholas exploring Richard's analysis and interpretation of Freire's emancipatory education and offering a contemporary example from their own experience – the American Indian Language Development Institute, in which Nicholas has participated since 1991 as student, co-instructor, research-apprentice, program coordinator and currently faculty instructor. This stirring introduction was followed by papers on Indigenous youth ideologies, practices and activism (Leisy Wyman), Indigenous Ĕbĕra children's schooling in Bogotá (Amparo Clavijo Olarte), and an innovative University of Arizona early childhood teacher education initiative involving pre-service Latina teachers in home and family engagements premised on families and communities as linguistic resources (Iliana Reyes and Cristina Iddings), all presented in thoughtful and heartfelt tribute to their mentor. All of these papers are published here in this volume for the first time.

As I listened and participated, the session brought back for me a bilingual session Richard and his student Vanessa Anthony-Stevens had organized at the American Anthropological Association meetings of 2013. The session, *Interculturality and Indigenous Education in the Americas: Engaging Intercultural Knowledge through Reflections on Practice and Policy*, with session participants representing perspectives from Native America (Apache and Osage), Northern Mexico (Yoreme and Raramuri) and South America (Aymara), was strikingly and symbolically organized, with presenters and audience members all seated in a large circle, and printed session description and oral discussion accomplished bilingually in Spanish and English in a dialogue highlighting 'cross-border collaborations among Indigenous and non-Indigenous scholars, graduate students, and Indigenous educators working throughout the Americas to engage the concept of "interculturality" in the practice of bringing Indigenous knowledges to the schooling process.' Here, as in the 2015 Lima Symposium honoring Richard, I was struck and moved by how thoroughly the session organization, respectful discussion and facilitating comments by Richard (in person in 2013 and through his students' voicing of his teachings in 2015), embodied the purpose and content of the session theme.

Colin Baker, my unfailingly encouraging and unerringly inspirational founding co-editor in this Bilingual Education and Bilingualism book series, concludes the volume with his inimitably pithy, perceptive and prophetic thoughts on Richard's person and power. Thank you, Colin, for welcoming and facilitating the creation of this volume, from the first inklings of a promising possibility to its fulfillment here.

I have just re-read Richard's (2011) 'Cooking with Nancy' and am reminded once again of his wonderful knack for making everyone else look, and feel, good – a generosity of spirit all too rare in our world. *Descanse en paz*, Richard, you will be greatly missed and affectionately remembered.

16 April 2016
Philadelphia, PA, USA

Note

(1) He generously credits me and another few of his PhD students for inspiring him to modify his original problem-resource dichotomy to a three-part model including

language rights (Ruiz, 2010b: 167; 2011: 176–177). If that is the case, I was unaware of it at the time.

References

Charalambous, C., Charalambous, P., Khan, K. and Rampton, B. (2015) Sociolinguistics and security. Working Paper in Urban Language and Literacies No. 177. London: King's College London.

Fishman, J.A. (1991) *Reversing Language Shift: Theoretical and Empirical Foundations of Assistance to Threatened Languages*. Clevedon: Multilingual Matters.

Hornberger, N.H. (2006) Voice and biliteracy in Indigenous language revitalization: Contentious educational practices in Quechua, Guarani, and Maori contexts. *Journal of Language, Identity, and Education* 5 (4), 277–292.

Krauss, M. (1992) The world's languages in crisis. *Language* 68, 4–10.

Moll, L. and Ruiz, R. (2005) The educational sovereignty of Latino/a students in the United States. In P. Pedraza and M. Rivera (eds) *Latino Education: An Agenda for Community Action Research* (pp. 295–320). Mahwah, NJ: Lawrence Erlbaum.

Rampton, B., Charalambous, P. and Charalambous, C. (2015) Desecuritizing Turkish: Teaching the language of a former enemy, and intercultural language education. Working Paper in Urban Language and Literacies No. 137. London: King's College London.

Ricento, T.K. and Hornberger, N.H. (1996) Unpeeling the onion: Language planning and policy and the ELT professional. *TESOL Quarterly* 30 (3), 401–428.

Ruiz, R. (1983) Ethnic group interests and the social good: Law and language in education. In W.A. Van Horne (ed.) *Ethnicity, Law and the Social Good* (Vol. 2, pp. 49–73). Milwaukee, WI: University of Wisconsin System, American Ethnic Studies Coordinating Committee/Urban Corridor Consortium.

Ruiz, R. (1984a) *Language Teaching in American Education: Impact on Second-language Learning*. NIE Synthesis Report. Washington, DC: National Institute of Education.

Ruiz, R. (1984b) Orientations in language planning. *NABE Journal* 8 (2), 15–34.

Ruiz, R. (1990) Official languages and language planning. In K.L. Adams and D.T. Brink (eds) *Perspectives on Official English: The Campaign for English as the Official Language of the USA* (pp. 11–24). Berlin: Mouton de Gruyter.

Ruiz, R. (1991) The empowerment of language-minority students. In C.E. Sleeter (ed.) *Empowerment Through Multicultural Education* (pp. 217–227). Albany, NY: SUNY Press.

Ruiz, R. (1992/1996) The parable of the pigs. Unpublished.

Ruiz, R. (1995) Language planning considerations in Indigenous communities. *Bilingual Research Journal* 19 (1), 71–81.

Ruiz, R. (1997) Bilingual education. In C.A. Grant and G. Ladson-Billings (eds) *Dictionary of Multicultural Education* (pp. 29–31). Phoenix, AZ: Oryx Press.

Ruiz, R. (2000) Asymmetrical worlds: The representation of the ethnic in public discourse. Unpublished.

Ruiz, R. (2003) Jesus was bilingual. Unpublished.

Ruiz, R. (2006) Threat inversion and language policy in the United States. Unpublished manuscript.

Ruiz, R. (2008a) The knowledge base of bilingual education. Review of: The Encyclopedia of Bilingual Education (J. González, ed.). Boulder, CO: Education Review, National Education Policy Center.

Ruiz, R. (2008b) The ontological status of burritos. Unpublished.

Ruiz, R. (2008c) Paradox of bilingual education. In J. González (ed.) *Encyclopedia of Bilingual Education* (pp. 646–651). Thousand Oaks, CA: Sage.

Ruiz, R. (2010a) English language planning and transethnification in the USA. *Télescope* 16 (3), 96–112. (Citations here are from the draft English version.)

Ruiz, R. (2010b) Reorienting language-as-resource. In J. Petrovic (ed.) *International Perspectives on Bilingual Education: Policy, Practice, and Controversy* (pp. 155–172). Charlotte, NC: Information Age Publishing.

Ruiz, R. (2011) Afterword: Cooking with Nancy. In F.M. Hult and K.A. King (eds) *Educational Linguistics in Practice: Applying the Local Globally and the Global Locally* (pp. 173–178). Bristol: Multilingual Matters.

Trudgill, P. (1991) Language maintenance and language shift: Preservation versus extinction. *International Journal of Applied Linguistics* 1 (1), 61–69.

Woolard, K.A. and Schieffelin, B.B. (1994) Language ideology. *Annual Review of Anthropology* 23, 55–82.

Acknowledgments

My deepest gratitude goes to Richard's Arizona colleagues and former students for their scholarly and personal contributions to this volume. Their unfailing generosity and appreciation have been an inspiration as I completed this project originally started with Richard. Special thanks also to Marie Ruiz for providing photos.

I am grateful to my own former students, now professors, who served as external reviewers for this volume honoring their 'grand-mentor': Elaine Allard, Angela Creese, Bridget Goodman, Cynthia Groff, Francis Hult, David Cassels Johnson, Kendall King, Katherine Mortimer and Jamie Schissel provided valuable comments on the original contributions in Parts 5 and 6. My thanks are also due to current TESOL master's students Julia Carboni and Katie Barlow and Educational Linguistics PhD student Miranda Weinberg here at the University of Pennsylvania Graduate School of Education for their essential work in converting and proofreading Richard's pdf essays into Word documents; and to Educational Linguistics PhD student Coleman Donaldson for preparing the volume index.

Several colleagues came to my rescue in securing permissions to reprint some of Richard's work here. Primary among them are Ofelia García, who facilitated permission for his 1990 *Official Languages and Language Planning*, originally published by Mouton in the Contributions to Sociology of Language book series she now edits, and María Franquiz, who facilitated permission for his much-celebrated 1984 'Orientations in language planning', originally published in the *National Association for Bilingual Education (NABE) Journal/Bilingual Research Journal* she now edits.

Finally, my warm thanks go to the staff at Multilingual Matters and especially to Tommi Grover, Managing Director, whose enthusiasm and support for this project never faltered although it took years to bring to fruition. True to his parents' founding vision for Multilingual Matters, Tommi cares deeply about the scholarly – and human – enterprise of promoting and sustaining multilingualism in all its varied splendor around the world. I am fortunate to have worked with them for so many years and grateful for the opportunity to contribute this book to the Bilingual Education and Bilingualism series.

Permissions

Orientations in Language Planning was previously published in (1984) *NABE Journal* 8 (2), 15–34. Permission kindly granted by Taylor & Francis.

Official Languages and Language Planning was previously published in (1990) In K. Adams and D. Brink (eds) *Perspectives on Official English: The Campaign for English as the Official Language of the USA* (pp. 11–24). Berlin: Mouton. Permission kindly granted by Mouton de Gruyter.

Language Planning Considerations in Indigenous Communities was previously published in (1995) *Bilingual Research Journal* 19, 71–81. Permission kindly granted by Taylor & Francis.

English Language Planning and Transethnification in the USA was previously published in (2010) *Telescope (Aménagement linguistique de l'anglais et la transethnification aux États-Unis)*, Autumn. Permission kindly granted by Télescope.

Language Teaching in American Education: Impact on Second-Language Learning was previously published in (1984) Report for the National Institute of Education, Washington. Washington, DC. Permission kindly granted by National Institute of Education, Washington.

Bilingual Education was previously published in (1997) In C. Grant and G. Ladson-Billings (eds) *The Dictionary of Multicultural Education*. Phoenix: Oryx Press – Greenwood. Permission kindly granted by Oryx Press.

Paradox of Bilingualism was previously published in (2008) In J. Gonzalez (ed.) *Encyclopedia of Bilingual Education* (pp. 645–650). Thousand Oaks, CA: Sage. Permission kindly granted by Sage.

The Knowledge Base of Bilingual Education was previously published in (2008) *The Education Review*, 8 November. Permission kindly granted by *The Education Review*.

Ethnic Group Interests and the Social Good: Law and Language in Education was previously published in (1983) In W. Van Horne (ed.) *Ethnicity, Law and the Social Good* (pp. 49–73). Milwaukee, WI: American Ethnic Studies Coordinating Committee. Permission kindly granted by American Ethnic Studies Coordinating Committee (Uni Wisconsin Press)/Board of Regents of the University of Wisconsin System.

The Empowerment of Language Minority Students was previously published in (1991) In C. Sleeter (ed.) *Empowerment Through Multicultural Education* (pp. 217–227). Albany, NY: SUNY Press. Permission kindly granted by SUNY Press.

The Educational Sovereignty of Latino/a Students in the United States by L. Moll and R. Ruiz was previously published in (2005) In P. Pedraza and M. Rivera (eds) *Latino Education: An Agenda for Community Action Research* (pp. 295–320). Hillsdale, NJ: Lawrence Erlbaum.

Part 1

Language Planning

'Language Planning is Social Planning': Reflections on the Language Planning Contributions of Richard Ruiz
Teresa L. McCarty

Orientations in Language Planning
(1984) *NABE Journal* 8 (2), 15–34

Official Languages and Language Planning
(1990) In K. Adams and D. Brink (eds) *Perspectives on Official English: The Campaign for English as the Official Language of the USA* (pp. 11–24). Berlin: Mouton

Language Planning Considerations in Indigenous Communities
(1995) *Bilingual Research Journal* 19, 71–81

Threat Inversion and Language Policy in the United States
(2006) Unpublished

English Language Planning and Transethnification in the USA
(2010) *Telescope (Aménagement linguistique de l'anglais et la transethnification aux États-Unis)*, Autumn

Richard and Terri visiting the Spindlers at their home in Calistoga, CA, in connection with the 1996 American Anthropological Association meetings in San Francisco
Courtesy of Yvonne Gonzalez/Teresa L. McCarty.

'Language Planning is Social Planning': Reflections on the Language Planning Contributions of Richard Ruiz

Teresa L. McCarty

Like many of the contributors to this volume, I was drawn into the field of language planning and policy through the mentorship and scholarship of Richard Ruiz. Having an office adjacent to his for the first years of my academic career helped. In the same way that Nancy Hornberger, in the Introduction to this volume, recalls sitting with Richard in his University of Wisconsin office as he articulated his now-classic formulation of language orientations, I remember him stopping by my office to chat, or vice versa, or talking with him in the hallway (the walls of which he and his wife, Marie Ruiz, had decorated in a lovely shade of green), or sitting next to him in a taxi en route to a national meeting. In these informal settings, I would listen as Richard casually but cogently elaborated the orientations (Ruiz, 1984), the 'official' versus 'national' policy typology (Ruiz, 1990), and his application of the endoglossic-exoglossic-mixed policy types to Indigenous bilingual education (Ruiz, 1995). Sequentially, these notions anchor the first three essays of this section. Underlying all three are the 'threat inversion' and 'safe/dangerous' conceptions about which he would write years later, and that appear in the fourth and fifth chapters in this section (Ruiz, 2006, 2010).

In a footnote to the fifth chapter, 'English Language Planning and Transethnification in the USA,' Richard suggests that notions of 'safe' versus 'dangerous' cultural differences and their implications for language planning had been brewing in his work for nearly 25 years (p. 1). Yet I suspect he had been contemplating – and negotiating – these language ideologies all his life. This realization came to me in the form of a story told to me after Richard's passing by his beloved life partner, Marie Ruiz. With her permission, I share the story here, as it places the essays in this section, and indeed the entire volume, in the context of Richard's life journey. As Marie related: 'I was so

3

struck by hearing Richard tell it, that the whole emotion of the story seemed to come alive.'[1]

Marie Ruiz and Terri McCarty at the 2016 American Educational Research Association Division G (Social Context of Education) Awards Ceremony, where Richard was honored with the Lifetime Achievement Award
Courtesy of Nancy H. Hornberger.

The story begins around September 1953 – coincidentally, the eve of the US Supreme Court's landmark school desegregation ruling in *Brown v. Board of Education*.[2] Richard would have been five or six years old at the time. 'Richard grew up in a predominantly Mexican community,' Marie explained. 'There were some Hopi children he remembers playing with but he had very little interaction with "White folk".' She continued:

> [H]e remembers his Mom getting him up early one morning, getting him dressed [and taking] his hand as she led him on a walk. She didn't say where they were going and Richard didn't ask. But eventually they got to the elementary school and his mother found the classroom where Richard would start first grade.

Richard did not attend kindergarten, and this was his first encounter with school. He watched as his mother spoke with the teacher, 'a tall White woman' named Mrs Yates. What were they saying, he wondered, since 'his mother didn't speak English and he wasn't sure Mrs Yates spoke Spanish'? But he remembered that at one point his mother, 'still holding Richard's hand, placed his hand in Mrs Yates' hand, and for a few moments, the three hands were clasped together.' Then:

his mother left the classroom and Richard [thought] to himself, 'She's giving me away – what did I do this time?' ... Still holding Richard's hand, Mrs Yates led him to a desk where he was seated.

As Marie explained the significance of this story:

This is such a strong image of a parent willing to entrust the education of her child to a teacher who is a different color but has knowledge that can build upon the values and cultural ideologies and diversity that each child brings to the classroom. Teachers make choices all the time on what they choose to include and ignore. ... Teachers have a world of colors and diversity to build on and that should never be considered a problem, but rather a resource for the good of all.

'Oh, and by the way,' she added, 'Richard's mother did come back for him at the end of the day and every day, and pretty soon Richard became acquainted with the routines of public school'.

Richard aged eight
Courtesy of Marie Ruiz.

I return to Marie's comment and the core lesson of the story: Diversity is 'a resource for the common good.' It is a lesson that rings loudly and clearly through every aspect of Richard's life work. Like all children, Richard Ruiz entered school with an abundance of linguistic, intellectual, cultural and experiential knowledge – resources that, as Marie Ruiz points out, educators can choose to build upon or ignore. This fundamental insight is, I believe, the bedrock of Richard's work – from his penetrating analysis of the 'complex of dispositions' toward languages and their role in society that he called language orientations, to his assessment of the risks to democracy posed by dominant-language officialization, to his calls for Indigenous linguistic self-determination, to his critiques of the discursive and ideological processes that structure linguistic inequality.

In his path-breaking 'Orientations' article (Ruiz, 1984), Richard asks in what way *is* language a resource? Building on Joshua Fishman's argument that 'monolingualism is bad for business' (1978: 46), Richard first suggests the economic and societal benefits. Yet, perhaps reflecting memories of his first day at school, his concern always returns to the children and the families who entrust their children to the public school. Pointing to scholarship on the relationship between bi/multilingualism and enhanced cognitive growth, Richard obaserved that 'bilingualism can aid in general concept learning and skill (especially reading) development' (Ruiz, 1984: 28). On the question of affording *both* societal and individual benefits, he maintained that the 'language-as-problem orientation offers no hope' and the language-as-right orientation 'has had mixed results' (Ruiz, 1984: 28). While not without problems, a resource orientation constitutes the best hope for affording universal multilingual opportunities – a policy stance that 'can only contribute to a greater social cohesion and cooperation' (Ruiz, 1984: 28).

Here, we see a second, closely related Ruizian insight: planning language is, in effect, planning society (Ruiz, 2010: 2; see also Ricento & Hornberger, 1996: 415). It is therefore essential, Richard emphasized, 'to keep in mind this larger social context as we try to understand the role of language in it' (Ruiz, 2010: 2). In his 1990 essay, 'Official languages and language planning,' he put it this way: '[W]hile language planning is *at least* about language, it is rarely *only* about language' (Ruiz, 1990: 14). Taking to heart Richard's call for contextually conscious scholarship, in the remainder of this introduction I link his work explicitly to the social and political context in which he lived and wrote.

Although Richard's research was international in scope, he came of age and spent the bulk of his career in the borderlands of the southwestern United States, a geographic, social and political setting that figured prominently in his work. In 1966, when Richard was 18, the National Education Association (NEA) published *The Invisible Minority*, an influential report intended to make visible the conditions of teaching and learning for Spanish-speaking students in the southwestern states of Arizona, California, Colorado, New Mexico and Texas. Tucson educator Maria Urquides led the NEA study,[3] and at the NEA's request, the research was undertaken by bilingual, mostly Mexican American teachers in Tucson schools. Presaging Richard's language-as-resource orientation, the teacher-researchers 'recognize[d] the Spanish-speaking ability of Mexican-American students as a distinct asset ... to build on ... rather than to root out,' and called for programs that 'relate closely to the needs, interests and ability' of Mexican American students in public schools (NEA, 1966: v,

27). The survey is credited with providing a key evidentiary base for the Bilingual Education Act (BEA), passed two years later as a Title VII amendment to the 1965 Elementary and Secondary Education Act (ESEA). Richard would both interrogate and actively seek to improve the BEA (and the ESEA) throughout his career.

In 1986, two decades after publication of *The Invisible Minority*, California voters approved Proposition 63, a constitutional amendment declaring English the state's official language. Part of the US English Movement, the California initiative gave rise to a parallel referendum in Arizona, where Richard had recently joined the faculty at the University of Arizona (UA). In 1987, Professors Karen Adams and Daniel Brink of Arizona State University (ASU) convened a conference there, with the goal of 'bringing some light to the heat that will doubtless be generated … as U.S. English continues' (Adams & Brink, 1990: vi). The papers in the conference focused on four states represented in the NEA study: Arizona, California, New Mexico and Texas. Richard was an invited speaker, and there I had the privilege of hearing him deliver an early version of the second essay in this part, 'Official Languages and Language Planning' (Ruiz, 1990).

In that essay, he brilliantly lays out a concise description of the multidisciplinary field of language planning – 'a literature that is not generally well-known in the United States' (Ruiz, 1990: 12) – followed by his 'national' - 'official' language typology and five propositions that constitute 'the beginnings of a conceptual framework' for language officialization (Ruiz, 1990: 22). Reminding us again of the importance of social context, he suggests that during 'a period of unparalleled English hegemony domestically and internationally,' the quest to make English an official (as opposed to national) language was driven by 'matters much broader than language itself' (Ruiz, 1990: 14, 22). This 'is a puzzle,' he said, leaving readers to ponder, with him, 'why the U.S. should disrupt a 200 year history of relatively successful linguistic tolerance by imposing language officialization' (Ruiz, 1990: 22, 24).

This paper and the larger environment it reflects were harbingers of policy developments to come. Increasingly harsh language restrictionism would characterize the sociopolitical context for all of Richard's remaining work. In this context we see him, in the third essay in this section, urging Indigenous communities to 'begin now' to implement endoglossic, community-driven policies 'that will reinforce past efforts in bilingual education while simultaneously stabilizing community heritage languages' (Ruiz, 1995: 71). At the time of that writing, Fishman had recently published his seminal treatise, *Reversing Language Shift* (Fishman, 1991), in which he presented the Graded Intergenerational Disruption Scale (GIDS), an empirically informed theoretical framework for language loss and revitalization. Indigenous concerns about those very issues were growing, nowhere more so than in the US Southwest, motivating the special issue of the *Bilingual*

Research Journal, 'Indigenous language education and literacy,' in which Richard's 1995 essay appears (McCarty & Zepeda, 1995). A long-time ally of UA's American Indian Language Development Institute (AILDI) (which he helped to fund), Richard was well aware of Indigenous community concerns. Examining the 'mixed history' of the BEA, which, for many years, had supported AILDI participants and their bilingual education programs, Richard cautioned that the BEA was 'a monolingual policy with the goal of anglification. For American Indian and other language minority communities,' he warned, 'this is an explicitly exoglossic policy':

> If, in fact, federally funded bilingual education programs in American Indian communities have served the purposes of language renewal ..., it is testimony to the ingenuity and dedication of the staffs of those programs, not the policy itself. ... I suggest starting now on the development of endoglossic language policies that can serve to reinforce and stabilize community languages ... the language planning decisions that are made now will help communities achieve the continuity of tradition that has served them so well up to now. (Ruiz, 1995: 79)

How prescient were those words! Just six years later, under the ultra-conservative administration of President George W. Bush, the word 'bilingual' would be expunged from the newly reauthorized ESEA known as No Child Left Behind (NCLB), high-stakes English-only testing would become the chief measure of student achievement, and federal funding for bilingual education programs would cease. The question posed by Richard at the 1987 ASU conference reverberates in these policy developments: How and why, in 'a period of unparalleled English hegemony,' did such a policy shift come about? 'It suggests, perhaps,' as he wrote years before the passage of NCLB, 'that the actual "risk" perceived by [dominant policymakers] is something beyond language' (Ruiz, 1990: 22).

This brings us to threat inversion. In the fourth (2006) essay, Richard argues that inverted threat discourses – claims that powerful English must be protected from 'smaller' languages through officialization and language restrictionism – 'reverse the normal logic where the weakest who are in real danger menace the strongest' (p. 1). He offers an 'A-to-H' typology of linguistic threat, where type A – the *genuine* threat faced by minoritized speakers in contact with speakers of dominant-aggressive languages – leads to minority-language death, and type H – *perceived* threats to linguistic hegemons – leads to the (further) oppression of minoritized communities. Subtractive language education policies (e.g. NCLB) are key mechanisms through which threat inversion discourses become normalized. 'We cannot be seen to be oppressive of minority communities merely because their cultural practices are exotic to us,' Richard pointed out. 'Somehow, these have to be perceived as dangerous':

This is the beginning of [threat inversion] discourse. It is only by show-ing that the common good is threatened by linguistic and cultural frag-mentation that such discourses are not only accepted but convincing. The consequence is a mobilization of extremely strong political and eco-nomic forces against very weak ones. (Ruiz, 2006: 7)

We come now to the safe/dangerous analysis presented in Richard's 2010 article, 'English Language Planning and Transethnification in the USA.' Let us recall the sociopolitical climate in Arizona and the nation at the time. Under NCLB, the former BEA had been renamed the English Language Acquisition, Language Enhancement, and Academic Achievement Act. By 2010, NCLB was in its eighth year of implementation, with growing cri-tiques of its withering effects on bi/multilingualism (Hornberger, 2006; Wiley & Wright, 2004), its discriminatory assessments and promotion of narrow 'teach-to-the-test' pedagogies (Heilig & Darling-Hammond, 2008; Solórzano, 2008), and its debilitating impacts on speakers of endangered Indigenous languages (Beaulieu *et al.*, 2005; McCarty, 2008; Wyman *et al.*, 2010). In Arizona, the state legislature had just approved anti-immigrant legislation that a federal judge later ruled encouraged racial profiling, along-side a ban on Mexican American Studies in public schools on the grounds that such classes promote the 'overthrow of the United States government' (Hull, 2010, para 8). During the week in which the anti-immigration law and the ethnic studies ban were approved, the state superintendent of public instruction ordered school districts to remove teachers with 'accents' from teaching English. Meanwhile, as part of a successful 2000 'English for the Children' initiative (Arizona Proposition 203), English learners were (and remain) segregated for much of the school day in mandated English language development classes where they are prohibited from using their mother tongue to learn.[4]

This is the context for 'English Language Planning and Transethnification in the USA' (Ruiz, 2010), in which Richard argues that cultural difference deemed 'safe' – for example, the presence of 'foreign' students in mainstream classrooms (i.e. students who will soon return to their home countries) – is tolerated and even viewed as an advantage 'to advance peace in the world through understanding and good will' (p. 5). In contrast, the linguistic and cultural knowledge of immigrant minorities – the 'Juan Josés' of the USA, as Richard writes – is perceived as a threat to national interests and hence a problem to be remediated:

Juan José is not an individual; he is ... representative of his community. His 'problems' [demonstrate] what ails his community. ... next year, his little brother or cousin will come into our classroom ..., and ... we will start again at zero, because that is all we think these children bring with them. (Ruiz, 2010: 6)

For the Juan Josés, says Richard, transethnification – the subordination of their linguistic and cultural capital for the sake of 'being American' – is an overweening official policy goal. In his earlier publications Richard analyzed such monolingualist ideologies as a source of puzzlement. Perhaps precisely *because* of the social context in which he wrote in 2010, with its growing anti-bilingual/anti-immigrant extremism, in this publication he condemns those ideologies as a sin. 'Unfortunately,' he writes, 'complete confession and renunciation of the sin of inveterate and aggressive and oppressive monolingualism' does not appear close; 'quite the contrary' (Ruiz, 2010: 9).

Richard was a man of science, but also of faith. Although this last essay ends on a note of grim reality, I believe Richard always saw light through darkness, redemption in the face of discrimination and loss. His unshaken belief in the power – and goodness – of linguistic and cultural pluralism, and the policy openings a resource orientation presents, continued to undergird his scholarship and activism.

In keeping with this anchoring Ruizian orientation, I close by returning to a 1991 essay included in Part 4 of this collection, 'The Empowerment of Language-Minority Students' (Ruiz, 1991). In that essay, Richard urges us to adopt a 'language of possibility' (Giroux, 1986), seeking not only to understand the causes of linguistic inequality, but to devise 'strategies by which we can take advantage of the transformative possibilities that exist even in the worst cases' (Ruiz, 1991: 224). The language restrictionist environment in which he labored over many years does indeed constitute a 'worst case.' In order to move around and through such a policy environment, he insisted, we must join our individual voices 'with other voices to effect social action on behalf of the community' (Ruiz, 1991: 224). In a very real sense, this volume exemplifies that multivocalic effort.

Richard possessed a distinctive voice, seeded in his experience as the son of Mexican immigrants, and strengthened through his pursuit of education, his love of family, his academic life and his faith. Through it all, he joined his voice with the voices of others who fight for equality and justice. A scholar of global vision and scope, he simultaneously sustained a clear-eyed view of the lesson behind a single child's hand clasped between that of his parent and his schoolteacher. Keeping that intimate yet far-sighted vision within our grasp, we may yet find ways to plan language by valorizing the resources of each child placed in our trust, and thereby build a more just, inclusive and diversely flourishing society for all.

Acknowledgments

It is a profound honor to be invited to provide these comments on Richard Ruiz's work. I thank Nancy Hornberger for bestowing that honor, and for her patience and support as I prepared the manuscript. Richard was an esteemed mentor, colleague and friend for much of my adult life. It was he who headed the search committee that hired me for my first academic job, and he guided me patiently and faithfully through my first 15 years in academe. Through his example he taught me how to be a professor and to mentor others; he offered a hand up when I needed it most, and he demonstrated what principled leadership and accountability to community look like in everyday practice. These are debts that can only be paid forward, and I thank Richard for teaching that lesson, too. I am deeply grateful to Marie Ruiz for taking the time to talk with me about Richard's life's work, to share the moving story of his first day at school, and to provide photographs from the family collection. Finally, I thank Yvonne González-Lewis for spending hours culling the photographic archives of UA's Program in Language, Reading and Culture so that we might share precious images of Richard with the readers of this book.

Notes

(1) The source of all quoted material relating to Richard Ruiz's early schooling is Marie Ruiz (personal communications, 12–13 October 2015).
(2) The fact that the story begins a few months before the Supreme Court would hear, for the second time, the case of *Brown v. Board,* is, in retrospect, telling. This is not only because of the enormous significance of the case in banning racial segregation in public schools, but also because, 50 years later, as head of social justice for the American Educational Research Association, Richard would co-found the organization's annual *Brown* Lecture. The lecture commemorates the important role of social science research in the Supreme Court's historic decision. Richard's research is foundational to that legacy.
(3) It is fitting that, three decades after *The Invisible Minority* was published, Richard was recognized for his outstanding contributions to language minority students with the University of Arizona College of Education María Urquides Laureate Award.
(4) For illuminating, if troubling, discussions of these policies and practices in Arizona, see Arias and Faltis (2012), Gándara and Hopkins (2010) and Moore (2014).

References

Adams, K.L. and Brink, D.T. (eds) (1990) *Perspectives on Official English: The Campaign for English as the Official Language of the USA.* Berlin: Mouton de Gruyter.
Arias, M.B. and Faltis, C. (eds) (2012) *Implementing Educational Language Policy in Arizona: Legal, Historical and Current Practices in SEI.* Bristol: Multilingual Matters.
Beaulieu, D., Sparks, L. and Alonzo, M. (2005) *Preliminary Report on No Child Left Behind in Indian Country.* Washington, DC: National Indian Education Association.
Fishman, J.A. (1978) Positive bilingualism: Some overlooked rationales and forefathers. In E.A. James (ed.) *Georgetown University Round Table on Languages and Linguistics 1978* (pp. 42–52). Washington, D.C.: Georgetown University Press.
Fishman, J.A. (1991) *Reversing Language Shift: Theoretical and Empirical Foundations of Assistance to Threatened Languages.* Clevedon: Multilingual Matters.
Gándara, P. and Hopkins, M. (eds) (2010) *Forbidden Language: English Learners and Restrictive Language Policies.* New York: Teachers College Press.
Giroux, H.A. (1986) Radical pedagogy and the politics of student voice. *Interchange* 17 (Spring), 48–69.

Heilig, J.V. and Darling-Hammond, L. (2008) Accountability Texas-style: The progress and learning of urban minority students in a high-stakes testing context. *Educational Evaluation and Policy Analysis* 30 (2), 75–110.

Hornberger, N.H. (2006) *Nichols* to *NCLB*: Local and global perspectives on US language education policy. In O. García, T. Skutnabb-Kangas and M.E. Torres-Guzmán (eds) *Imagining Multilingual Schools: Languages in Education and Glocalization* (pp. 223–237). Clevedon: Multilingual Matters.

Hull, T. (2010) Arizona teachers claim law against Mexican-American studies unconstitutional. *Courthouse News Service*, 21 October. See https://firstamendmentcoalition. org/2010/10/arizona-teachers-claim-law-against-mexican-american-studies-uncon stitutional/ (accessed 25 March 2016).

McCarty, T.L. (guest ed.) (2008) American Indian, Alaska Native, and Native Hawaiian education in the era of standardization and NCLB – An introduction. Special issue, *Journal of American Indian Education* 47 (1), 1–9.

McCarty, T.L. and Zepeda, O. (guest eds) (1995) *Introduction: Indigenous Language Education and Literacy*. Special issue, *Bilingual Research Journal* 19 (1), 1–4.

Moore, S.C.K. (ed.) (2014) *Language Policy Processes and Consequences: Arizona Case Studies*. Bristol: Multilingual Matters.

NEA (National Education Association) (1966) *The Invisible Minority*. Report of the NEA-Tucson Survey on the Teaching of Spanish to the Spanish-Speaking. Washington, DC: Department of Rural Education, National Education Association.

Ricento, T.K. and Hornberger, N.H. (1996) Unpeeling the onion: Language planning and policy and the ELT professional. *TESOL Quarterly* 30 (3), 401–427.

Ruiz, R. (1984) Orientations in language planning. *NABE Journal* 8 (2), 15–34.

Ruiz, R. (1990) Official languages and language planning. In K.L. Adams and D.T. Brink (eds) *Perspectives on Official English: The Campaign for English as the Official Language of the USA* (pp. 11–24). Berlin: Mouton de Gruyter.

Ruiz, R. (1991) The empowerment of language-minority students. In C.E. Sleeter (ed.) *Empowerment Through Multicultural Education* (pp. 217–227). Albany, NY: SUNY Press.

Ruiz, R. (1995) Language planning considerations in indigenous communities. *Bilingual Research Journal* 19 (1), 71–81.

Ruiz, R. (2006) Threat inversion and language policy in the United States. Unpublished manuscript.

Ruiz, R. (2010) English language planning and transethnification in the USA. *Télescope* 16 (3), 96–112. (Citations here are from the draft English version.)

Solórzano, R.W. (2008) High-stakes testing: Issues, implications, and remedies for English language learners. *Review of Educational Research* 78 (2), 260–329.

Wiley, T.G. and Wright, W.E. (2004) Against the undertow: Language-minority education policy and politics in the 'age of accountability'. *Educational Policy* 18 (1), 142–168.

Wyman, L., Marlow, P., Andrew, C.F., Miller, G., Nicholai, C.R. and Rearden, Y.N. (2010) High stakes testing, bilingual education and language endangerment: A Yup'ik example. *International Journal of Bilingual Education and Bilingualism* 23, 701–721.

Orientations in Language Planning

Richard Ruiz (1984)

*Basic orientations toward language and its role in society influence the nature of language planning efforts in any particular context. Three such orientations are proposed in this paper: language-as-problem, language-as-right, and language-as-resource. The first two currently compete for predominance in the international literature. While problem-solving has been the main activity of language planners from early on (language planning being an early and important aspect of social planning in 'development' contexts), rights-affirmation has gained in importance with the renewed emphasis on the protection of minority groups. The third orientation has received much less attention; it is proposed as vital to the interest of language planning in the United States. Bilingual education is considered in the framework of these orientations. Many of the problems of bilingual education programs in the United States arise because of the hostility and divisiveness inherent in the problem- and rights-orientations which generally underlie them. The development and elaboration of a language-resource orientation is seen as important for the integration of bilingual education into a responsible language policy for the United States.**

There are few conceptual models or principles which serve to orient the language planning literature. After fifteen or so years of trying to delimit and elaborate the field, we have not moved far beyond the point of adapting basic typologies like that of Haugen (1966) or Neustupný (1970) to new field situations; many of the very important early works, with titles like "Some comments on..." and "Toward a definition of ...", intended as starting points to the international debate on the nature and uses of language planning, still await integration into a more comprehensive theory.

Some notable exceptions to this contention come to mind: Neustupný's (1970) policy-cultivation distinction; Kloss' (1969) discussion of corpus and

* Research for this paper was supported partly by a Rockefeller Foundation Fellowship in the Social Sciences. I am also grateful to Andrew Cohen and Alicia Oman for useful suggestions and encouragement

status planning; McRae's (1975) territoriality-personality principles; and Tollefson's (1981) notions of centralized and decentralized language planning have emerged as important approaches to the basic issues of the field. However, there is still another level of conceptual integration in which orienting models are lacking; what is needed are meta-models which would serve to focus attention on the nature of the basic concepts with which language planning specialists work. It is in considering that kind of question that we can assess the usefulness of any particular model or language plan.

Orientations

In this paper, the concept of *orientations* is proposed as a heuristic approach to the study of basic issues in language planning. *Orientation*, as it is used here, refers to a *complex of dispositions toward language and its role, and toward languages and their role in society.* These dispositions may be largely unconscious and pre-rational because they are at the most fundamental level of arguments about language; yet, the argument here is that an important role of the metatheoretician of language planning is to make these orientations obvious. One way to do this is to discover them in policies and proposals which already exist; another is to propose or advocate new ones. Both of these are attempted in this paper.

Orientations are basic to language planning in that they delimit the ways we talk about language and language issues, they determine the basic questions we ask, the conclusions we draw from the data, and even the data themselves. Orientations are related to *language attitudes* in that they constitute the framework in which attitudes are formed: they help to delimit the range of acceptable attitudes toward language, and to make certain attitudes legitimate. In short, orientations determine what is thinkable about language in society.[1]

An example of how planners holding different orientations come to different policy positions will serve as a preliminary illustration of the importance of this concept. Tauli (1974) writes from an orientation which he would call "language as a means"; in the same argument he refers to language as a "tool." He contends that as tools some languages can be more useful than others, and that this usefulness is measurable.

> From the fact that language is a means follows that a language and its components can be evaluated, altered, corrected, regulated, improved, and replaced by others and new languages and components of a language can be created at will. Thus all languages or the components of a language, as constructions, words or morphemes, are not equal in efficiency in every respect. The efficiency of a language or a component of a language as a means of communication can be evaluated from a point of

view of economy, clarity, redundancy, etc. with objective scientific often quantitative methods. (Tauli, 1974: 51)

From this basic idea of "language-as-means" Tauli generates a definition of language planning as "the methodical activity of regulating and improving existing languages or creating new common, regional, national or international languages" (1974: 56). He goes on to propose the development of super-languages, which he calls "interlanguages", which would serve the communications needs of many different language communities. As evidence for the need of such interlanguages, he cites what he calls the "highly irrational" translation procedures of international bodies, and the difficulties of scientists in reading work in a variety of languages. "The ideal situation would be that all people all over the world who need to communicate with the people who have another mother tongue learn the same interlanguage as a secondary language" (1974: 66).

Others, proceeding from an orientation which Kelman (1972) might call "language as sentimental attachment", would be reluctant to create language policies from such a strictly "instrumental" point of view. After all, language is an important aspect of self-expression and self-identification; the value of these considerations must be measured by standards other than those of efficiency, clarity, redundancy, and others like these. Language policies based on these criteria can have devastating social consequences.

> Since language is so closely tied to group identity, language-based discrimination against the group is perceived as a threat to its very existence as a recognizable entity and as an attack on its sacred objects and symbols. The issue is no longer merely a redistribution of power and resources, but it is self-preservation of the group and defense against genocide. The conflict becomes highly charged with emotion and increasingly unmanageable. Genocide, after all, is not a matter for negotiation but for last-ditch defense. (Kelman, 1972: 199–200)

It is precisely for these kinds of reasons that some nations have conferred official status on previously subordinate indigenous languages; no one can suggest reasonably that it was for reasons of efficiency that Malaysia recently declared Malay an official language for government and education. It is this sort of consideration, as well, at the basis of much of the advocacy for bilingual education in the United States. In the international sphere, the problems of mutual intelligibility that Tauli bemoans are, from this orientation, merely technical; it is worth the effort to try to solve them on their own terms if the only other alternative is the abandonment of ethnic language.

In the following pages, two orientations in language planning are described which have had a significant impact on policy formulation; these two, called "language-as-problem" and "language-as-right", are healthy competitors in the planning literature (though as suggested above, advocates of each position may not recognize at what level their disagreement lies). A third is proposed, called "language-as-resource", which, although suggested by a number of others before, has benefitted from almost no conceptual elaboration at all. It is recommended as a potentially important redirection for language planning. At the same time, one should realize that these are competing but not incompatible approaches (here, the comparison to Kuhn's "paradigm" breaks down): while one orientation may be more desirable than another in any particular context, it is probably best to have a repertoire of orientations from which to draw.

Language-as-problem

The bulk of the work of language planners and those who have written in the field of language planning has been focused on the identification and resolution of language problems (Neustupný, 1970; Rubin and Shuy, 1973; Fishman, 1975). Karam, in reviewing the work of Haugen, Rubin and Jernudd, and Fishman, concludes that "the terms reviewed [for language planning] refer to an activity which *attempts* to solve a language problem" (1974a: 105). Fishman himself delimits language planning as "the organized pursuit of solutions to language problems, typically at the national level" (1974a: 79; 1975). Karam even implies that language problems are a necessary ingredient to any language planning at all: "Theoretically, wherever there is a communication problem concerning language, language planning is possible" (1974: 108). Mackey suggests that language problems are inherent in the multilingual situation: "the more languages there are to choose from, the more complex the problems tend to become" (1979: 48).

There are probably many reasons for this focus. One of the most obvious is that language planning activities have been carried out in the past predominantly in the context of national development, as Fishman points out:

> The sociology of language planning tends to be largely the sociology of organized change processes vis-à-vis non Western languages. The focus on the non-West is related to a corresponding focus on "newly developing" entities. (1975: 84)

Neustupný's (1970) examples of language problems—code selection, standardization, literacy, orthography, language stratification—suggest overwhelmingly a development context, as well.[2] In a framework so constituted, one must conclude that language is merely another of the problems of modernization.

Given this context, the emphasis on language problems is perhaps reasonable. This also may be a partial explanation of the lack of conceptual models in language planning: early specialists were interested less in the conceptual articulation of an academic area of research than in the treatment of practical and immediate field problems of policy-makers.

There are other explanations, as well, for the preponderance of problem-oriented language planning approaches. One of these certainly must be the unique sociohistorical context of multilingual societies. In the United States, for example, the need for language training of large numbers of non-English speaking Americans coincided, in the late 1950s, with a general societal concern for the disadvantaged. The importance of this coincidence lies in language issues becoming linked with the problems associated with this group—poverty, handicap, low educational achievement, little or no social mobility. The sorts of programs designed in the 1960s to address these socially undesirable conditions treated language as an underlying problem. Thus, the Bilingual Education Act (BEA) of 1968 and the State statutes on bilingual education which have followed start with the assumption that non-English language groups have a handicap to be overcome; the BEA, after all, was conceived and formulated in conjunction with the War on Poverty. Resolution of this problem—teaching English, even at the expense of the first language—became the objective of school programs now generally referred to as transitional bilingual education.

There is ample evidence that this connection of non-English language heritage and bilingualism with social problems has become entrenched in popular thought. Consider this passage from *U.S. v. Texas* (1971), in which Judge Justice delimits the Mexican American group.

> Mexican American students exhibit numerous characteristics which have a causal connection with their general inability to benefit from an educational program primarily designed to meet the needs of so-called Anglo Americans. These characteristics include "cultural incompatibilities" and English language deficiencies—two traits which immediately and effectively identify those students sharing them as members of a definite group whose performance as norm habitually will fall below that of Anglo American students who do not exhibit these traits. It would appear, therefore, ... that it is largely these ethnically-linked traits—albeit combined with other facts such as poverty, malnutrition, and the effects of past educational deprivation—which account for the identifiability of Mexican American students as a group ... (del Valle, 1981: 1)

This is a remarkable statement; for the purposes of the court, the Mexican American group has been identified on the basis of a number of criteria—all of them negative. Language is one of those. This statement is almost equivalent in its effects to another contained in a recent controversial report on the effectiveness of bilingual education programs.

[E]ducational policy makers should recognize the complexity of the needs of language-minority children. The source of their educational difficulties may warrant the types of approaches that have been developed in compensatory education programs (smaller class sizes, more individual attention, more structured curricula, etc.) for other children from economically disadvantaged backgrounds. (Birman and Ginsburg, 1981: 12)

Again, there is here an implicit understanding that economic disadvantage is inherent in the language-minority situation (the key word in the passage is "other").

Perhaps these examples suggest another explanation for the linking of language-minority persons with social problems; this explanation would be less arbitrary than those we have offered thus far, since it points to a central tendency, an essential tension, in all social systems: in any society, a sociolinguistic Darwinism will force on us the notion that subordinate languages are problems to be resolved. That is why, as Fishman (1978) says, it is the speakers of the "little" languages who are thought to need bilingualism: "they" need "us".

Whether it is General Motors or the American Federation of Teachers or the Interethnic Brotherhood of Deracinated Intellectuals, the pious view is advanced that "proper" monolingualism is the only sane solution to poverty, backwardness, and powerlessness. If only all those wild little people out there would speak English ..., they could solve all their problems. (1978: 45)[3]

Maintenance of a subordinate first language and bilingualism involving one of those "little languages" is therefore associated in a pre-rational way with intellectual limitation, linguistic deficiency (always defined from the perspective of English-speakers [Lawerence, 1978: 310]), provincialism, irrationalism, disruption, so that "the escape from little languages is viewed as liberating, as joyful, as self-fulfilling, as self-actualizing" (Fishman, 1978: 47).

This attitude obscures the current debate over whether transitional or maintenance-oriented bilingual programs are the more desirable. The question has already been decided: if the programs are acceptable at all, they are only to the extent that they are effective as transitions. Notice in the second sentence of this passage the obvious indifference to language loss:

Underlying this paper is the assumption that the ultimate goals of bilingual education programs are to learn English and keep up with English speaking peers in subject matter. While bilingualism per se is a laudable and worthwhile outcome, we judge benefit in terms of English acquisition and subject matter learning. The 1978 amendments embodied this assumption. (Birman and Ginsburg, 1981: 5n)

If these comments are suspect because of the attitudes of the authors toward bilingual education (see Gray's criticism in Babcock, 1981), they are not inconsistent with the views of even those who are thought to be in favor of the program generally. Shirley Hufstedler, Secretary of Education in the Carter Administration, sees the goals of bilingual education as exactly those two cited by Birman and Ginsburg, though her concern is as much the program regulations established following *Lau v. Nichols* (1974) as the 1978 BEA. As to the question of language loss, her response is that "the Lau regulations are *not* designed to maintain any language or subculture in the United States" (Hufstedler, 1980: 67).

The transition-maintenance controversy has been kept alive by a few dedicated advocates of language maintenance like Fishman and Hernández-Chávez, but even they concede that, in practice, alternatives to transitional language programs in the public schools are not viable ones (Hernández-Chávez, 1978). Again, it is as if nothing else is thinkable. This emphasis on transition, and the problem-orientation to language for which it stands, has been embodied in federal and state legislation from the beginning. The original BEA made poverty a requirement for eligibility in bilingual programs, and although this was dropped in the 1974 version, it remains a popular notion that bilingual education is for the poor and disadvantaged. The state statutes reinforce this attitude. The Massachusetts law is called "Transitional Bilingual Education"; the Wisconsin Statute is located in the state code in the chapter on "handicapped children," and proceeds to define the target population on that basis (see Ruíz, 1983). Even in California, where the code is considered more progressive than most, the transitional quality of the programs is obvious from the language of the Education Code (Section 5761):

A primary goal of such programs is, as effective and efficiently as possible, to develop in each child fluency in English so that he may then be enrolled in the regular program in which English is the language of instruction. (AB 1329, Chapter 576: 1978)

The major declarations of the courts, as well, do nothing to encourage anything other than transition.[4] Hufstedler herself says that the essential purpose of the Lau Regulations is to identify the best services for treating English-limited students and "to determine when those services are no longer needed and the students can be taught exclusively in English" (1980: 66).

Perhaps the perception most compelling—the connection of language and language diversity with social problems—is that multilingualism leads ultimately to a lack of social cohesiveness; with everyone speaking their own language, political and social consensus is impossible. The view is implicit in Hufstedler's statement:

> Cultural diversity is one of America's greatest strengths. We could not suppress it if we would; and we should not suppress it if we could. But unity is also America's strength. And the ability of every citizen to communicate in our national language is the keystone of unity. (1980: 69)

Hufstedler creates a false distinction between diversity and unity; it is based, as Fishman (1978: 43) points out, on the identification of unity with uniformity; it becomes, as well, an important element in the justification of monolingualism as an ideal. Whether or not the distinction is false, the conviction is strongly held nonetheless, possibly at a level beyond argument; President Reagan's rejection of maintenance programs as "absolutely wrong and against the American concept"[5] seem to strike a chord resonating deep in the US consciousness.

The orientation that language is a social problem to be identified operationally and resolved through treatments like transitional bilingual education may be more pervasive than we think. Whether the orientation is represented by malicious attitudes resolving to eradicate, invalidate, quarantine, or inoculate,[6] or comparatively benign ones concerned with remediation and "improvement," the central activity remains that of problem-solving. And, since language problems are never merely language problems, but have a direct impact on all spheres of social life (Karam, 1974: 108), this particular orientation toward language planning may be representative of a more general outlook on cultural and social diversity.

Language-as-right

Alan Pifer has written that "bilingual education has become the preeminent civil rights issue with Hispanic communities" (1975: 5). Pousada, as well, sees the current efforts on behalf of bilingual education for Hispanics as "a result of the civil rights movement" (1979: 84). These statements are representative of a strong movement, both within the United States and internationally, which would advocate consideration of language as a basic human right. How can language be fitted into a general conception of rights? What is meant by those who construe language as a right?

Several researchers give examples of language rights. For del Valle (1981), the right to "effective participation in governmental programs" has several aspects: provision of unemployment insurance benefits forms in Spanish for Spanish monolinguals; bilingual voting materials like ballots and instructional pamphlets; and interpreters.[7] Hernández-Chávez adds to these the right to the use of ethnic language in legal proceedings and the right to bilingual education (1978: 548n); he also mentions other things which a language-minority community might demand, like the use of the dominant language in the media, medical services, and in commercial contracts, but it is not clear that he offers these as examples of rights. Macías suggests two kinds of language rights: "the right to freedom from discrimination on the basis of language" and "the right to use your language(s) in the activities of communal life" (1979: 88–89). More specifically, the Committee on the CCCC Language Statement (1978) affirms "the right of students to their own language," by which is meant primarily whatever *variety of English* the students happen to speak. Also in the domain of education, Zachariev proposes as his Seventh Principle of Language Policy that mother tongue instruction is an inalienable right (1978: 271).

The wide range of statements proposed as language rights is explained in part by the pervasive nature of language itself: since language touches many aspects of social life, any comprehensive statement about language rights cannot confine itself to merely linguistic considerations. By extension, this means that discrimination as to language has important effects in many other areas, as several writers assert.

> Deprivations resulting from language discrimination may be devastating for skill acquisition. Language barriers have all too often worked to frustrate and stifle the full development of latent capabilities. When people are deprived of enlightenment and skill, their capabilities for effective participation in all other value processes are correspondingly diminished. (McDougal, Lasswell and Chen 1976: 155; see also del Valle, 1981)

It is not only access to formal processes like voting, civil service examinations, judicial and administrative proceedings, and public employment which are influenced; the right to personal freedom and enjoyment is also affected.[8] It is for this reason that an exhaustive list of language rights is difficult to compile.

The development and persistence of the rights-orientation is influenced by several factors. One of the most important is the nature of the U.S. legal system, in which the protections provided for minority groups are central (Lamb, 1981: 13; Burke, 1981: 166). A host of language-related cases—*Meyer v. Nebraska* (1932), *Yu Cong Eng v. Trinidad* (1925), *U.S. v. Texas* (1971), and *Lau v. Nichols* (1974), among others—have served to highlight the importance of the protection, more specifically, of *language*-minority groups in U.S. law, as well (Leibowitz, 1971; Teitelbaum and Hiller, 1977). It seems, however, that the basis of those protections and the nature of the entitlements which flow from them are still a source of some confusion. For example, some would contend that there is a connection between national origin and language; that, in fact, Congress and federal agencies have acted in a variety of ways based on an acknowledgement of that connection; discrimination on the basis of language, therefore, violates basic constitutional guarantees (del Valle, 1981). Other arguments deny such a connection (see the discussion in

Garcia v. Gloor [1980]). These sorts of confusions indicate that the debate on the legal status of language rights may continue indefinitely.

Another factor contributing to the emergence of a language-rights orientation is the concern for rights on a trans-national level (Van Dyke, 1976; McDougal, Laswell and Chen, 1976; Buergenthal, 1977; Zachariev, 1978; Macías, 1979). The charters of the League of Nations and, later, the United Nations, included the first significant protection of minority groups in the trans-national community; other internationally-recognized documents like the Universal Declaration of the Rights of Man and the Helsinki Final Act contain important statements on language-based discrimination. Zachariev, using many of these documents for support, puts language rights in the larger context of human and educational rights; he sees the necessity of linking language planning with social and educational planning:

> Language planning is an integral part of social and economic planning in a given society. Consequently, the formulation of a language policy for education and the realization of linguistic rights are inherent to a global vision of society and its corresponding national educational system.

Along with this general concern with human rights and the protection of minority groups, a most important development has been the emergence of ethnic researchers as prime movers in the effort to affirm language-identification as both a legal entitlement and a natural endowment. The kinds of arguments that have carried so much weight in other areas of discrimination have been adopted for language issues. Indeed, major ethnic agencies like the Mexican American Legal Defense and Education Fund (MALDEF) and the Centro de Estudios Puertorriqueños have devoted a great deal of their resources to resolving the legal status of language rights. One expects that these efforts will only intensify as the non-native-English-speaking population continues to grow and other issues, like the persistent question of the status of Puerto Rico, become less easily ignored. The clear implication of all of this is that the language-as-right orientation in language planning can only gain in importance.

What should be our attitude toward this orientation? To be sure, the importance of the legal argument in U.S. society is not to be denied. It is essential that for short term protections and long term guarantees, we be able to translate the interests of language-minority groups into rights-language; agencies like MALDEF should receive our support for performing this valuable service.

Yet, one cannot deny the problems of this approach. The most important of these could be that terms included in the legal universe of discourse do not incline the general public toward a ready acceptance of the arguments. Terms like "compliance", "enforcement", "entitlements", "requirements", and "protection" create an automatic resistance to whatever one is talking about. Their use creates confrontation.

Confrontation, of course, is what the legal process is all about. More generally, rights-affirmation is also confrontation, since the nature of a full-fledged right is that it is not a mere "claim-to" something but also a "claim-against" someone (Feinberg, 1970).[9] Even common-sense justifications of non-compliance do not go unchallenged: "Plaintiffs should be allowed to probe the validity of any defense made on the basis of administrative burden, and, courts should weigh such burdens as against the rights involved and available alternatives" (del Valle, 1981: 2). This atmosphere creates a situation in which different groups and authorities invoke their rights against each other: children vs. schools; parents vs. school boards; majority vs. minority groups; some minority groups vs. others; state rights vs. federal authority; and so on. In the case of language rights, for example, the controversy could be seen as one where the rights of the few are affirmed over those of the many.

Under these circumstances, a widespread response is non-compliance. Ignoring federal regulations, like those following *Lau*, for example, continues to be a common practice in which school districts engage with impunity, for the most part: a variety of factors conspire to make enforcement almost totally ineffective (Pousada, 1979: 89). Legal manipulation is another way of avoiding compliance, and it has a long history. Sapiens, for example, cites the arguments of the California State Attorney General in 1930 that Chicanos were Indians; this identification was important for social policy toward Chicanos because of the state law permitting the segregation of Indians (1979: 77).[10] See, also, González' contention that Judge Justice in *U.S. v. Texas* (1971) declared Title VI—where one must show the *effect* of discrimination-and the Fourteenth Amendment—where one must show *intent*—"coextensive." This particular maneuver, if successful, could mean that language discrimination cases would be harder to bring forward (NIME, 1981:6–7).

Other problems haunt the language-rightists: How does one delimit the affected class? (Macías, 1979: 91, 98) How important is the criterion of *numerosity*, mentioned by each Justice giving an opinion in *Lau*, and clearly the deciding factor for at least one of them? (Carter, Brown and Harris, 1979: 300; del Valle, 1981: 2, Pousada, 1979: 90). How are rights-claims to be articulated, given that some are more "immediate" than others? (Macías, 1979: 89). How are allegedly incompatible rights dealt with? For instance, while some see an "inherent inconsistency" between bilingual education requirements and desegregation orders (Burke, 1981: 167; Glazer, 1983), others deny the inconsistency (Pousada, 1979: 90; Arias, 1979). How are rights-standards at different levels (international, national, state, personal) integrated? (Macías, 1979: 90). How are rights which are conceptualized in different forms (e.g., individual vs. group rights) reconciled? (Williams, 1981: 62).

These are not simple questions. It is important to recognize that their formulation is peculiar to a rights-orientation: they are not of the sort that would emerge from a problem-orientation. Thus, one would expect answers to *those* questions to be sought in the universe of discourse appropriate to rights. Certainly, consideration of language rights must remain a central activity of language planners, as Williams suggests:

> ... before detailed language policies are formulated, it behooves us to question the relationship between language planning and language rights and to suggest the manner in which planning can realize the fulfillment of individual and group based rights. (1981: 62)

One might also consider, however, whether a rights-orientation, given the problems it faces, is sufficient as a way of addressing our language planning needs. Yet another language planning perspective is proposed in the following pages.

Language-as-resource

After reviewing several well-known typologies of language planning, Thompson concludes that another, a "resources-oriented typology may provide a more suitable approach" for language planning in the United States (1973: 227). He goes on to sketch a few ideas of what would be involved in this approach. These are not developed very extensively in his brief report, though his work can be considered a good starting point for the elaboration of such a typology. (Compare, as well, Karam's [1974: 113] characterization of the work of Jernudd and Das Gupta.) Greater development of a language-resources approach to language planning has not been forthcoming, possibly because of the sort of intractability perceived by Fishman: "language is certainly an odd kind of resource for current cost-benefit theory to handle, precisely because of the difficulty in measuring or separating 'it' from other resources" (1974a: 83).

As a justification for turning to other approaches in language planning, this criticism is weak. It is as applicable to others, as well: a language "problem" is no easier to distinguish from other "problems", for example (in another place, Fishman recognizes this [1974b: 261]). A closer look at the idea of language-as-resource could reveal some promise for alleviating some of the conflicts emerging out of the other two orientations: it can have a direct impact on enhancing the language status of subordinate languages; it can help to ease tensions between majority and minority communities; it can serve as a more consistent way of viewing the role of non-English languages in U.S. society; and it highlights the importance of cooperative language planning. Let us now turn to a consideration of language-resource planning.

Among observers of language use in the United States, there is almost unanimous agreement that this country has a great deficiency in language capability (Keller and Roel, 1979; President's Commission on Foreign Language and International Studies, 1979; Simon, 1980a, 1980b; Thompson, 1980; Tsongas, 1981).[11] Not only are we not developing language skills in the population to any great extent; we are doing almost nothing to encourage non-English language maintenance. The result could well be a pattern of language loss over just a few generations (Hernández-Chávez, 1978). The variety of proposals to remedy this situation indicates the urgency with which these issues have been approached recently in the literature.

Thompson (1980), for example, places his emphasis on the development of more and better language skills. He recommends a national teacher training program, longer sequences in language classes, development of better language aptitude measures, and a diversification of school approaches— including "bilingual-schools-for-all-Americans" and international high schools. The report of the President's Commission on Foreign Language and International Studies (1979) includes similar recommendations, and adds specific ones related directly to schools and universities. Among other things, the reestablishment of language requirements at the university level (the exact form of which was the subject of some controversy—see Rep. Fenwick's dissent in the addendum) is singled out as an important step influencing offerings throughout the educational system. Simon (1980b) is also concerned with the development of greater language capability, especially because of its usefulness in the areas of foreign affairs and international trade.

Development, obviously, is an important aspect of any resources-oriented policy, but what is missing in these proposals is a direct concern with resource *conservation*; what is worse, there seems to be no acknowledgement of the fact that existing resources are being destroyed through mismanagement and repression. This is true even where language communities are recognized as important reservoirs of language skills:

> Because of our rich ethnic mix, the United States is home to millions whose first language is not English. One of every 50 Americans is foreign born. We are the fourth largest Spanish-speaking country in the world. Yet almost nothing is being done to use these rich resources of linguists to train people in the use of a language other than English. (Simon, 1980b: 33; cf. Thompson, 1973: 227)

The irony of this situation is that language communities have become valuable to the larger society in precisely that skill which the school has worked so hard to eradicate in them! "National programs in the past have tended to encourage the study of foreign languages in the schools while at the same time discouraging continued study of languages represented by those ethnic minorities" (Rudolph Troike, in Thompson, 1973: 229). Consider, for example, Eddy's (1979) report of a national survey showing overwhelming support for offering foreign language courses in schools and universities, and considerable support for *requiring* such study. This is all true in a country where non-English speakers are *expected* to lose their first language (Macías, 1979: 96), and have suffered considerably and directly when that expectation was not fulfilled (see the discussion of school-language discriminatory practices in Ruiz, 1983). How is this explained? Could it be that the nature of the prevailing problem-orientation allows this seeming-contradiction as a basic tenet? After all, it is the "world standard" languages which one is expected to learn in school for personal enrichment or international understanding or foreign service, not the inferior vernaculars spoken by ethnic groups. For them, the best course would be to forget their "little" language, with the hope that one day they will be able to relearn it in a more acceptable form in school.

This is the way things are. But the situation could be different. A fuller development of a resources-oriented approach to language planning could help to reshape attitudes about language and language groups. In what way is language a resource? We can start with the common arguments for the benefits of language capability. Those of most interest involve trans-national considerations. Military preparedness and national security are issues which receive immediate attention; Tsongas, in fact, suggests to those concerned with language capability and training that "we must phrase the debate in terms of American interest and national security" (1981: 115; cf. President's Commission on Foreign Language and International Studies 1979 and the discussion on Conant in Valverde and Brown, 1978: 287). Also prominent is the importance of language skills for diplomatic functions: Thompson argues that language is an important aspect of "enlightened leadership" in foreign policy (1980: 47), and Gwertzman (1977) and Wooten (1977) record an embarrassing incident in Poland created by the inadequate language skills of the State Department.

Other trans-national concerns are also central to the new efforts at reviving language training in the U.S. In an economically interdependent world, Fishman claims that "English monolingualism is bad for business" (1978: 46); he is seconded by Dugan (1981), Pincus (1980), Simon (1980a), and Valverde and Brown (1978). Keller and Roel see linguistic diversity as an important part of the future of international communications: "In the process, the United States may be forced to reshape its system of communications as an integral, rather than dominant, component of a world language and information system" (1979: 110).

Not all arguments in favor of language training are of this sort. We have now, for example, a considerable body of literature on the positive effects of multilingual capacity on the social and educational domains. Timpe's (1979) study showed a relationship between declining ACT scores and decreased foreign language study. We are only now starting to see, on the domestic scene, the long-term effects of our incipient monolingualism. Kessler and Quinn (1980) show how improved conceptual skills in science are also related to multilingual ability. Hernández-Chávez (1978) holds that bilingualism can aid in general concept learning and skill (especially reading) development.

More generally, others argue for the social value of language competence. Lambert considers it important for the "deparochialization" of the student (in Thompson, 1973: 228). By this he seems to be saying, along with Sharp (1978: 3), that language study creates an awareness in students "that their own way of thinking and living is not the only reasonable possible one; and that some cultures are often keenly perceptive in areas in which others are short-sighted." Drake considers that bilingualism might help in blunting intergroup conflict and in making ethnic communities "better equipped to cope with ... modernity" (1978: 10). Keller and Roel (1979) are critical of U.S. mass media, which are largely ineffective in making the population aware of foreign cultures; greater access to non-English language communities would help.

Language planning efforts which start with the assumption that language is a resource to be managed, developed and conserved would tend to regard language-minority communities as important sources of expertise. Not only could language-competent community members be used to train others; the whole community itself could afford multilingual opportunities for language students. For example, students of Japanese being prepared for foreign service could benefit from an internship in a Japanese community center in San Francisco sponsored by the State Department. This would begin to address several problems. It would help to give students a more "natural" language training experience; it would give balance to language training programs dominated by written language (Pincus [1980] shows that spoken language training is generally poor, and Garvin [1974] implies that written language is the common focus of most language planning); it would help with any status problems the language and the community might have; and it would give something back to the community by encouraging the persistence of language maintenance institutions like community centers. This sort of consideration demonstrated in language plans can only contribute to a greater social cohesion and cooperation. On the question of affording that benefit, the language-as-problem orientation offers no hope; the rights orientation has had mixed results.

Conclusion

To be sure, a resource orientation in language planning is not without its problems, and the development of a more comprehensive model based on it is a matter for consideration elsewhere. For now, however, perhaps the best approach would be to encourage the compilation of a strong literature with an emphasis on language as a resource; this could create an atmosphere where language planning is seen as important in social planning. As it stands at present, the assumption of English monolingualism as the only acceptable social condition means that most people will see language planning as a meaningless activity (cf. Bailey, 1975: 156). Practically speaking, this implies a reluctance to acknowledge the importance of alternative linguistic behavior; ultimately, as in other parts of the world, this leads to social conflicts which, if ignored, can have disastrous effects (Deutsch, 1975: 7).

What is proposed in this paper is that language planning can benefit from a variety of approaches, and that in some circumstances some approaches are better than others. This is a call for the articulation of a new orientation in which language issues are framed and language attitudes developed. This orientation holds promise for a kind of cooperative language planning effort rarely seen anywhere. Indeed, in the United States, any meaningful language planning may not be possible without it.

Notes

1. Readers will recognize the similarities of "orientations" to other concepts current in language planning and social science more generally. Heath's (1977) idea of "language ideology" seems very close; the brevity of the discussion of this concept there makes me reluctant to claim a perfect match, however. Kuhn's (1970) "paradigm" is a reasonable comparison, though his claims for it (especially his criterion of incommensurability) are larger than what is proposed here for orientation. Perhaps the best comparison is that of Boulding's (1956, 1959) "image", especially as he might have focused it on language ("the image of language") in the way he did on other aspects of social life. Most interesting in his discussion is the way he sees the "image" determining the range of possible behavior: "people whose decisions determine policies and actions of nations do not respond to the 'objective' facts of the situation, whatever that may mean, but to their 'image' of the situation. It is what we think the world is like, not what it is really like, that determines our behavior" (1959: 120).
2. These problems are associated with the "policy" approach to language planning, which Neustupný says prevails in developing societies. Neustupný also lists other problems (correctness, efficiency, style, etc.) aligned with a "cultivation" approach predominant in modern nations. This latter concern seems less central to the work of language planners, with some notable exceptions (e.g., Haugen).
3. Fishman's cutting ridicule is aimed at Noel Epstein's analysis of bilingual education (1977).
4. In *Lau v. Nichols* (414 U.S. 563 [1974]), for example, Justice Douglas states that "no specific remedy is urged upon us." Still, this decision relied heavily on the 1970 HEW regulations (35 Fed. Reg. 11595) which held that any program for this population "must be designed to meet these language skill needs as soon as possible and must not operate as an educational deadend or permanent track."
5. See *The Washington Post*, March 4, 1981, and the discussion in Ruiz, 1983.
6. This term was suggested by Jim Cummins.
7. Del Valle's comments are most relevant to Puerto Ricans, who are citizens of the United States and who live in a commonwealth where Spanish is the official language.

The legal argument for provision of materials in the non-English dominant language for this group is perhaps more compelling than it would be applied to other groups.

8. Del Valle discusses *Hernández v. Erlenbusch* (1974), where a tavern rule against non-English language use at the bar abridged the "rights of Spanish-speaking patrons to buy, drink, and enjoy what the tavern had to offer on an equal footing with English-speaking patrons" (1981: 2).

9. Mere "claims-to" certain benefits or guarantees (fair housing, freedom from employment discrimination, etc.) could constitute what Feinberg would call a "manifesto right". Presumably, clear and purposeful action on the claim could not be taken until the identification of whomever were denying or inhibiting the guarantee. The presence of a valid "claim-to" and a valid "claim-against" constitutes a "full-fledged right". See the discussion of this adapted to ethnicity and language in Ruíz, 1983.

10. cf. *Gong Lum v. Rice,* 275 U.S. 78 (1927), where orientals were taken to be "negroes"; and *Ross v. Eckels,* 434 F. 2d 1140 (5th Cir. 1970), where Chicanos were not differentiated from whites for desegregation purposes: combining Chicanos with Blacks would therefore constitute minimum compliance.

11. But, see Pincus (1980: 82ff), whose report for the Rand Corporation found "no general market shortage" of language-trained specialists; he recognizes, however, that "market shortage" is not necessarily the same as "need."

References

Arias, M. Beatriz (1979). Desegregation and the rights of Hispanic students: the Los Angeles case. *Evaluation Comment* 6 (1):14–18.

Babcock, Charles R. (1981). Studies disavow U.S. focus on bilingual education. *The Washington Post.* September 29.

Bailey, Charles-James N. (1975). The new linguistic framework and language-planning. *Linguistics 158*:153–157.

Birman, Beatrice F. and Alan L. Ginsburg (1981). *Addressing the Needs of Language-Minority Children: Issues for Federal Policy.* Mimeo. Oct. 5.

Boulding, Kenneth E. (1956). *The Image: Knowledge in Life and Society.* Ann Arbor: University of Michigan Press.

Boulding, Kenneth E. (1959). National images and international systems. *Conflict Resolution* 3:120–131. June.

Buergenthal, Thomas, ed. (1977). *Human Rights, International Law, and the Helsinki Accord.* Montclair, New Jersey: Allanhead, Osmun & Co.

Burke, Fred G. (1981). Bilingualism/biculturalism in American education: an adventure in Wonderland. *The Annals of the American Academy of Political and Social Sciences 454*:164–177. March.

Carter, David G., Frank Brown, and J. John Harris III (1978). Bilingual/bicultural education: a legal analysis. *Education and Urban Society X* (3):295–304. May.

Committee on the CCCC Language Statement (1978). Students right to their own language. In: *A Pluralistic Nation: The Language Issue in the United States,* edited by Margaret A. Lourie and Nancy Faires Conklin. Rowley, Massachusetts: Newbury House Publishers. 315–328.

del Valle, Manuel (1981). Hispanics' language rights and due process. *New York Law Journal 186* (22):1–2. July.

Deutsch, Karl W. (1975). The political significance of linguistic conflicts. In: *Multilingual Political Systems,* edited by Jean-Guy Savard and Richard Vigneault. Quebec: Les Presses de l'Universite Laval.

Drake, Glendon (1978). Ethnicity, values and language policy in the United States. *NABE Journal III* (1):1–12. Fall.

Dugan, J., Sanford (1981). World languages and trade opportunities. *Foreign Language Annals 14* (4 & 5):287–292.

Eddy, Peter A. (1979). Attitudes toward foreign language study and requirements in American schools and colleges: results of a national survey. *ADFL Bulletin 11* (2):4–9. November.

Epstein, Noel (1977). *Language, Ethnicity, and the Schools: Policy Alternatives for Bilingual-Bicultural Education.* Washington, D.C.: Institute for Educational Leadership.

Feinberg, Joel (1970). The nature and value of rights. *Journal of Value Inquiry* 4:243–257.

Fishman, Joshua A. (1974a). Language modernization and planning in comparison with other types of national modernization and planning. In: *Advances in Language Planning,* edited by Joshua A. Fishman. The Hague: Mouton. 79–102.

Fishman, Joshua A. (1974b). Language planning and language planning research: the State of the art. In: *Advances in Language Planning,* edited by Joshua A. Fishman. The Hague: Mouton. 15–33.

Fishman, Joshua A. (1975). Some implications of 'the International Research Project on Language Planning Processes (IRPLPP)' for sociolinguistic surveys. In: *Language Surveys in Developing Nations: Papers and Reports on Sociolinguistic Surveys,* edited by Sirarpi Ohannessian, Charles A. Ferguson, and Edgar C. Polome. Arlington, VA.: Center for Applied Linguistics. 209–220.

Fishman, Joshua A. (1977). Social science perspective. In: *Bilingual Education: Current Perspectives* (vol. 1: Social Science). Arlington, Va.: Center for Applied Linguistics. 1–49.

Fishman, Joshua A. (1978). Positive bilingualism: some overlooked rationales and forefathers. In *Georgetown University Round Table on Languages and Linguistics 1978,* edited by James E. Alatis. Washington, D.C.: Georgetown University Press. 42–52.

Garvin, Paul L. (1974). Some comments on language planning. In: *Advances in Language Planning,* edited by Joshua A. Fishman. The Hague: Mouton. 69–78.

Glazer, Nathan (1983). The school and the judge. In *Ethnicity, Law, and the Social Good,* edited by W.A. Van Horne. Milwaukee: American Ethnic Studies Coordinating Committee.

Gwertzman, Bernard (1977). Interpreter's gaffes embarrass State Department. *New York Times.* December 31.

Haugen, Einar (1966). *Language Conflict and Language Planning: The Case of Modern Norwegian.* Cambridge: Harvard University Press.

Heath, Shirley Brice (1977). Social history. In: Bilingual Education: Current Perspectives (Vol. I: Social Science). Arlington, Va.: Center for Applied Linguistics. 53–72.

Hernández-Chávez, Eduardo (1978). Language maintenance, bilingual education, and philosophies of bilingualism in the United States. In: *Georgetown University Round Table on Languages and Linguistics 1978,* edited by James E. Alatis. Washington, D.C.: Georgetown University Press. 527–550.

Hufstedler, Shirley M. (1980). On bilingual education, civil rights, and language minority relations. *NABE Journal V* (1):63–69. Fall.

Karam, Francis X. (1974). Toward a definition of language planning. In: *Advances in Language Planning,* edited by Joshua A. Fishman. The Hague: Mouton. 103–124.

Keller, Edward and Ronald Roel (1979). Foreign languages and U.S. cultural policy: an institutional perspective. *Journal of Communication 29* (2):102–111. Fall.

Kelman, Herbert C. (1972). Language as an aid and barrier to involvement in the national system. In: *Advances in the Sociology of Language,* Vol. II, edited by Joshua A. Fishman. The Hague: Mouton. 185–212.

Kessler, Carolyn and Mary Ellen Quinn (1980). Positive effects of bilingualism on science problem-solving abilities. In: *Georgetown University Round Table on Languages and Linguistics 1980,* edited by James E. Alatis.

Kloss, Heinz (1969). *Research possibilities on group bilingualism: a report* (Quebec: International Center for Research on Bilingualism).

Kuhn, Thomas S. (1970). *The Structure of Scientific Revolutions*. Chicago: University of Chicago (International Encyclopedia of Unified Science).

Lamb, Charles M. (1981). Legal foundations of civil rights and pluralism in America. *Annals of the American Academy of Political and Sciences 454*:13–25. March.

Lawerence, Gay (1978). Indian education: why bilingual bicultural? *Education and Urban Society X* (3):305–320. May.

Leibowitz, Arnold (1971). *Educational Policy and Political Acceptance: The Imposition of English as the Language of Instruction in American Schools*. Arlington, Va.: Center for Applied Linguistics.

Macías, Reynaldo F. (1979). Language choice and human rights in the United States. In: *Georgetown University Round Table on Languages and Linguistics 1979*, edited by James E. Alatis. Washington, D.C.: Georgetown University Press. 86–101.

Mackey, William F. (1979). Language policy and language planning. *Journal of Communication 29* (2):48–53. Spring

McDougal, Myres S., Harold D. Lasswell, and Lung-chu Chen (1976). Freedom from discrimination in choice of language and international human rights. *Southern Illinois University Law Journal 1*:151–174.

McRae, Kenneth D. (1975). The principle of territoriality and the principle of personality in multi-lingual states. *Linguistics 158*:33–54.

National Institute for Multicultural Education (NIME) (1981). *Interview with Dr. Josue González*. (Unabridged edition). Mimeo. June 25.

Neustupný, J.V. (1970). Basic types of treatment of language problems. *Communications 1*:77–98.

Pifer, Alan (1979). *Bilingual Education and the Hispanic Challenge* (the Report of the President). Reprinted from *The Annual Report*. New York: The Carnegie Corporation.

Pincus, John (1980). Rand meets the President's Commission: the life cycle of a non-event. *Annals of the American Academy of Political and Social Science 449*:80–90. May.

Pousada, Alicia (1979). Bilingual education in the U.S. *Journal of Communication 29* (2):84–92. Spring.

President's Commission on Foreign Language and International Studies (1979). *Strength Through Wisdom: A Critique of U.S. Capability* (A report to the President). Washington, D.C.: U.S. Government Printing Office.

Rubin, Joan and Roger Shuy, eds. (1973). *Language Planning: Current Issues and Research*. Washington, D.C.: Georgetown University Press.

Ruíz, Richard (1983). Ethnic group interest and the social good: law and language in education. In *Ethnicity, law, and the social good*, edited by W.A. Van Horne. Milwaukee: American Ethnic Studies Coordinating Committee.

Sapiens, Alexander (1979). Spanish in California: a historical perspective. *Journal of Communication 29* (2):72–83. Spring.

Sharp, John M. (1978). Foreign language as a means of introduction to the study of minority group cultures in the United States. In: *Problems in Applied Educational Sociolinguistics: Readings on Language and Culture Problems of United States Ethnic Groups*, edited by Glenn E. Gilbert and Jacob Ornstein. The Hague: Mouton. 1–8.

Simon, Paul (1980a). Foreign language study: political, economic, and social realities. *Foreign Language Annals 13* (5):355–358.

Simon, Paul (1980b). The U.S. crisis in foreign language. *Annals of the American Academy of Political and Social Science 449*:31–44.

Tauli, Valter (1974). The theory of language planning. In: *Advances in Language Planning*, edited by Joshua A. Fishman. The Hague: Mouton. 49–67.

Teitelbaum, Herbert and Richard J. Hiller (1977). The legal perspective. In: *Bilingual Education: Current Perspectives* (Vol. 3: Law). Arlington, Va.: Center for Applied Linguistics.

Thompson, Richard T. (1973). Language resources and the national interest. In: *Georgetown University Round Table on Languages and Linguistics 1973,* edited by Kurt R. Jankowsky. Washington, D.C.: Georgetown University Press. 225–231.

Thompson, Richard T. (1980). New directions in foreign language study. *The Annals of the American Academy of Political and Social Science 449*:45–55.

Timpe, Eugene F. (1979). The effect of foreign language study on ACT scores. *ADFL Bulletin 11* (2):10–11.

Tollefson, James W. (1981). Centralized and decentralized language planning. *Language Problems and Language Planning 5* (2):175–188.

Tsongas, Paul E. (1981). Foreign languages and America's interests. *Foreign Language Annals 14* (2):115–119.

Valverde, Leonard A. and Frank Brown (1978). Equal educational opportunity and bilingual-bicultural education: a socioeconomic perspective. *Education and Urban Society X* (3):277–294.

Van Dyke, Vernon (1976). Human rights without distinction as to language. *International Studies Quarterly 20* (1):3–38.

Williams, Colin H. (1981). The territorial dimension in language planning: an evaluation of its potential in contemporary Wales. Language Problems and Language Planning 5 (1):57–73.

Wooten, James T. (1977). Carter in Warsaw on six-nation tour. *The New York Times,* 1:4. Dec. 30.

Zachariev, Z. (1978). Droits linguistiques et droits à l'éducation dans les sociétés plurilingues. *International Review of Education XXIV* (3):263–272.

Official Languages and Language Planning

Richard Ruiz (1990)

1. Introduction

In November, 1986, voters in California approved a Constitutional amendment declaring English to be the official language of the state. This has significance for several reasons. In recent years, proponents of an English Language Amendment (ELA) to the Constitution of the United States have failed on a number of occasions to persuade the Congress of the need for such a measure; partly as a result of those failures, lobbying groups such as *U.S. English* turned their attention to the states. The states held out the promise that constitutional amendments could be considered directly by the electorate, rather than by legislators who may be reluctant to vote on such a controversial and potentially divisive issue. Furthermore, passage of an ELA at the state level would encourage the argument that, perhaps, the country as a whole is ready to entertain such an amendment to the federal constitution.

The California amendment is also important for another reason: It is intended as a means by which substantive changes can be made in public policy and service delivery; specifically, it was aimed at the provision of bilingual education and bilingual ballots, although other aspects of the state's official business were also of concern (Diamond n.d.; Tomás Rivera Center 1986). While California was not the first state to adopt an ELA, most of the previous amendments (such as in Indiana) were largely regarded as symbolic – on the order of adopting a state flower or bird. Finally, the 1986 passage in California was significant because of both the magnitude of the victory and the demographics of the election. The measure received more than 70% of the votes; perhaps more significant, it attracted a large percentage of the Hispanic vote: Even if one doubts the claims of *U.S. English* that a majority of voters within all ethnic groups voted in favor (Diamond n.d.), it is clear that the California campaign was enormously successful.

What arguments for making English the state's official language could be so compelling? We can represent them here in broad outline:

- Ethnic groups today are less willing to assimilate, with respect to language behavior or anything else (cf. Lambert and Taylor 1987). The social fragmentation that results from this poses a threat to national unity;
- Non-English language groups are being encouraged to maintain their insulated enclaves through public policies such as bilingual ballots and bilingual education;
- These services are inordinately expensive to the (predominantly non-ethnic) taxpayers of the state;
- The primacy of English as the language in which the state does its official business is at risk; a measure ensuring the status of English is a way to discourage the development of competing "official" languages.

This last point draws attention to what may be the most pervasive effect that the ELA movement has had on U.S. society. Its very existence informs the citizenry that what the great majority of us had taken for granted was a myth: English is not now, nor has it ever been, the official language of the United States. Acknowledgement of this fact leads to a series of questions: Why has English never been so designated? What would officialization entail? What, after all, is meant by "official"? The first question is a matter of historical interpretation; various writers have provided us with their views (Heath 1981; Edwards 1985), and we have time to do little more than mention them here. The remaining questions are treated best by referring to a literature that is not generally well-known in the United States – a body of work collectively referred to as "language planning." The next few pages will be a general introduction to language planning; included in the discussion of its basic processes will be an attempt to answer the question of what is entailed in the officialization of languages. Next, I will discuss the development of policy about the status of languages. Finally, I will present five propositions about language officialization. The available examples of this process are international; an elaboration of the five propositions will pay special attention to language planning activities – particularly ELA movements – in the United States.

2. Language Planning and Language Policy

This section presents definitions of language planning, discusses its major dimensions, and outlines its basic processes. (For a more complete review, see Eastman 1983).

2.1. Definitions of language planning

Language planning as a professional field and as a scholarly literature is relatively young; its major contribution has been in our understanding of the role of language in nation-building. Many of the early language planning texts (e.g. Fishman et al. 1968; Rubin & Jernudd 1971) served as much to report on the activities of "developing" nations as to introduce a new area of academic research. This emphasis on "development contexts" is no doubt a reason many in the U.S. have not heard of language planning, much less thought of it as having relevance to western societies (Fishman 1975: 84, passim). This emphasis also helps to explain why the greater part of the language planning literature, even now, consists of case studies; the work of language planners is more practice than theory, since they are concerned with solving real, everyday language problems, sometimes in very trying circumstances, rather than developing a conceptual literature. Still, valuable theoretical contributions have been made by writers such as Jyotyrindra Das Gupta, Charles Ferguson, Joshua Fishman, Einar Haugen, Bjorn Jernudd, Joan Rubin, and others. Linguists and sociolinguists are attracted somewhat naturally to this field; scholars from other areas such as economics, political science, history, anthropology, education, and law have made language planning a multidisciplinary field.

The multidisciplinary nature of the field makes a unitary definition difficult. Rubin and Jernudd define language planning as "decision making about language," especially about *"deliberate* language change" (1971: xiii, xvi). Jernudd and Das Gupta describe it as "a political and administrative activity for solving language problems in society" (1971: 211). Similarly, Fishman thinks of it as the "organized pursuit of solutions to societal language problems" (1975: 210). Karam, in an attempt to synthesize early language planning work, also focuses on the activities of problem identification and resolution (1974: 105). Another perspective on language planning, one that draws attention to its relationship with a more general social planning, is offered by Eastman: "Language planning is the activity of manipulating language as a social resource in order to reach objectives set out by planning agencies which, in general, are an area's governmental, educational, economic, and linguistic authorities" (1983: 29).

Definitions of language planning vary because of differences in the disciplinary traditions from which the expositors come, as well as the exigencies of the particular work contexts in which they might find themselves. For the moment, it is enough for us to note that these definitions all suggest that while language planning is *at least* about language, it is rarely *only* about language.

2.2. Dimensions of language planning

The idea that language planning is a form of social or national planning is illustrated in the following list of some of the concerns of language planners:

language officialization
foreign language education
alphabet development ("graphization")
usage problems ("language purification")
language and technology ("language modernization")
dictionary/grammar development ("language standardization")
orthography problems
education of language minority groups
language and business
plain language legislation
interpretation services
language and the law ("forensic linguistics")
document design
readability formulas
literacy
language testing
voting rights
gender-neutrality in language
language revival
immigration/citizenship requirements
censorship
media access
language maintenance and shift
computer languages

The language planner is directly concerned with the resolution of techni-cal and technological problems, to be sure; these include developing alpha-bets, adapting lexicons to new domains of social experience (e.g. technology), and dictionary-making. It should be noted, however, that even these activi-ties that deal explicitly with the language itself have been preceded by deci-sions about matters much broader than that: Economics, aesthetics, ideology, politics, culture, law, and education.

2.3. Language planning processes

I will distinguish between those activities of language planners that have primarily to do with change in the language itself (lexicon, orthography, and so on) and those that have primarily to do with the place or role of the lan-guage or language variety within the society (its designation as an "official" language, for example). This distinction has come to be known most com-monly as one between "corpus planning" and "status planning" (Eastman 1983: 70–76, passim; Cobarrubias 1983; Keller 1983). Within these basic cat-egories of language planning activity, Fishman (1974), drawing on the work of other sociolinguists, identifies five major processes:

(i) *Policy formulation* results in a decision about language in the society – whether to officialize one or several languages, whether to promote one over others, whether to permit the limited use of one or some, and so on. Policy formulation is the product of deliberations that ideally include the following dimensions: sociolinguistic assessment (in which a survey is made of the varieties spoken, their distribution, attitudes held toward them and toward any kind of change, and so on); needs assessment (in which an appraisal is made of why a language change is necessary); impact assessment (in which planners anticipate as best they can how a language policy change will address the identified needs); articulation plan (in which the new policy is fitted into others that already exist or are anticipated); and finally the formulation itself (which is an explicit statement of goals, plans, purposes, and so on).

(ii) *Codification* is often necessary in the case of a language selected to function in a domain in which it had previously not served. The choice of a local vernacular as a medium of instruction in school may do little good if it has not been reduced to writing or standardized to some degree. Codification includes graphization (the development of a writing system) and grammatication (the development of a system of structural rules for the production of language).

(iii) *Elaboration* is a process whereby a language is extended and adapted for use in new domains. This could include lexical elaboration (the development of new words, forms, and conventions) sociolinguistic extension (stretching the meaning of terms into new domains of experience) and what is sometimes called "modernization" (the calibration of a language system with that of one with more technical or technological usefulness).

(iv) *Implementation* includes plans and strategies for carrying out the new policy. It is, therefore, a process that spans the division between corpus and status planning. It includes a system of enforcement, promotion, capacitation, and sanctions designed to allow the policy to be sustained and developed.

(v) *Evaluation*, finally, allows language planners and policy-makers to monitor, adjust, or change the policy if it is not successful. Evaluation requires the development of a set of criteria by which to measure the effects of the policy. It is a process that continues throughout the life of the policy.

The distinction between corpus planning and status planning, along with the processes we have just discussed, can be represented as in figure 1.

Three points should be made about these processes. First, it is important that corpus planning and status planning be considered more or less simultaneously. To declare and promote an official language, with little regard to whether or not there is anything for speakers of the language to read (cf. Hornberger 1985), is a symbolic gesture, at best; at worst, it is a cruel hoax

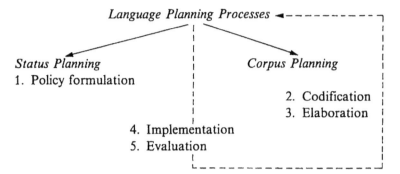

Figure 1 Language planning processes

played out by government agents for crassly utilitarian reasons. Second, the line between corpus and status planning is fuzzy precisely because it is difficult in practice to make strict delineations in this area (Fishman 1974: 23). The nature of the writing system (characters as opposed to letters, etc.), for example, could have much to do with the development of the status of a particular language. Third, the process outlined above represents an ideal pattern of activity; rarely does language policy develop in this way – but it would be better if it did.

2.4. Language planning orientations

In an earlier paper (Ruiz 1984), I suggest that language planning and policy development proceed within one or more "orientations," which are defined as a "complex of dispositions toward language and its role, and toward languages and their role in society" (1984: 16). My contention is that the process of language policy development is embedded in one or more of three basic orientations, language-as-problem, language-as-right, and language-as-resource:

(i) *Language-as-problem* construes the targets of language policy to be a kind of social problem to be identified, eradicated, alleviated, or in some other way resolved. Local vernaculars and their communities are the most common "beneficiaries" of language policies aimed at moving them into the dominant mainstream. In the officially received view, in the view of the outside community, and frequently in the view of the local community itself, the local vernacular is an important determinant of poverty and disadvantage; doing away with the problem involves doing away with the local language and replacing it with the dominant standard. The policy of subtractive bilingualism is often regarded as benign by the dominant society – a way of providing for equality of opportunity.

(ii) *Language-as-right* often is a reaction to these sorts of policies from within the local communities themselves. It confronts the assimilationist tendencies of dominant communities with arguments about the legal, moral, and natural right to local identity and language; it refutes the notion that minority communities are somehow made "better" through the loss of their language and culture. The language-as-right orientation is most visible, however, when the dominant language-as-problem orientation is taken to extremes: When language diversity is seen as a problem *in itself*, calling for language eradication *as a condition of individual and social betterment*, legal and quasi-legal remedies are regarded by minority communities as the last step before war or surrender (Kelman 1971: 36).

(iii) *Language-as-resource* is an orientation that has received very little emphasis, either in the literature or in actual language policy development (see, however, Jernudd and Das Gupta 1971 and Ozolins 1985 as valuable contributions to this orientation). It presents the view of language as a social resource; policy statements formulated in this orientation should serve as guides by which language is preserved, managed and developed. The tendency to view resources in purely utilitarian terms, however, should be resisted: Language is, after all, a human quality that cannot be treated as just another commodity. To the extent that the language-as-resource orientation draws attention to the social importance of all communities and their languages, and to the extent that it promotes tolerance and even acceptance of minority languages, it holds promise for reducing social conflict in a way that the other two cannot match.

3. Language Status

We need now to address questions of language status: What is an "official" language? How does it gain that status? What is the difference between an "official" language and a "national" language, if any?

3.1. Official language

This term is difficult to define because of its many uses in the literature. For example, Asmah (1985) discusses the Malayan National Language Policy of 1957 that established Bhasa Malaysia the official language of the country, although English was to remain official as well for a period of ten years. In 1967, with the Revised National Language Act, Malay was declared the sole official language in peninsular Malaysia, except in the courts where English is still the "operational language" (Asmah 1985: 41; see, also, Davey, 1990). In this case, English seems to have attained a kind of permanent "limited-official" status. Similarly, Conrad and Fishman (1977) have trouble listing countries by official language because of the many different designations and procedures. They make a useful distinction between policy and practice: A language is official because it has been declared so in authoritative policy statements, or because it is used for official purposes (1977: 8–10). Keller (1983) illustrates this second usage of "official" when he suggests that Spanish has attained a "sort of official status" because of its use in certain domains, especially education, media, civil rights, and voting (1983: 255).

We can summarize by formalizing these two conceptions of "official language" as follows:

(i) *Official language-(d)* refers to a language *declared* official for public governmental functions by an administrative authority.
(ii) *Official language-(p)* refers to a language used for official governmental *purposes.*

The criticism that Cobarrubias (1983) brings against Keller's use of official language-(p) is justified, it seems to me; judged by the criterion of use, any language, theoretically, can be considered "official" in the United States, since the provision of public bilingual education, interpretation services, voting materials, and the like is at least possible in many languages. One might say that the purpose of *U.S. English* and other ELA proponents is to take us away from the commonsense notion of "official-(p)" toward the more formal "official-(d)."

Yet another category of "official language" is worth noting. Cobarrubias discusses "endoglossic," "exoglossic," and "mixed" states (1983: 43). An "endoglossic" state is one where the official language-(d) is, or is considered to be, indigenous: Quechua in Peru, Bahasa Malaysia in Malaysia, Pilipino in the Philippines, and so on. An "exoglossic" state is one where the official language-(d) has been imported – the situation that exists in colonial situations, frequently even after independence (Conrad and Fishman 1977). A "mixed" state combines an indigenous with an outside official language-(d). While the endo/exoglossic distinction is difficult to hold very strictly (Ness 1987, for example, demonstrates the problem of classifying the Vietnamese "national language" within this dichotomy, since both indigenous and outside agents have contributed to its construction over centuries), it helps to explain the differences between a language-as-problem and language-as-resource orientation discussed earlier: Exoglossic and mixed states predominate in the third world, while endoglossic states are the norm in the west.

3.2. National language

"National language" appears to be used in two different ways in the language planning literature, as well. For example, Asmah (1985) argues that it is natural that Malay be the official language of Malaysia since, as the "national language," it is symbolic of nationhood:

> To the Malays and the *bumiputra* people, that the choice fell on Malay was the most natural thing. It is the language of the soil. … Superficially, it would have been fair to choose a language which is not identifiable with any community – fair and square. However, traditions die hard. The Malays, as a race, would rather die than lose their language to a foreign one. The motto *Bahasa Jiwa Bangsa* (Language is the soul of a nation) is deeply ingrained in them. … Besides, the national language not only has a utility role; it also has a symbolic function. It exudes emotion – one that gives the feeling of pride and attachment to one's country. (1985: 45–46)

Similarly, Edwards (1985: 17) and Kelman (1971: 194) discuss the role of language as a symbol of nationalism.

Ness (1987: 91) uses "national language" to mean a language the use of which is geographically or functionally extensive; it is in this sense, I think, that people in the United States speak of English as the "national language." It is in contrast to "regional" or "limited" languages.

We can set out the difference in these two senses of "national language" in the following way:

(i) *National language-(s)* is a language *symbolic* of national identity.
(ii) *National language-(g)* is a language *geographically* or functionally widespread.

It should be noted that "national language" and "official language" are frequently used interchangeably. This is evident in discussions about "choosing a national language" (Eastman 1983: 36). The adoption of "national language" in either of the senses presented above renders such locutions unfelicitous. One can *choose, designate,* or *declare* an "official language" (and certainly there is nothing to preclude one from choosing a "national language" as an "official language"), but it is better to say that one can do little more than *promote* a "national language."

4. Types of Language Policies in Relation to Language Status

Given our analysis above of "official" and "national" languages, we can proceed to a modest typology of language policies in relation to the status of the languages. This will lead, in time, to a discussion of the language policy change proposed for the United States and an assessment of its impact.

4.1. A national language-(s) is an official language-(d)

This arrangement – a declared, but symbolic official language – is the situation for Burmese in Burma (Allott 1985: 147–148), Quechua in Peru (Hornberger 1985), Swahili in Kenya and Tanzania (Larmouth 1987; Conrad and Fishman 1977), Bahasa Malaysia in Malaysia (Asmah 1985), among others. In the relatively few cases in which this situation obtains, these tend to be "mixed" rather than purely "endoglossic" states in which the indigenous language shares official status with a language of wider communication. In such an arrangement, the national language community has likely conceded some of its ethnic identity in the interest of a more general national integration.

4.2. A national language-(s) is not an official language-(d)

This pattern – an undeclared, symbolic official language – is the classic exoglossic state, which is the most common legacy of colonialism. Examples are Nigeria, Gambia, Ghana, and Sierra Leone (Conrad and Fishman 1977). There are, of course, pragmatic arguments to justify such situations; but it is also difficult to deny the effects of a history of language oppression.

4.3. A national language-(g) is an official language-(d)

This situation – a declared national language of wide geographic and functional distribution – is common in powerful centralized states such as the USSR and China (PRC), although it is also true of other nations that emphasize strong language-nation linkage (such as Spain, France, and Mexico) (Edwards 1985). These can be arrangements full of language conflict since minority groups sometimes perceive their language to be a barrier to social advance (see Fought 1985; Woolard 1985).

4.4. A national language-(g) is not the official language-(d)

The United States and the United Kingdom are perhaps the most obvious examples of this language policy type – an undeclared official language of wide geographical and functional distribution. The reluctance to legislate in matters of language is partly an idiosyncrasy of Anglo-American jurisprudence (Heath 1981), partly a result of the recognition, at least up to now, that the technological and commercial power of English was enough to sustain its status. The effect of promoting no language in particular in these states has been a perception on the part of non-English communities of linguistic tolerance, at least on the part of governmental authorities; the relative lack of linguistic conflict which has been the result is its own recommendation for such a language policy.

4.5. An official language-(d) is not a national language-(g)

Such cases – a declared official language with only limited distribution – are rare. Examples include Romansch in Switzerland and Quechua in Peru, two regional, limited languages. They result (at least in the case of Peru) from a perception on the part of governmental functionaries that the time was right for movement toward a language-as-resource orientation (Hornberger 1985). It remains to be seen whether merely extending official status to a long-oppressed language, without much consideration for problems of implementation, will be more than symbolism.

5. Language Policy Change in the United States

U.S. English and other advocates of an ELA in the United States are proposing a significant language policy change. At the moment, U.S. policy approximates the fourth of the five possibilities listed above: A geographically widespread national language-(g) which is not the declared, official language-(d). It is my contention that this policy, in comparison with the other types listed, has had the most success in avoiding serious language conflict. The burden falls on the ELA movement to explain what benefits would result from the proposed policy change, and how those benefits would outweigh the problems created by disengaging the present very successful policy.

6. Five Propositions About Language Officialization

By way of summary and conclusion, I offer the following propositions as the beginning of a conceptual framework by which we might understand language officialization and its problems.

6.1. Language officialization is generally associated with nation-building

This suggests that officialization movements are evidence of the perception of instability. This is understandable within emerging nations struggling to establish a national identity. Ayto (1983) demonstrates that such language planning concerns were also a feature of the early United States. The emergence of language officialization movements in the 1980s, however, a period of unparalleled English hegemony domestically and internationally, is a puzzle. It suggests, perhaps, that the actual "risk" perceived by ELA movers is something beyond language.

6.2. Language officialization is usually attended by some corpus planning

This is merely a restatement of the language planning axiom that status planning and corpus planning should proceed more or less simultaneously; there are numerous examples of such simultaneous development (Allott 1985; Whiteley 1969). It is, therefore, important to ask what corpus planning activities are proposed by ELA advocates in the United States. I have found none. I explain this by suggesting that this language officialization movement is not really about language at all, but about society. Language serves as a symbol for diversity and the diffusion of power; the perceived threat is not language, but language communities and their potential to disturb existing power relations in the society. This sort of movement has correlates in other societies (cf. Tollefson 1986).

6.3. Language officialization is usually poorly planned as to articulation and implementation

In the best language planning circumstances, articulation and implementation are problematic. Here, the literature gives us little help, since it usually presents policy statements and their results, but we seldom see how they got there (Fishman 1974: 20). One of the best descriptions of policy implementation is that for Burmese (Allott 1985); in that case, much thought was given to how the policy was to be carried out, as well as its anticipated effects. An important failure of ELA movements in the United States is the lack of thought as to how language officialization can be made consistent with our jurisprudential traditions (especially those dealing with free speech) and on what the anticipated effects of the policy change might be.

6.4. Language officialization proceeds generally from three language planning orientations: Language-as-problem, language-as-right, and language as resource

Several writers demonstrate that it is common for a language policy over time to endorse all three of these positions (Bowcock 1985; Hornberger 1985; Ozolins 1985). Sometimes language policies aimed at different languages and their communities vary in their underlying orientations. In the United States, for example, ELA movements advocate a policy discouraging public promotion of ethnic languages through bilingual education, but they endorse public support of foreign language study. Ethnic languages are treated as problems, on the one hand, foreign languages as resources, on the other.

6.5. Language officialization imposes status, not legitimacy

Movements for language officialization need not result in language conflict. Even critics of linguistic hegemony see that a language of wider communication can have a proper role in local communities (Afolayan 1984; Phillipson, Skutnabb-Kangas, and Africa 1986), and that its promotion can be legitimate. But such promotion cannot be harsh; it cannot be perceived as a threat to the survival of local languages, or conflict is almost a certain result (Adler 1977; Haugen 1985; Weinstein 1983). Proponents of an ELA in the United States profess a concern for national unity; to that end, they seek to constrain the language behavior of non-English speakers. They could benefit from the advice of H. C. Kelman, a thoughtful student of language conflict:

> Although my bias against deliberate attempts to create national identity derives from my value position, I also believe that this is not a very effective way of promoting national unity. I would propose … that a sense of national identity is more likely to develop when it is not forced but allowed to emerge out of functional relationships within the national society. (Kelman 1971: 38)

There is still no adequate explanation forthcoming as to why the United States should ignore this advice and disrupt a 200 year history of relatively successful linguistic tolerance.

References

Abramson, H.J. 1980 Assimilation and pluralism. *Harvard Encyclopedia of American Ethnic Groups,* 150–60. Cambridge, MA: Harvard University Press.

Adler, M.K. 1977 *Welsh and the Other Dying Languages in Europe: A Sociolinguistic Study.* Hamburg: Helmut Buske.

Afolayan, A. 1984 The English language in Nigerian education as an agent of proper multilingual and multicultural development. *Journal of Multilingual and Multicultural Development* 5:1–22

Agar, M. 1983 Political talk: Thematic analysis of a policy argument. *Policy Studies Review* 2:601–14.

Akutagawa, M. 1987 A linguistic minority under the protection of its own ethnic state: A case study in an Irish Gaeltacht. In *Third International Conference on Minority Languages: Celtic Papers,* ed. G. MacEoin, A. Ahlqvist, and D. O'hAodha, 125–46. Clevedon, Avon: Multilingual Matters.

Allardt, E. 1979 Implications of the ethnic revival in modern, industrialized society. *Commentationes Scientiarium Socialium* 12. Helsinki: Societas Scientiarium Fennica.

Allott, A.J. 1985 Language policy and language planning in Burma. In *Language Policy, Language Planning and Sociolinguistics in South-east Asia,* ed. D. Bradley, 131–54. Papers in South-east Asian Linguistics 9. Canberra: Australia National University, Department of Linguistics.

Amastae, J. 1982 Language maintenance and shift in the Rio Grande Valley of South Texas. In *Bilingualism and Language Contact: Spanish, English, and Native American*

Languages, ed. F. Barkin, E.A. Brandt, and J. OrnsteinôGalicia, 261–77. Bilingual Education Series 3. New York: Teacher's College, Columbia University Press.

American Institutes for Research 1978 *Evaluation of the Impact of ESEA Title VII Spanish/ English Bilingual Education Programs*. Los Angeles: National Dissemination and Assessment Center, California State University, Los Angeles.

Anderson, B. 1983 *Imagined Communities: Reflections on the Origin and Spread of Nationalism.* London: Verso

Annamalai, E. 1979 *Language Movements in India*. Mysore: Central Institute of Indian Languages.

Annamalai, E. 1986 Comment: legal vs. social. *International Journal of the Sociology of Language* 69:145–151

Arizona Department of Education 1985 *Bilingual Programs and English as a Second Language Programs. Annual Report, 1984–1985*. Phoenix, AZ: Arizona Department of Education, Bilingual Unit.

Arizona Department of Education 1986 *Bilingual Programs and English as a Second Language Programs. Annual Report, 1985–1986*. Phoenix, AZ: Arizona Department of Education, Bilingual Unit.

Arizona Department of Education 1987 *Statistics on Adult Education, Basic Education, and ESL*. Phoenix, AZ: Arizona Department of Education, Division of Adult Education.

Arizona Department of Education 1989 *Bilingual Programs and English as a Second Language Programs. Annual Report, 1987–1988*. Phoenix, AZ: Arizona Department of Education, Bilingual Unit.

Arizonans Against Constitutional Tampering 1988 Proposition on 106 loses more ground. Press release (October 20). Phoenix, AZ: Arizonans Against Constitutional Tampering.

Arocha, Z. 1988 Dispute fuels campaign against 'Official English'. *The Washington Post* (November 6), A, 20–21.

Asmah, H.O. 1979 *Language Planning for Unity and Efficiency*. Kuala Lumpur: Penerbit Universiti Malaya.

Asmah, H.O. 1985 The language policy of Malaysia: A formula for balanced pluralism. In *Language Policy, Language Planning and Sociolinguistics in South-east Asia,* ed. D. Bradley, 39–49. Papers in South-east Asian linguistics 9. Canberra: Australian National University Department of Linguistics.

Australia: Commonwealth Department of Education 1982 *Towards a National Language Policy*. Canberra: Australian Government Printing Service.

Ayto, J. 1983 English: Failures of language reforms. In *Language Reform: History and Future,* ed. Istvan F. and C. Hagege, 1:85–100. Hamburg: Helmut Buske.

Badia i Margarit, A. 1969 *La llengua del Barcelonins*. Barcelona: Editions 62.

Baetens Beardsmore, H. 1980 Bilngualism in Belgium. *Journal of Multilingual and Multicultural Development* 1,2:145–154

Baetens, Beardsmore, H., and R. Willemyns 1986 Comment. *International Journal of the Sociology of Language* 60:117–128.

Baker, K. and A. de Kanter 1986 Assessing the legal profession's contribution to the education of bilingual students. *La Raza Law Journal* 1:295.

Barkin, F., E.A. Brandt, and J. Ornstein-Galicia, eds. 1982 *Bilingualism and Language Contact: Spanish, English, and Native American Languages*. Bilingual Education Series 3. New York: Teachers College, Columbia University Press.

Barthes, R. 1972 Mythologies. New York: Hill & Wang.

Beebe, J., and M. Beebe 1981 The Filipinos: a special case. In *Language in the USA*, ed. C.A. Ferguson and S.B. Heath, 322–338. Cambridge: Cambridge University Press.

Beer, W.R. 1980 *The Unexpected Rebellion: Ethnic Activism in Contemporary France*. New York: New York University Press.

Beer, W.R. 1985 Toward a theory of linguistic mobilization. In *Language Policy and National Unity*, ed. W.R. Beer and J.E. Jacob, 217–35. Totowa, NJ: Rowan and Allanheld.

Beer, W.R., and J.E. Jacob, eds. 1985 *Language Policy and National Unity*. Totowa, NJ: Rowan and Allanheld.

Bikales, G. 1986 Comment: the other side. *International Journal of the Sociology of Language* 60:77–85.

Bikales, G., and G. Imhoff 1985 *A Kind of Discordant Harmony: Issues in Assimilation*. Washington, D.C.: U.S. English.

Bills, G., and A. Hudson-Edwards 1980 Intergenerational language shift in an Albuquerque barrio. In *Festschrift for Jacob Ornstein*, ed. E.L. Blansitt and R.V. Teschner, 139–58. Rowley, MA: Newbury House.

Binder, D. 1983 1983 election: A trend toward conservatism must still await 1984 for confirmation. *The Pettit Report* 4:23–24.

Bowcock, D.C. 1985 Educational language planning in Gambia. Unpublished doctoral dissertation, University of Wisconsin-Madison.

Brandt, E.A. 1988 Applied linguistic anthropology and American Indian language renewal. *Human Organization* 47,4:322–329.

Browning, M. 1980 Antibilingual backers celebrate early. *The Miami Herald* (November 5), A:11.

Buckley, W.F., Jr. 1988 On the right. Bilingualism promotes separatism, does immigrants no favors. *Albuquerque* Journal (November 9), 11A.

Burrows, T., J. Clark, and S. Klein 1980 What students know about their world. *Change* 12:10–17, 67.

Cardoza, D., L. Huddy, and D. Sears 1984 *The Symbolic Attitudes Study: Public Attitudes toward Bilingual Education*. Study for the National Center for Bilingual Research. Washington, D.C.: National Institute of Education.

Castro, M. 1988 Racism and the official language movement. Ms. Miami: Greater Miami United.

Central Statistics Office 1976 *Census of Population of Ireland 1971. Irish Language, with Special Tables for the Gaeltacht Areas, 8*. Dublin: Stationery Office.

Central Statistics Office 1984 *Census of Population of Ireland 1981. Bulletin No. 41-Ireland*. Dublin: The Stationery Office.

Chafe, W. 1962 Estimates regarding the present speakers of North American Indian languages. *International Journal of American Linguistics* 28:162–171.

Cheng, L.-R.L. 1987 *Assessing Asian Language Performance: Guidelines for Evaluating Limited-English-Proficient Students*. Excellence in Practice Series. Rockville, MD: Aspen Publishers.

Christian, J.M. and C.C. Christian, Jr. 1966 Spanish language and culture in the Southwest. In *Language Loyalty in the United States*, ed. J.A. Fishman et. al., 280–317. The Hague: Mouton.

Clyne, M. 1984 *Language and Society in the German Speaking Countries*. Cambridge: Cambridge University Press.

Coates, J. 1986 *Women, Men and Language*. London: Longman.

Cobarrubias, J. 1983 Ethical issues in status planning. In *Progress in Language Planning: International Perspectives*, ed. J. Cobarrubias and J.A. Fishman, 41–85. Contributions to the Sociology of Language 31. Berlin: Mouton.

Coimisiún um Athbheochan na Gaeilge [Commission on the Restoration of the Irish Language] 1964 *An Tuarascáil Dheiridh [Final Report]*. Dublin: The Stationery Office.

Collier, R., and C. Sowers 1988 State Worker 'afraid to speak Spanish' sues 'official English'. *Arizona Republic* (November 11), A:1,11.

Collier, V.P. 1987 Students and second language acquisition. *NABE News* 11:4–5.

Combs, M.C., and J. Trasvina 1986 Legal implications of the English language amendment. *The "English Plus" Project*, 24–31. Washington, D.C.: LULAC.

Commission on Declining Enrollments 1978 *Working Paper* 22:37–8. Ottawa: Government of Ontario, Commission on Declining Enrollments.

Commissioner of Official Languages 1978 *Report 35.* Ottawa: Government of Canada, Commissioner of Official Languages.

Committee on Irish Language Attitudes Research 1975 *Report.* Dublin: The Stationery Office.

Comrie, B., ed. 1987 *The World's Major Languages.* New York: Oxford University Press.

Conklin, N.F., and M.A. Lourie 1983 *A Host of Tongues: Language Communities in the United States.* New York: Free Press.

Conrad, A.W., and J.A. Fishman 1977 English as a world language: The evidence. In *The Spread of English: The Sociology of English as an Additional Language*, ed. J.A. Fishman, R.L. Cooper, and A.W. Conrad, 3–76. Rowley, MA: Newbury House.

Corbeil, J.-C. 1980 *L'Amenagement linguistique au Québec.* Montreal: Guerin.

Craddock, J.R. 1981 New World Spanish. In *Language in the USA*, ed. C.A. Ferguson and S.B. Heath, 196–211. Cambridge University Press.

Crawford, J. 1986 Immersion method is faring poorly in bilingual study. *Education Week* 5,31 (April 23):1,10.

Crawford, J. 1987 Group challenges U.S. English. *Education Week* 6,38 (June 17):15.

Crawford, J. 1988a Official English/English only: More than meets the eye. Washington, D.C.: English Plus Information Clearinghouse.

Crawford, J. 1988b Official English/amendment 11: Should English become Florida's official language? No. *The Miami Herald* (October 16), C:1.

Crawford, J. 1988c Official English would promote ethnic disunity. *Mesa [AZ] Tribune* (October 23), D-3.

Crawford, J. 1988d Split tongue: Self appointed guardians hide official English's real agenda. *Arizona Republic* (October 30), C:1,3.

Crawford, J. 1989 *Bilingual Education: History, Politics, Theory and Practice.* Trenton, NJ: Crane Publishing.

Crystal, D. 1987 *The Cambridge Encyclopaedia of Language.* Cambridge: Cambridge University Press.

Cuban American National Council, Inc. 1988a *America's English Need Not Divide Nor Censor.* Washington, D.C. and Miami, FL: Hispanic Information Center.

Cuban American National Council, Inc. 1988b Miami's Latin Business. Ms. Miami, FL: Cuban American National Council, Inc.

Cummins, J. 1981 The role of primary language development in promoting educational success for language minority students. *Schooling and Language Minority Students: A Theoretical Framework*, 3–49. Los Angeles: California State Department of Education, Office of Bilingual/Bicultural Education.

Curtis, E. 1919 The spoken languages of medieval Ireland. *Studies* 8:234–54.

Dale, C.V. 1983 *Legal Analysis of H.J.R. 169 Proposing to Amend the U.S. Constitution to Make English the Official Language of the United States.* Washington, D.C.: Congressional Research Service, Library of Congress.

Dale, C.V. 1985 Legal analysis of Senate Joint Resolution 167 proposing an amendment to the U.S. Constitution to make English the official language of the United States. *The English Language Amendment: Hearing before the Subcommittee on the Constitution of the Committee on the Judiciary, United States Senate, Ninety-Eighth Congress, Second Session on S.J. Res. 167, June 12, 1984, 32–35.* Washington, D.C.: U.S. Government Printing Office.

Datar, K.K. 1983 *Malaysia: Quest for a Politics of Consensus.* New Delhi: Vikas Publishing House.

Davey, W.G. 1990 In K. Adams & D. Brink (eds) *Perspectives on Official English: The Campaign for English as the Official Language of the USA* (pp. 95–104). Berlin: Mouton.

Davies, J. 1962 Toward a theory of revolution. *American Sociological Review* 27:5–19.

Davis, F.J. et al. 1962 Law as a type of social control. In *Society and the Law*, ed. F.J. Davis, et al., 39–64. Glencoe: Free Press.

de Certeau, M., D. Julia, and J. Revel 1975 *Une politique de la langue. La Revolution française et les patois*. Paris: Editions Gallimard.

DeLamater, J., D. Katz, and H.C. Kelman 1969 On the nature of national involvement: a preliminary study in an American community. *Journal of Conflict Resolution* 13.

de la Rosa, D. 1989 English literacy grants zero funded. *EPIC Events* (Newsletter of the English Plus Information Clearinghouse) 1,6 (March/April):1,10.

Detroit Free Press, February 14 1989 Petoskey doctor leads English-only crusade. 6a.

Deutsch, K.A. 1975 The social significance of linguistic conflicts. In *Les états multilingues*, ed. J.-G. Savard and R. Vigneault, 7–28. Quebec: Laval.

Diamond, Stanley n.d. Proposition 63 – English language initiative: A brief history. Mimeo. San Francisco: California English Campaign.

Dinstein, Y. 1976 Collective human rights of peoples and minorities. *International and Comparative Law Quarterly* 25:102.

Dwivedi, S. 1981 *Hindi on Trial*. New Delhi: Vikas.

Dyer, J., and K. Casteel 1987 3 of 4 Texans favor English-1st plan. *El Paso [TX] Times* (June 6), A:1.

Eastman, C.M. 1983 *Language Planning: An Introduction*. San Francisco: Chandler and Sharp.

Edwards, Congressman D. 1986 Bilingual ballots. *The "English Plus" Project*, 1–3. Washington, D.C.: LULAC.

Edwards, J. 1984 Irish and English in Ireland. In *Language in the British Isles*, ed. P. Trudgill, 480–98. Cambridge: Cambridge University Press.

Edwards, J. 1985 *Language, Society and Identity*. Oxford: Basil Blackwell.

English Plus 1988 Questions and answers about language enforcement. Ms. Washington, D.C.: English Plus Information Clearinghouse.

EPIC Events, March/April 1988 English Plus Information Clearing House Launched! 1,1:1.

Epstein, N. 1977 *Language, Ethnicity, and the Schools: Policy Alternatives for Bilingual Education*. Washington: Georgetown University Institute for Educational Leadership.

Esman, M.J. 1985 The politics of official bilingualism in Canada. In *Language Policy and National Unity*, ed. W.R. Beer and J.E. Jacobs, 45–66. Totowa, NJ: Rowman and Allanheld.

Estrada, L.F. n.d. *California's Non-English Speakers*. Claremont, CA: The Tomás Rivera Center.

Evan, W.M. 1980 Law as an instrument of social change. In *The Sociology of Law*, ed. W.M. Evan, 554–63. New York: Free Press.

Faber, M. 1987 ¿Inglés solamente o Inglés y más? Washington, D.C.: *NEA Today* 5,6 (March):6.

Falch, J. 1973 *Contribution à l'étude du Statut des langages en Europe*. Quebec: Laval University Press.

Fennell, D. 1981 Can a shrinking linguistic minority be saved? Lessons from the Irish experience. In *Minority Languages Today*, ed. E. Haugen, J. McClure, and D. Thomson, 32–39. Edinburgh: Edinburgh University Press.

Ferguson, C. 1959 Diglossia. *Word* 15:325–40.

Field Institute 1986 Prop. 63, the initiative which would declare English as the state's official language has very large majority support. The California Poll (August). San Francisco: Field Institute.

Fishman, J.A. 1960 The Systematization of the Whorfian Hypothesis. *Behavioral Science* 5:323–379.

Fishman, J.A. 1966 Some contrasts between linguistically homogeneous and linguistically heterogeneous polities. *Sociological Inquiry* 36:146–158.

Fishman, J.A. 1967 Bilingualism with and without diglossia; diglossia with and without bilingualism. *Journal of Social Issues* 32:29–38.

Fishman, J.A. 1968 Nationality-nationalism and nation-nationism. *In Language Problems of Developing Nations*, ed. J.A. Fishman, C. Ferguson, and J. Das Gupta, 39–51. New York: John Wiley and Sons.

Fishman, J.A. 1972 *Language and Nationalism: Two Integrative Essays*. Rowley, MA: Newbury House.

Fishman, J.A. 1974 Language planning and language planning research: The state of the art. In *Advances in Language Planning*, ed. J.A. Fishman, 15–33. The Hague: Mouton.

Fishman, J.A. 1975 Some implications of "The International Research Project on Language Planning Process (IRPLPP)" for sociolinguistic surveys. In *Language Surveys in Developing Nations: Papers and Reports on Sociolinguistic Surveys*, ed. S. Ohannessian, C.A. Ferguson, and E.C. Polomé, 209–20. Arlington, VA: Center for Applied Linguistics.

Fishman, J.A. 1980 The Whorfian hypothesis: varieties of valuation, confirmation and disconfirmation. *International Journal of the Sociology of Language* 26:25–40.

Fishman, J.A. 1981 Language policy: Past, present and future. In *Language in the USA*, ed. C.A. Ferguson and S.B. Heath, 116–26. Cambridge: Cambridge University Press.

Fishman, J.A. 1983 The sociology of English as an additional language. *In The Other Tongue: English Across Cultures*, ed. B.B. Kachru, 15–22. Oxford: Pergamon.

Fishman, J.A. 1985a Language, Ethnicity and Racism. In *The Rise and Fall of Ethnic Revival*, ed. J.A. Fishman et al., 3–13.

Fishman, J.A. 1985b Mother-tongue claiming in the United States since 1960: Trends and Correlates. *In The Rise and Fall of Ethnic Revival*, ed. J.A. Fishman et al., 107–194. Contributions to the Sociology of Language 37. Berlin: Mouton.

Fishman, J.A. 1985c Positive bilingualism: some overlooked rationales and forefathers. In *The Rise and Fall of Ethnic Revival*, ed. J.A. Fishman et al., 445–55. Contributions to the Sociology of Language 37. Berlin: Mouton.

Fishman, J.A. 1985d Whorfianism of the third kind: Ethnolinguistic diversity as a world-wide societal asset. In *The Rise and Fall of Ethnic Revival*, ed. J.A. Fishman et al., 473–87. Contributions to the Sociology of Language 37. Berlin: Mouton.

Fishman, J.A. 1986 Bilingualism and separatism. *Annals of the American Association of Political and Social Science* 487:169–80.

Fishman, J.A. 1988 "English only": Its ghosts, myths, and dangers. *International Journal of the Sociology of Language* 74:125–140.

Fishman, J.A. et al., eds. 1985 The Rise and Fall of Ethnic Revival. *Contributions to the Sociology of Language 37.* Berlin: Mouton.

Fishman, J.A., C.A. Ferguson, and J. Das Gupta, eds. 1968 *Language Problems of Developing Nations*. New York: Wiley.

Fishman, J.A. and J.E. Hofman 1966 Mother tongue and nativity in the American population. In *Language Loyalty in the United States*, ed. J.A. Fishman et. al., 34–50. The Hague: Mouton.

Fishman, J.A. and F. Solano 1988 Cross polity perspective on the importance of linguistic product. *Proceedings of the Heslington Conference on Sociolinguistic and Social Change.* Heslington: University of York.

Fishman, J.A. and F. Solano 1989 Cross polity perspective on the importance of linguistic heterogeneity as a 'contributing factor' in civil strife. In *Language and Ethnicity in Minority Sociolinguistic Perspective*, ed. J.A. Fishman, 605–26. Clevedon, Avon: Multilingual Matters.

Fiske, E.E. 1985 Education Department seeking to alter bilingual efforts. *New York Times* (September 26), A:1,2.

Fought, J. 1985 Patterns of Sociolinguistic inequality in Mesoamerica. In *Language of Inequality*, ed. N. Wolfson and J. Manes, 21–39. Berlin: Mouton.

Frost, R. 1949 *The Complete Works of Robert Frost*. New York: Holt.

Furet, F. and J. Ozouf 1977 *Lire et écrire. l'Alphabétisation des français de Calvin à Jules Ferry*. Paris: Les Editions de Minuit.

Gandhi, K.L. 1984 *The Problem of Official Language in India*. New Delhi: Arya.

Gee, J.P. 1986 Orality and literacy: From the savage mind to ways with words. *TESOL Quarterly* 20:719–47.

Genessee, F. 1987 *Learning through Two Languages: Studies of Immersion and Bilingual Education*. Rowley, MA: Newbury House.

Gilmer, P. 1986 Judeo-Spanish in Turkey. Unpublished doctoral dissertation, University of Texas at Austin.

Grimes, B.F. 1988 *Ethnologue*, 11th ed. Dallas: Summer Institute of Linguistics.

Grosjean, F. 1982 *Life with Two Languages: An Introduction to Bilingualism*. Cambridge, MA: Harvard University Press.

Gusfield, J. 1981 *The Culture of Public Problems: Drinking-Driving and the Symbolic Order*. Chicago: University of Chicago Press.

Hakuta, K. 1985 *The Causal Relation between the Development of Bilingualism. Cognitive Flexibility and Social-Cognitive Skills in Hispanic Elementary School Children*. Washington, D.C.: National Clearinghouse for Bilingual Education.

Hamers, J., J.-D. Gendron, and R. Vigneault, eds. 1984 *Du disciplinaire vers l'interdisciplinaire dans l'étude du contact des langues*. Quebec: Centre international de recherche sur le bilinguisme.

Handler, J.F. 1986 *The Conditions of Discretion: Autonomy, Community, Bureaucracy*. New York: Russell.

Hargreaves, D. 1984 *Improving Secondary Schools. Report of the Committee on the Curriculum and Organization of Secondary Schools*. London: Inner London Education Authority.

Harris, J., and L. Murtagh 1987 Irish and English in Gaeltacht primary schools. In *Third International Conference on Minority Languages: Celtic papers*, ed. G. MacEoin, A. Ahlqvist, and D. O'hAodha, 104–24. Clevedon, Avon: Multilingual Matters.

Haugen, E. 1985 The language of imperialism: unity or pluralism? In *Language and Inequality*, ed. N. Wolfson and J. Manes, 4–17. Berlin: Mouton.

Heath, S.B. 1977 Language and politics in the United States. In *Georgetown University Round Table on Languages and Linguistics*, ed. M. Saville-Troike, 267–96. Washington, D.C.: Georgetown University Press.

Heath, S.B. 1981 English in our language heritage. In *Language in the USA*, ed. C.A. Ferguson and S.B. Heath, 6–20. Cambridge: Cambridge University Press.

Heath, S.B., and F. Mandabach 1983 Language status decisions and the law in the United States. In *Progress in Language Planning: International Perspectives*, ed. J. Cobarrubias and J.A. Fishman, 87–103. Contributions to the Sociology of Language 31. Berlin: Mouton.

Hechter, M. 1975 *Internal Colonialism: The Celtic Fringe in British National Development, 1536–1966*. Berkeley: University of California Press.

Hertling, J. 1985 Bilingual policies have failed, need revisions, Bennett says. *Education Week* 5,5 (October 2):1,11,13.

Hill, C.P. 1986 Patterns of language use among Tanzanian secondary school pupils, 1970: a benchmark. In *Language in Education in Africa, Seminar Proceedings* 26. Edinburgh: Centre of African Studies.

Hirst, L. 1986 Native language promotes student achievement. In *NALI Proceedings*, ed. Suzanne Weryackwe, 47–50. Choctaw, OK: Native American Language Issues Institute (NALI) Planning Committee and Achukama Multicultural Indian Education (AMCIE).

Hitchen, R.C., and M.C. Combs 1986 The role of Spanish language media. *The "English Plus" Project*, 19–23. Washington, D.C.: LULAC.

Hornberger, N.H. 1985 Bilingual education and Quechua language maintenance in high-
     land Puno, Peru. Unpublished doctoral dissertation, University of
     Wisconsin-Madison.
Imhoff, G. 1987 Partisans of language. *English Today* 11:37–40.
Inglehardt, R. and M. Woodward 1967 Language conflicts and political community.
     Comparative Studies in Society and History 10,1:27–43.
Intertribal Council of Arizona 1987 Statement opposing the designation of English as the
     official language of Arizona. Press release (February 2). Phoenix, AZ: Intertribal
     Council of Arizona.
Irish Marketing Surveys, Ltd. 1969 *A Report on a Survey Conducted to Assess Public Reaction
     to "Buntús Cainte,"* 3 vols. Dublin: Irish Marketing Surveys, Ltd.
Irizarry, R. 1978 *Bilingual Education*. Technical Assistance Project, Center for the Study of
     Evaluation, Graduate School of Education, University of California, Los Angeles. Los
     Angeles: National Dissemination and Assessment Center.
Jernudd, B.H. and J. Das Gupta 1971 Towards a theory of language planning. *In Can
     Language be Planned? Sociolinguistic Theory and Practice for Developing Nations*, ed. J.
     Rubin and B.H. Jernudd, 195–215. Honolulu: University of Hawaii Press.
Kachru, B.B. 1983 Introduction: The other side of English. In *The Other Tongue: English
     Across Cultures*, ed. B.B. Kachru, 1–12. Oxford: Pergamon.
Kandiah, T. 1986 Comment. *International Journal of the Sociology of Language* 60:183–189.
Karam, F.X. 1974 Toward a definition of language planning. In *Advances in Language
     Planning*, ed. J.A. Fishman, 103–124. The Hague: Mouton.
Karst, K. 1986 Paths to Belonging: The Constitution and Cultural Identity. 64 *North
     Carolina Law Review* 304.
Keller, G.D. 1983 What can language planners learn from the Hispanic experience with
     corpus planning in the United States? *In Progress in Language Planning: International
     Perspectives*, ed. J. Cobarrubias and J.A. Fishman, 253–65. Contributions to the
     Sociology of Language 31. Berlin: Mouton.
Kelman, H.C. 1971 Language as an aid and barrier to involvement in the national system.
     In Can Language Be Planned? Sociological Theory and Practice for Developing Nations, ed.
     J. Rubin and B.H. Jernudd, 21–51. Honolulu: University of Hawaii Press.
Kloss, H. 1977 *The American Bilingual Tradition*. Rowley, MA: Newbury House.
Knoll, H. 1982 *Becoming Americans: Asian Sojourners, Immigrants and Refugees in the Western
     United States*. Portland, Oregon: Coast to Coast Books.
Krashen, S. 1981 *Principles and Practices in Second Language Acquisition*. Oxford: Pergamon.
Labov, W. 1972 *Sociolinguistic Patterns*. Philadelphia: University of Pennsylvania Press.
Lachapelle, R., and J. Henripen 1980 *La situation démolinguistique au Canada: évolution
     passée et prospective*. Montreal: Institute for Research on Public Policy.
Lagasse, C.E. 1982 *La Contre-réforme de l'état: Panorama des institutions de la Belgique*.
     Brussels: Ciaco éditeur.
Lambert, W.E., and E. Peal. 1962 The relation of bilingualism to intelligence. *Psychological
     Monographs* 76,27 (whole no. 546).
Lambert, W.E., and D. Taylor 1987 Language minorities in the U.S.: Conflicts around
     assimilation and proposed modes of accommodation. In *Ethnicity and Language*, ed.
     W.A. Van Horne, 90–123. Milwaukee: Institute on Race and Ethnicity.
Lambert, W.E., G.R. Tucker, and A. d'Anglejan 1973 Cognitive and attitudinal conse-
     quences of bilingual education. *Journal of Educational Psychology* 65:141–159.
Landry, W.J. 1986 Comment. *International Journal of the Sociology of Language* 60:
     129–138.
Laporte, P.-E. 1988 Where the majority is a minority: the difficulty of conflation in
     Quebec's language and education policies. Paper read at the conference on Minority
     Language Rights and Minority Education: European, Australian and North American
     Perspectives. Cornell University, Ithaca, NY, May 7–9.

Larmouth, D. 1987 Does linguistic heterogeneity erode national unity? In *Ethnicity and Language*, ed. W.A. Van Horne, 37–57. Milwaukee: Institute on Race and Ethnicity.

Las Cruces Sun-News, February 6a 1987 Carruthers opposes English as official language, 1A.

Las Cruces Sun-News, February 6b 1987 English language amendment killed, 1A.

Las Cruces Sun-News, February 15 1987 Letter to the editor, D. Shaw, 5A.

Las Cruces Sun-News, February 22 1987 Letter to the editor, M.B. Grothe, 5A.

Las Cruces Sun-News, March 10 1987 Panel OKs local senator's protection bill, 5A.

Las Cruces Sun-News, March 15 1987 Letter to the editor, Mr. and Mrs. R. Larsen, 5A.

League of United Latin American Citizens 1986 *The "English Plus" Program*. Washington, D.C.: LULAC.

Leap, W.L. 1981 American Indian languages. In *Language in the USA*, ed. C.A. Ferguson and S.B. Heath, 116–44. Cambridge: Cambridge University Press.

Leap, W.L. 1983 *Toward a Language Policy for Navajo Education: Background Considerations and Recommendations*. Albuquerque, NM: American Indian Bilingual Education Center, University of New Mexico.

Leap, W.L. 1988 Applied linguistics and American Indian language renewal: Introductory comments. *Human Organization* 47,4:238–291.

Leap, W.L., and D. Cissna 1984 *Final Report on the Makah Title VII Bilingual Program*. Neah Bay, WA.

Leap, W.L., and D. Cissna 1985 *Final Report and Evaluation on the Makah Title VII Bilingual Program*. Neah Bay, WA.

Lebon, A. 1986 Situation et avenir des jeunes issus de la migration: Une génération au centre des débats. *Working Paper, UNDP|ILO European Regional Project for Second Generation Migrants*. Geneva: ILO.

Lee, R.N., ed. 1986 *Ethnicity and ethnic relations in Malaysia*. DeKalb: Northern Illinois University Press.

Leibowicz, J. 1985 The proposed English language amendment: Shield or sword? *Yale Law and Policy Review*, 3:519–50.

Leibowitz, A. 1969 English Literacy: Legal Sanction for Discrimination. 45 *Notre Dame Lawyer* 7.

Leibowitz, A. 1976 Language and the law: the exercise of power through official designation of language. In *Language and Politics*, ed. W. O'Barr and J. O'Barr, 449–66. The Hague: Mouton.

Lent, J.A., ed. 1977 *Cultural Pluralism in Malaysia: Polity, Military, Mass Media, Education, Religion, and Social Class*. DeKalb: Northern Illinois University Press.

LePage, R.B. 1964 *The National Language Question: Linguistic Problems of Newly Independent States*. London: Oxford University Press.

Lewis, E.G. 1972 *Multilingualism in the Soviet Union*. The Hague: Mouton.

Lewis, E.G. 1978 The morality of bilingual education. *In International Dimensions of Bilingual Education*, ed. J. Alatis, 675–81. Georgetown University Round Table on Languages and Linguistics. Washington, D.C.: Georgetown University Press.

Lewis, E.G. 1980 *Bilingualism and Bilingual Education: A Comparative Study*. Albuquerque: University of New Mexico Press.

Li, C.N. 1988 *Minority Nationalities of China: Languages and Culture*. Berlin: Mouton DeGruyter.

Lieberson, S. and S. Hansen 1974 National development, mother-tongue diversity and the comparative study of nations. *American Sociological Review* 39,4:523–541.

Lijphart, A. 1977 *Democracy in Plural Societies*. New Haven: Yale University Press.

Lijphart, A. 1984 *Democracies: Patterns of Majoritarian and Consensus Government in Twenty-One Countries*. New Haven: Yale University Press.

Limage, L. 1984 Young migrants of the second generation in Europe: education and labour marker insertion prospects. *International Migration* 22:367–87.

Limage, L. 1985a Policy aspects of educational provision for children of migrants in western European schools. *International Migration* 23:251–62.

Limage, L. 1985b Multilingual educational provision in Belgium. In *Education and Intergroup Relations: An International Perspective*, ed. J.N. Hawkins and T.J. La Belle, 293–314. New York: Praeger.

Limage, L. 1987 Literacies and labor market prospects: migrant/minority youth. Paper presented at the Annual Conference of the Comparative and International Education Society, Washington, D.C., March 12–15.

Los Angeles Herald Examiner, October 21 1986 Vast majority polled back "English-only" initiative. A:1,7.

Mac Gréil, M. 1977 *Prejudice and Tolerance in Ireland.* Dublin: College of Industrial Relations.

Macnamara, J. 1971 Successes and failures in the movement for the restoration of Irish. In *Can Language be Planned? Sociolinguistic Theory and Practice for Developing Nations*, ed. J. Rubin and B. Jernudd, 65–94. Honolulu: University of Hawaii Press.

Magnet, J.E. 1986 The future of official language minorities. 27 *Cahiers de* Droit 189.

Magnet, J.E. 1988 Multiculturalism and collective rights. *In The Canadian Charter of Rights and Freedoms: Commentary, 2nd edition*, ed. E. Ratushny and G.-A. Beaudoin. Toronto: Carswell.

Maldoff, E. 1986 Comment: a Canadian perspective. *International Journal of the Sociology of Language* 60:105–114.

Margulies, P. 1981 Bilingual education, remedial language instruction, Title VI, and proof of discriminatory purpose: A suggested approach. *Columbia Journal of Law and Social Problems* 17:99–115.

Marshall, D.F. 1986a The question of an official language: language rights and the English language amendment; Rebuttal. *International Journal of the Sociology of Language* 60:7–75;201–211.

Marshall, D.F. 1986b English: an endangered language? *English Today* 6:21–24.

Marshall, D.F. 1988 Federal language rights in the United States. Paper read at the conference on Minority Language Rights and Minority Education: European, Australian and North American Perspectives. Cornell University, Ithaca, N.Y., May 7–9.

Marshall, D.F. 1989 Language spread and language preservation in China: problems in data and documentation. Paper read at the conference on Language Spread and Social Change: Dynamics and Measurement, Université Laval, Centre international de recherche sur le bilinguisme. Quebec, April 9–12.

Marshall, D.F. and Y. Chen, eds. 1990 The sociolinguistics of China. *International Journal of the Sociology of Language* 81.

McArthur, T. 1986 Comment: worried about something else. *International Journal of the Sociology of Language* 60:87–91.

McBee, S. 1985 English out to conquer the world. *U.S. News and World Report* (February 18), 49–52.

McCain, Congressman J. 1986 Bilingual education: The need for equity. *The "English Plus" Project*, 4–6. Washington, D.C.: LULAC.

McCarthy, D. 1968 Report of a speech by Dalton McCarthy at Portage la Prairie on August 5, 1889. In *The Manitoba School Question: Majority Rule or Minority Rights*, ed. L. Clark, 36–38. Toronto: Copp Clark.

McCarthy, K.F., and R.B. Valdez 1986 Current and future effects of Mexican immigration in California. *The California Roundtable*, May. Santa Monica, CA: Rand Corporation.

Mejias, H., and P. Anderson 1984 Language maintenance in southern Texas. *Southwest Journal of Linguistics* 7:116–24.

Mendoza, N. 1986 Bilingual education. *Phoenix [AZ] Gazette* (February 6), Opinion Page.

Metro-Dade Planning Department 1986 *Dade County's Hispanic-Origin Population, 1985.* Miami, FL: Research Division, Metro-Dade County Planning Department.

Miami Herald, August 17 1987. Se habla Espanol: Bilingualism becomes an economic issue, A:15.

Milan, W.G. 1986 Comment: undressing the English language amendment. *International Journal of the Sociology of Language* 60:93–96.

Milne, R.S. and D.K. Mauzy 1986. *Malaysia: Tradition, Modernity, and Islam.* Boulder, CO: Westview.

Moran, R.F. 1986 Foreword – the lessons of Keyes: How do you translate "The American dream"? 1 *La Raza Law Journal* 195: 211–12.

Moran, R.F. 1987 Bilingual education as a status conflict. 75 *California Law Review* 321,329.

Morokvasic, M. 1985 Aspiration au changement des femmes migrantes et vecu des jeunes filles de la 'seconde génération': le cas des jeunes Yougoslaves. *Working Paper. UNDP|ILO European Project Regional Project for Second Generation Migrants.* Geneva: ILO.

Mosher, E., A. Hastings & J. Wagoner, Jr. 1979 Pursuing Equal Educational Opportunity. New York: Institute for Urban and Minority Education, Teachers College, Columbia University.

National Center for Education Statistics 1978 Geographic distribution, nativity, and age distribution of language minorities in the United States, Spring 1976. *Bulletin*, NCES 78–134 (August 22).

National Council of La Raza 1986 *The Education of Hispanics: Status and Implications.* Washington, D.C.: National Council of La Raza.

Navajo Nation 1988 *Navajo Facts.* Window Rock, AZ: Navajo Nation, Division of Economic Development.

Ness, E. 1987 Language policy and education in Vietnam during the French colonial period. *University of Pennsylvania Working Papers in Educational Linguistics* 3:75–91.

Neustupny, J.V. 1970 Basic types of treatment of language problems. *Linguistic Communications* 1:77–98.

Newsweek, February 20 1989 Say it in English, 22–23.

New York Times, August 27 1987 Saying no to bilingual education, A:14.

Nichols, S.P. 1989 The official English movement in the United States with special reference to New Mexico and Arizona. Unpublished masters thesis, University of New Mexico.

Norman, J. 1988 *Chinese.* Cambridge: Cambridge University Press.

Nunberg, G. 1989 Linguists and the official language movement. *Language* 65,3:579–87.

O'Cinnéide, M., M. Keane, and M. Cawley 1985. Industrialization and linguistic change among Gaelic-speaking communities in the West of Ireland. *Language Problems and Language Planning* 9:3–16.

O'Domhnalláin, T. 1977 Ireland: The Irish language in education. *Language Problems and Language Planning* 1:83–96.

O'Domhnalláin, T. 1979 An Ghaeilge san oideachas [The Irish language in education]. *Teangeolas* 9:25–28.

Rubin, J. and B.H. Jernudd, eds. 1971 *Can Language Be Planned? Sociological Theory and Practice for Developing Nations.* Honolulu: University of Hawaii Press.

Ruiz, R. 1984 Orientations in language planning. *NABE Journal* 8:15–34.

Ryan, N.J. 1965 *The Making of Modern Malaya.* Kuala Lumpur: Oxford University Press.

St. Clair, R., and W. Leap 1982 *Language Renewal among American Indian Tribes: Issues, Problems, and Prospects.* Rosslyn, Virginia: National Clearinghouse for Bilingual Education.

San Miguel, G. 1986 *One Country, One Language: An Historical Sketch of English Language Movements in the United States.* Pomona, CA: The Tomás Rivera Center.

Savard, J.-G. and R. Vigneault, eds. 1975 *Les etats multilingues.* Quebec: Laval.

Schmidt, P. 1989 'English Only' advocates target bill on Puerto Rico. *Education Week* 9,8 (October 18):23.

Schmitt, E. 1989 English-only bill ignites debate and fear on L.I. *The New York Times* (February 14), B 3.

Shaffer, M. 1988 State tribes fighting 'English': Indian schools, business at stake. *Arizona Republic* (November 6), B:1,2.

Simon, Senator P. 1986 Expanding language horizons: "English Plus". *The "English Plus" Project,* 7–10. Washington, D.C.: LULAC.

Scollon, R. 1981 *Human Knowledge and the Institution's Knowledge.* Final report on National Institute of Education Grant No. G-80–0185, October 1, 1980 to December 31, 1981: Communication in patterns and retention in a public university.

Skutnabb-Kangas, T. 1986 Who wants to change what and why – conflicting paradigms in minority education research. In *Language and Education in Multilingual Settings,* ed. B. Spolsky, 153–81. Clevedon, Avon: Multilingual Matters.

Skutnabb-Kangas, T. 1988 Multilingualism and the education of minority children. In *Minority Education: From Shame to Struggle,* ed. T. Skutnabb-Kangas and J. Cummins, 9–44. Clevedon, Avon: Multilingual Matters.

Skutnabb-Kangas, T. and J. Cummins, eds. 1988 *Minority Education: from Shame to Struggle.* Clevedon, Avon: Multilingual Matters.

Skutnabb-Kangas, T. and R. Phillipson 1989. Wanted: linguistic human rights. *ROLIG-papir* 44. Roskilde: Roskilde University Centre, Linvistgruppen.

Stanton, S. 1989 Corbin calls 'English' law legal, flexible. *Arizona Republic* (January 25), A:1,6.

Sundberg, T.J. 1988 The case against bilingualism. *English Journal* 77:16–17.

Tapp, J.L., and F.F. Levine 1980. Legal socialization. In *The Sociology of Law,* ed. W.M. Evan, 121–34. New York: Free Press.

Teik, G.C. 1971 *The May Thirteenth Incident and Democracy in Malaysia.* Kuala Lumpur: Oxford University Press.

Thernstrom, A. 1988 Affirmative Action and Minority Voting Rights, 175–95. *Twentieth Century Fund.*

Tohono O'odham Tribal Council 1986. Language Policy of the Tohono O'odham. Sells, AZ: Tohono O'odham Tribal Council.

Tollefson, J.F. 1986 Language policy and the radical left in the Philippines: The New People's Army and its antecedents. *Language Problems and Language Planning* 10:177–89.

Tomás Rivera Center 1986. Are English language amendments in the national interest? An analysis of proposals to establish English as the official language of the United States. Mimeo. Pomona, CA: Tomás Rivera Center.

Troike, R. 1982 Testimony before the Illinois State Board of Education Policy and Planning Committee, October 7.

Trombley, W. 1986a Prop 63. backer will try to defeat opposing candidates. *Los Angeles Times* (October 1), I:3,25.

Trombley, W. 1986b English-only proposition kindles minorities' fears. *Los Angeles Times* (October 12), I:1,29–30.

Trudgill, P. 1983 *On Dialect: Social and Geographical Perspectives.* New York: New York University Press.

Tucker, G.R. 1986 Implications of Canadian research for promoting a language competent American society. *The "English Plus" Project,* 11–18. Washington, D.C.:LULAC.

Turk, A.T. 1980 Law as weapon in social conflict. In *The Sociology of Law,* ed. W.M. Evan, 105–21. New York: Free Press.

U.S. Commission on Civil Rights 1981 *The Voting Rights Act: Unfulfilled Goals.* Washington, D.C.: U.S. Government Printing Office.

U.S. Department of Commerce, Bureau of Census 1973 *American Indians: PC(2)-1F.* 1970 Census of Population, Subject Reports (June). Washington, D.C.

U.S. Department of Commerce, Bureau of Census 1983a *1980 Census of Population. Volume 1: Characteristics of the Population.* Washington, D.C.: U.S. Government Printing Office.

U.S. Department of Commerce, Bureau of Census 1983b The demographic dilemma of the Soviet Union (R. Crisostomo). *International Research Document No. 10* (ISP-RD-10). Washington, D.C.: U.S. Government Printing Office.

U.S. Department of Commerce, Bureau of Census 1984 *Current Population Survey.* Washington, D.C.: U.S. Government Printing Office.

U.S. Department of Commerce, Bureau of Census 1988a *We, the First Americans.* Washington, D.C.: U.S. Government Printing Office.

U.S. Department of Commerce, Bureau of Census 1988b *1980 Census of Population, Subject Reports, Volume 2: Asian and Pacific Islander Population in the United States: 1980,* PC80-2–1E (January). Washington, D.C.: U.S. Government Printing Office.

U.S. Department of Education 1986 *Update on Adult Illiteracy, Commissioned and Conducted in Fall 1982. Revised by U.S. Department of Education, April 14, 1986.* Washington, D.C.: U.S. Government Printing Office.

U.S. English 1989 Official Navajo? *U.S. English Update* 7,2 (March/April): 1–2.

U.S. English 1988 Official English claims victory in three more states *U.S. English Update* 6,6 (November/December), 5.

Vasil, R.K. 1980 *Ethnic Politics in Malaysia.* New Delhi: Radiant Publishers.

Veltman, C. 1983 *Language Shift in the United States.* Berlin: Mouton

Veltman, C. 1986 Comment. *International Journal of the Sociology of Language* 60:177–181.

Viglucci, A. 1988 Petition pros spark English drive. *Miami Herald* (March 11), D:1.

Von Drehle, D. 1988 Dad language fight continues as post-landslide celebration. *Miami Herald* (November 9), A:18.

Webb, K., and E. Hall 1978 *Explanation of the Rise of Political Nationalism in Scotland.* Glasgow: University of Strathclyde Center for the Study of Public Policy.

Weihofen, H. 1979 *The Urge to Punish.* New York: Farrar, Straus and Cudahy.

Weinstein, B. 1979 Language strategists: redefining political frontiers on the basis of linguistic choices. *World Politics* 31,3:345–64.

Weinstein, B. 1983 *The Civic Tongue: Political Consequences of Language Choice.* New York: Longman.

Whited, C. 1987 We can't force English out of anyone's throat. *Miami Herald* (March 28), B:1.

Whiteley, W. 1969 *Swahili: The Rise of a National Language.* London: Methuen.

Willemyns, R. 1981 Die Sprachsituation in Belgiën unter soziolinguistischen Aspekten. *Linguistische Berichte* 75:41–59.

Willemyns, R. 1984 La standardization linguistique en dehors des centres de gravité de la langue: la Flandre et le Québec. In *Du disciplinaire vers l'interdisciplinaire dans l'étude du contact des langues,* ed. J. Hamers, J.-D. Gendron, and R. Vigneault, 52–70. Québec: Centre international de recherché sur le bilinguisme.

Williams, L.E. 1976 *Southeast Asia: A History.* New York: Oxford University Press.

Willig, A. 1985 A meta-analysis of selected studies on the effectiveness of bilingual education. *Review of Educational Research* 55:269–317.

Wirth, T.E. 1988 Commentary: Official English contrary to America's Ideal. *EPIC Events* (Newsletter of the English Plus Information Clearinghouse) 1,2 (May/June):3.

Witherspoon, G. 1977 *Language and Art in the Navajo Universe.* Ann Arbor: University of Michigan Press.

Woolard, K. 1985 Catalonia: The dilemma of language rights. In *Language and Inequality,* ed. N. Wolfson and J. Manes, 91–109. Berlin: Mouton.

Yngve, V.H. 1986 *Linguistics as a Science*. Bloomington: Indiana University Press.

Zentella, A.C. 1981 Language variety among Puerto Ricans. In *Language in the USA,* ed. C.A. Ferguson and S.B. Heath, 218–38. Cambridge: Cambridge University Press.

Zentella, A.C. 1988a Language politics in the USA: The English-only movement. In *Literature, Language, and Politics,* ed. B.J. Craige, 39–53. Athens, GA: University of Georgia Press.

Zentella, A.C. 1988b English-only laws will foster divisiveness, not unity: they are anti-hispanic, anti-elderly, and anti-female. *Chronicle of Higher Education* 2 (November 23), 1.

Zeydel, E.G. 1964 The teaching of German in the United States from colonial times to the present. *German Quarterly* 37:315–92.

Language Planning Considerations in Indigenous Communities

Richard Ruiz (1995)

Federally-funded bilingual programs for American Indian/Alaska Native students are addressed from a language planning perspective. The discussion identifies three language policy types – endoglossic (community-oriented), exoglossic (externally-oriented), and mixed policies – and their relationship to American Indian/Alaska Native bilingual education. Federally-funded bilingual education represents an exoglossic policy for indigenous communities and as such, can lead to language loss. The recommendation here is that indigenous communities begin now to develop endoglossic policies that will reinforce past efforts in bilingual education while simultaneously stabilizing community heritage languages.

Introduction

There has been considerable recent interest in language planning and policy development directed at the various indigenous communities in the United States and Canada (Leap, 1988; Zepeda and Hill, 1990; Zepeda, 1990). That interest has focused alternatively on developments within the communities themselves and those outside, especially at the federal level. Leap (1988) lists a number of indicators of language interest from within the communities, including the development of tribal language policies and education standards, attendance at summer institutes designed to develop the capacity to maintain the various languages, participation in language conferences aimed specifically at indigenous communities, and the expansion of federally funded bilingual education programs for Indian students. In this article, I will touch on all of these briefly; my focus, however, will be on the possible effects of the last indicator, expanded participation in federal bilingual programs, from a language planning perspective. My conclusion will be that while such participation can present an opportunity for language renewal, it must be approached cautiously lest the trend toward language loss be reinforced.

Federal Bilingual Education Policy

The first federal Bilingual Education Act (BEA) was enacted in 1968; its official was Title VII of the Elementary and Secondary Education Act of 1965. The primary targets of the early programs resulting under the BEA were Spanish-speaking children of elementary school age; more specifically, the programs were aimed at the Mexican-American population of the Southwestern states, with limited participation by Puerto Ricans in the northeast and American Indians and Alaska Natives (Crawford, 1989; Ruiz, 1994).

The initial version of the BEA had a very general design, having been fashioned after the Great Society programs of the Johnson administration; its main emphasis was more on general academic achievement rather than language proficiency as such. This general aspect changed radically in the 1974 version, which introduced a definition of bilingual education which has persisted with no significant alteration until the present time; the program was to be "transitional" in its direction, with the native language used only until such time as the student could perform ordinary class work in English. The centrality of the goal of English proficiency was clear; bilingual programs were not aimed at developing or advancing the capacity to use a language other than English.

The BEA has had a mixed history, owing in large part to the administrations in charge at the time of the enactment of its various versions. The narrowing of focus to a concern with English proficiency in the 1974 reauthorization, for example, should be understood as a reaction on the part of the Nixon administration to what it considered misguided generosity from Lyndon Johnson's War on Poverty. Similarly, the accelerated funding levels for Title VII programs in the late 1970s testifies to the need expressed by the Carter administration to correct the underfunding of the BEA under Nixon-Ford. Financial support for federal bilingual programs peaked in 1980. Since the very beginning of the Reagan-Bush era, allocations for Title VII were severely cut; program expenditures for 1992 were the same as those for 1978, for example. Estimates on the growing size of the non-English speaking school-age population notwithstanding (Waggonner, 1988; Stanford Working Group, 1993), budget constraints will likely make any significant funding increases for Title VII in the near future difficult. The requests for 1993 and 1994 from the Office of Bilingual Education and Minority Languages Affairs represented increases that could lead to a significant upward trend in spending for bilingual education. Of major significance, however, is the conservative takeover of Congress in the 1994 elections. Since many of those in authority to set the agenda for education (for example, the newly elected Chair of the House Committee on Education and Labor) are openly critical of bilingual education programs, it is more likely that authorization levels will be lowered to something more like those of the 1980s.

Even more significant than the funding levels, however, is the trend in the last two administrations and in the 1994 Congress to intensify the goal of English proficiency, to the point of promoting English-only instructional programs under the aegis of Title VII. This was accomplished most effectively by William Bennett, Secretary of Education under Ronald Reagan (San Miguel, 1988; Crawford, 1992). Bennett expressed an early concern with what he considered the cultural-separatist nature of bilingual programs, and with the lack of priority on learning English as quickly as possible. Early in 1982, the administration introduced its own version of the BEA, scheduled for reauthorization in 1983 or 1984. It contained a variety of new elements aimed at focusing on the neediest students, but the most controversial proposal was one in which a small percentage of Title VII funds would be set aside for "special alternative programs," programs of "structured immersion" in English where the child's native language would not be used for any instructional purpose. These explicitly monolingual programs were based on the assumption that maximum exposure to English would result in higher and more rapid proficiency in English. Even while the predominant research studies (including those sponsored and funded by the Department of Education itself) demonstrated that this assumption had no validity (see, e.g., Ramirez, 1991), both the 1984 and 1988 versions of the BEA set aside funds for English immersion programs, up to 25% of the total allocation; the current Act, passed in 1994, contains the same provision.

This history clearly indicates a trend toward an increasingly English-centered BEA. With the momentum that has been built up by the English immersion advocates in past administrations, in both budgetary and policy development, it will be very difficult to develop programs designed to maintain, much less to renew indigenous languages (cf. Crawford, this issue). This can have a substantial impact on efforts within indigenous communities to maintain and develop their cultural resources. In the following section, I present some language policy concepts that should be used in our consideration of such efforts.

Language Policy Types

I will deal presently with policy goals. For the moment, I am concerned with the types of language policies that indigenous communities have to choose from. Here, the simple typology presented by Cobarrubias (1983) is helpful. He distinguishes *endoglossic, exoglossic,* and *mixed* policies. Endoglossic policies are those that give primacy to and promote an indigenous language of the community. In situations where the indigenous language is also a language of wider communication (LWC) with high prestige value inside and outside native contexts, endoglossic policies pose no particular practical or political problem. Thus, it seems only natural for the French or the Spanish that their languages have official status, even in the face of linguistic diversity in both Spain and France (Limage, 1990). On the other hand, cases such as that of Malaysia create great concern about endoglossic policies. Bahasa Malaysia was declared the single official language of Malaysia in 1963. The National Language Act that contained the declaration is generally explained as a measure designed to reinforce a sense of national identity following independence from British rule in 1957. But, while Bahasa Malaysia is justifiably classified as a regional lingua franca, its association with the ethnic Malays, the *bumiputras* ("sons of the soil"), in Malaysia is unquestioned; what resulted was significant social and political conflict with the large ethnic Chinese and Indian communities, who saw their life chances diminished by the new language policy (Davey, 1990). Such tensions are characteristic of pluralistic, non-LWC states that enact exclusively endoglossic policies. This may be the reason very few such states exist in the world.

Exoglossic policies are those that give primacy and promote an outside, frequently a former colonial language; the adoption of a language in a non-native context is a major indication of LWC status. This happens frequently in multilingual states where none of the indigenous languages is an LWC, and where there is a history of prolonged contact with an LWC state. The ironic political fact is that even after colonies have been able to gain their independence, they often find it necessary to adopt the former colonial language for official and public purposes, since the former colonial power and its institutions have pervaded the life of the colony. Many of the still-emerging states of western Africa, even while they struggle for recognition of their national identities, nevertheless enact policies that recognize the status and power of LWCs (see, e.g., Akinnaso, 1989, on Nigeria; Bowcock, 1985, on Gambia; Macedo and Freire, 1987, on Sao Tome and Cape Verde; Tollefson, 1994).

Mixed policies are essentially bilingual policies; they accommodate and promote both indigenous and outside languages. There are numerous examples of mixed states, but very few in what is commonly called the West. Quechua was declared an official language in Peru, co-equal with Spanish, in 1975 (Hornberger, 1988), yet tremendous problems of policy implementation remain. Guaraní and Spanish are both official languages in Paraguay (Rubin, 1985), yet the dominance of Spanish for the higher prestige functions is generally recognized in all language communities. The only example of a mixed Western state where the LWC has historically predominated is Australia, whose recent National Language Policy promotes English along with a number of other languages, including aboriginal languages (Lo Bianco,

1987). The new policy has been facilitated by the National Institute on Languages and Literacy, with headquarters in Canberra and research and dissemination centers throughout Australia. The unusual case of Australia will no doubt be monitored closely by those interested in language policy development.

Language Policy Development in Minority Communities

Given the three types of language policy just described, how should minority (non-LWC) communities orient themselves to them? My attempt at an answer to this question will be preceded by a series of observations drawn from international case studies relevant to minority communities.

(1) **Most non-LWC communities are either exoglossic or mixed states.** This situation arises because of a pre-rational association between the LWC and "modernization" (and, by implication, the indigenous language with "primitivity"), attributed by Fishman (1990) to a western social science that has convinced us that "modernization and authenticity preoccupations cannot go together, just as authenticity preoccupations and rationality cannot go together" (p. 9). From a purely pragmatic perspective, minority language communities have made the decision to take advantage of the economic and technological power associated with the LWCs, even while making efforts to retain their indigenous languages for identificational purposes (see Crawford, this issue). In Kelman's (1971) formulation, the one represents an instrumental attachment, the other a sentimental attachment to language. In the case of mixed states, even while there may be a genuine effort to promote both languages equally, real parity is rarely achieved. More often than not, the LWC is reserved for public and powerful subjects and functions, the indigenous local language for private, community-based functions. This asymmetry is easily perceived by the children, whose motivation for learning the languages is affected by the perceived status associated with them.

(2) **Exoglossic language policies contribute to language shift.** These sorts of policies reinforce the already favored position of the LWC. And, because language policies tend to be diffused into informal contexts within the society, their influence is felt throughout the community. Recall the previous discussion about the trend toward English primacy in federal bilingual education policy. Translated into language planning terms, such a policy pushes minority language communities toward exoglossic policies favoring the LWC; thus, it reinforces the already overwhelming power and attractiveness of English for these

communities, and diminishes the value of the local languages. In this atmosphere, language renewal and efforts to reverse language shift become very difficult.

(3) **There are few stable mixed states.** That is, mixed or bilingual language policies for non-LWC communities lead toward language shift. For minority communities, bilingualism is often a transitional state between monolingualism in the indigenous language and monolingualism in the LWC. Bilingualism itself tends to be transitory and unstable unless definite diglossic norms are reinforced by strong instrumental and sentimental attachments to the languages involved. Where diglossia is weak, and where neophyte speakers do not associate language behavior with vital societal functions, the attraction of especially the younger generations to the LWC will tend to overwhelm interest in retaining or learning the local language, thus leading to its demise. This is the process described by Trudgill, who calls the LWCs "killer" languages because of their effects on language communities in contact (Trudgill, 1991).

(4) **Language maintenance and efforts to reverse language shift in non-LWC communities require endoglossic policies.** These policies, by themselves, will have little effect on language behavior. The implementation plans that accompany them must work to strengthen both instrumental and sentimental functions for the indigenous language in the community. They also must be comprehensive in scope. Generally, the more formal the contexts in which the language policy is implemented, the less effect it will have in language maintenance. Since languages live in communities, the common life activities of the community must be the targets of language policies. This means that the electronic and print media, social activities, social service providers, and other everyday centers of community life must be included in the implementation strategies by which language policies are promoted. In this way, our language policies have more of a chance to become more closely associated with our language behavior.

Conclusion

I began this analysis by characterizing federal bilingual education as essentially a monolingual policy with the goal of anglification. For American Indian and other language minority communities, this is an explicitly exoglossic policy. In combination with local initiatives, however, these communities may find a considerable amount of opportunity to intensify language maintenance efforts within federal policies such as Title VII. What I offer here is a caution. If, in fact, federally funded bilingual education programs in American Indian communities have served the purposes of language renewal and reversal of language shift, it is testimony to the ingenuity and dedication of the staffs of those programs, not the policy itself. In economic hard times, monitoring of the basic goals of federal programs such as Title VII is more likely to decrease funding and increase the pressure to conform to its basic orientation. American Indian communities may well find in those times that the demands to implement exoglossic (i.e., English-only) policies becomes overwhelming (cf. Holm and Holm, this volume).

I suggest starting now on the development of endoglossic language policies that can serve to reinforce and stabilize community languages. For the time being, federally funded bilingual education appears able to be fitted into such policies. If the time comes when this is no longer possible, the language planning decisions that are made now will help communities achieve the continuity of tradition that has served them so well up to now.

Richard Ruiz
The Bilingual Research Journal Winter 1995, 19 (1), 71–81.

References

Akinnaso, F.N. (1989). One nation, four hundred languages: Unity and diversity in Nigeria's language policy. *Language Problems and Language Planning, 13*(2), 133–146.

Bowcock, D. (1985). Language and education in the Gambia. Unpublished Ph.D. dissertation, University of Wisconsin, Madison.

Cobarrubias, J. (1983). Ethical issues in status planning. In J. Cobarrubias and J.A. Fishman (Eds.), *Progress in language planning: International perspectives* (pp. 41–85). Berlin: Mouton de Gruyter.

Crawford, J. (1989). *Bilingual education: History, politics, theory and practice.* Trenton, N.J.: Crane Publishing Co.

Crawford, J. (1992). *Language loyalties.* Chicago: University of Chicago Press.

Davey, W.G. (1990). The legislation of Bahasa Malaysia as the official language of Malaysia. In K. Adams and D. Brink (Eds.), *Perspectives on Official English: The campaign for English as the official language of the USA* (pp. 95–103). Berlin and New York: Mouton de Gruyter.

Fishman, J.A. (1990). What is reversing language shift (RSL) and how can it succeed? In D. Gorter et al. (Eds.), *Fourth international conference on minority languages, Vol. I: General papers* (pp. 5–36). Clevedon and Philadelphia: Multilingual Matters.

Hornberger, N. (1988). Language planning orientations and bilingual education in Peru. *Language Problems and Language Planning, 12*(1), 14–29.

Kelman, H. (1971). Language as an aid and barrier to involvement in the national system. In J. Rubin and B.H. Jernudd (Eds.), *Can language be planned? Sociological theory and practice for developing nations* (pp. 21–51). Honolulu: University of Hawaii Press.

Leap, W. (1988). Indian language renewal. *Human organization, 47*(4), 283–291.

Limage, L. (1990). Language policies in Western Europe and the Union of Soviet Socialist Republics. In K. Adams & D. Brink (Eds.), *Perspectives on official English: The campaign for English as the official language of the USA* (pp. 83–94). Berlin and New York: Mouton de Gruyter.

Lo Bianco, J. (1987). *National policy on languages.* Canberra: Government of Australia.

Macedo, D. & Freire, P. (1987). *Literacy: Reading the word and the world.* South Hadley, MA.: Bergin and Garvey.

Ramirez, J.D. (1991). *Final report: Longitudinal study of structured English immersion strategy, early-exit and late-exit transitional bilingual education programs for language minority children.* Report to the Department of Education, Contract #300-87-0156, Washington, D.C.

Rubin, J. (1985). The special relation of Guaraní and Spanish in Paraguay. In N. Wolfson and J. Manes (Eds.), *Language of inequality* (pp. 11–20). Berlin: Mouton de Gruyter.

Ruiz, R. (1994). Language policy and planning in the United States. *Annual Review of Applied Linguistics, 14,* 111–125.

San Miguel, G. (1988). Bilingual education policy development: The Reagan years, 1980–1987. *NABE Journal, 12,* 97–109.

Stanford Working Group (1993). *Federal education programs for limited-English-proficient students: A blueprint for the second generation.* Stanford, CA: Stanford Working Group.

Tollefson, J. W. (1994). *Planning language, planning inequality.* London & New York: Longman.

Trudgill, P. Language maintenance and language shift: Preservation vs. extinction. *International Journal of Applied Linguistics, 1*(1), 61–69.

Waggonner, D. (1988). Language minorities in the United States in the 1980s: The evidence from the 1980 census. In S. McKay and S.C. Wong (Eds.), *Language diversity: Problem or resource?* (pp. 69–108). New York: Harper and Row.

Zepeda, O. (1990). American Indian language policy. In K. Adams and D. Brink (Eds.), *Perspectives on official English: The campaign for English as the official language of the USA* (pp. 247–256). Berlin and New York: Mouton de Gruyter.

Zepeda, O. & J. Hill (1990). The condition of Native American languages in the United States. Tucson: University of Arizona Department of Linguistics (mimeo).

Threat Inversion and Language Policy in the United States

Richard Ruiz (2006)

Language policy development in the United States is characterized by "threat inversion." The threats to the existence of some languages in the United States, or to the vitality of the languages, are grounded in real circumstances of language endangerment; a number of indigenous languages, for example, have already been lost, and many others are moribund. Unfortunately, language policy development at all levels pays very little attention and offers very few resources to these situations. Language loss for these communities is regarded with indifference, at best. Instead, the predominant language policy discourses aim at "protecting and enhancing" English against the threat of multilingualism that a host of other "little" languages poses. In other words, speakers of the most powerful language in the world feel the urgent need to protect themselves from those who have very little with which to fight it, and who have shown very little inclination to do so. This has been effected in large measure by political movements that have constructed threat-discourses that reverse normal logic where the weakest who are in real danger menace the strongest. Furthermore, large majorities within various states have been convinced of the imminent danger posed by these languages. The paper will explore how these discourses have been constructed, why they have been successful, and how they have been put into action in schools and the larger society.

Introduction

The literature on language threat and endangerment has now produced vast data sets on stages of language vitality. For example, the work of the Summer Institute of Linguistics (SIL) is among the leaders in cataloging the status of languages based on dimensions proposed by UNESCO and others (Lewis, 2006; Showalter, 2006, et al.). Ethnologue, the world's largest database on languages, has used these dimensions (intergenerational transmission, number of speakers in households, age distribution of speakers, modes of language use, and so on) as a way to understand where languages are on the continuum between long-term stability and imminent extinction. Similarly, organizations such as the Endangered Languages Foundation (Ostler, 2004), and independent scholars (Krauss, 1991; Leonard, 2006; Snow, 2006) have developed their own scales based on similar factors.

This work is valuable but limited if we are to understand what is meant by language threat and endangerment. In the overwhelming majority of cases, language threat and endangerment focuses on the status and future of minority or minoritized languages, especially indigenous languages – an obviously justified focus given the number of extinct and moribund languages in this situation. Still, there are other cases not treated in the literature on threat and endangerment. In this paper I try to fill some of the holes in this literature by proposing a typology of threat and endangerment that includes the extreme ends of these cases. First, I suggest some definitions of basic terms; these are often assumed in the literature. Second, I outline a possible typology for categorizing the situation of particular languages in their macro-sociolinguistic contexts. Finally, I offer some comments on how such an analysis can be useful for those interested in working in the area of language endangerment. Within the argument, I coin the term "threat inversion" to characterize those situations where the perceived threat appears to be ungrounded if not irrational, and elaborate the process by which such irrationalities become credible.

Defining Basic Terms

¿What does it mean for a language to be threatened? ¿Are all "threatened" languages also "endangered"? The definitions offered here make a distinction between threats as mere perceptions and threats that have some objective grounding.

> **Language threat$_1$ (θ1):** Within a language community, a perception of impending loss of or change in language resources, usually as a result of outside intervention
> **Language threat$_2$(θ2):** Contact between or among languages such that one or more of them are likely to experience imminent (whether gradual or precipitous) loss or change in language resources.

Notice that there can be a strong relation between θ1 (theta-one) and θ-2. That is, it is possible that the perception within the community that its language (and much more) is in danger of some sort of loss corresponds to a more or less objective condition of contact with larger, more powerful languages. Nevertheless, the fact that the perception may exist in the absence of such conditions justifies the conceptual distinction between θ1 and θ2.

Threat and endangerment are conceptually and practically connected. Even when a threat is not perceived (when we are surprised by incidence of language loss), it could nevertheless have real conditions associated with it that we can at least see post hoc, if not predict.

> **Language endangerment$_a$:** Language threats that are likely to lead to extinction of the language or variety
>
> **Language endangerment$_b$:** Language threats that create changes in the roles and functions that language plays in social life, such that the cultural vitality of the group is diminished
>
> **Language resources:** internal (codes, discursive practices, conventions, etc.) and external ("language maintenance institutions" – churches, media, schools, family practices) structures within a language and language community that facilitate the use and development of the language

Threat inversion (1/θ)

Threat inversion happens when a community of powerful, sometimes very powerful, language speakers claims that smaller, sometimes extremely small, languages and their users threaten them. The threat is not articulated as one against the life of the language (θ1 in the definitions above), but rather against their way of life (i.e. the relations of power that exist between and among the different societal groups). The most spectacular example of threat inversion has been playing itself out at the turn of the 21 case; we have the users of what is unarguably the most powerful language in the history of the world, English, within the context of what is arguably the most powerful nation in the history of the world, the United States, insisting that it needs protection against the cultural invasion of smaller, sometimes very small, language communities.

Examples are found throughout its history (see Crawford, 2000; Wiley, 2000; Ricento & Wiley, 2006, among many others). When newly-arrived German immigrants to mid-western cities in the early 19th century sought to preserve some of their cultural and religious heritage by establishing private German Lutheran and Catholic schools, school boards sought ways to curtail the "Germanization" of their communities; the earliest versions of ELAs were the 1889 twin Bennett and Edwards Laws in Wisconsin and Illinois, respectively. The laws were intended to require children to attend school for a certain amount of time during the year, but they defined a school as a place where basic subjects were taught in English. The laws created an uproar among the German communities, and eventually the laws were repealed. Still, the impetus for such legal restrictions on non-English language use was strong. The introduction of "new immigrant" communities from Eastern and Southern Europe between 1880 and 1920 intensified attitudes toward cultural and political assimilation, and language was a central issue. The new immigration, coupled with the hostilities of the first world war, created the momentum for increasingly restrictive immigration and language laws: between 1918 and 1928 half the states passed laws against the use of non-English languages in schools. The most well-known of these measures, the Siman Law in Nebraska and the Bartels Law in Iowa, were found to be unconstitutional by the Supreme Court in Meyer v. Nebraska (1923), but Nebraska's law was passed later that year in a slightly revised form; it is still on the books.

More recently, the 1980s saw a resurgence of conservative and nativist sentiment in the United States, and it was strengthened with the election of an ultra-conservative president. New versions of anti-immigrant legislation and English Language Amendments were introduced early in the decade. Although efforts to pass a federal ELA failed, the impetus was created for a new strategy – working through the initiative process to pass such laws at the state level. The first such law was passed in California in 1986; several other states passed laws subsequently, including Arizona in 1988. This was essentially a language policy for the state designed to "protect and enhance the status of English" by requiring its use, and prohibiting the use of other languages, for all government functions. While the measure was eventually found to be unconstitutional because it was a broad restriction of first amendment rights to free speech, the attitude that English somehow had to be protected remained strong. As has always been the case with such measures in US history, the language policy was coupled with a particular view of immigration that saw these communities as problems for the welfare of the larger society. The argument has these elements: these people are a drain on our welfare and health systems; whatever money they earn here they send back to their relatives in other countries; they form enclaves in which they can live without needing to learn "our" ways and values and language; and, perhaps most disturbing, they have no allegiance to the country in which they are guests.

The argument is immediately compelling in border states such as Arizona and California where a great many of the population see immigration as a major societal problem. Even the most liberal politicians in those states call for "securing our borders" and requiring illegal immigrants who want citizenship to learn English. But the attitudes are not limited to border states; some of the most vocal critics of proposals for enfranchising immigrants through guest worker programs or pathways to eventual citizenship are legislators from mid-western states. Estimates that the number of illegal immigrants in the United States range from 11 to 20 million create panic in the general population that we are being overrun, that we are not sure who is coming across, and that the present wave of terrorism aimed at the United

States requires us all to be concerned about the security of our borders. Such arguments are coupled with issues of language, just as they were for earlier immigrants who were forced to abandon their language (and often their names) to show their loyalty. Counter-arguments that these immigrants come to work, and thus help the economy; that they overwhelmingly learn English in a generation or less; that they serve in our military; that they have no inclination, nor would they have even the slightest hope, to engage in any hostility toward the United States – all are lost in our concern that we are in a war to keep our way of life, including our language.

Schools have become a major battleground in this war. All of the major restrictions on language use in the history of the United States has included schools. In the present cases, the laws severely curtail the judgment of teachers and the wishes of parents with respect to the education of children. While research on best practices in the education of English learners clearly favors the development of the child's first language as an important foundation for subsequent linguistic and cognitive development, Proposition 203 in Arizona is designed to proscribe anything but the use of English as medium of instruction. The conservative state Superintendent of Schools has declared publicly his commitment to discourage any use of non-English languages in schools, even in the exceptional cases where they are allowed by the law. The fact that there is no general uproar against a law aimed at prohibiting best practices by teachers and free choice of educational approaches by parents is evidence of the strength of the inverted threat discourse that has pervaded discussions of social policy in the past decade. Given current discussions about the use of national guard military troops along the border, and an emboldened conservative congress in the midst of election-year posturing, the situation is not likely to improve soon.

Threat inversion is a process in which a threat discourse is developed that eventually convinces a critical mass of people in the society that its claims have legitimacy. Such discourses objectify the threat and demonize the threateners by portraying them as parasites, aliens without allegiance to their immediate surroundings, and having no regard for the country that has served them as host.

Threat inversion is similar to what has been called the "racial threat hypothesis" (Barker & Giles, 2002; cf. Giles & Buckner, 1993; Key, 1949; Quillian, 1996; [for official English] Tatalovich, 1995; Tolbert & Hero, 1996) where members of a dominant racial group view "an influx of minorities as a threat to their power and status. This results in outright racism and repression." (Barker & Giles, 2002, p. 355). The perceived linguistic vitality of minority groups is mediated through a "linguistic landscape" in

"As individuals move out of their neighborhoods and into the city, they may feel a 'symbolic threat' to group identity; thus, it may not be just perceptions about group vitality and awareness of diverse languages in the immediate vicinity that fuel concerns" (p. 367).

The authors conclude the paper arguing that the "role of subjective perceptions about changing group vitality, linguistic landscape, and the concomitant relationships to group identity appear to be part of the equation when it comes to intolerance and language restriction" (p. 367).

Types of Threatened Languages

As stated earlier, quite a lot of research has been done on the vitality of languages, especially directed at minority or minoritized languages that have undergone large amounts of language loss. Much of this research focuses on indigenous languages, an alarming number of which have disappeared in the last several decades. Fishman (1991), Krauss (1991) and others have created scales by which we might gauge how strong the languages are and what prospects they have of survival. Such scales often assume an internal relationship between threat and endangerment, often using these terms interchangeably. I propose that we see these terms as conceptually distinct if practically related so that we can understand how different language communities experience language threat. Ultimately, my goal is to use the typology below to advance the notion of threat inversion.

The table below is intended to characterize all cases of language threat normally included in this literature. It therefore includes what I regard as the extreme cases, as well as those that are less easily recognized as instances of language threat.

Types of threatened languages

	Description	Evidence	Danger
A	Uni-centric minority/indigenous Ls in significant contact with an aggressive majority L/LWC	Significant L1 → L2 disappearance of L1 (GIDS regression)	Language death
B	Stigmatized or minoritized varieties of pluricentric LWCs in large multilingual states (**e.g. US Spanish varieties**) where the LWCs are not in danger of extinction	Significant L1 → L2 Diminished vitality (cf. Krauss)	Displaced and diminished L1 functions; cultural disruption
C	Majority minoritized languages in stable states in contact with LWCs but not in danger of either extinction or significant shift (**Spanish in PR**)	Anti-L2 LP: legislation, rules, sanctions, etc.	Isolation, political polarization

D	Indigenous Ls in multilingual states **(Xhosa in South Africa)** not in imminent danger of language death	Pro-L1 LP: status, corpus and acquisition planning	Limited use of L1 in P-domains
E	Majority Indigenous languages in small states in contact with LWCs **(Netherlands Antilles Papiamento)**	L1/L2 functional differentiation	L1 confined to non-P domains: devaluing of L1
F	LWCs in small states that are threatened by LWCs in adjacent states (French in Quebec)	Political separation; endoglossic LP	Political antagonisms and isolation; gradual L1 → L2
G	Non-LWC majority languages that perceive threats from LWCs in adjacent states (Catalan in Spain)	Endoglossic LP	Political antagonisms and isolation
H	LWCs in large states that perceive threats From multilingualism consisting of "smaller" languages (French Creole, Vietnamese) or other LWCs (Spanish in the USA, English in France)	Anti-L1 LP	Oppression of minority Ls and their speakers; or co-optation of L1 community by providing certain forms of subtractive schooling

Most of our concern in the literature on threat and endangerment, justifiably so, is with Type A cases. Indigenous languages undergoing massive amounts of language shift as a result of contact with a powerful language, where the community is the only source of language production, and where intergenerational mother tongue transmission is limited if not absent clearly need immediate attention if they are to survive.

We must concede, however, that not all indigenous languages are in that situation. Papiamento in the Netherlands Antilles, for example, identified here as a Type E case, is not used outside the three islands (each with its own variety) and has had significant contact with major colonial languages for hundreds of years. Spanish, English and Dutch are languages that are in major use for public commerce and some civic and governmental functions; until very recently, Dutch was used exclusively as a medium of instruction in schools beyond kindergarten. Yet, Papiamento remains vital, with very little erosion of use in indigenous Aruban households (Emerencia, 2006)[1]. It appears that this indigenous community has been able to absorb the impact of language contact with powerful languages through a strategic diglossic approach. However, we should note that while the language itself does not appear to be in imminent danger, it is clear that its domains of use have been severely restricted. It remains to be seen whether the recent introduction of Papiamento into higher levels of schooling in Aruba will lead to its diffusion into other functions.

Another interesting case is that of the Type D languages. They are indigenous languages embedded in multilingual countries that appear to be stable, though again their uses are restricted. Heugh (1993) suggests an ironic conclusion for the South African languages: it could very well be that the same apartheid system that marginalized and isolated the indigenous languages also insulated them from the influence of English. It will be interesting to see whether the increased use of English in South African schools leads to more instability in the indigenous languages.

Other cases, such as that of Spanish in Puerto Rico (Carroll, 2006), also demonstrate remarkable stability and vitality in the face of significant, sometimes hostile, influence from English. There, not only does the language thrive in households, but it is also the major language of public affairs.

My main interest in the typology, however, is in the extreme case of Type H language groups, those that, because of their social, economic, political and technological predominance in the world, are in no obvious danger of any resource loss; yet, they engage in aggressive defensive activities characteristic of languages in danger of imminent demise. Clearly the perception of threat from smaller languages is there; as I have explained above, it is not a new attitude in the United States, but one that emerges and intensifies in times of national crisis. It is then that we see the elaboration of new forms of inverted threat discourses where the victims of oppression are seen as the causes of unrest. We have obviously not learned much from our previous campaigns against minority communities. When we show a willingness to be inclusive and practice our democratic values of equity and fairness, as happened in the case of the post-civil rights era of the 1970s, relations tend to be more mutually supportive and stable. When, on the other hand, we turn on those who are the least able to defend themselves as the cause of our problems, the conflicts intensify.

Conclusion

It could be argued that such inverted θ-discourses are required in societies such as the United States that have extended rights to minorities, that have in fact founded their basic political ideals on constitutional guarantees for the well-being of minorities in the framework of majority rule. The debate in 2006 on whether immigrant minorities should have rights and what they should be is at its root a debate about legal standing and its effects on "American culture." Giving standing to those who are perceived to have their loyalties elsewhere (because they retain their native languages, because they are proud enough of their heritage to fly a foreign flag on occasion) is for some an erosion of the assimilation ideal in which we all blend into one cultural mass. It means that they can remain "aliens among us" with impunity. Any move toward the liberalization of laws against undocumented workers thus becomes the first step on the slippery slope toward amnesty and citizenship – the ultimate legal standing.

Thus, inverted θ-discourses are not incidental to the political rhetoric of the United States, they are essential to it. We cannot be seen to be oppressive of minority communities merely because their cultural practices are exotic to us; somehow, these have to be perceived as dangerous. This is the beginning of inverted θ-discourse. It is only by showing that the common good is threatened by linguistic and cultural fragmentation that such discourses are not only accepted but convincing. The consequence is a mobilization of extremely strong political and economic forces against very weak ones. This is reflected in language policies, and translated into school practices and programs, designed to minimize the effect of minority presence; indeed, these policies re-invigorate ancient notions of the polluting effects of immigrants on the society. Ultimately, it leads to a situation that exists now in the United States, but that has also existing in a number of bygone eras there and elsewhere: curtailment of minority civil rights, disenfranchisement, and efforts to restrict if not eliminate immigration from non-English speaking countries. While the present situation could be attributed to the events of September 11, 2001 and their aftermath, they are neither new nor unique to the United States: we have had our 911s in the past, and they have always been pretexts for the oppression of minority voices. Perhaps a recognition of these tendencies in us could prevent the same reaction to future tragedies.

Note

(1) Ruiz refers here to Emerencia's 2006 unpublished paper presented on the same panel with him at the Georgetown Roundtable on Language and Linguistics, Washington, D.C. 5 March, 2006.

References

Barker, V. & Giles, H. (2002) Who supports the English-only movement?: Evidence for misconceptions about Latino group vitality. Journal of Multilingual and Multicultural Development 23(5), 353–370.

Carroll, K. (2006) Perceived threats toward Spanish in Puerto Rico. Paper presented at the Georgetown University Round Table on Languages and Linguistics, Washington DC.

Fishman, J. A. (1991) Reversing language shift. Philadelphia and Clevedon: Multilingual Matters

Giles, M. W. and Buckner, M. A. (1993) David duke and black threat: An old hypothesis revisited. Journal of Politics 55, 702–713.

Heugh, K. (1993) The Place of English in Relation to Other Languages in South Africa. Per Linguam, 9(1), 2–10.

Key, Vladimer O. (1949) Southern politics in state and nation. Knoxville, Tennesee: University of Tennessee Press.

Leonard, W. Y. (2006) No longer "extinct"—A classification system for sleeping (and other highly endangered) languages. Paper presented at the Georgetown University Round Table on Languages and Linguistics, Washington, DC.

Lewis, P. (2006) Evaluating endangerment: Proposed metadata and implementation. Paper presented at the Georgetown University Round Table on Languages and Linguistics, Washington, DC.

Monaka, K. C. (2006) Speakers living and languages dying: The endangeredness of !Xoo and #Hua in Botswana. Paper presented at the Georgetown University Round Table on Languages and Linguistics, Washington, DC.

Nover, S. (2006) Is ASL endangered? Paper presented at the Georgetown University Round Table on Languages and Linguistics, Washington, DC.

Quillian, L. (1996) 'Group Threat and Regional Change in Attitudes towards African Americans', American Journal of Sociology 102, 816–60.

Schiffman, H. (2006) When is an endangered language not an endangered language? Paper presented at the Georgetown University Round Table on Languages and Linguistics, Washington, DC.

Showalter, S. D. (2006) The endangered languages of Burkina Faso. Paper presented at the Georgetown University Round Table on Languages and Linguistics, Washington, DC.

Snow, P. (2006) What about the creoles? Language ideologies and the classification of "endangered" languages. Paper presented at the Georgetown University Round Table on Languages and Linguistics, Washington, DC.

Tatalovich, R. (1995) Nativism reborn? The official English language movement and the American states. Lexington: University of Kentucky Press.

Tolbert, Caroline J. and Rodney E. Hero (1996) Race/Ethnicity and Direct Democracy: An Analysis of California's Illegal Immigration Initiative. Journal of Politics 58 (3), 806–818.

Toth, C. R. (1990) German-English bilingual schools in America: the Cincinnati tradition in historical context. New York: Peter Lang.

Villanueva, M., Bishop, M. & Meyer, K. N. (2006) American Sign Language: Endangered and endangering? Paper presented at the Georgetown University Round Table on Languages and Linguistics, Washington, DC.

English Language Planning and Transethnification in the USA[1]

Richard Ruiz (2010)

The primary thesis presented here is that language planning in the USA is carried out within a general vision of transethnification, a process by which minority groups are expected to subordinate their language and culture to a larger sense of 'being American.' Transethnification therefore differs from classic assimilation in that ethnic groups do not have to abandon completely their cultural identities in order to be integrated into the nation-state; what is necessary is that their political allegiance must be transferred completely to the multinational state, even while their local cultural and language practices retain a semblance of authenticity. In fact, such local practices are seen as contributing to the strength of the nation-state, so long as they do not reflect a competing political identity.

While language planning as an activity of societies and individuals is perhaps as old as language itself, language planning as a professional field of work and systematic study did not establish itself until the mid-1900s (see the discussion in Kaplan & Baldauf, 1997, esp. pp. ix and following). The initial purposes of pioneers in language planning, perhaps most easily exemplified by the work included in early volumes such as *Language Problems of Developing Nations* (Fishman *et al.*, 1968) and *Can Language Be Planned?* (Rubin & Jernudd, 1971), centered primarily on solving specific 'language problems' that coincided with the development of new nations emerging out of decades, sometimes centuries, of colonialism (cf. Tollefson, 2002); in spite of the titles of these volumes, it was clear from the outset that the issues involved were not merely linguistic, but had much broader societal implications. Thus, the field quickly was populated and informed by researchers from a wide variety of disciplines besides language and linguistics, including anthropology (Heath, 1972), economics (Coulmas, 1992; Jernudd, 1971), education (Andersson & Boyer, 1970; John-Steiner, 1971), law (Leibowitz, 1969; Turi, 1977), political science (Kelman, 1969 [1971]; Pool, 1972; Weinstein, 1983), psychology (Lambert & Tucker, 1972; Macnamara, 1971), and sociology (Lieberson, 1971). Research and publication has persisted and expanded in all of these areas up to the present. Language planning therefore has become a vast multidisciplinary field that potentially touches on all dimensions of public life, as demonstrated by the following short list of some of the activities and concerns of language planners:

- Literacy campaigns
- Media of various sorts
- Language and economic opportunities (the 'linguistic marketplace')
- The social and political status of language minority communities
- Language maintenance, shift and revitalization
- Orthographic development and spelling reform
- Production of dictionaries, grammars, and style manuals
- Medium of instruction policies in schools
- Language policy development
- Language rights
- Court interpretation
- Terminological elaboration
- The language of technology
- Language standardization
- Preparation of teachers
- Bilingual and foreign language education
- Language and cultural identity
- Language and political integration
- Language officialization

It is evident from this brief list that language planning reaches far and wide into the public life of a society. In short, language planning is, as many writers have noted, social planning. It is therefore important to keep in mind this larger social context as we try to understand the role of languages in it. In this regard, Spolsky's (2004) advice is useful; he warns against a 'linguicentrism,' an approach to the study of language and language policy that ignores the larger social forces at play: '… language policy exists within a complex set of social, political, economic, religious, demographic, educational and cultural factors that make up the full ecology of human life. … language and language policy need to be looked at in the widest context and not treated as a closed universe. Language is a central factor, but linguicentrism … imposes limited vision' (Spolsky, 2004: ix–x).

The development of language planning as a discipline corresponds roughly to that of the broader field of sociolinguistics, and specifically the sub-field of the politics of language. Even after a half-century of elaboration, there are still a number of important, even basic questions to be pursued. In this article my purpose is to discuss a few of these with the hope of clarifying how the field of language planning can help us understand some of our most important issues.

The focus of this brief article is language planning in the US, but this cannot be easily divorced from developments elsewhere. A number of publications have contained much more complete discussions of these topics than I can possibly include in this small space; among the most recent of these are Gándara and Hopkins (2010) and Menken and García (2010). Both of these books concern how language planning and policy affects schools; the former deals exclusively with developments in the US, especially in a few key states, and the latter examines the issue internationally. The controversies inherent in the intersection of language and society have been exacerbated recently with demographic changes and political developments in the United States. My specific interest is to try to explain why these conflicts have surfaced now; I will concentrate on questions of political identity and integration by looking at English officialization movements in the US.

Language Planning and Transethnification

Movements toward the officialization of English in the United States are consistent with the tendency in large multinational states to promote a transethnified public culture that requires political allegiance to the administrative nation-state; further, it expects that allegiance to be demonstrated in at least a few of the major dimensions of public life (language behavior being one such dimension).[2] In Fishman's (1968) terms, the self-interest of states impels them to act to ensure their preservation by promoting 'nationism' over 'nationalism' and instrumental over sentimental attachments to the political system (Kelman, 1969).

Fishman's early distinction between 'nationalism' and 'nationism' is still useful, especially as we try to understand the role that language plays in these dynamics. His purpose was to illuminate the complex situations in which ethnic-language groups ('nationalities') find themselves within larger nation-states ('nations').[3] His analysis makes clear that characterizing all cases of nation-building with one term ('nationalism') is not only simplistic but misleading. The process by which ethnic groups become a nationality is very different from that undergone by various nationalities gaining an identity-attachment to the nation-state, yet we refer to these processes by the same term.[4] 'Nationalism' ultimately emphasizes local, ethnic attachments; it can stand quite apart and opposed to the ethos of the state, it can be in substantial if not complete alignment with it (Edwards' 'nation-state'), or, as we shall explore presently, it can be seen somewhere in between. It is important, however, not to minimize the importance that such local ethnic attachments play in identity. So, in the US, one might see oneself as Navajo or African American or Chicano first; when language becomes a factor in these attachments, then it is seen as another mechanism for the development and elaboration of identity. The challenge of nationalism for the state, then, is to devise strategies whereby these groups start to move their allegiance toward it.

One possible avenue for such a move is for the state to hold out to its citizens a quid pro quo – allegiance and commitment to its values and practices in exchange for a piece of the pie, whether that is economic reward in the form of access to education and jobs, social status in the form of official recognition, or some combination of sanctions. Such an arrangement promotes the view that the goods that the state can provide are at least as satisfying as those that can be gained by the sentimental relationships of the local clan. Eventually, after a few generations of cultivating such an instrumental arrangement, the state may begin to attract some of the sentimentality traditionally reserved for the clan, and therefore start a migration into the larger social circle that erodes ethnic group solidarity. This adaptation of Kelman's view of the relation of ethnicities to the state is similar to the idea of 'civic nationalism' proposed by Smith (2007) and contested by Edwards (2009). See also Conversi's (2007) discussion of instrumentalism and its relation to ethnic attachments. Below I suggest ways in which states proceed to create ethnic allegiance; my discussion is not incompatible substantively with the ideas of Smith and Kelman as I understand them, rather my purpose is to understand the processes involved in their realization.

The attempt to erode ethnic ties is not necessary to preserve the state, as Smith (2007) and a number of others contend; large states could tolerate, perhaps even encourage, local ethnic attachments and cultural pluralism and remain not only viable but vibrant. Smith envisions 'a civic ideal of nationhood ... predicated on the union of nation and state, and on a political type of nationalism ...' (Smith, 2007: 325). But the rule, established and reinforced over many centuries of insensitivity toward the needs of small ethnic communities, is broken in only a few instances – and there are still significant doubts that the modern exceptions will have much long- term success (see, as an example, the short-term official status for Australian aboriginal languages embodied in the National Policy on Languages [LoBianco, 1987] confronted shortly thereafter by a new government intent on giving priority to English and the powerful Asian languages [Dawkins, 1991]).

Transethnification can be described as follows: in the hierarchy of allegiances that characterizes identification (everyone has multiple identities, and these compete for priority by circumstance), individuals and communities are transethnified when local (ethnic) attachments are subordinated (if not suppressed in relation) to national ones. The iconography of these attachments may be largely codified in political values – individualistic capitalism, democracy, and the various freedoms of the Bill of Rights are examples from the United States. Transethnification allows the possibility that one will 'fight for one's country' (actually or symbolically) even in the face of an egregious history of oppression by that country. The fact that African Americans continue to distinguish themselves in US military service is understandable given their allegiance to the state (or its ideal). But it is also important to note that African Americans, along with other minority groups, tend to be over-represented in the US military relative to their percentage of the population. Members of these groups continue to distinguish themselves in military service and in their patriotic commitment toward a society that still, even in the so-called 'post-racial' period with a Black President, does not know how to acknowledge this loyalty, much less how to compensate them as they deserve. Some of these are in service to a country to which they have not yet gained citizenship.

Such apparently anomalous attitudes are not unknown in other parts of the Americas, as well. In the face of great injustice toward indigenous groups in Mexico and Guatemala and Peru and Bolivia, one still sees evidence of the loyalty, even love, of native groups for their beloved countries: schoolchildren in Chiapas stand outside every morning before class to salute the flag and sing the national hymn with great enthusiasm; crowds in Santa Cruz and Chichicastenango and Lima and hundreds of other communities march and dance in celebration of their independence days or because their national team has beaten the US in soccer.

What all of these cases demonstrate is a strong and pervasive ethic in a country, as imperfect as it has been, that demands allegiance to its central ideals, and for the most part receives it from even those who would be more than justified in rejecting it. But such loyalty is not evidence that they do not also cherish their own cultural distinctiveness; this also is important to them. But they have appropriated, through their own initiative or through imposition, a political identity that affirms their connection to their homeland. We cannot deny, however, that there are also other cases, in these and other times, in which these loyalties are in conflict; occasional disruptions of such public allegiance (e.g. the Los Angeles riots in the 1960s and 1990s) are significant as evidence that such public/private identity formations are delicate, but they nevertheless stand in sharp contrast to the actions of minority communities in other states (e.g. pre-Mandela South Africa) where acts of public disobedience are a constant reminder of the political fragmentation of civil authority where transethnification has not been realized. What we can say is that states can create conditions under which ethnic attachments and allegiance to the state can co-exist.

One should ask what differentiates transethnification from classical definitions of assimilation. The main difference is that, in transethnification, it is not necessary to 'lose' one's ethnicity to be useful to the state. Local attachments are not only permissible, but entirely desirable, so long as they have a certain aspect that qualifies them for acceptance in the public culture. Nor is it necessary, as it is in the full assimilation described by Gordon (1964), that one's attachment to the state have any 'sentimental' aspect (in Kelman's sense of historicity and authenticity). It is minimally sufficient that one's public actions convey acceptance of the legitimacy of the state and its ideals, even though these are not always (or even often) realized. The hope is that such public displays of allegiance will be convincing to our enemies that the union is strong, and to the younger generations of minority children that their successful futures lie in giving in to the majoritarian ethos. I propose the following propositions as a way to explain the case of the USA; whether they apply to other cases will be left for another time.

(1) To the extent that we value cultural differences, we tolerate 'cultural diversity' rather than 'cultural pluralism.'
(2) To the extent that we value cultural pluralism, we tolerate it as a private rather than a public pluralism.
(3) To the extent that we tolerate a public pluralism, it is symbolic and ceremonial rather than personal and political.

I will explain these in order.

The priority of diversity over pluralism

Proposition (1) contains a distinction between diversity and pluralism. Simply stated, I suggest it as a distinction between individual (though not idiosyncratic) and group differences. These appear to be practically if not conceptually indistinct ideas, and they are used interchangeably by many writers. When Sonia Nieto (2004), for example, speaks of 'affirming diversity,' or when Eugene Garcia (1995) asks that we consider how we might meet 'the challenge of cultural and linguistic diversity' in our schools, they are really talking about pluralism as I use the terms. Diversity is exemplified by the Mexican (from Mexico) or Chinese (from China) or Portuguese (from Portugal) student who sits in classrooms like the one I visited in Chicago. They have all been in school in their countries, and none knows English at all, but their parents, students at the university, want them there to learn it. They pose a challenge in approach and technology. About such students we ask, 'how can I teach them, given that they don't understand me?'. This is a technical problem, resolved relatively quickly, with the solicited aid of their parents, who will likely go back in a few years to Mexico or China or Portugal. The families live among us for a while, perhaps in ethnically separate communities, perhaps not; it would not be surprising to see them living and shopping in the same neighborhood as their child's teacher. We think of them as interesting and enriching (if complicating) additions to our classroom and school. To the extent that they represent anything beyond themselves, they are at most reluctant ambassadors of far-off lands (this is what I meant when I said that they are individuals, but not idiosyncratic); if we ask them to contribute something of their culture to the experiences of the other students, it is because we value the foreign qua foreign as academically enriching, but not because our goal is somehow to appropriate the foreign in school or society. We often go beyond merely appreciating this sort of cultural difference, to the point of seeking it out and cultivating it (in foreign exchanges and the adoption of sister cities, for example). Such differences are never the object of proselytization; in these circumstances, it would be a shame to detract from the exoticism of this kind of 'other.'

This is safe cultural difference: encouraging, even affirming 'diversity' of this sort makes us feel somehow as if we are doing something to advance peace in the world through understanding and good will; at the very least we are giving our children one more useful experience. We have no qualms about tapping into their prior knowledge, that rich storehouse of cultural and linguistic wealth we never doubt they bring with them. I suspect that many of the strategies we have developed for teaching English language learners have been significantly informed by these students; some of our innovations in teaching may have even started with them in mind.

This is hardly the situation facing Juan José in South Tucson, Arizona. His family has lived in this neighborhood for generations. His parents speak Spanish to him, as do many of his friends and family. He is bilingual, although he has some trouble reading and writing in English. His teacher drives ten miles from across the river to the school every day. She would like to have more contact with 'JJ's' parents, but they speak little English, and they hardly ever come to the school. His teacher, along with many of the teachers and administrators of the school, are sympathetic, but they are frustrated with his lack of progress. They express concerns about the neighborhood and his non-English environment, and in their candid moments decry the existence of the barrio as the real obstacle to achievement for these kids. This is not the sort of cultural difference to be encouraged and invited into the classroom, even for the sake of ceremony or 'cultural appreciation'; it is risky to try to domesticate this sort of 'otherness.' It is, instead, to be ignored, at best, perhaps even rooted out so that these kids can get ahead.

Juan José is not an individual cultural actor. He is a representative of his community, past and future; he is the same child who has walked into our classrooms for generations, and will continue doing so into the indefinite future. Even though they are among us, these families are still considered aliens and foreigners. Galindo and Vijil (2004) call this a 'Latino-as-foreigner phenomenon in which long-term residents and recent immigrants are perceived as foreigners' (Galindo & Vijil, 2004: 38). This form of nativism is more virulent than that which affected earlier European immigrant groups because Latinos are more easily identifiable as different through skin color and language. They are a persistent problem. The best we expect is to rescue one of them, and thus validate the schooling that we have provided, the only kind we know. The question we ask of Juan José is, '¿how quickly can we get him away from his community so that he can achieve?' Further, we ask, '¿If we teach him in Spanish so that he can understand, will we not be promoting the ghettoization that is the cause of his disadvantage?'

Juan José is not an individual; he is a token, a representative of his community. His 'problems' are not his uniquely: they are a demonstration of what ails his community. His disadvantage is existential, not circumstantial. He is not an 'immigrant' who will leave us soon so we can be done with his problem, which will never leave us. Tomorrow or next year, his little brother or cousin will come into our classroom as he did, and whatever minimal progress we saw in Juan José will be a distant memory: we will start again at zero, because that is all we think these children bring with them. This is how we conceptualize the problems of pluralism, as opposed to the advantages of diversity.

The priority of private over public

The second proposition is an acknowledgement that we do not like cultural pluralism, but that there may be times and circumstances in which we have to tolerate and cope with it. If we have to have it, it should be restricted to the private domains of family and community. Although there are some who would deny ethnic communities the right to identify themselves and raise their children as they would like, these are often rebuked as extremists or anti-immigrant (a label which itself distorts the debate, since quite often immigrant status is not involved). But when common, public resources are involved, the resistance to the promotion of programs of ethnic identification becomes broad based and more easily voiced. This is the reason that bilingual education, to the extent that it is regarded as a program that encourages ethnic identifications, is resisted with such hostility. If it is in public schools, it is using public money to subsidize what is regarded as essentially a private matter. This is also a rationale for including bilingual education, bilingual ballots and other aspects of public life as targets for elimination in official English legislation.

Although a number of states, including Colorado, Massachusetts and Florida, have recently considered measures some might call anti-immigrant, Arizona has been by far the most visible. Since 2000, the legislature and the electorate have passed laws in several versions against bilingual education, amendments to the constitution making English the official language of the state (Fitzsimmons-Doolan, 2009), and restrictions against public financing of English classes for illegal aliens. Most recently, the State Superintendent of Schools in Arizona has launched a campaign and promoted legislation for the purpose of eliminating public funds for courses in ethnic studies in the state's second largest school district. House Bill 2281 prohibits public school classes that 'promote the overthrow of the United States government, … promote resentment toward a race or class of people, … are designed primarily for pupils of a particular ethnic group, [and] … advocate ethnic solidarity instead of the treatment of pupils as individuals.' The bill allows the Superintendent to decide whether a public school is in compliance with the law, and to lower financial sanctions if it is not (State of Arizona, House of Representatives, 2010). He has also declared his intention to enforce a rule that principals should terminate teachers who speak English with an accent (Jordan, 2010). While one might argue that no one speaks any language without an accent, this particular measure is widely perceived to reflect a pervasive anti-Hispanic attitude in official state agencies, especially in the Department of Education. These are all instances of a pervasive atmosphere in Arizona and increasingly in other states; it views any public accommodation of ethnicity and languages other than English as a promotion of ethnic nationalism and prejudice instead of commitment to an idealized general will; publically-funded ethnic studies programs are anti-American and 'promote ethnic chauvinism.'

It is noteworthy that the legislation and regulations in question are aimed at public (including charter) schools. There appears to be little concern about heritage language schools and other efforts to maintain language and culture, as long as they are privately financed.

The priority of symbolic over committed ethnicity

Finally, the third proposition accepts the possibility that a public cultural pluralism may be acceptable, and even valuable for the public good, but only if it represents an occasional, tip-of-the-hat acknowledgment of ethnic heritages and works to advance the cultural and economic interests of the greater community. Publicly subsidized displays of ethnic identification may be especially valuable in the economic and artistic life of the dominant community. The fact that in Chicago 'everyone is Irish' on 17 March, and that a wide variety of people in Tucson celebrate Cinco de Mayo (even if they are not sure what it means) suggests that symbolic and ceremonial public ethnicity is valuable to dominant communities, as well as to the state.

The value of language diversity is not lost on the economic community. To the extent that it can take advantage of a bilingual workforce, the economic sector promotes ethnic communities. What would Boston's North End be without 'authentic' Italian restaurants and businesses, staffed by real Italian-Americans? Would San Francisco be the same without Chinatown? What is the economic impact of Olvera Street in Los Angeles? Would Miami be as charming without Little Havana? Can Tucson survive economically without the restaurants on South Sixth Street and the Mariachi Festival? These are questions that can be repeated for countless cities and towns throughout the country. Similarly, large corporations understand that ethnic communities that have retained language and culture can be real assets. Executives from such companies as CitiBank, Sears and Afni sound like multiculturalists when speaking on these issues: 'This is becoming a bilingual nation, with Spanish speaking people now accounting for 10 to 15 percent of the population and growing. It's an important part of our culture and who we are as Americans. So, it's important to us, because to speak in someone's native tongue is the definition of customer service' (Moore, 2006). Cultural diversity and language proficiencies are good when they are good for capitalism.

In addition to their usefulness, these are also nice, safe expressions of cultural difference. They become problematic, however, if they lead people within ethnic communities to rejuvenate their commitments to social justice – if these become the icons that index the history of oppression and discrimination that has characterized the dominant and the subaltern in North America. This would be a retrogression to nationalism, whereas transethnification is conceived of as a progressive step to the future that accommodates the needs of the administrative state (cf. Roosens' [1989] discussion on 'ethnogenesis').

Conclusion

This analysis leads to the conclusion that languages other than English (LOTEs) are perfectly acceptable in US society as long as they are mediated through individuals and not communities; if they are community languages, they should be confined to the private sector and not make demands for public subsidy; if there is to be public subsidy, their use should be for the common public good, and not signal competing allegiances.

This last proposition suggests the critical role that instrumentalism plays in our language ideology. As mentioned above, Herbert Kelman (1971) contrasted different modes of identifying with the national system by distinguishing 'sentimental' and 'instrumental' attachments. He describes the distinction as follows.

> An individual is sentimentally attached to the national system to the extent that he sees it as representing him – as being, in some central way, a reflection and an extension of himself. The system is legitimate and deserving of his loyalty because it is the embodiment of a people in which his personal identity is anchored. ... An individual is instrumentally attached to the national system to the extent that he sees it as an effective vehicle for achieving his own ends and the ends of members of other systems. For the instrumentally attached, the system is legitimate and deserving of his loyalty because it provides the organization for a smoothly running society, in which individuals can participate to their mutual benefit and have some assurance that their needs will be met. (Kelman, 1971: 25)

The instrumental orientation serves the interests of transethnification in several ways. In general, it urges us beyond local to system-wide and global considerations. We might perhaps say that attending to the usefulness of things beyond our community makes those things better in the long run because, by nullifying our incapacitating sentimentalities, we encourage the progress that is the result of a free market of goods and ideas. While we recognize the conservative call to 'buy American' as a competing tendency, the value placed on open competition in the marketplace is still dominant (Conservative Pat Buchanan drove a Mercedes Benz during his 'America First' 1992 presidential campaign). More specifically with respect to ethnicity and language, we perceive a sort of hierarchical stratification of languages in society where some are better because they are more useful, some are small and invalid because there is little return for the investment of learning and using them. This is the image of a sociolinguistic Darwinism that ensures the perpetuation of strong (Trudgill [1991] calls them 'killer') languages, the languages of wider communication (LWCs), often at the expense of the weak. This results in relative indifference on the part of LWC speakers in the face of massive and rapid loss of the 'little' languages. After all, while languages might be lost, it is primarily because they have been replaced with something else; when the 'something else' is a LWC, this may be cause for celebration not dismay, since the new that has come is much more useful to these speakers. Indeed, we should wonder whether 'little' language communities do not more often encourage their own demise if the reward is gaining the advantages of a more powerful language (Edwards, 1984).

The prior discussion on ethnicity and transethnification needs to be more directly tied to language if we are to understand the movement to officialize English in the US. Language is historically (if not conceptually) tied to national origin in the US. The idea of 'a nation of immigrants' is a 19th-century image of non-English speaking European ethnicities – Italians, Greeks, Hungarians, Norwegians, Germans – all of whose collective names as a people are the same as the names of their languages. More recently, Japanese, Chinese, Mexicans and the Hmong have also brought with them ethnicities not easily divorced in our minds from their languages. Language is therefore one of those 'major dimensions of public life' mentioned above. Change in language behavior is demonstrable, and it serves to index change in identity, or at least in loyalty: the transfer of allegiance from old country to new is signaled most visibly by the switch from the ethnic language to English. The switch from speaking Italian to speaking English is the switch from *being* Italian to *being* American (or from being Italian to being Italian-American to being 'just American').

The tendency to tie language to nation and to insist on allegiance to a dominant language ideology is not new, nor is it confined to the US. Mackey's (2004: 68) contention that 'subsuming all sister languages under a politically dominant tongue has long been the practice of nation-states' is well documented. Similarly, Schlyter (2004) cites the influence of the Soviet and western traditions on Central Asian policy makers in 'making language one of the main components in definitions of ethnicity and nation …' (Schlyter, 2004: 166). This is also the predominant ideology in the US, although it could be otherwise, as Morris (2004) suggests:

> A linguistically diverse USA, in which the large Spanish-speaking minority would be regarded as an asset, would likely be much more supportive of a linguistically diverse North America. On the other hand, powerful forces within the USA regard monolingualism and cultural homogeneity as essential for national unity, and ascendancy of these forces within the country would likely exert powerful pressure on other North American partners to join the Anglophone bandwagon. (Morris, 2004: 155)

The movement to officialize English in the United States must seem quite strange to outside observers. While states such as Arizona pass laws in order to 'preserve, protect and enhance the role of English,' a large part of the language planning activities of many countries is dedicated to protecting its own languages from the encroachment of English, even while they understand the need for their citizens to acquire it. The US has no official language as a nation, yet the overwhelming power of English seems to have convinced many of its citizens that it can live as if it does. In a world where multilingualism is the norm, such isolationism can be a risky gamble. In an extraordinary passage on the sociology of English under the equally extraordinary heading of 'The Parochialism of World Languages,' Fishman sounded an early alarm:

> The very factors that we have found to foster the international and intranational use and spread of English – economic relations with the Anglophone world, social status (whether reflected via income or education), and interaction with modern technology and mass media – also tend to insulate most Anglophones from learning the languages and cultures of other peoples of the world, precisely because of Anglophone predominance in these crucial respects. The parochialism engendered by such insulation is ultimately deleterious in technology, science, and industry per se and may erode the very superiority that leads the world to English today, thereby leading it to turn to other superior languages tomorrow. Only if the massive worldwide efforts to learn more English are increasingly matched by Anglophone efforts to learn a bit more of the languages (and values, traditions, purposes, etc.) of the rest of the world, might the current extraordinary position of English as an additional language be any more firmly established than were those of the previous lingua francas of world history. In an increasingly interacting world, the acceptance *of* English may be increasingly related to the acceptance of others by native speakers of English. Unfortunately, we know far more about how to help the world learn English (little though that may be),

than we do about how to help native speakers of English learn about the world. (Fishman, 1977: 334–335)

Fishman's insight should be the centerpiece for language planning and policy development in the United States. It points us to a society where everyone gains the perspective of another's language, another's culture. Instead of running away from our natural multilingual communities, we should embrace them for the resources they are, and ask them to help us enter the new millennium. Instead, we have yielded the ground to those with a 'persistent aversion to ... multiculturalism ... who have seen legendary political unifications or those under way as a kind of gilded cage' (Colomines, 2005: 211). Without a complete confession and renunciation of the sin of inveterate and aggressive and oppressive monolingualism, the US runs the risk of losing all of the advantages it has gained for itself and the world. Unfortunately, no such development appears close; quite the contrary.

This paper is the original manuscript and has not been revised or edited.

For the final version, see the French translation, (2010) L'aménagement linguistique de l'anglais et transethnification aux États-Unis, *Télescope* 16 (3), 96–112

Notes

(1) Portions of this paper have been read as early as 1986 at the Annual Meeting of the American Anthropological Association in San Francisco and as recently as the 2nd International Congress of Applied Linguistics in Costa Rica in 2009. I wish to acknowledge helpful comments and conversations with Brendan O'Connor, Janelle Johnson, Leila Varley Gutierrez and the members of the Language Planning seminars at the University of Arizona.

(2) This tendency most often works to the detriment of 'small' languages in relation to more powerful ones. See the opening remarks of the Director of the UNESCO Centre of Catalonia at an international conference on language promotion in Europe and Russia: '... the predominance of the traditional nation-states means that the official languages of these states come to dominate and that the languages of stateless nations are endangered by the *weak* protection they receive. This is even worse in the case of multinational and plurilingual states, which nevertheless rank their languages in a hierarchy and only make one of them the official language of the state on the grounds that it is the majority language demographically or for reasons of power' (Colomines, 2005: 207). Similar statements can be found throughout the language planning literature; see the papers in Maurais and Morris (2004) and Brock-Utne and Hopson (2005) for some recent examples.

(3) There is, as always, considerable argument and contestation of terms in this area. See, for example, Edwards' (2009) review of nationalism and its relation to ethnicity. He is especially critical of the term 'nation-state' when it is used as a synonym for 'country' or merely 'state.' Nation, for him, is 'a subjective or "imagined" community in Anderson's sense,' while the state is an administrative unit attached to a territory (Edwards, 2009: 171ff); the term 'nation-state' would require that these two constructs be coterminous, which they almost never are. What Edwards calls 'nation,' Fishman calls 'nationality,' and the state in Edwards' lexicon would be Fishman's 'nation.' I am not for the moment ready to argue against Edwards; for our purposes

here, Fishman is making the same distinction with different terms, and so we will see where that leads.
(4) Historical examples of civic identity-convergence between different ethnic groups abound. One might see a similar pattern of political convergence between Mexican-Americans, Puerto Ricans and some Central American immigrant groups into 'Latinos' as a political entity. While this term (as well as Hispanic) is contested with considerable justification, it can also function as a way to concentrate political interests.

References

Andersson, T. and Boyer, M. (1970) *Bilingual Schooling in the United States*, Vols 1 and 2. Washington, DC: US Government Printing Office.

Brock-Utne, B. and Hopson, R.K. (eds) (2005) *Languages of Instruction for African Emancipation: Focus on Postcolonial Contexts and Considerations*. Cape Town: Centre for Advanced Studies of African Society.

Colomines, A. (2005) Minority languages promotion and planning in Europe. In *Language Promotion and Planning in Europe and Russia: Acts of the International Seminar, 28–29 September 2004, Elista, Republic of Kalmykia, Russian Federation* (pp. 205–211). Elista: Kalmyk State University.

Conversi, D. (2007) Mapping the field: Theories of nationalism and the ethnosymbolic approach. In A.S. Leoussi and S. Grosby (eds) *Nationalism and Ethnosymbolism: History, Culture and Ethnicity in the Formation of Nations* (pp. 15–30). Edinburgh: Edinburgh University Press.

Coulmas, F. (1992) *Language and Economy*. Oxford: Blackwell.

Dawkins, J. (1991) *Australia's Language: The Australian Language and Literacy Policy*. Canberra: Australian Government Publishing Service.

Edwards, J. (ed.) (1984) *Linguistic Minorities, Policies and Pluralism*. London: Academic Press.

Edwards, J. (2009) *Language and Identity: An Introduction*. New York: Cambridge University Press.

Fishman, J. (1968) Nationality-nationalism and Nation-nationism. In J. Fishman, C. Ferguson and J. Das Gupta (eds) *Language Problems of Developing Nations*. New York: John Wiley & Sons.

Fishman, J. (1977) English in the context of international societal bilingualism. In J.A. Fishman, R.L. Cooper and A.W. Conrad (eds) *The Spread of English: The Sociology of English as an Additional Language* (pp. 329–336). Rowley, MA: Rowley House Publishers.

Fishman, J. (1991) *Reversing Language Shift: Theoretical and Empirical Foundations of Assistance to Threatened Languages*. Clevedon: Multilingual Matters.

Fishman, J.A., Ferguson, C.A. and Das Gupta, J. (eds) (1968) *Language Problems of Developing Nations*. New York: John Wiley & Sons.

Fitzsimmons-Doolan, S. (2009) Is public discourse about language policy really public discourse about immigration? A corpus-based study. *Language Policy* 8, 377–402.

Galindo, R. and Vijil, J. (2004) Language restrictionism revisited: The case against Colorado's 2000 Anti- Bilingual Education Initiative. *Harvard Latino Law Review 7*, 27–61.

Gándara, P. and Hopkins, M. (eds) (2010) *Forbidden Language: English Learners and Restrictive Language Policies*. New York: Teachers College Press.

Garcia, E.E., McLaughlin, B., Spodek, B. and Saracho, O.N. (1995) *Meeting the Challenge of Linguistic and Cultural Diversity in Early Childhood Education*. New York: Teachers College Press.

Gordon, M. (1964) *Assimilation in American life: The Role of Race, Religion and National Origins*. New York: Oxford University Press.

Heath, S.B. (1972) *Telling Tongues: Language Policy in Mexico, Colony to Nation*. New York: Teachers College Press.

Jernudd, B.H. (1971) Notes on economic analysis for solving language problems. In J. Rubin and B.H. Jernudd (eds) *Can Language be Planned? Sociolinguistic Theory and Practice for Developing Nations* (pp. 263–276). Honolulu: University of Hawaii Press.

John-Steiner, V.P. (1971) *Early Childhood Bilingual Education*. New York: Modern Language Association.

Jordan, M. (2010) Arizona grades teachers on fluency: State pushes school districts to reassign instructors with heavy accents or other shortcomings in their English. *Wall Street Journal*, 30 April.

Kaplan, R.B. and Baldauf, R.B. (1997) *Language Planning from Practice to Theory*. Clevedon: Multilingual Matters.

Kelman, H. (1969) Language as aid and barrier to involvement in the national system. *Consultative Meeting on Language Planning Processes, East-West Center, Honolulu*. Also in J. Rubin and B. Jernudd (eds) (1971) *Can Language Be Planned?* Honolulu: University of Hawaii Press (pp. 21–51).

Lambert, W.E. and Tucker, G.R. (1972) *Bilingual Education of Children: The St. Lambert Experiment*. Rowley, MA: Newbury House.

Leibowitz, A. (1969) *Educational Policy and Political Acceptance: The Imposition of English as the Language of Instruction in American Schools*. ED047321. Washington, DC: Educational Resources Information Center (ERIC).

Lieberson, S. (with T.J. Curry) (1971) Language shift in the United States: Some demographic clues. *International Migration Review* 5 (Special Issue on Language Maintenance and Language Shift in Migration and Immigration), 125–137.

Lo Bianco, J. (1987) *National Policy on Languages*. Canberra: Australian Government Publishing Service.

Mackey, W. (2004) Forecasting the fate of languages. In J. Maurais and M.A. Morris (eds) *Languages in a Globalizing World* (pp. 64–81). New York: Cambridge University Press.

Macnamara, J. (1971) Successes and failures in the movement for the restoration of Irish. In J. Rubin and B.H. Jernudd (eds) *Can Language be Planned? Sociolinguistic Theory and Practice for Developing Nations* (pp. 65–94). Honolulu: University of Hawaii Press.

Maurais, J. and Morris, M.A. (eds) (2004) *Languages in a Globalizing World*. New York: Cambridge University Press.

Menken, K. and García, O. (eds) (2010) *Negotiating Language Policies in Schools: Educators as Policymakers*. New York: Routledge.

Moore, P. (2006) Tucson call centers booming; bilingual workforce is key. *Inside Tucson Business*, 10 March. See http://www.azbiz.com/articles/2006/03/16/news/news02.txt, (accessed 9 June 2010).

Morris, M.A. (2004) Effects of North American integration on linguistic diversity. In J. Maurais and M.A. Morris (eds) *Languages in a Globalizing World* (pp. 143–156). New York: Cambridge University Press.

Nieto, S. (2004) *Affirming Diversity: The Sociocultural Context of Multicultural Education* (4th edn). White Plains, NY: Longman.

Pool, J. (1972) National development and linguistic diversity. In J.A. Fishman (ed.) *Advances in the Sociology of Language*, Vol. 2 (pp. 213–230). The Hague: Mouton.

Roosens, E. (1989) *Creating Ethnicity: The Process of Ethnogenesis*. Newbury Park, CA: Sage Publications.

Rubin, J. and Jernudd, B. (eds) (1971) *Can Language be Planned? Sociolinguistic Theory and Practice for Developing Nations*. Honolulu: University of Hawaii Press.

Schlyter, B.N. (2004) Sociolinguistic changes in transformed Central Asian societies. In J. Maurais and M.A. Morris (eds) *Languages in a Globalizing World* (pp. 157–187). New York: Cambridge University Press.

Smith, A. (2007) The power of ethnic traditions in the modern world. In A.S Leoussi and
    S. Grosby (eds) *Nationalism and Ethnosymbolism: History, Culture and Ethnicity in the
    Formation of Nations* (pp. 325–336). Edinburgh: Edinburgh University Press.
Spolsky, B. (2004) *Language Policy*. Cambridge: Cambridge University Press.
State of Arizona, House of Representatives (2010) *House Bill 2281*. Forty-ninth Legislature,
    Second Regular Session. Phoenix, AZ.
Tollefson, J.W. (2002) Limitations of language policy and planning. In R.B. Kaplan (ed.)
    The Oxford Handbook of Applied Linguistics (pp. 416–425). New York: Oxford University
    Press.
Trudgill, P. (1991) Language maintenance and language shift: Preservation versus extinc-
    tion. *International Journal of Applied Linguistics* 1 (1), pp. 61–69.
Turi, J.-G. (1977) *Les dispositions jurido-constitutionelles de 147 états en matière de politique
    linguistique*. Québec: CIRB, Université Laval.
Weinstein, B. (1983) *The Civic Tongue: Political Consequences of Language Choices*. New York
    and London: Longman.

Part 2

Bilingual Education

Richard Ruiz and Bilingual Education
Norma González and Eric J. Johnson

Language Teaching in American Education
(1984) NIE report. Washington, DC: National Institute of Education

Bilingual Education
(1997) In C. Grant and G. Ladson-Billings (eds)
Dictionary of Multicultural Education
(pp. 29–31). Phoenix, AZ: Oryx

Paradox of Bilingualism
(2008) In J. González (ed.) *Encyclopedia of Bilingual Education* (pp. 645–650)
London: Sage

The Knowledge Base of Bilingual Education
(2008) Review of González (2008) *The Encyclopedia of Bilingual Education.*
Education Review, 8 November

Richard in front of his bookshelf, University of Arizona, date unknown
Courtesy of Marie Ruiz.

Richard Ruiz and Bilingual Education

Norma González and Eric J. Johnson

Richard Ruiz often wore many hats. One hat that he never removed was that of a steadfast supporter and advocate for bilingual education. His support, however, was nuanced by his incisive and keen insights into how policy in bilingual education was shaped by political exigencies rather than the research base on how English learners could become truly emergent bilinguals. One short story illustrates this point. The Dean of the College of Education at the University of Arizona, Ron Marx, relates the following:

> Richard had apparently attended a series of meetings at the state capital regarding bilingual education. The State Superintendent of Education at the time was not a supporter of bilingual education and had enacted a series of provisions that many found to be harmful to English learners. Dean Marx related that 'At one point the State Superintendent said to me something like: There is a faculty member in your college who comes to these meetings, sits in the back, and has an inscrutable look on his face. I don't think he agrees with what we are doing and I don't think he likes me very much. What is he doing and what can I do about him?' The Superintendent clearly was nervous about this faculty member attending these meetings and acting as a foil to the Arizona Department of Education policies and practices on bilingual education. After a little back and forth to get an idea about who this might have been, Dean Marx responded. 'That is most likely Richard Ruiz. You are right, he does not agree with what you are doing in bilingual education, and I suspect he does not like you very much. He is a tenured faculty member with expertise in this area and he is doing what he is supposed to be doing.' Without question, Richard's attendance at the meetings was a burr in the Superintendent's side, and Richard's demeanor evidently made him nervous. He would have preferred that Richard not be present.

But present he was, not only in a physical presence, but in his extensive and penetrating scholarship on how students best acquired a second language while developing their first language.

Richard's scholarship led him to pinpoint early on (see his 1984 article) that there are several paradoxes in what we call bilingual education. First of all, bilingual education is really not about *bilingualization* (his term for the development of bilingual proficiency in students – see his 1997 article) and the acquisition of two languages. It was first and foremost a vehicle for the acquisition of English. This assertion was confirmed with the 2001 Reauthorization of ESEA which eradicated all mention of bilingual education in favor of the terminology of English acquisition. The second paradox, which is the basis for his 2008b 'Paradox of bilingualism,' is that 'Other languages are to be pursued by those who don't have them, but they are to be abandoned by those who do.' This paradox is brilliantly illustrated by his painstaking and detailed scholarship into the historical documentation of publically funded bilingual education in the United States, most dramatically exemplified by the contrast between German language programs in the Midwest and Spanish language programs in the Southwest. Ruiz traces the paradox to underlying ideologies that fall into two categories:

(1)   A highly instrumentalized view of language that views language as a tool and an instrument for obtaining social goods. 'To the extent that it does that, we see language as valuable; to the extent that it does not, we devalue it' (Ruiz, 2008b).
(2)   Language as a part of the identity, history, tradition, culture and personality of a community.

These two perspectives on the role of language in the life of communities belie widely divergent expectations on how language is learned and the policies that undergird language learning in schools. The paradox restated is then: Spanish (or French or German or any other non-English world standard foreign language) is to be pursued by those who do not have it, but Spanish (or French or German or any other 'little' non-English community language) is to be abandoned by those children and youth who do. Spanish uplifts and enhances and builds up; Spanish tears down and fragments and holds back all who maintain it (Ruiz, 2008b).

With great clarity, Richard's work cinches together an array of topics that comprise significant tenets of bilingual education; nowhere is this more evident than in his review of the *Encyclopedia of Bilingual Education* (2008a). His emphasis on the politicized nature of language minority education can be seen as a conceptual hub that guides his perspectives on the complex facets of bilingual education. Ruiz used his review of the *Encyclopedia* as a platform for discussing themes like language acquisition, medium of instruction, culture, family engagement, and assessment. Although not explicitly stated in his review, Ruiz's stance on these topics resonates with his paradoxical view noted above. By looking at the dichotomous relationship between the predominant trends in academic research versus policy development, Ruiz penetrated the prevailing ideological assumptions about language minority communities that continue to drive programmatic responses to shifting demographic landscapes in education.

Richard used a policy narrative to highlight strengths in language minority communities while calling attention to weaknesses in political decision making processes. His advocacy for language minority students is reflected in his points on providing bilingual support programs for students at any age, and for an extended timeframe. He raises multiple forceful points about the contradictory nature of promoting additive language programs for students from privileged backgrounds around the world (usually in private school settings) while restricting opportunities for programs that promote bilingualization in the US. In his discussion of federal education policy developments, Ruiz mentions how increased standardized assessment requirements adversely affected language minority students and communities (e.g. increased dropout rates, special education placements and remedial compensatory programs). Although ever aware of the weightiness of the significance of bilingual education programs, his keen and wry humor was one of his weapons in skewering programs and policies that purported to be something they were not (see Parable of the Pig).

On a state level, living in Arizona provided Richard with extensive exposure to the anti-bilingual education policies promoted by Ron Unz's group, English for the Children. As an ardent opponent of these types of policies, he indicates the fallacies of the one-year timeframe for acquiring English, as fabricated by opponents of bilingual programs. While his refutation draws from scholars from the field of language acquisition, he is also quick to point out the role of the political ideologies espoused by anti-bilingual education groups. In this case, these opponents to bilingual education align with an instrumentalized view of language that not only posits English as the *sine qua non* for success in school, it simultaneously discredits the inherent value of minority languages, essentially targeting them (as vehicles of cultural transmission) for eradication. Again, the paradox rings true: abate minority languages within minority communities while promoting foreign language learning in majority language communities.

While much of Richard's work on bilingual education is dedicated to foregrounding the political nature of language policies as driven by broader social forces, he consistently prioritizes the important role that cultural practices play in working with language minority students. This slant is twofold. First, educators and politicians operate within an educational framework that prioritizes certain sets of knowledge and skills – resulting in the development of programs, curricula and classroom practices that serve to perpetuate and advance the interests of those in positions of power within a given cultural context. By recognizing systemic inequities, educators can potentially modify their own professional practices to honor language minority students' background knowledge and experiences. Secondly, Richard's perspective emphasized patterns of 'home-school isomorphism' that abound in American schools. So important is this particular topic that Ruiz dedicates a substantial part of his review to illustrating the need for re-conceptualizing how educators engage language minorities and communities with a view toward acknowledging their strengths, resources and resiliency.

Ruiz's discussion of the underlying home-school isomorphism that has molded educators' perceptions of minority communities reflects his profound understanding of the cultural dynamics inherent in the process of schooling. This is particularly noteworthy considering that the *Encyclopedia* does not contain an entry solely focused on this topic. Instead, he uses this publication as a venue to caution us to be mindful of the cultural assumptions entailed in the loaded, yet predominant, notion of 'parental involvement.' The prevailing perspective of parents who are unable to attend school functions or dedicate time to tutor their children with homework every night tends to cast such family practices in a negative light – i.e. something that requires intensive remediation. More often than not, this view of families parallels a mindset that minority students' background knowledge is of little value in school settings. Ruiz urges educators to push back against the deficit orientations that perpetuate asymmetrical relationships between schools and the minority families and communities they serve.

Rather than seeing language minority students' background experiences as incongruous with academic contexts, Ruiz endorses the opposite – i.e. 'that the children bring many strengths with them to school, having learned a lot from home and community about how to learn and act' (Ruiz, 2008a). Once again, this claim is grounded in understanding the way cultural practices shape interactions between teachers and students, teachers and parents and, most importantly, between parents and their children. Richard underscores the concept of cultural capital to illustrate the potential for valuing students' Funds of Knowledge as a means of enhancing academic experiences. Not only does espousing a Funds of Knowledge approach in the classroom contribute to the students' academic progress, but home–school partnerships are strengthened and wider avenues of communication allow 'mutual sharing of valuable knowledge that leads to an enhanced learning environment for children' (Ruiz, 2008a).

Ruiz's passion for bilingual education is evident in the way he describes minority students' (and families') lived experiences as assets. The way he chronicles political processes sheds light on the broader forces that ultimately affect children, families, communities and educators. His historical accounts of bilingual education policies in the United States demonstrate how particular language orientations are manifested out of deeper, underlying tensions between different cultural groups. Richard's writings are a powerful reminder of the significant role that schools play, especially when language policies are developed, in expediting the assimilation of minority groups at the expense of academic progress, and more disturbingly, their cultural identities.

Honoring language minority communities, rather than disparaging them, is among the most significant threads woven throughout all of Richard's work on bilingual education. His fervent defense of bilingual education at all levels was a source of strength for those demoralized by the political contexts of language policy in Arizona. He was unwavering and unbroken in seeing the promise.

Resources

Ruiz, R. (1984a) Language teaching in American education: Impact on second-language learning. Synthesis report for the National Institute of Education, Washington, DC.

Ruiz, R. (1997) Bilingual education. In C.A. Grant and G. Ladson-Billings (eds) *Dictionary of Multicultural Education* (pp. 29–31). Phoenix, AZ: Oryx Press.

Ruiz, R. (2008a) The knowledge base of bilingual education. Review of: The Encyclopedia of Bilingual Education (J. González, ed.). Boulder, CO: Education Review, National Education Policy Center.

Ruiz, R. (2008b) Paradox of bilingual education. In J. González (ed.) *Encyclopedia of Bilingual Education* (pp. 646–651). Thousand Oaks, CA: Sage.

Language Teaching in American Education: Impact on Second-Language Learning

Richard Ruiz (1984)

Introduction

The purpose of this report is to address some basic questions about language teaching and the education of language minority populations in the United States. The end of this effort is to serve as background for important policy decisions on such topics as bilingual education, foreign language programs, and the development of language policy statements.

The report is divided into two parts. The first is a presentation of a brief history of language study and teaching beginning in the middle of the last century. Several key questions guide this discussion: What factors have influenced the variable interest in language study and bilingual education? Who and what have influenced language education practices? How have language minority students been treated in schools? How have court decisions and state and local laws affected language education and policy? What efforts have been made to formulate a national consensus (or a national policy) on language use and language education? The result of this discussion will be a general picture of the sociolinguistic context in which language policy decisions are made in the United States.

The second part of the report relates directly to the issue of second-language teaching. It comprises a review of the most important concepts and theories on second-language acquisition, an outline of some methods of second-language teaching arising from these theories, and an examination of the assumptions, goals, and effects of progress of second-language teaching like bilingual education and immersion. Also in this section, some suggestions on the relationship among the different language teaching approaches are offered. A final section of the report presents some policy implications arising out of the review.

PART I: LANGUAGE POLICY AND PRACTICE IN U.S. SCHOOLS

The United States has a particular sociolinguistic history which must be considered in any examination of language and education policy formation. That history is formed by many influences. Perhaps the most important are traditional practices; the fact, for example, that the school "has always done things that way" itself is sometimes treated as a tacit policy. Also important have been court decisions and opinions regarding language minority communities and their education. Setting legal precedent has far-reaching and relatively long-term effects on the development of policy. At times the messages sent by the court have transcended the legal text itself: the opinions offered by judges and justices can convey embedded attitudes about what is the proper course for social and educational policy, regardless of the court's explicit decision. Finally, we should keep in mind that language and education policy are matters which reach far beyond the school. These are issues of political ideology as much as ones of academic research. Whatever decisions are reached in this area, there is sure to be a pervasive social and political effect. The purpose of this section is to present some of this historical background, and to work through some of the difficulties of language policy formulation given this context.

The Historical Context

1850–1880: An uneasy tolerance

The United States has experienced waves of language interest throughout its history. It is fair to say, however, that the factors affecting this interest seldom if ever had anything to do with the languages themselves; rather, the crucial elements related to the perceived status of the language groups involved. To the extent that these groups were viewed as socially, politically, or economically threatening, tolerance of their language was greatly diminished.[1] Various factors have worked to determine the social status of non-English language groups. Generally, characteristics which have combined to generate negative evaluations of a group include the following: non-white racial traits, non-western cultural traditions, provenance from authoritarian/totalitarian states, political-military hostility of the native country toward the United States. Conversely, those who are white, well-to-do, western in orientation, and from friendly democratic states have been well received.

The schools tend to respond to and reflect these sociopolitical considerations. In the case of language study, the nature of curricular offerings and the composition of school staffs have changed almost immediately with a significant shift in social climate. The correspondence between the inclusion of language study in school and the social perception of language communities in the larger society is demonstrated most dramatically in the U.S. in the case of German in the mid-19th and early 20th centuries. Most of the Northern and Western European groups were accepted in urban neighborhoods and in the schools, as they were seen generally as hard-working and productive members of the community. They met with resistance only to the extent that they became intrusive or hostile to what by that time was the main purpose of the public school—Americanization.

The 1860s and 70s saw a dramatic rise in the study of German in the public schools, accompanying the enhanced political status of Germans in the communities of the midwest. By midcentury, Germans in St. Louis constituted one quarter of the population and formed "a considerable portion of [the] active business and manufacturing community, holding a great amount of wealth of [the] city, and contributing largely to its revenues."[2] Advocates for including German in the public schools, responding in part to mounting pressures to increase public school enrollments[3], argued that German study would encourage German parents to send their children to public school; this was especially true of the earlier grades, where "the absence of German instruction … induced a large number of German families to send their children first to private schools."[4] These arguments finally prevailed; in 1864–65, 450 elementary students (about 5% of the total student population) in 5 schools studied German under the tutelage of 5 specially trained teachers (who had been "furnished" by the Cincinnati school district, which had by then some 25 years of experience in German teaching). By the end of that year, the Office of German Assistant Superintendent was established. The increase in public resources allocated to German instruction in subsequent years was dramatic. By 1870, 37% of the students studied German; in 1875, 73% studied German with 73 teachers in 45 schools, and the numbers kept increasing into the 1880s.[5]

This pattern was mirrored at this time in other large cities of the midwest. In Chicago, German instruction was introduced in 1865, due largely to the efforts of influential Germans in the community and on the school board; by 1878, German teaching was being coordinated through the Special Teacher of German, Dr. Gustav A. Zimmerman.[6] In Milwaukee, German teaching in the public schools was a common practice as early as the 1840s; various state laws starting in 1848 gave this practice official sanction. By 1870, more than 46% of the students were studying German.[7] In 1878, the National German-American Teachers' Seminary was established "to fit young ladies and gentlemen for teaching in both English and German … according to the most approved methods of modern pedagogy adapted to American institutions."[8] Even as late as 1907, when the study of German was made optional, about 70% of Milwaukee students were enrolled in German classes. This pattern persisted until 1915 in Milwaukee.[9]

It is too simple to say that Germans, Norwegians, and other groups were accepted into these communities and their languages included in the schools because they were white and sought to better themselves. While their situation was obviously better than that for Blacks or Hispanics or the Eastern and Southern Europeans that would follow them, their non-Anglo status was still troublesome. Indeed, those very characteristics which helped them gain access to the schools—their numerosity, their political influence, and their economic power base—were sources of friction: sporadic at first, then more widespread. This can be seen early, as when a few complained of the "Germanizing" of Chicago schools in 1865,[10] or when Wisconsin residents demanded that an 1848 law which allowed the teaching of "other languages" in the schools be amended to require that all fundamental courses would be taught in English.[11] There was an uneasiness with any group that tried too hard to preserve its old world language. This did not go unnoticed by the groups themselves, who did not want to appear overly resistant to the Americanizing efforts of the public schools. The Scandinavian groups, among others, protested the inclusion of German in Chicago schools and affirmed the primacy of English in their new country.[12] This was a common public posture for many immigrant language communities, especially in times of social agitation, as the pressures then to shake off the old ways and become "fully American" became urgent.[13]

1880–1920: The new immigration and the push for Americanization

While it is true that German instruction persisted in public schools into the first part of the twentieth century, the nature of intergroup relations changed significantly in the 1880s with a renewed push for Americanization. Several factors combined to intensify this emphasis. Perhaps the most important is the fact that immigrants of the 1880s were different from those who had preceded them: of the 23 million coming into the United States between 1880 and 1920, 20 million of these would be from Eastern and Southern Europe.[14] Add to these the Asians and the Latin Americans (Puerto Rico became officially an American "problem" in 1898), and the situation had become intolerable for some. There was a general public outcry: these people had strange customs, spoke foreign languages, did not have the American sense of decency or respect for democratic institutions, and tended to be poor. The English historian James Bryce summarized the growing apprehension of many Americans:

> Swarms of European immigrants have invaded America, drawn from their homes in the eastern parts of Central Europe by the constant cheapening of ocean transit and by the more thorough drainage, so to speak, of the inland regions of Europe which is due to the extension of railways. These immigrants ... come from a lower stratum of civilization ... and, since they speak foreign tongues, are less quickly amenable to American

influences ... There seems to be some danger that if they continue to come in large numbers they may retain their own low standard of decency and comfort, and menace the continuance among the working class generally of that far higher standard which has hitherto prevailed in all but a few spots in the country.[15]

Americans felt menaced on all sides. The culmination of the Mexican War in the late 1840s had left the United States with what many perceived as a mixed blessing: a vast land with untold natural resources but with a considerable number of poor, Spanish-speaking tenants generally resentful of their new status; in addition, the end of the war left a hostile neighbor to the south which, though thoroughly defeated, still held potential for mischief. On the west coast, Asians had been valuable as a source of labor for the railroads; now, with the completion of that project, they posed a major problem. A series of nuisance laws, designed largely to hinder Aslan small business efforts, served as background to the Chinese Exclusion Act of 1882.[16] With the arrival in large numbers of these new immigrant groups in the 1880s, American xenophobia, which had remained just below the surface earlier in the century, now threatened to become an epidemic.

Many of the new immigrants were also Catholics. This added another element to the problem of social unrest. But it also was a factor in the new attitudes toward language and language study: for many, their religion, if not language-specific, was at least intertwined with their language. This could be most forcefully expressed by the German Catholics, whose social position was relatively strong: "German children, if Anglicized, by some strange fate generally become alienated from Catholic life."[17]

The strong push for Americanization in the public schools of the 1880s brought with it a concern for Anglicization, as well. The President of the Milwaukee School Board expressed the charge this way in 1888: "Our children must first and foremost be taught to read, write, and speak English with facility and correctness ... And although we may yield to the local interest of the community in regard to the instruction in a special foreign language, we must not forget that the schools are, first of all, American schools ..."[18] This set the stage for social conflict. Catholics faced a hard choice: they could send their children to private school to preserve the integrity of language, religion, and cultural tradition, but risk being accused of anti-American parochialism; or, they could send them to the public schools, becoming vulnerable to attack from their own community as "lax Catholics." The situation was exacerbated in 1889 when state legislatures in several midwestern states, most notably Illinois and Wisconsin, tried to regulate the practices of the parochial schools as well. Early in 1889, Wisconsin state Senator Pond introduced a bill which would have required annual statistical reports from both public and private schools "to enable the state to judge whether sufficient English instruction was provided."[19] The bill was defeated, due largely to pressure on the legislators from the German communities and press.

Later that year, the Edwards Law in Illinois and the Bennett Law in Wisconsin were enacted. On their face, these two identical laws were designed to curb the exploitation of child labor by requiring, under penalty of fine, that children between 7 and 14 attend a school a minimum number of days a year. The problem arose in the legislators' definition of a school: "No school shall be regarded as a school under this act unless there shall be taught therein, as part of the elementary education of children, reading, writing, arithmetic and United States history in the English language." In 1889, the conservative Wisconsin Synod of the Lutheran Church administered 164 parochial schools, many of which used German exclusively. About 4,000 children were served by these schools.[20] These German communities convinced Lutherans throughout the midwest, as well as the powerful Catholic Church in Wisconsin, that the ultimate goal of this legislation was "to place the parochial and private schools under the control of the state," with the "further objective of entirely eliminating the parochial schools."[21] The effect on the local elections of 1890 was, by all accounts, devastating for the incumbent Republicans, as Lutherans, Catholics, and the German press[22] formed a strong alliance encouraging the defection of German communities from the Republican party.[23]

In Illinois, the Superintendent of Public Instruction predicted that the controversy would attenuate as private schools were given time to adjust to the new rules: "the hostility of the parochial schools is rapidly disappearing where they find that the law is not leveled at them so long as they teach in English the primary studies of the public schools."[24] This was a serious miscalculation of the public mood. The fate of Republicans in Illinois was the same as in Wisconsin.

In spite of the quick repeal of these laws (in 1891), they had a chilling effect on the parochial schools and on foreign language instruction in the public schools.[25] The survival of the private schools depended on their filling a role different from that of the public schools. Instead, after the Bennett law controversy, parochial schools in Wisconsin, "under pressure from public school men and Irish Catholics, became increasingly American in form and content."[26] Thus, as Kellogg suggests, it appears that, even as the Bennett Law was being defeated, "the principle of the law triumphed." The sentiment in favor of these kinds of laws was becoming more public throughout the midwest in the 1880s and 90s.[27]

Two other developments have been significant to a change in public mood toward ethnic communities in the 1880s. One has to do with the practical concerns of the public schools. Earlier in the century, school officials courted ethnic communities because of the need to make their institutions viable;[28] whatever concessions they had to make in the area of language instruction seemed reasonable given the advantage of large enrollments.

In the 1880s, this need was no longer urgent. Attention could now be turned to assimilating the immigrant in order to eliminate the hostile "foreign element" invading the society. Teaching English to the immigrant was considered an indispensable first step toward assimilation: school books of the time, like Sara O'Brien's English for Foreigners (1909), showed the intimate connection perceived between learning English and becoming "fully American." At the same time, changing the foreigner through school was not enough; measures which would exclude anyone not meeting certain minimum standards were proposed. In 1897, for example, the House of Representatives recommended a bill excluding for admission to the United States "all persons physically capable and over sixteen years of age who cannot read and write the English language or some other language."[29] While this particular measure was vetoed, it showed that the mood of the country had changed toward immigration and the value of ethnic communities to its social institutions. The national attitude toward exclusion which culminated in 1924 can trace its roots to the 1880s.

Another development contributing to this shift in mood, significant for the schools, is something of a historical irony. The 1880s are the beginning of what some have called the Modern Languages movement. The benefits of including modern languages in the curriculum had been debated since at least the early republic (Thomas Jefferson urged his nephews to learn the "travelling" languages like Spanish, which he was sure would become politically important, and even established the first American professorship in modern languages)[30]; nevertheless, formal study until the mid-19th century was still based on the British trivium which, with its emphasis on "mental discipline," was dominated by courses in logic, rhetoric, and the classical languages. The shift to modern spoken languages no doubt was due to a combination of factors. The increase in school and college enrollments and the prevalence of the elective system in courses of study were perhaps most significant. An emphasis on popular education which would produce practical professionals rather than merely cultured gentlemen was also important; this is demonstrated by the remarkable number of state-technical-land grant universities established in the second half of the 19th century. Whatever the reasons, more than one-third of high school students were studying modern languages by 1915.[31]

What appears to distinguish this era from the preceding one is an emphasis on formal foreign language study. Earlier, Germans, Italians, Norwegians, Poles, and others studied their own languages in school, informally at first, then more systematically. While there is evidence that Anglo-American students were enrolled in these classes, that was almost certainly an incidental side effect of bilingual instruction aimed at the ethnic community. In the late 70s and early 80s, organizations dedicated to more formal teaching and study of modern languages emerged. The most notable of these is the Modern Language Association, established in 1883. It is perhaps here that we can see the genesis of a most important distinction in language study, as Ferguson and Heath suggest: "From at least the time of World War I and possibly as far back as the Modern Languages movement of the 1880s, there has been a sharp distinction in the attitudes toward non-English languages between the languages of immigrants and the foreign languages (FL) taught in school."[32] Immigrant and ethnic languages are discriminated against in the school domain, while foreign languages are encouraged as a formal subject. This is consistent with the Americanization focus of the schools of this time: language study as a means of ethnic preservation and solidarity was dangerous and to be discouraged; but studying a foreign language, so long as it remained a foreign language, was a perfectly acceptable subject.[33] This fundamental distinction underlies even now the conflicts involved in some of the most important language issues: teaching the standard language or the vernacular; establishing maintenance or transitional programs; using dialects as media of instruction. Certainly it is at the center of the cleavage which exists between foreign language and bilingual education teachers. The formalization of foreign language study between 1880 and 1920, while it was accompanied by a tremendous increase in language course enrollments, changed radically the nature of language education in the United States.

1920–1950: Dropping the language curtain

By the 1920s, the "language curtain" is fully dropped in the United States.[34] All of the advantages which Germans and their language had in the society and the schools were now overshadowed by Germany's hostility towards the United States. The schools, once again the mirrors of public sentiment, almost completely dismembered their German instructional programs by the end of the war. Between 1916 and 1918, for example, the number of students enrolled in German classes in Milwaukee schools dropped from 30,000 to 400, and the number of German teachers from 200 to one. By the end of the 1919 school year, German teaching was completely discontinued in the elementary schools.[35] The same pattern was repeated in cities throughout the country.[36] At the same time, advocates for the use of other languages took advantage of the decline of German in school to promote their interests; the American Association of Teachers of Spanish, established in 1917, highlighted the commercial utility of Spanish, apparently a novel justification of modern language study: "having not yet gained academic recognition of the importance of Hispanic literatures, they successfully called attention to the importance of Spanish for anyone interested in trade with the opening markets of Latin America. A new argument for studying modern languages had been advanced."[37] Spanish, along with French, now became the principal languages of interest for school study.

However, while German was the focus of hostility in both school and society, laws and official pronouncements immediately following World War

I reflected a general antagonism toward foreigners and their languages; the urge to Americanize and anglicize the schools was stronger than ever. The Americanization Department of the federal Bureau of Education issued the following statement in 1919: "We recommend urgently to all states to pre-scribe that all schools, private and public, be conducted in the English lan-guage and that instruction in the elementary classes of all schools be in English."[38] More drastic measures were taken by the states, almost half of which passed legislation hostile to foreign language instruction between 1918 and 1925.[39] The most famous of these is Nebraska's Siman Law of 1919, which proscribed foreign language instruction in both public and private schools below the ninth grade. This law was declared unconstitutional in Meyer v. Nebraska (1923); however, the opinions of the Justices in this and other similar cases betray a sympathy for the ultimate ends of such laws.[40] Consider this statement in Meyer from Justice McReynolds: "The desire of the legislature to foster a homogeneous people with American ideals pre-pared readily to understand current discussions of civil matters is easy to appreciate." Compare this to the dissenters' opinion in Bartels v. Iowa of the same year:

> We all agree, I take it, that it is desirable that all the citizens of the United States should speak a common tongue, and therefore that the end aimed at by the statute is a lawful and proper one ... I cannot bring my mind to believe that in some circumstances, and circumstances existing it is said in Nebraska, the statute might not be regarded as a reasonable or even necessary method of reaching the desired result.

In spite of the repeal of most of these laws, local antagonisms and fear within the ethnic communities served to alter radically the nature of language study in the schools after 1920. Of course, the calls for removing language alto-gether from the school curriculum continued, justified at times by arguments perhaps best described as xenophobic, at other times by what at least appeared to be more utilitarian considerations.[41] More often, the trend was away from eradicating language programs and toward making them more formal. As a result, modern language teaching in the United States came to stress literacy, while speaking skills languished badly. This tendency was reinforced by the Coleman Report of 1924, one of a series of reports commis-sioned by the "Modern Foreign Language Study" supported by the Carnegie Corporation. It found that the vast majority of high school students studied foreign languages for 2 years or fewer. Since it was impossible to become proficient in all language skills in that short time, the report concluded that the reading skill should be emphasized over others since it is the most easily attainable in a limited time.[42]

Furthermore, the trend toward formalization was strengthened by removing almost all language teaching from the elementary schools and assigning it to high schools and colleges. But even there, the situation was bleak. With high schools unable to find qualified American-born language teachers, and constrained by the short time in which to have students attain proficiency, many chose to drop or minimize language study. This put pressure on colleges which survived by competing for students. It was practical for many to drop foreign language requirements; others were forced to compromise these requirements in order to accommodate otherwise well-prepared students.[43]

The decline in foreign language study in the United States between the world wars was dramatic, as the following table shows:

Year	Total H.S. Enrollment	% Latin	Modern languages	% French	% German	% Spanish
1915	1,328,984	37.3	35.9	8.8	24.4	2.7
1922	2,230,000	27.5	27.4	15.5	0.6	11.3
1928	3,354,473	22.0	25.2	14.0	1.8	9.4
1934	5,620,625	16.0	19.5	10.9	2.4	6.2
1949	5,399,452	7.8	13.7	4.7	0.8	8.2

Source: W.R. Parker, The National Interest and Foreign Languages. Washington, D.C.: Department of State, U.S. Government Printing Office, 1961, p. 86.

German has not recovered from the impact of World War I on American society and its consciousness. This period virtually guaranteed that language, even if it were to regain its popularity as a course of study in American schools, would never again be appropriate for study in school as an ethnic language. This remains a legacy of the 1920s language scare.

1950–1965: A new motivation

While there were some efforts on the local level in the 1930s to revive instruction in ethnic languages in the elementary schools,[44] they were undermined once again by a world war. However, the result of the second war with respect to language study was radically different from that of the first: at least officially, Americans began to acknowledge the weakness of an educational system without foreign languages. In the late 1940s and early 1950s, the country began to mobilize around an old idea: languages are militarily and diplomatically important. Language centers developed after the war, such as the one at the University of Michigan with Charles Fries and Robert Lado, were based on an awareness of our lack of linguistic resources.[45]

At the popular level, there were still practical problems with the implementation of the new idea. A whole generation of GIs, many of whom had interrupted their schooling to enter the war, was in need of immediate training. The emphasis on vocationalism and the concern for accommodating the returning soldier resulted in a reduction in language teaching in colleges immediately after the war; foreign language study declined steadily from the end of the war until the early fifties.[46]

With the problem of training the returning GI having abated, and with a new international outlook which was wary of a return to a pre-war isolationist position, the new mood toward the benefits of foreign languages began to expand.[47] By 1952, the U.S. Commissioner of Education, who had earlier consistently minimized the importance of language study, reversed his position, asserting that not only colleges and universities but even elementary schools had a role in the retraining of Americans in languages. Other prominent citizens throughout the society also declared publicly their support of foreign language study. After 1953, college enrollment in foreign language courses began to expand, and many institutions restored the foreign language requirement. Especially interesting in this period is the phenomenal growth in the study of the uncommonly-taught languages, most notably Russian. This testifies to the effectiveness of concern for national security as a motivation for language study.[48]

By the early 60s, language study was a pervasive and essential element in American education; the rise in high school enrollments was as dramatic at midcentury as had been its decline after the first world war, as the following table shows:

Year	Total US enrollment	% Latin	Modern languages	% French	% German	% Spanish
1949	5,399,452	7.8	13.7	4.7	0.8	8.2
1954	6,582,300	6.9	14.2	5.6	0.8	7.3
1958	7,897,232	7.8	16.4	6.1	1.2	8.8
1959	8,155,573	7.9	19.1	7.4	1.5	9.8
1964	11,056,639	5.4	26.2	10.8	2.6	12.3

Source: W.R. Parker, The National Interest and Foreign Languages, 3rd ed., Washington D.C.: Department of State, U.S. Government Printing Office, 1961, p. 94.

The sharp increase between 1958 and 1959 no doubt was influenced by the Sputnik launch and subsequent media accounts of the education of Russian children; also of significance was the National Defense Education Act of 1958, which provided funds for the study of modern foreign languages. However, other important influences may have been just as strong. In 1952, for example, the modern language teachers of the United States organized themselves in order better to address the language study needs of the country. In addition, the rediscovery of the "Army method" of teaching foreign languages, which had demonstrated impressive results by emphasizing speaking skills, held promise as a technique easily adaptable to schools.

This approach to language teaching, also called the "New Key" and the audio-lingual method (ALM), was designed to immerse children in a new linguistic milieu, thereby giving them a more "natural" language-learning experience. Generally, it did not tolerate any use of the first language. Its methods were essentially behavioristic, emphasizing patterned drills, memorization, and the imitation of a speaking model. It gave primacy to spoken language, since "language is what issues from the mouths of living speakers. Language on paper is a derived and secondary form of language."[49]

The development of ALM, along with new research suggesting that younger children learn languages best, impelled the resurgence of a movement for teaching foreign languages in the elementary schools (FLES). While its beginnings were in the midwest in the 1920s, its visibility was at a peak in the 1950s; by 1960, about 1,227,000 pupils were enrolled in more than 100 FLES programs throughout the country.[50] FLES programs were developed at the local level largely because of community enthusiasm; they seemed to satisfy almost everyone's conception of a good education: academically challenging, personally enriching, culturally sensitive, and pedagogically effective. These were principally enrichment programs for middle-class communities.

By 1970, however, only a few isolated FLES programs existed. The failure of this movement can be attributed to a complex of conditions: there were few qualified teachers, and, in some communities, no training or recruitment programs; there was a lack of "teachable" materials in foreign languages adapted to the elementary level; there was relatively little planning and evaluation of programs, so that some communities were caught by surprise as to cost. Perhaps most important was its failure to deliver on its fairly lofty promises. This failure is attributed by some to a flawed approach to second-language learning which emphasized production over understanding, learning over communication; the enthusiasm of students, along with their achievement levels, tended to wane after the first few years of repetitive drills. This was exacerbated, no doubt, by a miscalculation of the potential of young children for language learning; but this is understandable, given the prevailing research findings of the time.[51]

The FLES experiments of the 1950s and early 60s are an interesting chapter in American language interest. While some may see them as faddish, it may be that they reveal a new underlying attitude toward language learning: where the program is explicitly non-political; where the goal is personal enrichment; where there is promise for significant language learning; and where the curriculum is academically rigorous, local communities tend to be supportive, and school districts tend to be responsive. The failure of FLES lies in its broken promises: the theory at its center was insufficient to satisfy public expectations.

Nevertheless, even with better results, it is still possible that the fate of this movement was sealed by its historical position: the 1960s were a time not for personal enrichment but political idealism and commitment, not for strict adherence to a rigid program of habit-formation but for academic freedom and experiential learning. Above all, it was a time when attention was directed at the fate of those who had become disenfranchised within their own society, at those who were positionally disadvantaged, whose rights needed affirmation, and not at those who were trying to enhance their already privileged position through school enrichment programs. FLES was ill-suited to the ethos of the decade. It should have been predictable that it would have given way to a more appropriate approach to language curriculum.

1965–1981: The paradox of bilingual education

The conflict over bilingual schooling which has persisted until the present time has its roots in the ambivalence of Americans toward minority groups in the 1960s. In the first place, bilingual education became associated with world-wide anti-colonialist efforts; in the U.S., this was translated into a concern for "internal colonialism"—the subjugating effects of American institutions on minority groups. Our attention turned to the protection of minority rights and the affirmation of ethnic identity; this entailed, as to language, the need for programs which would maintain the mother tongue or, at least, would not work toward its eradication.[52] In the second place, a concern that these groups not be left behind, that they be integrated into the American mainstream, suggested the need for school programs that would allow a transition between the ethnic community and the larger society. This placed a primacy, as well, on learning the language of the larger society.

This ambivalence between "maintenance" and "transitional" attitudes has grown into a full-blown controversy representing two great ideologies: cultural pluralism and assimilation. But this present polarization obscures the fact that both tendencies are present in early bilingual programs. This, indeed, is what makes the conflict so complicated: the two tendencies are not mutually exclusive, and the two sides, at different times and places, often use the same arguments.

The initial arguments in favor of bilingual education legislation revealed an apprehension that use of the native language for instruction not suggest to ethnic communities that they could with impunity neglect the importance of learning English.[53] This was in keeping with the theme that ran throughout the first hearings—that bilingual instruction would be good in that it would ultimately mean the entrance of non-English speakers into mainstream American society. At the same time, Senators heard those who advocated cultural and linguistic pluralism, and apparently accepted the validity of these comments.[54] Indeed, the principal sponsor of the Senate bill, Ralph Yarborough of Texas, affirmed repeatedly that a main purpose of this bill was the development of bilingual competence: "We have a magnificent opportunity to do a very sensible thing—to enable naturally bilingual children to grow up speaking both good Spanish and good English ..."[55] Early manuals of project applicants developed by HEW also reveal a mixture of "maintenance" and "transition" ideas. On the one hand: "a complete program develops and maintains the children's self-esteem and a legitimate pride in both cultures"; and "the goal of bilingual education is a student who functions well in two languages on any occasion." On the other hand, the use of the mother tongue seems to be purely as a means to an end: "Though the Title VII, ESEA program affirms the primary importance of English, it also recognizes that the use of the children's mother tongue in school can have a beneficial effect upon their education. Instructional use of the mother tongue can help to prevent retardation in school performance until sufficient command of English is attained."[56]

Initial drafts of what came to be known as the Bilingual Education Act (BEA) were aimed at specific constituencies. Yarborough was responding to the needs of Spanish speakers in his own state. Others wanted to expand the bill to include non-Spanish-speakers as well. Politically, this was important, as it created a broader base of support for the proposed legislation. Yet, through all the modifications, the ambiguities associated with this bill remained: what was to be its purpose?

One purpose would have to be compensatory—that much was clear. The testimony at the hearings—the testimony, at any rate, which seemed to create the strongest impression—had focused on the consequences of ignoring the linguistic difference of these children in school: high drop-out rates, low achievement scores, high rate of illiteracy, eventual problems of unemployment and poverty. Simply to go on doing nothing was intolerable. Heavy emphasis was placed on correcting this problem: the poorest children in the poorest neighborhoods would be targeted. In 1968, that meant that only children from families where the annual income was $3,000 or lower were eligible for the new programs; only school districts with high concentrations of such families could apply for federal start-up funds for these projects. Of course, the principal criterion for eligibility was that the child be of "limited English-speaking Ability" (LES); however, children whose dominant language was English were not automatically excluded from the program, although their primary role seems to have been one of providing cultural and linguistic variety: "Children whose dominant language is English and who attend schools in the project area should be encouraged to participate, and provision should be made for their participation in order to enhance the bilingual and bicultural aspects of the program."[57] Still, this was an important provision since it allowed for the possibility that the programs would stand for more than merely teaching English skills to limited English-speakers.

As to the instructional dimension of the program, the language of the legislation was vague, perhaps because expertise in bilingual education was limited.[58] The 1968 version of the BEA did not even include a definition of or a range of programmatic alternatives for what was called "bilingual education." Instead, the legislators gave a general charge to local education agencies (LEAs) to "develop and carry out new and imaginative elementary and secondary school programs" designed with this special population in mind. This resulted in a wide gamut of school-based activities funded as bilingual education: the Spanish Dame project in San Jose, California, which taught parents of Spanish-speaking preschoolers techniques of tutoring their children in preparation for kindergarten; elementary schools in Milwaukee which taught Spanish literacy skills to Puerto Rican and Chicano children; Project Bilingualism for Cultural Democracy at Mountain View (California) High School, which was essentially an enrichment experience for Chicano and Filipino students; the Gonzales (California) High School bilingual program, which offered intensive ESL classes and electives in Spanish literature to children of Mexican farmworkers who decided to stay in California after the termination of the bracero program; these are examples of the variety of projects called "bilingual education" resulting from the act.[59] Thus, it would seem, at least judging from the sorts of proposals that were funded in the early years, that personal enrichment, cultural pluralism, and language maintenance were also goals of the BEA.

This variety in interpretations of the law was problematic to those who saw the need as one of trying to integrate non-English speakers into American society as quickly as possible. For them, the definition of bilingual education, at least insofar as federal programs were concerned, needed to be narrowed. Especially influential were officials high in the Nixon administration who wanted bilingual education to be essentially a temporary, transitional program.[60]

This narrow conception of bilingual education as a program to teach English to LES students was reinforced in 1974 with the Supreme Court's decision in Lau v. Nichols.[61] Here, the San Francisco school system was found to be in violation of section 601 of the Civil Rights Act of 1964 based on its failure to provide special instruction to 1800 Chinese children who did not speak English. This decision popularly is thought to have given impetus to the development of bilingual education programs and to the enactment of state laws providing for bilingual instruction. Indeed this is true. Of the almost thirty states that have passed such legislation, the vast majority did so since 1974. But Lau, as much as anything, solidified for American educators and in the public mind the narrow view of bilingual education as teaching English to limited English-speakers. As the landmark case dealing with linguistic minority groups, it perpetuates the peculiarly American view that bilingual education, when successful, leads ultimately to English monolingualism.[62]

The 1974 amendments to the BEA reflected the views of those who origi-nally had supported the legislation out of a concern for providing assistance to non-English speakers; they were clearly upset that so much emphasis was being placed on cultural pluralism and mother tongue maintenance and not enough on English. The 1974 revisions were specific as to appropriate ends and acceptable approaches in schooling the LES student. Title VII funds were to be used explicitly for transitional purposes, "to demonstrate effective ways of providing, for children of limited English-speaking ability, instruction designed to enable them, while using their native language, to achieve com-petence in the English language." The native language was clearly portrayed as merely a means by which the child would keep up in subject areas until sufficient English was learned to enter the all-English regular curriculum. As for the role of anglophones in bilingual education, they were allowed in the programs on a voluntary basis, but only for the cultural benefits which might accrue to them; language-learning was not an acceptable intention on their part. "In no event shall the program be designed for the purpose of teaching a foreign language to English-speaking students."[63]

Nor was there much encouragement to promote the cultural aspects of these programs. While the 1974 amendments refer to "appreciation for the cultural heritage" of LES children, this component is clearly subordinated to English learning; there is little indication of what this "appreciation" might entail. The explicit position of government policy analysts and consultants was that these programs were not intended to promote cultural pluralism, nor should they require a cultural component in the curriculum.[64] On these ques-tions, the revisions of 1978 provided no significant changes. The objective remained, and remains even now, teaching English to LES students: "The objective of the program shall be to assist children of limited English profi-ciency to improve their English language skills, and the participation of other children in the program must be for the principal purpose of contributing to the achievement of that objective." The prospect that bilingual education may become a vehicle for bilingualization has been effectively discouraged and officially disowned. The primacy of English and the indifference to language loss is viewed by some as central to the BEA, as recent reports by staff mem-bers within the Department of Education demonstrate:

> Underlying this paper is the assumption that the ultimate goals of bilin-gual education programs are to learn English and keep up with English-speaking peers in subject matter. While bilingualism per se is a laudable and worthwhile outcome, we judge benefit in terms of English acquisi-tion and subject matter learning. The 1978 amendments embodied this assumption.[65]

While some, like Steven Grant, express some optimism that our attitude toward linguistic diversity and bilingual education is becoming more tolerant, most advocates of the broader view toward these issues are discouraged. Joshua Fishman, who has long chastised Americans for their short-sightedness with respect to language resources, has gone beyond "maintenance" to "enrichment" bilingual education where both LES and English-speaking students have an opportunity to add to their linguistic repertoires. But, apparently, this is not possible through the BEA, which he says is "primarily an act for the Anglification of non-English speakers and not an act for BILINGUALISM." And again, more forcefully, he says that "the act is basically not an act for bilingualism, but, rather, an act against bilingualism."[66]

This is the paradox of bilingual education in the United States: that, while in some isolated programs, and in the minds of a few hopeful cultural pluralists, it may at times have stood for bilingualization, almost always its purpose and its outcome have been the reverse. The German communities of the last century were ignorant of the machinations of school officials who, through German language and German teachers, were working to make them a little less German, a little more "American." The most recent official expression of bilingual education policy, with its emphasis on transition and its indifference to cultural integrity, aims at the same result. The BEA is illustration par excellence of false advertising; it would be more honest to repeal it and pass another measure more appropriately titled—Language Training for Limited English Speakers, perhaps, or simply English as a Second Language. But this could be unnecessary, as Fishman suggests, since transitional bilingual education is already inherently self destructive: "It is damned if it does and damned if it doesn't. If it does bring about a rapid transition to English, then it will no longer be needed. If it does not, it will also no longer be needed."[67] This double-bind is not unique to bilingual education, but it does contribute its own curious wrinkle to the essential paradox: in America, "bilingualism" has come to mean not proficiency in two languages, but deficiency in English, and "bilingual" education has come to stand for the opposite of its name. The preceding sociolinguistic history is an attempt both to explain the paradox, and to understand why so few in the United States see it as paradoxical.

Toward a National Language Policy?

The United States has no comprehensive language policy. It has never declared an official language; in fact, there has been from the early republic a reluctance to impose status on any language or to create agencies which might regulate language decisions and behavior. The prevailing status of English as the dominant national language derives from its widespread use, from social sanctions on language behavior, from the initiative of individuals or private agencies concerned with language standardization, and from legal and quasi-legal attempts on the local level to restrict non-English language behavior; it does not derive from any official pronouncement.[68]

There are various explanations possible for the fact that English has never been given official status. One is that those in power in the early republic inherited the British tendency for tolerance and individual choice on those matters.[69] Another is the recognition, in more recent times, of the extreme complexity of the officialization process. The act of designating an official standard is only one, possibly the least problematic of the dimensions of language planning: generally, the most important of these is the nature and means of elaboration for the new official language, the acceptable orthographic representation of it, the measures taken to cultivate its use, some determination as to the pervasiveness of the policy, the agencies assigned to regulate language decisions and behavior, and the articulation of the language policy with other national policies.[70] Another explanation for the unofficial status of English is that the need for a special designation has not been seen as urgent. Recent developments reflected in media editorials and proposed legislation may signal a change in this attitude. This change suggests that the push for officializing English could lead in the near future to efforts to develop a comprehensive language policy.

If there is to be a policy of this sort, many groups and individuals will be concerned to influence it, and many already existing policies will have to be considered. In the next few pages, a brief examination of some of the more important of these considerations will be attempted.

State laws

Any national policy must be delimited by the fact that the United States is a federal system where the states and local authorities have considerable power of jurisdiction, both legal and traditional. As to the nature of a general language policy in this context, Grant says the following:

> [I]n almost every case it is the state and local governments that have the right to set language policy and that will do so. The federal government should set down some very broad guidelines in specific areas involving language; it may also state its own language policy. But in a federal system like ours, the smaller communities are always the final arbiters of taste and culture. To achieve language standardization in English throughout this country may be impossible or undesirable, or both.[71]

There have been problems of disarticulation between federal and state policy in the past; this is especially true in the area of education, the provision and regulation of which have traditionally been the responsibilities of the states. The most obvious recent example of this is the conflict created by court-imposed desegregation orders, based on guarantees of the federal constitution, and the rights of state and local authorities to the control of education.

Generally, where official pronouncements have concerned language education, these conflicts have not arisen. State laws on bilingual education have run parallel to the federal tendency toward transition.[72] The first such law in Massachusetts (1973), which served as a model for those to follow, was explicitly entitled "Transitional Bilingual Education." Others were less explicit, though the effect of the law was the same. Texas (1974) provided for a "compensatory program of bilingual education" where the LES child could be enrolled "for a period of three years or until he achieves a level of English language proficiency which will enable him to perform successfully in classes in which instruction is given only in English, whichever occurs first." The Wisconsin statute makes a similar provision, and includes its bilingual education law in a chapter on handicapped children. Even the California law, more progressive than most, cites as its primary goal the rapid development of child fluency in English "so that [the child] may be enrolled in the regular program in which English is the language of instruction." This is not to say that discrepancies between federal and state laws do not exist. But the general orientation of these laws is similar enough so that the specifics are reconcilable. (In Wisconsin, for example, investigators found differences in the strength of the mandates, the enforcement procedures followed, provisions for parental consent, and the terminology used [LES in Wisconsin, instead of the broader LEP—limited English proficient—found in the federal statute]. Having been identified, these discrepancies are easily resolved.)[73]

Most of the controversies arising out of bilingual education emerge not so much from legislative conflicts as from differential interpretations of constitutional principles. The Lau remedies, for example, were essentially guidelines derived from basic issues resolved in that case; the decision itself mandated no particular method of remediation. States and LEAs have complained that too much emphasis was placed on bilingual methods in the Lau remedies, to the point where anything other than such a program was seen as being in non-compliance with federal law. Since 1981, these guidelines have been rescinded; the mood in the present administration is to relax the requirement of bilingual education, and to allow other approaches which do not use non-English languages as media of instruction. Still, we should not make more of this controversy than what it is—a disagreement over the best method to teach English to LES students. In other words, it is a disagreement over the use of the mother tongue in transitional bilingual education, not one over whether maintenance or transitional programs should prevail. As to the general orientation of our language policy, federal and state laws are in substantial agreement.

The most recent concern for excellence in education could have some effect on language policies. In some states, there has already been some agitation that foreign languages be an integral part of the public school curriculum.

In Washington, for example, community support was instrumental in amending the state's Basic Skill act to designate foreign language as a basic skill.[74] Whether this becomes a widespread result of the movement for quality in education is questionable.[75] At any rate, in the area of foreign language study, the states have generally been more active in promoting legislation than the federal government, which has not so much mandated as <u>encouraged</u> it through the provision of funds for special projects. This is not an area of language policy where state and federal authorities would likely clash.

Commission reports on language study

Two important reports written in the last five years have concerned the nation's language policy.[76] The first is by a national commission which was assembled by President Carter and charged with assessing the need in the United States for specialists in foreign languages and area studies and with recommending the means for improving the nation's language resources. The second is a study by the Modern Language Association and the American Council of Learned Societies (MLA-ACLS) on the decline of foreign language study in the United States. While the MLA-ACLS study group was formed independently and prior to the President's Commission, it did have a chance to present many of its recommendations to the Commission, which also had the benefit of the full MLC-ACLS report by the time it had finished its deliberations. Each report will be examined briefly; an analysis of their potential impact will be offered.

The report of the President's Commission on Foreign Language and International Studies, entitled <u>Strength Through Wisdom,</u> is dramatic in tone, highlighting the importance of foreign language skills in an interdependent world. It depicts nothing short of a national crisis brought on by "Americans' scandalous incompetence in foreign languages." The most obvious concerns of the Commission are the consequences for national security created by this weakness, as the introductory statement by the Chairman demonstrates:

> Nothing less is at issue than the nation's security. At a time when the resurgent forces of nationalism and of ethnic and linguistic consciousness so directly affect global realities, the United States requires far more reliable capacities to communicate with its allies, analyze the behavior of potential adversaries, and earn the trust and sympathies of the uncommitted. Yet, there is a widening gap between these needs and the American competence to understand and deal successfully with other people in a world of flux.

The military/diplomatic emphasis in the report recalled the agitation over foreign language competence in the late 1950s; it seemed to herald a new language scare, as expressed by the editor of the foreign language division of a major textbook publisher: "attention has been focused on our work at least briefly in a way we have not experienced since the launching of Sputnik set off a flurry of interest in Russian (and, to a lesser extent, other languages)."[77]

Two other major emphases involve the economic and. educational benefits of foreign language study. All of the recommendations of the Commission regarding economic questions deal with international business and export trade. This is perhaps understandable, given its name and its charge. However, it seems an oversight to neglect to mention the domestic importance of non-English language competence, at least in two areas. The first is that business will have to play a role in attracting large groups of students into foreign language/international studies programs by offering incentives to attain these competencies. Not enough of these students will be motivated by the prospects of a job abroad; they will be motivated by the knowledge that their prospects for getting a job in any aspect of business will be enhanced by foreign language capability and international experience. The second area is a major deficiency of the report. It completely overlooks the importance of non-English language markets within the United States. Though it does cite the need to involve minority businesses in the international arena, and the potential value of ethnic communities to foreign language training, it does not encourage business to gain better access to areas having large concentrations of non-English speakers. This is hard to explain, since the areas involved, especially large metropolitan markets, would be potentially profitable, without the large expenditures normally associated with international investment; furthermore, many businesses have lost customers due to insensitivity to and ignorance of ethnic and linguistic difference in the community.[78]

As to the educational benefits it cites, the most important seem to be a more well-rounded curriculum and the creation of an international or global outlook starting in the early years. This is in keeping with the central theme that we now live in an interdependent world where those who are able to understand and communicate with those around them best will survive. Those who made presentations to and commented on the Commission and its report also see this benefit. Sven Groennings, staff member of the Senate subcommittee on Education, Arts, and Humanities, sees international education as an important ingredient in educational quality:

> There are numerous indications that the most significant education issue during the 1980s will be educational quality, which may join "access" and "equity" as one of the dominant justifications of Federal educational policies. … It would be natural, … given the strongly national justification for encouraging international education, for the Department to make international education one of its major contributions to the enhancement of educational quality.[79]

Other advocates of foreign language study have also noted the importance of the connection with "global" or "international" education.[80] It should be noted, however, that this approach seems to minimize the value of ethnic languages and communities, and places a heavy emphasis on the formal study of standard "foreign" languages. Witness to this is the call for reestablishing foreign language requirements, for developing international high schools, for lengthening the courses for study available to students of foreign language, and for international travel and scholarly exchanges as ways of addressing our lack in foreign language resources; at the same time, bilingual education, the strengthening of ethnic language institutions (films, newspapers, radio, etc.), and the potential value of local ethnic communities as language training sites are hardly mentioned. The connection of foreign language study with international education highlights the importance of training or retraining for language competence, but not the importance of retaining it.

This report ends with a proposal for a national commission which would serve as "catalyst, energizer, public educator, and public conscience" with regard to foreign languages and international understanding. This would insure that the work of the first commission not be left without appropriate public attention. This sort of commission would probably have little effect on the development of language policy, since its work would be of limited duration and constrained by the scope of the initial commission. Better would be a standing commission whose work would continue across administrations and would be concerned with the articulation of language policy decisions with the linguistic needs of the country. Apart from this sort of permanence, presidential commissions will survive only until the next administration.

The MLA-ACLS report is larger in scope than that of the President's commission, including reports on less-commonly taught languages, classical studies, and the role of the media in the development of international understanding and language competence. It also offers an analysis of language policy development in the United States. Many of the concerns here are similar to those of the President's commission; the military importance of foreign language capability, for example, has high visibility, especially in Grant's paper on language policy ("if foreign language training and other education programs can be made to sound like military expenditures rather than schooling proposals, the federal government is more likely to fund and maintain them"). The recommendations, especially as to pedagogy and the administration of school language programs, are more specific here, which is understandable given the sponsoring agencies.

Interestingly, possibly the most important of the papers included in this report is the one by Keller and Roel on the media. It demonstrates, more than any of the others, the appalling lack of information on other cultures in American society. Prime-time television is dominated by American scenes and American actors; very few non-English radio and television programs exist for the general public; the "international" news that is provided on American television is limited, mainly bunched into four categories: military-defense, foreign relations, domestic government politics, and crime-justice-terrorism. This creates a highly distorted view of world affairs, and no doubt explains the "relationship between increased television viewing and a tendency toward isolationism on the part of the viewing public."

This is instructive; it suggests that our conception of "education," when it comes to foreign language and international understanding, is too narrow. Recommendations which aim at the school, without consideration of the role of mass communications and access to information, aim too low. A rise in foreign language/international studies enrollments in the schools, motivated by interests more general than military preparedness or economic mobility, will likely accompany, but not precede, a general reorientation of attitude toward America's own diversity and its relationship to the rest of the world.

Federal legislation

If a national language policy is attempted, existing and proposed legislation will likely form its contours; articulation of these legislative pronouncements will be a major activity of the policy-makers. Steven Grant, in the paper cited above, has done an excellent analysis of some of these, especially the National Defense Education Act of 1958 and the Voting Rights Act of 1965. The discussion below will be much briefer and more selective.

There are two pieces of legislation which might be called "positive law"— acts which target not the remediation of some perceived deficiency as to language, but the maintenance of language and cultural diversity; these are seen as goods in themselves, as opposed to social problems. The Ethnic Heritage Studies Program (1974) provides funds for curriculum materials and special projects related to the contributions of ethnic groups to American society. The American Folklife Preservation Act of 1975 states that "the history of the United States effectively demonstrates that building a strong nation does not require the sacrifice of cultural differences; ... it is in the interest of the general welfare of the Nation to preserve, support, revitalize, and disseminate American folklife traditions and arts." It also provides for an American Folklife Center which would present these traditions to the public.

These acts have received very little attention in recent years, perhaps because of a general reluctance to fund programs in liberal education and the humanities, perhaps because it would seem like too strong an endorsement of cultural pluralism—about which we have always been ambivalent, at best. Nevertheless, if they were to have an influence on a national language policy, they would probably tend only to strengthen the attitude that formal, knowledge-about language and culture study is the most appropriate approach; they do little to encourage the <u>use</u> of these languages in the public at large.

Predictably, the legislation which gains considerable support is that which deals with national security and international business matters (for some, these are intimately related). The revised Title VI of the Higher Education Act, for example, provides matching grants to universities establishing links between international/area studies and business.[81] Similarly, a newly-introduced piece of legislation, H.R. 2708, Foreign Language Assistance for National Security Act, is in response to the "very substantive" losses to American business abroad because of the lack of foreign language skills. It authorizes $50,000,000 per year for three years to schools and colleges to upgrade foreign language instruction. The act has been called "essential to the national security agenda."[82]

One important area of legislation which holds potential to influence language policy in the coming decade is immigration reform. Great pressure has been placed on the Congress in recent years to address the issues created by the rapidly changing demographic patterns in the United States. Specifically, with respect to language, the dramatic increase in the Hispanic population has prompted legislators to include language provisions in proposals for immigration reform. Perhaps the most important of these proposals in the past year was the Senate version of a legislative package known commonly as Simpson-Mazzoli—S. 529, the Immigration Reform and Control Act of 1983.[83]

Most of the provisions of this bill related to the difficult problems of restricting immigration, and only indirectly to language issues. But section 406, added to the end of the bill as a general provision, was a direct statement of language policy: "It is the sense of the Congress that– (1) the English language is the official language of the United States, and (2) no language other than the English language is recognized as the official language of the United States." This section included no elaboration or explanation. The companion bill in the House, H.R. 1510, included no such provision. The Senate version passed easily with wide bipartisan support; the House bill also passed, but only after a bitter debate. The compromise reached in the conference committee did away with the language section, though it did include an amendment which would have required undocumented aliens seeking amnesty to study English. The bill was eventually rejected, but for reasons other than the language provision. The lesson to be learned from Simpson-Mazzoli is that the Congress may now be ready for an action it has always actively rejected: the designation of an official language.

If such legislation is enacted, the process of language policy formulation will only have begun. Difficult questions remain: will use of non-English languages as media of instruction be proscribed for public schools? Will knowledge of English become a requirement for voting? What of the use of interpreters in judicial and administrative proceedings? And what will it mean for the nature of education on reservations and in territories like Puerto Rico and Guam? These questions are not likely to be addressed in the legislation. Until they are, the declaration of an official language will cause many problems not anticipated by the Congress, and will be still quite far from a comprehensive language policy.

Revision of the Bilingual Education Act

In 1983, the Department of Education, with the support of the administration, submitted a bill to the Congress for consideration as the "Bilingual Education Improvements Act of 1983."[84] It proposed four major changes in emphasis or language: it provided for a program of basic grants for the purpose of building the capacity of LEAs in treating children of limited English proficiency; it encouraged the involvement of SEAs in the review and evaluation of projects; it targeted funding for those programs serving primarily children "whose usual language is not English" and, it broadened the range of instructional alternatives fundable under Title VII.

The last two of these provisions have generated much debate.[85] Critics of the administration proposal contended that the "usual language" provision could have the effect of excluding many children who have been served by bilingual programs up to now; this would involve, as examples, many American Indian children from communities where the traditional language has been subordinated to English and children of various communities where the parents are bilingual to some degree. It also may be seen as undercutting the 1978 amendment specifying the target population as limited-English proficient (LEP). This designation is broader than the earlier LES since it allows for those children who have oral skills but lack reading and writing proficiency. However, "usual language" suggests an oral context; literacy skills are not always part of the home domain for many of these children. This could have the practical effect of having programs revert to the earlier, more restricted eligibility criterion.

The bill asserted that "no one educational technique or method for educating children of limited English proficiency through programs of bilingual education has been proven uniformly effective"; therefore, it would have given LEAs more of a free hand in developing programs which at the local level are deemed warranted for meeting the needs of this population. This includes approaches which do not use non-English languages as media of instruction. With this in view, the definition of bilingual education would be changed as follows: "The term 'bilingual education' means a program of instruction, designed for children of limited English proficiency in elementary or secondary schools, in which ... there is instruction for the acquisition of English language skills and such instruction ... is designed to provide such children an opportunity to progress effectively through the educational system; and ... is given with appreciation for the cultural heritage of such children."

This would have been a substantive departure from earlier conceptions of bilingual education expressed in the BEA. While it is true that at least since 1974 the law has emphasized transition, it nevertheless saw the use of both English and the native language as media of instruction as the essential ingredient in bilingual education. Without this, and without the objective of bilingualization, what is it that would make this education "bilingual"?

This question and others like it were the focus of the criticisms of this bill during deliberations for the 1984 authorization. Had this provision been enacted in this form, it would have crystallized within the statute the intuition about bilingual education that Ricardo Otheguy perceives in the general population, that "any deviation from the regular school curriculum for students whose native language is not English is frequently labeled bilingual education, even if no element of the native language is involved." It also would have gone far in setting the tone for a national language policy in which English has primacy, and ethnic languages are valued only to the extent that they contribute to English proficiency.[86]

The politics of language in the United States

Setting any sort of national policy is essentially a political process. It involves not merely articulating existing laws and social conventions with the new policy or taking prevailing scholarly opinion into account, but also assessing the potential impact on particular constituencies. As we have already seen, the original BEA was aimed at Spanish-speakers, especially those of Mexican and Puerto Rican heritage; in fact, the first Senate draft was called the "Bilingual American Education Act," highlighting a specific target population as opposed to a program. Senator Tarborough eventually was persuaded by those, like Senator Randolph from West Virginia, who argued that a broader bill would pass more easily than one aimed at one language group.[87]

Issues involving language and language education have formed the basis of organizations with considerable political influence. The National Education Association, the American Federation of Teachers, the Modern Language Association, the National Association for Bilingual Education, those representing the various language professions, and others will certainly have an important voice in the development of a language policy. The extent to which these groups agree on issues like language education will determine how much political compromise will be necessary. Beyond these groups, ethnically-identified associations like the League of United Latin American Citizens, the Puerto Rican Legal Defense and Education Fund, the Mexican American Legal Defense and Education Fund, and the National Council of La Raza form significant lobbying efforts, especially when they are able to cooperate on a particular issue. The fact that bilingual education appropriations have not yet been included in President Reagan's block grant program, for example, is due largely to the political leverage of these and other groups.

However much importance we might attach to the impact of policy changes on particular interest groups, it is perhaps most important to assess the general response to such an action. Within the U.S. political and bureaucratic structure, significant time and effort are given to polls and surveys on specific issues. The difficulty of relying solely on these measures of public sentiment for the development of policy is that, even when they are properly constructed, the results are often ambiguous. For example, in a media survey of attitudes on a variety of language-related questions, Clark and Rudolph found "a general belief in the value of foreign language study in public schools and a desire to extend such study."[88] However, this general belief was tempered by a reluctance to commit resources to this subject in times of economic constraint. While conceding the importance of foreign language competence, some of those polled suggested that giving time to foreign languages would mean that English skills could suffer: "Whether we can justify taking the time from teaching basic English communication skills to teach basic communication skills in a foreign language is indeed a perplexing question." But another contended that this was a false distinction, that the knowledge of other languages actually enhanced competence in English. One can see the difficulties of trying to synthesize these disparate opinions into a political statement.

Surveys on bilingual education suffer from the same ambiguity. Reports from a Columbia University project reveal widespread support for bilingual education programs. But the reasons for that support differ markedly between Hispanics and non-Hispanics. Generally, the former group projects "maintenance" attitudes, valuing these programs because of their potential for cultural and linguistic continuity and integrity; the latter sees the benefits of a transitional program which "prevents Hispanic children from falling behind in their studies and therefore will help them be upwardly mobile."[89] These sorts of results can create confusion in the policy-making process.

The politics of language as it is focused on bilingual education and second-language acquisition has also had an influence on the conduct of scholarly research. This may be unfortunate, but it is not unexpected given the highly charged atmosphere surrounding these topics. Advocates of bilingual education in the past have felt compelled to answer longstanding criticisms that bilingualism resulted in a variety of cognitive, educational, and social disorders. Those arguments having been effectively countered, the predominant research activity has now switched to demonstrating the pervasiveness of the benefits of bilingualism.[90]

The criticisms of bilingual education, however, continue. That is because of the peculiar United States view of the purpose of bilingual education, as we have already argued: that is, whether or not bilingualism itself is a good thing may already have been resolved as a research question, but it is irrelevant in arguments about bilingual education, which has nothing to do with bilingualism. What it does have to do with, the critics contend, is learning English; and it is on that basis that these programs have been evaluated negatively. This is the central argument in the recent reports from staff members of the Department of Education, who give the following reasons for such views: "The justification for this viewpoint is that in the United States, any successful education program must prepare the students to participate in an English-speaking society. Therefore the overriding concern in evaluating instruction for bilingual students is how well they learn English."[91] Other researchers make similar arguments and come to similar conclusions as to the ineffectiveness of bilingual education programs.[92] Predictably, these views have been countered by others who, while treating the same evidence, come to strikingly different conclusions. Rudolph Troike, for example, surveys twelve programs from throughout the country and reports that "enough evidence has now been accumulated to make it possible to say with confidence that quality bilingual programs can meet the goal of providing equal educational opportunity for students from non-English speaking backgrounds."[93]

These variations in scholarly opinion could certainly arise because of important differences in the treatment of the data by the research teams. Perhaps more likely, however, is a difference in political or ideological views which itself shaped the treatments in question. At the most general level, the assumption that English learning should be the sole criterion for the effectiveness of a program could rest on prior assumptions: that English is (or should be) the language of the United States, that English proficiency promotes economic and social mobility, and others. It is possible to uncover these assumptions, and to argue about their validity; but in the end, we must concede that, however much they might determine the nature of empirical research, they are nonetheless conceptually prior to it.[94]

It should come as no surprise that the critics of bilingual education and their views now are in the ascendant position, at least politically. It would be curious indeed if staff researchers working under a president who has declared that programs designed to maintain language and culture in school are "absolutely wrong and against [the] American concept" were to find that these very programs are effective and desirable. While these views have been criticized from a technical-methodological point of view, the debate, if it is to be an honest one, must ultimately be about ideology and politics.[95]

The conflicts surrounding bilingual education and the potential for a language policy are intense, much more so than if the questions involved were about merely effectiveness of instruction or the costs of these programs. Perhaps we have begun to recognize that this political debate, unlike most, can have important implications for what this nation is to become. Studies of language planning around the world have demonstrated what Shirley Heath articulates, that "any language policy is, in effect, a cultural policy which calls for changes in the quality of life and cultural developments of specific groups in the nation." Glyn Lewis goes a bit further in saying that "a theory of instruction is essentially a theory of social morality":

> Whether or not we are willing to envisage a pluralist society, and how we regard the part bilingual education should play in such a society, are value judgments, and imply the use of moral criteria.[96]

This political question is something more than merely a political question. At the root of any new language policy will be some fundamental assumptions about the future of the United States: that it will marshal its public and private resources to create a more viable and tolerant cultural pluralism, or not; that the nation's considerable language resources will be actively developed and conscientiously maintained, or not; that ethnic-linguistic communities will be valued as important to the strength of the nation, or not; that equal educational opportunity and quality of education will be seen as compatible or competitors; that the nation will begin to recognize its interdependence with the rest of the world, or remain relatively isolated, hopeful that its military and technological influence and the power of its language are sufficient to maintain its preeminence. The posture that the United States takes toward the language question may well signal the orientation it brings to these other, more general social concerns.

PART II: APPROACHES TO LANGUAGE LEARNING IN THE SCHOOLS

In this section, we will review some of the more important concepts and theories on second language acquisition and teaching. First we will examine major trends in the literature, demonstrating how theories have been developed, modified, and adapted to the classroom. Our second consideration will be how these theories have generated methods of second-language teaching. Then, we will describe some of the major school programs that have been developed to promote language learning for various populations. Studies on the effects of these programs for different students will be reviewed. Finally, we will present some observations on the potential for cooperation among these programs.

Research on Second-Language Acquisition and Teaching

In this section, we will address the question of teaching method and programmatic structure as these have been designed for the LEP/NEP student. We will be concerned with the reported effects of using the first and second language of the child for instructional purposes, the effectiveness of bilingual programs along various dimensions, and the interrelationships of the many kinds of language teaching programs which exist in schools. Preliminary to that discussion, however, will be a review of the important trends in research on second-language acquisition (SLA) and some of the most important concepts which emerge from that research.

Sociolinguistic and psycholinguistic emphases

The problems associated with second-language acquisition and teaching are multifaceted. They also involve different levels of analysis. Initially, one should make a distinction between those studies which approach SLA as if it were primarily a linguistic or <u>psycholinguistic</u> phenomenon and those approaching it primarily as a societal or <u>sociolinguistic</u> phenomenon. The former generally treat language behavior from the point of view of the individual; they deal with such topics as comprehension strategies, linguistic interference, the influence of stress on language acquisition, coordinate versus compound bilingualism, and language attitudes. The latter place a primacy on the collective nature of language behavior; their topics include language status and prestige, code alternation and interpersonal cues, diglossic norms in both society and classroom, and language loyalty.

While these two types of emphases are conceptually distinct, they are intimately related in the area of SLA. For example, while the problems associated with anglophones learning Spanish in a bilingual program could be thought to be merely technical-linguistic ones (how to prevent interference; what the best age is to introduce the second language; whether to drill the child in formally correct dialogue or concentrate on natural speech forms; etc.), the critical factors sometimes are not technical or even strictly linguistic at all, but social (or, more properly, sociolinguistic). Various researchers have found that anglophones acquire vary little Spanish in U.S. bilingual programs.[97] In most cases, this is not difficult to explain, as the great majority of programs in the United States are designed to promote English language skills for the non- or limited-English proficient (NEP/LEP) student. However, even where the explicit goal is bilingualization for both groups, anglophones learn comparatively little Spanish.[98] This is explained sociolinguistically by Edelsky and Hudelson.[99] They suggest that motivations and strategies for SLA are influenced strongly by the fact that Spanish is a "marked" language in the United States. In the school context, this means that special arrangements must be made for Spanish to be used in the curriculum, since Spanish is not the "usual language" of the school. These evaluations of markedness rarely have anything to do with qualities thought to inhere in the language itself (its beauty, efficiency, and others); rather, they have at their basis the sociopolitical status of languages in relation to English.[100] It is this status difference, especially in the Southwestern and

Northeastern United States where Spanish-speakers have been perceived to be of lower social status, which influences the attitudes of anglophones toward Spanish acquisition. This explanation can be applied to other vernacular languages as well since, as Edelsky and Hudelson contend, "even under highly favorable conditions, acquiring a marked language as a second language is going to be problematic."[101]

Another illustration of the interrelatedness of sociolinguistic and psycholinguistic behaviors is that cited by Spolsky and Irvine. They found that some American Indian communities tended to reject vernacular literacy, perhaps as a way of maintaining cultural integrity; that is, literacy was seen as an intrusion, an alteration of the traditional language: "when the introduction of literacy is associated with a second language, an alien culture, and modern technological functions, literacy in these new domains is preferred in the alien, second, or standard language."[102] In this case, an important factor in the acquisition of literacy could have been missed had this phenomenon been treated merely linguistically.

Even those concepts which appear to be most fundamentally linguistic are not strictly so. Language "proficiency" is one such concept. It creates problems of definition precisely because it cannot be confined to the area of individual psychological development.[103] Higher degrees of proficiency would involve, among other things, what can be called sociolinguistic competence, as McLaughlin states: "Full communicative competence requires ... not only mastery of the formal and semantic aspects of language but control of the various styles of speaking that characterize how different people talk to each other under differing circumstances."[104] Cummins makes a similar point, noting that it has been especially difficult to understand the nature of language proficiency in school contexts; that is, we still cannot be sure of the relationship between proficiency in everyday communication and that in academic language skills. The first of these is characterized by what Cummins calls "context-embedded" language skills; this is where the participants in face-to-face communication can actively negotiate the meaning of their language (by asking questions, for example) and have access to paralinguistic cues, such as intonation and gestures, as aids to comprehension. Academic language skills, on the other hand, are "context-reduced," meaning that the sorts of cues available are primarily linguistic (the narrative context is an obvious aid in reading comprehension, for example, but it is limited compared to the social context involved in personal conversation). Failure to make this distinction can be harmful to NEP/LEP students. Those who show a general ("context-embedded") competence in English may be placed in a regular classroom where they will be expected to exhibit academic ("context-reduced") language skills such as test-taking and reading. When these children fail to achieve at these tasks, the school may assume that other kinds of things (mental deficiency, "cultural deprivation," and others) account for this failure, since the problem of English proficiency has been resolved.[105]

While it is possible to look at certain phenomena from one or the other of these perspectives with some profit, it is probably misleading to regard bilingualism and language acquisition in a unidimensional way. Bernbaum goes further, suggesting that we may do this only at considerable peril: "to examine bilingualism without due regard for the wider socio-cultural, economic, and political considerations would lead to superficial and possibly dangerously inaccurate conclusions."[106] A proper study of these questions, then would be necessarily multidisciplinary, involving linguists, sociologists, political scientists, economists, and others.

The relation of first and second language acquisition

An important question in language teaching deals with the relation between learning a first and second language. Are these qualitatively different processes? The answer to this question is significant for the development of language teaching programs. In this section, we will be concerned with various topics bearing on the relation of first and second language acquisition.

Learning versus acquisition

Recently, various researchers have tried to elaborate the distinction between learning and acquiring a second language. Generally, language learning is conceived of as gaining "conscious knowledge of a second language, knowing the rules, being aware of them, and being able to talk about them" whereas acquisition is a "subconscious process," the result of which is communicative competence.[107] One can also think of language acquisition as a nonformal, natural-language process. McLaughlin suggests that the critical difference lies in the conditions of exposure to a second language: acquisition implies a "natural environment" in which language is picked up in the normal course of social development, while learning requires a formal context in which technical errors are corrected and exercises are engaged in.[108]

The natural language-acquisition environment is described below by Penfield, who conceived of the development of language ability as an innate urge resulting from the need to interact with one's surroundings:

> For the child at home, the learning of language is a method of learning about life, a means of getting what he wants, a way of satisfying the unquenchable curiosity that burns in him almost from the beginning. He is hardly aware of the fact that he is learning language, and it does not form his primary conscious goal.[109]

One might infer from this statement that age is also an important factor in the distinction between natural and formal contexts of language exposure: that is, children acquire a language while adults learn it. However, as we shall see in a later section, the present consensus among language researchers is that age is of relatively little consequence in language acquisition, and that both children and adults can acquire and learn language.

Another possible inference from this distinction, related to the age question, is that second-language acquisition is qualitatively different from first-language acquisition. While conclusions vary among recent researchers,[110] the prevalent finding is that the two are not different in kind. This is an important conclusion, since it calls attention to the question of appropriate teaching approaches. If the second-language acquirer perceives and needs explicit language rules for acquisition, as those following Chomsky have suggested, then this learner will require more systematic instruction than the first-language learner. But if there is no difference in kind, it could be that the ideal classroom would be one that duplicated or approximated the natural language-acquisition environment.

The relation of learning to acquisition is critical to an understanding of the theories upon which most approaches to second-language teaching have been based. The view that a consciously-learned language rule will eventually be internalized and become a part of automatic language behavior (i.e. that learning leads to acquisition) has been an important part of modern linguistic theory;[111] it has now been called into question. A number of researchers have demonstrated that, while consciously learning a rule may aid acquisition, the role that this kind of learning plays in acquisition is very limited.[112]

Any analysis of effective teaching is inadequate without attention to this distinction. For the purposes of this review, primacy will be given to second-language acquisition (SLA) rather than second-language learning. Most especially in the area of language, any approach which results in the mere learning of rules, without an internalization of them so that they become "second nature," must be seen as inherently inferior to one where real acquisition takes place. It is with this assumption that effective language teaching approaches will be examined.

Age and second-language acquisition

The relation of age to SLA was mentioned briefly above. It will be treated separately here because of its centrality in the literature. This relation is what has come to be known as the "critical period hypothesis." This is a general notion that language is learned best at certain periods or within certain age ranges, outside of which the ability is diminished. The question of the optimum age for SLA is an old one (some researchers have traced it to the ancient Egyptians);[113] but the focus here will be on research conducted since the 1950s which has had an impact on modern foreign language teaching and programs.

A number of researchers have concluded that young children are better acquirers of language than are older children and adults. The evidence given for this position is of two sorts. One is information gathered from neurophysiological experimentation. Especially important was the work by Lenneberg on brain lateralization and Penfield on the "uncommitted cortex."[114] Both of these researchers contended that the natural process of cerebral dominance, where specific functions like language are allocated to one or the other of the brain hemispheres, is complete by about the time of puberty. Before this time, the brain's plasticity had allowed the child to acquire language easily and automatically, even where exposure to the language was merely informal; the structures of the adult brain, on the other hand, have lost their flexibility and therefore are less receptive to language acquisition. Andersson, whose work has had considerable impact on modern language teaching programs, draws on these sorts of studies for his own theories:

> [The] optimum age for the beginning of the continuous learning of a second language seems to fall within the span of ages four through eight, with superior performance to be anticipated at ages eight, nine, ten. In this early period the brain seems to have the greatest plasticity and specialized capacity needed for acquiring speech.[115]

Andersson concludes that language-acquisition for the adult is different in kind than that for children: the childhood experience is dominated by what he calls "conditioned learning," which is at its peak at infancy and diminishes in capacity with age; in adults, "conceptual learning," which attends to more formal aspects of language acquisition, predominates and is enhanced with maturity.

Others advance arguments for a critical period based on their conception of the nature of language itself and its relation to other developmental processes. Ervin-Tripp, for example, argues for introducing languages between the ages of 7 and 9, before which the memory span is probably not well enough developed to aid in acquisition. Saville-Troike suggests the age of ten, when the problems caused by interference are lessened because the first language has had a chance to develop. Snow holds that adolescents might be the most motivated language learners because their study would be more a matter of personal choice than would be the ease for children.[116]

In addition to the question of the optimum age for beginning second-language study, the critical period hypothesis implies two other important and related questions: Does adult language acquisition entail different processes than child language acquisition? And, is first-language acquisition different in kind from second-language acquisition? Many modern approaches to language teaching are based on Chomsky's largely conceptual research which demonstrates that adults acquire language differently than do children because of the attention to rules in the adult. This has led to systematic teaching programs generally associated with what is called the "cognitive code" approach. More recently, however, these conclusions have been challenged; the consensus among researchers and applied linguists now seems to be that there is no essential difference between first and second language acquisition.[117] Furthermore, the assumption that children are more skilled language acquirers than adults, whether because of a biological pre-disposition or some other factor, is a misconception. Krashen summarizes the most recent view on the relation of age to SLA:

- Second language development proceeds through the early stages more quickly in adults than children.
- Older children are faster acquirers than younger children.
- The earlier the exposure to the second language, the higher the degree of second-language proficiency.[118]

These statements suggest that adults and older children are better acquir-ers than young children in the short run; in the long run, especially as to the phonological dimensions of second-language acquisition, it is better to have been exposed to the language as a child. They lead as well to the conclusion that both children and adults can be proficient language acquirers.

In the final analysis, it appears that despite its central place in the literature, age is not a very important factor in SLA. Burstall sees the time spent studying and being exposed to the language as more important. Similarly, Krashen holds that the quality and quantity of second language input in a comfortable, non-inhibiting context is critical for SLA, age notwithstanding.[119]

Natural order of acquisition

A language acquirer's first language (L1) has traditionally been regarded as the main influence on the learning of the second language (L2). Early research tended to show that many of the problems students had with L2 resulted from linguistic interference, the tendency to confuse L1 and L2 structures.[120] Many of the errors observed were phonological, as in the inabil-ity to trill the Spanish /r/; these, of course, were the most obvious indicators of a potential conflict between L1 and L2 in the acquirer. However, more subtle structural errors were also observed (confusion in verb-subject order, for example).

These observations led to a comparative approach in the study of SLA, in which the structures of two languages were put up against each other in order to predict where interlingual errors would most likely occur. The pri-mary assumption of this approach (known as "contrastive analysis") is that the basic processes of SLA are dependent on the structure of L1. The peda-gogical implications of this assumption were that the teacher would have to be conscious of the differences between the two languages involved, and that the students would be drilled in the structural patterns of L2.

More recently, researchers have suggested that the influence of L1 on L2 in SLA is minimal. Dulay and Burt, for example, found that only about 5%

of children's errors resulted from interference; instead, the overwhelming majority (almost 90%) were developmental errors of the sort that first-language learners exhibit. Moreover, speakers of different languages tended to make the same kinds of error and acquire linguistic structures in generally the same order when the target language was the same. This has led to the conclusion that, for any particular language, there is a natural order of acquisition. Many different researchers, studying different language learners, have reached the same conclusion.[121]

The natural order of acquisition hypothesis has considerable support, although it is still undergoing study and modification. It represents a completely new way of viewing SLA, and has important effects on teaching. In the first place, it negates the validity of comparing the structures of languages to see where interlingual errors will occur. These errors tend not to be significant; furthermore, this type of comparison has proven not to be a reliable predictor of error or performance.[122] In the second place, the natural order hypothesis implies that the processes of acquiring the L2 are not qualitatively different from those of acquiring the L1. Instead of trying to establish new habit patterns in the child, the teacher should work to develop as close to a natural language-acquisition environment as possible. In a later section, we will examine what this environment entails.

Classifying theories of second-language acquisition

Research in SLA continues to result in new theories and models with potential usefulness to the classroom. We should be careful not to overestimate the validity of our present knowledge, since it has evolved out of old theories which have also been strongly held. In this section, we will review some of this history in an effort to understand how current ideas on SLA are related to older ones, and to speculate on where we might be headed.

Behavioristic theories. Early research in SLA was influenced heavily by behavioral models of human behavior.[123] Central to this paradigm was the notion of habit acquisition through the early reinforcement of certain behaviors. The child learned how to behave appropriately by being rewarded for some actions and punished (or not rewarded) for others. Similarly, structural linguists theorized that children learned to speak in a particular language by being encouraged in some language habits and discouraged from others; the rules of the language were internalized eventually through the repetition of appropriate behaviors.

This inductivist theory of language acquisition gave rise in the 1940s to the audiolingual method (ALM) of teaching a second language. In this approach, primacy was placed on the spoken language, since it was considered to be the dimension of language which was acquired naturally through habit formation. Reading and writing, considered a secondary, derived form of language, would have an important place, but would come relatively late in the curriculum.

The development of ALM was supported by the work of structural linguists who studied languages comparatively. Most prominent among these were those engaged in "contrastive analysis" in which predictions about difficulty in language acquisition were based on knowledge of the structural differences between the two languages. Curriculum materials were produced with this knowledge in mind; the aim of teaching was to attend to the errors the students would most likely make and reinforce in them habits appropriate to the L2. This is put quite clearly by Banathy and his colleagues:

> Our initial assumption is that learning means changing behavior. Learning a foreign language, thus, means changing one's native language behavior to that of speakers of the target language. ... the change that has to take place in the language behavior of a foreign language student can be equated with the differences between the structure of the student's native language and culture and that of the target language and culture. The task of the linguist, the cultural anthropologist, and the sociologist is to identify these differences. The task of the writer of a foreign language teaching program is to develop materials which will be based on a statement of these differences; the task of the foreign language teacher is to be aware of these differences and to be prepared to teach them; the task of the student is to learn them.[124]

The period of greatest popularity for ALM and contrastive analysis was from the end of World War II to the early 1960s. While ALM is still in use in foreign language teaching programs, it has undergone modifications. These resulted from some important criticisms: patterned drills produced considerable and unnecessary anxiety; students had difficulty using the dialogues outside the classroom, so that this language learning had limited usefulness; above all, the processes were too mechanistic, so that students had little personal attachment to their new language. While the basic principles of ALM and contrastive analysis are still exhibited in some classrooms, there is more attention to the relevance of the language forms for personal use and the creation of a more relaxed language learning environment.[125]

<u>Mentalistic theories</u>. The late 1950s saw a revolution in linguistics spearheaded by Noam Chomsky. The assumption that children acquired language through habit formation was discarded in favor of the hypothesis that human beings have an innate language capacity. This capacity, called the language acquisition device (LAD), is extended through testing the environment. Essential to this process is the opportunity to make mistakes about appropriate language use and to learn from them. This leads to an understanding of the underlying structure of the language being learned, and an internalization of the rules of that language. These rules are generative in that they serve as a heuristic for the production and comprehension of speech forms which the child has never heard.[126]

The teaching program which has arisen from these ideas is commonly called the "cognitive code" approach to SLA.[127] Central to this approach is direct teaching of the rules of grammar and an engagement of the student's reasoning abilities in grasping these rules. Here, literacy skills in the second language are introduced relatively early since they help to illustrate some of the grammatical structure of the language and provide another source for comprehension. At the same time, it is important to allow children the freedom to use their new language regardless of their degree of proficiency, since hypothesis-testing could proceed only to the extent that they actively produced utterances. This implied that teachers encouraged short exchanges as an inducement to further use, and that curriculum writers relied less on pre-formed dialogues as models for appropriate speech.

Some have suggested that the ALM and cognitive code approaches need not be strictly separated for pedagogical reasons. Carroll, for example, suggests that teachers find it convenient to use both methods alternatively for different functions and at different times in the same classroom.[128] This is probably because of the intuition that language consists of both learned habits and structural rules, and that both conditioned and conceptual learning contribute to SLA.[129] Nevertheless, it is probably important to understand the differences between the two approaches, since curriculum materials vary widely depending on the approach underlying them.

Communicative theories. Behavioristic approaches tended to subordinate conscious learning of language forms to the acquisition of good language habits; mentalistic theories concentrated on the direct learning of grammatical rules, since these engaged the child's reason in language acquisition and allowed him or her to internalize the structure of the language. Both sorts of theories have been criticized for fostering an artificial environment for language acquisition; the emphasis was on the production of a correct form of language, rather than on the activity of sending and receiving meaningful messages through language.

In communicative approaches, the second language becomes less a learning target than a means by which communication of meaningful pieces of information takes place.[130] The principle underlying these approaches can be stated as follows: A language is more readily acquired when it is used as a medium for the communication of meaningful messages than when it is used as a target for learning.

This approach is based on the assumption that language learning and teaching must take account of the social context in which the language is produced. That is, it places an emphasis on the way in which language is actually used by native speakers, rather than on notions of "correct" or ideal usage which are the concern of grammarians and some language professionals. In a helpful analysis of this issue, H.G. Widdowson proposes a contrasting set of concepts which define the distinction between formal and communicative (or "functional") approaches to language teaching:

Linguistic concepts	Communicative concepts
usage	use
correctness	appropriateness
sentence	utterance
signification	value
cohesion	coherence

This contrast points the way toward a language pedagogy that views language as a system of communication, rather than a formal set of rules which students learn more or less well. The communicative approach is the major modern influence on theories of language teaching. The bulk of the literature in this area has been developed by European and Canadian researchers; it has already had a significant impact on the development of language teaching programs, especially in Europe.[131]

Most prominent among the theorists who have tried to adapt a communicative approach to the U.S. are Terrell, Krashen, and Cummins, though there are many others.[132] Three major points are common to the work of these writers: (1) SLA is most effectively achieved when there are large quantities of comprehensible input in the L2; mere exposure to the new language, without regard to whether the child understands or can engage in strategies for understanding the message, is of little consequence in SLA. (2) The input must be purposeful and relevant to immediate experience; phrases created merely for the purpose of practicing a particular language form tend to inhibit real acquisition. (3) Acquisition should not be anxious; to the extent that the environment creates tensions in the students, achievement in SLA will be diminished.

In a later section, we will examine how various writers working within this paradigm for SLA propose to achieve a teaching environment consistent with these principles.

Sociolinguistic theories. In their 1977 article, Hakuta and Cancino offer a more or less chronological review of SLA theories, from the early contrastive and error analyses to the more recent trends in performance and discourse analysis. When they look to the future, they see a greater concern for sociocultural variables which may influence SLA. This added factor, they contend, represents an approach that "would give greater acknowledgment to the complexity of the second-language acquisition process."[133] Of course, these sorts of elements have already been evident, especially in what we have called "communicative approaches." But the concern with sociolinguistics offers a much broader context for the analysis of the problems of SLA.

The sociolinguist would argue that a concentration on the micro-level in our analysis—the classroom, for example—without regard to macroscopic social processes misrepresents the complexity of SLA. The motivation to learn a second language may be influenced heavily by extra-linguistic and extra-school factors: language attitudes, toward both the L1 and L2; prestige levels and power relationships among ethnic groups and their languages; evaluations of markedness for some languages; these and other similar variables can have an important impact on achievement levels in SLA, as well as generally in school.

A sociolinguistic perspective on SLA draws attention to the political nature of language in society. It brings together matters of pedagogy and matters of policy. In developing a position on language teaching in the United States, it is not enough to find the "best" classroom technique or pedagogical approach. At least, one must show how the school program interacts with social and political circumstances, and how that interaction effects certain goals. Various writers demonstrate, for example, that school programs called "bilingual education" can be used for goals from one extreme to the other, from language maintenance and pluralism to language shift and assimilation.[134] The crucial factor in these different effects is not the nature of the school program itself, but its relationship to social circumstance. A responsible approach to policy-making in language education must be mindful of the larger social context of school programs.

The use of the first and second language in teaching

Some of the controversy over bilingual education in the United States focuses on the role that L1 and L2 should have in instruction. Many school programs are based on the assumption that use of L1 as a medium of instruction is essential to the achievement of LEP/NEP students. Indeed, the very definition of bilingual education, at least until very recently, required that both L1 and L2 be used for instructional purposes.[135]

Researchers draw two kinds of conclusions as to the benefits of L1-use as an instructional medium: that it is necessary academically so that the child not fall behind in subject matter while he or she is learning English; and that it is important symbolically and psychologically, alleviating some of the problems of minority culture depreciation and low self esteem in the child. Skutnabb-Kangas and Toukomaa, for example, try to demonstrate that school language programs which neglect the use of L1 can impair learning in both L1 and L2.[136] Similarly, Tikunoff and Vazquez-Faria, in summaries of their work on effective bilingual instruction, conclude the following:

> It is clear that use of both L1 and L2 are necessary, that a focus on language development is required throughout instruction, and that use of cues from a LEP student's culture contributes significantly to effective bilingual instruction.[137]

It seems clear, however, that recently much more weight has been given to psychological and sociocultural justifications for the substantive use of L1 to teach LEP students. This is stated most forcefully by Rudolph Troike: "... while the use of the student's language as a medium in a bilingual program may indeed promote the development of cognitive abilities, its chief value may be symbolic, by helping to legitimize the positive valuation of the student's culture, social group, and self."[138] L1-use thus works to alter perceptions of markedness which, as reported above, can have an important influence on language acquisition.

Critics of L1-use contend that this practice has done little but disadvantage these children academically: it does not foster general learning to any great extent, and, most important, it takes away from English mastery, which is the key to school achievement.[139] These contentions are disputed, on the grounds of both empirical results from bilingual education experiments and conceptual-psychological research on language development and bilingualism. Cummins, for example, argues that these criticisms are based on erroneous assumptions about language proficiency, achievement, and the relation between two languages in the bilingual.[140] Specifically, he argues against what he calls the Separate Underlying Proficiency (SUP) model of bilingual competence, which implies that (1) proficiency in L1 is separate from that in L2; and (2) there is a direct relationship between exposure to a language and proficiency in that language. These assumptions would lead us to predict that students exposed only to L2 in the curriculum would achieve a higher degree of L2 proficiency than students undergoing instruction in both L1 and L2. This does not seem to be the case; generally, after only three or four years of instruction, children taught bilingually tend to surpass children with comparable characteristics taught exclusively in L1 in both L1 and L2 proficiency levels. In fact, there is a growing body of literature which links bilingual proficiency with enhancement of even more general, nonlinguistic skills like problem-solving and conceptualization.[141]

Working from what he calls the "interdependence hypothesis", Cummins posits an alternative view of bilingual competence, which he calls the Common Underlying Proficiency (CUP) model. He suggests that basic language skills are transferable from one language to another; therefore, proficiency attainment in one language has a positive effect on proficiency attainment in another. It is important to keep in mind, however, his discussion of "proficiency," which is more complicated than it seems (see the review above). There is a significant difference between "context-reduced" and "context-embedded" proficiency. The crucial factor in the child's development of these skills is the nature of the linguistic interaction available to him or her. The greater the number of opportunities the child has for meaningful interaction in a comfortable environment, the greater the chances for more complete proficiency attainment. In general, this means that early use of L1, the language with which the child is most comfortable, is crucial for the development of proficiency in any language. Moreover, since psychological and sociocultural factors are strong influences on language achievement, it is beneficial to continue exposure in and encourage maintenance of L1 for an extended period in the curriculum, perhaps throughout the elementary years.

Cummins' work, adapted to the United States, suggests that the common intuition that language minority students attain English language skills best through direct instruction is based on a too-simple view of language development. His is another way of justifying a position that bilingual education advocates have long held: the surest and quickest way to attain English proficiency is through the child's native language. He implies what Harrington says directly, that the transition/maintenance distinction in bilingual education, viewed correctly, is a false distinction: "the best transitional program is one which provides a maintenance of learning in L1."[142]

This point is also pertinent to another argument made by the critics of L1-use for instruction, mentioned above: that English mastery is the key to school achievement for LEP/NEP students. For the record, many researchers, including Troike, Cummins, and others, consider English proficiency by itself to be much overrated as a factor in school success. More important are "extrinsic and intrinsic social and cultural factors (including such things as the Pygmalion effect of self-fulfilling teacher expectations)."[143] However one resolves this question, it may well be that any attempt at linking English-language capacity and school and social achievement may be premature. This effort must wait until we have a clearer idea of what factors help or hinder English-language skills development for the LEP/NEP child. Up to now, there is much evidence to suggest that attempting to foster such development without regard for L1 is dysfunctional. At the same time, we have much to make us hopeful that an instructional approach with L1 at its center can yield a lasting and more general benefit.

Methods of Second-Language Teaching

Theories of acquiring a second language are not yet usable pedagogical methods. Our task now is to show how these ideas have been translated into systematic teaching programs. Interested readers can find detailed reviews of a variety of teaching approaches in works by Stevick, LaForge, Bernbaum, Cornejo and Cornejo, McLaughlin, and Krashen.[144] Here, I will merely give some of the broader outlines of the more recent methods, and attempt to see how they are related.

The Silent Way. One of the more innovative and controversial approaches to second-language teaching is what Gattegno calls the "silent way."[145] Here, the activity of the teacher is always to be subordinated to that of the learner, who is encouraged to experiment with the new language without significant interference from the teacher. The material aspects of this curriculum are very simple: a set of colored rods, which form the center of the lessons; a word chart; a phonic chart; workbooks and other reading matter. Initially, the role of the teacher is to introduce each new element in the curriculum (a word, phrase, or structure, for example) clearly and forcefully; subsequently, the students do 90% of the talking, with the teacher giving mostly nonverbal feedback to them. Student talk is always accompanied by behaviors appropriate to it, for example the manipulation of the rods as a visual representation of what is being talked about. Teacher silence is indispensable to the success of this method, which Gattegno regards as a general pedagogy, suited for more than just language teaching. This silence allows the student time to try the new language at his or her own pace; in addition, it allows for a period of internalization and introspection needed in order to assimilate the new language. The greatest virtue of the silent way is perhaps that it emphasizes that the students themselves must be the principal active agents in learning a new language.

Total Physical Response Course. James Asher and his colleagues have developed a technique in which physical responses characterize initial contact with a foreign language.[146] Here, students do not speak in the early stages of their exposure, but rather respond physically to commands from the teacher ("raise your bands", for example, or "everyone stand up"). Asher expects that students will spend about 70% of their time listening (perhaps more in the very early phases), 20% speaking, and 10% reading and writing in a typical Total Physical Response (TPR) course. Allowing students a silent period in which they are not required to produce any utterances in the new language is central to TPR; it is essential, from this point of view, to make sure that the students themselves indicate when they are ready to start speaking. This silent period is not lost time, by any means; it provides a student a chance to absorb and internalize the new language in a non-threatening atmosphere. Students exposed to language in this way have shown superior achievement compared with students who have been forced to speak immediately. It could also be that the effort to speak interferes with hypothesis-testing in the early stages, thereby hindering to a degree the creative aspects of language acquisition. TPR is perhaps the best example of methods which emphasize communication over rule-learning (or function over form) in language acquisition. The approach highlights the fact that language behavior naturally generates messages of relevance in the immediate environment.

Community Language Learning. Community Language Learning (CLL) is an approach, developed and elaborated most notably by Charles Curran, which applies the concepts and techniques of counseling to language teaching.[147] In this approach, every effort is made that the class become a little community. The students sit, usually in a circle, and speak to one another in their native language about any subject they wish. The teacher, acting more as a counselor and resource, translates the sentences into the target language; sometimes the teacher also writes down key words and phrases, which become topics for later discussion. The teacher must never act in such a way that the student feels on guard; tone of voice and gestures must be consonant with the teacher's role as counselor. This is important for what Stevick regards as a basic principle underlying foreign language learning; "the human person learns new behavior rapidly if the learner is not busy defending himself from someone else."[148]

The learning-counseling sessions are tape recorded to provide an opportunity for self-reflection and feedback. These also are occasions on which the students can become more conscious of the mutually-supportive atmosphere which is supposed to characterize their learning experience. In other words, they come to understand that they are learning not merely a new language, but also a new principle of learning: it happens best in the context of a community in which the members respect and cooperate with each other. CLL thus has the quality of an alternative to traditional education in general, rather than being restricted to any particular subject.

The Input Hypothesis. Stephen Krashen's work in second-language acquisition has had a wide-reaching impact on this literature. Briefly, his Input Hypothesis can be stated as follows: Second-language acquisition takes place best when the linguistic messages available to the acquirer (input) are (1) comprehensible, (2) interesting and relevant to the student, (3) not grammatically-sequenced, (4) provided in sufficient quantity, and (5) provided in a context and manner that minimizes anxiety for the student.[149] The first two conditions, comprehensibility and relevance, imply an emphasis on communication in the language acquisition environment. If the purpose of the language exchange is merely to learn some form of the language, without a concern for conveying some meaningful message, acquisition is hindered. Here, Krashen has in mind approaches characterized by drills and mimicry which place great importance on the duplication of a formally correct model. Examples of this follow, both taken from a level one Spanish lesson in an ALM manual (but they could have come from a number of other programs, as well). This series of exercises is intended to test the student's knowledge of vocabulary and sentence structure by selection of the most likely rejoinder:

(1) El cielo está nublado.
    A. Sea lo que sea, está cansado.
    B. Vamos, siempre lo ha sido.
    C. Si, hace buen tiempo.
    D. Seguro que va a llover.
(2) Torea bien Arruza?
    A. Si, es muy malo.
    B. Si, es muy valiente.
    C. Si, es un loro.
    D. Si, es un toro.[150]

These test items exemplify how form prevails over function in many language teaching programs. Number (1) is representative of a good many conversations which likely exist only in textbooks, but hardly ever in life. There are, perhaps, occasions on which we might exchange the words "The sky is cloudy"/"It is sure to rain", but this is not natural, everyday speech. The fact that it is not nonsense (i.e. we can recognize it as a possible exchange in Spanish) does not make it meaningful or interesting. Number (2) means even less to us, both because it is a strained exchange much like (1), and because it is taken from a highly restricted cultural context with which most students of Spanish would be completely unfamiliar. In fact, one could probably expect that even most native Spanish speakers would have to hear this question at least twice before making any sense of it.

The third condition mentioned above aims at the provision of as close to a natural language environment as possible. Children develop language capacity by attending to natural speech in their environment. That speech is intended as a complex of meaningful messages; almost never do language speakers consciously monitor their speech so that neophytes will be exposed only to those forms which are appropriate to their stage of development.

This condition works in concert with the first two and with the fourth: the more conscious the speaker is of the correctness or appropriateness of the form of speech being used, the less comprehensible input be or she will provide to the acquirer. No one is sure how much input is sufficient to develop high levels of proficiency; that is an empirical question which as yet requires further investigation. The only point to be made as to quantity is that, in general, more is better, particularly if we are talking about meaningful exchanges in which the student is free to test the linguistic environment and receive feedback.

Finally, we should be concerned with what is sometimes called the "affective filter." This concerns the role that affective variables play in language acquisition. These variables include relatively long-term ones like motivation and self-esteem, as well as those related more directly to the immediate environment like test anxiety. As we have suggested previously, concerns of the first sort are perhaps more appropriately addressed within a discussion of the role of macroscopic forces like economic deprivation and social isolation in language acquisition. Krashen quite properly confines himself to the atmosphere of the classroom. His conclusion is that any approach which heightens anxiety in the classroom is a hindrance to language acquisition, and any approach which lowers anxiety is a help. This is comparable to Stevick's principle previously stated, that a student learns best when not on the defensive. We can identify a good number of activities common to many language classrooms which contribute to this problem: forcing children to speak in a new language before they feel ready; requiring exact duplication of dialogues and other models; correcting the form of speech, sometimes publicly and in an embarrassing way; popping quizzes. The strength of the affective filter can determine how much input actually becomes accessible to the student and may explain why some students who are in a position to receive large amounts of input still do not become very proficient.[151]

Krashen's work represents a theme running through the literature on SLA which urges a communicative approach to language teaching. The Input Hypothesis is not so much a method as a model by which to evaluate the potential effectiveness of aspects of any approach. Other models and approaches, like Terrell's Natural Approach and Cummins' Common Underlying Proficiency model, fall within this tradition. As Krashen himself says, it is probably less important to identify the "best" method than to outline important principles by which we can evaluate certain practices of the language classroom:

> ... there is no one way to teach, no one method that is clearly the best. Some methods are clearly more effective than others, however, and the claim made here is that the same underlying principles will hold for any successful second language teaching program ...[152]

The methods that we have outlined here are not necessarily tied to any specific program type. Any one or combination of approaches could be used in a bilingual program, an immersion program, or a traditional foreign language classroom. They have as a common theme the concern for communication and comfort in the language acquisition environment. We should turn now to programs designed to address the needs of the LEP/NEP student. There, we will try to show how the ideas underlying the methods discussed above are usable.

Programs of Second Language Teaching

In this section, a review of some of the major language-oriented school programs is presented. We will be most interested in the assumptions inherent in the programs, their goals, and their perceived effects—for the LEP/NEP student and in a more general sense. Finally, we will explore the requirements for program interrelation and cooperation. Definitions and explanations are difficult in this area because the distinctions among programs are not clear-cut. We will see, for example, that while "immersion" programs are sometimes offered as alternatives to "bilingual education" programs, they are at other times recognized as a type of bilingual education. We will try to indicate where strict distinctions should be avoided.[153]

Submersion

"Submersion" is not so much a program as the absence of a program. It is sometimes called "sink-or-swim", which suggests the nature of the treatment and support afforded the LEP/NEP student. All subject matter is taught in English. There is no effort to teach in or develop student skills in the non-English language. The students are expected to keep up their work largely on their own. In some areas, school officials, most concerned about the influx of immigrant NEP children, have instituted English-as-a-second-language (ESL) classes; the usual procedure is for children to be pulled out of certain class periods (physical education, art, and other "nonacademic" subjects) in order to receive special intensive English language training. Again, there is no instruction in the mother tongue; this would be difficult, since many different language groups may be represented in the class. The purpose of the program is to teach the child English as quickly as possible.

Several assumptions in submersion approaches can be identified:

- The child should receive as much exposure to English as possible in the early years, since this is the fastest way in which the child will learn English.
- The child will not fall too far behind in subject matter learning because children learn many things without understanding the medium of instruction.
- Learning English is the key to successful school achievement.

We have already shown that many researchers would regard these as serious miscalculations. The first is more naive than wrong. It misses the fact that the language experience must provide not just a large quantity of input, but input of a certain quality. Much of the input for the LEP/NEP child in this classroom will not be comprehensible, and therefore would not help in acquisition. As for the second, while it is true that children learn many things through nonverbal cues and other contextual variables, this kind of learning represents proficiency of a particular sort ("context-embedded"); learning academic subjects requires other, "context-reduced" skills, as well. Furthermore, learning is frequently complicated by a tacit understanding on the part of the student that the home language and culture (and therefore the student) are not very valuable in school. These sociocultural variables are perhaps a stronger influence on learning than a mismatch in language between home and school. The third assumption is one we have already addressed; it is clear that English proficiency, even English monolingualism, has been negligible as a factor in school success for some groups.

Generally, submersion approaches have met with little success. The ineffectiveness of simply doing nothing has been documented by a number of investigators. This conclusion is most forceful in the case of ethnic groups like American Indians and Chicanos. A series of reports by the United States Commission on Civil Rights in the late 1960s and early 1970s chronicled the failure of regular school programs in extending equal educational opportunities to these groups. Even worse, it revealed that students in some schools were publicly humiliated because of their language background. A survey of Southwestern schools showed that administrators took measures against Mexican American children who were "caught" speaking Spanish. The following student comments reveal how the "no Spanish rules" were enforced:

> "If we speak Spanish we had to pay 5 cents to the teacher or we had to stay after school ..."

> "In the sixth grade, they kept a record of which if we spoke Spanish they would take it down and charge us a penny for every Spanish word. If we spoke more than one thousand words our parents would have to come to the school and talk with the principal ..."

> "If you'd be caught speaking Spanish you would be sent to the principal's office or given extra assignments to do as homework or probably made to stand by the wall during recess and after school ..."[154]

Most of these practices have now been ruled illegal, but the attitudes which engendered them have not entirely disappeared. Alan Pifer suggests that there are many ways in which the school can convey a sense of inferiority to non-English speakers: tracking them into low achievement classes, denigrating their heritage, labelling them mentally retarded, and otherwise "giving them the message that they cannot, or are not expected to, succeed."[155] The attraction of special programs like bilingual education for language minority communities is that at least these programs make a conscious effort to respect the child's language and culture. Otheguy characterizes the school where no bilingual education exists, where there is only submersion, as follows:

> Experience has shown that where no bilingual program exists, Hispanic parents are less likely to approach the school and talk with teachers, that children are neglected by their teachers and tend to drop out, and that little effort is made to teach them English, preferring instead to classify them as slow learners and retarded.[156]

We should add that, in most instances, a submersion program would probably be found to be a violation of the child's civil rights. The principle that students must have access to the curriculum by understanding the language of instruction is embodied in Lau, but it has prior expressions as well.[157] We turn now to some alternatives to submersion.

Bilingual bicultural education

The usual conception of bilingual education includes two distinguishing characteristics: (1) use of both L1 and English as a medium of instruction, and (2) a concern for the appreciation of the cultural heritage of the language-minority children. It is not merely a language-teaching program, but one conceived of as a complete curriculum. Beyond these general features, the range of programs which are called "bilingual" is very great: they vary in the ratio of L1/L2 use, the nature and extent of the cultural component, the goals of the program, the staffing patterns and classroom organization, student composition of the classrooms, and others. In this section, we will present different categorizations of bilingual education, then try to assess some of the effects of this program.

Types of bilingual bicultural education

One of the major problems in evaluating the effectiveness of bilingual education is the variety of activities included under that label. This is one of the factors cited for the lack of reliable data regarding these programs. One solution to this problem would be to define bilingual education more narrowly to isolate particular variables more efficiently. Another approach would be to typologize programs using a few key dimensions; in this way we might be able to compare evaluation results by program type. A number of researchers have opted for the latter approach.

In 1967, Wallace Lambert distinguished between additive and subtractive bilingualism. The first situation is one where the acquirer is retaining and developing the L1 while adding the L2 to his or her linguistic repertoire; the situation is construed by the student as one where both L1 and L2 have relatively high prestige. In the second, L2 acquisition is accompanied by a loss of L1; L1 in this situation is perceived as having a lower social status than L2. As to the role of schooling in these situations, Lambert says that there are school programs which foster one or the other sort of bilingual capacity. Where the school emphasizes full development of language skills only for L2; where teachers are proficient only in the child's L2; where the goal of the program is to transfer the child's language dominance from L1 to L2; and where the child is moved out of L1 instruction as quickly as possible; conditions are favorable for the development of subtractive (sometimes also called "replacive") bilingualism. But where language development goals are specified for both languages; where teachers are native speakers of the child's L1; where the goal is bilingualization by maintenance of the L1; and where L1-instruction may continue indefinitely in the curriculum; this is a program which fosters additive bilingualism. The development of these two types of bilingualism is more complex than this, of course, but Lambert contends that the school's contribution to this development is major. Lambert's bias is in favor of additive programs, since he finds these beneficial for both the child and the society: "The challenge for social planners and educators in this decade, then. is to help transform instances of subtractive bilingualism into additive ones."[158]

The effect of this sort of distinction is to show that school programs called "bilingual" can have very different, even contradictory, goals and effects. Rolf Kjolseth has the same intent in positing the distinction between programs fostering <u>linguistic pluralism</u> and those fostering <u>linguistic assimilation</u>. But his typology places a greater emphasis on sociolinguistic variables than does Lambert's. Central to his analysis is the concept of diglossia. This term describes a situation where different languages or language varieties are used in different social domains and for different purposes within the society or speech community. This differential use is normative; that is, it is regulated or influenced by social rules, usually tacit, which are understood and shared by members of the speech communities involved. The domains in which these diglossic norms operate are of different sorts. Switzerland is perhaps the most obvious case in which the domains are largely <u>geographical</u> or <u>territorial</u>; in other cases they are primarily <u>functional</u> (using one language for education and another for religious practice, for example). In societies where diglossic norms are strong, it has become a matter of course that, as one moves from one domain dominated by one set of language-behavior rules to one dominated by another, one's change in language behavior is natural and automatic. Using our territorial case to provide an example, as one moves from Basel to Geneva, it is expected that one's language behavior will also change. Kjolseth refers to this as a "multilingual opportunity structure." Therein lies the importance of this concept: to the extent that each of two languages has an important function or role to play in the society and is seen as valuable for that reason, individual bilingualism will be long-term and stable; to the extent that these norms do not exist, bilingualism is not sustained.

Kjolseth's two-pronged typology is based on the interaction between school program and social situation. The program which works for the development of diglossic norms in the larger society fosters linguistic pluralism because it contributes to stable bilingualism; the program unconcerned about such development fosters linguistic assimilation since diglossic norms must be cultivated if they are to be developed or kept from eroding. Kjolseth contends that more than 80 percent of United States programs approximate the linguistic assimilation type.[159]

Joshua Fishman and John Lovas have given us a slightly more expanded typology of bilingual schooling. They suggest four types: transitional, monoliterate, partial, and full bilingual programs. A <u>transitional</u> program is one where the L1 is used only for the purpose of providing a bridge between home and school and to allow the child to keep up in subject matter learning while learning English. There is no concern for the identification or development of mother tongue skills in the student; goals are specified only for English acquisition. The children are moved into the all-English curriculum as soon as their English proficiency seems suited to performing ordinary classwork at their grade level. A <u>monoliterate</u> program is designed so that both L1 and L2 are used as media of instruction. Conversational skills are developed and encouraged in both languages, but literacy skills are taught only in English. Fishman and Lovas suggest that this program has promise for sustaining bilingualism in the short run; but in the long run, bilingualism could be unstable and eventually eroded. That has been the case already with many American Indian languages. As the younger members of the community have become linguistically assimilated, the language dies with the older generations; without literacy skills in those languages, it is almost impossible to revive them. A partial bilingual program specifies goals for language development in both L1 and L2, but restricts L1-use to certain subjects in the curriculum. Usually, these are the "ethnically encumbered" subjects, or at least those where ethnic content is likely to be high, like social studies, history, art, music, and others. While this is valuable, it still tends to convey the message that the child's mother tongue has restricted usefulness: it is appropriate for "cultural" subjects, but not those associated with "power" like science and mathematics. Finally, the full bilingual program is one where both languages are developed for conversational and literacy uses and where there is no restriction in the way languages are distributed through the curriculum. There is still, to be sure, a concern that each language has its own substantive function, but this need not imply any allocation prejudiced by social status. This typology draws our attention once again to the fact that bilingual programs can achieve a wide variety of aims.[160]

William Mackey has outlined the most extensive and detailed typology of all. It is not possible in this short summary to represent it fully. Only the general idea and a few examples will be offered. His model of program types is based on the interaction of school and social variables. The typology relates three general factors: the language background of the student in relation to the school, the nature of language use in the curriculum, and the status and allocation of languages in the community and larger society. As to the first, the student's home language experience is compared with the school language pattern; for example, the student could come from a single-language home into a bilingual curriculum in which one or neither language is the language of the home, or from a bilingual home where both languages are used in the curriculum, and so on. He identifies five kinds of learners from this mix. The next factor, curricular language use, has a variety of dimensions (whether one language or two are used as media of instruction, whether the goal is language maintenance or language transfer, and others) which generate 10 possible curriculum patterns. One such pattern, for example, he labels Single medium-Accultural-Transfer (SAT); this is where the classroom uses only one language as the medium of instruction (the other is presented as a subject) and the goals are to transfer the child's language capability from L1 to L2 (in the direction of acculturation). Another example is called Dual medium-Equal distribution-Maintenance (DEM), where two languages are used relatively equally and the goal is the preservation of L1. Eight other patterns are presented. The third factor concerns the status of the languages. Here, he is concerned with whether or not the language of the home is used in the school, the community, and the nation, and to what degree it is used. He outlines nine different relationship patterns on the status of languages in society.

Combining these factors, Mackey generates ninety different types of bilingual schooling (10 curriculum patterns x nine language status patterns); going further, he combines this number with the 5 types of learner to get 450 possible types of programs which a student might encounter in school. While it would be cumbersome to derive public policy based on such detail, the typology is potentially useful in specifying more precisely the points of comparison among programs for evaluation purposes.[161]

For the purposes of public discussion of bilingual education, the many possible differences among programs have been condensed into a simple dichotomy: today, programs are commonly classified as either <u>transitional bilingual education</u> (TBE) or <u>maintenance bilingual education</u> (MBE).[162] TBE generally corresponds to Fishman's category of the same label; its purpose is to teach English to the student and to move him or her into the regular all-English curriculum as quickly as possible. MBE has the general goal of maintaining the L1 while adding English to the child's language capacity. Central to these goals are language arts activities in L1 and intensive ESL instruction, usually by a teacher specially certified for such a purpose. As we have said previously, the overwhelming majority of the bilingual education programs in the United States are transitional in nature. Although we will discuss briefly some of the effects of MBE programs, it should be kept in mind that they are very few in number. That amounts to the same as saying that to speak of bilingual education in the United States is to speak to TBE.

The effectiveness of bilingual education

An evaluation of the effectiveness of bilingual education turns on two key issues: the goals and assumptions of the program, and the determination of what is a valid research finding. Both of these issues are at the center of the present controversy over bilingual education.

As noted in an earlier section, there are basic disagreements over what the goal of a bilingual education program should be. On the one hand, some like Baker and deKanter contend that its overriding goal should be English language skill development. Others like Willig and Troike argue that its purpose has been from the beginning the provision of equality of educational opportunity; therefore, the extent of the evaluation of effectiveness must go beyond testing for English mastery.[163]

Even when agreement is reached on goals, problems emerge. For example, many advocates of bilingual education concede that <u>a</u> goal of the program is the teaching of English. How do different investigators view its effectiveness on that point? Baker and deKanter see little positive effect: "the bilingually instructed child will not do any better in English than the child instructed only in English and often will do worse."[164] On the other hand, Troike and others, examining many of the same projects as those discussed by Baker and deKanter, demonstrate that these children in fact make significant gains in English skills.[165] How is this discrepancy explained? Earlier, we suggested that it might best be viewed as an ideological struggle which influences the selection and treatment of the data. Troike also complains that it is difficult to draw wide-ranging conclusions about bilingual education, since the funds allocated for its evaluation have been totally inadequate to such determinations. There is another possible explanation which relates to the earlier discussion on the variety of program types. If we view TBE and MBE as two poles of a continuum, the range and clustering of the programs selected for examination along the continuum can affect dramatically the general conclusions we draw. It could be that the range of program types in one sample is larger than in another.

This relates to the second issue, that of determining what are valid research findings. Researchers will sometimes have slightly different criteria in mind in making these decisions. Dulay and Burt eliminated 95% of the reports and studies available to them in their survey of bilingual education because of improper sampling procedures and problems with control.[166] Baker and deKanter rejected the great majority of the studies they reviewed for similar reasons. They have been criticized by Willig, Tates and Ortiz, and others for being inconsistent in their procedures. These suggest that many of the programs that were included could have been eliminated by the same criteria suggested by Baker and deKanter.[167] These problems serve merely to make more difficult a dispassionate analysis of the effectiveness of bilingual education.

Recently, the literature on the effectiveness of the bilingual school program has gone in a new direction. Instead of criticizing or praising different projects for the results they achieve, some have been charged with the task of identifying those features of the bilingual classroom that are effective in promoting student learning. This addresses some of the problems raised earlier. To eliminate a program because it does not on average appear to some to have significant benefit may be inefficient public policy; it is better to see which dimensions of the program seem to work and promote those throughout the school system.

Identification of these dimensions is an important aspect of the Significant Instruction Features (SIF) studies conducted by William Tikunoff and others. Here, projects that have shown positive results were investigated to ascertain what features of them seem to lead to student success. The researchers assumed that effective instructional approaches in general are applicable to the bilingual classroom. They isolated three central components of effective teaching: (1) Active teaching: the teacher has clear goals, and spends most of classtime on their achievement; the teacher makes clear presentations; paces instruction; gives immediate, academically-oriented feedback; promotes and maintains high student engagement in academic tasks; and creates a serious yet relaxed learning environment. (2) Academic learning time (ALT): "the time a student spends in a particular content area engaged in learning tasks with a high degree of accuracy." This component has three dimensions: the amount of time allocated for the particular task; the degree of student engagement in the task; and the accuracy rate of the student in performing the task. The accumulation of ALT requires all three of these dimensions. "The more ALT accumulated by a student during instruction, the more the student is learning." (3) Student participation: this implies an active understanding of what the tasks of the classroom are and how they are to be completed; it also suggests that the student be given the impression that he or she is expected to be engaged in the task to a high degree. These three components are essential aspects of any classroom.

SIF researchers were also concerned with what features peculiar to bilingual classrooms contribute to high achievement levels. There are many, but three main factors were identified:

- Use of both L1 and L2 effectively for instruction. Non-use of L1 has two different effects. In the first place, it diminishes the prospects of high student engagement and participation, which is essential for learning: "participation in instructional work activity requires that a student understand what is going on. … When instruction is delivered in a language a child only minimally can understand, the result frequently is frustration, boredom, hostility, or withdrawal. Thus, access to learning is impeded at the very least, resulting in failure or falling behind in school work." In the second place, using L1 only for nonacademic purposes can affect the child's motivation for learning: "there is a relationship between the confidence possessed by a NES/LES in learning a second language and the self-esteem which results and the self-concept which develops."
- Integration of English language acquisition with academic skills development. This is consistent with SLA theories which we have presented previously which hold that language is learned best when it is used as a medium in meaningful interaction, as opposed to when it is the direct target of instruction.
- Use of the culture of the child as a mediator for instruction in the classroom. This is an application of the old principle of using what is familiar to teach what is novel. But it also implies two other effects. In the first place, it conveys a sense of legitimacy for the home experience of the child; as we have already said, this is invaluable in motivation for learning. In the second place, it has the effect of lowering the "affective filter"; to the extent that the child is comfortable in the classroom, the possibility for learning is enhanced.[168]

Others have also tried to delineate criteria for a good bilingual education program. Harrington[169] has perhaps the longest list of these:

- A high degree of commitment to bilingual education by the district level staff (indicated by resource allocation and long-term planning).
- Community support.
- Coordination and cooperation between the program and school.
- Voluntary participation in the program.
- Linguistically (and culturally) integrated classrooms.
- Initial literacy training in L1.
- Accommodation of a variety of teaching styles.
- Long-range evaluation of student performance.
- Teachers who (a) are bilingual, (b) are sensitive to cultural differences, (c) are certified as bilingual teachers, (d) reflect the ethnicity of the students and live in the community, and (e) receive inservice training.

This list draws attention to the fact that the goals of bilingual education are numerous; this is because of the comprehensive nature of the curriculum and the general goal of academic achievement. It is probably unreasonable to emphasize the importance of English mastery, as important as this objective is, to the exclusion of all others in evaluating the effectiveness of bilingual education. What is needed is a broadened framework which may include, in addition to student academic characteristics, questions of how the programs have affected community involvement, absentee rates and disciplinary problems, student self-esteem and cultural appreciation, and teacher training and morale.[170]

Critics of TBE contend that the mixed results of bilingual education should lead us away from that program as the only remedy for language minority children. Baker and deKanter propose experimentation with immersion programs to see if the results prove more beneficial. Others, also, see TBE as ineffective, but their alternatives are away from the direction of immersion. Harrington and Lambert say that non-effective programs tend to be those which foster subtractive bilingualism.[171] Rotberg argues that "current findings do not indicate that the transitional bilingual-bicultural approach advocated by the Lau remedies and Title VII is better on the average than other models" and calls for a national research study on these questions.[172] And Fishman, perhaps the most visible advocate of bilingual education, also gives TBE falling marks: "Generally speaking, on the basis of nationwide inquiry, transitional compensatory bilingual education has not been conspicuously successful in imparting English skills to marked student populations."[173] But Fishman is not arguing for a movement away from bilingual education, but toward more extensive bilingual approaches. This seems reasonable. All of the criticism of bilingual education is directed at TBE. If alternatives are to be proposed, perhaps our approach should be more comprehensive. A national experiment investigating the effects of real main-tenance (or even enrichment!) programs would reveal more of the potential of bilingual education than moving away from L1 teaching altogether. In this way, we might be able to make more informed policy decisions based on experimentation on a greater variety of programs. We will now turn to what is entailed by one of the frequently-mentioned alternatives to bilingual education.

Immersion

In an immersion program, students are taught exclusively in their L2. Teachers may understand the student's native language, and may even use it for non-instructional purposes. Special L2 language arts instruction is pro-vided. The most famous of these programs are those in Canada in which anglophones are taught in French medium schools. Only a handful of such programs exist in the United States. We will be concerned in this section with reviewing some of the types of immersion programs and with the pros-pects for adapting this approach to classrooms in the US.

Types of immersion programs

The different types of immersion programs emerge mainly from experi-ments conducted in Canada since the 1960s. The initiative of these programs came from Anglophone parents who were dissatisfied with the level of French proficiency attained by their children in traditional classrooms.[174] Programs usually fall into four types: (1) early immersion where instruction is completely in French (the child's L2) starting as early as kindergarten; L1 instruction is gradually introduced, so that by the end of the elementary years there is approximate equality in the use of the two languages.[175] (2) Late immersion is offered as an option to students who are in the higher grades and who desire French instruction. Instruction begins in the L2 in 6th or 7th grade, after the student has had some exposure to the language in more traditional classrooms.[176] These two types are also sometimes referred to as Total Immersion programs. (3) Partial early immersion provides for L2-instruction for part of the day and L1-instruction for the rest, the time divided more or less evenly for both languages. The programs typically begin in kindergarten or grade one. The different parts of the day may be taught by the same teacher or different teachers; the primary requirement is that teachers have a native or native like command of the languages in which they teach.[177] (4) Partial late immersion appears to be the most varied of the different types of programs. These start at grade 7 or 8 after a short period of initiation into French instruction in earlier grades. Up to 75% of the school day can involve instruction in L2.[178]

All of these programs show very impressive results in the attainment of both French and English proficiency and in the learning of subject matter. Students in early immersion programs appeared to achieve best in cognitive learning; but even late immersion students showed gains superior to those attained by students in traditional language classrooms. Moreover, these students appeared to gain positive attitudes toward the L2 and L2-speakers; this could be an extremely important outcome, given what we have said about the influence of affective factors on language attainment.[179]

Adapting immersion to the United States

Some writers, such as Baker and deKanter, are very impressed with the results of Canadian immersion programs. They propose experimenting with "structured immersion" in the United States. However, the adaptability of that model to the United States is problematic, as many writers note. They cite the following concerns:

- The purpose of Canadian programs is bilingualization; in the U.S., it is generally language transfer.
- The sociolinguistic dynamics of the countries are very different; in Canada, French and English are both officially recognized and have high prestige; in the U.S., there is no official language policy, but in terms of social status all languages are marked in relation to English.
- Canadian programs are a high prestige, noncompensatory activity designed for the middle and upper classes; in the U.S., they would be designed for economically disadvantaged minority children.
- Canadian programs are long-term; in the U.S. there is a concern for moving these children out of the program as quickly as possible.
- In Canadian programs, teachers tend to have high expectations of their students; in U.S. compensatory programs, teachers generally have low expectations.
- In Canada, English-speakers do not achieve the same levels of French proficiency as do francophones, nor are they expected to; in the U.S., students are judged on how well they do compared to native English speakers. [180]

In fact, those who report the strongest evidence in favor of immersion programs in Canada at the same time offer the strongest cautions against their introduction into the U.S. Richard Tucker, for example, draws this conclusion: "We have not previously and we will not in the future recommend, on the basis of these careful, critical, and longitudinal studies, that Mexican-American, Franco-American, or other non- or limited English-speaking youngsters in the United States be submerged in English medium programs. We believe that the appropriate inference to be drawn is exactly the opposite."[181]

Still, many different researchers are impressed with the gains in L2 language achievement in immersion programs. The calls for a U.S. adaptation have significant support. What are needed are guidelines for implementation of a U.S. version which take into account the list of discrepancies above. The following suggestions are adapted from Lambert and Tucker.[182]

- Priority should be given to the language <u>least</u> likely to be developed outside the school.
- Since English is the socially prestigious language, Anglophones should be exposed to the non-English language until literacy skills are developed, then switched into English instruction.
- Non-English speakers have three options: (a) partial immersion in an English language curriculum for half days, the other half devoted to native language instruction; (b) instruction in L1 until literacy skills are well-developed; (c) bilingual instruction.

There is no reason to shy away from experimentation in immersion for NEP/LEP students, provided we do not ignore the problems outlined here. Perhaps the best approach would be to have researchers who are very familiar with both the Canadian and U.S. contexts (Mackey, Lambert, Tucker, Cummins, or others) oversee the experiment in U.S. immersion. That would no doubt satisfy those who would fear that the model would be adapted inappropriately.

Foreign language education

Foreign language study in schools has been popular in the United States since the end of the last century. Knowledge of a foreign language has been valued in this society for instrumental and academic reasons. But, as explained in a previous section, the emphasis has been placed on <u>foreign</u> as opposed to <u>ethnic</u> languages. This emphasis persists in the most recent wave of language interest; this can be seen by the fact that many who advocate the development of foreign language capacity are indifferent to or even hostile toward bilingual education which aims to preserve the native language.

The recent reports on language capacity and development in the United States are evidence enough of this attitude. For example, the American Council on Teaching of Foreign Languages and the National Council for the Social Studies made a joint statement to the President's Commission on Foreign Language and International Studies in which they recommended the creation of model programs for foreign language teaching. They mention several possible alternatives: <u>early language training</u> (the functional equivalent of LFES); <u>immersion</u>; <u>exploratory courses</u>; and <u>"alternative intensive experiences in the United States."</u> The preservation of language through bilingual methods is not even mentioned.[183] Similarly, the MLA-ACLS Language Task Forces continually use the term "foreign language" when they actually mean "non-English language"; emphasis is clearly placed on language development rather than on preservation. For example: "all students in American schools should have the opportunity to study at least one <u>foreign</u> language. Every American college graduate should be able to read and converse in a <u>foreign</u> language. All students in the United States should have readily available opportunities to acquire or improve knowledge of a <u>foreign</u> language." (emphasis added)[184] Finally, the report of the President's Commission on Foreign Language and International Studies includes no substantive discussion of the potential for bilingual education programs to maintain or improve U.S. language capacity. Moreover, they explicitly exclude from consideration ethnic communities for which bilingual education is intended and which could serve as resources in language training.[185]

There are other aspects of foreign language education that distinguish it from programs intended for the NEP/LEP child:

- Foreign language study is considered an elite, academic pursuit; LEP/NEP language programs are compensatory in that they are designed to remedy some social problem.
- <u>Foreign</u> language study and capacity is associated with national security; ethnic languages and bilingual education are associated with national divisiveness.
- Foreign language study is frequently seen as compatible with a concern for <u>quality</u> of education; ethnic languages and bilingual education are associated with <u>equality</u> of education (which is sometimes seen as the opposite of quality),
- Foreign language study is aligned with global education; ethnic languages and bilingual education are community-based concerns,
- Foreign language study aims at adding to the student's language repertoire; bilingual education primarily aims at a transfer in language capacity.

In times of national and international crisis, foreign language study has been regarded as alleviating some of our problems; but in those same periods, ethnic language communities have been seen as a threat. It could be, as the president of one association of foreign language teachers has said, that "the time is right and the public is ready … to increase and enhance foreign language and international studies,"[186] but the same is not true of bilingual education. Only by finding an accommodation between these programs is bilingual education in the public schools likely to survive much longer.

Program interrelations

"The study of second languages by nonspecialists can have the effect of reducing linguistic isolationism, preventing parochialism, developing intellectual flexibility, strengthening skills in the mother tongue, and learning how to learn a language. But nothing short of restructuring the role of language in America will have much effect on educating the citizenry at large in the field of foreign language."[187] The testimony of this Peace Corps official before the President's Commission on Foreign Language and International Studies was a call to a new orientation toward language and language study in the United States. He might also conclude that any attempts at cooperation among the different language teaching programs mentioned here may well require such a reorientation. In the first place, the role of non-English languages in U.S. society must be cultivated. We must begin to see ethnic communities and their languages as resources to be developed and managed rather than problems to be solved. With this change, many difficulties could be resolved. For example, the hostility which exists between foreign language and bilingual educators is frequently associated with status differences between foreign and ethnic languages; the new orientation would allow us to regard all languages as potential resources. Similarly, it would encourage a more tolerant attitude toward the wish of ethnic communities for language maintenance programs; this in turn would alleviate some of the tension among different communities and clear up longstanding misconceptions. One of the most pervasive of these is that ethnic communities use bilingual education for politically separatist purposes. Nothing could be further from the truth, as a recent survey report out of Columbia University shows: "Rather than foster cultural or political separatism ... efforts to involve Hispanic parents in the bilingual education movement have contributed to their cultural and social integration. What is to be feared is not bilingual education but rather the separatism which will result if bilingual education is rejected."[188]

There are a few instances of program cooperation which make us hopeful. A Spanish language teacher in New York reports on a class of fourth year Spanish students who spend one afternoon a week with a Hispanic partner in a bilingual school.[189] In Washington state, "bilingual programs have affected positively the enrollment in regular foreign language classes. ... Foreign language teachers must support the efforts of bilingual teachers and vice versa, because we can accomplish a great deal together."[190] Examples like these are few and isolated. But perhaps they can serve as models of what can be accomplished in combining the efforts of the foreign language and bilingual education communities.

Policy Implications

Conclusions about an area as broad as language study and teaching are difficult to formulate. They would be necessarily general and somewhat tentative. It is desirable, however, to identify a few implications which we might draw from this review. Selected from a large number of possible statements, the following list represents those most directly related to the development of policy.

- Language policy decisions must be informed by sociolinguistic and historical research.
- While relevant research is important and instructive to policy-makers, language policy should be recognized as essentially political decisions.

- A variety of factors can influence public interest in language study. Recently, as in the past, economic and national security considerations are the main factors behind the promotion of language study.
- Language policy in the United States is formed by a constellation of factors; potential jurisdictional conflicts (e.g. federal versus state authority in education) hamper the development of a comprehensive national language policy.
- To the extent that there is a national language policy, it is negative toward ethnic language communities and their languages (i.e. it aims at remedying some perceived language or educational deficiency) and positive toward foreign languages (i.e. it aims at their promotion in the general population). It is aimed at the creation, not the preservation, of language resources.
- Bilingual education policy in the United States aims at the development of English proficiency for NEP/LEP students, not the bilingualization of the society or any part of it.
- Submersion approaches to the education of NEP/LEP students have had disastrous effects on the school achievement of those populations.
- Programs which use the L1 for instructional purposes, which engage the child in learning tasks in a non-threatening environment, and which respect and use the child's culture to mediate instruction tend to have the best effects on student achievement.
- Experiments in a wide range of bilingual approaches, from "structured immersion" to full maintenance and even enrichment, should be attempted and carefully monitored to provide reliable information on the effects of different programs on different populations.
- Experiments in immersion should be carefully designed to minimize problems of language markedness and student self-esteem.
- The viability of bilingual education in the long run depends on reorienting our conception of the role of non-English language in the United States from that of national "problem" to that of natural "resource." Such a national reorientation is also a prerequisite for general and meaningful cooperation between the foreign language and ethnic language/bilingual education communities.

Acknowledgments

Research for this report was undertaken with the support of a Rockefeller Foundation Fellowship in the Social Sciences. I would also like to acknowledge the contributions of Carl Kaestle and Julia Richards, who made valuable suggestions for revising the manuscript, and Cheryl Roberts and Susan Quatrini for their technical assistance.
Richard Ruiz
A Synthesis Report for the National Institute of Education

Notes

1. S. B. Heath, "English in our language heritage," in C. A. Ferguson and S. B. Heath (eds.), Language in the USA (New York: Cambridge University Press, 1981), p. 10; A. Leibowitz, Educational policy and political acceptance: the imposition of English as the language of instruction in American schools (Washington, D.C.: Center for Applied Linguistics, 1971), p. 4.
2. Annual report of the Board of Directors of the St. Louis public schools for the year ending August 1, 1875 (St. Louis: St. Louis Public Schools, 1876), p. 114. (Hereafter cited as St. Louis Report 1875.)
3. Heath, op. cit., pp. 12–13.
4. St. Louis Report 1875, p. 117
5. St. Louis Report 1875, p. 113.
6. Bessie Pierce, History of Chicago (New York: A.A. Knopf, 1936), pp. 385–386.
7. C. E. Patzer, Public education in Wisconsin (Madison: State Historical Society, 1924), pp. 65–66; P. Donnely, "German in the schools," in J. W. Stearns (ed.), Columbian history of education in Wisconsin (Milwaukee, 1893), pp. 458–460; B. Still, Milwaukee—the history of a city (Madison: State Historical Society, 1948).
8. In Stearns, op. cit., pp. 317–318.
9. J. A. Watrous, Memoirs of Milwaukee County, Vol. I (Madison: Western Historical Society, 1909), p. 393; Proceedings of the Board of School Directors of Milwaukee (Milwaukee, 1915), p. 434.
10. Pierce, op. cit., p. 385.
11. Patzer, op. cit., p. 66 ff.
12. Pierce, op. cit., p. 386.
13. Asians were especially anxious about their status in America. See, for example, K. K. Kawakami, Asia at the door: a study of the Japanese question in the continental United States, Hawaii, and Canada (New York: Revell, 1914).
14. F. Cordasco, Bilingual schooling in the United States: a sourcebook for educational personnel (New York: McGraw-Hill, 1976).
15. The American commonwealth, Vol. II (New York: Macmillan, 1888), pp. 709–710.
16. For discussion of the anti-oriental agitation at this time, see M. Konvitz, The alien and the asiatic in American law (Ithaca: Cornell University Press, 1946); H. Hill, "Anti-oriental agitation and the rise of working class racism," Society 10 (January/February, 1973), pp. 43–54; Y. Ichihashi, Japanese in the United States (New York: Arno Press, 1969; Reprint of the 1932 edition). In pages 234–244, Ichihashi discusses the segregation ordinance passed by the San Francisco Board of Education, effective October 15, 1906. The reasons for segregating Japanese children relate explicitly to the essential immorality of their culture: lying is a universal trait among the Japanese; there is no word which corresponds to "sin" in Japanese, and no word corresponding to "home". These sorts of arguments persisted well into the twentieth century, and were the basis of anti-oriental legislation of the 20s. The media played a significant role in this activity. V. S. McClatchy, editor of The Sacramento Bee, wrote a series of court briefs and pamphlets in the late teens and early 20s on the peril posed by the Japanese in California (see, for example, Four anti-Japanese pamphlets. 1919–1925 (New York: Arno Press, 1978) and "Japanese in the melting-pot: can they assimilate and make good citizens?" The annals of the American Academy of Political and Social Science CXIII (January, 1921)). Here, McClatchy reiterates some old objections to the Japanese: they are non-assimilable, they are inordinately fecund, they have great advantages in economic competition. Representatives of the Japanese-American communities were at pains to refute these allegations. As to their being non-assimilable, they went so far as to suggest that even oriental racial

characteristics were starting to change: "Their hair, formerly jet black, is toning toward the brown and their skin is losing its darker pigment." The Japanese themselves made the learning of English a high priority even in their own, segregated language schools (Ichihasi, op. cit., p. 328).

17.   T. G. Walch, Catholic education in Chicago and Milwaukee. 1840–1890 (Evanston, Ill.: Northwestern University unpublished Ph.D. dissertation, 1975), p. 92. Walch is quoting Anthony Urbanek, a missionary priest of the 1840s.

18.   Walch, op. cit., pp. 116–117.

19.   R. Jensen, The winning of the midwest; social and political conflict (Chicago: University of Chicago Press, 1971), p. 123.

20.   Jensen, op. cit., p. 124.

21.   Milwaukee Journal (March 12, 1890).

22.   L. P. Kellogg, "The Bennett Law in Wisconsin," The Wisconsin magazine of history 2 (September, 1918). Kellogg implies that the German press was interested in the controversy mainly for practical reasons: "The too rapid growth of the knowledge of English meant a decrease in subscriptions and a consequent loss of income ... (they regarded) the Bennett Law with suspicion ..." (pp. 10–11).

23.   For the political impact of the Bennett Law, see R. E. Wyman, "Wisconsin ethnic groups and the election of 1890," Wisconsin magazine of history 51 (Summer, 1968), pp. 269–293, and W. F. Whyte, "The Bennett Law campaign in Wisconsin," Wisconsin magazine of history 10 (June, 1927), pp. 363–390.

24.   Walch, op. cit., p. 80.

25.   H. Kloss, The American bilingual tradition (Rowley, Ma.: Newbury House Publishers, 1977), pp. 69–71. Kloss suggests that a secret nationalist organization, the American Protective Association (APA), may have been behind some of the agitation against ethnic parochial schools of this time.

26.   Welch, op. cit., p. 123.

27.   This sentiment is summarized by a German-American quoted by Kellogg: "It is by unity of speech and harmony of thought that the ultimate American is to be the light of civilization." (p. 25). Similar attitudes emerge in other cities of the midwest, even those where German enclaves were strong and public school instruction in German was a long-standing practice. The controversies among ethnic groups in Chicago have already been mentioned (Pierce, op. cit., p. 385 ff). Perhaps more surprising are the conflicts in St. Louis and Indianapolis. In 1890, the St. Louis Republic boasted that it "led the fight for a single language of instruction—and that language English—in the public schools of St. Louis. The fight was won, and the public schools are the better for it." (In "Public Opinion", a pamphlet collected In C. Koerner (ed.), The Bennett Law and the German protestant parochial schools of Wisconsin [Milwaukee: Germanic Publishing Company 1890]). The Indianapolis Journal, which had lent strong support to German language instruction in the public schools earlier in the century, became uncharacteristically silent in the late 80s and early 90s when opponents of this instruction introduced a series of local anti-German ordinances. (Frances Ellis, "Historical account of German instruction in the public schools of Indianapolis 1869–1919, Indiana magazine of history 50 [September, 1954], pp. 251–276)

28.   Heath, op. cit., pp. 12–13.

29.   Heath, op. cit., p. 14.

30.   R. J. Honeywell, The educational work of Thomas Jefferson (New York: Russell and Russell, Inc., 1964), pp. 113–114.

31.   W. R. Parker, The language curtain, and other essays on American education (New York: Modern Language Association of America, 1966), p. 112. Cf. Heath, op. cit., passim.

32. C. A. Ferguson and S. B. Heath, "Introduction," in C. A. Ferguson and S. B. Heath (eds.), op. cit., p. xxxiv.

33. Enrollment figures for selected school districts indicate a growing interest on the part of non-German students in German study. For example, for both 1909 and 1916, Indianapolis schools enrolled almost twice as many non-German as German students in their program (F.H. Ellis, op. cit., p. 371.) Kloss also notes a trend starting in the 1880s "away from demanding German as a subject for lower-grade children of German-speaking parents and toward advocating German instruction for the children of Anglo-American parents as well" (op. cit., p. 90). This points to a growing acceptance of foreign language as opposed to ethnic language study.

34. Parker, op. cit. Parker's essay, entitled "The language curtain", was first delivered as a speech at Middlebury College in 1953. In it, he suggests that American ignorance of foreign languages and international affairs has the same effect as the restricted flow of public information in countries behind the "Iron Curtain."

35. Still, op. cit., pp. 461–462.

36. See Kloss, op. cit., esp. p. 71 ff. and Ellis, op. cit.

37. Parker, op. cit., p. 153; cf. W. R. Parker, The national interest and foreign languages (Washington, D.C.: Department of State, U.S. Government Printing Office, 1961), p. 131.

38. Cited in Kloss, op. cit., p. 71.

39. The exact number of states passing such laws is a matter of some debate and interpretation; see, e.g., B. McLaughlin, Second-language acquisition in childhood (Hillsdale, N.J.: Lawrence Erlbaum Associates, Publishers, 1978), pp. 134–135; Parker, 1966, p. 113.

40. Meyer v. Nebraska, 262 U.S. 390 (1923). A similar case was Bartels v. Iowa, 262 U.S. 404 (1923). For a discussion of these and other language cases, see S. B. Heath and F. Mandabach, "Language status decisions and the law in the United States," In J. Cobarrubias and J. A. Fishman (eds.), Progress in language planning: international perspectives (Berlin: Mouton Publishers, 1983), pp. 87–105.

41. Parker notes the decline of language interest between the wars and attributes it in part to the "New Education"—education for all children regardless of social status. Parker saw this as a revolt against the cultural/traditional and toward the practical. Furthermore, reports on education by agencies like the American Youth Commission found that the academic curriculum was "causing" a lot of school failure through subjects like science, mathematics, and foreign languages. This and other similar reports of the time recommended instead course work with an emphasis on personal development, occupational training, and civic competence. (Parker, 1966, pp. 143–145.)

42. Parker (1966), pp. 141–142.

43. Idem.

44. See e.g., Still, op. cit., p. 462.

45. R. J. Cornejo and L. O. Cornejo, Theories and research on second language acquisition (Las Cruces, N.M.: ERIC Clearinghouse on Rural Education and Small Schools, 1981), pp. 38–40.

46. Parker (1966), p. 147.

47. McLaughlin, op. cit., p. 135.

48. Parker (1966), pp. 135, 148–149; Parker (1961), pp. 7 ff.

49. A-LM Spanish level one, teacher's manual (New York: Harcourt, Brace, and World, Inc., 1964), p. 4.

50. T. Andersson, Foreign languages in the elementary school (Austin: University of Texas Press, 1969); H. B. Dyess, "FLES supports bilingual education and vice versa in the Louisiana experiment," In Bilingual education and FLES: keeping the children in focus (New Orleans: American Association of Teachers of French, 1975).

51. For example, Mary Finocchiaro, in <u>Teaching children foreign languages</u> (New York: McGraw-Hill, 1964), calls the idea that children are better than adults at language learning a "self-evident truth" (p. 4). Compare the findings of E. H. Lenneberg, <u>Biological foundations of language</u> (New York: Wiley, 1967); W. Penfield and L. Roberts, <u>Speech and brain mechanisms</u> (Princeton, N.J.: Princeton University Press, 1959); T. Andersson, "The optimum age for beginning the study of modern languages," <u>International review of education</u> VI (1960), pp. 296–306; J. Carroll, "The contributions of psychological theory and educational research to the teaching of foreign languages," In A. Valdman (ed.), <u>Trends in language teaching</u> (New York: McGraw-Hill, 1966), pp. 93–106. See also the discussion In G. Bernbaum, <u>Bilingualism in society</u>, Bilingual Education Monographs, No. 2 (Fall River, MA: National Assessment and Dissemination Center for Bilingual Education, 1979) and McLaughlin, <u>op. cit.</u>, pp. 137–138.
52. Bernbaum, <u>Bilingualism in society</u>, p. 2.
53. <u>Hearings before the special subcommittee on bilingual education ... on S. 428</u> (Washington, D.C.: U.S. Government Printing Office, 1967). See, especially, the exchange between Sen. Fannin and J. Monserrat p. 79.
54. <u>Idem.</u> See, among others, the statements by Gaarder (pp. 46–59), Andersson (pp. 221–226), and Fishman (pp. 120–142).
55. <u>Idem.</u> p. 19; cf. p. 16.
56. <u>Programs under Bilingual Education Act (Title VII, ESEA), manual for project applicants and grantees</u> (Washington, D.C.: U.S. Department of Health, Education, and Welfare, 1971), pp. 1, 21.
57. <u>Idem.</u> p. 8.
58. See A. M. Thernstrom, "Language: issues and legislation" In S. Thernstrom (ed.). <u>Harvard encyclopedia of American ethnic groups</u> (Cambridge: Harvard University Press, 1980), p. 619: "In 1968, when the act was passed, nobody knew or had the authority to decide precisely what bilingual education meant." This view is a bit overstated, to be sure.
59. On the San Jose project, see T. Owens, <u>Final evaluation report for the Spanish Dame School Project</u> (San Jose: Center for Planning and Evaluation, 1972); on the Milwaukee programs, see V. Masemann, W. Cooley, J. Richards, <u>Bilingual education in Milwaukee: an interdisciplinary study</u> (Madison: Department of Educational Policy Studies, University of Wisconsin-Madison, 1977); on the Mountain View High School program, see <u>Proposal for Project Bilingualism for Cultural Democracy</u> (Mountain View, CA: Mountain View High School, 1973); on the Gonzales program, see T. Owens, R. Hernandez, and R. Ruiz, <u>Final evaluation report for the Gonzales ESL/Bilingual Project</u> (San Jose, CA: Center for Planning and Evaluation, July, 1972). In spite of the apparent diversity represented by these programs, there were important influences working to homogenize these projects. Possibly the most important was the procedure for continuing a project from year to year. In the application for continuation, a preliminary evaluation report was to be included by December of each year which demonstrated the project's potential for success. Some project managers took this as a signal that it might be best to concentrate on a few important and measurable skills, especially English and mathematics. This served as a negative incentive for innovation.
60. See A. Thernstrom, <u>op. cit.</u>, p. 623 ff.
61. <u>Lau v. Nichols</u>, 414 U.S. 563 (1974).
62. While the guidelines issued by D/HEW specifying remedies to the curricular deficiencies outlined in <u>Lau</u> allowed for both liberal and conservative interpretations of the decision, <u>English language Limitation</u> and "overcoming language barriers" was nevertheless what the case was all about (see, especially, Justice Blackmun's concurring opinion). Very few argue that the case is a mandate for <u>maintenance</u> of

bilingual education. Shirley Hufstedler, Secretary of Education in the Carter admin-istration, and herself a strong supporter of bilingual education, concedes that "the Lau regulations are <u>not</u> designed to maintain any language or subculture in the United States." ("On bilingual education, civil rights and language minority regula-tions," <u>NABE journal</u> V [Fall, 1960], p. 67). The clear message is that, whatever the form of the programs and whether or not the native language is used for instruc-tion, the ultimate criterion of success is the child's English language proficiency.

63. R. Padilla sees the 1974 amendments as a "basic shift" in federal policy on the treatment of language minority groups: "... it is probably correct to say that the era of equity through innovation had passed and a new era of equity through mastery of English had arrived." ("Federal policy shifts and the implementation of bilingual education programs," a paper presented at the annual meeting of the National Association for Chicano Studies [Ypsilanti, MI, April, 1983], p. 8.) On this point, Thernstrom's contention that the 1974 act included "a definition of bilingual education that distinctly favored maintenance" (<u>op. cit.</u>, p. 623) is hard to understand, unless by "maintenance" she means here something different than her own definition—"the preservation of the language and values of a foreign culture." (p. 619).

64. See Frank Calucci, Memorandum to the assistant Secretary of Health, Education, and Welfare, December 2, 1974: "It is clearly the intent of Congress that the goal of federally funded capacity building programs in bilingual education be to assist chil-dren in English so that they may enjoy equal educational opportunity—and not to require cultural pluralism." Interestingly, the cultural activities—ethnic dance groups, traditional celebrations, etc. —are frequently the most popular parts of the projects; they also are important, since they provide visibility for the program in the community at large.

65. B. F. Birman and A. L. Ginsburg, <u>Addressing the needs of language-minority children: issues for federal policy</u> (Washington, D.C.: unpublished manuscript, October 5, 1981), p. 5n; cf. K. A. Baker and A. A. deKanter, "Effectiveness of bilingual education: a review of the literature. Final draft report." (Washington, D.C.: Office of Technical and Analytic Systems, U.S. Department of Education); and K. Baker and A. A. deKanter (eds.), <u>Bilingual education: a reappraisal of federal policy</u> (Lexington, MA: D.C. Heath, 1983).

66. J. A. Fishman, "Language policy: past, present, and future," in C. A. Ferguson and S. B. Heath (eds.), <u>op. cit.</u>, 1981, pp. 517–518; cf. J. A. Fishman, "Sociolinguistic founda-tions of bilingual education," <u>The bilingual review/La revista bilingue</u> 9 (January–April, 1982). For the optimistic view, see S. Grant, "Language policy in the United States," in R. I. Brod (ed.), <u>Language study for the 1980s: reports of the MLA-ACLS language task forces</u> (New York: Modern Language Association, 1980), p. 104. In contrast, R. F. Roeming represents those skeptical of the BEA from the beginning: "... the sponsors of the Bilingual Education Act found it a good means for nailing down votes. It represents no commitment at all to bilingualism any more than the National Defense Education Act of recent memory was a national commitment to support the study of foreign languages." ("Bilingualism and the national interest," In J. Alatis [ed.], <u>Georgetown University round table on languages and linguistics 1970</u> [Washington, D.C.: Georgetown University Press, 1970], p. 372.)

67. Fishman, 1981, p. 518.

68. S. B. Heath, <u>op. cit.</u> There is some disagreement in the literature as to what consti-tutes "official status" for a language. G. Keller maintains that Spanish now has offi-cial status in certain domains in the United States which is "traceable back to the Voting Rights Act of 1965 and the Bilingual Education Act of 1968." ("What can language planners learn from the hispanic experience with corpus planning in the

United States?", in J. Cobarrubias and J. Fishman [eds.], <u>Progress in Language Planning: International Perspectives</u> [Berlin: Mouton, 1983], p. 253. J. Cobarrubias, in his introduction to the same volume, disagrees that such important but isolated pronouncements can qualify to officialize a language. His position is more in line with the bulk of the language planning literature (see, e.g., Kloss, <u>op. cit.</u>, p. 140) than is Keller's.

69.   S. B. Heath, "Bilingual education and a national language policy," In J. Alatis (ed.) <u>Georgetown University round table on languages and linguistics 1978</u> (Washington, D.C.: Georgetown University Press, 1978), p. 58.

70.   A few of the basic works in language planning give an idea of the complexity of the processes involved: R. B. LePage, <u>The national language question: linguistic problems of newly independent states</u> (London: Oxford University Press, 1964): J. A. Fishman, et al., (eds), <u>Language problems of developing nations</u> (New York: Wiley, 1968); E. Haugen, <u>Language conflict and language planning</u> (Cambridge: Harvard University Press, 1966); J. Rubin and R. Shuy (eds.), <u>Language planning: current issues and research</u> (Washington, D.C.: Georgetown University Press, 1973).

71.   S. Grant <u>op. cit.</u>, p. 105.

72.   The Massachusetts, Texas, Wisconsin and California laws can be found at the following: <u>Ann. Laws Mass.</u>, Ch. 71A (Supp. 1973); <u>Texas Codes Ann.</u>, Education Code Subchapter L. (Vernon Supp. 197*1–5); <u>Wisconsin Statutes Chapter 115, Subchapter VII</u> (1976); <u>California A.B. 1329</u> (1976).

73.   Wisconsin Advisory Committee to the U.5. Commission on Civil Rights, <u>Falling through the cracks: an assessment of bilingual education in Wisconsin</u> (Washington, D.C.; U.S. Commission on Civil Rights, 1982).

74.   R. Royer, "Promoting foreign languages," <u>Foreign language annals</u> 12 (October, 1979), p. 395.

75.   C. Putnam suggests that the "back-to-basics" movement may have influenced the reinstitution of foreign language requirements in some instances; later, she says that, in times of economic constraint, foreign language classes may suffer because they are seen as "frills". The concern with "basics" is obviously unpredictable when it comes to foreign language education. ("Assessing the assessment: a review of the President's Commission report," <u>Foreign language annals</u> 14 [1981], pp. 13, 14).

76.   The President's Commission on Foreign Language and International Studies, <u>Strength through wisdom: a critique of U.S. capability</u> (Washington, D.C.: U.S. Government Printing Office, 1979); R. I. Brod (ed.). <u>Language study for the 1980s: reports of the MLA-ACLS language task forces</u> (New York: The Modern Language Association of America, 1980).

77.   Putnam, <u>op. cit.</u>, p. 11.

78.   Two recent examples of litigation involving the relationship of business to ethnic communities illustrate this problem. In <u>Hernandez v. Erlenbusch</u>, 368 F. Supp. 752 (D. Oregon 1973), Mexican Americans filed a claim of racial discrimination against a tavern with a policy prohibiting the use of any non-English language at the bar; Mexican Americans made up one-fourth of the tavern's potential customers. In <u>Garcia v. Gloor</u>. 628 F. 2nd 264 (1980), a bilingual Mexican American employee was dismissed from his job at a lumber company for speaking Spanish to another employee. The company rules prohibited the use of Spanish during business hours unless the customer preferred it. In spite of the fact that Hispanics made up more than 75% of the population in the business area served by the Gloor Lumber Company (Brownsville, Texas), "and many of Gloor's customers wish to be waited on by a salesman who speaks Spanish," Gloor offered what it said to be sound business reasons to justify the rule. These reasons related mainly to improving the competence of their employees on the job and as citizens; it apparently did not see the

business deficiency in the fact that its top managers and supervisors did not speak Spanish, nor would they feel the need to learn it, given this rule.

79. S. Groennings, "Developments and prospects following the President's Commission on Foreign Language and International Studies." Foreign language annals 13 (December, 1980), p. 449.

80. See, especially, American Council on the Teaching of Foreign Languages and the National Council for the Social Studies, "Recommendations to the President's Commission on Foreign Language and International Studies," Foreign language annals 12 (February, 1979), pp. 29–34.

81. Groennlngs, op. cit., p. 447.

82. See the discussion in "Foreign aid endorsed by experts," Education daily 16 (April 28, 1983), p. 4.

83. Congressional Record-Senate. May 18, 1983.

84. The bill was introduced in the Senate (S. 1041) on April 13, 1983, by Orrin Hatch (R-Utah) and in the House (HR 2682) on April 21, 1983 by John Erlenborn (R-Illinois) and William Godling (R-Pennsylvania).

85. See, for example, the discussions in Education daily, March 28, June 8, June 29, and April 19, 1983; see also J.J. Lyons, "Bilingual education: the past and the new year," NABE news VI (3) (January, 1983).

86. "Thinking about bilingual education: a critical appraisal," Harvard educational review 52 (August, 1982), p. 304. The final version of the 1984 Bilingual Education Act was enacted in October, 1984—too late for analysis in this report. It should be noted, however, that all four of the mentioned changes have been incorporated in the new legislation. And, while the explicit definition of bilingual education was not changed as proposed, a small amount of money for "special alternatives" which do not use the child's first language was authorized (98th Congress, House of Representatives, Education Amendments of 1984. October 2, 1984).

87. Hearings ... on S. 428, p. 58.

88. M.L. Clark and M. H. Rudolph, "Why or why not foreign languages," Foreign language annals 14 (September–October, 1981), p. 317.

89. See the discussion of this survey in Education daily 16 (July 21, 1983), p. 2.

90. For a review of the criticisms and a reply, see W. E. Lambert, "Bilingualism: its nature and significance," in W. E. Lambert et al., Faces and facets of bilingualism. Bilingual Education Series 10. Papers in applied linguistics (Washington, D.C.: Center for Applied Linguistics, 1981). On some of the positive effects, see C. Kessler and M. Quinn, "Positive effects of bilingualism on science problem-solving abilities," In J. Alatis (ed.), Georgetown University round table on languages and linguistics 1980 (Washington, D.C.: Georgetown University Press, 1980); J. Cummins, "Linguistic interdependence and educational development of bilingual children," Review of educational research 49 (1979); W. Lambert, "Some cognitive and sociocultural consequences of being bilingual," in J. Alatis (ed.), Georgetown University round table on languages and linguistics 1978 (Washington, D.C.: Georgetown University Press, 1978); S. Lieberson and L. Hansen, "National development, mother tongue diversity, and the comparative study of nations," American sociological review 39 (1974).

91. K. A. Baker and A. A. deKanter, "Federal policy and the effectiveness of bilingual education," In K. A. Baker and A. A. deKanter (eds.), Bilingual education: a reappraisal of federal policy (Lexington, MA: D.C. Heath, 1983), p. 36.

92. See, for example, M. N. Danoff, Evaluation of the impact of ESEA Title VII Spanish/English Bilingual Education Program: overview of study and findings (Palo Alto: American Institutes for Research, 1978); N. Epstein, Language, ethnicity, and the schools: policy alternatives for bilingual-bicultural education (Washington, D.C.: Institute for Educational Leadership, 1977); N. Glazer, "The school and the judge,"

In W. Van Horne (ed.), <u>Ethnicity, law, and the social good</u> (Milwaukee: American Ethnic Studies Coordinating Committee, 1983).

93. "Research evidence for the effectiveness of bilingual education," <u>NABE journal III</u> (Fall, 1978), p. 15.

94. Fishman comments on these assumptions: "Currently, bilingual education is conducted in the context of an implicit view of a uniform, Anglified society. Given this view, it is only natural that English achievement alone becomes the prime criterion of bilingual education's "success" and that corpus planning within the marked languages remains minimal, based on the assumption that they will not be around for long. Both of these issues profit from sociolinguistic scrutiny." (J.A. Fishman, 1982, pp. 11–12.) Otheguy (<u>op. cit.</u>, p. 306) also criticizes as naive the view that English proficiency by itself adds significantly to social and economic opportunity: "Moreover, English monolingualism has meant little in terms of economic advantages to most blacks and to the masses of poor descendants of poor European immigrants. Hispanics who now speak only English can often be found in as poor a state as when they first came. English monolingualism among immigrants tends to follow economic integration rather than cause it."

95. For an attempt at a methodological critique, see A.C. Willig, "The effectiveness of bilingual education: review of a report," <u>NABE journal</u> 6 (Winter-Spring, 1981–1982); for a review of the Baker-deKanter studies as representing political-ideological bias, see S.S. Seidner, "A matter of academic integrity," <u>NABE news 6</u> (January, 1983). President Reagan's remark is reported in <u>The Washington Post</u>, March 4, 1981.

96. E. G. Lewis, "The morality of bilingual education," in J. Alatis (ed.), <u>Georgetown University round table on languages and linguistics 1978</u> (Washington, D.C.: Georgetown University Press, 1978), p. 675. The citation from Heath is in the same volume, p. 63.

97. A. D. Cohen, "The Culver City Spanish immersion project: the first two years," <u>Modern language journal 58</u> (1974), pp. 95–103; C. Edelsky and S. Hudelson, "The acquisition (?) of Spanish as a second language," in F. Barkin <u>et al.</u> (eds.), <u>Bilingualism and language contact: Spanish, English, and Native American languages</u> (New York and London: Teacher's College Press, 1982), pp. 203–227.

98. W. F. Mackey and V. N. Beebe, <u>Bilingual schools for a bicultural community: Miami's adaptation to the Cuban refugees</u> (Rowley, MA: Newbury House Publishers, 1977); Edelsky and Hudelson, <u>op. cit.</u>

99. <u>Idem.</u> Cf. J. A. Fishman, "Sociolinguistic foundations of bilingual education," <u>Bilingual review/revista bilingue IX</u> (January–April 1982), pp. 1–35.

100. Evaluations of language status can be made for different varieties of one language as well as for totally unrelated languages. The primacy of English in relation to all other languages in the United States is indisputable; the fact that regional vernaculars like Chicano Spanish are also marked in relation to recognized standard varieties (World Standard Spanish, as an example) may be less generally perceived, but no less salient (see T. Andersson, "Popular and elite bilingualism reconciled," <u>Hispania 59</u> [1976]). Indeed, an important sociolinguistic question in bilingual education is not just what role the non-English mother tongue should play, but <u>which variety</u> of that language should be used. If bilingual education is designed in part to address problems of self-esteem in the NEP/LEP child (see U.S. Commission on Civil Rights, <u>A better chance to learn</u> [Washington, D.C.: Government Printing Office, 1975]), then it must deal directly with the lower status of the child's vernacular. This is a difficult question, even once the political issue of whether or not to use the local vernacular for instruction has been resolved. On the practical level, a considerable amount of corpus planning could be involved: the development of curricular materials, the availability of assessment instruments, the elaboration of the lexicon for use in its new domain, and other considerations could slow up implementation substantially.

101. Edelsky and Hudelson. op. cit., p. 225. Cf. W. E. Lambert, "A social psychology of bilingualism," Journal of social issues 23 (1967); J. Cummins, "The language and culture issue in the education of minority language children," Interchange 10 (3) (1979–80), pp. 79–80; T. Skutnabb-Kangas and P. Toukomaa, Teaching migrant children's mother tongue and learning the language of the host country in the context of the socio-cultural situation of the migrant family (Helsinki: The Finnish National Commission for UNESCO, 1976).

102. B. Spolsky and P. Irvine, "Sociolinguistic aspects of the acceptance of literacy in the vernacular," in F. Barken et al., (eds.), Bilingualism and language contact: Spanish, English, and Native American languages (New York and London: Teacher's College Press, 1982), p. 76. Maintaining this kind of distinction can be even more important when the traditional language is also a sacred language. After the most recent Iranian revolution, for example, proscriptions on the use of English—up to then the language of technology—resulted in no lexical elaboration of Farsi to adapt it to this new domain; this would have implied both westernization and desacralization (see K. Brown, "Language loss in Iran: de facto language policy implementation," paper presented at the International Conference on Language Policy and Social Problems, Curacao, 1983).

103. For some attempts at definition, see E. Hernandez-Chavez, M. K. Burt, and H. C. Dulay, "Language dominance and proficiency testing: some general considerations," NABE journal III (1978); J. W. Oller, Language tests at school: a pragmatic approach (New York: Longman, 1979),

104. B. McLaughlin, op. cit., p. 43. "Communicative competence" and "proficiency" are not the same thing (proficiency implies more than communication: problem-solving is an illustration of this); but since the former can be said to be a dimension of the latter, these aspects of communicative competence would also apply to proficiency more generally.

105. J. Cummins, "The role of primary language development in promoting educational success for language minority students," in Schooling and language minority students: a theoretical framework (Los Angeles: Evaluation, Dissemination and Assessment Center, California State University, 1981). Cf. M. Saville-Troike, "What really matters in second language learning for academic achievement?" TESOL quarterly 18 (2) (June, 1984), pp. 199–219.

106. Bernbaum, op. cit., p. 15. For a fuller examination of the issues from these two perspectives, see E. Hatch, Second language acquisition: a book of readings (Rowley, MA: Newbury House, 1978); E. Hatch, Psycholinguistics: a second language perspective (Rowley, MA: Newbury House, 1983); N. Wolfson and E. Judd (eds.), Sociolinguistics and language acquisition (Rowley, MA: Newbury House, 1983).

107. S. Krashen, Principles and practice in second language acquisition (Oxford: Pergamon Press, 1982), pp. 10 ff.

108. B. McLaughlin, op. cit., p. 9. There are contexts in which this distinction, strictly held, may not be useful for our purposes (a general discussion on the development of language abilities, for example); for such instances, Teschner suggests the conflated term "language-getting." (R. V. Teschner, "Second-language acquisition and foreign language teaching: Spanish language programs at a university on the U.S.–Mexican border," in F. Barkin et al. (eds.), op. cit., p. 228.

109. W. Penfield and L. Roberts, Speech and brain mechanisms (Princeton, NJ: Princeton University Press, 1959), p. 241.

110. J. Guskin, "Understanding bilingual teachers: a sociolinguistic analysis," a paper presented at the annual meeting of the American Educational Research Association, Washington, D.C. 1975; S. M. Ervin-Tripp, "Is second language learning like the first?," TESOL Quarterly 8 (1974); N. Chomsky, Aspects of the theory of syntax (Cambridge, MA: MIT Press, 1965).

111. See, e.g., Carroll, op. cit., (at note 51 above)
112. Krashen, op. cit., 1982.
113. Cornejo and Cornejo, op. cit., p. viii.
114. E. H. Lenneberg, Biological foundations of language (New York : Wiley, 1967); Penfield and Roberts, op. cit.
115. T. Andersson, "The optimum age for beginning the study of modern languages," International review of education VI (3) (1960), p. 304. Cf. T. Andersson, "Bilingual education and early childhood," Hispania 57 (1974).
116. Ervln-Tripp, op. cit.; M. Saville-Troike, Bilingual education (Arlington, VA: Center for Applied Linguistics, 1973); Snow is cited in Bernbaum, op. cit., p. 9.
117. Guskin, op. cit. 1975; McLaughlin, op. cit.; Cummins, "The role of primary language development ...".
118. Krashen, op. cit. 1982, p. 42. Research continues on this important question. See, for example, R.C. Scarcella and C.A. Higa, "Input and age differences in second language acquisition," In S. Krashen, R.C. Scarcella, and M.H. Long, Child-adult differences in second language acquisition, (Rowley, MA: Newbury House, 1982).
119. C. Burstall, "An 'optimum age' for foreign language learning," English teacher's journal (Israel) XIV (November 1975), pp. 23–26; Krashen, op. cit., 1982.
120. C. Fries, Teaching and learning English as a foreign language (Ann Arbor: University of Michigan Press, 1945); R. Lado, Linguistics across cultures (Ann Arbor: University of Michigan Press, 1957).
121. H. Dulay and M. Burt, "Natural sequences in child second language acquisition," Language learning 24 (1974); A. Fathman, "The relationship between age and second language productive ability," Language learning 25 (1975); S. Krashen, "Some Issues relating to the Monitor Model," In H. D. Brown et al. (eds.), On TESOL '77: Teaching and learning English as a second language: trends in research and practice (Washington, D.C.: TESOL, 1977). Note, however, some important qualifications to the natural order hypothesis offered by K. Hakuta and B. Cancino, "Trends in second language acquisition research," Harvard educational review 47 (3) (August, 1977), pp. 294–316. Other work in progress suggests that the order of acquisition of a second language involves complicated processes with many dimensions; see, e.g., E.E. Tarone, "The interlanguage continuum," a paper presented at the Conference on Current Approaches to Second Language Acquisition, Milwaukee, March 29–31, 1984.
122. Hakuta and Cancino, op. cit., p. 302.
123. For this section, I have found the following works helpful: W. M. Rivers, "Psychology and linguistics as bases for language pedagogy," In F.M. Grittner (ed.), Learning a second language. Seventy-ninth yearbook of the National Society for the Study of Education, Part II (Chicago: University of Chicago Press, 1980); Cornejo and Cornejo, op. cit.; Hakuta and Cancino, op. cit.; McLaughlin, op. cit.
124. B. Banathy, E. C. Trager, and C. D. Waddle, "The use of contrastive data in foreign language course development," in A. Valdman (ed.) Trends in language teaching (New York: McGraw-Hill, 1966), p. 37.
125. For an examination of some of these early criticisms, see W. M. Rivers, The psychologist and the foreign-language teacher (Chicago: University of Chicago Press, 1964).
126. N. Chomsky, op. cit., p. 58: "It seems plain that language acquisition is based on the child's discovery of what from a formal point of view is a deep and abstract theory— a generative grammar of his language—many of the concepts and principles of which are only remotely related to experience by long and intricate chains of unconscious quasi-inferential steps."
127. J. B. Carroll, "The contributions of psychological theory and educational research to the teaching of foreign languages," Modern language journal 49 (May 1965), pp. 273–281. Carroll appears to have been the first to use this phrase.

128. Idem.
129. M. Anisfeld, "Psycholinguistic perspectives on language learning," In A. Valdman (ed.), op. cit., pp. 107–119; Andersson, op. cit. 1960, p. 304.
130. R. Gingras, "Second-language acquisition and foreign language teaching," in R. Gingras, Second-language acquisition and foreign language teaching (Washington, D.C.: Center for Applied Linguistics, 1978), pp. 93–85.
131. H. G. Widdowson, Teaching language as communication (Oxford: Oxford University Press, 1978); H.H. Stern, Fundamental concepts of language teaching (Oxford: Oxford University Press, 1983); C.J. Brumfit and K. Johnson (eds.), The communicative approach to language teaching (Oxford: Oxford University Press, 1979).
132. The general theories for each of these writers are outlined in Schooling and language minority students: a theoretical framework (Los Angeles: California State University, 1981). See also a review of other theories in Krashen, op. cit. 1982; H. Winitz (ed.), The comprehension approach to foreign language instruction (Rowley, MA: Newbury House, 1981); M.H. Long, "Input, interaction, and second language acquisition," paper presented at the New York Academy of Sciences Conference on Native Language and Foreign Language Acquisition, New York, January 15–16, 1981; S.J. Savignon, Communicative competence: an experiment in foreign language teaching (Philadelphia: Center for Curriculum Development, 1972); M. Canale and M. Swain, "Theoretical bases of communicative approaches to second language teaching," Applied linguistics 1 (Spring 1980) pp. 1–47.
133. Hakuta and Cancino, op. cit., p. 312. See, as an example of work which treats SLA as both a psychological and social process John Schumann's Acculturation Model in Gingras, op. cit.
134. R. Kjolseth, "Bilingual education programs in the United States: for assimilation or pluralism?" In B. Spolsky (ed.), The language education of minority children (Rowley, MA: Newbury House Publishers, 1972); J. Fishman and J. Lovas, "Bilingual education in a sociolinguistic perspective," In B. Spolsky, op. cit., 1972.
135. See U.S. Commission on Civil Rights, op. cit., 1975, pp. 3, 29, et al. The idea that bilingual education may not include L1 instruction is part of the Reagan Administration's proposed amendments to the BEA, discussed above.
136. Skutnabb-Kangas and Toukomaa, op. cit.; cf. C. Harrington, Bilingual education in the United States: a view from 1980 (New York: ERIC Clearinghouse on Urban Education, 1980).
137. W. Tikunoff and J. Vazquez-Faria, "Components of effective instruction for LEP students." Chapter four of W. Tikunoff (ed.), Part I of the study report volume IV, Teaching in successful bilingual instructional settings (San Francisco: Far West Laboratory for Educational Research and Development, March, 1983), p. 86. See also W. Tikunoff and J. Vazquez-Faria, "Successful instruction for bilingual schooling," Peabody journal of education 59 (4) (July, 1982), pp. 234–271.
138. R. C. Troike, "Zeno's paradox and language assessment," in S.S. Seidner (ed.). Issues of language assessment: foundations and research (n.l.: Illinois State Board of Education; disseminated by the National Clearinghouse for Bilingual Education, Rosslyn, VA., 1982), p. 4. This is also recognized by Tikunoff and Vazquez-Faria, though they are more concerned with how it affects second-language acquisition (op. cit. 1982, pp. 253–254).
139. See the discussion on bilingual education in D. Ravitch, The troubled crusade: American education, 1945–1980 (New York: Basic Books, 1983), pp. 271–280. For more specific criticisms, see articles in Baker and deKanter, op. cit. 1983.
140. The discussion of Cummins' work which follows is taken from his article in Schooling and language minority children: a theoretical framework (1981). See also J. Cummins, "The construct of language proficiency in bilingual education," a paper

presented at the Georgetown University Round Table on Languages and Linguistics, Washington, D.C., March, 1980. For a practical adaptation of his CUP model to bilingual classrooms, see D. Legarreta-Maroaida, "Effective use of primary language in the classroom," in Schooling and language minority students (1981), pp. 83–116. For critical commentary on his linguistic interdependence hypothesis, see R. Troike, "Social and cultural aspects of language proficiency," paper presented at the Language Proficiency Assessment Symposium, Warrenton, Virginia, March 15–17. 1981

141. See Lambert, op. cit., 1978, 1981; Kessler and Quinn, op. cit.; and Cummins, op. cit., 1979, among others (all cited at note 90 above).

142. Harrington, op. cit., 1980, p. 12.

143. H. Troike, op. cit. 1982, p. 4. Cf. Cummins, op. cit., 1981. More generally, Otheguy (op. cit., pp. 305–306) notes that linguistic assimilation historically has meant little for the social mobility and economic viability of some minority groups in the U.S.

144. E. W. Stevick, Memory, meaning, and method: some psychological perspectives on language learning (Rowley, MA: Newbury House Publishers, 1976); E.W. Stevick, Teaching languages: a way and ways (Rowley, MA: Newbury House Publishers, 1980); P.G. LaForge, Counseling and culture in second language acquisition (Oxford: Pergamon Press, 1983); Bernbaum, op. cit., 1979; Cornejo and Cornejo, op. cit.: McLaughlin, op. cit.; Krashen, op. cit.. 1982.

145. C. Gattegno, Teaching foreign languages in schools: the silent way (New York: Educational Solutions, 1972).

146. J. Asher, Learning another language through actions: the complete teacher's guide-book (Los Gatos, CA: Sky Oaks Productions, 1977); J. Asher, J. Kusudo, and R. de la Torre, "Learning a second language through commands: the second field test," Modern language journal 58 (1974), pp. 24–32

147. C. Curran, Counseling-learning in second languages (Apple River, Ill.: Apple River Press, 1976).

148. Stevick, op. cit., 1976, p. 128.

149. Krashen, op. cit., 1982.

150. A-LM Spanish level one, teacher's manual (New York: Harcourt, Brace and World, Inc., 1964) pp. 178, 201.

151. See the discussion on the distinction between "input" and "intake" in Gingras, op. cit., p. 96.

152. Krashen, op. cit., 1982, p. 160. For a recent compilation of language teaching methods, see J.W. Oller and P. Richard-Amato, Methods that work (Rowley, MA: Newbury House, 1984).

153. For some brief definitions of many of these terms, see L. Leann Parker, "Current perspectives," in Bilingual education: current perspectives. Volume 5: Synthesis (Arlington, VA: Center for Applied Linguistics, 1977).

154. United States Commission on Civil Rights, The excluded student: educational practices affecting Mexican Americans in the southwest. Report III (Washington, D.C.: U.S. Government Printing Office, May, 1972), pp. 14–20. For similar treatment of other groups, see A. B. Gaarder, "Language maintenance and language shift," in W. F. Mackey and T. Andersson (eds.), Bilingualism in early childhood (Rowley, Mass.: Newbury House Publishers, 1977): "teachers in the public schools ... threatened the pupils with punishment for speaking Norwegian on the playgrounds." (p. 414).

155. A. Pifer, "Bilingual education and the Hispanic challenge" (Report of the President), reprinted from The Annual Report, Carnegie Corporation of New York, 1979.

156. Otheguy, op. cit., p. 313.

157. Perhaps the best known of these is the Memorandum from Stanley J. Pottinger, director of the Office for Civil Rights, entitled Identification of discrimination and denial of services on the basis of national origin. May 25, 1970. Commonly referred

to as the May 25th Memorandum, it reads in part: "Where inability to speak and understand the English language excludes national origin-minority group children from effective participation in the educational program offered by a school district, the district must take affirmative steps to rectify the language deficiency in order to open its instructional program to these students."

158. W. E. Lambert, "Bilingualism: its nature and significance," In W. E. Lambert, Faces and facets of bilingualism. Bilingual Education Series 10. Papers in Applied Linguistics (Washington, D.C.: Center for Applied Linguistics, 1981), p. 5. See also W. E. Lambert, "A social psychology of bilingualism," Journal of social issues 23 (2) (1967), pp. 91–109.
159. R. Kjolseth, op. cit., 1972.
160. J. Fishman and J. Lovas, op. cit., 1972
161. W. Mackey, "Typology of bilingual education, in T. Andersson and M. Boyer (eds.), Bilingual schooling in the United States, 2 volumes (Washington, D.C.: Government Printing Office, 1970).
162. To these, Fishman and others have added "enrichment bilingual education" which aims at teaching second language skills to both majority and minority children. (See Fishman, op. cit., 1982.)
163. A. Willig, op. cit., 1981– 1982; Troike, op. cit., 1978.
164. Baker and deKanter, op. cit., 1983, p. 44.
165. Troike, op. cit., 1978; M. J. Fulton-Scott and A. D. Calvin, "Bilingual multi-cultural education vs. integrated and non-integrated ESL Instruction," NABE journal VII (3) (Spring, 1983).
166. H. Dulay and M. Burt, Why bilingual education? A summary of research findings (San Francisco: Bloomsbury West, 1978).
167. Willig, op. cit.; J. R. Tates and A. A. Ortiz, "Baker-deKanter review: Inappropriate conclusions on the efficacy of bilingual education," NABE Journal VII (3) (Spring, 1983).
168. Tikunoff and Vazquez-Faria, op. cit. 1982, pp. 244–253.
169. C. Harrington, op. cit., 1980.
170. For more discussion of such an expanded framework for evaluation, see L. S. Orum, "The question of effectiveness: a blueprint for examining the effects of the federal bilingual education program," NABE News VI(5) (June, 1983).
171. Harrington, op. cit., 1980, p. 12; W. E. Lambert and G. R. Tucker, Bilingual education of children: the St. Lambert experiment (Rowley, MA: Newbury House Publishers, 1972).
172. I. Rotberg, "Some legal and research considerations in establishing federal policy in bilingual education," Harvard educational review 52(2) (May, 1982), p. 157.
173. Fishman, op. cit. 1982, p. 23.
174. H.H. Stern, "French immersion in Canada: achievements and directions," Canadian modern language review 34 (5) (1978), p. 836; G.R. Tucker, "Implications for U.S. bilingual education: evidence from Canadian research." Focus No. 2 (National Clearinghouse for Bilingual Education) (February, 1980) p. 1.
175. D. Kaufman and S. Shapson, "Overview of secondary and post-secondary French immersion: issues and research," Canadian modern language review 34 (3) (1978), pp. 604–620.
176. F. Genesee, E. Polich, and M. Stanley, "An experimental French immersion program at the secondary school level 1969–1974," Canadian modern language review 33 (3) (1977) pp. 318–332.
177. M. Swain, "French immersion: early, late, or partial?" Canadian modern language review 34 (3) (1978), pp. 577–585.
178. Idem. Cf. the discussion of these different types in H.M. Stone, "Immersion bilingual education in Canada and its implications for the United States," Canadian ethnic studies XV (2) (1983), pp. 25–41.

179. G. R. Tucker, "Summary: research conference on immersion education for the majority child," Canadian modern language review 32 (5) (1976), pp. 585–591.
180. McLaughlin, op. cit., p. 163; Troike, op. cit., 1978, p. 21. Edelsky and Hudelson, op. cit., p. 226n; R. L. Venezky, "Non-standard language and reading—ten years later," In J. Edwards (ed.). The social psychology of reading (Silver Spring, MD: Institute of Modern Languages, 1981), pp. 199–200; M. Swain and H. Barik, "Bilingual education in Canada: French and English," in B. Spolsky and R. L. Cooper (eds.), Case studies in bilingual education (Rowley, MA: Newbury House Publishers, 1978), pp. 22, 33, et passim.
181. G.R. Tucker, op. cit., 1980, p. 2.
182. Lambert and Tucker, op. cit., 1972.
183. American Council on the Teaching of Foreign Languages and the National Council for the Social Studies, "Recommendations to the President's Commission on Foreign Language and International Studies," Foreign language annals 12 (5) (October, 1979), p. 388.
184. H. I. Brod, op. cit., p. 20.
185. President's Commission on Foreign Language and International Studies, op. cit., 1979.
186. R. Royer, "Promoting foreign languages," Foreign language annals 12(5) (October, 1979), p. 395.
187. R. L. Hayden, "Toward a national foreign language policy," Journal of communication 29(2) (Spring, 1979), p. 98
188. J. DeWind, The organizing of parents to support bilingual education (New York: Columbia University Center for the Social Sciences, c. 1983), p. ii.
189. G. S. Nussenbaum, "Foreign language teaching and bilingual education–a natural alliance," Foreign language annals 13(2) (April, 1980), p. 125.
190. Royer, op. cit., p. 395.

Selected annotated bibliography

Alatis, J.E. (ed.) 1978. Georgetown University round table on languages and linguistics 1978. Washington, D.C.: Georgetown University Press
Articles selected from the annual conference held at Georgetown. The 1978 theme was "International dimensions of bilingual education." This volume comprises more than forty papers on theoretical constructs, language policy, problems of second language learning and literacy, strategies for implementing bilingual education, and problems of assessment in the second language. Authors include Shirley Heath, Joshua Fishman, William Mackey, Joan Rubin, Glyn Lewis, Robert Cooper, Wallace Lambert, Charles Ferguson, and William Leap.
Alatis, J.E. (ed.) 1980. Georgetown University round table on languages and linguistics 1980. Washington, D.C.: Georgetown University Press.
Articles selected from the annual conference held at Georgetown. Especially useful are papers by Reyes, Medina-Seidner, Perez, and Mazzone on language-in-education policies and assessment procedures in various states.
Andersson, T. and M. Boyer. 1970. Bilingual schooling in the United States (2 vols.). Washington, D.C.: U.S. Government Printing Office.
The standard work on bilingual education in the United States. It outlines some of the features of early programs, and gives a brief historical sketch of language teaching in the U.S. It also includes conceptual papers on models of bilingual instruction and evaluation. This book has served as a model for later works on bilingual education, most notably F. Cordasco's book of the same title.
Baker, K.A. and A.A. deKanter. (eds.) 1983. Bilingual education: A reappraisal of federal policy. Lexington, MA: Lexington Books (D.C. Heath & Co.)

A collection of papers intended to demonstrate the need for a change in federal bilingual education policy. The editors were employees of the Department of Education at the time the information for the book was being compiled; some of the authors are still employed within the Department. The book, which includes papers by Baker and deKanter, Birman and Ginsburg, and Milne treats critically four assumptions on which putatively federal bilingual education policy rests: that as many as 3.6 million children need special language services; that the non-English language background of the children is the cause of their school failure; that transitional bilingual education is an effective treatment for these children; and that practical constraints (lack of teachers, high program costs, etc.) can be ignored in setting federal policy.

Barkin, F. et al (eds.) 1982. Bilingualism and language contact: Spanish, English, and Native American languages. New York and London: Teacher's College Press
A collection of papers representing empirical and conceptual research in second-language acquisition, literacy, and language contact. Especially important are papers by Edelsky and Budelson on the prospects of acquiring a socially marked language as a second language, Teschner on language programs on the U.S.–Mexican border, and Spolsky and Irvine on sociolinguistic problems of vernacular literacy among some Native Americans.

Brod, R. I. (ed.) 1980. Language study for the 1980's: report of the MLA-ACLS language task forces. New York: The Modern Language Association of America.
A collection of reports on the current status of language study and its prospects in the United States. The reports contain recommendations and resolutions aimed at enhancing the role of language throughout U.S. society. Topics are indicated by the names of the five task forces: Institutional Language Policy, Commonly Taught Languages, Less Commonly Taught Languages, Public Awareness, and Government Relations. Also included were supplemental reports, the most notable of which were by Keller and Roel on media and Grant on language policy in the United States.

California State Department of Education (Office of Bilingual Bicultural Education) 1981. Schooling and language minority students; a theoretical framework. Los Angeles: Evaluation, Dissemination, and Assessment Center.
The five papers in this collection represent brief syntheses of some of the theoretical work of the authors. James Cummins, in "The role of primary language development in promoting educational success for language minority students," discusses his ideas of language proficiency and his conclusion that English language proficiency has been exaggerated as a factor in school achievement for language minority students. Other articles are by Krashen (on his input hypothesis of second language acquisition), Terrell on the "natural approach" in bilingual programs, Lagarreta-Marcaida on the primacy of native language instruction, and Thonis on implementation strategies for biliteracy.

Cohen, A. and M. Swain. 1976. Bilingual education: The "Immersion" model in the North American context. TESOL quarterly 10: 45–53.
Cohen and Swain investigate the practices and effects of "immersion" language programs in various contexts in Canada and the United States. They put forth some tentative observations on the role these programs might play within bilingual education. Especially important are the characteristics they offer as important for a successful immersion program.

Cornejo, R.J. and L.O. Cornejo. 1981. Theories and research on second language acquisition. Las Cruces, N.M.: ERIC Clearinghouse on Rural Education and Small Schools.
A review of the theoretical literature on second-language acquisition. The monograph goes into considerable historical detail. For contemporary research, the authors use the categories posited by Hakuta and Cancino (1977) as a framework for their own discussion.

Ferguson, C.A. and S.B. Heath (eds.) 1981. Language in the USA. New York: Cambridge University Press.

This is intended as a contribution to the growing literature on language planning and language studies in the United States. The papers deal with the different varieties of English in the U.S., its role in the country's history, the politics of language and the problems of pluralism, the status of non-English languages and the communities associated with them. Fishman's paper on U.S. language policy as well as the editors' introduction frame the issues and offer some observations on the future of language in the U.S.

Fishman, J.A. 1982. Sociolinguistic foundations of bilingual education. The bilingual review/la revista bilingue 9 (1): 1–35.

A self-review of some of Fishman's basic ideas on bilingual education. It includes reprises on his discussions elsewhere of language maintenance-language shift, language planning and bilingual education, types of bilingual education, the nature and role of "immersion" programs in bilingual education, and the role of speech communities in a bilingual education program. This is an important, though brief, summary of Fishman's work in bilingual education.

Gingras, R. (ed.) 1978 Second Language acquisition and foreign language teaching. Washington, D.C.: Center for Applied Linguistics.

This volume presents two papers on the basic processes of second-language acquisition (SLA): one by Krashen on the "monitor model," the other by Schumann on the "acculturation model" of SLA. Sajavaara, Saville-Troike, and Valdman offer critical comments on the two papers. Finally, Gingras presents a brief summary of some practical implications for language teaching of these two models.

Gray, T. 1981. The current status of bilingual education legislation: an update. Bilingual Education Series: 9. Papers in Applied Linguistics. Washington, D.C.: Center for Applied Linguistics.

Critical annotations on bilingual education legislation at different administrative and legislative levels. Especially helpful is the update on state language policy and education.

Grittner, F.M. (ed.) 1980. Learning a second language. (Seventy-ninth yearbook of the National Society for the Study of Education, Part II). Chicago: University of Chicago Press.

The 1980 Yearbook contains papers on the history of second-language teaching and bilingual education in the United States, the contribution of linguistics and psychology to language teaching, the relation of foreign language teaching and bilingual education, and problems of teacher training and supervision.

Hakuta, K. and H. Cancino 1977. Trends in second language acquisition research. Harvard educational review 47 (3): 294–316.

An important synthetic paper on various approaches to the study of second-language acquisition (SLA). The authors classify this study into four types: contrastive analysis is an investigation of the grammatical features of two languages; error analysis is an examination of errors that depart from the norm for the second language; performance analysis concerns proficiency in usage; and discourse analysis, which is the study of the use of linguistic features in spontaneous conversation. These types also represent a general chronological pattern. The authors suggest that the most recent discourse studies could be overshadowed by an emphasis on more general sociolinguistic approaches in the future.

Harrington, C. 1980. Bilingual education in the United States: A view from 1980. New York: ERIC Clearinghouse on Urban Education.

A review of some of the research evidence on the effectiveness of bilingual education programs. Harrington is an acknowledged advocate of these programs, and refutes arguments against bilingual education based on lack of results. He distinguishes, as does Lambert, between those programs promoting "additive" and those promoting "subtractive" bilingualism, and asserts that negative results are generally associated with the latter kind. He offers a long list of criteria which characterize effective bilingual education programs.

Heath, S.B. and F. Mandabach. 1983. Language status decisions and the law in the United States. In Progress in language planning: international perspectives, edited by J. Cobarrubias and J.A. Fishman. 87–105. Berlin: Mouton Publishers.
The authors present a historical analysis of language law in the United States. Especially important is their discussion of court cases and state language policies in the 1910s and 1920s. Their contention is that any discussion of the development of language policy must be informed by a knowledge of the history of language law and education in the United States.

Kloss, H. 1977. The American bilingual tradition. Rowley HA: Newbury House Publishers.
One of the most comprehensive works on language diversity and its effects on U.S. institutions, including schools, courts, the media, churches, and community organizations. He distinguishes between "promotive" and "acquiescent" language rights, and frames his historical discussion around these concepts. Languages discussed include French, Spanish, German, Dutch, Italian, Portuguese, Norwegian, Hawaiian, some Native American languages, and others representing relatively small communities. Attentive to the nature of the U.S. as a federal system, he also gives considerable space to the role of the states in the development of language policy.

Krashen, S.D. 1982. Principles and practice in second language acquisition. Oxford: Pergamon Press.
Krashen develops his "comprehensible input" model of second-language acquisition (SLA) in this book. He also details his ideas on what conditions are favorable for SLA and which seem to have a detrimental effect. Finally, he provides a very useful summary of some of the major theories of SLA and language teaching, and assesses them in the context of his own model.

McLaughlin, Barry. 1978. Second-language acquisition in childhood. Hillsdale, NJ: Lawrence Erlbaum Associates, Publishers.
A review of major theories of second-language acquisition (SLA) and related concepts (learning-acquisition distinction, the critical period hypothesis, and others). It also gives considerable attention to language teaching programs like FLES, bilingual-bicultural education, and immersion programs.

Padilla, R.V. (ed.) 1979. Ethnoperspectives in bilingual education research: bilingual education and public policy in the United States. Ypsilanti, MI: Eastern Michigan University Department of Foreign Languages and Bilingual Studies.
Selected papers from a series of working conferences held at Eastern Michigan University. Topics range from broad social policy implications of bilingual education to specific strategies for implementation of local programs. The political dimensions of language policy are discussed, mainly in the context of state laws and ordinances. There is also an important concluding section on the involvement of the local community in school programs.

Parker, W.R. 1961. The national interest and foreign languages (a discussion guide prepared for the U.S. National Commission for UNESCO). 3rd edition. Washington, D.C.: U.S. Government Printing Office.
One of a series of monographs commissioned by the U.S. government on the history and current state of language study in the United States. This edition is especially helpful in providing historical context for the critical period after the second World War. It contains sections on the NDEA, FLES, the development of language training

centers, the role of languages in American society, and the problems of teacher training.

Parker. W.R. 1966. The language curtain, and other essays on education. New York: Modern Language Association of America.

A book of essays and speeches on language study in the United States. Some of these, or parts of them, also appeared in his 1961 monograph. Parker argues for the importance of language study—both English and foreign languages—throughout the American system of education. He discusses the role of language study in the humanities, the centrality of Latin, and the need for a broadened curriculum. This volume includes his famous speech, "The Language Curtain."

The President's Commission on Foreign Language and International Studies. 1979. Strength through wisdom: a critique of U.S. capability. Washington, D.C.: U.S. Government Printing Office.

The report of a commission appointed by President Carter to assess the current state and future prospects of language capability in the U.S. The report is an alarm that the country is in danger on many fronts because of our "scandalous incompetence in foreign languages." It calls for a series of reforms, including the development of international high schools, the reestablishment of foreign language requirements in universities, business incentives for foreign language competence, and the appointment of a national commission on language issues.

Seidner. S.S. (ed.) 1982. Issues of language assessment; foundations and research. Springfield, IL: Illinois State Board of Education (Disseminated by the National Clearinghouse on Bilingual Education).

This volume contains papers presented at the Language Assessment Institute held in 1981 in Evanston, IL. Papers are arranged under three headings: foundations, assessment approaches, and research and policy. While the central topic is assessment, the papers run the gamut from conceptual discussions to involved analyses of technical questions.

Spolsky, B. and R.L. Cooper, (eds.) Case studies in bilingual education. Fowley, MA: Newbury House Publishers.

A collection of papers on language and bilingual education in the United States and other parts of the world. It is designed to give an outline of the broad range of language situations which are addressed by bilingual education. Most helpful are articles by Swain and Barik on immersion and bilingual programs in Canada and by Blanco on the implementation of bilingual education in the United States. (This is one of a variety of important works on language policy and bilingual education published by Newbury House Publishers.)

Tikunoff, W.J. and J.A. Vazquez-Faria. 1982. Successful instruction for bilingual schooling. Peabody journal of education 59 (4): 234–271.

In this article, Tikunoff and Vazquez present some of their findings from an extensive project funded by the National Institute of Education designed to isolate important features of the successful bilingual program. Their general conclusion is that effective bilingual instruction has many of the same features as any effective classroom, with the additional dimensions of using the child's native language and being sensitive to use the child's culture to mediate instruction. The authors also offer recommendations for policy implementation of bilingual education.

Bilingual Education

Richard Ruiz (1997)

Bilingual education can be defined simply as the use of two languages as the media of instruction. While *bilingualization* (the development of bilingual proficiency in students) may or may not be the goal of bilingual education, this definition implies that the issue of language proficiency development is secondary to the learning of subject matter through language. In other words, bilingual education is an approach to the teaching that uses two languages; it is not primarily an approach to the teaching of languages. It should be distinguished from English as a second language (ESL), the purpose of which is to teach English. Nevertheless, the connection between subject matter learning and language development, especially that of the first language, has been shown by various researchers to be extremely strong. The relatively early work of Wallace Lambert, Richard Tucker, and Lily Wong Fillmore is still being developed; more recent work by Kenji Hakuta, Virginia Collier, David Ramirez, Eugene Garcia, Barry McLaughlin, Catherine Snow, Stephen Krashen, Jim Cummins, and others has further extended our knowledge of basic language development processes in bilingual contexts.

Bilingual education in the United States has been controversial because it has been linked with the political and ideological conflicts stereotypically associated with liberals and conservatives, especially since 1968 when Congress passed Title VII of the Elementary and Secondary Education Act of 1965, commonly known as the Bilingual Education Act (BEA), allowing federally sponsored public school bilingual programs. Because bilingual education is most often associated with the education of culturally diverse populations (in the United States it is frequently labeled *bilingual-bicultural education*), its definition has generally included a cultural dimension, as in the following: "The term 'program of bilingual education' means a program of instruction … in which … there is instruction given in, and study of, English and, to the extent necessary to allow a child to progress effectively through the educational system, the native language of the children of limited English-speaking ability, and such instruction is given with appreciation for the cultural heritage of such children" (PL 93-380, Sec. 703a4A). This is seen as both reasonable and natural; language is part of culture, and language behaviors and proficiency should be developed in a cultural context, rather than divorced from it. This theoretical and pedagogical point is lost in the debate about whether public school programs should encourage cultural and ethnic maintenance in diverse populations.

The classic legislative conceptualization of bilingual education is that of *transitional bilingual education*, first codified into federal law by the 1974 revision of the BEA. According to the law, the purpose of a bilingual program should be to teach the non- or limited-English-proficient student enough English to allow a transfer into the all-English classroom as soon as possible and to use only enough of the native language to ensure that he or she does not fall behind peers in subject matter learning. This version of bilingual education was reinforced in the 1984 and 1988 reauthorizations, which allowed that a certain amount of money appropriated for bilingual programs could fund approaches that used nothing but English as a medium of instruction—the so-called special alternative instructional programs. This provision was based on a largely intuitive sense that children learn English fastest and best in an environment that gives it maximum exposure by excluding all other languages from the classroom. While this intuition is disputed by all the major researchers in second language acquisition, bilingualism, language development, and bilingual education (see e.g., Collier, 1995; Snow and Hakuta, 1992; McLaughlin, 1987; Ramirez, et al., 1991), these programs continue to be allowed in the 1994 reauthorization of the BEA. However, it should be noted that the latest enactment removed much of the old language surrounding bilingual education that portrayed bilingualism as a deficit or a problem to be solved, promoting instead the view that it is a national resource that must be cultivated, not merely for the benefit of ethnic communities, but for the good of the nation as a whole (Stanford Working Group, 1993). It remains an open question whether a policy that portrays bilingualism and bilingual education positively will remain in force for long, and, if it does, whether it will make any real programmatic and pedagogical difference.

Richard Ruiz
* *See also* Bicultural Education; Code-Switching; Limited English Proficiency (LEP)

References

Collier, V. P. (1995). *Promoting academic success for ESL students: Understanding second language acquisition for school.* Elizabeth, NJ: New Jersey TESOL/Bilingual Educators.

Cummins, J. (1989). *Empowering minority students.* Sacramento, CA: California Association for Bilingual Education.

Garcia, E. (1994). *Understanding and meeting the challenge of student cultural diversity.* Boston: Houghton Mifflin.

Hakuta, K. (1986). *Mirror of language: The debate on bilingualism.* New York: Basic Books.

Krashen, S. (1991). *Bilingual education: A focus on current research.* Washington, DC: National Clearinghouse for Bilingual Education.

Lambert, W. E., & Taylor, D. M. (1990). *Coping with cultural and racial diversity in urban America.* New York: Praeger.

Mackey, W. F. (1978) The importation of bilingual education models. In J. Alatis (Ed.), *Georgetown University round table: International dimensions of education.* Washington, DC: Georgetown University Press.

McLaughlin, B. (1987). *Theories of second language learning.* London: Edward Arnold.

Ramirez, D., Yuen, S. D., Ramey, D. R., & Pasta, D. J. (1991). *Final report: National longitudinal study of structured-English immersion strategy, early-exit and late-exit transitional bilingual education programs for language minority children (Vol. 1–2). Technical Report.* San Mateo, CA: Aguirre International.

Snow, C., & Hakuta, K. (1992). The costs of monolingualism. In J. Crawford (Ed.), *Language loyalties: A source book on the official English controversy* (pp. 384–94). Chicago: University of Chicago Press.

Stanford Working Group. (1993). *Federal education programs for limited-English-proficient students: A blueprint for the second generation.* Stanford, CA: Stanford Working Group.

Tucker, G. R. (1990). Second language education: Issues and perspectives. In A. Padilla, H. Fairchild, & C. Valadez (Eds.), *Foreign language education: Issues and strategies.* Newbury Park, CA: Sage.

Wong Fillmore, L. (1991). Second language learning in children: A model of language learning in social context. In E. Bialystok (Ed.), *Language processing in bilingual children* (pp. 49–69), Cambridge: Cambridge University Press.

Paradox of Bilingualism

Richard Ruiz (2008)

Essay

Editor's Note: *This essay is an abridged version of the Du Val Lee Lecture delivered by the author as part of the Community Faculty Lecture Series of the University of Arizona, in 1999.*

There is an essential paradox, a contradiction, in the way we have conceived of the role of languages other than English in public life in the United States. This paradox can be stated simply as follows: *Other languages are to be pursued by those who don't have them, but they are to be abandoned by those who do.* This paradox, now embedded in laws and pervading our norms, has led to a number of other strange and seemingly contradictory ideas that are the engines for much of U.S. public policy.

Many others have also noted this paradox and have described it in various ways. For example, Kurt Müller, in 2002, stated it in this way:

We prevent first-generation natives from developing competence in the language and culture of their heritage, and we require those already assimilated into the common culture to begin learning another language later than their competitors abroad. At its worst, in many school systems we limit the choice of languages to the very one that the objectors do not want the immigrants to maintain, (p. 10)

Müller sees it as our "self-imposed handicap in international affairs." Sandra McKay and Sau-Ling Wong, in 2000, made much the same point, characterizing existing language education policy as "curtailing mother-tongue maintenance among immigrants and then providing foreign-language programs for Anglophone monolinguals (many of whom are former bilinguals)" (p. 3). Patricia MacGregor-Mendoza goes further, suggesting that the number of cases in which Spanish speakers have been punished by the courts constitutes the "criminalization" of Spanish in the United States, but it is clear she is talking about local, "ethnic" varieties of Spanish. James Crawford, among many others, also analyses the paradoxical nature of policies on bilingual education.

Arizona is a state full of beautiful natural culture and linguistic diversity, yet its people are full of ambivalence with respect to it. We treasure our natural wonders yet see with suspicion efforts by environmentalists to preserve them for our children and grandchildren. Phoenix has been for a long time a "suburb" of Los Angeles, and California is the tail that wags the dog called Arizona. As previously mentioned, in 1988, Arizona passed a law making English the official language of the state by constitutional amendment; that was 2 years after California passed much the same law for the second time in its history. In 2000, just a few months after California passed a law by which teachers are told how best to teach bilingual students, Arizona did the same. Parts of Arizona have a long, established identity and a sense of purpose; as a state, we do not yet know what we are or where we are going. This is especially true with respect to cultural and linguistic diversity.

Finally, we are, in the United States, a country that has for more than two centuries resisted the idea of an official language at the national level— yet has a long history of embracing restrictionist policies and laws with respect to the public use of languages other than English. The proposals for immigration reform discussed in the U.S. Congress after the 2006 elections make it clear that from one extreme of the political spectrum to the other, whatever disagreements there might be on other details, the primacy of English must be an absolute requirement in the law.

The historical and political contexts in which we live help to shape how we think about language and its role in our public life. Let us discuss briefly in more detail some of the principal historical developments that have influenced our perceptions. But there must be some dispelling of historical myths at the outset; in some ways, these are more powerful than any actual data that might be brought to bear.

One often hears on talk radio and reads in letters to the editor statements such as the following: "My ancestors came here from (wherever, usually Europe), and they didn't have bilingual education, but they still got ahead. Why do the Spanish speakers need it?" We are about to see how wrong this perception among the general public is, but it is even more disturbing when it is held by those who should know better. One example, for instance, is the *New York Times* editorial by Joan Keefe, in 1985, who at the time was a member of the National Advisory and Coordinating Council on Bilingual Education of the U.S. Department of Education. She was described as a teacher of English as a Second Language (ESL) and French at Washington area universities. Keefe asked whether bilingual education is needed. She asserted,

> If it had existed earlier in the century, some of today's leading educators, scholars, and entertainers would have been placed in classes in languages their immigrant parents spoke. Would they have gained their present prominence—or have stagnated in cultural and linguistic ghettos? (p. A27)

There are many approaches to answering this question, which is why at universities we give whole courses devoted to addressing it. But for now, let us disabuse ourselves of some of this particular historical myth. At the time of Keefe's editorial, some 182,000 children were being served in federally funded bilingual education programs. While it is true that many more were enrolled in state and locally supported programs, the number of children affected by these programs was extremely small as a percentage of total school population. Keefe implied that these were unprecedented numbers. Nothing could be further from the truth.

German language in the Midwest

The heyday of publicly funded bilingual education in this country was from about the middle of the 19th century to the second decade of the 20th, roughly 1840 to 1920. These programs primarily served western and northern European groups, the largest of which were the Germans. While there was some concern expressed early in the development of these programs that schools were spending too many public resources on non-English instruction (e.g., see work by Conrad Patzer and Bessie Pierce), these communities generally tended to be well received in urban neighborhoods and the schools. They met resistance to the extent that they were perceived as hostile to what was by that time the main purpose of the public schools—Americanization. The 1860s and 1870s saw a dramatic rise in the study of German in the public schools, and also study conducted in German. This accompanied the enhanced political status of Germans in the communities of the Midwest. By the middle of the century, Germans in St. Louis, for example, constituted one quarter of the population and according to St. Louis Public Schools, in 1876, had "a considerable portion of the active business and manufacturing community, holding a great amount of the wealth of the city, and contributing largely to its revenues" (p. 114). The political status of Germans in the Midwest accompanied their heightened economic interest and weight, suggesting that the accommodations that could be made with public funds for the education of ethnic communities were proportional to the general perception of their economic benefit to the larger society. Advocates for including the German language in public school curricula argued that German study would encourage German parents to send their children to public schools, at that time a tenuous institution because of the strength of competing Catholic and Lutheran parochial school systems. These arguments prevailed: In 1864 and 1865, in St. Louis, 450 elementary students, about 5% of the school population in 5 schools, studied German under the tutelage of 5 specially trained German teachers furnished by the Cincinnati schools. By the end of that year, the Office of German Assistant Superintendent was established. The increase in resources allocated for German instruction was dramatic. By 1870, 37% of the students studied German; in 1875, 73%

studied German, with 73 teachers in 45 schools; and the numbers increased into the 1880s. This pattern was mirrored throughout the Midwest, especially in the so-called German triangle (St. Louis-Milwaukee-Cincinnati). Pierce and the St. Louis Public Schools state that in Milwaukee as late as 1907, some 70% of Milwaukee high school students were enrolled in German classes. The national statistics on foreign-language study in high school also show this interest in language study.

The historical context is important to keep in mind. The great majority of the teachers in these programs were not proficient in English, at least not to the extent that they could teach basic subjects in English. John Sterns and Jerome Watrous confirm that many of them had been prepared at German seminaries such as those in Milwaukee and Chicago, having only recently arrived from Germany for the purpose of teaching basic subjects in German. In other words, while many of these students were studying the German language, it appears that many of them were also using the German language to learn other subjects. In effect, they were experiencing German immersion, a form of bilingual education, in public schools. The figures in Table 1 demonstrate the popularity of such study.

The table also illustrates the precipitous decline of German study throughout the country after 1915. In Milwaukee, for example, between 1916 and 1918, enrollment in German classes dropped from 30,000 to 400, and the number of German teachers from 200 to 1; by the end of the 1919 school year, the teaching of German was completely discontinued in elementary schools. Heinz Kloss and Bayrd Still maintain this was a common pattern throughout the Midwest in this period. This is understandable given the ethos of the time. Much had happened in the world to make people and institutions in the United States suspicious of anyone of German ancestry who wanted to study German. It became a sign of disloyalty and disrespect to maintain the language of a people at war with the United States. This association of language and political loyalty was to be ingrained in the public mentality from that period to the present. William Parker claims that from 1918 to 1925, about half the states passed anti-foreign-language laws, many of them aimed at schools. Shirley Brice Heath and Frederick Mandabach claim that perhaps the most remembered of these laws were the twin Siman and Bartels Laws, in Nebraska and Iowa, respectively; these became the subject of one of the most famous U.S. Supreme Court cases, Meyer v. Nebraska, in 1923. The arguments of the justices in these cases mirrored much of the sentiment in the country: Even while, in some instances, such as Meyer, they were compelled to find the laws unconstitutional, they nevertheless made it evident that states could find ways to restrict the public use of languages other than English. In Meyer, the justices even gave guidance on how that could happen, and the state quickly took its advantage: Nebraska's official English law is the oldest in the country, dating from 1923.

Year	Total high school enrollment	% Latin	Modern languages	% French	% German	% Spanish
1890	202,963	34.7	16.3	5.8	10.5	
1895	350,099	43.9	17.9	6.5	11.4	
1900	519,251	50.6	22.1	7.8	14.3	
1905	679,702	50.2	29.3	9.1	20.2	
1910	915,061	49.0	34.3	9.9	23.7	0.7
1915	1,328,984	37.3	35.9	8.8	24.4	2.7
1922	2,230,000	27.5	27.4	15.5	0.6	11.3
1928	3,354,473	22.0	25.2	14.0	1.8	9.4
1934	5,620,625	16.0	19.5	10.9	2.4	6.2
1949	5,399,452	7.8	13.7	4.7	0.8	8.2
1954	6,582,300	6.9	14.2	5.6	0.8	7.3
1958	7,897,232	7.8	16.4	6.1	1.2	8.8
1959	8,155,573	7.9	19.1	7.4	1.5	9.8
1964	11,056,639	5.4	26.2	10.8	2.6	12.3

Source: Adapted from Parker (1966, pp. 139, 140, 150).

Spanish language in the Southwest

The early situation of German Americans stands in stark contrast to the way in which, at the very same time, new Mexican citizens were being treated in the territorial Southwest. Not only was there no accommodation for their language and culture needs in schools, but they were viewed with considerable suspicion, to the extent that they were actively discriminated against in all aspects of the public sector. After numerous Mexicans were incorporated into the United States after the Mexican War in 1848, their lands were confiscated, their culture was undermined, and their language suppressed, sometimes in ruthless fashion. According to reports prepared by the U.S. Commission on Civil Rights on the Education of Mexican Americans clear into the 1960s, Spanish was proscribed in many schools of the Southwest. No-Spanish rules were notorious in Texas, Arizona, and parts of California. Arizona developed a segregated system of education for Mexican Americans called the "1C Program" some researchers compare it to the segregated schools for Blacks in the South of the same period, as Mary Carol Combs and her colleagues explain.

What accounts for this difference? It is part of the paradox of bilingualism and bilingual education in the United States.

The paradox restated

When Arizona was passing Proposition 106 in 1988, making English the official language of the state and targeting bilingual education, the state's department of education was promulgating rules, with much popular support, that would provide for every student in every grade level in every school in Arizona the opportunity to study a foreign language. Ironically, but predictably, Arizona follows the same pattern at the present time: The constitutional amendment passed in 2000 outlawing most instances of bilingual education is accompanied by initiatives in local districts to promote foreign-language study. In 2007, the Arizona Department of Education has been pushing legislation by which the state would fund international schools promoting the study of foreign languages. In its most recent iteration in 2007, a bill to create three international schools failed to pass the state legislature amid criticisms from some legislators that such schools would be "un-American."

This apparent contradiction has to do in part with the ideas we have about language, about the roles that languages should play in our public life, and about the communities that use these languages, for example,

- We have a highly instrumentalized view of language. We see it as essentially a tool, an instrument for getting social goods. To the extent that it does that, we see a language as valuable; to the extent that it does not, we devalue it.
- This is in contrast to a view of language that sees it as part of identity, as part of the tradition and history and culture and personality of a community. While language can still be seen instrumentally, that is not its essence.

Ethnicity is seen as a sort of sentimentality, an allegiance toward community, toward local attachments, and toward intimate relationships, rather than toward the public, transethnified needs of the bureaucratic state. When we see ethnicity, we see a breakdown of the state based on a faulty commitment toward sentimentality demonstrated by the concern to maintain heritage languages other than English and the cultures of which they are a part. As a society, we devalue these groups, and we see their languages as equally depreciated. Even worse, we see these groups as threats to our way of life.

Language study that deemphasizes commitment to local community, that urges us toward allegiance toward the larger public state, and that promotes the instrumental values that fuel a capitalist system are those that are valued. Others are seen as at best inadequate, perhaps even threatening to the public good.

So, the paradox mentioned by Müller and others above is not perceived as a contradiction. Foreign languages are academic, not intimate. They do not form part of our personal identities, and they do not impel us to any sort of political action. They are not attached to a local community of which I am, or am becoming, a part. Their purpose is to enhance my academic or social status, and perhaps to allow me to travel with a little more ease. One studies them for a year or two, but they are rarely if ever completely mastered, at least not through the current ways of teaching them employed by public schools, except perhaps to read; they are tools to be used on occasion, not a means to attach or reattach individuals to communities. This is precisely what local community languages are, or are perceived to be. Therefore, bilingual education is seen as the agent of irredentism, of maintaining or bringing back into the fold those who could be transformed by a severe acculturation into *real Americans*, loyal not to their parochial interests, but to those of the commonweal, the state.

The paradox described at the outset can thus be restated as such: Spanish (or French or German or any other non-English world standard foreign language) is to be pursued by those who do not have it, but Spanish (or French or German or any other "little" non-English community language) is to be abandoned by those children and youth who do. Spanish uplifts and enhances and builds up; Spanish tears down and fragments and holds back all who maintain it. If this is a paradox, it is easily accommodated by those who see these as quite different languages.

But there is an even more fundamental and puzzling paradox: Publicly funded, especially federally funded public school bilingual education, has never really been about bilingualism or about bilingualization. Although we have had a bilingual education law in the United States since 1968, there was very little in any of its pronouncements to allow us to infer that its purpose was true bilingualization. Those whose purpose it has been to implement these laws at the federal level have been consistent in their insistence that they were designed to promote the teaching and learning of English; all else is secondary. This position is stated explicitly in policy and position papers commissioned by federal education offices. Beatrice Birman and Alan Ginsburg, in 1981, provided the following prime example:

> Underlying this paper is the assumption that the ultimate goals of bilingual education programs are to learn English and to keep up with English-speaking peers in subject matter. While bilingualism is a laudable and worthwhile outcome, we judge benefit in terms of English acquisition and subject matter learning, (p. 5n)

The United States is unusual if not unique in the world in this: Bilingual education is not designed to create bilinguals, but rather monolinguals in English out of those who previously spoke another language. Joshua A. Fishman, a leading researcher and advocate for bilingual education in the world, has been blunt in his criticism of the U.S. law. According to Fishman, in 1981, it is "primarily an act for the Anglification of non-English speakers and not an act for bilingualism. … The act is basically not an act *for* bilingualism, but, rather, an act *against* bilingualism" (pp. 517–518). This is the irony of the present controversy in this state and in this country. Opponents of bilingual education argue against it because it promotes other languages over English. Proponents of bilingual education argue against most of what we have up to now called bilingual education because all it does is promote English over all other languages.

If we truly had bilingual education in this country, we might then be able to realize the great potential of those children who come to our schools speaking all those many and varied languages, build on those experiences to learn English and much more, and use their language proficiencies to make the world better. The present sociolinguistic and political dynamics in the United States preclude that bright future.

Encyclopedia of Bilingual Education
Editors: Josué M. González
Book Title: Encyclopedia of Bilingual Education
Chapter Title: "Paradox of Bilingualism"
Pub. Date: 2008
Access Date: August 24, 2015
Publishing Company: SAGE Publications, Inc.
City: Thousand Oaks
Print ISBN: 9781412937207
Online ISBN: 9781412963985
DOI: http://dx.doi.org/10.4135/9781412963985.n244
Print pages: 646–651
©2008 SAGE Publications, Inc. All Rights Reserved.

See also
- Language Education Policy in Global Perspective
- Language Rights in Education
- U.S. Bilingual Education Viewed from Abroad
- Views of Bilingual Education
- Views of Language Difference

Further readings

Birman, B. E., & Ginsburg, A. L. (1981, October 5). Addressing the needs of language-minority children: Issues for federal policy. Unpublished manuscript for the Department of Education, Washington, DC.

Combs, M. C., Evans, C., Fletcher, T., Parra, E., and Jiménez, A. Bilingualism for the children: Implementing a dual-language program in an English-only state. Educational Policy, 19 (2005). 701–728. http://dx.doi.org/10.1177/0895904805278063

Crawford, J. (2000). Language politics in the United States: The paradox of bilingual education. In C. J. Ovando, ed. & P. McLaren (Eds.), The politics of multiculturalism and bilingual education: Students and teachers caught in the crossfire (pp. 107–125). Boston: McGraw-Hill.

Fishman, J. A. (1981). Language policy: Past, present, and future. In C. A. Ferguson, ed. & S. B. Heath (Eds.), Language in the USA (pp. 516–526). New York: Cambridge University Press.

Heath, S. B., & Mandabach, F. (1983). Language status decisions and the law in the United States. In J. Cobarrubias, ed. & J. A. Fishman (Eds.), Progress in language planning: International perspectives (pp. 87–105). Berlin, Germany: Mouton.

Keefe, J. (1985, October 24). An alternative to bilingualism. New York Times, p. A27.

Kloss, H. (1977). The American bilingual tradition. Rowley, MA: Newbury House.

MacGregor-Mendoza, P. (1998). The criminalization of Spanish in the United States. In D. Kibbee (Ed.), Language legislation and language rights (pp. 55–67). Amsterdam: Benjamins.

McKay, S. L., ed., & Wong, S.-L. C. (Eds.). (2000). Introduction. New immigrants in the United States: Readings for second-language educators (pp. 1–7). New York: Cambridge University Press.

Meyer v. Nebraska, 262 U.S. 390 (1923).

Müller, K. E. Addressing counterterrorism: U.S. literacy in language and international affairs. Language Problems and Language Planning, 26 (2002). 1–21.

Parker, W. R. (1966). The national interest and foreign languages. The language curtain and other essays on American education. New York: Modern Language Association of America.

Patzer, C. E. (1924). Public education in Wisconsin. Madison, WI: State Historical Society.

Pierce, B. (1936). History of Chicago. New York: Knopf.

Ruiz, R. (1984). Language teaching in American education: Impact on second-language learning. Unpublished synthesis report for the National Institute of Education, Washington, DC.

St. Louis Public Schools. (1876). Annual report of the Board of Directors of the St. Louis Public Schools for the year ending August 1, 1875. St. Louis, MO: Author.

Steams, J. W (1893). The Columbian history of education in Wisconsin. Milwaukee: State Committee on Educational Exhibit for Wisconsin.

Still, B. (1948). Milwaukee: The history of a city. Madison, WI: State Historical Society.

U.S. Commission on Civil Rights. (1971–1974). The Mexican American education study (Reports 1–6). Washington, DC: U.S. Department of Health, Education and Welfare.

Watrous, J. A. (1909). Memoirs of Milwaukee County (Vol. 1). Madison, WI: Western Historical Society.

The Knowledge Base of Bilingual Education

Richard Ruiz (2008)

We know a lot about bilingual education. In large part, that is because we know a lot about those subjects that inform it—first language development, second language acquisition, bilingualism and bilingualization, pedagogy, the relation of parents, communities and schools, the management of policy to program to practice, literacy and biliteracy, and assessment. It is important to recognize this, since a popular objection to moving ahead with what we know are best practices is that we need more studies, that "the experts disagree" on how best to educate English learners. No one is opposed to more studies; these would continue even if we were. But what is clear is that there is little if any disagreement among researchers on the answers to the major questions about what is best for these students. The just-released *Encyclopedia of Bilingual Education* compiled and edited by Josúe González is the latest piece in a growing body of evidence that we not only know a lot, but we know, and have known for some time, more than enough to move ahead. We might call this the knowledge base of bilingual education, and we can visualize that it rests on the following principles:

- Bilingualism enriches; bilinguals and language diversity are resources that benefit the society as a whole.
- For all students, first language development is crucial for language development in general, and significant for further cognitive development.
- Language is best acquired when it is not the target of direct instruction.
- The best conditions for the promotion of language development in classrooms are those that (a) provide many and varied opportunities to use the language for significant purposes; (b) emphasize communication over form; (c) are not rigidly organized; (d) are based on student interests; and (e) are challenging without producing anxiety in students.
- In situations where students are acquiring a second or additional language, the most promising pedagogy is one that (a) recognizes and takes advantage of the cognitive and linguistic capacity that the child already possesses through the first language; (b) provides and promotes a variety

of linguistic opportunities; (c) integrates language and subject matter teaching and learning; and (d) uses the cultural background of the child as an educational resource.

There is overwhelming consensus on these principles among researchers; yet, what passes for policy and practice on the education of bilinguals and English learners in the United States presents a different picture. I will go further and say that what researchers in this field say should prevail in our development of policy and programs serves to tell the policymakers what *not* to do: there is an inverse relation between research and policy development in bilingual education in the United States. I can illustrate it using the following table.

The relation of research to policy development in bilingual education in the US

Predominant research trend	↔	Predominant policy trend
Primacy of L_1 development for all students	L_1 development	Primacy of L_1 development for Anglophones, L_2 for all others
Longer for academic development	Timeframe	As short as politically possible
Mediation and appreciation	Role of Culture	Neglect, if not acculturation
All students	Targets	Non-anglophones
Multiple/strength-based/ongoing	Assessment/ID	One-shot/high stakes
$L_1 + L_2 + L_x$	Medium	L_2 (English) predominantly
Enrichment/Additive	Character	Compensatory/Subtractive
Home ↔ School	Home ↔ School	Home → School
Resource/Right	Orientation	Problem
Colin Baker Virginia Collier/Wayne Thomas Jim Cummins Eugene Garcia Kenji Hakuta Stephen Baker Wallace Lambert Lily Wong-Fillmore	Principals	Keith Baker/Adriana de Kanter William Bennett Linda Chavez Rosalie Pedalino Porter Ronald Reagan Ron Unz

I will comment on the final row in the table after a discussion of the various topics. As a basic framework for my review, all of the references for my discussion will come exclusively from the authors included in the *Encyclopedia*. The following sections are ample support for my contention that we have a sufficient knowledge base to proceed with the establishment of programs that benefit students, programs that unfortunately are precluded for many of us.

L₁ Development

The research on this critical aspect of the education of English learners is considerable and growing. It proceeds from a variety of disciplines—linguistics, psychology, education, anthropology, cognitive science, and others—and all of these are represented in the *Encyclopedia*. The early research on brain plasticity and lateralization by Lenneberg, Penfield and others was important in shaping our view of how the brain processes linguistic data. Chomsky later introduced the concept of the *language acquisition device*, essentially a black box input/output model designed to help visualize how language proficiency is a process internal to the mind, as opposed to earlier behaviorist models that saw language learning as habit formation. Those researchers interested in bilingualism and second language acquisition used Chomsky's cognitive approach to construct theories of bilingual development. Much of this research, as in the early work of Lambert, Troike, Wong-Fillmore and others has been elaborated and largely confirmed by later researchers such as Thomas and Collier, Hakuta, Cummins, and Krashen; these and other writers have also pointed out how their work relates to the education of children growing up in multilingual contexts.

As Iliana Reyes (pp. 78–81) concludes, this whole body of research is clear in its implications that first language development is crucial for further language and cognitive development; yet, there are those who have influenced the formulation of school policies who insist that this need not be a concern for language minority children. At best they are indifferent to first language development for non-Anglophones, suggesting that the acquisition of English is the *sine qua non* for school success; often, they are hostile to the possibility that these children may retain their first language since this would indicate lack of political assimilation. Therefore they could advocate a policy that would emphasize English acquisition over all else, including retention and further development of the first language. A catalyst for development and implementation of this policy at the national level were the rules and regulations promoted by William Bennett, Secretary of Education under Ronald Reagan, who had declared that bilingual education was "wrong and against the American concept." Bennett's view that alternatives to bilingual education, alternatives that used only English as a medium of instruction, needed to be encoded in law created the impetus for movements calling for English immersion curriculum for language minority students (see the entry on Bennett by Gregory Pearson, pp. 57–58).

Entries on English Immersion (Kellie Rolstad, pp. 259–264) and the English for the Children campaign (Eric Johnson, pp. 256–259) describe the arguments used by proponents for an all-English or English-predominant curriculum for non-Anglophones. Ron Unz, a California scientist who is the most visible of the English immersion advocates, clearly had no research or theoretical basis for advancing his argument. He aligned himself closely with US English, an organization founded by Senator S. I. Hayakawa and briefly headed by Linda Chavez, a conservative activist appointed by President Reagan to several positions (see her entry by Gregory Pearson, pp. 127–128). Since the mission of US English is to make English the official language of the United States, Unz' ties with it is seen as evidence that his was more a political and ideological agenda than an academic one. Keith Baker and Adriana de Kanter, two analysts at the US Department of Education in the late 1970s and early 1980s, did offer research support for their advocacy; however, their argument appears to be based on a misinterpretation of the Canadian experience of French immersion for English speaking children. While they cite research for their views, they misapply it to the case of the United States. Rosalie Pedalino Porter also cites the Canadian immersion programs as evidence of the superiority of English immersion in the United States (see the entry by Sarah Catherine Moore, pp. 660–661, especially the reference to Porter's "declaration"). Many of these authors also refer to the "success" of programs after the passage of Proposition 227 in California, an argument that is directly refuted by Stephen Krashen (see his entry by Jeff MacSwan, pp. 413–414) among others included in the *Encyclopedia*. Jim Crawford, a journalist and bilingual education advocate (see Mary Carol Combs, pp. 183–185) has included an exhaustive compilation of the arguments and counterarguments on the question of first language development and the putative successes of English-immersion education on his website.

The *Encyclopedia* presents a clear picture on the question of first language development: research urges us to give it the highest possible priority for all children, while the predominant policy in the United States, promoted by English-only and English immersion advocates, accepts this as a principle but only for English-speaking students. All others can forego their L_1 as long as they are replacing it with English.

Research on first language development has been critical for the advance of bilingual education research and theory. Some of the central concepts in the bilingual literature that derive from that on first language are discussed in the following subsections.

Critical period. A number of researchers have contributed to our understanding of how language is best acquired at certain times in the life cycle. This research is commonly referred to collectively as the *critical period hypothesis*. In his lead entry on this topic, John Petrovic (pp. 194–197) discusses the work of some of the early neurolinguists such as Lenneberg and Penfield, and extends his analysis to the more recent work of Steven Pinker. While the work is controversial because of the constraints on experiments with children, Petrovic suggests that the research points to a period between age 6 and puberty in which normal language acquisition becomes increasingly difficult. Perhaps even more tenuous are conclusions about a critical period for the acquisition of a second language (L_2). He, along with other researchers such as Hakuta and colleagues, recommend that we think in terms of an optimal period rather than an inflexible critical period for L_2 acquisition. Still, while most agree that language acquisition would be best started at an early age, there is much evidence in the research that adults are quite efficient learners of language (cf Eric Johnson's discussion, pp. 303–304): we should not use age as an excuse to keep language learning opportunities from anyone of any age.

Code-switching. Code-switching (CS) is one of the most prevalent and natural behaviors among "natural" bilinguals. Concepts such as parallel-channel processing and matrix language and distinctions such as that between inter- and intra-sentential CS have been formulated, debated and refined from very early on. In his entry, Rudy Troike (pp. 142–147) describes the research on this phenomenon and corrects the record with respect to its character and significance: CS is not only prevalent, but, contrary to popular conception as well as some of the earliest writings about it, it is evidence of a high level of proficiency and extreme linguistic sophistication in *both* languages. This is so because bilinguals exhibit great sensitivity to the rules of the languages in and out of which they are switching; these switches are possible only if there is also deep competence in both languages. Troike gives examples from various languages and cites many studies (e.g. by Rodolfo Jacobson, Carol Myers-Scotton, Shana Poplack and others) to support his claim. Jo Anne Kleifgen's analysis (pp. 226–229) that CS is a skill that continues to develop in bilinguals as they mature is consistent with Troike's discussion. Iliana Reyes (pp. 78–81) also notes that CS is common in the development of bilingual proficiency, and highlights its social significance as a way to reinforce group identity. Likewise, a number of other writers, including Chris Faltis (pp. 161–163), Josué González (pp. 238–240), and Kathy Escamilla and Susan Hopewell (pp. 713–719) discuss CS as a central phenomenon in bilingual development; they also all agree that it is an indicator of expanded language resources rather than some sort of deficit. At the very least what this body of research tells us is that we can dismiss claims that CS is somehow an indicator of some kind of linguistic or cognitive deficiency. CS should be recognized by teachers and the society at large as the valuable skill that it is; we then need to construct learning approaches that take advantage of it.

Interlanguage. Interlanguage is the system of communication used by bilinguals as they become competent speakers of a second or additional language. Research on interlanguage has focused on the nature and rate of acquisition of the "target" language—the language the learner is in the process of acquiring. However, it also contains features of the L_1, and can even have unique features of its own. Interlanguage is a meta-state in which there is dynamic movement in the development of the first language and acquisition of the second. At the same time, Peter Sayer's entry on the concept (pp. 404–406) explains the phenomenon of fossilization, where progress in the interlanguage toward acquiring the target language has become stuck; he cautions that bilingual pedagogy and curriculum development should consider how the language development needs of these students can be met.

Timeframe

Over the past twenty years, as ideological battles over bilingual education have shifted the emphasis away from the use of first language as a medium of instruction for non-Anglophones toward straight-for-English approaches, willingness to use public funds for long-term bilingual programs has waned significantly. Currently, many states have limits on the amount of time a student can be served by a special curriculum using the L_1 while developing competence in L_2. In states such as Arizona and California, voter initiatives promoted by anti-bilingual education advocates limit most children to one year in most cases (see entries on Proposition 203 in Arizona by Wayne Wright [pp. 684–688] and Kate Mahony [pp. 688–691] and on Proposition 227 in California by Grace McField [pp. 691–696] and Margarita Jimenez Silva [pp. 696–699]). These limits are based on no identifiable research, but rather on anecdotes about real or imagined cases of immigrant ancestors or friends who learned English quickly once immersed in the society. Instead, the best research available points strongly to a longer timeframe for developing language proficiency necessary for higher-order language tasks and school success. The work of Virginia Collier and Wayne Thomas (see the entry by Judith Munter and Josefina Tinajero, pp. 153–154) and Jim Cummins (entry on Cummins' BICS/CALP distinction by Kellie Rolstad and Jeff MacSwan, pp. 62–65]) suggests that perhaps as much as 6 years or longer, depending on a variety of social factors, could be required for students to acquire sufficient language skills to succeed in an all-L_2 classroom.

In her entry on how long it takes a non-English speaker to learn English, Michelle Kuamoo (pp. 249–253) refutes the notion that these students are able to become proficient in English enough to compete with age-level peers in as little as a year. Her discussion includes the work of Genessee on brain research and Stephen Krashen on the difference between first and second language acquisition. The arguments for a limited time frame are countered not merely by these theorists, but also by evidence that post-227 (California) and post-203 (Arizona) English immersion programs have failed miserably to reclassify students as fluent English speakers in one year. Yet, since this notion fits well with the ideology of the day, these programs continue, bolstered by declarations by advocates who claim their success even as the data show otherwise.

Role of Culture

In their work on "funds of knowledge" for teaching, Luis Moll and his colleagues (see Mary Carol Combs' entry at pp. 558–559) promote the view that the cultural knowledge of the child should be an essential building block in school curriculum. They advocate a Vygotskian socio-cultural approach that sees the culture of the child as an important mediating structure for the construction of further knowledge in the learner. These notions are also at the heart of what are sometimes called "culturally-responsive pedagogy" or "culturally competent teaching" (see this discussion by Heriberto Godina at pp. 203–206). Such approaches to pedagogy construct curriculum from the prior experiences of the children, and create the possibility for the local community to be an important part of the teaching and learning experience. This is effected by both inviting people from the community (parents, local citizens, others) into the classroom and by having teachers and others from the school explore the communities around the school in which they are largely strangers. The resulting inter-penetration creates a partnership for learning in which students reinforce their own identities and understand and appreciate the role of school in their education. An important dimension of this learning experience based on cultural mediation is the language of the child. To the extent that it is valued and used in the school for important functions, the mediating role of culture is enhanced. To the extent that it is devalued and excluded, it created anxiety, ambivalence, and conflict that militates against learning.

These important insights from research on schools and their communities are frequently negated by the practice of schools that are influenced by negative attitudes toward multiculturalism. Josúe González (pp. 200–203) explains some of this mentality in his entry on cultural deficit and cultural mismatch theories. The view that language minority children bring a "culture of poverty" with them to school, a culture encoded in their non-English language, reinforces the promotion of pedagogies designed to erase the handicap. The notion that we may want to "affirm diversity," as firmly asserted by Sonia Nieto in her writings (see entry by Marietta Saravia-Shore, pp. 603–604), is alien to that way of thinking—sometimes inspired by xenophobia, sometimes by a genuine misunderstanding of the value of the cultural knowledge brought into the school by these children.

Targets

The United States has been slow to recognize the importance of multilingual proficiency in a rapidly globalizing world. We are hard-pressed to find a genuinely monolingual context anywhere, yet the United States still lags behind much of the world in providing language learning opportunities to its citizens. Foreign language study, as Elsie Szecsy points out (pp. 554–558), has not kept up with higher education enrollments in the US. And even so, our collective lack of interest in such study translates into dismal fluency levels. Larisa Warhol (pp. 497–501) attributes much of our problem in this area to a "lack of commitment to language diversity." The resulting monolingual mentality reinforces the idea that only English is needed to succeed in the world; this in turn gives legitimacy to the attitude that only non-English speakers need to be involved in bilingual education, since its primary purpose should be to teach English to those who do not have it. So, while researchers extol the virtues of "dual language" or "two way" or "double immersion" bilingual programs in which everyone, everyone, has the best opportunity to become proficient in a second language (see Grace McField, pp. 229–232), our ideology limits the targets of these programs to non-Anglophones. When such a limitation exists, where we create programs for the "needy" among us, those programs are almost always treated as compensatory, and are therefore less successful than they would be otherwise.

Assessment

Kate Menken, in her entries on High Stakes Testing (pp. 350–353) and on federal testing requirements (pp. 604–607), as well as her recent book on US policy, chronicles the effects of these tests on language minority children: higher failure and drop-out rates, higher assignments to remedial groups, placements in special needs classrooms, higher subscriptions to GED programs, and others. In large part this is because of testing in the child's second language, administered by those who have no expertise in the child's first language. The enactment of the Bush administration's education law, No Child Left Behind (NCLB), accelerated the proliferation of state accountability systems that had high stakes tests at their center. Unfortunately, while NCLB placed extreme demands on children and their schools, it did not provide the adequate resources that would constitute a real opportunity to learn for them. As an example, the criteria promulgated on highly qualified teachers (HQTs) used by most states for certification purposes say nothing about knowledge, proficiency or promotion of the child's non-English language. This is understandable since, as Wayne Wright reminds us (pp. 607–616), NCLB has totally expunged the word "bilingual" from the federal lexicon: "Absent from Title III [Formerly Title IV—the Bilingual Education Act] are any recognitions of the benefit of bilingual education and bilingualism, issues of cultural differences, or the need for multicultural understanding." The result is the certification of teachers for these students who need know nothing about their language needs. At a time when researchers call even more urgently for assessment for all children that is continuous, formative, "authentic," on-going, and multiple, especially for children learning English, the nation is rushing headlong toward one-shot tests that have harsh effects on the lives of these families.

Medium

We have already mentioned the rapid movement toward English-only or English-predominant education for language minority students in the

US. This development is the opposite of what the research demonstrates are superior approaches, and the opposite of what is happening in much of the rest of the world. As societies in Asia, Africa, the Caribbean and other parts of North America pursue opportunities for all of their citizens to develop greater and more formal capacities in multiple languages, the US has aggressively promoted, sometimes through legislation with harsh sanctions, English-only media of instruction for all, including language minority students. State laws in California and Arizona, passed by voter initiative, are among the strictest in the country in this regard (see entries on Proposition 203 and Proposition 227 in Arizona and California, respectively). Researchers such as Wallace Lambert and Richard Tucker pioneered programs of 2-way, also called dual-language, bilingual education in North America in the early 1960s. From that time, studies consistently show positive results for both language and content learning. Exemplary programs such as those at the Oyster School in Washington DC (see Paquita B. Holland's discussion at pp. 638–643) and Coral Way Elementary School in Miami, the first Spanish-English public school bilingual program in the country, have a long history of high student performance in both bilingual proficiency and academic success. The common characteristics of these programs are (1) use of two or more languages as media of instruction in more or less equal proportion; (2) both minority and majority students learning together, each receiving instruction in their first and second languages; (3) language and cultural awareness and appreciation goals, with strong parental and community support (see Grace McField's entry, pp. 229–232). It remains to be seen whether the accumulation of such results will eventually change the mood of the states toward language proficiency opportunities for all.

Character

Much bilingual education in the world is in private schools for elites (see Colin Baker's essay, pp. 871–878). These groups have discovered, perhaps only intuitively, what the research shows, that there are cognitive, social, academic, cultural, and economic advantages that come with multiple language proficiency (see the entry by Geri McDonough Bell, pp. 149–153). This is what Wallace Lambert perceived in his early studies in the 1960s of students in the St. Lambert School immersed in a bilingual program. He called this phenomenon "additive" because he saw that many non-language advantages came along with gaining a minority language for majority students. The opposite of this, "subtractive" bilingualism, attended programs where the object was to supplant the first language of language minority students with a second language. Josúe González' discussion of additive and subtractive programs (pp. 10–13) focuses on the treatment of the first language: when it is viewed as a deficit, a handicap, it follows that the school program will have the goal of its subordination, if not elimination; as an advantage, the purpose of the program will be to cultivate and expand it. One is a compensatory program for the "needy," the other an enrichment program for the gifted. As already mentioned, while the research from around the world points us to enrichment, our policies and program development in bilingual education reflect an increasingly compensatory character.

Home-School Isomorphism

The previous discussion on the role of culture is closely related to this topic. The predominant view of the role of parents and the community in schools is reflected in the phrase "parental involvement." This conveys the sense that what is important for the success of children, especially minority children, is that their home experiences start to reflect and reinforce their experiences in school. What's more, the learning structures of school should be transported to the home and community. In other words, since all of the educational value lies in what happens in school, the home should do its best to imitate it. For example, the practice of formal reading and the provision of a definite study space for children is considered an important part of parenting designed for academic success. This is an asymmetrical relationship in which the home and community are in the subordinate position, and where the required change is one-way. To the extent that this is a characteristic of bilingual programs, the approach to parental involvement is consistent with the view that there is little of value in the homes of language minority children. The opposite view is that the children bring many strengths with them to school, having learned a lot from home and community about how to learn and act. The social networks that are part of this community can be used with profit by the school if only they started with another attitude. Heriberto Godina's discussion of cultural capital (pp. 197–199) is useful in this regard, as is the previously mentioned discussion of the funds of knowledge approach. This latter view creates a greater sense of partnership and mutual sharing of valuable knowledge that leads to an enhanced learning environment for children.

Policy Orientation

All we have said so far about the role of research in policy development in bilingual education points to a clear conclusion: as much as researchers overwhelmingly demonstrate the superior results of programs of first language development that treat the first language of children as an advantage to cultivate within a new context that values parents and communities, the policies and programs that we have developed reflect an opposite view—that the language and cultural backgrounds of the child are problems to be solved, if not handicaps to be eradicated. This view is deeply embedded in policies directed at the education of language minority students. In those states where bilingual education is still allowed, it is transitional and largely subtractive in nature. Luis Javier Rangel-Ortiz relates such policy orientations to relations of power (pp. 472–476). In his discussion of the development of national education policy during his tenure in Washington, Gene Garcia (pp. 377–386), Director of the Office of Bilingual Education and Minority Language Affairs (OBEMLA) during the Clinton Administration, assesses the effect of policy developments on programs and practice. It should be noted that, for the brief period between 1994 and 2001, the Bilingual Education Act characterized language diversity in the United States as a "national resource." Unfortunately, in spite of the hopes that many of us had for support for bilingual education from the Bush Administration, what became Title III of NCLB was highly disappointing. Essentially, the word bilingual was absent from the law and from the priorities of the new Department of Education: OBEMLA was replaced by the Office of English Language Acquisition, signaling an ominous move towards English-only instruction for language minority students. It represents a reversal from viewing non-English languages as "national resources" to seeing them as "problems" as they had for much of our legal history. One of the hopes some of us have in a change of administrations in Washington is that we might once again see the value of language diversity and act to create better educational experiences for language minority students in that spirit.

Final Notes

There are many topics I have not been able to cover and many authors I have not been able to cite in this short review. Students of bilingual education interested in history, critical court decisions, curricular design, language revitalization, pedagogical approaches, specific cases and bilingual program characteristics and a host of other issues will find them in this valuable resource. There is an extensive and very helpful index at the end of the second volume. Most of the entries have fairly standard titles, so they can be easily found in the alphabetical layout. As a person interested in bilingual education as a global phenomenon, I was disappointed that there was only one entry (by Colin Baker) that dealt extensively with this topic. But in an encyclopedia of more than 1000 pages it may be unfair to complain about a lack of entries. I found the appendices at the end, many of them comprising original texts of historical documents, very useful; I also enjoyed reading the biographies of some of the important figures in bilingual education.

The *Encyclopedia of Bilingual Education* is a massive undertaking; the editor, who is also an author of many entries, has created a valuable resource for those of us who have desired a comprehensive repository of essential information in our field. It represents an important advance in the continuing development of the knowledge base of bilingual education.

About the reviewer

Richard Ruiz received degrees in French Literature at Harvard College and in Anthropology and Philosophy of Education at Stanford University. He was Head of the Department of Language, Reading and Culture in the College of Education of the University of Arizona from 1993 to 1999; he is currently a professor in that department, with faculty affiliations in the Interdisciplinary Graduate Program in Second Language Acquisition and Teaching and in the Program on Comparative Cultural and Literary Studies. He has been a consultant to the governments of Mexico, Australia, Guatemala, Bolivia, the Federated States of Micronesia, the Netherlands Antilles (Aruba and Curaçao), Israel, South Africa, and native communities in the United States and Canada. He was editor of the *Bilingual Research Journal* for three years, and serves on the editorial boards of *Urban Education, Teaching Education, Journal of Teacher Education*, and the *Review of Educational Research*. He has been Chair of the Standing Committee on the Role and Status of Minorities in Educational Research and Development and Chair of the Social Justice Action Committee of the American Educational Research Association (AERA). In June 2001, he was appointed Director of Social Justice of the American Educational Research Association.

González, Josúe (Ed.) (2008) *The Encyclopedia of Bilingual Education*
(2 volumes). SAGE Publications
Pp. xvi + 1008   ISBN 978-1412937207
Reviewed by Richard Ruiz
University of Arizona
November 8, 2008

Part 3

Language Fun

Taking 'Language Fun' Seriously
Perry Gilmore, Brendan H. O'Connor and Lauren Zentz

The Parable of the Pigs
(1992/1996) unpublished

Jesus Was Bilingual
(2003) unpublished

The Ontological Status of Burritos
(2008) unpublished

Team building with Indigenous teachers from Mexico, Project SEED (Scholarships for Education and Economic Development), University of Arizona, Tucson, AZ 2011
Courtesy of Janelle Johnson.

Taking 'Language Fun' Seriously

Perry Gilmore, Brendan H. O'Connor
and Lauren Zentz

Richard Ruiz loved to play. He played with words, ideas, puzzles and on intramural sports teams with players half his age. He also kept a steady supply of chocolate (M&Ms were prized) in his office to tempt and delight any passersby or visitors. In this section, three previously unpublished papers reveal a side of Richard that many of his colleagues, friends and students cherished, but that was not always obvious in his scholarly works.

Richard was an extraordinarily funny person! An erudite scholar recognized for his inspiring writings and the breadth of his knowledge in a broad range of disciplines and subjects, Richard was also widely known for his unique, understated, dry, deadpan, wonderful, and – many would say – quirky humor. It was often difficult to know if he was joking. His sophisticated, wry scholarly wit could catch his audience by surprise. His playful twists of thought were softly spoken, subtle and always delivered in a quiet, matter-of-fact, casual way. Occasionally one might catch a glimpse (he was usually looking down with his head turned slightly away) of his slightly expanding smile and telling wrinkles forming around the corners of his eyes, cues that hinted that he had just made, or was about to make, a joke. His apparent delight in his own play with words, ideas and scholarship was obvious in those small facial signals, frequently accompanied by his quintessential soft chuckle.

Similarly, in the unpublished papers collected in this section, Richard was joking – or was he? Deeply committed to social justice, language equality and bilingual education, in each of the papers that follows he skillfully uses play, humor, satire, parody and his wonderful wit to critique societal ills, expose hypocrisy, and present alternative perspectives that provide new insights and inspire change. Richard had a unique way of using fun and play to turn things around, to highlight contradictions, and to argue for very powerful issues and policies. His humor brings very serious controversial issues to his audiences in very playful and noncontroversial ways.

Throughout history, humor, comedy, parody, irony, exaggeration and satire have been used as social corrective – to illuminate and make visible injustices and to suggest how we might improve the way we live (Combs

& Nimmo, 1996). From comedy in ancient Greece that scorned leaders and gods, to European court jesters in the Middle Ages who performed mocking critiques, from the satirical writings of Jonathan Swift to the modern parodies and social commentaries of Jon Stewart and Stephen Colbert, humor and comedy have provided acceptable ways to confront and ridicule dominant powers.

Richard, following this comedic tradition, had a unique way of using fun and play to argue and advocate for language policy change, to educate, and to build a better community (from university intramural teams to global international education institutions). For him, play was inquiry; fun was an educational tool for provoking new ideas and fresh thought, both within his own intellectual 'in-groups' (cf. Malmqvist, 2015 and Simpson, 2003 on 'humor communities') as well as with potential new members.

One example of the latter was a course he taught, 'Language, Culture and Education through Word Puzzles.' In the syllabus, he writes:

> We will learn some formal linguistics and sociolinguistics in the context of solving, creating, and re-creating (through re-cluing) word puzzles. ... how language play can enhance our proficiency in language and cognition in general ... [we] will draw on constructs in anthropology, linguistics and socio-linguistics such as semantic and lexical alternatives, homonyms, paronyms, homographs, contrast sets, metaphor and metonym ... As far as we know [this is] *the only course on crossword puzzles in the universe.*

In the papers that follow in this section, Richard uses many of these same elements to play with and educate us, his 'humor community,' a group that he felt connected to through 'likemindedness' and 'political affiliation' (Simpson, 2003). The fact that we are so tickled with these pieces indicates that Richard intended them for an audience who generally agreed with him on the importance of bilingual education, cultural diversity, and our professional commitment to reassessing constantly the concepts we create as we attempt to understand the world(s) we study. For those not in on the joke, 'the utterance remains ambivalent, and anxiety and uncertainty follow' (Simpson, 2003: 34).

Richard liked to play, but he was also a truly serious thinker in a world where it is increasingly rare to encounter such a person. He thought deeply and earnestly for a long time about topics he considered important and, once he'd made up his mind, was generally convinced of his conclusions – although, he was willing to admit, someone else might see the matter very differently. He was also thought provoking. He'd ask the most unexpected, original, probing questions of students, colleagues and friends. In all of this, he used his humor to make his reader/listener unpack multiple layers of meaning, digging more deeply into each turn of phrase, metaphoric (and often esoteric) reference, and semantic twist.

His playfulness created a safe space for exploring controversial, challenging and sometimes dangerous ideas. A Batesonian master of play and paradox, he not only signals the iconic message 'this is play'; he also makes us wonder 'is this play?' (Bateson, 1972). To be sure, this was often profound play. At its best it was paradigm-shifting play. It was play that spoke truth to power, a sort of Foucauldian parrhesiastic play. Richard's papers can be viewed as a kind of fearless speech that confronts power for the common good (Foucault, 2001; Gilmore, 2008). But this brand of boldness is clothed in teasing jest, not anger.

Without meaning to sound blasphemous, Richard's parables put us in mind of a famous teller of parables from the ancient Near East, whose sense of the absurdity of human foibles (to wit: 'He sighed deeply and said, "Why does this generation seek after a sign? Truly I say to you, there will be no sign given to this generation"'; Mark, 8: 12) was likewise leavened by deep compassion and understanding. We hope we are not out of place in mentioning that Richard was, among other things, a person of deep faith, a quality that might have surprised some people even more than his sense of humor. In this, he followed the lead of that other great jester of the poor and outcast, St Francis of Assisi, who urged his companions, 'Preach always. If necessary, use words.' To use words in a heavy-handed manner was not Richard's way. He did indeed preach a message of justice, equity and respect in his writings, but rather than being didactic or self-righteous, preferred to use 'turned-over words,' as Bambi Schieffelin (1986) observed of the Kaluli of Papua New Guinea – expressions whose surface meaning may be obscure, but whose true force is apparent to the intended audience. A largely self-taught scholar of theology and biblical translation, Richard's mastery of genres such as the parable is striking, making his wit shine all the more brightly.

In 'Jesus Was Bilingual,' Ruiz invokes the paramount parable-teller himself – in part, to lament the misuse of his message and legacy in the service of intolerant agendas and ideologies, past and present, according to which (English) language hegemony is interpreted as evidence of divine will. Characteristically, instead of speaking ill of Christian friends who, he implies, have been led to vote against bilingual and heritage language education because of misinformation, he merely admits to being 'confused and deeply disappointed' at his own ineffectiveness as a bilingual education advocate (p. 216). Then, just as characteristically, in 'turning over' the formulaic phrase 'What Would Jesus Do?,' he gently pushes us to consider where we might find Jesus today, were we courageous enough to look for him, and what his stance on language diversity might be:

His life was spent with the poor and disenfranchised, with the peasants and the sick, with the lepers and blind and other outcasts from society; he railed against the established order, and insisted that the powerless and faceless have access to him. ... While he learned the languages of commerce and of government and of formal religion, he never stopped using his heritage language. He did not insist on a language requirement for entrance into the citizenship of his kingdom. … He should be the poster child for bilingual education.

Richard's brand of satire does not allow us, as proponents of linguistic and cultural diversity in education, to sit comfortably back as he mocks the xenophobia and ignorance of those with the power to shape monoglossic language policies. Rather, he turns the oft-parodied cliché ¿WWJD? (putting his usual translingual spin on things with Spanish question notation) into an opportunity for us to take stock of our lives and consider what it would take to bring them into closer alignment with Jesus's impossible example, whether or not we call ourselves Christians. For, he implies, promoting language diversity and opposing linguistic hegemony can only be seen as a small part of a much, much larger movement toward social justice, one that involves questions of poverty, disenfranchisement, citizenship and access to economic and social capital.

In our efforts to make sense of Richard's multilayered language fun, a continuing challenge is the fact that Richard was über-smart and incredibly well-read and knowledgeable in a wide array of fields, genres and languages. This means that despite the fact that we think we are a part of the in-group that he was writing these pieces for, we still won't always 'get it.' We may only appreciate a portion of his many-layered meanings and double-entendres. As coauthors of this introductory essay, we sought interpretive help from a range of distinguished colleagues and friends who are quite sophisticated in their knowledge of these areas and knew Richard well. Not surprisingly, the people we asked had a wide range of responses and professed little certain insight into the particulars that were stumping us. We all projected our own understandings of Richard and our own research and experiences onto our interpretations of his texts, and we invite you, the reader, to do the same.

'The Parable of the Pigs,' in particular, posed numerous conundrums of interpretation: What are the Wisconsin cheeseheads doing there? Who does Prince William represent? Nevertheless, all among those asked agreed that in this little satirical gem, Richard makes a powerful case that US bilingual education policy is too often bilingual in name only and that authentic bilingual programs are sorely needed. Nancy Hornberger (personal communication) suggests that this parable, originally dated 1992 but revised as late as 1996, refers specifically to changes to US bilingual education policy in the late 1980s, when the Bilingual Education Act (BEA) was amended to allow up to 25% of funding to be used for Special Alternative Instructional Programs (SAIP), which would not necessarily involve any use of students' first language.

Whether or not Ruiz was referring to this particular development, it is clear that the parable skewers what Kenji Hakuta called the problem of 'bad labeling' in bilingual education, according to Hornberger: in other words, calling programs 'bilingual' when they are no such thing (see Hinton, 2015, for a recent, troubling example), and – even worse – supporting monolingual and homogenizing programs with funding designated for bilingual education. Luis Moll (personal communication) points out that the teachers placed in programs funded under the amended BEA were often not bilingual at all. Calling a cow a pig doesn't make it so – or does it? If it happens gradually enough, will people just come to accept the new definition of 'cow' or 'bilingual education'?

As with all worthy parables, however, the most obvious or direct meaning is just the tip of the iceberg. We would argue that the 'The Parable of the Pigs,' while it may refer to historical developments in US language policy, is also a cutting and prescient commentary on the abuse of power/knowledge in education reform (and, perhaps, in human conduct more generally). *Cogito ergo scum*, Richard glosses the cow-to-pig transformation: I know, therefore (I'm) scum. With power and just a little knowledge (a dangerous thing, in the absence of wisdom) I transform an unclean animal – to cite Biblical precedent – into a clean one.

With all that in mind, one need not be familiar with Biblical parables to engage fruitfully with Richard's. In the one-page 'Parable of the Pigs,' Richard took us all on a journey of trying to figure out exactly what he was talking about, as we looked for clues in his professional histories in Wisconsin and Arizona. Readers with histories in both states saw this parable as acerbically appropriate to the past and present contexts that they knew intimately. For example, our consulting colleagues appealed to Richard's work on bilingual education in Wisconsin in the 1970s (Marie Ruiz, personal communication); teacher strikes in Wisconsin in the 1980s (Elizabeth Hubbs, personal communication); the US House of Representatives' passing of HR123, the English Language Empowerment Act; and Richard's publications regarding the nature of 'empowerment' (Ruiz, 1991). Amid all our competing interpretations of this piece, perhaps the best interpretation is simply as Mary Carol Combs (personal communication) put it: 'One of the main points is that no matter how much we might want to retitle or rename something, it nevertheless remains what it is.'

Thus, in his language games, Richard slyly directs our attention to the disruptive consequences of the language games played by those in power. Relabeling a thing cannot, in fact, transform it into something it is not; even a whitewashed tomb may look beautiful on the outside, but it is still full of old bones and uncleanness (Matthew, 23: 27). Empowerment is not empowerment if it does not, in fact, empower; bilingual education is not bilingual if it is monolingual; a cow is not a cow if it is a pig. The problem is that, over time, people might indeed '[get] used to the new streamlined look of their cows' – i.e. their pigs – start to prefer bacon to beef, and so on, because the language games of those with power and voice (Blommaert, 2005; Hymes,

1996) can refocus our view of the world, even if they really can't change one thing into another.

This line of critique is consistent with a broader theme in Richard's scholarly writings, especially his trenchant essay 'The empowerment of language-minority students' (1991), where he takes issue with the arrogance of thinkers or pedagogues, however well-intentioned, who would seek to bestow 'empowerment' as a gift on marginalized people. Richard quotes Paolo Freire to the effect that a movement for *true* educational reform – not the rotted tomb that masquerades as a palace – can come only from within the people themselves, and might entail approaches or solutions that are politically unpopular or counterintuitive to those who presume to turn cows into pigs, *in loco vaca*. Again, in satirizing the politics of language, he prods his readers, the scholarly community, to consider the limits of our own wisdom: How can anyone claim to be 'empowering' disenfranchised people by reducing them to a condition of passivity?

Throughout the pieces in this section, Richard regularly relies on satire, play, his own personal history, and his personal connections with his scholarly community in order to question ideas from the very mundane to the most scholarly. Traveling from the questionable status of the burrito as a sandwich to the life of Jesus, Richard echoes his own published works intended for broader audiences and, throughout, leaves us pondering a series of questions related to voice: Who has the power and responsibility to call out injustice and to work toward justice? How do our naming practices as scholars contribute to or detract from social justice, polyglossic and multicultural education and true empowerment? And how do orientations to language shape the ways in which we understand even the most mundane things of our everyday worlds, such as burritos? We believe that Richard's voice calls us to keep his legacy alive while carrying on this work, as he wryly challenges us to continue to hone our craft and to aim to change our world for the better.

References

Bateson, G. (1972) A theory of play and fantasy. In *Steps to an Ecology of Mind* (pp. 183–198). Chicago, IL: University of Chicago Press.

Blommaert, J. (2005) *Discourse: A Critical Introduction*. New York: Cambridge University Press.

Combs, J.E. and Nimmo, D. (1996) *The Comedy of Democracy*. Westport, CT: Praeger.

Foucault, M. (2001) *Fearless Speech* (ed. J. Pearson). Los Angeles, CA: Semiotext(e).

Gilmore, P. (2008) Engagement on the backroads: Insights for anthropology and education. *Anthropology & Education Quarterly* 39 (2), 109–116.

Hinton, K.A. (2015) 'We only teach in English': An examination of bilingual-in-name-only classrooms. In Y. Freeman and D. Freeman (eds) *Research on Preparing Inservice Teachers to Work Effectively with Emergent Bilinguals* (pp. 265–289). Bingley: Emerald Books.

Hymes, D. (1996) *Ethnography, Linguistics, Narrative Inequality: Toward an Understanding of Voice*. London: Taylor & Francis.

Malmqvist, K. (2015) Satire, racist humour and the power of (un)laughter: On the restrained nature of Swedish online racist discourse targeting EU-migrants begging for money. *Discourse and Society* 26 (6), 733–753.

Ruiz, R. (1991) The empowerment of language-minority students. In C. Sleeter (ed.) *Empowerment Through Multicultural Education* (pp. 217–228). Albany, NY: State University of New York Press.

Ruiz, R. (1992/1996) The parable of the pigs. Unpublished.

Ruiz, R. (2003) Jesus was bilingual. Unpublished.

Ruiz, R. (2008) The ontological status of burritos. Unpublished.

Schieffelin, B. (1986) Teasing and shaming in Kaluli children's interactions. In B. Schieffelin and E. Ochs (eds) *Language Socialization Across Cultures* (pp. 165–181). New York: Cambridge University Press.

Simpson, P. (2003) *On the Discourse of Satire: Towards a Stylistic Model of Satirical Humour.* Amsterdam and Philadelphia, PA: John Benjamins.

The Parable of the Pigs
A Story in the Development of US Bilingual Education Policy

Richard Ruiz (1996)

The King of Wisconsin had a dilemma: He hated cows. (Anybody who knows anything about Wisconsin understands immediately how this is a dilemma.) He hated cows and everything about them – how they looked, how they smelled, what they did, the messes they made (iyuch!), and the people who dealt with them. Yet, there were cows everywhere, and the milk-mongers and cheese heads were rapidly increasing in numbers (not so much from within but from without – there was no security at the western and southern borders) and concentrating in their squalid chocolate milk-infested ghettoes.

He called together his closest advisors, his princes and his magicians. They were at a loss on a course of action because Wisconsin was the Land of Enmilkment and the Holy See of Cheese; its motto, seared at birth into the rumps of all animals (four-footed or two-footed) was 'Smell our Dairy Air': Wisconsinites were proud of their kingdom, and they did whatever they needed to keep the yogurt fanatics and margarine peddlers out; they named their sons 'Bull' and 'Chip' and their daughters 'Daisy.' The solution to the dilemma finally came from young Prince William, the King's favorite son. And so the King acted on the brilliant plan.

He told the farmers to replace all cows with pigs (he liked pigs), in the following way: when a cow was eliminated from the herd, by sale or slaughter or some other form of natural or artificial termination, in its place the farmer was to insert a pig. But the genius of William's plan was this: the pigs were not just to hold the cow's place (*in loco vaca*), they were (henceforth and for all eternity) to be called (and therefore to become) 'cows' (*cogito ergo scum*). For each transmogrified 'cow' the King would pay a healthy subsidy.

Wisconsinites soon got used to the new streamlined look of their cows, and after a time developed the technology for extracting milk from them; they even started to favor bacon and oink over beef and moo. Thus, in a generation, Wisconsin had eliminated all cows, but the King could still say he had 'cows.' The King was happy, while the bulls plotted their return.

Jesus Was Bilingual

Richard Ruiz (2003)

International Perspectives on Heritage Language Education[1]

Jesus was bilingual.[2]

First, the statement makes reference to the so-called 'historical Jesus' about which much has been written. Perhaps the best-known among the recent works is John P. Meier's *A Marginal Jew: Rethinking the Historical Jesus*, in two volumes (1991). His is a purely secular treatment, although he makes extensive use of a wide range of literature from historical to archaeological to theological to poetic. His cautious conclusion, found in a section of Volume I called 'What language did Jesus speak?', is that Jesus spoke his heritage language, Aramaic, for most purposes, but that he also had some knowledge of Hebrew and Greek: 'In a quadrilingual country, Jesus may indeed have been a trilingual Jew. ...' (p. 268). While he is not completely convinced on this question, he cites many others who have more definite views on Jesus' language proficiency. There is strong evidence – historical, sociological, and exegetical – that Jesus knew and used a number of languages beyond his native Aramaic, including Greek (Argyle, 1955–1956; Taylor, 1944–1945) and Hebrew (Birkeland, 1954; Lapide, 1972–1975); the evidence is less strong for his knowledge of Latin, the lingua franca of most of the Roman Empire of which his native Palestine was a part (see 'The languages of Palestine in the first century A.D.' in Fitzmyer, 1979: 29–56). Recent scholars, re-evaluating the sociolinguistic context in which Jesus lived, characterize him more definitely as trilingual: 'Although it is very likely that Jesus could speak Greek as a second language and possible that he debated with the scribes in Hebrew, he seems to have done most of his teaching in Aramaic' (Fiensy, 1996: 83).

Secondly, I use the term 'bilingual' loosely, in keeping with popular convention: it means more than one language, regardless of how many. Consider the number of 'bilingual' (or 'dual' language) programs in the US that use more than two languages as media of instruction as evidence of this. The phrase makes use of synecdoche and understatement, but that is very much in keeping with biblical traditions and the teachings of Jesus himself. Perhaps I should say that Jesus was at least bilingual, but that is a cumbersome phrase and even more so as a title of a talk or paper. More etymologically correct would be 'Jesus was a polyglot,' but hardly anyone knows, much less uses, that term. As it is, the title, flawed as it might be, has the desired effect (see below).

Thirdly, since I may be criticized by my conservative and orthodox Christian friends for being theologically incorrect, I should reiterate that the phrase refers to the historical Jesus in his human aspect: he was born at a certain place and time that gave him a particular heritage language, with other languages important enough to his earthly existence to be known and used by him to some degree. He had what looks by all accounts to be a typical Jewish upbringing for the time. He grew up in the family business in Galilee, and (except for an early excursion out of country that an infant would hardly remember) did not travel much until his last few years, when he became a very public speaker. His audiences, by account of the historians, were mainly poor and working-class Arameans, though he also had significant interactions with Greek and Hebrew speakers as well. We can infer, and the consensus of the academics and theologians seems to be, that he spoke and taught principally in Aramaic, but that he also knew and used Greek and Hebrew. His bi- (tri-) lingualism was a result of what Krashen (Ramos & Krashen, 1997) calls *de facto* bilingual education, and it appeared to serve him well. Of course, in the context of orthodox Christian belief, to say that Jesus *was* anything is infelicitous if not completely wrong: 'Jesus *is* bilingual' is the better phrase, since he is not only still alive but he speaks to every person and language group in their own language. We should note that John's gospel refers to Jesus as The Word of God, and the Bible is often called 'the Word of God in the words of men.' What this implies is that the differences in the experience that human communities have of God is influenced by the differences in their languages, which are a dimension of their cultural traditions. The fact that the Bible has been translated into numerous languages, and continues to be so, suggests acceptance of the notion that a diversity of languages allows for the possibility of multiple perspectives on God. As an example, the term λογος, translated 'Word' in most English Bibles, is rendered 'Verbo' in most Spanish translations, suggesting action in a way obscured by the English.

Fourthly, I should explain how this title came to be. I used this phrase in remarks I made in September of 2000 in my role as respondent at a Symposium in Tucson on the subject of a school program in that state once known as '1c' (about which my colleague Mary Carol Combs and her collaborators have written much; Combs *et al.*, 2005). Several people had told their stories about how they felt when they and their Hispanic schoolmates were segregated in their own classrooms because they spoke Spanish. The program operated in Southern Arizona for some 40 years from the early

1920s. A major motivation for the symposium was to discuss whether the effect of passing Proposition 203 (which would end bilingual education and place non-English speaking children in separate classrooms in order to 'immerse' them in English) would be to return to the days of 1c. Since it was less than a month before the election, the political atmosphere was thick with sloganeering and campaign rhetoric ('English for the Children,' 'Blessed with Bilingual Brains,' etc.). I recalled the sorts of slogans attributed to Senator Hayakawa, founder of US English and first mover of the initial federal English Language Amendment in 1981. In his efforts to rally the official English/English-only troops to pass a Constitutional English Language Amendment through the Congress, he borrowed a phrase from H.L. Mencken: 'If English was good enough for Jesus Christ it's good enough for me.' Although popularly attributed to Mencken, I have not yet been able to find this quote in any of his writings. Regardless of attribution, it has been used several times by members of Congress (including the late Sonny Bono of California) and others who are opposed to bilingual education and in favor of making English the official language of the nation. While this retort can be viewed as whimsical, the amount of space devoted to the discussion of the religious, spiritual and moral implications of English use in Mencken's *The American Language* (1919) testifies to the seriousness with which the connection has been made. These early discussions should be seen in the context of the colonial power of England up to the middle of the 20th century and the role that English played in the hegemony that resulted. Simon Winchester, in his re-telling of the tales of intrigue and murder in the writing of the *Oxford English Dictionary* (1998), relates a series of discussions within the British Philological Society surrounding the development of the OED in 1857. These were led by the Dean of Westminster, Dr Trench, who 'firmly believed ... that some kind of divine ordination lay behind what seemed then the ceaseless dissemination of the English language around the planet. God, who in that part of the London society was of course firmly held to be an Englishman, naturally approved the spread of the language as an essential imperial device; but he also encouraged its undisputed corollary, which was the worldwide growth of Christianity. The equation was really very simple, a formula for undoubted global good: the more English there was in the world, the more God-fearing its peoples would be' (Winchester, 1998: 68). More recently, researchers such as Heath (1981) and Baron (1982) show that the connection between English use and moral standing is still a significant underpinning of the language ideology of English speakers. Although used tongue-in-cheek by Hayakawa, the phrase itself neatly makes the point that many of us have been trying to drive home to the public at large: the most persuasive arguments of the anti-bilingual education lobby are based on historical myths and distortions. Perhaps the most persistent of these is that other groups never received bilingual education, so ¿why should we provide them for Spanish-speakers? Any number of historical works can be cited to refute this historical distortion, yet the myths persist, perhaps because they fit with an ideology that sees the present demographic shifts as undesirable compared to those of the past.

Of course, as a well-established linguist himself, Hayakawa must have understood the irony of using such slogans for his own political purposes. He was known for using other such zingers in other contexts. During the Panama Canal debates during the Carter Administration, he argued against devolvement of the Zone by saying that 'we stole it fair and square.' Mencken also relates another interesting story about Hayakawa when the latter was a young linguist at the Illinois Institute of Technology. Apparently, a young woman who was interested in using linguistics to elevate the status of her profession wrote to Mencken to ask him to come up with an alternative for 'stripteaser.' He wrote back that he could think of no appropriate substitutes, but he suggested a few possibilities, including 'ecdysiast,' which he coined as an adaptation of the Greek *ekdysis*, meaning to molt or shed one's skin. Not pleased with this, the young lady consulted other academics who had become known in the popular press as linguists. Hayakawa, who had just published *Language in Action*, apparently declined the offer to comment. Mencken speculates that it is because 'he had never seen a stripteaser in action and hence had nothing to offer.' With no other possibilities, the young woman chose 'ecdysiast,' a term that remains until the present time as the formal referent for stripteaser. (This discussion can be found in Mencken, 1945: 585).

I must admit to another motivation for the title of my presentation and paper. During the long debates in California and Arizona on official English, bilingual education, and the effects of laws on minority and immigrant populations, one important group has been largely silent: the clergy. What's more, those conservative Christians I have spoken with have been persuaded by their secular conservative friends to vote for initiatives banning bilingual education and heritage language programs. While I understand the political dynamics of such trends in thought, I have been confused and deeply disappointed that my arguments have been so ineffective. Perhaps if we could relate it to that modern phrase, ¿What Would Jesus Do? (¿WWJD?), we might be more persuasive. The answer to that question is best arrived at by seeing what Jesus *actually did* according to the historical and scriptural accounts we have: His life was spent with the poor and disenfranchised, with the peasants and the sick, with the lepers and blind and other outcasts from society; he railed against the established order, and insisted that the powerless and faceless have access to him. He had parents and brothers and uncles and aunts and cousins. Among all of these people he spoke the heritage language of the communities. While he learned the languages of commerce and of government and of formal religion, he never stopped using his heritage language. He did not insist on a language requirement for entrance into the citizenship of his kingdom. He became bilingual in the course of his life by retaining his heritage language and learning others around him. ¿WWJD? He should be the poster child for bilingual education. Perhaps some T-shirts and bumper stickers and buttons hailing the fact that Jesus was bilingual will begin to bring the churches into alignment with the life of Christ and change their answer to the question of WWJD?

Finally, I should explain why the title is appropriate for a discussion of international efforts to use and preserve heritage languages. I attended a conference on language policy in Israel in November 1999. That conference began and ended with the issue of the religio-historical importance of the study of language use practices and policy. It began with an introduction using the Biblical image of the Tower of Babel as way to project the problems we would be dealing with in the symposium. During the three days, we heard about a number of cases of heritage language preservation throughout the world, including South Africa, Australia, Eritrea, Paraguay, Israel, Ireland, Taiwan and various countries in Europe and North America. The last session was highlighted by Christina Bratt Paulston's paper on the languages of 1st-century Palestine (cf Paulston, 2001). She started it by asking the question, 'Why did Jesus speak Aramaic?' Of course, she went on to explain how he probably needed to speak other languages as well, but the interesting question for her was how a minority heritage language in a subjugated country managed to remain the language of everyday life for the inhabitants. What conditions allowed such a language to be transmitted from one generation to another? How was such an additive bilingual environment constructed? The lessons of first century Palestine are perhaps instructive for us as well.

Notes

(1) This is a revision of several presentations: A keynote address to the annual meeting of the California Association for Bilingual Education, Los Angeles, 2 February 2001; a presentation at the University of Arizona Faculty Fellows Speakers Series, Tucson, 8 October 2003. A number of scholars have helped me with references and commentary over the years, most notably Stephen Krashen of the University of Southern California, George [Editor's note: though he did not specify further, Richard undoubtedly refers here to George Spindler, his long-time mentor and friend]

(2) This statement needs some clarification.

References

Argyle, A.W. (1955–1956) Did Jesus speak Greek? *Expository Times* 67, 92–93.

Baron, D. (1982) *Grammar and Good Taste: Reforming the American Language*. New Haven, CT and London: Yale University Press.

Birkeland, H. (1954) *The Language of Jesus*. Oslo: Dybwad.

Combs, M.C., Evans, C., Fletcher, T., Parra, E. and Jimenez, A. (2005) English for the children: Implementing a dual language program in an English-only state. *Language Policy* 19 (5), 701–728.

Fiensy, D. (1996) *The Message and Ministry of Jesus: An Introductory Textbook*. Lanham, MD: University Press of America.

Fitzmyer, J. (1979) *The Semitic Background of the New Testament. Volume II: A Wandering Aramean: Collected Aramaic Essays.* Biblical Resource Series (3rd edn). Grand Rapids, MI: Eerdmans.

Heath, S.B. (1981) English in our language heritage. In C.A. Ferguson and S.B. Heath (eds) *Language in the USA* (pp. 6–20). Cambridge: Cambridge University Press.

Lapide, P. (1972–1975). Insights from Qumran into the languages of Jesus. *Revue de Qumran* 8, 483–501.

Meier, J.P. (1991) *A Marginal Jew: Rethinking the Historical Jesus, Vol. I.* New York: Doubleday.

Mencken, H.L. (1919) *The American Language: An Inquiry into the Development of English in the United States.* New York: Alfred A. Knopf.

Mencken, H.L. (1945) *Supplement I. The American Language: An Inquiry into the Development of English in the United States.* New York: Alfred A. Knopf.

Paulston, C.B. (2001) Multilingualism in Palestine in the first century. In R.L. Cooper, E. Shohamy and J. Walters (eds) *New Perspectives and Issues in Educational Language Policy – a Festschrift for Bernard Dov Spolsky* (pp. 133–143). Amsterdam: John Benjamins.

Ramos, F. and Krashen, S. (1997) Success without bilingual education? Some European cases of de facto bilingual education. *CABE Newsletter* 20 (6), 7, 19.

Taylor, R.O.P. (1944–1945) Did Jesus speak Aramaic? *Expository Times* 56, 95–96.

Winchester, S. (1998) *The Professor and the Madman: A Tale of Murder in the Making of the Oxford English Dictionary.* New York: Harper Collins.

The Ontological Status of Burritos

Richard Ruiz (2008)

A few months ago, a judge in Massachusetts declared that a burrito was not a sandwich.

It is not clear what his credentials were to make this decision. His name (Jeffrey Locke) does not lead me to conclude that he had the kind of intimate personal experience with Mexican food that I and many others like me have had, although I fully acknowledge that names are not a good way to determine national origin or ethnic identification (I went to school with a Mexican American named Plunkett and I work with a Puerto Rican who counts Schwartzkopf as one of his family names). The judge's decision was explicitly legal, but it still brings us to question what social and cultural considerations might have gone into this determination.

It is not new that judges and courts decide questions for which their background may be deemed inadequate. Some of these decisions are much more important than resolving the ontological status of burritos. In 1896, a court decided that a law requiring Black and white people to use separate public facilities was constitutional; the plaintiff was Homer Plessy, a man who was one-eighth Black. In 1927, in a test case challenging the Plessy decision in the area of school segregation, a court decided that a Chinese girl was legally black (actually 'negro,' the term of the day). In 1954, a court in Texas declared that Mexican Americans were Caucasians. (I now know the cause of the brief bout of cold shivers resulting from the chemical reorganization I went through when I became white as a young boy.) In retrospect, many of us would now agree that the judges had no special qualification to decide these questions, and that they were just wrong to boot.

But let me return to the important issue of burritos.

I should have placed the phrase 'Mexican food' in quotation marks in the paragraph above. It is not that I am an essentialist or a culinary snob; I never classify food as 'authentic Chinese' or 'real Mexican.' I eat food; if I like it, I tend to eat it again, even if it's 'not the way my mother made it' or it doesn't fit with my idea of 'what Japanese people really eat.' I figure that if I am eating Chinese food in Tucson, it's probably going to be different from eating it in Shanghai. (Come to think of it, even Chinese people who eat food in Shanghai are probably having a different experience from Chinese people eating Chinese food in Beijing or Hong Kong or Taipei. It makes you wonder what 'Chinese food' is, or whether it is even important to classify food in these ways.) Even further, I have a strong suspicion that if I actually did eat what some would call 'authentic' or 'real' Chinese or Japanese or Nepalese food, I would not like it or, even if I did, my stomach might reject it. This is a strong suspicion not only because I occasionally watch television programs that feature strange and exotic foods from around the world, usually focused on how the US globetrotting gourmet TV host was able to choke down a sea cucumber or a sheep's lung. In fact, the sea cucumber has a special place in my dietary memory. Sometime in the fall of 1992, Kenji Hakuta picked me up at Dulles Airport; I had arrived early for a meeting of his Stanford Working Group that would start the next day. He offered dinner, and we headed to a small restaurant in Chinatown he knew well. He proceeded to order the most outrageous stuff on the menu – chicken feet, pig testicles, crab eyes. He was testing me. We both did ok until we got to the sea cucumber, at which point I excused myself and declared him the winner. It took me a while to recover.

When I was a reservist protecting my country from the communist hordes in a transportation unit located under the Golden Gate Bridge, my friend and fellow reservist Louie Yu took a few of us to lunch at the restaurant of a family friend. There was no menu. Louie ordered for us. I knew what Chinese food was, and I was an expert with chopsticks; further, as a budding ethnographer, I welcomed such an 'authentic' experience. I did not get past my first bite before knowing that if I took a second I might die. I grew up in a home where my mother would chew on a raw jalapeño as a snack, and where it was a sign of great respect and cultural pride that we all ate the hottest chile (now called salsa). But I had never eaten anything approaching the hotness of this food. I am now a little more conscious of where I am on the scale of hot-food eaters.

Talking about my mother gets me back to why I should have placed 'Mexican' in quotes. I never ate a burrito in my home. At least we did not call anything we ate that. A typical mealtime routine in my family would be for us to grab a flour tortilla, fill up the bottomside[1] with beans, add some chile, roll it up and eat it. To the beans, or in their place, we could have added hamburger meat or shredded chicken or any of a number of meat-vegetable combinations. I recognize that some of you reading this would say that I was, in fact, eating a burrito. Fine. Call it what you like. But in my house, this was just a taco, if we called it anything. I know that this is not what they call a taco at Jack-in-the-Box, which I guess requires the following: a corn tortilla, ultra-dry and machine-folded and molded into a shape that easily fits into your hand and into the boxed packaging; some sort of meat and/or vegetable. Cheese is almost always added, as are onions and some salsa – but these are optional as to meeting the basic requirements of taco-ness.

In fact, many Mexicans in my circle would say that 'taco' is metaphorical (actually metonymic – the Mexicans I know tend to be precise in their use of classical root-words), an icon that stands for much more than a piece of food. *Vamos a echarnos un taco*, literally 'let's go throw a taco on ourselves,' means something like 'let's do lunch' or, more liturgically, 'let us break bread together.' Here, no one is really talking about bread. It is a way of indicating an interest in establishing or reinforcing a friendship beyond whatever formal roles the participants may be playing. In this, 'taco' may be sociolinguistically unique; you don't hear people inviting someone to throw an enchilada or tamale (sic) on each other, thankfully. (If they did, I imagine it would be taken as an invitation to some sort of kinky Mexican duel – but that would be different.)

When I was a kid, if someone had told me to eat my burrito, I would have looked at them with bewilderment and perhaps disdain (respectful, if they were older): had I even known where to get one, I certainly knew that a little ass was not for eating. As I grew up and started going to 'Mexican' restaurants, I noticed a number of words on the menu, presumably referring to things to eat, that I had never heard of. 'Tamale' was not hard to figure out, and I have come to accept it as a gringoistic generalization of some English grammatical rule that merely drops the –s if you want to move from plural to singular (in Spanish the singular is 'tamal,' and the pluralization rule in this case is to add –es for phonological and aesthetic reasons). 'Tamale' is now found on the menus of even the most 'Mexican' of restaurants, a concession to popular ignorance, or perhaps another indication of how the colonizers have taken over even our own intimate culture talk. If 'the way to a man's (sic) heart is through his stomach,' then it stands to reason that a major dimension of establishing the colonial mentality is to rename our food: phonology recapitulates psychology (and cardiology).

As for 'mojito' on the menu, I could only guess reluctantly and with much soul searching that it was somehow related to 'mojon,' but I could not imagine that something so scatalogically disgusting could be on a menu.

This all seems to be a digression, but it is not. The judge said that a burrito is not a sandwich. ¿Does that decide the issue? ¿Who decides? ¿Is a burrito, by any other name, still a burrito? Since this is a question about culture and language, perhaps my background in anthropology can help. As a graduate student at Stanford I took some courses with Charles Frake, a well-known cognitive anthropologist (also called an ethnosemanticist). Cognitive anthropologists are interested in what people call things; they go to exotic places like Borneo and New Guinea and Texas to find out local terms for plants and animals and snow; they ask what you call your mother's sister's half-brother's nephew. They do this not only to find out if anyone actually knows the terms, but also to see how important these categories are in the everyday lives of actual people. They see the linguistic code as a reflection of the cognitive code: by studying how we talk, especially how we name things, ethnosemanticists say they can discover how we think, and ultimately how we see the world. So, it seems this is a relevant area for deciding questions about what to call a burrito and if it is significant that we call it a sandwich or something else; in fact, it appears that the case of *Burrito v. Sandwich* drew a few such academic types (including some cooks and other popular culture thinkers) as expert witnesses – Frake unfortunately was not among them, although some blogs included pseudo-philosophical references to Wittgenstein and his ilk.

Frake does not know this, but his course changed my view of the academic life. Up to then I thought academics were strange little people who spent their time in cells thinking about serious but relatively insignificant things and writing books about them. Frake changed all that. He walked in the first day of class dressed like a 60s hippie-surfer, hair barely combed and clothes thrown on to his body directly from a pile somewhere on his floor, I imagined. (I should note, to be fair, that this was in the early 70s, and pretty much everybody looked like that, so it should not have seemed so strange to me.) In the next few weeks he told us that he was an anthropologist because it allowed him to go sailing and drinking in faraway places. He was bewildered as to why Stanford administrators paid him to do these things, and wondered whether he would soon be exposed for the academic goof-off he was. He took to extremes the adage that my friend Bill Trent takes as his guiding motto: If you love what you do, you will never work a day in your life. I can imagine that this is on the Frake coat of arms. Think of this: his most famous article is a linguistic analysis of how to ask for a drink at a bar on a remote island in the Philippine archipelago. Combine this with what all academic researchers know – that the data that appear in our articles represent perhaps 10% of what we actually collect – and you get a sense of how seriously he took his work. I try to think about this in my own work.

That first day of class, he came in lugging a big boxful of obviously heavy stuff. After what then seemed like an uncharacteristically routine period of checking the class roll, he started pulling things out of the box – a tall glass, a Styrofoam cup, a coffee cup, a beer stein, and so on. As he did he asked us to name the items. 'That's a glass.' Right, but then he wanted to know what characteristics of this object 'made' it a 'glass.' The class got into it quickly:

'it's made of glass'
'it has a cylindrical shape'
'its function is to hold liquid'
'it's easy to drink from.'

As we went on and on, he would write things on the blackboard in a kind of shorthand:

'glass' → made of glass + cylindrical + for drinking + for holding liquid + …

When it seemed we had exhausted the category, he took out another item: an object of the same shape and size as the previous one, but with a handle. 'That's a mug.' OK, but ¿what about this object made us call it something different? 'The handle.' More writing on the board:

'glass' → [...] + handle → 'mug'

He took out an object the same shape and size as the previous one, but opaque: 'That's still a mug.' ¿But why, since it is not transparent?

'glass' → [...] +/– made of glass + handle → 'mug'

Another one: same shape, no handle, opaque, Styrofoam – 'That's a cup.' The crucial thing for us here was what it was made of, not necessarily the shape: nobody calls this a 'Styrofoam glass.' All the examples were not as easy as these; the class was divided on whether a 'stein' was different from or a kind of 'mug.' Somebody suggested that it might depend on whether you use it to drink beer or koolaid.

This all went on for a while longer until we started to get his point: what we call things may be somewhat intuitive, but on reflection there may be some structure to all of this. The 'structure' is what he wanted to get at – the cognitive code that unlocks the secret of how we think.

We then discussed the distinction between syntagmatic and paradigmatic conceptions, but I think most of us were lost there. This is what he might have meant: cups, mugs and steins stand in some continuous relation to one another, but glasses and cups diverge enough to be totally different units. The one relation is syntagmatic, the other paradigmatic. (It could be the other way around, or this could be totally off – I am just reporting what I remember. But it could be useful to decide the burrito question, so let's keep it on the table.)

This all has to do with the wonders of structuralism (it was too early in the 1970s to talk of post-structuralism – it might still be too early to talk about it). We got totally into these questions, and we thought the answers had profound consequences for life. ¿Why do brides in Yakan try to grab the house posts as the groom is taking her away after the ceremony, as if she does not want to go (it did not occur to us that she might not)? ¿Why is it important for Lincoln Keiser's vice lords to distinguish between 'humbugging' and 'hustling'? ¿How are sisters metonymic dogs (pets)? ¿Why does one morpheme sometimes represent two phonemes (cat_s and boy_s)? Frake thought this was important, and he told us that Levi-Strauss did too (we found out later that this was not the blue jeans guy). It is important because there is no way to know what people are really doing unless you know what they think, and you find out how they think by how they talk – that's what the ethnosemanticist would say.

Maybe we can now get back to burritos again. Our conclusion could well be that the judge was asked to decide the wrong question: instead of sandwiches and burritos being two different elements in a contrast set, they might better be thought to be instantiations of the same overall concept. Thus, 'sandwich,' 'burrito,' 'taco,' 'torta,' 'antojito,' and perhaps others may be said to participate in the same conceptual universe, what one may call the universe TACO. (Frake would put a lot of triangles on the board, although I was not always sure what they were; I am following his example below, but you will have to figure it out yourself.)

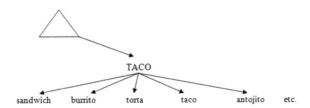

Still, since we feel the need to use different words, the ethnosemanticist would say that therefore we are describing two different realities. The idea that 'a burrito by any other name is still a burrito' is ludicrous: if you call it a burrito, I taste a burrito (actually, a taco); call it a sandwich and my head flips over to gringolandia and I take it with some chai tea or Perrier. Sticks and stones will break my bones, but words will change my taste buds.

So, while burritos are not sandwiches paradigmatically, they are syntagmatically. The judge was only half-right: Burritos are not sandwiches and, at the same time, they are. QED

(Worcester, Massachusetts-AP) November 10, 2006 – This is not generally the stuff of legal scholars. But a Massachusetts judge is using wisdom worthy of Solomon to settle a major dispute.

The question at hand: Is a burrito a sandwich? The judge's ruling: No.

Panera, a popular chain of bakery-cafes, brought the case over one of its locations in a suburban Boston mall. Panera tried to stop Mexican restaurant chain Qdoba Mexican Grill from moving into the mall, arguing its lease bans rival sandwich shops.

Lawyers for Panera went into court insisting a flour tortilla is bread, so a burrito is a sandwich. Qdoba brought in a respected chef who calls that 'absurd.'

Citing the testimony – plus Webster's Dictionary – the judge is ruling in Qdoba's favor.

Arguments spread thick
Rivals aren't serving same food, judge rules

By Jenn Abelson, Globe Staff | November 10, 2006

A burrito is not a sandwich.

That's the culinary ruling of a Worcester judge, ending, for now, a food fight between Panera Bread Co. and Qdoba Mexican Grill.

In issuing his decision, which blocks Panera Bread's attempts to keep the burrito maker off its turf, Worcester Superior Court Judge Jeffrey A. Locke relied on testimony from Cambridge chef Chris Schlesinger and a former high-ranking USDA official, not to mention the Webster's Third New International Dictionary.

The burrito brouhaha began when Panera, one of the country's biggest bakery cafes, argued that owners of the White City Shopping Center in Shrewsbury violated a 2001 lease agreement that restricted the mall from renting to another sandwich shop. When the center signed a lease this year with Qdoba, Panera balked, saying the Mexican chain's burritos violate its sandwich exclusivity clause.

Not so, Qdoba countered, submitting affidavits from high-profile experts in the restaurant and food industry. 'I know of no chef or culinary historian who would call a burrito a sandwich,' Schlesinger said in his affidavit. 'Indeed, the notion would be absurd to any credible chef or culinary historian.'

In his ruling, Locke cited Webster's definition of a sandwich and explained that the difference comes down to two slices of bread versus one tortilla: 'A sandwich is not commonly understood to include burritos, tacos, and quesadillas, which are typically made with a single tortilla and stuffed with a choice filling of meat, rice, and beans,' he wrote.

Panera spokesman Mark Crowley declined to discuss the matter or say whether the St. Louis company planned to appeal the ruling. Mitchell Roberts, manager of the franchise group that runs the Shrewsbury Panera, could not be reached for comment yesterday.

'We were surprised at the suit because we think it's common sense that a burrito is not a sandwich,' said Jeff Ackerman, owner of Qdoba franchise group, known as Chair 5 Restaurants, which plans to open the eatery next year. 'We're just delighted that the experts and judge saw it the same way we did.'

The case, observers say, is less about common sense and more about the high stakes of the Massachusetts restaurant market. Panera Bread, as the established player in the region with 31 locations, is trying to fend off upstart Qdoba, which plans to build at least nine new stores in the market next year, up from eight now. Panera serves up fresh-baked artisan breads and sandwiches, while Qdoba is known for its signature burritos.

'It shows you how competitive the business is when a bakery cafe feels like it's in direct competition with a Mexican chain,' said Ron Paul, president of Technomic Inc., a restaurant consulting firm in Chicago. 'They're fighting for a share of the stomach.'

The fight began earlier this year when Panera learned that the owners of White City Shopping Center were in negotiations to lease space to Qdoba. Panera, citing the exclusivity clause in its lease, sought assurances that White City would not rent to the Mexican chain, saying its burritos, tacos, and quesadillas were all types of sandwiches, according to court papers.

But the landlords refused, and in August they agreed to lease about 2,100 square feet to Qdoba, which planned to spend more than $300,000 on construction. A month later, the landlords sought a court ruling that renting to Qdoba would not breach its lease with Panera.

In turn, Panera filed a counter-claim trying to stop Qdoba from moving into the neighborhood. Qdoba rolled out an all-star line-up of food experts to testify that a burrito is just a burrito.

Schlesinger explained that a sandwich is of 'European roots' and generally recognized as 'two pieces of leavened bread,' while a burrito is 'specific to Mexico' and typically contains hot ingredients rolled into a flat unleavened tortilla.

Schlesinger, whose All Star Sandwich Bar includes items such as the Pastraminator and Meat Loaf Meltdown, also features hot dogs – though they are on the menu with this disclaimer: 'not a real sandwich, but a close friend.'

Judith A. Quick, who previously worked as a deputy director of the Standards and Labeling Division at the US Department of Agriculture, said in her affidavit: 'The USDA views a sandwich as a separate and distinct food product from a burrito or taco.'

Panera, in court filings, argued for a broad definition of sandwich, saying a flour tortilla qualifies as bread and a food product with bread and a filling is a sandwich.

Ultimately, the judge ruled against Panera's request to stop Qdoba from moving into the shopping center. In his eight-page ruling released last week, Locke said Panera had not stipulated that burritos and tacos be covered in the exclusivity clause. Moreover, Panera failed to show that its survival was dependent on preventing Qdoba from opening.

Panera has up to 30 days to file an appeal.

'This was a very important case for us,' said Lawrence Green, a lawyer with Burns & Levinson LLP, which represented Qdoba. 'Panera frankly got a bit greedy here. What are they afraid of?'

Jenn Abelson can be reached at abelson@globe.com.

Note

1   For those of us who know the difference between the top and the bottom of a tortilla, no explanation is necessary.

Part 4

Language Minority Education

Introductory Reflection
Luis C. Moll and D. Lane Santa Cruz

Ethnic Group Interests and the Social Good
(1983) In W. Van Horne (ed.) *Ethnicity, Law and the Social Good* (pp. 49–73).
Milwaukee, WI: American Ethnic Studies Coordinating Committee

The Empowerment of Language Minority Students
(1991) In C. Sleeter (ed.) *Empowerment Through Multicultural Education*
(pp. 217–227). Albany, NY: SUNY Press

Asymmetrical Worlds (2000) unpublished

The Educational Sovereignty of Latino/a Students in the United States
L. Moll and R. Ruiz (2005) In P. Pedraza and M. Rivera (eds) *Latino
Education: An Agenda for Community Action Research* (pp. 295–320). Hillsdale,
NJ: Lawrence Erlbaum

Richard and Luis Moll at Department of Language, Reading and Culture, University of Arizona, Tucson, AZ, May, 2008
Courtesy of Yvonne Gonzalez/Teresa L. McCarty.

Introductory Reflection

Luis C. Moll and D. Lane Santa Cruz

This introduction presents a summary of key ideas or concepts found in the chapters in this section. We will not recapitulate all of Richard's arguments; after all, the chapters that follow are eloquent and brief. But we do want to highlight selectively ideas that capture his emphasis on social justice in education, in our view, a major theme of his body of work. We also present an example of current research, which was inspired by Richard's mentoring and the writings in this section, taken from Santa Cruz's dissertation on 'deschooling' as a form of empowerment and social justice action in education.

But first, a word about the authors of this introduction and their relation to Richard. Luis met Richard when they both arrived at the University of Arizona (UA) in 1986, forming part of the Department of Language, Reading and Culture in the College of Education. They not only became fast friends but also close colleagues and had offices on the same floor of the college for almost 30 years. Lane, in turn, was one of Richard's last doctoral students who first met him as an undergraduate in 2004. He was the faculty fellow at the UA's Chicano/Hispano Student Affairs, where he always did his best to make students feel at home. From Richard's mentorship, Lane remembers his humble wisdom spoken matter of factly, genuinely, sincerely, with a touch of humor.

The section starts with one of his earlier writings (Ruiz, 1983), on language, the law and the social good, that emphasizes the importance of supporting language diversity, especially bilingual education, not only for personal development but also for how it enriches and contributes positively to the broader social good. This orientation stands in sharp contrast to extant coercive assimilation policies, such as those found in mandated English-only educational programs that prohibit the use of Spanish, which Richard condemns as oppressive.

Richard makes the point forcefully in the following passages, quoted from the article. He proposes the importance of developing a 'resource language,' that is, ways of identifying, discussing, appropriating and using the resources and assets that exist within minority communities, including its language. 'What is wrong with most educational and social policy designed to improve the lot of ethnic groups by equalizing opportunity,' he warns, 'is that these ideas have always tended to deprecate the resources which already existed within ethnic communities and individuals' (p. 63). As an example, consider the massive dismissal of Black teachers and principals after the *Brown* decision (Toppo, 2004), and with them the relations of trust with families, and the sense of intimacy and advocacy that these teachers had established with students (Walker, 2013).

'What are needed most urgently,' Richard added, 'are policies aimed at developing and managing the resources which exist in ethnic communities – not their eradication. … In the cases I have elected to discuss, language is to be seen as just such a resource. And as a resource, we should consider it in our planning and management, always seeking the benefit of the greater collectivity' (p. 63). His call for building on community assets is quite clear.

In his next chapter, Richard advances a similar argument about native language instruction (Ruiz, 1991), that it is good for the kids and good for the country, but also proposes the strategic use of such instruction for political advancement by the (subordinate) communities involved. His point is made succinctly: 'Native language instruction in schools can be an important factor in ethnic communities shedding their minority status by sharing power with the dominant group' (p. 217). But how does he propose this empowerment might take place? As he points out: 'Teachers do not empower or disempower anyone, nor do schools. They merely create the conditions under which people *empower themselves*, or not' (p. 223, emphasis in the original). An important aspect of these conditions is that of students conducting inquiry into social issues that matter within their communities or families, and by informing and engaging with families about what they are learning. Here is how a teacher working in a social justice-oriented program at a local high school explained it:

> As a literature teacher, it was crucial for me to find engaging, provocative literature that was relevant to the lives and experiences of my students. … As students became fully engaged in the curricular experiences, the dialogue in the classes centered around how the students were perceiving the literature and how they applied it to their own lives and the world around them. Thus, critical inquiry and pedagogy became the way for students to push each other toward developing social consciousness rooted firmly in themes of social justice. Literature study in our classes became a lens to analyze our *barrio*, school, or world and the platform for students to generate ideas for taking action to transform the inequalities in their lives. (Acosta & Mir, 2012: 20–21)

As Richard points out, the power to define the nature of lived experiences, which of them are an asset or which are problematic, or we could say, which are marked or unmarked, is a key aspect of the power of language. An important challenge in bilingual programs, for instance, is how to make

Spanish, alongside English, an unmarked language in school for both academic and social purposes. In our experience, this takes special care, and teachers and administrators must be cognizant of constraining language ideologies, which always play a role in students' definitions of self, as persons and as learners. But it also may entail how to make (working-class) Funds of Knowledge pedagogically useful in schools, which is a process of authentication, of making worthy, explicit and viable what is usually deemed unworthy, for both classroom study and life.

But Richard also went beyond these claims by emphasizing the distinction between language and voice, the latter, he wrote, being central to any critical approach. To deny people their language, he points out, is clearly to deny them voice; but to allow them their language, is not necessarily to allow them voice. By voice he is referring the actions where people empower themselves, initiating and establishing changes favorable to their welfare; it is agency for self-determination. In education, it is the students' voice being developed and used in the educational experience; it represents not only a pedagogical but also a political achievement. As he put it: '… voice is the central ingredient of critical pedagogy; without its consideration, there is no radical reform of curriculum' (p. 220).

In the co-authored article Luis wrote with Richard (Moll & Ruiz, 2005), we seek to elaborate on the idea of voice, we could say, in the sense of community control of education. We use the term 'educational sovereignty' not as a call for separation but for developing educational programs that are responsive to the needs and resources found in the students' communities. As we wrote, we mean it as: '… the strength and power a social setting like a school can garner by developing strategic social networks to create "cultural spaces," [both local and transnational, we should add] that will enhance its autonomy, mediate ideological and programmatic constraints, and provide additive forms of schooling for its students' (p. 300). The term educational sovereignty was inspired by the work of Native Americans who are seeking tribal sovereignty, or de-colonization, including autonomy and community control over their education. Richard provides an excellent overview of some of that literature in this article. The article also summarizes three educational projects with a strong community orientation as a pedagogical strategy. From our perspective, then, 'Educational sovereignty requires that communities create their own infrastructures for development, including mechanisms for the education of their children that capitalize on rather than de-value their cultural resources' (p. 317).

Richard reminds us in his 2000 paper, however – a brief presentation entitled Asymmetrical Worlds – that the possibilities for developing any such educational innovations, especially in regard to language, must always be considered in their particular social and political context. Consider the following example. In a successful dual-language (Spanish/English) immersion program that Luis and colleagues studied, where all students graduated elementary school fluent and literate in both languages, parents were active in supporting the academic and cultural program of the school, including its strong Spanish immersion component, and came to the program's rescue when threatened with closure for its emphasis on Spanish. They had voice and clout, no doubt about it, and so did the teachers, who were regularly consulted by school administrators when making decisions to modify the program. But this program was also fragile, in the sense that its additive policies and practices were constantly under attack.

Of course, not all immersion or bilingual programs are targeted politically; it depends on the race/ethnicity and social class status of the families and children. For example, the largest school district in Tucson, Arizona, where we work, has a (working-class) Latino or Hispanic enrollment of close to 65% with white enrollment at about 20%; yet, it is under siege, proscribed by the state for offering bilingual programs and a culturally relevant curriculum to Latino students (see Acosta & Mir, 2012: 24). Tellingly, the bilingual programs (including one in Mandarin) offered by a wealthy district in Tucson, where 85% of the students are white, are unencumbered by the state. For instance, in contrast to the attacks by conservative politicians on the academically successful Mexican American Studies Program in Tucson (Cabrera et al., 2014), considered by them as un-American and seditious, no-one is accusing the teachers or administrators of this wealthy enclave of being communists or seditious for offering bilingual education in Mandarin, the dominant language of China. These are the asymmetrical worlds to which Richard referred. The Mandarin program is lauded as innovative and important, and a wonderful opportunity for the youngsters to learn an important language; the Mexican American Studies Program, in turn, is considered dangerous and was subsequently dismantled by the state.

That can change, of course. Richard reminds us of the demise of once thriving German bilingual programs in the US, in the context of political hostilities and war with that country, where even the public use of German was condemned. And no doubt the changing demographics in Arizona and the US are behind the hostility toward Spanish and its users, even if they are little children learning how to read and write in two languages.

Beyond Sovereignty: The Virtue of Deschooling

As one of Richard's doctoral students, I (Santa Cruz) had the privilege of experiencing his work through his mentorship. He helped nurture the environment where I could develop my voice and sense of agency which not only offered a critique of compulsory schooling and its deculturalizing effect on Chicanx/Indigenous youth but also a 'language of possibility' (Giroux, 1986, cited in Ruiz, 1991) in which I could actively participate in bringing education back to the community and the home. My work in raising awareness about deschooling (also known as unschooling) in a State that defines cultural/historical knowledge as seditious was inspired by works like Moll and Ruiz's (2005) declaration of sovereignty or decision-making authority in education by Latinx/Chicanx families.

Although for myself, earlier idealism around sovereignty came from a place of claiming Indigenous autonomy, or control over tribal/communal life, I now see the limitations of seeking self-determination through the expressions of sovereignty – a Western and neoliberal function of creating social order and political normativity. Aihwa Ong (2006) writes about the multiple functions of sovereignty in capitalist societies whose role is to serve as the bureaucratic administration of populations or the sociopolitical order that defines, disciplines and regulates individual and collective life (human activities) within a nation-state. Although this perceived independence fueled the idea behind the right to self-determination of Indigenous people in the 1960s as well as a central theme within many civil rights movements of the time, unfortunately, treaties between the US and Indigenous nations require that recognized tribal reservations mirror the sovereignty and governmentality of the US – an entity that displays ultimate sovereignty through its unparalleled military power (Ong, 2006).

So Native Nations, by mirroring the US model, reproduce and replicate the very colonial/imperial institutions and logic it used to subjugate Indigenous peoples. We must then ask: is this true sovereignty and self-determination? Are Native Nations truly democratic and/or using traditional and egalitarian modes of governance that would better embody a true sovereignty? But I digress, because I agree that as people with histories of colonization, we seek to have 'control' of the education of our children. But what seems to be limiting us is the power of the dominant language, which defines our lived experiences in physical and material ways (Ruiz, 1991). According to Ivan Illich (1970), this language has characterized our worldviews:

> Rich and poor alike depend on schools and hospitals, which guide their lives, form their worldview, and define for them what is legitimate, and what is not. Both view doctoring oneself as irresponsible, learning on one's own as unreliable, and community organization, when not paid for by those in authority, as a form of aggression or subversion. (Illich, in Hern, 2008: 14)

Similarly to the language surrounding sovereignty, school reforms aimed at cultural and language inclusion will continue to limit our agency around education (although, as Ruiz argues, it is a necessary fight). Ruiz (1991: 225) advocates for language maintenance and authentic empowerment through the strategy of being 'more conservative than the conservatives by developing the power of privatization'.

> Privatization implies two things: developing the resources readily available to minority communities to increase what the cultural theorist calls their own 'cultural capital,' and minorities taking control of their own lives in such a way that their communities can act positively in their own interests (Ruiz, 1991: 227)

I am sure that when Richard wrote about the power of privatization, he was not directly thinking about deschooling, but this is where I, as a mother and community educator, have found my voice as I see homeschooling as, 'the ultimate in cultural self-determination, that often touted but poorly observed human right. Keeping our children out of governmental institutions can be a way of keeping them in our community's cultural commons' (Swidler, n.d.). On paper, deschooling looks like homeschooling, but in practice deschooling does not reproduce school culture at home; on the contrary, it is 'a cooperative exploration of power, society, and the natural world' (Lyn-Piluso & Lyn-Piluso, in Hern, 2008: 83). In my quest to decolonize education/childrearing for my children, I found the possibilities outside the framework of compulsory schooling.

I operate the term deschooling (rather than unschooling) through the lens of how Linda Tuhiwai Smith (1999) uses decolonization: as an ongoing process that engages with imperialism and colonialism as it involves knowingness and naming of the colonizer. Furthermore, it entails the time before colonization (pre-colonized time) and colonized time as one that continues to this day. The process of naming and knowing the colonizer in the case of schooling is also a claim to an alternative system of knowledge that is the foundation for 'alternative ways of doing things' (Smith, 1999: 34), as is the process of deschooling. Deschooling is a process of unlearning coercion, capitalism, and Western accounts of histories by 'acknowledging it [deschooling] as a lifelong, cooperative project of questioning and discovery, thinking and rethinking' (Lyn-Piluso & Lyn-Piluso, in Hern, 2008: 84).

Making the shift away from the dominant systems of knowledge that guide our lives is not as simple as saying we are living 'off grid' because we still make negotiations with how we *choose* to interact with institutions of power – an expression of self-determination. Deschooling is a way of life that not only encompasses the school-age years but how we think about birth, child rearing, family arrangements, housing, labor, community, health, education – life. It is the critique of how we have 'professionalized' life to where we believe we can only learn about it through institutions like schools. According to Daniel Grego (in Hern, 2008), education is

> a process by which people become responsibly mature members of their communities. In non-industrial cultures, this education process is inseparable from the life of the community. Children are 'educated' by example

of their elders, by stories, by initiation rituals, and by performing the daily tasks required for subsistence (Grego, 2008: 79)

Deschooling begins to sound a lot like Indigenous education as described by Greg Cajete, 'learning about life through participation and relationship in the community, including not only people but plants, animals, and the whole of Nature' (Cajete, 1994: 26).

A friend and fellow unschooling parent recently shared with me that she believes all children can benefit from unschooling, but that not all parents are capable to provide the environment to unschool. I thought about this for a moment and agreed. The choice to deschool (or unschool), like decolonization, as stated above, implies knowingness and naming of the colonizer. For deschooling to work, parents would have to engage with the process of conscientization themselves. For myself, knowing what I knew about the history of compulsory schooling and how it continuously fails children of color, I decided to expand my cultural capital by learning to network with other people who have similar hopes; meanwhile, knowing that the majority of children are in schools, I will continue to support and advocate for curricula that include our stories, language and, as Eva Swidler (n.d.) articulates:

> We want the schools that do exist to give all their children as good a life as possible. We want schools to be nurturing, caring and inclusive. We want them to be exciting, stimulating and thought-provoking. We want them to confront race and class and gender, to promote social and ecological justice. And we want them to be free and public, not accessed by tuition or run by corporate and religious sponsors.

Until the day compulsory schooling is eradicated, I, like many other mothers of color, will keep supporting community agency over the education of children of color. In the meantime, critical educators working in schools can also learn from the critical education that is taking place outside of schools and incorporate some of these cooperative and anti-authoritarian modes of being within their cultural and language empowerment frameworks.

Resources

Acosta, C. and Mir, A. (2012) Empowering young people to be critical thinkers: The Mexican American studies program in Tucson. *Voices in Urban Education* 34 (Summer), 15–26.

Cabrera, N.L., Milem, J., Jaquette, O. and Marx, R. (2014) Missing the (student achievement) forest for all the (political) trees: Empiricism and the Mexican American studies controversy in Tucson. *American Educational Research Journal* 51 (6), 1084–1118.

Cajete, G. (1994) *Look to the Mountain: An Ecology of Indigenous Education*. Durango, CO: Kivakí.

Grego, D. (2008) From untouchables to conscientious objectors. In M. Hern (ed.) *Everywhere All the Time: A New Deschooling Reader* (pp. 73–81). Oakland, CA: AK Press.

Illich, I. (2008) Deschooling society. In M. Hern (ed.) *Everywhere All the Time: A New Deschooling Reader* (pp. 13–16). Oakland, CA: AK Press.

Lyn-Piluso, G. and Lyn-Piluso, G. (2008) Challenging the popular wisdom: What can families do? In M. Hern (ed.) *Everywhere All the Time: A New Deschooling Reader* (pp. 82–90). Oakland, CA: AK Press.

Moll, L. and Ruiz, R. (2005) The educational sovereignty of Latino/a students in the United States. In P. Pedraza and M. Rivera (eds) *Latino Education: An Agenda for Community Action Research* (pp. 295–320). Mahwah, NJ: Lawrence Erlbaum.

Ong, A. (2006) *Neoliberalism as Exception: Mutations in Citizenship and Sovereignty*. Durham, NC: Duke University Press.

Ruiz, R. (1983) Ethnic group interests and the social good: Law and language in education. In W.A. Van Horne (ed.) *Ethnicity, Law and the Social Good* (Vol. 2, pp. 49–73). Milwaukee, WI: University of Wisconsin System American Ethnic Studies Coordinating Committee/Urban Corridor Consortium.

Ruiz, R. (1991) The empowerment of language-minority students. In C. Sleeter (ed.) *Empowerment Through Multicultural Education* (pp. 217–227). Albany: SUNY Press.

Ruiz, R. (2000) Asymmetrical worlds: The representation of the ethnic in public discourse. Unpublished.

Smith, L.T. (1999) *Decolonizing Methodologies: Research and Indigenous Peoples*. London and New York: ZED Books; Dunedin, NZ: University of Otago Press.

Swidler, E. (n.d.) Re-imagining school public educators & unschoolers may have much in common. See http://www.life.ca/naturallife/1002/unschoolers_re-imagine_schools.htm (accessed 2 February 2016).

Toppo, G. (2004) Brown vs. Board of Education: Thousands of Black teachers lost jobs. *USA Today*, 28 April.

Walker, V.S. (2013) Black educators as educational advocates in the decades before *Brown v. Board of Education*. *Educational Researcher* 42 (4), 207–212.

Ethnic Group Interests and the Social Good: Law and Language in Education*

Richard Ruiz (1983)

The question at issue is broad, so I have chosen to focus it in a way that draws attention to the complexities of cultural diversity in the United States. This question is: How are ethnic group interests in education promoted by law, and what relation might this promotion have to the "larger social good"? There is much discussion of the problems raised by school desegregation, affirmative action, and the role of the judiciary in resolving these; there is sometimes also a tendency to concentrate on issues of race and its importance in our representation of "ethnicity." This emphasis is important, and I do not mean to minimize it. (After all, Homer Plessy was only one-eighth black—a fact which attests to the tremendous salience of black-white distinctions in society and in law.) My objection is that we tend to forget other aspects of ethnic identification which, indeed, may be as significant as race in the context of schooling.

I am referring here to language. Our census enumerators tell us that the largest minority group in the country will soon be non-English speaking. By the end of this century, blacks will be overtaken numerically by Hispanics, by which is meant primarily Chicanos, Puerto Ricans and Cubans, though other Latin Americans and Europeans are also sometimes included in this category. Moreover, while the general school enrollment is decreasing, greater numbers of Hispanic children are attending public schools. This means that the demands on the school to address linguistic diversity will intensify. There is already a large body of codified state and federal policy, as well as court decisions, dealing with the responsibility of the school in this area. Before proceeding, however, let me elaborate our primary question.

What Are Interests?

A debate about ethnic group interests, whether they relate to race, language, national origin, or some other dimension of ethnicity, has little value without first sorting out what is meant by "interests." The articulation, aggregation and promotion of interests involve first a determination of what interests are; only then might we turn to the question of how law promotes them, and how this relates to the "larger social good."

Are "interests" to be construed as social goods by those who hold them? Is everything which I think will benefit me "in my interest"? Or are there other, more general standards by which we can evaluate whether something we consider desirable is actually an interest? How and by whom are my interests determined? Let us suppose that a group of us who are Hispanics would like our children to speak Spanish as we and our parents do, because it would strengthen the familial bond and allow succeeding generations to retain something of their heritage. No claims are made that our children will be better citizens, achieve at a greater level in school, get better jobs, or in any other way "improve themselves" as a result of that ability. How can I investigate if such language facility is "in our interest"? One might postulate that because we hold it as a social good, it is therefore in our interest. In this view, interests are social constructions to be evaluated by the group in which they emerge. Implicit in this argument is the assumption that the group itself determines what is in its interest, regardless of perceptions to the contrary from the outside.

On the other hand, we might decide that interests sometimes do not correspond neatly to socially determined desirability; that what is truly in one's interest will have to be measured by the eventual benefit it has for the whole group. Besides, it is seldom true that even small social groups can agree on what is desirable. When there are conflicting perceptions of what is desirable, interest must be evaluated by some external criterion. At any rate, none of this implies that one must create laws to promote one's interests, however they may be determined. That is because an "interest" is not compelling in the context of law. The concept must be translated (or at least translatable) into language forms which are. It may be possible, for example, to reformulate "interests" as "rights," a word which forces itself on the legal and legislative system.

Can an "interest" be construed as a "right"? If so, what kind of right is it? A human right?[1] A cultural right? An individual right?[2] A moral right? A legal right? And, as a right, what is its ontological status? Is it natural, and therefore inalienable? Or is it conferred on one by one's "group, and thus inalienable?[3]" Are not some aspects of human experience sometimes weakly represented as "interests" when they should be strongly affirmed as "rights"?

These questions are significant when asked in the face of what appear to be ethnic group demands. Some arguments for bilingual education, for example, are based on the premise that some interests are actually rights. Thus, bilingual education programs are demanded for reasons in addition to the belief that they will accommodate the legal (if not moral) right of children to equal educational opportunity, without discrimination based on national origin. Such programs are also linked to the right of self-expression and self-identification—construed as a natural and inalienable right—which is denied by not allowing the use of one's native language in school. This is a significant dimension to the argument identifying "interests" with "rights," for even where opportunities are equalized and discrimination has disappeared, the justification for bilingual education is not weakened. Advocated in this way, bilingual education—in its role of institutionalizing language maintenance—takes on the force of a natural right.

At the heart of the concept of rights is the question of claims. To have a right, according to Feinberg,[4] is to have at least a "claim-to" something. This claim-to can be justified in a variety of ways, depending on the substance of the claim. For example, if it is a claim about some legal entitlement, appeal to legal rules or principles (as opposed to, let us say, moral precepts) can make the claim valid. For Feinberg, however, this is not enough to make the claim constitute a "full-fledged right"; what is needed are both a valid claim-to and a valid claim-against.[5] To restrict oneself to a claim-to is to diminish what could be a full-fledged right into a "manifesto right." In terms we have already used, to affirm a manifesto right may be tantamount to expressing an interest, at least for the purpose of legal persuasion. Neither a mere claim-to nor an interest appears to have much legal weight. It is important to consider whether the demand for bilingual education constitutes merely a manifesto right, or whether it can be expressed more forcefully.[6]

Can an interest (and therefore a right) change with the passage of time and the advancement of knowledge? Apparently so, judging from the way the Supreme Court has overturned its own seemingly immutable principles concerning rights. Take the *Brown* decision nullifying the "separate but equal" doctrine. Did this mean that the interest of blacks was now different because of the judicial pronouncement? Or had the interest been there all along, denied or obscured by the Court's ignorance and misapplication of constitutional principles? On this point, Frederick Wirt and Michael Kirst say:

> History threw little clear light on what the intent of the framers of the Fourteenth Amendment had been in this respect, but certainly the scope and importance of education had changed since then. Separation of children in this important aspect of their lives "generates a feeling of inferiority as to their status in the community that may affect their hearts and minds in a way unlikely ever to be undone." While such psychological knowledge may not have been available in 1896, it [is] today, so its weight should not be denied.[7]

So, an important justification for overturning long-standing judicial principles is that we now understand something about the human condition about which we were previously ignorant. In these cases, new knowledge about human development processes allows us to reassess what the ethnic group interest is: while before the Brown decision it was separate facilities, it is now propinquity.

The importance of *Lau v. Nichols* twenty years later lies in its reformulation of the principles underlying *Brown*. Its most startling pronouncement is that "there is no equality of treatment merely by providing the students with the same facilities, textbooks, teachers, and curriculum; for students who do not understand English are effectively foreclosed from any meaningful education."[8] This is no small thing; it calls into question the very framework which sustains *Brown*. Where *Brown* emphasized the importance of physical proximity in alleviating educational disadvantage and discrimination, *Lau* subordinates all this to the nature of the treatment, saying that disregarding such cultural variables as language can do as much harm as segregation.

In these changes, the Court has been reasonable. The fundamental tenet of *Brown* is that intentional separation of the races under state authority is unacceptable because it results in a radical disparity in resource allocation. *Lau* constitutes a refinement of that principle, rather than a negation of it. Sharing the same facilities is not enough to insure equal access to education; there must also be a reasonable attempt to provide services to children in light of their differences. To treat them all the same is, under *Lau*, to treat them unequally. Once again, we see here that judicial decisions based on new knowledge—in this case, about linguistic difference and access to curricular information—changed our conception of what constituted ethnic group interest.

If an interest is not a right, how does it relate to rights? Does it, should it, *inform* rights? These are not pointless questions for the world of schools today. In the case of bilingual education, the sociolinguistic literature on language attitudes and their importance in establishing a school program[9] may throw some light on the question of interests and rights. The critical point made by sociolinguists is that the general goals of the school program—either toward language maintenance or language shift and, indeed, the establishment of any program in the first place—should be determined primarily by the attitude of the parents of prospective participants. Consider two communities, one where the attitudes of parents are favorable toward a maintenance-bilingual program, and one where the parents want no special program at all. Does this mean that the right for a bilingual program has been created, or at least influenced, by the interest of the first group; while for the second—lacking the self-determined interest—no such right exists?[10]

This question is not farfetched. It is consistent with many of the arguments favoring bilingual education for some groups, but not for others, and it is a response to the contention that providing bilingual services in schools for one or two groups will open the floodgates of demand for such benefits from every conceivable language group even though it is possible that many, maybe most, of these groups do not see these services as "in their interest," preferring over anything else that their children learn English. Gaarder's characterization of the Norwegian attitude at the turn of the century indicates this lack of support from school-based language teaching:

"Norwegian-Americans—most of them—cherished their mother tongue, but Haugen found that they stoutly resisted those who advocated parochial or other schools that would have segregated their children from other Americans."[11] Whether or not one believes that rights should be informed by interests in this way, it is unsound public policy to insist on this benefit for those who would see it as a hindrance. The objection, then, that the costs for providing all these groups with bilingual education would be astronomical, because of the number of language groups potentially involved, distracts us from more pertinent questions about bilingual education. (Arguments that nativist rights should take precedence over immigrant rights are intimately related to this line of reasoning; it is to be expected, after all, that voluntary immigrants would make fewer demands for language and cultural mainte-nance than would conquered or colonized nativist groups.)

Underlying most of the formulations of "interest" and "right" discussed here is the notion that the particular interest and the general interest are natural competitors; the implication for policymakers is that the primary task is to choose between a particular interest and the greater social good. This is unfortunate. While in order to provide for the possibility of legal remedy "interest" language should perhaps be translated into "rights" lan-guage, a more beneficial approach would be to develop a language repertoire, the most important of which could be a "resource language." If instead of insisting on this or that right we were able to demonstrate the resource potential of cultural and linguistic diversity, the arguments about bilingual education would take on a completely different character. Questions of whether this or that linguistic group should be offered the privilege of lan-guage instruction in the schools would be subordinated to questions of resource development and management; more importantly, policy formula-tion would include strategies for using these resources in the best possible way, rather than arguments about whether we need them at all.

Just what is involved in developing such a resource language shall be discussed in the last section of this chapter. What we must remember is that if we continually regard interests as either particular or general, then we fail to ask the right questions about interests.

How Does the Law Promote or Hinder Interests?

Wirt and Kirst see the role of the judiciary in promoting or hindering interests as greater than merely that of arbiter in legal disputes. The Supreme Court, in particular, is important in that it gives not only laws but norms and values as well:

The Supreme Court legitimizes national policies and values they reflect … In the process, the judiciary provides signals to litigants, general public, and political subsystems and their actors (including their own local courts) as to the policy-value output it will reinforce. ... However such decisions are derived, they constitute outputs for society. They are something more than a statement of which litigant won and lost. Rather, they instruct a larger circle as to the value norms that the judicial subsystems seek to impose upon the environment.[12]

In the realm of language, judicial decisions as well as laws and legislative declarations contribute to the development of what Shirley Heath calls a language ideology.[13] The ideology is developed explicitly in the language of the pronouncement or implicitly in the orientation conveyed in making this pronouncement. Several examples of each will help to clarify this concept.

Both federal and state legislation on bilingual education is overwhelmingly transitional and compensatory, being aimed at children with identifiable "limitations."[14] The original version of Title VII in 1967 specified not only a non-English primary language but also poverty (that is, less than $3,000 income per year per family) as eligibility criteria for bilingual programs. Thus, the association between non-English language ability and poverty was embodied in a national declaration of policy.[15] This is not to say that the association was not already present in American language ideology, but the program language served to make the connection explicit.

Another example is the language of the Massachusetts Transitional Bilingual Education Act of 1972, the first such law and a model for many other states: "The General Court believes that a compensatory program of transitional bilingual education can meet the needs of [limited English-speaking] children and facilitate their integration into the regular public school curriculum." The law associates a lack of English language ability with a need for remediation, expressly stating that the program will no longer be necessary once a child has mastered enough English to become integrated with the "regular" school program.

Wisconsin's Bilingual-Bicultural Education Law (1975) is very similar to the Massachusetts law in this respect, even though it does not contain the word "transitional": "It is the policy of this state that a limited-English speaking pupil participate in a bilingual-bicultural education program only until such time as the pupil is able to perform ordinary classwork in English." Also noteworthy for our discussion of language ideology are two more things in the Wisconsin law. First, it is probably not insignificant that this statute appears in the Wisconsin Code as a subchapter to a larger section on handicapped children. The negative association with special education conveyed in the context of bilingual education is not at all subtle; it shows a definite attitude on the part of the legislators toward this kind of school program.

Second, in a list of definitions, most of the people involved in the programs are referred to as "bilingual": bilingual teacher, bilingual counselor, bilingual teacher's aide, bilingual counselor's aide. In the context of the statute, however, "bilingual" does not refer to language ability; it is merely a status marker conferred through certification. At the same time a student participant in the program is called "limited-English speaking ... because of the use of a non-English language in his or her family or in his or her daily, non-school surrounding ..." This is ironic, suggesting the possibility of a classroom where the only person who has a natural bilingual experience is called "limited," while others—who are not necessarily bilingual but have passed courses and achieved a minimum test score, though not necessarily a minimum level of functional language use—are called "bilingual."

Here one observes an aspect of American language ideology which is as of yet merely an intuition: *adding* a foreign language to English is associated with erudition, social and economic status and, perhaps, even patriotism (consider that the military has been our most vigorous language trainer in the last thirty years—most of the trainees being native English speakers); but *maintaining* a non-English language implies disadvantage, poverty, low achievement and disloyalty (it promotes biculturalism and irredentism, both potentially politically dangerous). One's intuition is strengthened by the fact that evaluations of bilingual education programs show a tendency to be disproportionately impressed with relatively meager gains in Spanish language scores by English-speaking children when compared to the much greater gains on English test scores by non-English-speaking children. "Additive" bilingualism is acceptable when the second language is not English, but "subtractive" bilingualism is our goal when it is. Gaarder's contention that almost all Spanish-English bilinguals in the United States are mother-tongue speakers of Spanish[16] is probably adaptable to any non-English language speech community.

One comes away with the attitude that it would be a shame indeed if one's child were even *thought* to need a program of this sort. It is designed for people who have a problem—the ability to speak a non-English language. Moreover, the specific associations that one is invited to make direct one to conceptualize a dilemma on the horns of which only non-English language speakers are caught: one can retain one's language and culture, and thereby virtually insure economic and social marginality, or one can discard the old for the new and find oneself on the crest of the wave toward modernity, economic viability and social status. The Wisconsin statute reminds us that this is "a society whose language is English,"[17] and President Reagan insists that "it is absolutely wrong and against [the] American concept to preserve native language and culture in school programs."[18] This is in keeping with what Charles Ferguson says about the perceived incompatibility of indigenization and modernization from the point of view of the English-speaking nations. Certainly a non-Western indigenous language like Thai or Fula is in itself incapable of representing technological advances to its speakers; the vernacular must be subordinated to a Western language—perhaps even eliminated—in the interest of progress.[19] Haugen makes the same point in saying about U.S. immigrants that "if individuals or groups rejected English ... they handicapped themselves, because they limited their chances for socioeconomic mobility and valuation as good citizens."[20] This is an assumption not shared by industrialized non-Western nations of which Japan is a notable example.

Imbedded orientations as an important aspect of language ideology are not always easily recognized partly because, since they frequently reflect prevailing social sentiment, they are not seen as "marked." A good example of this is the tone of the Supreme Court in *Meyer v. Nebraska*. A German teacher in a parochial school was convicted of violating a state law prohibiting instruction in a non-English language. The Supreme Court found that a Nebraska Supreme Court decision upholding the conviction was in violation of the due process clause of the Fourteenth Amendment, and reversed; but the attitude of the Court was tolerant of the social judgment at the basis of the law: "The desire of the legislature to foster a homogeneous people with American ideals ... is easy to appreciate."[21] The simple message is that one cannot really be an American and advocate linguistic diversity.

Heath finds this orientation in judicial decisions throughout the twenties, when every state passed language laws, and extending into the antisubversive movement of the fifties. During World War I, knowledge of a foreign language was believed to be "clearly harmful." Between 1919 and 1925, more than one thousand people, mostly aliens, were sentenced to jail for "subversive speech"; Heath attributes this to the idea of "inchoate crime," where "words were said which made people fear something would happen, although no action ensued. The speech people used made them socially dangerous."[22]

Furthermore, Heath finds that judicial decisions in this period were "based on the view that language is a predictor, or at least an indicator, of behavior."[23] This view is illustrated in the following passage from the Nebraska Supreme Court's affirmation of Meyer's conviction:

The legislature had seen the baneful effects of permitting foreigners who had taken residence in this country to rear and educate their children in the language of their native land. The result of that condition was found to be inimical to our own safety. To allow the children of foreigners who had emigrated here, to be taught from early childhood the language of the country of their parents, was to rear them with that language as their mother tongue. It was to educate them so that they must always think in that language, and as a consequence, naturally inculcate in them the idea and sentiments foreign to the best interest of this country.[24]

We might interpret this perceived threat in one of two ways. The first has to do with the impression that some groups of people were ill-suited to living peacefully in a democracy because either the political and social circumstances prevailing in their country of origin inclined them toward attitudes harmful to American society, or they possessed biogenetic qualities which were considered undesirable and dangerous. This is the thrust of E. B. Cubberley's well-known statement: "Illiterate, docile, lacking in self-reliance and initiative, and not possessing the Anglo-Teutonic conceptions of law, order and government, their coming has served to dilute tremendously our national stock, and to corrupt our civic life."[25] Allowing "foreigners" to teach these social traits and to reinforce their own language in the schools could be seen as against the best interests of a democratic society.

Yet another interpretation is possible. One might conclude that the encouragement of ethnic identification through the institution of school was itself a social evil because collective diversity of any sort—regardless of the perceived similarity of the ideologies at its base—would eventually work to weaken a democracy. Instead, the country needed to process its immigrant stock socially, through the schools and other institutions, in order to develop a common and fundamental sense of identity. In this view, the eradication of the distinctive—cultural, linguistic, biogenetic, political or otherwise—in order to create a basic commonality is essential for the maintenance of democratic institutions.[26]

Some may argue that this latter interpretation is exaggerated, that if it ever existed, it surely does not have much force now. On the contrary, it is a possible explanation for the inordinate amount of controversy that language issues—bilingual education in particular—have generated in this country. Surely, if we were concerned merely with the cost of the program, or even its educational merits, the arguments would not be as impassioned as they now are. *Meyer v. Nebraska*, after all, involved language instruction in a private school; funding did not emerge as an issue. The same was true of the Bennett and Edwards Law controversies in Wisconsin and Illinois. Yet it is hard to find a case in the first part of this century to compare with those in passion.

Nor does this orientation confine itself to another era. A recent manifestation of our concern of our concern for linguistic diversity outside the public funding issue is *Garcia v. Gloor.*[27] Hector Garcia was an employee of Gloor Lumber and Supply Company in Brownsville, Texas. The company had a rule prohibiting employees from speaking Spanish on the job unless they were communicating with Spanish-speaking customers. Gloor employed some workers who were Spanish monolinguals, and the rule did not apply to them. Also, the rule did not apply during breaks. In 1975, Garcia was dismissed from his job for violating the rule; he had been asked by another Mexican American employee about an item requested by a customer, and he responded in Spanish. Alton Gloor, a company officer, overheard the exchange. Representatives of Gloor argued that there were sound business reasons for the rule, and that the question of discrimination on the basis of national origin was irrelevant to the case. These business reasons included:[28]

- English speaking customers objected to hearing Spanish spoken because they could not understand the entire transaction.
- All of the trade literature and pamphlets were in English; not Spanish.
- Employees would improve their English skills by being compelled to speak English where they otherwise would not; this would not only improve their efficiency as employees, but would expand their opportunities as citizens.
- The rule would permit supervisors, "who did not speak Spanish," to oversee their employees' performance better.

Other factors, however, are also important. More than 75 percent of the population in the business area served by Gloor are Hispanic, "and many of Gloor's customers wish to be waited on by a salesman who speaks Spanish."[29]

The determination of the court entailed a relatively narrow legal argument: "An employer's rule forbidding a bilingual employee to speak anything but English in public areas while on the job is not discrimination based on national origin. [Garcia] was discharged because having the ability to comply with his employer's rule, he did not do so."[30]

The court left the issue there, but more questions have to be asked. What kind of business is it that would discourage the use and maintenance among its employees of a language which 75 percent of its potential customers speak? There are ways to encourage speakers of other languages to speak English on the job without so drastic a measure. Devising some system (or encouraging bilingual employees like Garcia to devise it) in which employees would have an opportunity to use both of these commercially important languages in the work place would surely be better business.

And what of the fact that none of the supervisors at Gloor spoke Spanish? Would it not have helped them improve the business by encouraging bilingual exchanges, so that those overseeing the operation could become at least superficially familiar with the predominant language of communication in the area? Besides, since one could assume that a relatively large percentage of the transactions would be in Spanish, how could the supervisors possibly oversee, let alone evaluate, the performance of the employee?

These and other peculiarities of *Garcia* lead one to think that other factors are at work here. Without a better idea of the particulars of the case and the specific situation being litigated, one can only speculate. The fact that the court confined itself to the narrow constitutional issue is not in itself unreasonable, but some comment on oddities in a case is not uncommon. Nor was this decision completely devoid of such comment. In a statement of justification for the finding that Garcia voluntarily and intentionally violated a perfectly acceptable rule, the court showed its lack of expertise on the issue of bilingualism: "the language a person who is multilingual elects to speak at a particular time is by definition a matter of choice."[31] Apart from the fact that this statement can be true by reason of circularity (whatever anyone *elects* to do is of course a matter of choice), the court fails to recognize the importance of sociolinguistic cues in the speech behavior of bilinguals. It is not necessarily true that a bilingual person has a choice of language codes regardless of the context (bilinguals whose linguistic knowledge is balanced in every domain of social experience are very rare), and it is true that one can distinguish between the cognitive choices available to an individual as a result of knowledge of more than one code and the sociolinguistic options available to the individual within the particular context. In the case of Garcia speaking with another Spanish-speaking employee, one can well imagine that the choice involved is a much more difficult one than the court suggests.

The point of this discussion is to suggest that orientations toward languages—their acceptability in certain domains or generally, their relative status, their extra-linguistic concomitants, their political and ideological uses—and toward the people who speak them are frequently implicit in the decisions reached involving them. These orientations can have consequences for the kinds of policy advanced relating to ethnic and linguistic minority groups. We tend to remember the xenophobic reaction of the Court in *Meyer v. Nebraska* more than the fact that Meyer's conviction was reversed. The way the court says what it wants, regardless of the decision it may feel compelled to reach, can affect the way those involved in these decisions are seen and treated in the public domain.[32]

How Is the "Greater Social Good" Identified?

How have judicial decisions helped us to identify what is the "greater social good"? It is fair to say that the Court's concept of this "good" has varied in time. In some cases, it is clear that the arguments reflected prevailing sentiments (as in *Plessy* and *Meyer*), while in others, most notably *Brown*, the Court's decision caught the general public by considerable surprise. Some of the decisions create distinctions and conceptualizations which are significant for the affected classes, although they may go virtually unnoticed by the general public. In *Gong Lum v. Rice* in 1927, for example, the Supreme Court accepted the finding of a Mississippi court that, for the purposes of the public education laws, all those who were not white belonged to the "colored race." Lum had contended, following the argument in *Plessy*, that since there were no schools for Mongolians, she should be allowed to go to the white school.[33] The court's denial of her petition rendered her legally a "Negro" for the purpose of education.

More recently, in *Pete Hernandez Petitioner v. State of Texas* in 1954, Mexican Americans were established legally as "Caucasians";[34] in *Ross v. Eckels* in 1970, Chicanos were not differentiated from whites in a Houston school desegregation case.[35] This means that school officials could, following *Gong Lum*, classify non-Anglos as black; before *Brown* this classification served the interests of radical segregationists. After *Brown*, in a practice alleged on numerous occasions, blacks could still be excluded from Anglo schools by combining them with Chicanos to fulfill desegregation orders. One's inference, cynical and distasteful as it is, must be that the Court still cannot bring itself to eradicate a long-held conception that separation of the races constitutes a big part of the "greater social good," even after *Brown*. Modern formulations of this pervasive orientation are just more subtle than before *Brown*. Earlier, social mood allowed judges to be more direct, as were Justices McReynolds and Butler in their dissenting opinion in *Missouri ex. rel. Gaines v. Canada* in 1938. Here the Court considered the Missouri Law School's denial of admission to Gaines (a black man):

> For a long time, Missouri has acted upon the view that the best interests of her people demand separation of whites and negroes in schools. Under the opinion just announced, I presume she may abandon her law school and thereby disadvantage her white citizens without improving petitioner's opportunities for legal instruction; or she may break down the settled practice concerning separate schools and thereby, as indicated by experience, damnify both races.[36]

It is not only the Supreme Court and the federal legislative bodies that influence the development of these orientations in policy and ideology. Local authorities can and do play an important role in the development of policy regarding ethnic groups. Consider these few examples:

(1) "No Spanish" rules in Southwestern schools (especially in Texas), where children are punished in a variety of ways if found speaking Spanish to anyone anywhere on the school grounds, were in effect well into the 1960s, and endure in isolated cases even now.[37]

(2) Sterilization laws have been aimed at, among others, poor black women. Between 1907 and 1928, twenty-one states passed laws for involuntary eugenic sterilization; at that time, these were considered one aspect of progressivism, and some important historical figures were prominent in the movement. The "greater social good" deriving from these policies had a number of dimensions: it would allow the society to rid itself of the "defective germ plasm" which was threatening to destroy the social fabric of the country in the wake of the new immigration; it would display the effectiveness of the new scientific efficiency in social human engineering; and it would be in the best interests of the "inferior races"

as well. Henry Garrett explains this last concept in his pamphlet *Breeding Down*:

You can no more mix the two races and maintain the standards of white civilization than you can add 80 (the average I.Q. of Negroes) and 100 (the average I.Q. of Whites), divide by two and get 100. What you would get would be a race of 90s, and it is that 10 percent differential that spells the difference between a spire and a mud hut; 10 percent—or less—is the margin of civilization's profit; it is the difference between a cultured society and savagery. Therefore it follows that if miscegenation would be bad for white people, it would be bad for Negroes as well. For, if leadership is destroyed, all is destroyed.[38]

Clarence Karier asserts that Garrett's arguments were not out of line, in nature or in tone, with the prevalent social and scientific attitudes of the time.[39] He considers the work of many prominent scientists and statesmen— Thorndike, Terman, Jordan, Van Hise, Ross and others—to have contributed most to this orientation. The motivation for advocates of the eugenics movement seems to have been a belief that genetic engineering was indicative of greater scientific and social efficiency. Garrett's comment implies that the "greater social good" is best served by at least a strict separation of the races, if not the complete eradication of non-whites.

(3)   Finally, the rash of legislation attempted and passed during the period of anti-Oriental agitation in the Western states aimed at a similar view of the social good. The Chinese Exclusion Act of 1882, the Alien Land Laws and the Immigration Act of the 1920s,[40] and a variety of local ordinances—such as the one passed by the San Francisco School Board in 1906[41]—which were designed to keep Orientals out of schools, if not out of jobs[42] and out of the country, demonstrated the judicial and legislative determinations of the "greater social good."

How Do We Develop A Resource Language?

Garrett's argument contains an important central idea which has become prominent in public policy formulations of the last twenty years: The "greater social good" *includes* the promotion of ethnic and racial group interests. According to Garrett, it was in the interest of the black man that he be kept in subordination to the white society, which was his protector and benefactor, since he had nothing of value—and quite a lot of harm—to contribute to it. This is only the most obvious formulation of the "trickle-down theory" of public policy; in it, the distinctiveness of ethnic and linguistic groups *in itself* is never seen as a resource, the promotion of which is important in any conceptualization of the greater social good.

I agree that ethnic group interests are an important part of the general welfare, but I take issue with the motivation which has propelled public policy based on it. What is wrong with the "separate but equal"[43] doctrine; what is wrong with most educational and social policy designed to improve the lot of ethnic groups by equalizing opportunity; is that these ideas have always tended to deprecate the resources which already existed within ethnic communities and individuals. At the basis of enforced separation is the assumption of inferiority rather than the right to voluntary association with familiars; behind "integration" frequently is the paternalistic attitude cited by Levin: "Many blacks reject integration as a solution not because it is identified with false promises but also because it has ideological overtones that are an affront to Black dignity. As Floyd McKissick has suggested, the view that quality education can only take place in an integrated school seems to be based upon the degrading proposition: Mix Negroes with Negroes and you get stupidity."[44]

Even recent concerns with educational opportunity and bilingual education have behind them the view that the targeted populations have little of value in themselves. We have mistakenly tried to remedy what we took to be deficiencies in culture or language or social orientation through promotive policies based on erroneous assumptions. What are needed most urgently are policies aimed at developing and managing the resources which exist in ethnic communities—not their eradication. This can only promote the "greater social good" since it aims at the integration of the strengths of each group. In the cases I have elected to discuss, language is to be viewed as just such a resource. As a resource, we should consider it in our planning and management, always seeking the benefit of the greater collectivity.

But what, actually has been our position toward language diversity? We have already seen some of that. Perhaps one of the strongest statements about our language attitude is made by Gerald Johnson. "No polyglot empire of the world has dared to be as ruthless in imposing a single language upon its whole population as was the liberal republic dedicated to the proposition that all men are created equal."[45] Charles Ferguson, a bit less passionately, says about the same thing: "America is the world's leader in quality research in first and second language acquisition, but it is probably the world's poorest consumer of that research."[46]

One might well ask at this point, so what? What harm have we done to ourselves by discouraging and actively eradicating non-English languages and non-Anglo American cultures? Is this not overwhelmed by the good it has brought us—political unity, technological advance, military superiority, social cohesion, educational achievement, economic strength, all beyond compare? The fact is that we may not now see the pervasive and long-term damage that oppressive homogenization has had, even in the areas just mentioned. Fishman, in a rousing call for bilingual education, suggests that heavy-handedness in the cultural realm may be more dangerous than abuse of the ecological balance. His are not arguments based solely on the affirmation of "manifesto rights" or on the importance of natural symmetry: "... any argument that bases itself only on the ethics and esthetics of diversity is, in our more advanced day and age, only half an argument. If natural diversity is so central to a truly human existence, then there must be some demonstrable loss or damage when and if the balance of nature is disturbed."[47]

What are some of these demonstrable losses? There have been indications here and there in the last twenty years that our ability to cope with the demands of a diverse world has diminished. Paul Simon cites an example of this which is intriguing yet terrifying in its implications.[48] He asks us to recall the incident which, in many of our minds, set the tone for the Cold War and, more generally, made reasonable the anti-Soviet sentiments which remain even now: Nikita Krushchev's threat, "We will bury you." Simon points out, however, that this is a distorted representation of what was said. "We will survive you" is more accurate. This is similar to, though much less humorous than, the embarrassment suffered by President Carter some years ago when his interpreter showed his ignorance of acceptable Polish usage before a group of dignitaries. The language resources at hand in each case were inadequate to meet the demands of important international situations. Simon sees this as a worsening national problem which can have serious consequences. He points to some obvious indicators that something has gone wrong:

- In 1974, only 4 percent of our high school graduates had two years of foreign language training.
- Before our involvement in Vietnam, there was no American-born specialist on Indochinese languages available to the military.
- The Foreign Service has no foreign language requirement. Simon notes that even most of those who patrol for the Immigration Service along the Mexico-Texas border cannot speak Spanish. "Is this a rational way to run that kind of operation?" he asks.[49]

We must remember that this is true at a time when we are classifying natural bilinguals as "handicapped" and developing school programs designed to eliminate their "language problem." It could not be more obvious that the "greater social good" is best approached by preserving these important and fragile resources. We must now take up the challenge Ferguson outlined for us in 1978:

> ... the time is ripe, and perhaps long overdue, for some Americans ... to devote thought and effort to the formulation of a national language policy or set of policies which could move us toward conservation of our present resources and the strengthening of our resources where necessary, to meet the foreseeable language needs of our nation, for its internal strength and for its proper role in the family of nations.[50]

These resources cannot be neglected much longer without lasting negative effects. While we have introduced here the idea of a "resource-language" to talk about cultural and linguistic maintenance, we must see the differences between these and material resources like coal and oil. We can leave the oil in the ground and it will still be there to use in a hundred years; the more we use it, and the more we use it unwisely, the less we have of it later. Just the opposite is true of language and culture. The more we use these, the more we have of them; but the longer we neglect their use, the closer we are to extinguishing them. That has already happened for some languages, and we may be starting to see the consequences. The world will end one day, and the overriding cause is more likely to be a shortage of such human resources as language and culture, which could aid in promoting international understanding, than a shortage of such physical resources as coal and oil.

Whether the policies resulting from this orientation toward human resources embody bilingual education as we now know it, or some other institutional program, is not in itself the crucial issue. Ultimately, what is surely necessary are laws and legislative pronouncements which give status to precious resources like language. As yet, the most liberal policy does not approach this orientation.

Notes

*   This chapter has profited greatly from my discussions with Shirley Brice Heath (to whom I am also indebted for giving me a copy of her 1979 paper) and Andrew Cohen. It would have been a better work had I talked with them more. I would also like to acknowledge the invaluable technical assistance of Sharon Lorusso and Marie Ruiz.

(1)   For an elaboration of this concept and how it relates to "cultural rights," see United Nations Educational, Scientific, and Cultural Organization (UNESCO), *Cultural Rights as Human Rights*, Vol. 3, *Studies and Documents on Cultural Policies* (Paris: UNESCO, 1970). Cf. also Vladimir Kudryavtsev, "The Truth About Human Rights," *Human Rights*, 5 (Winter 1976): 199. The political rhetoric about human rights, especially in the last five years, makes a dispassionate analysis of this concept very difficult. Tibor R. Machan, in "Some Recent Work in Human Rights Theory" (*American Philosophical Quarterly*, 17 [April 1980]: 103–115), makes a good attempt at this review and analysis.

(2)   See Ronald Dworkin, *Taking Rights Seriously* (Cambridge, Mass.: Harvard University Press, 1977). Dworkin conceives of rights as based on individual dignity and respect rather than on collective concerns. He describes rights as "trumps over collective goals" (p. xv).

(3)   UNESCO, op. cit., p. 85. Yehudi Cohen contends that "people do not derive their rights from the very fact that they are human. There are no inalienable individual human rights; people have always derived their rights from their groups." (Ibid., p. 80.) Yet the distinction between individual and group rights may be misleading, as these two sorts of rights are intimately connected. The distinction underlies Cohen's later statement that "one of the first things the Nazis had to do was to declare all the people that they were slaughtering as 'non-humans.' First, they deprived them

of their citizenship, and citizenship is the social definition of being human in a particular group." (Ibid., p. 85.)

It is also probable that affirmation of group over individual rights is culturally, ideologically and politically determined. See Kudryavtsev, for example, for a Soviet view of human rights. "There are no human rights in the abstract, in isolation from society. A right is an opportunity guaranteed by the state to enjoy the social benefits and values existing in a given society. For this reason the one and the same right (for instance, the right to education) has an entirely different content in different historical and social circumstances." (Kudryavtsev, op. cit., p. 199.)

(4) Reviewed in Rex Martin and James W. Nickel, "Recent Work on the Concept of Rights," *American Philosophical Quarterly*, 17 (July 1980): 165–180.

(5) This point is disputed by McCloskey in Martin and Nickel, ibid. McCloskey sees positive entitlements as the basis of rights. "Rights are explained positively as entitlements to do, have, enjoy, or have done, and not negatively, as something against others, or as something one ought to have."

(6) There is another kind of right, which may be called a "negative right," that may be relevant here. See A. Bruce Gaarder, "Language Maintenance or Language Shift?" in W. F. Mackey and T. Andersson, eds., *Bilingualism in Early Childhood* (Rowley, Mass.: Newbury House Publishers, 1977), p. 10. Gaarder asserts that cultural pluralism entails "the right not to assimilate." For this to be a right in Feinberg's sense, it would have to be translated into a statement of affirmation. The right not to assimilate becomes, for example, the (positive) right to affirm and maintain a distinct cultural and linguistic identity. Even then, however, it would be difficult to develop a "claim-against" formulation for cultural pluralism in Gaarder's sense.

(7) Frederick M. Wirt and Michael W. Kirst, *Political and Social Foundations of Education* (Berkeley, Cal.: McCutcheon, 1975), p. 179.

(8) *Lau v. Nichols*, 414 U.S. 566 (1974).

(9) Joshua A. Fishman and John Lovas, "Bilingual Education in a Sociolinguistic Perspective," in Bernard Spolsky, ed., *The Language Education of Minority Children* (Rowley, Mass.: Newbury House Publishers, 1977). For an extensive examination of the issues surrounding the concept of language attitude more generally, see the collection of essays in Roger Shuy and Ralph W. Fasold, *Language Attitudes: Current Trends and Prospects* (Washington, D.C.: Georgetown University Press, 1973).

(10) McCloskey (in Martin and Nickel, op. cit., p. 169) would argue that the right (or "entitlement" in his terms) continues to exist quite apart from anyone's will, including that of the right-holder. From the perspective of public policy, however, one might hold that in that case there is no compunction to provide the entitlement, which under the circumstances might be seen as an imposition.

(11) Gaarder, op. cit., p. 413.

(12) Wirt and Kirst, op. cit., pp. 175–176.

(13) Shirley Brice Heath, "Social History," *Bilingual Education: Current Perspectives*, Vol. 1, *Social Science* (Arlington, Va.: Center for Applied Linguistics, 1977).

(14) This is as true today as it was in 1967. See, for example, Alan Pifer, "Bilingual Education and the Hispanic Challenge," *The Annual Report, Carnegie Corporation of New York* (New York: Carnegie Corporation, 1979), p. 11. He says that bilingual education is a "means of correcting English language deficiencies in primary school children, with the rationale that it could help them make the transition from the mother tongue to English and promote assimilation into mainstream education ... It has not had as its central aim the fostering and maintaining of competence in two languages ...."

(15) Joshua Fishman in *Bilingual Education: An International Sociological Perspective* (Rowley, Mass.: Newbury House Publishers, 1976), p. x, strongly criticizes this aspect of the

law. "I note the totally unnatural, shameful, and indeed, slanderous relationship between bilingual education and poverty or other societal dislocation which is still required by much of the Bilingual Education legislation in the United States."

(16) Gaarder, op. cit., p. 418.

(17) See also the language in *Lau v. Nichols*, 483 F. 2nd 799 (9th Cir. 1973).

(18) *Washington Post* (March 4, 1981), p. 5. Numerous examples of this attitude have appeared in the popular media since the enactment of bilingual education legislation; these show, perhaps, that the President's statement is representative of a relatively large segment of the American population. See, for instance, Ernest Cuneo, "Bilingual Teaching Is A Grave Error," *Long Island Press* (June 19, 1975), p 18. He writes, "If the parents of these children are too lazy or too ignorant to learn the American language, they ought not to be voting citizens ... The emphasis, therefore, should be upon teaching their children the American language to overcome the disadvantage of their parents. The object of American schooling is to teach them to think as Americans, not to continue the customs of a different culture."

(19) Charles A. Ferguson, "Language and Global Interdependence," in E. Michael Gerli, James E. Alatis, and Richard I. Brod, eds., *Language in American Life: Proceedings of the Georgetown University – Modern Language Association Conference*, October 6–8, 1977 (Washington, D.C.: Georgetown University Press, 1978).

(20) Cited in Shirley Brice Heath and Frederick Mandabach, "Language Status Decisions and the Law in the United States," a paper prepared for *Progress in Language Planning: International Perspectives* (Wayne, N.J.: William Paterson College of New Jersey, 1979), pp. 21–22.

(21) *Meyer v. Nebraska*, 262 U.S. 402 (1923).

(22) Heath and Mandabach, op. cit., p. 18.

(23) Ibid.

(24) Cited in Herbert Teitelbaum and Richard J. Hiller, "The Legal Perspective," *Bilingual Education: Current Perspectives*, Vol. 3, *Law* (Arlington, Va.: Center for Applied Linguistics, 1977), p. 3.

(25) Quoted in Milton Gordon, *Assimilation in American Life: The Role of Race, Religion and National Origins* (New York: Oxford University Press, 1964), p. 98.

(26) See Joshua Fishman, et. al. *Language Loyalty in the United States: The Maintenance and Perpetuation of Non-English Mother Tongues by American Ethnic and Religious Groups* (The Hague: Mouton and Co., 1966), pp. 29ff, for some explanations of the loss of ethnic and linguistic distinctiveness in American society.

(27) *Garcia v. Gloor*, 628 F. 2nd 264 (1980).

(28) These "business reasons" are remarkably similar to the justification given by school administrators in the Southwest for "no Spanish" rules in the schools: English is the standard language in the United States and all citizens must learn it. The pupil's best interests are served if he speaks English well; English enhances his opportunity for education and employment while Spanish is a handicap. Proper English enables Mexican Americans to compete with Anglos. Teachers and Anglo pupils do not speak Spanish: it is impolite to speak a language not understood by all. (United States Commission on Civil Rights, *The Excluded Student: Educational Practices Affecting Mexican Americans in the Southwest, Report III* [Washington, D.C.: U.S. Government Printing Office, May 1972], p. 14.)

(29) This is a factor of some importance in a similar case in Oregon, *Hernandez v. Erlenbusch*, 368 F. Supp. 752 (D. Oregon 1973). Here, the district court found grounds for a claim of racial discrimination against Mexican Americans in a tavern's policy prohibiting the use of any foreign language at the bar. In this case, the fact that Mexican Americans made up one-fourth of the tavern's potential customers was an important aspect.

(30) *Garcia v. Gloor*, op. cit.

(31) Ibid.

(32) There is another way to explain the Court's apparent ambivalence in the decisions it reaches, especially those relating to controversial social issues. Some on the Court have seemingly held that there is, or should be, a difference between "equality before the law" and a more general social equality; the argument is that the Court should rule in strictly legal terms, without any consideration of the social and practical consequences. Note this tension in, for example, the expression of the Court in *Plessy v. Ferguson* (1896): "The 'Object' and purpose of the Fourteenth Amendment, according to the court, was to secure the 'absolute equality of the two races before the law.' But, wrote Justice Henry Billings Brown, 'in the nature of things it could not have been intended to abolish distinctions based on color, or to enforce social, as distinguished from political equality, or a commingling of the two races upon terms unsatisfactory to either'!" (Albert P. Blaustein and Clarence Clyde Ferguson, *Desegregation and the Law: The Meaning and Effect of the School Segregation Cases* [New York: Vintage Books, 1962], p. 96.)

(33) *Gong Lum v. Rice*, 275 U.S. 78 (1927). Cf. *Cummings v. Board of Education*, 175 U.S. 528 (1899), the first Supreme Court school segregation case. Black plaintiffs, also using *Plessy*, asked for an injunction closing white schools in Richmond County, Georgia, until a separate black school could be provided. The suit was dismissed, the Court contending that the proposed remedy would do harm to everyone and good to no one.

(34) Cited in Gaarder, op. cit., pp. 411–412.

(35) *Ross v. Eckels*, 434 F. 2nd 1140 (5th Cir. 1970).

(36) *Missouri ex. rel. Gaines v. Canada*, 305 U.S. 337 (1938).

(37) See Manuel Ramirez III and Alfredo Castaneda, *Cultural Democracy, Bicognitive Development and Education* (New York: Academic Press, 1974), pp. 21–24; and United States Commission on Civil Rights, op. cit., pp. 14–20. The second source reports the findings of a survey of Southwestern schools which included information on measures taken against students caught speaking Spanish. The following comments are a sample of some of these measures: "If we speak Spanish we had to pay five cents to the teacher or we had to stay after school ...;" "In the sixth grade, they kept a record of which if we spoke Spanish they would take it down and charge us a penny for every Spanish word. If we spoke more than one thousand words our parents would have to come to school and talk with the principal ...;" "If you'd be caught speaking Spanish you would be sent to the principal's office or given extra assignments to do as homework or probably made to stand by the wall during recess and after school ..." There was similar treatment for other language groups. See, for example, Gaarder's reference (op. cit., p. 414) to "teachers in public schools ... threatening the pupils with punishment for speaking Norwegian on the playgrounds." Nor have these practices been limited to a concern with language. Alan Pifer (op. cit., p. 10) cites other contributions of the school to discrimination against Hispanics: tracking Spanish speakers into low achievement classes: "classifying them as mentally retarded and emotionally disturbed"; "denigrating their Hispanic heritage"; "giving them the message that they cannot, or are not expected to, succeed."

(38) Quoted in Clarence J. Karier, "Testing for Order and Control in the Corporate Liberal State," *Educational Theory*, 22:2(1972): 154–180.

(39) Ibid.

(40) The printed media were important in this agitation. V. S. McClatchy, publisher of the *Sacramento Bee*, spent considerable time and resources fighting Japanese immigration in California. In a brief delivered to the State Department on behalf of the Japanese

Exclusion League of California (See Valentine Stuart McClatchy, *Four Anti-Japanese Pamphlets, 1919–1925* [New York: Arno Press, 1978], he cites the League's "Declaration of Principles," the first of which is: "Absolute exclusion for the future of all Japanese immigration, not only male, but female, and not only laborers, skilled and unskilled, but 'farmers' and men of small trades and professions as recommended by Theodore Roosevelt." In support, he points to Roosevelt's autobiography: "Let the arrangement between Japan and the United States be entirely reciprocal. Let the Japanese and Americans visit one another's countries with entire freedom as tourists, scholars, professors, sojourners for study or pleasure, or for purposes of international business, but keep out laborers, men who want to take up farms, men who want to go into the small trades, or even in professions where the work is of a non-international character: that is, keep out of Japan those Americans who wish to settle and become part of the resident working population, and keep out of America those Japanese who wish to adopt a similar attitude. This is the only wise and proper policy." (McClatchy, op. cit., pp. 104–105.)

(41) Yamato Ichihashi, *Japanese in the United States* (New York: Arno Press, 1969), pp. 234–244. See also Harry H. Kitano, *Japanese Americans: Evolution of a Subculture*, 2nd ed. (Englewood Cliffs, N.J.: Prentice Hall Publishers, 1976).

(42) Herbert Hill, "Anti-Oriental Agitation and the Rise of the Working Class Racism," *Society*, 10(January/February 1973): 43–54. Hill shows how organized labor was instrumental in diminishing the opportunities of Asian Americans in the work force. He chronicles mass meetings of otherwise competing groups like the Knights of Labor, the Anarcho-Communists of the International Working People's Association, and trade unions, whose purpose was Chinese expulsion from the labor force. He also describes the workings of the League of Deliverance whose boycott of Chinese-made goods and lobbying helped in the passage of the Chinese Exclusion Act of 1882. While these were grass roots efforts, they were facilitated by the support of such well-known labor leaders as Samuel Gompers.

(43) Wirt and Kirst would prefer the word "desegregation" in this context. Their distinction between desegregation ("an administrative, physical act") and integration ("the emotional and spiritual belief of men") is taken from *United States v. Texas*, 342 F. Supp. 28 (E. D. Texas 1971). (Wirt and Kirst, op. cit., p. 200.)

(44) Henry M. Levin, ed., *Community Control of Schools* (Washington, D.C.: The Brookings Institution, 1970), p. 7.

(45) Gerald W. Johnson, *Our English Heritage* (Philadelphia: J.P. Lippincott, 1949), pp. 118–119.

(46) Ferguson, op. cit., p. 31.

(47) Fishman, *Bilingual Education: An International Sociological Perspective*, op. cit., p. 6. Pifer calls for the same kind of demonstration more specifically about bilingual education. "Its very vulnerability to criticism on political grounds makes it especially incumbent upon this experiment to justify itself educationally. Nothing less will do justice to the needs of children from linguistic minorities and to the meaning of equal educational opportunity." (Pifer, op. cit., p. 5.)

(48) Paul Simon, "Language and National Policy," *Language in American Life*, op. cit., p. 109.

(49) Ibid., pp. 110–112.

(50) Ferguson, op. cit., p. 30.

References

Blaustein, Albert P. and Ferguson, Clarence Clyde. *Desegregation and the Law: The Meaning and Effect of the School Segregation Cases*. New York: Vintage Books, 1962.

Cummings v. Board of Education, 175 U.S. 528, 1899.

Cuneo, Ernest. "Bilingual Teaching is a Grave Error." *Long Island Press*, June 19, 1975, p. 18.

Ferguson, Charles A., "Language and Global Interdependence." In *Language in American Life* (Proceedings of the Georgetown University-Modern Language Association Conference, October 6–8, 1977), E. Michael Gerli, James E. Alatis and Richard I. Brod (eds.) Washington, D.C.: Georgetown University Press, 1978.

Fishman, Joshua A. *Bilingual Education: An International Sociological Perspective*. Rowley, Massachusetts: Newbury House Publishers, 1976.

Fishman, Joshua A., et al. *Language Loyalty in the United States: The Maintenance and Perpetuation of Non-English Mother Tongues by American Ethnic and Religious Groups*. The Hague: Mouton & Co., 1966.

Fishman, Joshua A., and Lovas, John. "Bilingual Education in a Sociolinguistic Perspective." In *The Language Education of Minority Children*, Bernard Spolsky (ed.). Rowley, Massachusetts: Newbury House Publishers, 1977.

Gaarder, A. Bruce. "Language Maintenance or Language Shift." In *Bilingualism in Early Childhood*, W. F. Mackey and T. Anderson (eds.). Rowley, Massachusetts: Newbury House Publishers, 1977.

Garcia v. Gloor, 618 F. 2d 264, 1980.

Gong Lum v. Rice, 275 U.S. 78, 1927.

Gordon, Milton. *Assimilation in American Life: The Role of Race, Religion, and National Origins*. New York: Oxford, 1964.

Heath, Shirley Brice. "Social History." In *Bilingual Education: Current Perspectives* (Volume 1: Social Science). Arlington, VA.: Center for Applied Linguistics, 1977.

Heath, Shirley Brice, and Mandabach, Frederick. "Language Status Decisions and the Law in the United States" (paper prepared for Progress in Language Planning: International Perspectives, William Paterson College of New Jersey), 1979.

Hernandez v. Erlenbusch, 368 F. Supp. 752, D. Ore., 1973

Hill, Herbert. "Anti-Oriental Agitation and the Rise of Working Class Racism." *Society 10* (2): 43–54, January/February, 1973.

Ichihashi, Yamato. *Japanese in the United States*. New York: Arno Press, 1969 (orig. 1932)

Johnson, Gerald W. *Our English Heritage*. Philadelphia: J.P. Lippincott, 1949.

Karier, Clarence J. "Testing for Order and Control in the Corporate Liberal State." *Educational Theory 22* (2): 154–180, 1972.

Kitano, Harry H. *Japanese Americans: Evolution of A Subculture* (2nd. Edition). Englewood Cliffs: Prentice-Hall, 1976.

Kudryavtsev, Vladimir. "The Truth About Human Rights." *Human Rights 5:* 193–199, 1976.

Lau v. Nichols, 483 F. 2d 791, 9th Circuit, 1973.

Lau v. Nichols, 414 U.S.: 563, 1974.

Levin, Henry M. (ed.). *Community Control of Schools*. Washington D.C.: The Brookings Institution, 1970.

Machan, Tibor R. "Some Recent Work in Human Rights Theory." *American Philosophical Quarterly 17* (2): 103–115, April, 1980.

McClatchy, Valentine Stuart. *Four Anti-Japanese Pamphlets* (1919–1925). New York: Arno Press, 1978.

Martin, Rex, and Nickel, James W. "Recent Work on the Concept of Rights." *American Philosophical Quarterly 17* (3): 165–180, July, 1980.

Meyer v. Nebraska, 262 U.S. 390, 1923.

Missouri ex rel Gaines v. Canada, 305 U.S. 337, 1938.

Pifer, Alan. "Bilingual Education and the Hispanic Challenge" (The Report of the President). Reprinted from *The Annual Report, Carnegie Corporation of New York*, 1979.

Ramirez III, Manuel and Castaneda, Alfredo. *Cultural Democracy, Bicognitive Development, and Education*. New York: Academic Press, 1974.

"Reagan Denounces Carter's Proposed Rules on Bilingual Education." *Washington Post*, c5, March 4, 1981.

Ross v. Eckels, 434 F. 2d 1140, 5th Cir., 1970.

Shuy, Roger and Fasold, Ralph W. *Language Attitudes: Current Trends and Prospects*. Washington D.C., Georgetown University Press, 1973.

Simon, Paul. "Language and National Policy." In *Language in American Life* (Proceedings of the Georgetown University Modern Language Association Conference, October 6–8, 1977), E. Michael Gerli, James E. Alatis, and Richard I. Brod (eds.). Washington D.C.: Georgetown University Press, 1978.

Teitelbaum, Herbert and Hiller, Richard J. "The Legal Perspective." In *Bilingual Education: Current Perspectives* (Volume 3: Law). Arlington, VA.: Center for Applied Linguistics, 1977.

United Nations Educational, Scientific, and Cultural Organization (UNESCO). *Cultural Rights as Human Rights* (Volume 3: Studies and Documents on Cultural Policies). Paris: UNESCO, 1970.

United States v. Texas, 342 F. Supp. 24, E.D. Texas, 1971.

United States Commission on Civil Rights. *The Excluded Student: Educational Practices Affecting Mexican Americans in the Southwest*, Report III. Washington D.C.: U.S. Government Printing Office, May, 1972.

Wirt, Frederick M. and Kirst, Michael W., *Political and Social Foundations of Education*. Berkeley: McCutcheon, 1975.

The Empowerment of Language-Minority Students

Richard Ruiz (1991)

A central and early tenet of bilingual education advocates was that inclusion of the child's language and culture in the curriculum would lead to greater school achievement. The claims for the benefit of native language instruction were broad, including not only an increase in language proficiency, but also enhancement of more general, nonlinguistic skills such as problem solving and conceptualization (Lambert, 1978; Cummins, 1979; Kessler and Quinn, 1980). More recently, this discussion has turned from a consideration of merely cognitive and academic consequences of mother tongue instruction and bilingualism to their sociolinguistic and political consequences as well. This goes beyond suggestions that being bilingual can be of some economic or commercial advantage: it entails a general reordering of prevailing societal patterns of stratification. In other words, native language instruction in schools can be an important factor in ethnic communities shedding their minority status by sharing power with the dominant group.

The focal concept in these arguments is 'empowerment'. In the following pages, I will try to explain the general connection between language and power, the arguments concerning school language programs and empowerment, the problems and limitations of those arguments from the perspective of a critical pedagogy, and some possibilities for the role that school language programs can play in the authentic empowerment of minority students and their communities.

Language and Power

Frantz Fanon begins his book *Black Skin, White Masks* with an essay titled "The Negro and Language." He is concerned with the psychological consequences of colonialism and the role that language suppression and domination play in it: "The problem that we confront in this chapter is this: The Negro of the Antilles will be proportionately whiter—that is, he will come closer to being a real human being—in direct ratio to his mastery of the French Language" (Fanon, 1967, p. 18). By "the French Language," he means to say "the French of France, the Frenchman's French, French French" (p. 20). Fanon illustrates the relationship between language and power in society: not merely social position, but ontological status, can be inferred from the language one speaks. The colonializing power of language has a long history and a large literature; the overt political effects of linguistic and cultural dominance are well documented (for a recent treatment of such questions, see, for example, *Language of Inequality*, 1985, edited by Wolfson and Manes). I am more interested in exploring aspects of this relationship that are less obvious.

A major dimension of the power of language is the power to define, to decide the nature of lived experience. In social relations, the power to define determines dominance and subordination, as Moreau (1984) says: "In social discourse, the dominated are defined (collectively) as incomplete, while the dominant are singularized and defined as the incarnation of achieved human nature" (p. 46). Put another way, subordinate minority groups are those who are named and defined by majority groups. Consider that most ethnic minority communities in the United States are known by names not of their own choosing: "Asians" and "Hispanics" are lumped into categories that deny the distinctiveness of the groups they comprise; American Indian nations usually are distinguished by names ("Papago" or "Stockbridge," for example), but those names generally are not the ones by which they refer to themselves. And, when groups do try to define themselves—when Mexican Americans become "Chicanos," when Negroes become "Blacks," or Blacks propose for themselves "African Americans"—there is resistance, not just because of the inconvenience and confusion created for the rest of us, but because of a deep-felt sense that this sort of self-definition by these groups lacks legitimacy: who has given them the right to change their name?

This concern with whether a person or group is allowed the power of self-definition is closely related to another dimension of the relation of language and power: the distinction between *language* and *voice*. The link between language and voice is put forward by Girouxi (1986): "Language represents a central force in the struggle for voice ... language is able to shape the way various individuals and groups encode and thereby engage the world" (p. 59).

As much as language and voice are related, it is also important to distinguish between them. I have become convinced of the need for this distinction through a consideration of instances of language planning in which the "inclusion" of the language of a group has coincided with the exclusion of their voice. Guadalupe Valdes (1987) has conducted a series of important studies on the Spanish language classes designed for U.S. Hispanics. She find that "a surprising number of Spanish-speaking students in the American Southwest are still being placed in beginning Spanish classes for non-speakers to help them 'unlearn' their 'bad' habits and begin anew as foreign speakers" (p. 7). She cites an attitude study of Texas Spanish teachers in which a common sentiment expressed was that "Spanish-speaking students should be provided with grammar explanations which show them why their way of speaking is wrong" (p. 6). This is a case of a language class designed to show speakers of that language that theirs is not really that language—perhaps is not really *any* language. This is similar to my personal experiences with teachers in "maintenance" bilingual education programs, where the explicit goal is to conserve the language of the child. What I frequently find, however, is that the language of the child is rarely spoken in the classroom, much less taught in formal lessons. There are two important explanations for this. In the first place, teachers in these classrooms rarely speak the language of the child; either they have learned a textbook language that no one actually uses in everyday conversation, or they confine their speech to standard forms because of their sense of what is proper or acceptable classroom behavior. In the second place, even if they themselves speak or are familiar with the language of the child, they have appropriated the view that it is not proper language and therefore not to be encouraged in the classroom. They attain their goal of language "maintenance" to the extent that they eradicate *lonche* and replace it with *almuerzo*. One might properly ask why this called "language maintenance."

One other case of language planning will help illustrate the distinction between language and voice. In Peru, Quechua was made an official language, "coequal" with Spanish, in 1975. This policy was hailed at the time as an enhancement of the status of the indigenous language communities to be a significant part of the nation. The problem with Quechua's officialization was the relatively minor role that the Quechua communities themselves played in the decision and its implementation. Almost fifteen years later, there is little hope that Quechua will fulfill any substantive role as an official language, or that Quechua-Spanish bilingual programs in the Highlands will have any impact on Quechua language maintenance (Hornberger, 1988).

I have offered these examples to illustrate the distinction between language and voice. *Language* is general, abstract, subject to a somewhat arbitrary normalization; *voice* is particular and concrete. *Language* has a life of its own—it exists even when it is suppressed; when *voice* is suppressed, it is not heard—it does not exist. To deny people their language, as in the colonial situations described by Fanon (1967) and Macedo (1983), is, to be sure, to deny them voice. Indeed, this may be the most evil form of colonialism, because everyone, even the colonizers themselves, recognize it as just the opposite. To have a voice implies not just that people can say things, but that they are heard (that is, that their words have status, influence). Giroux (1986) argues that "schools do not allow students from subordinate groups to authenticate their problems and experiences through their own individual and collective voices" (p. 65). Nichols (1984) makes a similar point regarding adult-to-child and male-to-female speech dynamics: "Children talking with adults and women talking with men are consistently and frequently interrupted by their speaking partners, as well as ignored or unsupported when they attempted to choose the topic of conversation" (p. 25). The *language* of these situations is largely irrelevant; let us assume that everyone was speaking in his or her own conversational mother tongue. What is important is that some groups consistently impose their *voice* on others. When sociolinguists carry out their investigations of language use, they ask "Who says what to whom in what language?" When we investigate the issue of voice, we should ask, "Who says?"

The question of voice will be taken up again presently. We might anticipate my conclusion: voice is the central ingredient of critical pedagogy; without its consideration, there is no radical reform of curriculum. I would like now to turn to a recent proposal for curricular reform aimed directly at the language-minority student. My evaluation of it will be based on this concern for voice.

School Language and Empowerment

Jim Cummins's 1986 article in the *Harvard Educational Review,* "Empowering Minority Students: A Framework for Intervention," has become one of the most influential works in the literature on the education of minority students. He has since expanded his ideas into the book *Empowering Minority Students* (1989). His use of the term *empowerment* is already a stock item in the lexicons of various areas within the education literature, most notably bilingual education and special education. Any treatment of the concept of empowerment in education would be incomplete without consideration of Cummins's work. Let us turn to that now.

Cummins's argument runs as follows. First, the failure of minority students is not completely, perhaps not even in major part, an academic or school matter. Instead, one should examine their subordinate status in the larger society, and the ways in which the school reinforces or reproduces that status: "Status and power relations between groups are an important part of any comprehensive account of minority students' school failure" (Cummins, 1986, p. 21). Such failure will persist so long as school reformers fail to take into account these extraschool factors. Second, school and curricular reform must involve the inclusion of the students' home cultural experiences. Here, Cummins is most concerned with four aspects of school structure: "incorporation of minority students' culture and language, inclusion of minority communities in the education of their children, pedagogical assumptions and practices operating in the classroom, and the assessment of minority students" (p. 24). To the extent that schools consistently exclude the child's home experiences from the curriculum, alienate their families and discourage their participation in the education of the children, transmit in an authoritarian way a standardized curriculum, and bias their assessment of minority children to ensure that some "problem" will be found in them, minority students will be disabled. Empowerment comes when schools are inclusionary, when their pedagogy encourages critical, independent thinking, and when they aim to find and build on a child's strengths rather than identify weaknesses. Third, and finally, in the same way that school failure is not merely a school matter, student empowerment cannot be confined to the school. There is a dynamic interrelation between home and school: real school reform and authentic student empowerment will contribute to the transformation of societal power relations as well.

This argument is significant for language-minority students because it describes deep structural reasons for school failure. The language difference of the child is no longer of primary concern; or, more precisely, particular language differences are indicators of class differences, and these are where our examination of school failure should focus. The argument is also significant because it bypasses the usual concern for cognitive or academic justifications for using the first language of these children. One might even say that Cummins's argument makes irrelevant the research on the effectiveness of various methods to use with language-minority students.

I have chosen to be critical of Cummins's work for a specific reason. Few doubt his personal commitment to the betterment of education for language-minority students or the significance of his scholarship. I judge that Cummins is one of only a handful of academics whose work consistently determines the direction of the literature in this area. It is precisely for that reason that I offer this criticism. What I will try to demonstrate is that, even for those among us who are the most sympathetic to the concerns of minority communities and who are the most conscious of the effect of our public statements, our words sometimes betray what we intend.

Let me now take up this criticism at its most central point. It has to do with the issue of voice. Note the use of "empowerment" in the following typical passages:

> Students from "dominated" societal groups are "empowered" or "disabled" as a direct result of their interactions with educators in the schools. (p. 21)

> Minority students are disabled or disempowered by schools in very much the same way that their communities are disempowered by interactions with societal institutions. (p. 24)

What disturbs me most about such usage is the passivity of the "empowered" groups. Empowerment appears to be an action performed by others on their behalf. This is put most directly in the following passage.

> Language minority students' educational progress is strongly influenced by the extent to which individual educators become advocates for the

promotion of students' linguistic talents, actively encourage participation in developing students' academic and cultural resources, and implement pedagogical approaches that succeed in liberating students from instructional dependence. (p. 35)

I do not see here any action on the part of those who are to be empowered. Instead, empowerment is portrayed as a gift to the powerless. This evokes several questions. If empowerment is a gift from those in power to those out, what kind of power would they be willing to give up? Will it be of a sort that might lead to the transformation of society? Could empowerment entail another sort of acculturation, by which we change the behavior of underachieving students to conform to that of high achievers? Are higher test scores the ultimate index of empowerment? Would empowered students become critical, or merely successful?

Beyond these important questions, we should ask, what has happened to student voice? Assuming that students' language has been included in the curriculum, whose voice is heard in it if they are not active participants? How can they be characterized as "empowered" when minority communities merely wait for schools to change in particular ways?

The radical pedagogue who treats empowerment as a gift is not yet radical. Teachers do not empower or disempower anyone, nor do schools. They merely create the conditions under which people can *empower themselves*, or not. It is certainly true that teachers impart skills—literacy, numeracy, and others; but these are not in themselves power. They are tools to be used or not, and, if used, for responsible or irresponsible ends. (If the proficiency in using a standard language to which I contributed becomes a means to denigrate the experience of nonstandard speakers, that is empowerment—but I would not boast about my connection with it.)

The idea that empowerment might be construed as a gift should be a central concern in the development or evaluation of a critical transformative pedagogy. It is one anticipated by Freire (1970), in his most famous work, *Pedagogy of the Oppressed*:

Not even the best-intentioned leadership can bestow independence as a gift. The liberation of the oppressed is a liberation of men [and women], not things. Accordingly, while no one liberates himself [or herself] by his [or her] own efforts alone, neither is he [or she] liberated by others ... The conviction of the oppressed that they must fight for their liberation is not a gift bestowed by the revolutionary leadership, but a result of their own *conscientização*. (pp. 53–54)

Freire avoids this problem, as well as the problem of voice, by eschewing an orientation of "inclusion." He does not suggest, as does Cummins, that the language and culture of the child should be "included" in the curriculum of the school; this would suggest that this curriculum is fundamentally sound but that it needs a few additions or modifications. Instead, for Freire, the language and culture of the child *constitute* the curriculum. The most dramatic example of this are the "generative words" he uses in adult literacy programs. These words are recorded in an initial period of observation in the village where the program is to take place. In the course of the training, these words are represented to the students as the basis for both decoding instruction and discussion. The discussion results in the development of more words, and these words eventually become themes for further study and discussion. In this way, student voice becomes the curriculum; furthermore, the discussion of themes with other students demonstrates how one's individual voice can be joined with other voices to effect social action on behalf of the community. This is the essence of what Freire calls *conscientização*, the development of critical consciousness. Although Freire's early work involved literacy training of peasant adults, he has gone on to show how his can be a more general pedagogy (Freire and Macedo, 1987).

Cummins can be criticized in his assumption that the school will contribute to its own transformation, with little active participation by the minority communities. Freire denies that this can happen, and asserts that the transformation of society will come when the oppressed empower themselves. We should now turn to a consideration of how this might happen, with special emphasis on language minority communities.

Privatization and Power

Henry Giroux (1986) chastises radical educators because they have concentrated on developing a "language of resistance" but not a "language of possibility." By this he means that we should not only understand society, its institutions, and the power relations that result in oppressed classes, but we should devise strategies by which we can take advantage of the transformative possibilities that exist even in the worst cases. In what remains of this essay, I would like to suggest a possibility for social transformation that exists in a conservative critique of bilingual education and cultural pluralism.

This critique is put forward most elegantly by John Edwards (1984). In its broadest terms, it contends that ethnic language and cultural identification are essentially private matters. To promote them in the public sector would be chaotic and fragmenting, since there is no objective measure by which to choose the ethnicities and languages to be subsidized. Besides, this is undesirable because the interest of the state is unity and coherence, and a public cultural pluralism leads to conflict. Therefore, to the extent that programs such as public school bilingual education are to be tolerated, it is only the narrowest form of transitional program that should receive public support. This would exclude "maintenance" programs designed to preserve ethnic language and culture. Presumably, this would also preclude funding proposals such as that by Cummins, not to mention Freire.

The conservative movement of the 1980s in the United States has placed such critiques at the basis of much public policy, including bilingual education policy. Instead of cultural pluralism, we have "cultural literacy" (Hirsch, 1987) as the guiding principle of curricular reform. This entails, among other things, a national culture and history to be appropriated by everyone as a result of public schooling. From the perspective of critical pedagogy, it means a total exclusion of student voice from the school. Such a state of affairs minimizes the prospects for the empowerment of language minority communities, if we are to believe Cummins and Freire. How can a language of possibility be fashioned from such a critique?

The key lies in the distinction between public and private life. The conservative argues for what I call the "privatization of pluralism," and makes a distinction between private pluralism and public unity. Some advocates of bilingual education see such arguments (rightly, I think) as a way to limit funding for and eventually suppress these programs. Their reaction is to increase the pressure in favor of public funding. Although I do not disagree with the effort to conserve such public school programs, I believe another strategy is advisable if language maintenance and authentic empowerment are the aims. This strategy is to be more conservative than the conservatives by developing the power of privatization.

My study of two contrasting cases has brought me to this point; I refer to them often in my classes and when I write, but it is only now that I articulate the essential lesson in them. These are the German communities of the Midwest in the latter half of the nineteenth century and the Mexican communities of the Southwest at precisely the same time. The Germans were afforded the most extensive programs of public school bilingual education in the history of the country. The public school districts in cities within the so-called German Triangle, Cincinnati, St. Louis, Milwaukee, Chicago, Indianapolis, and others, also developed formal offices of German instruction to supervise the programs. Seminaries and institutes established in part to train German teachers for both public and private schools flourished in Milwaukee and Chicago. In some school districts, as much as 70 percent of the school population took some of their instruction in German as late as 1916. This situation persisted until the beginning of World War I, when anti-German sentiment made German study unpopular. By 1920, the programs that had been so pervasive in the public schools virtually disappeared (Ruiz, 1988). This case is easily contrasted with that of the Mexicans. Not only did they not receive instruction in their own language, but their language was actively suppressed. In some districts, Mexicans were prohibited from attending public schools; when they were allowed, they were prohibited from speaking Spanish, even outside class. This situation persisted into the 1960s, when federally funded Spanish-English bilingual programs were allowed for the first time in the schools of the Southwest.

There is another important contrast to be made in these cases. Today, German communities have effectively lost their language: they are culturally but not linguistically German communities. On the other hand, in spite of much individual language loss, Spanish-speaking Mexican communities still flourish in the Southwest. How is that explained? How is it that publicly supported school programs have led to language loss, whereas linguistic discrimination has resulted in language maintenance? In large part, the explanation lies in the dynamics of privatization. The German communities had strong cultural maintenance institutions of their own—schools, churches, civic organizations—which were neglected in the period of public subsidy. When public support was suddenly withdrawn, those institutions weakened considerably. Along with that, the reversal of public sentiment toward Germans made those communities less willing to engage in activities of cultural and linguistic loyalty which would only intensify social conflict for them. The Mexicans, on the other hand, had no reason to believe that their cultural institutions would be supported outside their communities; they turned inward for support, thereby strengthening those very institutions— the church, the family, and neighborhoods—which would allow for long-term language maintenance. The difference in these two cases demonstrates the potential power of privatization.

I am not the first to suggest such a strategy for language-minority communities. Geneva Smitherman (1984) describes how traditional White education has pulled Black people away from Black language and community. She explores the possibilities for self-empowerment through the reclaiming of Black language within the Black community. Similarly, Shirley Heath (1985) makes a distinction between *maintenance* of language, or the efforts of those outside the community to preserve the language, and the *retention* of language, whereby the community itself acts out its language loyalty. This is put most forcefully by Kjolseth (1982), an advocate of bilingual education and cultural pluralism:

> Chicano families who desire the maintenance of their ethnic language *must* exercise their control over that single domain of language use where they do have effective and continuing control: the family. Parental insistence upon the use of Spanish by themselves and their children within the private family domain is the *only* realistic hope. (p. 25)

Privatization implies two things: developing the resources readily available to minority communities to increase what the critical theorist calls their own "cultural capital," and minorities taking control of their own lives in such a way that their communities can act positively in their own interests.

Such action may include pressure on the public sector for subvention of their activities, but it need not be dependent on such support. School programs that aim at these goals might very well resemble Mr. Hardcastle's English class, of which one student reported the following: "If the type of English work we have been discussing continues, then the possibility of taking control of our own lives, our own education, and becoming our own experts, is extremely exciting" (McLeod, 1986, p. 49). Privatization and "taking control" is another way of saying that the student's voice is developed and heard in the educational experience.

Let me conclude by suggesting two modifications to the lexicon of critical pedagogy. First, we should understand that when we say "language," we often mean "voice." I hope I have shown how we delude ourselves into thinking that because we include the first we include the second. And second, *empowerment* may not be desirable in English because of our tendency to use it as a transitive verb; this denies both voice and agency to students and communities. A convenient one-word substitute does not come readily to mind; *appropriation* is not exactly synonymous with *taking control.* Perhaps this discussion will provoke someone to think of something suitable. The point to be made is that voice and agency are central to critical pedagogy; without them there is no such thing as "empowerment."

References

Cummins, J. (1979). Linguistic interdependence and educational development of bilingual children. *Review of Educational Research, 49,* 222–251.

—— (1986). Empowering minority students: A framework for intervention. *Harvard Educational Review, 56,* 18–36.

—— (1989). *Empowering minority students.* Sacramento: California State Department of Education.

Edwards, J. (1984). Language, diversity and identity. In J. Edwards (Ed.), *Linguistic minorities, policies and pluralism* (pp. 277–310). Orlando, Fla.: Academic Press.

Fanon, F. (1967). *Black skin, white masks.* Translated by C. L. Markmann. New York: Grove Press.

Freire, P. (1970). *Pedagogy of the oppressed.* Translated by M. B. Ramos. New York: Continuum.

Freire, P., and Macedo, D. (1987). *Literacy: Reading the word and the world.* South Hadley, Mass.: Bergin and Garvey.

Giroux, H. A. (1986, Spring). Radical pedagogy and the politics of student voice. *Interchange, 17,* 48–69.

Heath, S. B. (1985). Language policies: Patterns of retention and maintenance. In W. Connor (Ed.), *Mexican Americans in comparative perspective.* Washington, D.C.: The Urban Institute.

Hirsch, E. D. (1987). *Cultural literacy.* Boston: Houghton Mifflin.

Hornberger, N. (1988). *Bilingual education and language maintenance: A southern Peruvian Quechua case.* Providence, R.I.: Floris.

Kessler, C., and Quinn, M. (1980). Positive effects of bilingualism on science problem-solving abilities. In J. Alatis (Ed.), *Georgetown University round table on languages and linguistics 1980.* Washington, D.C.: Georgetown University Press.

Kjolseth, R. (1982). Bilingual education programs in the United States: For assimilation or pluralism? In P. R. Turner (Ed.), *Bilingualism in the southwest* (2nd ed., rev., pp. 3–28). Tucson: University of Arizona Press.

Lambert, W. (1978). Some cognitive and sociocultural consequences of being bilingual. In J. Alatis (Ed.), *Georgetown University round table on languages and linguistics* (pp. 214–229). Washington, D.C.: Georgetown University Press.

Macedo, D. P. (1983, Winter). The politics of emancipatory literacy in Cape Verde. *Journal of Education, 165,* 99–112.

McLeod, A. (1986, January). Critical literacy: Taking control of our own lives. *Language Arts, 63,* 37–50.

Moreau, N. B. (1984). Education, ideology, and class/sex identity. In C. Karmarae, M.Schulz and W. M. O'Barr (Eds.), *Language and power* (pp. 43–61). Beverly Hills, Calif.: Sage Publications.

Nichols, P. C. (1984). Networks and hierarchies: Language and social stratification. In C. Kramarae, M. Schulz, and W. M. O'Barr (Eds.), *Language and power* (pp. 23–42). Beverly Hills, Calif.: Sage Publications.

Ruiz, R. (1988). Bilingualism and bilingual education in the United States. In C. B. Paulston (Ed.), *International handbook of bilingualism and bilingual education.* Westport, Conn.: Greenwood Press.

Smitherman, G. (1984). Black language as power. In C. Kramarae, M. Schulz, and W. M. O'Barr (Eds.), *Language and power.* Beverly Hills, Calif.: Sage Publications.

Valdes, G. (1981). Pedagogical implications of teaching Spanish to the Spanish-speaking in the United States. In G. Valdes, A. G. Lozano, and R. Garcia-Moya (Eds.), *Teaching Spanish to the Hispanic bilingual: Issues, aims, and methods.* New York: Teachers College Press.

Wolfson, N., and Manes, J. (Eds.). (1985). *Language of inequality.* Berlin: Mouton.

Asymmetrical Worlds: The Representation of the Ethnic in Public Discourse

Richard Ruiz (2000)

(i)

In an article on the shootings at Columbine High School, Courtland Milloy (1999) describes what he calls a 'parallel universe.' In the past when I have heard that phrase, I have associated it with the science-fictional experiences of a million light years from here: a doppelganger world, accessible only by way of a time warp or worm hole, in which everything is as it is here, but reversed – leftists are conservative, progressives oppress the poor, foul balls are in play, Mr. Spock is emotional, Republicans care about the environment, loyalists sit on the king's left, and clocks go counter-clockwise. These are mirror images – strange, yet totally commensurate and so predictable, a bit like driving in London.

This is a symmetrical isomorphism that does not characterize the ethnic experience of the world as I know it, or the one depicted by Milloy. He speaks of the manhunts of Black men following fictional assaults, and the later justification of those, based on the very believable sense of threat, even after the hoax had been exposed. We can just as easily sense the rationality our communities impose on acts of police overreaction to black men who might have guns or Latino gang members whose very existence threaten our sense of well-being. Even where the officers and the police chief and the mayor are black or Latino, we assume that the legitimacy of their actions cannot be secure without the consent of the dominant, non-minority power structure. These are not parallel universes as I conceive of them above, but two asymmetrical worlds that are not always predictable in the degree of their difference.

(ii)

In Tucson earlier this month, Kathy Morris, a middle-school science teacher, was shot in her classroom early in the morning before the start of the school day. She managed to get to a telephone. In her call to 911 she described her assailant as a Hispanic man of high-school age with a shaved head. Later that day, as the manhunt proceeded, she told investigators that she had been receiving threatening letters for about a month. She suspected one of the current students at the school, another Hispanic boy who was detained and questioned for about an hour by police. The truth is now known, since the case was on national news and on tabloid TV. In a style closely paralleling the Susan Smith case mentioned by Milloy, Morris invented the story of the two Hispanic boys in order to divert police attention: she shot herself for reasons that are still difficult to understand. She says she was trying to call attention to the lack of security at the school, but it appears she confirmed just the opposite; police were able to unravel the story in part because the school was closed up so tightly that it seemed to them highly unlikely that an outsider could have entered and left quickly enough to have done what she alleged.

But that is not the point of my retelling this story. The question here, as in several other notable cases, is why Morris decided that her story would be more believable with a Hispanic teenager with a shaved head as its protagonist. When I heard her description I imagined someone like Will Doty (sp?) and his Huron compatriots in *The Last of the Mohicans*: their heads were not completely shaved, but had a long dark strand tied behind that somehow made the Indians more sinister and menacing. This semester I am teaching a course for graduate students that deals in large part with the distortions of the received view of history and canonical explanations of minority–majority relations, but even I believed her, even though I am inclined, as is Milloy, to suspect such attributions without more evidence. In the asymmetrical world I know, Hispanic and Black boys are always guilty until proven innocent. What is more, there was no reason to disbelieve Morris (¿did I mention she is white?). In the days after the incident, there were a number of reports depicting her as a popular teacher and loving wife. Her husband said he never suspected anything, even though it was obvious she had been planning the incident for some time. She will no doubt lose her job and probably her teaching certification, and she has voluntarily entered a treatment center; in the few days that have transpired, there appears to be little sentiment to punish her further. She was, after all, a model teacher who apparently just snapped under pressure. Let's not kid ourselves about what would have happened in the asymmetrical world where the teacher would be a Hispanic man: even there, his best story would have a Hispanic or Black teenager at its center.

A further note that underscores the point: after she confessed to police that she had shot herself and there were no assailants, the School District apologized to the Hispanic students of the school and the Hispanic community at large. But it was not a unanimous sentiment on the school board. Two of its members chided the District and the Superintendent for having overreacted to the public outcry, and lectured the Hispanic community that they should not take her actions 'personally': all the evidence was not yet in on what she did, and besides it appears to be primarily an act of a disturbed person. Parents of some of the Hispanic students who were in the middle of writing sympathy cards to their beloved teacher when they heard of the ruse asked how else they should take it.

(iii)

Shirley Heath and Frederick Mandabach have written several histories of language law and politics in the United States. One that seems especially relevant for us is one in which they discuss first amendment cases that associate speech with physical action (Heath & Mandabach, 1983). They assert that hardly any cases, and none of any consequence, exist before 1919. What is significant about this date is that it is generally viewed as the beginning of the first significant language scare in the United States that resulted in both court decisions and legislation restricting public language use. The scare is seen as a reaction to the 'new immigration' of the previous 40 years in which the 'racial stock' and language behavior of this society had changed dramatically. They suggest that these are not unrelated considerations. At the same time that as many as half the states passed anti-foreign language legislation aimed primarily at schools (1919–1925), the courts jailed 1000 people for subversive speech. In their words, the courts were motivated by a public sense of 'inchoate crime' – the perception that the speech that people used could lead to violence. This is codified in Justice Holmes' phrase, 'clear and present danger.' The fears intensified during wartime, when subversive speech was considered major violence against the country. What makes this analysis relevant to an asymmetrical world view is what they say about differences in treatment of the language users. 'Until the late 1960s, a majority of those tried on subversive-speech charges were either aliens or individuals linked with "alien elements" of the society. Relatively few First Amendment cases went to court in the Vietnam protests of the late 1960s; protesters were children of the establishment, not foreigners. *They were seen as individuals who had gone astray, but who could (and probably would) move back into the main stream of American culture.*' (Heath & Mandabach, 1983: 100). The last sentence has my emphasis because it underscores what I think might be the core idea that separates the two worlds: mainstream kids 'go astray,' rebel against the older generations, have periods of stress in which they crack under pressure, but we always see them as corrigible. They will come back. And so, Kathy Morris is sent to a rehabilitation center, but the Hispanic boy, had he been 'caught,' or a Black teacher doing what she did would have been in jail.

(This all reminds me of the way we have historically dealt with the international cocaine problem: we send the users and abusers, the Hollywood crowd and their offspring, to treatment programs, but we wage war on the criminals in Colombia who produce it; in the same way, we assume a racial 'style' in using cocaine, either in powder or solid form ('crack'), and diversify the punishments accordingly.)

Fast forward to today – two cases in point. (1) The current Title I law identifies those 'at risk' of school failure as those for whom the law will be of most benefit. It includes a long list of characteristics of such people, including gang membership, history of drug use, vandalism, teen pregnancy, juvenile offenders and those whose first language is not English. Perhaps without being conscious of it, the framers of the law have reinforced in the public mind the idea that non-English language background and behavior is close enough to equate with socially undesirable, if not felonious, conduct. (2) Arizona is considering an initiative that would effectively end bilingual programs in the state. It is introduced in the aftermath of a twin law passed in California in 1998, which was enacted in the middle of one of the most racist, anti-immigrant campaigns in California history. Some idea of public sentiment is captured in letters to the editor that lecture Hispanics about the need to learn English to get ahead – that this is, after all, an English-speaking country. We err if we think these are isolated cases of public policy gone astray. Custodial workers at the University of Arizona have complained, quietly, for years, that they are prohibited from speaking Spanish on the job for fear of being fired for a more politically justifiable reason. Just two weeks ago, a local news reporter uncovered a 'policy' circulated to employees in the Pima County Court system proscribing the use of anything but English as 'rude' and 'offensive' and threatening to co-workers. No-one has said for sure how long these policies have been in effect, and what impact they have had on the composition of the workforce. We are in a situation, and have been in it for a long time, that rewards English speakers for their initiative in learning a 'foreign language,' but punishes those speakers of that same language for using it. These are asymmetrical worlds.

(iv)

Let me try to create some predictability in these two worlds. The following statements are intended to provoke a sense of the asymmetry I have tried to describe above. I am not sure that even as I write them I hold them completely. There are arguments to be had about them, to be sure. Perhaps that is the point: without arguments, whatever truth they contain will never surface. We have convinced ourselves that, fundamentally, the system is fair to everybody. Perhaps, as some liberals say, we need some compensatory action to ensure that the playing field is level before the game starts, but having done that, we assume everyone has the same opportunity. What I am saying is that the basic differences presented in the following statements point to two different world views that are not reconciled merely by tweaking the system here and there.

- Majority groups talk about law. Minority groups talk about justice.
- Majority groups say that no-one is above the law. Minority groups say that no-one is above the law, unless the law is too low.
- The motto of majority groups: 'Equal justice under law.' The motto of minority groups: 'Laws that are just.'

These are the ways in which members of minority groups struggle in their asymmetrical world to make sense of a society that has yet to live up to its ideals.

Richard Ruiz
Presentation to an Invitational Symposium on the Public Representation of Youth Violence, Annual Meeting of the American Educational Research Association, New Orleans, 25 April 2000.

References

Heath, S.B. and Mandabach, F. (1983) Language status decisions and the law in the United States. In J. Cobarrubias and J.A. Fishman (eds) *Progress in Language Planning: International Perspectives* (pp. 87–105). Berlin: Mouton.
Milloy, C. (1999) A look at tragedy in black and white. *Washington Post*, 2 May.

The Educational Sovereignty of Latino/a Students in the United States[1]

Luis C. Moll and Richard Ruiz (2005)

In one of his last papers, our late friend and colleague David Smith (Smith, 2000) reflects on research he conducted in Philadelphia and elsewhere, and mentions how ethnographic research has difficulty in addressing the "real" issues in education: disparities in relations of power. He wrote as follows:

> A challenge facing urban ethnography today is not only to surface the narratives of oppression, resistance and resilience [but to] develop approaches that put these narratives to use in addressing the oppressive equations. It is not enough to uncover local "funds of knowledge" … nor to incorporate these into our pedagogical repertoire, but they must become the basis for a radical new pedagogy, one that is based on and privileges these narratives and local knowledge. (p. 16 in manuscript)

In this chapter we want to present and elaborate a concept that attempts to respond, at least in some respects, to David's challenge. The concept is that of educational sovereignty. This is a term inspired by the work of colleagues doing research in and with indigenous communities, addressing the need to challenge a long history of control and coercion in the education of Indian students (e.g., Lomawaima, 2000; McCarty, 2002; Warner, 1999; see also Henze & Davis, 1999).

What is Educational Sovereignty?

We use the term "educational sovereignty" to capture the need to challenge the arbitrary authority of the "white" power structure and reestablish within the Latino/a communities themselves the structures and norms by which to determine the essence of education for Latino/a (and other minority) students (see Moll & Ruiz, 2002). It is, in other words, a term of both resistance and affirmation, signaling the recognition of a negative history to be challenged and the hope of a positive future to be grasped. But we are not proposing "sovereignty" in the sense of creating strict and arbitrary boundaries of separation, the way it is done to mark, chauvinistically, and often on the basis of conquest, the territory of a nation/state. That concept of sovereignty, despite the recent nationalistic rhetoric in the United States about "homeland defense," is becoming obsolete because of "the emergence of a new political order, one which would permit overlapping authority structures" (Wright, 2000, p. 79). This new order is being created in large part by the requirements of a global economy, the transnational character of immigration, and the emergence and strengthening within the past half century of supranational authorities intervening in the affairs of putatively sovereign states.

The obsolescence of the notion of territorial sovereignty, the purpose of which is to separate "us" from "them," is demonstrated clearly in the contradictions inherent in the juxtaposition of calls for border-free economic spaces, on the one hand, and insistence on strict border control to keep immigrants out, on the other. "The emergence of a new economic regime," Sassen (1999) writes, "sharply reduces the role of national governments and national borders in controlling international [economic] transactions." "Yet," she continues, "the framework for immigration policy in these countries remains centered on older conceptions of the nation-state and the national borders" (Sassen, 1999, pp. 4–5; cf. Held et al., 1999).

As important to the decline of the territorially sovereign nation-state is the growing importance of supranational and regional authorities such as the United Nations, the International Court of Justice, and the various regional and subcontinental conventions that compete for legitimacy with traditional nations. Indeed, such entities exist in large part to intervene in the affairs of states on behalf of individuals or groups, deriving their authority from the application of principles "higher" than those embodied in the laws of the state.

The International Nuremburg tribunal (1946 and following); the UN's International Bill of Human Rights (1948); the European Convention for the Protection of Human Rights (1950); the Helsinki Declarations of Human Rights (1992); and the UN International Criminal Court (1998) are powerful influences against the laws of individual states even though they have little if any enforcement capacity beyond public humiliation. These and similar authorities have been used to contravene long-standing sovereignty agreements between states, as well, as when the British House of Lords used the 1984 Torture Convention to justify the extradition of General Pinochet to answer charges of human rights abuses in Chile (Held, 1995; Wright, 2000).

The challenge to the traditional view of sovereignty as strict boundedness is captured nicely in the literature on interdisciplinarity and international education, and we can use it here to some advantage. In their edited book on boundaries and theoretical integration, Sil and Doherty (2000) include papers that argue against rigid divisions at the same time that core aspects of disciplinary traditions are both acknowledged and valued. Huntley (2000), for example, uses the term "threshold" (as opposed to boundary) to characterize the separation or compartmentalization of disciplinary traditions in the social sciences. "Whereas the concept of 'boundary' connotes forced separation and perhaps antipathy, the concept of 'threshold' inheres [*sic*] suggestions of both separation and joining—one 'crosses' a threshold" (p. 178). Nor does he bemoan the proliferation of thresholds, seeing it as a natural development of knowledge, what he calls the "geography of human knowledge":

> The emergence of thresholds is providing an ever more detailed map of this geography, viewing which requires only the development of our own capacity to rise above perceiving these thresholds as "boundaries." Our judgments as to topics of attention, epistemological viewpoints, and the like, thus can serve to locate us, rather than limit us, if only we can rise above the choices themselves. (Huntley, 2000, p. 197)

Other writers make similar distinctions. Fardon and Furniss (1994), for example, suggest the use of "frontiers," implying the "interpenetration of phenomena," rather than "boundaries," which suggest "exclusive and distinct phenomena," in discussions of language communities (p. 3). Such use of the concept of "frontier," although embedded, is also evident in work by Bixler-Márquez (1998), who describes how indigenous communities on both sides of the Mexico-U.S. border use electronic media to convey information on health, political reform, education, and language to each other. The control they have over the dissemination of essential information is an exercise in educational sovereignty: it affords them the opportunity to decide how and to what degree they will interact with the communities around them.

Perhaps the best examples of the type of educational sovereignty we are proposing can be found in the literature on indigenous schooling. One such example is provided by Vick-Westgate (2002), who presents a detailed history of the struggle for good schooling for Inuit children against the Quebec government. She describes a situation in northern Canada in which native communities have started to take control of the education of their children. By "control," she means having decision-making authority over curriculum, methods and materials, staffing, calendar, and assessment, among many other things—in other words, the essence of schooling. She describes the need for greater appropriation of schooling by the Inuit community with a quote from a 1992 task force report on Inuit schooling:

> The education system in Nunavik should be restructured and refocused to make it work for us, to ensure that it prepares us to handle the

problems and opportunities of living that we actually face—not just the ones the school board has been mechanically structured to deal with. We are not asking someone else to create this system for us. Creating it ourselves is a necessary step to self-government in Nunavik. Self-government and education go hand in hand just as independence goes with wisdom. (Vick-Westgate, 2002, p. 236)

The situation in Nunavik is different from those of most minority communities in North America in that they have retaken control of not only their social institutions but also their territory (Inuits selected "Nunavik" as the name of their territory in 1987, although the resolution of property rights and governmental structure is ongoing). Even here, however, it is important to note that the greatest obstacle to their independence, as in most colonial situations, is not territorial but psychological.

Even having control over a bordered piece of property does not ensure control of their educational and social institutions, as native communities in the United States are well aware. To help in the reorientation process and to objectify a sense of internal control, the community established a formal body, the Satuigiarniq Committee ("Satuigiarniq" is an Inuit word meaning "reclaiming"). The committee expressed the need for such an attitudinal change:

Community involvement and empowerment will come only from the development of a sense of ownership of the process. Our aim is not to do the consultation for the communities but rather to help them develop the leadership skills necessary to design and conduct their community's consultation and to develop the attitude of self-reliance and a level of competence which will truly lead to their community's reclaiming of the educational system. (Vick-Westgate, 2002, p. 229)

An essential dimension of educational sovereignty is the extent to which communities feel themselves to be in control of their language behaviors. The considerable recent work on language retention and revitalization from the inside (see, for example, Grenoble & Whaley, 1998; Ostler & Rudes, 2000; Fishman, 2001; May, 2001, and many others) is testimony to the salience of such issues. The multitude of examples precludes a comprehensive review of this work here. We will mention only two. Nora England's work among several Maya communities in Guatemala (in Grenoble & Whaley, 1998) reveals the difficult processes of language preservation in a highly minoritized community. She chronicles the work of the Mayan Language Academy (established in 1991) that established a number of principles and assumptions under which it proceeds: Mayan control of language decisions; standardization of Mayan languages; expansion of the domains of Mayan language use; use of Mayan languages in schools as media of instruction, not primarily as instruments of castellanization; and the eventual recognition of the Mayan languages as official within their regions. Although these communities recognize that the demarcation of formal borders around the areas they inhabit (territorial sovereignty) is not feasible nor perhaps even desirable, they do affirm their right and responsibility to take control of the development of their language (linguistic sovereignty) and the uses to which it is put in schools (educational sovereignty).

Similarly, Martinez (2000) describes the situation of native Pueblo communities in North America. She explains that the motivation of these people to teach children the heritage language is because this is valuable for their own reasons, not merely as a means to learning English: "The reason Pueblo adults wish for children to learn their heritage language has nothing to do with the acquisition of English. It is so that the children can participate knowledgeably and appropriately in the maintenance of their traditional culture and religion" (2000, p. 217) She also mentions the need for future leaders of the communities to know the traditional language and values of the people, and the importance of recognizing the "intrinsic value" of Pueblo languages. Finally, she makes the connection between linguistic and educational sovereignty: "... educators must understand that if Pueblo languages are taught in schools, they should be used in ways that are appropriate to the cultures they represent, and not as poor translations of English language curriculum" (p. 217).

It is important to reiterate that we are not using the term "educational sovereignty" to signal the need for an act of separation. We mean by it almost the opposite—the strength and power a social setting like a school can garner by developing strategic social networks to create "cultural spaces" that will enhance its autonomy, mediate ideological and programmatic constraints, and provide additive forms of schooling for its students. In relation to Latino/a children and their teachers, consonant with the international examples mentioned earlier, educational sovereignty also means reclaiming their language rights, in the midst of their oppression, and the aggression perpetrated by the dominant society (more on this later).

In particular, we emphasize the type of agency that considers the schooling of Latino/a children within a larger education ecology, with an eye toward the transnational potential of such schooling, and that respects and responds to the values of education possessed by Latino/a families (see, e.g., Goldenberg & Gallimore, 1995). This larger ecology, then, includes not only schools but also the social relationships and cultural resources found in local households and community settings, and the potential connections created with other schools and communities in the Americas.

What follows is, first, a somewhat cursory review of the status quo for hundreds of thousands of Latino/a students, very diverse in their own right, but mostly from low-income families (see Moll & Ruiz, 2002). It will seem very oppressive for those not familiar with the current conditions of Latino/a education. In fact, no White, middle-class child will ever face the pressures, abuses, and restrictive learning conditions imposed on these children.

Although emphasis of these comments is on the education of Latino/a children, there are many cognate issues with the situation of other marginalized groups, especially African American children. There are very few studies, however, that attempt to address jointly the education issues of these two groups. These studies are badly needed. Let us keep in mind that Latino/a and African American children now constitute the majority population in most urban school districts in the country.

This initial summary, then, will serve to highlight the "encapsulation" of these children's schooling, resulting in various forms of what Valenzuela (1999) has called "subtractive" schooling: forms of schooling that are not only forcibly (and punitively) assimilative, but that deliberately exclude the social, cultural, or linguistic resources of the students. We then present three promising responses, among many others that could be reviewed, to this encapsulation of schooling by dominant policies, practices, and ideologies, which illustrate attempts at educational sovereignty. Each example is taken from projects in which we have participated and in which an ethnographic understanding of issues plays a pivotal role. To conclude, we identify four areas of study essential to elaborating the concept of educational sovereignty.

The Status Quo Considered

All contemporary issues of education for Latino/a students must be understood, in one way or another, in the context created by demographic changes. Los Angeles is a case in point. For example, Rumbaut (1998; see also Portes & Rumbaut, 2001) has estimated that 62% of the population of Los Angeles, approximately six million people, is of "immigrant stock," most of them Latinos.[2] A current estimate is that the Latino/a population of the city and county of Los Angeles ranges from 40 to 45% of the total population. In the county this represents a total of over four million people, the majority population of Los Angeles, with about 40% between the ages of 0 and 17, or school age; moreover, about 63% of young children (ages 0–5) in the county are Latinos (Children Now, 1999). All issues in Los Angeles, then, political, economic, or educational, are now framed and mediated by this demographic reality (see Rocco, 1996).[3]

Furthermore, the great majority of this population, whether recent immigrants, second generation, or later, could be considered as either working-class or poor, and very likely to remain that way (see, e.g., López et al., 1996; Treiman & Lee, 1996). The Latino/a population nationally is also overwhelmingly working class and low income. Consider just two national indicators: In 2002, 28% of Latino/a children younger than 18 (school-age) live below the poverty level (compared to 9.5% for Whites); and 21.4% of Latinos were living in poverty (7.8% for Whites) (Ramirez & de la Cruz, 2002). The sociologist Vilma Ortíz (1996), in a study done of Latinos in Los Angeles, concluded that, given existing structural and economic conditions, this population would remain permanently in the low working class. Whether her prediction is accurate or not, the point is that this low social class status is a more or less stable, a more or less "fixed" structural condition of Latinos in urban settings. This socioeconomic standing, as is well known, has major implications for the schooling of children (Lee & Burkam, 2002).

The schools reflect these broader demographic changes. For example, the Latino/a population of the LAUSD (as of 2002–2003), according to District data, is well over half a million students (537,136), or 72% of the total student population (746,852); in contrast, the White student population is 9.4% (70,031).[4] Taking into account the other ethnic groups, this school district is approximately 90% "minority," if such a term is still applicable.

Furthermore, 75% of students in the district are eligible for free or reduced lunch services, the great majority of these students Latinos. In addition, of the total number of students in the District, about 43% are designated as English Learners (EL), about 300,000 of these students being Spanish speakers. Nearly all of these (EL) students are in the free or reduced lunch program, among the poorest students in the district.

The teaching corps, however, remains largely White (47.7%), with 27.2% Latino/a and 14% African American. Statewide in California, we should point out, the discrepancies are larger: the Latino/a student population is at 45% (34% White) whereas 74% of teachers are White and only 14% are Latinos. Thus, Latinos are the majority at LAUSD and statewide; students are mostly working class and poor, but the teaching corps is primarily White and middle class, and English monolingual as well.

The academic performance of Latino/a students is generally low. Without belaboring the point, the dropout rate (grades 9–12) for Latinos, and for African Americans, is very high;[5] for example, the 4-year derived rate, an estimate of the percent of students who would drop out in a 4-year period based on data collected for a single year (2002–2003), is 36% for Latinos, and 43% for African Americans. Furthermore, the academic achievement of these students is the lowest in the district. For example, Latinos have the lowest percentage (55%) of students passing the state's English language arts high school exit exam; the percentage of passing scores for the math exam are even lower (27%). These high dropout rates, combined with the low achievement, are a consistent finding in all school districts nationally with comparable socioeconomic profiles.

One would figure that in a school district with such a dominant Latino/a population, issues affecting these children would take precedence, but nothing could be further from the truth, which helps illustrate the neocolonial conditions of their schooling. If anything, Los Angeles Unified has become one of the most restrictive districts anywhere. Consider the following issues.

- Bilingual education is virtually banned (statewide), Spanish is banished as a language of instruction, under penalty of law, and the teachers threatened with lawsuits if they use Spanish in school.

A similar law was passed by initiative and is now in place in Arizona and Massachusetts, and is being considered in other states, such as New York and Texas. Consider the coercive ideological context that such a law perpetuates, establishing Spanish as a pariah language in the schools while privileging English exclusively, and showing how only the interests of the Anglo monolingual community can be represented in the schools. Sadly, this ideology is confined neither to California nor to the present context; see MacGregor-Mendoza's (1998) historical analysis of what she calls the "criminalization of Spanish in the United States."

- Highly restrictive and regimented reading curricula are put in place district wide, and without any evidence of their appropriateness, imposed on teachers by law, focusing primarily on the children pronouncing phonemes in isolation as the principal if not sole pedagogy of early reading, severely curtailing or prohibiting alternative (meaning-driven) instructional approaches.
- Mandatory mass (high-stakes) testing is implemented, despite the failure of such systems to narrow the gap between majority and minority students. These tests leave little to no room for more formative forms of assessment that may lead to increased professional development of teachers, precisely what is needed to address the needs of a diverse and largely poor group of students, and result in increased rote instruction of a narrow group of subjects.
- The referral of Latino/a students to special education increases with the onset of English-only practices. The most common reason for referral is early reading difficulties, particularly common when non-English speakers are being taught to read in English by English-monolingual teachers using mandated phonics methods. These lessons become, in essence, prolonged dialect correction lessons.
- The district implements a no-social-promotions policy, as part of the standards movement, with retention rates estimated as high as 50%.
- The district implements a mandatory class reduction program. A consequence, given a shortage of teachers, is that uncertified teachers are routinely assigned to teach in the poorest schools with large populations of English language learners.

Therefore, if you are a young Latino/a student entering the LAUSD, you are likely to (1) engage a low-level academic curriculum, befitting your low social class status, that will limit your opportunities for academic advancement; (2) suffer the indignity and psychological violence of having Spanish, your home language, banned in school by the edict of white strangers; (3) spend hours every week doing language drills on nonsense phonemes, with little time devoted to understanding what you read; (4) face the strong likelihood of being labeled retarded or learning disabled for the rest of your school career; (5) be flunked for not passing tests of questionable validity but that are politically expedient; or (6) risk being taught by teachers with limited or no qualifications.

The point is that these constraints are not just isolated issues that coincide. It is vital to recognize the organized political forces and language ideologies that guide these activities as part of a broader social and educational policy of control and coercion, in the context created by immigration and the changing demographics. Moreover, none of these structural and ideological conditions is likely to change in the near future; in fact, they are likely to become more oppressive, given the changing demographics of the school population.

Our claim is that the situation as described, although with considerable variation, represents the status quo for Latino/a students in the United States, a population that is overwhelmingly working class and poor, growing demographically, and suffering the consequences of their growth and their position in the social order.

The Status Quo Mediated: Three Approaches

What follows are examples taken from three projects, all featuring additive forms of agency that may mediate these constraints by tapping into existing cultural resources in both local and distant communities to situate and redefine teaching and learning within a broader educational ecology (see Moll & Ruiz, 2002).

Funds of knowledge

This work involves close collaboration with anthropologists and teachers to develop a pedagogical approach that builds on the cultural resources of local communities, mostly working-class, Latino/a neighborhoods. We refer to these cultural resources as "funds of knowledge," those bodies of knowledge that underlie the productive (and other) activities of households. We have been particularly successful in helping teachers, as well as others, approach, understand, and define their school's community in terms of these funds of knowledge. What characterizes the approach is the work of teachers conducting research in their students' households, and then discussing and analyzing their data in conjunction with other teachers and researchers as part of study-group settings. In contrast to other approaches that emphasize home visits, the teachers in our studies visit their students' households to learn from the families, and they enter households with a theoretical perspective that seeks to understand the ways in which people make sense of their everyday lives. The goal is to gain an appreciation and understanding of how people use resources of all kinds, most prominently their funds of knowledge, to engage life. We sustain that through firsthand research experiences with families, teachers come to develop a representation of their school's community as possessing ample resources for learning, which help create many possibilities for positive pedagogical actions (González et al., 2005).

In addition to the possibilities of forming new classroom practices, what is also important is that teachers come to know the households not only intellectually but also personally and emotionally. Moreover, just as important as the concrete social relations established through the visits, are the "imagined" relations that can be formed with other families in the school or community. The point is that it becomes easy to imagine that other families in the community also possess ample funds of knowledge. These *imagined communities,* a term we borrow from Anderson (1991), become important cultural artifacts, for they help us mediate in important ways our actions and our thinking about (low-income) children, their families, their lives, and their prospects within schools, even if we have not met them personally.

Therefore, the process of documenting funds of knowledge is not only an empirical but also a theoretical activity. The empirical information that teachers collect from households is the starting point; expanding and sharing insights from these visits with other teachers is part of the theoretical work done at the study-group settings. In other words, through the visits, and through the deliberate elaboration of the concept of funds of knowledge, we appropriate theoretically the families' lived experiences. As such, as with any theoretical enterprise, our conclusions are always tentative, temporary, and subject to revision by further study or scrutiny (for details, see González et al., 2005).

There is one additional point about this work that we want to emphasize for present purposes. Given the importance of social class in the schooling of children and the work of teachers, one could consider treating social class as a primary theoretical or conceptual tool, exactly the way we have treated funds of knowledge. In collaborating with teachers, we prepared diligently to conduct the work by doing the required theoretical and methodological readings to establish the ethnographic nature of the concept. As part of this preparation we highlighted the relation of funds of knowledge to the history of labor of the families and to the household economy, with the understanding that both were related primarily to the working-class segment of the labor market. Ideally, we could also have developed, as part of the same study-group discussions, a more sophisticated understanding of social class as it helps determine household and classroom dynamics, the production of knowledge, and the relationships between these settings.

That is, just as the teachers came to develop a theoretical language about funds of knowledge in the process of conducting research and in making their findings pedagogically viable, they (and we) could also have developed a language to talk about class relations as the major source of inequalities in education.

Additive schooling

In our most recent work we are extending our previous research by concentrating on two important aspects. One is the development of biliteracy, how young children become literate in two language systems and accomplish this feat routinely, as a mundane task. This is an important point. In the elementary school that is our study site, a Spanish-immersion school (K-5), all children, regardless of social and language background, graduate from the school literate in English and Spanish. Part of our analytic task is to document, through various means, but especially participant observations, the developmental trajectories of the students in each language. Our primary strategy has been to develop longitudinal case studies of twenty such students, what we call an integrated case-study analysis, out of a sample of 80 children.

We take biliteracy development in children, then, as the clearest index of additive schooling. Simply put: If you are a parent and your child is not graduating elementary school literate in two languages, you are being short-changed by the school system; the system is serving somebody else's needs and interests, but not yours. Although we emphasize this goal for all children, it is all the more to be expected for immigrant and other bilingual children—children who come to school with pre-existing proficiencies and cultural contexts for acquiring additional languages. That is, for those children whose first or heritage language is other than English, rather than lowering our expectations for them, as has been the norm, we should instead fully expect that their schooling experience would result in at least bilingualism and biliteracy. They are, after all, in the best position of all to develop into highly proficient bilinguals: their first language is supported by the home environment and their second by the social environment. It remains for the school to promote such advantageous conditions. But such promotion rests on a reorientation—a sense that these children have been gifted culturally and linguistically (Portes & Hao, 2002), and that they, their languages and culture, their communities, and their traditions are a great value that we squander unless we develop them fully (Ruiz, in press).

There is no magic in helping children learn to read and write fluently in two languages. It takes a committed principal, well-trained instructional staff, sound bilingual pedagogy, and the wherewithal to mediate constraints imposed on schools. For example, the school received complaints from parents that the levels of beginning Spanish reading were too low for Spanish speakers because these levels were tailored to the English-monolingual students. The school, with the participation of all teachers, responded by creating "Exito Bilingue" (EB), a series of cross-age Spanish reading groups (1½ hours a day; 3 days a week) into which the students were placed according to their reading proficiency in Spanish. The entire school staff participated in these sessions; there are currently about 14 such groups. We feared the program would turn into a static tracking program, but that has not been the case. The students are continually assessed, both formally and informally, and the groups rearranged accordingly. This innovation has allowed for prolonged and concentrated (meaning-based) literacy instruction in Spanish for all students. For the English-dominant speakers EB has provided extra support in their weaker language; for the Spanish-dominant students it has provided accelerated development in Spanish that has created a sort of "zone of proximal development" for their English reading.

A second aspect of study has been to analyze how language ideologies, an inescapable aspect of the schooling of Latino/a students, come to mediate the biliteracy development of students. Two unanticipated developments have shaped our work. One is that the voters of Arizona approved Proposition 203, the evil twin of a similar antibilingual education proposition in California that targets Latino/a children and families, and which has placed the school ideologically under siege. As in California, Latino/a (and American Indian) voters opposed the proposition by about the same proportion as Anglo voters favored it, around 65%.

During the whole campaign and election period we were able to document how the school became a site of resistance to such oppression. The campaign became a defining moment for the school, as teachers, students and their parents become political activists in defending their school. Even after passage of the proposition into law, the school, with the support of the parents, has remained a site of defiance, as it has continued to offer its curriculum, what they consider not only a pedagogical but also a moral choice for the students, while adjusting to the new legal conditions.

A second development is that we noticed, more than we had anticipated in designing the study, how the children develop their own versions of language ideologies, which influence their dispositions for literacy in one language or another. These ideologies, if we can call them that, may have little to do with their parents' attitudes or beliefs about language, but a lot to do with peer relations at the school. The following example illustrates how language ideologies do their work (from Moll, 2000). We have found how, especially for Latino/a children, language ideologies arouse strong feelings about Spanish and English from the very beginning of their formal education.

As we initiated the study we learned of a 5-year-old girl, Veronica, who while in kindergarten expressed quite clearly her feelings about English and Spanish (from Carmichael, 1998). Veronica, who was born in Tucson and lives in the barrio in which the school is located, is the oldest of four children. Her mother immigrated (legally), along with her parents, from Sonora, Mexico in 1986, when she (the mother) was 14; her father also was born in Mexico and immigrated (legally) when he was 14. Her parents married at the age of 17; her mother was, at the time of the interview, 27 years old and her father 28.

In an initial interview, this Spanish-monolingual girl told her teacher, Cathy, that she (Veronica) enjoyed speaking English more than Spanish, and predicted that she would soon stop speaking Spanish because she didn't like it much. In fact, this young girl imagined herself speaking only in English in just 3 or 4 years, when she would be in the intermediate grades. She also expressed that one can learn more in English, a stance based on her observation that most grown-ups speak English (Carmichael, 1998, pp. 7–11). In her view, a person who doesn't learn English will suffer dire consequences: "He has to be out on the street begging for food ... because when he went to school he didn't hear anything and he stayed dumb" (*"Tiene que andar en la calle pidiendo comidas ... porque cuando iba a la escuela no oía nada y luego se quedó burro"*).

We also found, however, that the sources of Veronica's and other children's ideologies did not depend on a lineal transmission model from adults to child. For example, Veronica's mother expressed very clearly that she wanted her child to retain her Spanish and become bilingual: "I don't want her to focus only on English, nor only on Spanish. I want both (languages) to go with her [in life] (*"No quiero que se enfoque no más en inglés, ni tampoco en el español. Yo quiero que los dos vayan."*). The mother also expressed that she considered Spanish the language of the family (something that Veronica acknowledged), and emphasized that Spanish was intimately tied to her Mexican cultural identity.

Nevertheless, even in the context of a Spanish-language immersion school, one that makes every effort to privilege Spanish in the school, in a classroom in which the teacher uses only Spanish in the school, in a classroom in which the teacher uses only Spanish and conveys through her actions and attitude the importance of knowing the language well, with a mother who wants her to retain her Spanish while developing her English, and who considers Spanish the language of their family and the language of their identity, this little girl was already planning to speak English and only English in the near future.

What was going on with Veronica? We had some hints from the initial interviews. One is that she was a limited English speaker (according to the school's language assessment instrument), and was eager to learn the language, for it is the first language of most of the children at school. As just one of four Spanish speakers in her class of 20 children, she considered English the language of the school for it dominated her peer relations, regardless of Spanish being the obvious language of instruction. She also felt that English is the language of grown-ups, of people on the street, that is, the public language, and people would understand her better if she spoke English, and even that one can learn more in that language. She knows that her mother did not learn English as a child and figures that is why she cannot speak English fluently now. And finally, she wanted to learn English to teach her little sister, who could not speak it very well.

Veronica already embodies and articulates competing language ideologies, as linked to the larger context of Spanish-speakers in the Tucson borderlands area, indeed to the larger context of Latinos in the United States, and to specific forms of life and schooling. We have suggested, as Luykx (1996) has asserted, that "rather than simply being inculcated with a prefabricated ideology, students bring their own meanings, practices, and values to the pedagogic situation, and the outcome is a conflictive mixture of what they bring and what they encounter there" (p. 264). Thus, it is important to consider how ideologies function as mediating devices, and how they help give meaning to the actions of becoming a biliterate in a school setting, with both positive or negative consequences for the children's learning, including their language development.

This key point needs a bit more elaboration. Central to our analysis is how language ideologies can be linked to several semiotic systems and social interactions central to the schooling processes, thus becoming inescapable for the students and teachers. Therefore, in a Vygotskian sort of way, language ideologies may function as "cultural resources" with differential influences on actions by adults and children. In particular, as van Dijk (1996) proposes, a key dimension of ideologies is their cross-situational potential as socially shared resources for thinking, for both groups and individuals, that can be drawn on (or not) and applied in different contexts. The example of Veronica, then a kindergarten student, illustrates how a child may come to restrict herself, determine her future, and delineate her identity by decisions she makes about language. Notice how she comes to consent, to acquiesce, to the dominant social ideologies about language, in this instance English, even before she can speak the language. As such, we are struck by how language ideologies, in several mediated ways, are always involved in the process of the students' personal production, that is, in the production of who they are becoming as persons.

Children, then, form their subjectivities, who they are as persons, and reconstitute them, using the cultural resources and social processes available to them. These subjectivities, which are always fluid, are simultaneously "deeply singular," for no two children have identical social histories, and "deeply social," for they are always embedded in the dynamics of particular systems of social interaction. In this respect, one must consider that children actively create and re-create themselves, within domains and communities not necessarily of their choosing, but with social, semiotic, and ideological aspects specific to their particular status as children, especially if they are minority children.

Norma González (2001), in her research with Mexican American children and families, also has addressed the identities that children construct when they use language(s) in particular ways. She does so in relation to what she calls the "emotion of subalternity," that is, how minority status itself provides an "infrastructure" for child language socialization, and mediates the children's construction of meaning and identity. She writes that "these evocative dimensions of race/class and minority status have been absent in language studies of children" (p. 54), yet they represent a formative force in language socialization. Thus, for Latinos, as for African American children, ambiguity and contradiction, and competing language ideologies, are always a backdrop to their language socialization and development, especially in relation to schooling.

Mediating structures

The third example (adapted from Moll, 2001) refers to work that attempts to create activities within community contexts as additional settings for the learning and development of children and adults. The example is from the work of Vásquez and colleagues, and the activity setting they refer to as "La Clase Mágica" (see Vásquez, 2003). This setting forms part of a group of related projects called the Fifth Dimension, all community-based, after-school programs (see, e.g., Cole, 1996). In brief, all of these projects share a particular social structure, combining play with educational activities, and containing a special set of rules, activities, artifacts, and relationships among participants, including work and computer-mediated connections with local universities.

The programs are all conducted after school, meeting in the afternoons, usually 3 days a week for 2 hours, at a community site such as a youth club, library, or other community setting. All of the participants are volunteers, including the school children that attend the program. The adults in the setting typically represent an intergenerational mix of undergraduate students, enrolled in psychology or education courses at local universities, who act as on-site tutors and research assistants; graduate students majoring in the social sciences; family members of the children in the program or local community members, and university faculty who supervise the implementation of activities and conduct research at each site.

La Clase Mágica is a bilingual setting (English and Spanish), so that children, or adults, can participate in all activities in either language, or in both. Vásquez (1993) explains it as follows:

> Transforming the Fifth Dimension was not a simple act of translation from English to Spanish but a fundamental change in the approach to

the organization of the pedagogical activity. Although informed throughout by traditional Mexican cultural knowledge, the Fifth Dimension's evolution into La Clase Mágica was not based solely on the children's home culture. Rather it tapped the multiple knowledge sources available in the children's everyday life. Whenever possible, content knowledge and skills from such learning domains as the family, church, sports, and dance groups were written into tasks accompanying the games. The goal was to build upon the background knowledge of the children at the same time that a new set of experiences and a second language were introduced. (p. 208)

La Clase Mágica represents, therefore, a fundamentally new cultural setting, one that borrows strategically but differs significantly from the children's home culture and from other institutional cultures such as the school. The children's experiences and background knowledge form part of the foundation of the site, something that is recognizable by all participants and validated daily through the routines and practices that constitute the setting. In this sense, perhaps the most notable characteristic of this site is the internal distribution of languages. An important consequence of the particular cultural arrangement of La Clase Mágica is that, to a remarkable extent, language designations, especially in relation to English fluency, which are so powerful in sorting children in schools, become irrelevant within the site. The specific language characteristics of the child, considered temporary, never become a barrier to full participation within the site, nor do they control or limit involvement because both languages are found everywhere, fostered, and used routinely in the performance of tasks.

Another consequence has to do with the connections created with the local community. La Clase Mágica is an open cultural system where the participation of local residents is encouraged and vital to the success of the site. The local residents, especially the children's families, represent not only an additional resource for teaching, contributing their knowledge and experiences, but help establish on a daily basis the cultural identity of the site, that is, how La Clase Mágica defines itself culturally through the nature and content of its routines. The long-term existence of such a nonschool setting depends crucially on the network of support it can generate, and how it can mediate existing constraints, especially given fluctuations in funding. The involvement of parents becomes an essential strategy to help perpetuate the site within its host setting, be it a local club, library, or church.

Future Research Themes

This section contains four issues or themes (there are certainly many more) that might help shape a future educational agenda (adapted from Moll

& Ruiz, 2002). All four themes take into account the growing population of Latinos in the United States, which serves as the broader context for education issues, and the need to create strategic alliances in enhancing the educational landscape and sovereignty of these students. These themes also hold considerable theoretical potential, for their investigation can motivate new concepts and propositions.

Interethnic relations

An important characteristic of the schooling of Latino/a children is their predominance in "minority dominant" schools. As such, the issues that we have summarized in this paper are also relevant to the schooling of other groups, in particular African American children. Put another way, the character and dimension of the schooling of Latinos should be analyzed not independently, as is usually the case, but in relation to the situation of African American children, for they both share similar political environments in urban areas. There are few recent studies in the literature addressing jointly issues of education for both Latinos and African Americans (but see Dávila & Rodríguez, 2000; Hout, 2001; MacDonald & Beck, 2004). There are, however, recent studies pointing to the negative interethnic perceptions and to potential serious conflict among these and other groups (see Johnson et al., 1999), although Latino/a and African American relations may vary considerably depending on urban area, political and economic history and arrangements, and specific social issues, as shown by Mollenkopf (1999) and Rodríguez (1999). Clearly, education is an issue that lends itself to intergroup analysis. Urban schools may have become mostly irrelevant to Whites, as it seems from the demographics. Nevertheless, these institutions remain crucial for both Latinos and African American communities, so that collaboration may be in both groups' mutual interest, and an important if undertheorized subject of study.

Transnational communities

This issue reflects one of the most interesting developments in Latino/a (and other immigrant) communities across the country. It refers to the social networks that facilitate more or less continuous links between the societies of origin and settlement. To be sure, this is not a new phenomenon, especially with Mexicans living in the borderlands, or among Puerto Ricans and their "circular" migration to and from the island, a dynamic popularly known as *"el vaivén."* However, as Portes (1996) has pointed out, contemporary transnational communities seem to have developed a new character, as defined by three features: (1) the large number of people involved and the variety or diversity of the Latino/a groups implicated in transnational enterprises; (2) the near instantaneous character of long-distance communications across national borders, as characterized by the constant use of cell phones and electronic mail for instant communication; and (3) that cumulative participation in this transnational process helps make it a "normative" phenomenon, instead of anomalous, among certain immigrant groups.

The social, economic, or political activities that these international social networks facilitate may be creating novel paths of adaptation (into U.S. society) unlike previous immigrations, with potential implications for the formation of identities and for education (see, e.g., Guerra, 1998). Note the possible variations in these transnational arrangements: (a) communities along the border (Texas-to-California), characterized by geographical proximity to Mexico, may be inclined to reduce transnationalism to actual physical contacts—shopping, shipping, working, and so on; (b) cyclical migrants (e.g., Puerto Ricans or Dominicans who travel back and forth to the island) may have political allegiances, sentimental attachments, and some economic interests in maintaining their ties; (c) economic elites with Internet and other technological connections may be able to establish such communities wherever they may be, even far from the traditional centers of Latino/a concentrations; (d) such communities may be more motivated to maintain and develop their first languages, thereby giving increasing perceptions of economic, cultural, and social threat among those who argue that such communities pose irredentist dangers.

One consequence of these transnational dynamics may be the creation of a strong "linguistic marketplace," where language proficiency is seen as real capital in the global economy (see, e.g., Skutnabb-Kangas, 1999). In the United States, perhaps the strongest case for the economic benefits of dual language proficiency has been made by Fradd and her colleagues (e.g., Fradd & Lee, 1998), who have documented the economic benefits of fluent bilingualism, especially in south Florida. These outcomes may help establish the desirability of bilingualism and biliteracy for all populations, but especially for Latinos. In a sense, these transnational activities extend the borders of the countries in question, and within these contexts, Latinos in the United States are hardly a minority, forming instead part of a much larger and international community.

The uses of technology

The rapid spread of new technologies in the home and workplace, and as the bases for economic development, has had a differential impact on the wealthy versus the poor. The use of computers in schools reflects the stratification of the system, with the wealthier schools doing the most interesting intellectual work with the technology. Similarly, the use of the Internet, for example, is mostly a middle-class phenomenon, hardly influencing working-class life and work; and even when social class is taken into account, there are differential uses of this resource by different ethnic groups. Few studies are available that analyze successful applications of technological solutions to the schooling of Latino/a children. The issue remains not how to adapt the technology to existing circumstances but, rather, how to use the technology to create fundamentally new circumstances for the children's schooling.

Linguistic human rights

The last few years of the 20th century have seen a virtual explosion in scholarly interest in the issue of how to extend rights to language minority communities, especially those in large, multinational states. This is evidenced by the number of books, chapters, and articles in scholarly journals (e.g., May, 2001; Kontra et al., 1999; Skutnabb-Kangas & Phillipson, 1995), new journals on the question (e.g., International Journal on Minority and Group Rights), international conferences and conventions (e.g., the Hague Recommendations Regarding the Educational Rights of National Minorities in 1996), and Web sites (e.g., terralingua.org). The issue has become so central and familiar to scholars in a multiplicity of fields, from language planning to law to sociology and political science, that it is known most popularly by its initials, LHRs (linguistic human rights). Although the interest emerged most dramatically out of concern for saving the world's dying indigenous languages (see, e.g., Krauss, 1998), it has been broadened to portray the language rights of immigrants and other minority communities as essential civil rights, regardless of the status of the languages (cf. Hernández-Chávez, 1995; Grin, 1995). This will surely be a matter of great concern with respect to Latinos in the United States as the Spanish-speaking population grows to be the largest minority group in the country.

Conclusion

We have proposed the concept of "educational sovereignty" to capture the agency needed to challenge the legacy of control and impositions that characterizes the education of Latino/a students in this country. Educational sovereignty requires that communities create their own infrastructures for development, including mechanisms for the education of their children that capitalize on rather than devalue their cultural resources. It will then be their initiative to invite others, including those in the academic community, to participate in such a creation (cf., Lomawaima, 2000). These forms of education must address Latino's self-interest or self-determination, while limiting the influence of the anglocentric whims of the majority that historically have shaped their schooling.

At a minimum, educational sovereignty must (1) attend to the larger historical structures and ideologies of schooling, with the goal of making educational constraints, especially those related to social class, visible and unstable;

and (2) develop social agency that situates teaching and learning as part of a broader education ecology and that taps into existing social and cultural resources in schools, households, and communities in promoting change.

Notes

(1)   This paper is a revised version of a keynote address delivered by L. C. Moll at the Ethnography Form, Graduate School of Education, University of Pennsylvania, March 1, 2002; it is also a revised version of Moll and Ruiz (2002).

(2)   Rumbaut defines "immigrant stock" as the sum of the first and second generations of the U.S. populations.

(3)   As of January 1, 2002, the population of the City of Los Angeles: 3,80,400: the County of Los Angeles: 9,824,800. Source: Office of the City Administrative Officer, 2003, City of Los Angeles Economic and Demographic Information; see http://www.cityofla.org/CAO/econdemo.htm.

(4)   All data about LAUSD were obtained from the following California Department of Education websites: see, http://www.ed-data.k12.ca.us/welcome.asp; http://www.lausd.k12.ca.us/; http://cahsee.cde.ca.gov/2002/

(5)   Beginning in 2002–2003, the California Department of Education (CDE) adopted the National Center for Educational Statistics (NCES) Dropout definition, which is as follows: [A student who] (1) Was enrolled in grades 7, 8, 9, 10, 11, or 12 at some time during the previous school year and left school prior to completing the school year and has not returned to school as of Information Day; or, (2) Did not begin attending the next grade (7, 8, 9, 10, 11, or 12) in the school to which they were assigned or in which they had preregistered or were expected to attend by Information Day.

References

Anderson, B. (1991). *Imagined communities: Reflections on the origin and spread of nationalism* (2nd ed.). London: Verso.

Bixler-Márquez, D. (1998). Multilingual, long-distance community education in Mexico's Sierra Tarahumara. *La Educación, Año XLII,* No. 129–131, I–III, pp. 121–139.

Carmichael, C. (1998). *Hablar dos veces: Talking twice: Language ideologies in a dual-language kindergarten.* Unpublished project paper.

Children Now (1999). *California county data book: How our youngest children are faring.* Los Angeles, CA. Available online at http://www.childrennow.org

Cole, M. (1996). *Cultural psychology.* Cambridge, MA: Harvard University Press.

Dávila, R., & Rodríguez, N. (2000). Successes and challenges of relations between African Americans and Latinos. In L. Huntley (Ed.), *Beyond racism: Embracing an interdependent future* (pp. 36–48). Atlanta, GA: The Southern Education Foundation.

Fardon, R., & Furniss, G. (Eds.). (1994). *African languages, development and the state.* London: Routledge.

Fishman, J. A. (Ed.). (2001). *Can threatened languages be saved? Reversing language shift revisited: A 21st century perspective.* Clevedon: Multilingual Matters.

Fradd, S., & Lee, O. (Eds.). (1998). *Creating Florida's multilingual global work force: Policies and practices in assessing and instructing students learning English as a new language.* Tallahassee: Florida Department of Education.

Goldenberg, C. N., & Gallimore, R. (1995). Immigrant Latino parents' values and beliefs about their children's education: Continuities and discontinuities across cultures and generations. In P. Pintrich, & M. Maehr (Eds.), *Advances in motivation and achievement* (Vol. 9, pp. 183–227). Greenwich, CT: JAI.

González, N. (2001). *I am my language: Discourses of women and children in the borderlands.* Tucson: University of Arizona Press.

González, N., Moll, L. C., & Amanti, C. (Eds.). (2005). *Theorizing practices: Funds of knowledge in households, communities, and classrooms.* Cresskill, NJ: Hampton.

Grenoble, L. A., & Whaley, L. J. (Eds.). (1998). *Endangered languages: Current issues and future prospects.* Cambridge: Cambridge University Press.

Grin, F. (1995). Combining immigrant and autochthonous language rights: a territorial approach to multilingualism. In T. Skutnabb-Kangas, & R. Phillipson (Eds.), *Linguistic human rights: Overcoming linguistic discrimination* (pp. 31–48). Berlin: Mouton de Gruyter.

Guerra, J. (1998). *Close to home: Oral and literate practices in a transnational Mexicano community.* New York: Teachers College Press.

Held, D. (1995). *Democracy and the global order.* Cambridge, UK: Polity.

Held, D., McGrew, A., Goldblatt, D., & Perraton, J. (1999). *Global transformations.* Cambridge: Polity.

Henze, R., & Davis, K. (1999). Authenticity and identity: Lessons from indigenous language education. *Anthropology and Education Quarterly, 30*(1), 3–21.

Hernandez-Chavez, E. (1995). Language policy in the United States: A history of cultural genocide. In T. Skutnabb-Kangas, & R. Phillipson (Eds.), *Linguistic human rights: Overcoming linguistic discrimination* (pp. 141–158). Berlin: Mouton de Gruyter.

Hout, M. (2001). Educational progress for African Americans and Latinos in the United States from the 1950s to the 1990s: The interaction of ancestry and class. *Working paper.* Survey Research Center, University of California, Berkeley.

Huntley, W. L. (2000). Thresholds in the evolution of social science. In R. Sil, & E. M. Doherty (Eds.), *Beyond boundaries? Disciplines, paradigms, and theoretical integration in international studies* (pp. 177–205). Albany: SUNY Press.

Johnson, Jr., J., Farrell, W. C. Jr., W., & Guinn, C. (1999). Immigration reform and the browning of America: Tensions, conflicts, and community instability in metropolitan Los Angeles. In C. Hirschman, P. Kasinitz, & J. DeWind (Eds.), *The handbook of international migration: The American experience* (pp. 290–310). New York: The Russell Sage Foundation.

Kontra, M., Phillipson, R., Skutnabb-Kangas, T., & Várady, T. (Eds.). (1999). *Language: A right and a resource. Approaching linguistic human rights.* Budapest: Central European University Press.

Krauss, M. (1998). The condition of Native North American languages. *International Journal of the Sociology of Language, 132,* 9–21.

Lee, V., & Burkam, D. (2002). *Inequality at the starting gate: Social background differences in achievement as children begin school.* Washington, DC: Economic Policy Institute.

Lomawaima, K. T. (2000). Tribal sovereigns: Reframing research in American Indian communities. *Harvard Educational Review, 27*(1), 1–21.

Lopez, D., Popkin, E., & Tellez, E. (1996). Central Americans: At the bottom, struggling to get ahead. In R. Waldinger, & M. Bozorgmehr (Eds.), *Ethnic Los Angeles* (pp. 279–304). New York: Russell Sage Foundation.

Luykx, A. (1996). From Indios to Profesionales: Stereotypes and student resistance in Bolivian teacher training. In B. Levinson, D. Foley, & D. Holland (Eds.), *The cultural production of the educated person* (pp. 239–272). Albany: State University of New York Press.

MacDonald, V. M., & Beck, S. (2004, April). *Paths of divergence and convergence in black and brown educational history.* Paper presented at the American Educational Research Association Annual Meeting, San Diego, CA.

MacGregor-Mendoza, P. (1998). The criminalization of Spanish in the United States. In D. Kibbee (Ed.), *Language legislation and language rights* (pp. 55–67). Amsterdam: John Benjamins.

Martinez, R. B. (2000). Languages and tribal sovereignty: Whose language is it anyway? *Theory into Practice* 39 (4), 211–220.

May, S. (2001). *Language and minority rights: Ethnicity, nationalism, and the politics of language.* Harlow, UK: Longman/Pearson.

McCarty, T. L. (2002). *A place to be Navajo: Rough Rock and the struggle for self-determination in indigenous schooling.* Mahwah, NJ: Lawrence Erlbaum Associates.

Moll, L. C. (2000, April). *Mediating matters: The importance of forms of life.* Paper presented at the symposium, Diversity matters: New perspectives from sociocultural theory, Annual Meeting of the American Educational Research Association.

Moll, L. C. (2001). Through the mediation of others: Vygotskian research on teaching. In V. Richardson (Ed.), *Handbook of research on teaching* (4th ed.) (pp. 111–129). Washington, DC: American Educational Research Association.

Moll, L. C., & González, N. (2004). Engaging life: A funds of knowledge approach to multicultural education. In J. Banks, & C. McGee Banks (Eds.), *Handbook of research on multicultural education* (2nd ed.) (pp. 699–715). New York: Jossey-Bass.

Moll, L. C., & Ruiz, R. (2002). The schooling of Latino students. In M. Suárez-Orozco, & M. Páez (Eds.), *Latinos: Remaking America* (pp. 362–374). Berkeley: University of California Press.

Mollenkopf, J. (1999). Urban political conflicts and alliances: New York and Los Angeles compared. In C. Hirschman, P. Kasinitz, & J. DeWind (Eds.), *The handbook of international migration: The American experience* (pp. 412–422). New York: The Russell Sage Foundation.

Ortíz, V. (1996). The Mexican-origin population: Permanent working class or emerging middle class? In R. Waldinger, & M. Bozorgmehr (Eds.), *Ethnic Los Angeles* (pp. 247–278). New York: Russell Sage.

Ostler, N., & Rudes, B. (Eds.). (2000). *Endangered languages and literacy* (Proceedings of the Fourth Foundation for Endangered Languages Conference). Bath, UK: Foundation for Endangered Languages.

Portes, A., & Hao, L. (2002). The price of uniformity: Language, family, and personality adjustment in the immigrant second generation. *Ethnic and Racial Studies, 25,* 889–912.

Portes, P. (1996). Globalization from below: The rise of transnational communities. In W. P. Smith, & R. P. Korczenwicz (Eds.), *Latin America in the world economy* (pp. 151–168). Westport, CT: Greenwood Press.

Portes, P., & Rumbaut, R. (2001). *Legacies: The story of the immigrant second generation.* Berkeley: University of California Press, and New York: Russell Sage Foundation.

Ramirez, R., & de la Cruz, P. G. (2002). *The Hispanic population in the United States: March 2002,* Current Population Reports, P20–545. Washington, DC: U.S. Census Bureau.

Rocco, R. (1996). Latino Los Angeles. In A. Scott, & E. Soja (Eds.), *The city: Los Angeles and urban theory at the end of the twentieth century* (pp. 365–389). Berkeley: University of California Press.

Rodriguez, N. (1999). U.S. immigration and changing relations between African American and Latinos. In C. Hirschman, P. Kasinitz, & J. DeWind (Eds.), *The handbook of international migration: The American experience* (pp. 423–432). New York: Russell Sage Foundation.

Ruiz, R. (in press). *Language as resource: Language planning and the wealth of nations.* Clevedon and Philadelphia: Multilingual Matters.

Rumbaut, R. (1998, March). *Transformations: The post-immigrant generation in an age of diversity.* Paper presented at the Annual Meeting of the Eastern Sociological Society, Philadelphia.

Sassen, S. (1999). *Guests and aliens.* New York: New Press.

Sil, R., & Doherty, E. M. (Eds.). (2000). *Beyond boundaries? Disciplines, paradigms, and theoretical integration in international studies*. Albany: State University of New York Press.

Skutnabb-Kangas, T. (1999). Linguistic diversity, human rights and the "free" market. In M. Kontra, R. Phillipson, T. Skutnabb-Kangas, & T. Várady (Eds.), *Language: A right and a resource. Approaches to linguistic human rights* (pp. 187–222). Budapest: Central European University Press.

Skutnabb-Kangas, T., & Phillipson, R. (1995). Linguicide and linguicism. In R. Phillipson, & T. Skutnabb-Kangas (Eds.), *Papers in European language policy* (pp. 83–91). ROLIG papir 53. Roskilde: Roskilde Universitetscenter, Lingvistgruppen.

Smith, D. (2002). The challenge of urban ethnography. In E. Trueba, & Y. Zou (Eds.), *Ethnography and schools: Qualitative approaches to the study of education* (pp. 369–387). Lanham, MD: Rowman & Littlefield Publishers.

Treiman, D., & Lee, H. (1996). Income differences among 31 ethnic groups in Los Angeles. In J. Baron, D. Grutsky, & D. Treiman (Eds.), *Social differentiation and social inequality: Essays in Honor of John Pock* (pp. 37–82). Boulder, CO: Westview.

Valenzuela, A. (1999). *Subtractive schooling: U.S.-Mexican youth and the politics of caring*. Albany: State University of New York Press.

van Dijk, T. (1996). *Discourse, racism and ideology*. Islas Canarias, Spain: RCEI Ediciones, Universidad de La Laguna.

Vásquez, O. (1993). A look at language as a resource: Lessons from La Clase Mágica. In M. B. Arias, & U. Casanova (Eds.), *Bilingual education: Politics, practice, and research* (pp. 199–224). (Ninety-second Yearbook of the National Society for the Study of Education, Part 2.) Chicago: University of Chicago Press.

Vásquez, O. (2003). *La Clase Mágica: Imagining optimal possibilities in a bilingual community of learners*. Mahwah, NJ: Lawrence Erlbaum Associates.

Vick-Westgate, A. (2002). *Nunavik: Inuit-controlled education in Arctic Quebec*. Calgary: University of Calgary Press.

Warner, S. (1999). Kuleana: The right, responsibility, and authority of indigenous peoples to speak and make decisions for themselves in language and cultural revitalization. *Anthropology and Education Quarterly, 30*(1), 68–93.

Wright, S. (2000). *Community and communication: The role of language in nation state building and European integration*. Clevedon: Multilingual Matters.

Part 5

Perspectives on Language Planning Orientations and Language Threat Inversion

Language Ideologies and Bilingual Realities: The Case of Coral Way
Erin Mackinney

Language Orientations in Guatemala: Toward Language as Resource?
Janelle M. Johnson and Julia B. Richards

'Language-as-Catalyst': Exploring the Role of Linguistic Landscapes in the Framework of Richard Ruiz's 'Orientations in Language Planning'
Olga Bever

Threat Inversion and Language Maintenance in Puerto Rico and Aruba
Kevin S. Carroll and Joyce Pereira

Language Ideologies and Bilingual Realities: The Case of Coral Way

Erin Mackinney

Language planning, which starts with the assumption that language is a resource to be managed, developed and conserved, tends to regard language-minority communities as important sources of expertise (Ruiz, 1984). Schools can serve as institutions that facilitate the use and development of language. In particular, schools with bilingual programs that recognize, promote and cultivate bilingualism and biliteracy send positive messages about the value of language and language speakers. Yet, even within additive (Lambert, 1975) schooling – where the learning of a second language adds to one's repertory of skills at no cost to one's first language – conflicting messages exist.

This chapter describes the language ideologies present within a Spanish-English dual language public neighborhood school in Miami, Florida. My role as a visiting teacher and researcher during the 2012–2013 academic year provided me with a particular lens to observe language use, promotion and development. Embedded in this chapter are the perspectives of students, educators and parents who participated in an ethnographic study exploring the Spanish speaking and writing practices of middle-school Latina/o youth enrolled in both the school's dual language and 'English for speakers of other languages' (ESOL) programs. This simultaneous enrollment afforded students a dynamic bilingual school experience, one that English language learners in mainstream programs or in states with English-only instructional policies are unlikely to receive.

Conceptual Framework

Language ideologies are sets of beliefs, feelings and conceptions about language that form a mediating link between social structures and language practices. They are not only about language; rather they envision and enact links of language to group and personal identity, and to epistemology (Woolard & Schieffelin, 1994). Socioculturally and historically contingent, language ideologies are constructed through one's own experiences and in the interests of a particular social or cultural group. They can promote, protect and legitimate group interests as well as rationalize and justify how one uses language (Kroskrity, 2010; Silverstein, 1979). Adding complexity, language ideologies are often unnoticed and taken for granted.

Language ideologies shape and are shaped by language policies as they are constructed in social practice (McCarty, 2011). This shaping makes language policies dynamic and active rather than stagnant and fixed. Language policies can be top-down, bottom-up, *de jure*, *de facto*, overt and covert. They can serve larger political, economic and national interests with their power to manage language. They can also serve ground-level interests in their recognition of the power of societal and local policy texts, discourses and discoursers (Hornberger & Johnson, 2011). The sociocultural process of negotiating language policies creates a space for language policy makers at all levels.

Schools provide a crucial context in which to explore the intersection of language ideologies and language policies. The day-to-day order and authority in US schools is visibly and invisibly present in scheduling, hierarchical relationships, and state-imposed accountability measures such as the Common Core State Standards and English Language Proficiency Standards. As McCarty (2011) notes, schools have 'language-regulating power' through the ways in which they make normative claims about legitimate and illegitimate language form and use.

One way schools exert their language-regulating power is through control of the complete linguistic repertoire of bilingual students. Bilinguals draw from multiple languages in their everyday communication, such as shifting from one language to another and mixing languages. They engage in translanguaging – a term originally discussed by Williams (1994) and further conceptualized to describe how bilinguals make meaning and shape experiences, understandings and knowledge through the use of two languages as one new whole (Baker, 2011; García & Wei, 2014). Schools regulate students' bilingualism through language compartmentalization, such as designating a particular language for instruction, assignments, testing and communication. Compartmentalization of languages is what Lippi-Green (1997: 109) highlights as separate-but-equal language policies. She explains, 'On the surface, these policies seem to be conciliatory: do not deny the home language of the student; instead, redirect the student's use of that language to those environments and circumstances in which it is appropriate.' This redirection of language reflects an institutional undermining of the complete linguistic repertoire of bilingual students.

In addition to compartmentalization, schools regulate language through perceptions of language quality. Language quality involves issues of ownership. Blommaert (1999: 433) argues:

> A 'good' language is one that is inherited through generations of speakers. And only when someone is part of the genealogy of the speech community, he or she will be able to speak the language 'well', 'correctly', or to understand it 'completely'.

Language quality evokes ideologies of linguistic purity. This purism is upheld through dividing and ranking language into standard and vernacular: the former is deemed dominant while the latter is categorized as subordinate. Standardizing language is an attempt to stop language change and unify linguistic distinctions between language varieties (Lippi-Green, 1997). Ideologies of standardization ignore languages as living and dynamic in favor of fossilized and unified notions.

Ruiz's conceptualization of 'orientation' (1983, 1984, 2010) as a set of dispositions or predispositions toward language and its social role has greatly contributed to understanding the intersection of language ideologies and language policies within multilingual communities. Ideologies are explicit in the language of the policy or implicit in the orientation in making the policy. In particular, Ruiz's language-as-resource orientation is a precursor to and exemplar of a pro-translanguaging perspective, supportive of policies that reflect the dynamic language behavior of language-minority speakers. Such policies, Ruiz (1995) asserts, give status to precious resources like language and generally have a greater effect on language maintenance than policies implemented in more formal contexts.

Context

Uncovering language ideologies within a dual language school serves as a formal setting in which to explore the notion of language as resource. The following sections present the larger sociohistorical, ethnolinguistic and institutional context of Miami and Coral Way Bilingual School.

A Pan-American city

Miami has continued its historical beginning as a refuge for immigrants. From the 1930s until today, immigrant groups from the Caribbean, Europe, Central America and South America have made Miami their home. Presently, 58% of its approximately 430,000 residents are foreign born, and among the city's 70% Latina/o population, 66% are foreign born (US Census, 2013). Large-scale Cuban migration began in 1959 after the rise to power of Fidel

Castro. Miami's Latina/o population has since expanded to comprise groups originating from 20 different Spanish-speaking countries, including Nicaragua, Honduras, Colombia, Puerto Rico and the Dominican Republic.

It does not take long for a newcomer to Miami to feel the presence of Spanish. The language is as much a part of the linguistic landscape (Shohamy & Gorter, 2009) as English, represented in the public sphere through audio and visual means. Spanish, in all its varieties, is seen on billboards, posters, window signs, graffiti, business and street names, and electronic displays. A quick rotation through the AM and FM dials generates more than 23 radio stations in Spanish. Basic TV includes at least 12 Spanish channels, and more than 14 Spanish newspapers and magazines are in circulation. The impact of these media sources is expansive, every day reaching tens of millions of homes in the US and throughout Latin America (Florida News Media Directory, 2013).

Described by locals as simultaneously a piece of the United States and a piece of Latin America, Miami links the Americas. Its interconnecting media, bilingual population and warm, coastal location have contributed to the flourishing industries of commerce, travel and tourism. Spanish has become an important language of exchange; it spans the public and private realms of daily life, from electronic and print media, to social activities, employment and school. Its status is one of social, political, economic and educational value.

Coral Way Bilingual School

Built in 1936 by noted Miami architect August Geiger, Coral Way is a Mediterranean-style two-story wrap-around building with classrooms that open onto a courtyard full of shady oak trees. The school is home to the oldest Spanish-English public bilingual program in the US. As part of the US government's 'Cuban Refugee Program,' Coral Way was selected to pioneer a Spanish-English dual language program for the 1963–1964 academic year. At the time, federal support of bilingual education was seen as a temporary effort that would end upon the overthrow of Fidel Castro's regime. Cuban refugees were then expected to return home. Coral Way was chosen because of three factors: (a) it was located in a neighborhood of approximately half Spanish-speaking and half English-speaking families; (b) the neighborhood was a stable middle-class community; and (c) administration, faculty, staff and parents were interested in the concept of bilingual education (Shaw, 1966). As part of a national Ford Foundation grant totaling $278,000 and serving Florida, New York and the southwestern United States, Coral Way sought to fulfill the funder's aim of improving the education of Spanish-speaking children who had come to live in the US (e.g. Cubans in Miami, Mexicans in Los Angeles and Puerto Ricans in New York). Hence, the school shifted its focus in 1963 to provide students with the opportunity to become bilingual, biliterate and bicultural through a Spanish-English dual language program, which has continued for more than 50 years.

Figure 1 First Grade Classroom – 1964
Source: Coral Way Bilingual Elementary School Oral History Project (2010).

Coral Way is part of Miami-Dade County Public Schools (M-DCPS), the fourth largest school district in the US. Since 1963, schools within M-DCPS have adopted various forms of additive bilingual programs such as dual language, extended foreign language, Spanish for Spanish speakers, and the

Figure 2 Coral Way Courtyard – 2008

International Studies Program – a joint collaboration between the district and the education ministries of France, Germany, Italy and Spain. With an initial focus on teaching Spanish and providing content-area instruction through Spanish, M-DCPS schools have expanded to offer French, Italian, Haitian Creole, Portuguese, Mandarin Chinese and German as languages of PK-12 instruction. In addition to district funding, a variety of sources support these bilingual programs, including active parent associations, intergovernmental collaborations and school-community partnerships (e.g. Spain-Florida Foundation 500 Years). Funding aids in hiring teachers, purchasing textbooks and materials, providing student scholarships and hosting cultural events, guest speakers, field trips and study-abroad experiences.

In 2004, Coral Way expanded to become a K-8 Center. Its school motto *'Dos idiomas, Dos mundos de oportunidad*/Two languages, Two worlds of opportunity' reflects essential aspects of its mission, vision and goals, such as academic and conversational bilingualism, biliteracy, multiculturalism, academic achievement and preparation of students as citizens of the future. Coral Way is unique in that it is the only public neighborhood dual language school in M-DCPS, meaning that it welcomes all students residing in its school boundaries, and all students participate in the dual language program. At the elementary level, students have two 'cooperating teachers,' one who instructs in Spanish and the other who instructs in English. Students spend the morning with one teacher and the afternoon with the other teacher. Spanish language arts and social studies are taught in Spanish, whereas English language arts, developmental language arts and science are taught in English. Mathematics is taught bilingually by the Spanish-instruction teacher. At the middle-school level, humanities, Spanish language arts and mathematics are taught in Spanish, whereas English language arts, developmental language arts, science and social studies are taught in English. Except for slight changes, the dual language program has remained consistent during its 50 years of operation. Coral Way's rotational schedule is such an ingrained aspect of its operation that teachers in the study often commented that the school 'runs by itself.'

Coral Way is a Title I school where 75% of students participate in the federally funded free and reduced price school lunch program. Of the school's 1500 students, 89% are Latina/o, 8% are White, 1% are Black and 2% are classified as Asian/Multiracial. The majority of students are of Caribbean, Central American and South American origin. Approximately 35% of students participate in the ESOL program. The majority of students in ESOL speak Spanish as a first language, with about 10% who speak a language other than Spanish (e.g. Portuguese, French, Italian and Arabic).

Walking the halls of Coral Way, one sees and hears both English and Spanish. Student work is displayed on the walls in both languages. Morning announcements include English and Spanish components. The majority of administrators, teachers and staff at Coral Way are Latina/o, while relatively few are African American and White educators. Most are bilingual, and many were raised in Miami or immigrated there as adults. It is common to meet administrators, teachers and staff who have worked at Coral Way for more than 10, 20 or even 30 years. For many, Coral Way is a 'family', an extension of home. In the next section, I unpack language ideologies embedded within language policies and practices at Coral Way.

Uncovering Language Ideologies

Nested within a US city where Spanish has status, Coral Way, with its mandatory dual language program for all students, serves as a poignant setting in which to explore the intersection of language beliefs. This section draws from school-wide classroom observations, and semi-structured interviews[1] with 23 participants including students, educators and parents, as well as students' written work. Students in the study were involved in both the dual language and ESOL programs, providing a unique lens through which to interrogate language ideologies. Students, together with influential adults, created and received messages about language – ideologies of language as evolving, standard and dynamic.

Language as evolving

The Coral Way community rejected the notion of an 'ideal Spanish.' Students in the study recognized that Spanish speakers differed in their ways of speaking, such as sentence structure, accent and vocabulary. They noted examples such as the accent from Spain and the multiple ways of saying *'crispetas'* (popcorn) and *'mamey'* (tropical fruit). Parents and educators also called attention to the differences in speaking: *'la importancia de la lengua es poder entenderse la persona, no la perfección del idioma en sí'* (the importance of language is to make oneself understood, not perfection of the language itself.), *'el lenguaje español en sí, ideal, no existe, existe una conversación adecuada según la persona que está hablando'* (the Spanish language itself, ideal, does not exist, what exists is an appropriate conversation according to the person who is speaking). In the responses of students, parents and educators, an ideology of communicative competence emerged in their recognition of a range of possibilities of speaking (Hymes, 1992). The Coral Way community had, as Hymes notes, 'systemic potential' in members' articulation of the way of life.

The idea of communicative competence seeped into conversations about correspondence in the current digital age. Rapid forms of communication (e.g. text, video chat and Twitter) have become a part of daily language practices for participants. Features like abbreviated words, creative spelling and symbols have shifted notions of linguistic purism. As one mother commented, *'Nadie escribe perfecto ni en inglés ni en español. La misma situación tecnológica, el escritura lo está poniendo como algo secundario. Ya la gente lo habla es de contarle que te entiendan o qué, aunque sea mal escrito.'* (No one writes perfectly in English or in Spanish. The very presence of technology is placing writing as secondary. Now people [use] language to make oneself understood, even if poorly written.). The impact of technological advances on language has created a space in which to explore language change and its convergence with ideas of standard language.

The borderlands of Miami not only include the convergence of speakers of various Spanish language varieties, they also represent a space where English and Spanish intersect. All students in the study drew from English and Spanish in speaking and writing. They indicated that they alternated between languages when they forgot a word in English or in Spanish or, as one student stated, 'cuz I know better words to say in Spanish, words that I know more in Spanish [than English].' In speaking with friends and family members, students described their language practices as 'bilingual,' 'Spanglish' and 'mixed.' Their articulation did not reference a stigmatized language; rather, students viewed translanguaging as a communicative tool in their everyday lives. As one student explained, mixing English and Spanish with loved ones is 'how we get along.'

Parents echoed students in their articulation of youth mixed language practices. As one father expressed:

Creo que va a haber un fenómeno ... que en la calle ser bilingüe dice Spanglish. Pero creo que es serio. Yo creo que los niños hoy hablan un idioma que no es inglés ni español. Es diferente cuando tú aprendes otro idioma. Si tú hablas alemán, tú hablas alemán e inglés. Italiano, tú hablas italiano e inglés pero cuando tú hablas inglés y español, sale una tercera lengua ... [los niños] se identifican con una lengua que no es inglés ni español ... no es inglés inglés ni español español.

(I believe that there is going to be a phenomenon ... that on the streets, they say being bilingual is [speaking] Spanglish. But I believe that it is serious. I believe that children today speak a language that is neither English nor Spanish. It is different when you learn another language. If you speak German, you speak German and English. Italian, you speak Italian and English, but when you speak English and Spanish, a third language emerges ... [the children] identify with a language that is not English nor Spanish ... it is not English English nor Spanish Spanish.)

According to this father, children growing up bilingual create a third language. This third language is not a clear amalgamation of English and Spanish that can be pulled apart to expose the languages of its makeup in pure form. Rather, this third language, in many ways, is the children's first language. It is their foundation for expression. These ideologies of language as evolving, including language variety, modernization and mixing, collided with ides of language as standard and pure.

Language as standard

Ideologies of language quality and 'full languageness' are consistently associated with structure and order (Blommaert, 1999). Within Coral Way's mandatory Spanish-English dual language program, a formal and informal ranking of languages exists. English is the dominant language of student placement and assessment. Students' proficiency in English determines inclusion in or exclusion from the ESOL program. Inclusion in ESOL signifies exclusion from an elective in middle school. Students' level of English proficiency indicates their particular English language arts class. Furthermore, mathematics placement tests are in English as well as all annual Florida Comprehensive Assessment Tests (FCAT).[2] These scores are also used to determine student placement. As observed, this process often resulted in ESOL participants concentrated together in content-area classes and placed below their academic level. Overall, students' perceived full English languageness, as determined by state-imposed test-based means, steered students toward certain classes and schedules.

Whereas English is used to formally test and place all students, the school uses a less formal process to place students in their Spanish-instruction classes, including Spanish language arts and Humanities. Most students are in regular Spanish language arts and humanities. Students in the honors-level International Studies Program (ISP) are typically those who have been nominated by their teachers during their elementary years and have maintained good grades. Distinct from the test-based means of full English languageness, full Spanish languageness is determined via past ISP participation, a type of Spanish language inheritance through an exclusive program. Unlike the exclusion from an elective in middle school for students enrolled in the ESOL program, participation in ISP does not have any adverse effects; instead, as observed in the study, students in ISP received more opportunities for in-school and out-of-school public language opportunities, such as choral concerts and field trips.

Teachers' ideologies of standard Spanish shaped and were shaped by macro-level policies that placed students into particular classes based on perceptions of students' full Spanish languageness. Teachers viewed students in ISP as having an advanced Spanish vocabulary level, possessing a strong ability to understand, read and write in Spanish, and being academically motivated. Teacher perspectives of students' Spanish proficiency in the regular classes differed. While the majority of teachers in the study did not support the notion of an 'español ideal' (ideal Spanish), their beliefs were more associated with Spanish speaking than with Spanish writing. Teachers viewed students' writing as 'malísimo' (awful) or 'una de las cosas que peor llevan' (one of students' worst [language] aspects), referring to students' difficulties with grammar (e.g. conjugation and gender), sound-spelling conventions (e.g. b and v), and syntax (e.g. using English ways of expression).

When students in the study spoke about their own Spanish writing, beliefs of standard language surfaced. They perceived writing to be their weakest ability in Spanish and expressed their difficulty in remembering complex sound-spelling conventions and tilde placement. One student articulated what she finds difficult about Spanish writing:

> The accents, the 's', 'c', cuz they all sound the same. When you say a word that starts with 's' or 'c,' you don't know the difference cuz they sound the same. And in English, I don't know why, but I'm able to separate the sounds. I don't know why, I just know it.

Students' ideologies of standard written language were shaped by teachers' pedagogical and assessment practices in Spanish language arts. Spanish lessons often focused on grammar, punctuation and spelling. Likewise, teacher feedback typically consisted of written comments highlighting these aspects. Limited attention was given to students' ideas, writing styles and conceptual knowledge.

Language as dynamic

As members of the ESOL and dual language programs, students in the study were in a unique position to problematize and critically reflect upon school language policies. Blackledge and Creese (2008: 537) comment on the active role of those on the receiving end of language transmission:

> Simply the process of 'passing on' [linguistic] resources will alter them … those who seek to preserve and pass on certain sets of resources may find that the next generation either rejects imposed subject positions, contests the validity or significance of resources, or appropriates them for other purposes.

Students aligned with resource-oriented language policies that recognized and favored their realities as bilinguals. On the other hand, students rejected attempts to manage language and define them as language speakers.

The mathematics class provided students in the study with a prime space in which to engage in fluid language practices. Students' dynamic bilingualism was influenced by language policies at multiple levels. The school district's provision of mathematics materials in English and Spanish, and the school administration's indication that mathematics should utilize bilingual instruction, created opportunities for language choice in the classroom. Teachers instructed in Spanish or frequently alternated between Spanish and English. On the overhead projector, they displayed definitions, textbook pages and FCAT practice problems in English. In addition, students chose the language of their workbook. This creation of a bilingual and biliterate space fostered translanguaging as an intermediary meso-level language practice among students and teachers. Teachers sought to facilitate students' mathematics understanding and appeared to accept students' Spanish or English oral and written responses. Students accessed their complete linguistic repertoires as they engaged in micro-level interactions, such as mirroring the language of instruction, codeswitching, parallel speech and parallel writing. Furthermore, students relied on modes other than language, such as images and gestures, to mediate their understanding of mathematics. While not a *de jure* language policy, translanguaging became a normative *de facto* policy of practice shaped by dynamic macro-level bilingual policy.

Whereas students' ideologies of language as dynamic aligned with mathematics learning, their beliefs clashed with ideologies that placed them in particular categories as language speakers. For example, students in the ESOL program were called 'stupid' and 'REF' (refugee) by their peers. Students recognized these institutionally created labels and sought to reposition themselves through language. As one student exclaimed:

> I don't get what [educators] want, really, it's just based on a test, it supposedly tells you if you know English or not, why can't a teacher just tell, 'Oh she knows how to speak English,' why does a test have to do it. It's a test, it's not gonna really test your understanding about anything. I don't think so, I don't think a test is gonna tell you how much you know, it's just impossible … just because you get an F in a test, it doesn't mean you're stupid.

In their expression, students in the study rejected narrow definitions of ESOL as associated with someone who lacks English and therefore intellect. Instead, they highlighted their multilayered identities as bilinguals and articulated cultural, communicative and economic benefits of their bilingualism (see Mackinney, 2014). In addition, students challenged macro-level language policies that placed them in certain classes (Developmental language arts) instead of electives and defined when students achieved English proficiency. Students verbalized suggestions for alternative macro-level policies for ESOL participants, such as one comprehensive English language arts class, inclusion of an elective, and ESOL program exit processes that emphasized teacher assessment of student's English proficiency.

Discussion

This case study highlighted dominant language ideologies within a Spanish-English dual language school. Explicit and implicit language policies shaped ideologies, and at the same time, were shaped by ground-level language practices of middle-school youth, educators and parents in the study. Embedded within these language ideologies were views of language as instrumental and sentimental (Ruiz, 1984), often woven together without clear delineation.

Language served an instrumental function in the school's designation of English or Spanish instruction for particular content areas. English served to formally place and assess students in all classes except for Spanish language arts and humanities, where Spanish was used for placement, albeit informally. As observed, use of the English proficiency exam as a criterion for students' 'full English languageness' was not without critique from students in the study. They questioned the policy's implicit message that passing the exam signaled one's designation as an English speaker.

With regard to sentimental views of language, students, educators and parents were aware of language variety among Spanish speakers and the importance of language for self-identification and expression. Furthermore, participants called attention to the influences of digital literacies and English on the Spanish language, countering notions of linguistic purism. The Coral Way community intertwined sentimental and instrumental views of language in their rejection of an 'ideal Spanish' and declaration of language for communicative competence. Why educators acknowledged and accepted the vernacular in spoken Spanish yet strove for standardization in Spanish writing is a matter of further inquiry.

Where Coral Way could strengthen its additive model of bilingual education is to leverage the bilingualism and biliteracy of its students, educators and parents in teaching and learning. Ruiz (1995: 78) notes, 'Since languages live in communities, the common life activities of the community must be the targets of language policies [...] In this way, our language policies have more of a chance to become more closely associated with our language behavior.' Coral Way can continue to embrace *de facto* language policies like the use of translanguaging for teaching and learning mathematics. Translanguaging links formal learning with freedom of expression. Accepting and supporting Spanish and English for meaning making is a way for educators to recognize students' bilingual realities.

In addition, Coral Way teachers should call greater attention to the notion of language variety. Students can learn that standard Spanish is one variety of many, and that all varieties have their own situated uses. Parents and community members can be invited to share how knowledge of language variety has served to benefit or limit opportunities in their own lives. An awareness and usage of multiple language varieties is a skill that educators should make explicit. Furthermore, Coral Way should continue to develop students' biliteracy through texts from different Spanish-speaking countries. Through exposure to a variety of literature, students and teachers can read, learn and share cultural references such as *refranes* (proverbs), *expresiones* (idioms) and *regionalismos* (regionalisms). Texts should also include national literature that explores Latina/o youth experiences in the United States. In this manner, students are exposed to content and language that may connect or contrast with their own experiences as bilinguals.

Last but not least, Coral Way should continue its Spanish-English dual language program and more actively promote student success to the community and nation. For example, the school offers AP Spanish in 8th grade, granting students the opportunity to receive college credit upon passing the AP exam. Over one-third of Coral Way students enroll in AP Spanish. Students' success contributes to the district's success. In M-DCPS, more individual Latina/o students score 3 or above on AP exams, in general, than anywhere else in the country (College Board, 2014). Equating bilingualism with intellect sends a positive message that counters the biting messages of verbal deprivation.

These recommendations would not have been possible without learning from the Coral Way community and recognizing its members as policy makers. The current era of schooling is one of migration, accountability and technological advances. Ochs (2002: 100) notes that ethnographers are faced with the challenge of 'articulating society and culture through the eyes of children as well as of those who attend to them.' Of importance in this challenge are opportunities for students to critically reflect upon their own language practices and for influential members, such as parents and educators, to share their insights. As this study demonstrated, matters of language are intertwined with language ideologies. Youth, together with those around them, create and receive messages about language. These messages are significant for the use, promotion and maintenance of language.

Notes

(1) In specific instances of transcription, I have utilized modified orthography (Ochs, 1979) to represent stylistic aspects of pronunciation that conventional spelling cannot capture.
(2) Depending on the grade level, students complete FCAT exams in English reading, English writing, Mathematics and Science.

Acknowledgments

I would like to extend my appreciation to my former graduate advisor, Richard Ruiz, for his insights on bilingual education, ideas on language policy and planning, and his open-door policy. Thank you, Richard, for speaking of Coral Way in seminars and supporting my interest in visiting the school. I am also deeply grateful to the community of students, educators and parents at Coral Way who extended their hospitality and furthered my understanding of dual language education.

Richard and Erin at University of Arizona Commencement, Tuscon, May 2014

References

Baker, C. (2011) *Foundations of Bilingual Education and Bilingualism* (5th edn). Bristol: Multilingual Matters.

Blackledge, A. and Creese, A. (2008) Contesting 'language' as 'heritage': Negotiation of identities in late modernity. *Applied Linguistics* 29 (4), 533–554.

Blommaert, J. (1999) *Language Ideological Debates*. Berlin: De Gruyter.

College Board (2014) 10 years of Advanced Placement exam data show significant gains in access and success; Areas for improvement. *CollegeBoard*, 11 February. See https://www.collegeboard.org/releases/2014/class-2013-advanced-placement-results-announced

Coral Way Bilingual Elementary School Oral History Project (2010) Tucson, AZ: Arizona Board of Regents. See https://uair.arizona.edu/item/273749

Florida News Media Directory (2013) Mount Doral, FL: News Media Directories.

García, O. and Wei, L. (2014) *Translanguaging: Language, Bilingualism and Education*. New York: Palgrave Macmillan.

Hornberger, N.H. and Johnson, D.C. (2011) The ethnography of language policy. In T.L. McCarty (ed.) *Ethnography and Language Policy* (pp. 273–289). New York: Routledge.

Hymes, D. (1992) The concept of communicative competence revisited. In M. Pütz (ed.) *Thirty Years of Linguistic Evolution: Studies in Honour of René Dirven on the Occasion of his Sixtieth Birthday* (pp. 31–57). Philadelphia, PA: John Benjamins.

Kroskrity, P.V. (2010) Language ideologies: Evolving perspectives. In J. Östman, J. Verschueren and J. Jaspers (eds) *Society and Language Use* (pp. 192–211). Herndon, VA: John Benjamins.

Lambert, W.E. (1975) Culture and language as factors in learning and education. In A. Wolfgang (ed.) *Education of Immigrant Students*. Toronto: Ontario Institute for Studies in Education.

Lippi-Green, R. (1997) *English With an Accent: Language, Ideology, and Discrimination in the United States*. New York: Routledge.

Mackinney, E. (2014) Spanish production among middle-school Latina/o emerging bilinguals in Miami, Florida. Unpublished doctoral dissertation, University of Arizona.

McCarty, T.L. (2011) Introducing ethnography and language policy. In T.L. McCarty (ed.) *Ethnography and Language Policy* (pp. 1–28). New York: Routledge.

Ochs, E. (1979) Transcription as theory. In E. Ochs and B.B. Schieffelin (eds) *Developmental Pragmatics* (pp. 43–72). New York: Academic Press.

Ochs, E. (2002) Becoming a speaker of culture. In C.J. Kramsch (ed.) *Language Acquisition and Language Socialization: Ecological Perspectives* (pp. 99–120). London: Continuum.

Ruiz, R. (1983) Ethnic group interests and the social good: Law and language in education. In W. Van Horne (ed.) *Ethnicity, Law and the Social Good* (pp. 49–73). Milwaukee, WI: American Ethnic Studies Coordinating Committee.

Ruiz, R. (1984) Orientations in language planning. *NABE Journal* 8 (2), 15–34.

Ruiz, R. (1995) Language planning considerations in Indigenous communities. *Bilingual Research Journal* 19, 71–81.

Ruiz, R. (2010) Reorienting language-as-resource. In J. Petrovic (ed.) *International Perspectives on Bilingual Education: Policy, Practice, and Controversy* (pp. 155–172). Charlotte, NC: Information Age.

Shaw, J.R. (1966) Dade County's bilingual school programs. *Florida School Bulletin* XXVIII. Tallahassee, FL: State Department of Education.

Shohamy, E. and Gorter, D. (2009) *Linguistic Landscape: Expanding the Scenery.* New York: Taylor & Francis.

Silverstein, M. (1979) Language structure and linguistic ideology. In P. Clyne, W. Hanks and C. Hofbauer (eds) *The Elements: A Parasession on Linguistic Units and Levels* (pp. 193–248). Chicago, IL: Chicago Linguistic Society.

US Census Bureau (2013) *American Community Survey.* See https://www.census.gov.

Williams, C. (1994) Arfarniad o ddulliau dysgu ac addysgu yng nghyd-destun addysg uwchradd ddwyieithog. Unpublished PhD thesis, University of Wales.

Woolard, K.A. and Schieffelin, B.B. (1994) Language ideology. *Annual Review of Anthropology* 23, 55–82.

Language Orientations in Guatemala: Toward Language as Resource?

Janelle M. Johnson and Julia B. Richards

Drawing from Richard Ruiz's (1984) language orientations and theories of language and power (Cummins, 2000; Fanon, 1967; Ruiz, 1991), in this chapter we apply the orientations lens to educational language planning and policies in Guatemala. Our analysis focuses on the discourses of orientation within official school policies and curricula as the 'most strategic institutional interface between the community and the state apparatus' (J.B. Richards, 1998: 100). We illustrate the racialized and colonized ideologies so prevalent in these language policy discourses across multiple eras, consistently maintained and reproduced despite substantially different political backdrops. Although language orientations have appeared to shift over time, underlying racism has been constant. The early iterations of Guatemala's bilingual education efforts took place during a time of assassinations, horrific massacres of entire communities, and the fleeing of hundreds of thousands of Mayas into Mexico, or to mountain hideaways or lowlands of Guatemala and to marginal areas of the capital city, cloaking themselves in the invisibility of shanty towns. We argue that although systemic racism and the ongoing marginalization of Indigenous peoples undergird contemporary Guatemalan language policies, there is hope that, despite uneven implementation of bilingual intercultural education at the school and classroom level, institutionalized language rights have proven to be instrumental in supporting a burgeoning language-as-resource orientation.

Language Orientations and Power

Richard Ruiz was extremely adept at pushing his colleagues, students and readers of his work to examine the underlying meaning of everyday language, ranging from signage at the Department of Motor Vehicles to the

316

wording of a textbook. He would initiate a dialog on the name of a food like 'burrito,' always playing devil's advocate to elicit deeper thinking from the group on a lighthearted or humorous topic, with a sense of humor so dry that many would often miss the joke. He would post optical illusions and ask the viewer to examine the different perspectives that were represented, and he would encourage reflection on *why* the viewer was able to see certain aspects over others. This was similar to the way in which he asked us to consider language orientations, and pressed us to carefully draw upon multiple theoretical lenses to analyze different types of language policies. Especially in the realm of education, language policies are often passionately contested due to deeper social, political and cultural positionalities, revealing the deeply human nature of specific contexts.

Richard, Alejandra Ramos and Janelle Johnson, Project SEED, Tucson, 2011

Richard Ruiz elaborated the conceptual model of language orientations as a contribution to the field of language planning and in support of multilingual education. He describes orientations as 'a complex of dispositions toward language and its role, and toward languages and their role in society' (Ruiz, 1984: 17). While such dispositions are generally unconscious, the process of language planning brings them to the level of discourse. This transition carves out space for addressing historical inequities of access to culturally and linguistically relevant education among marginalized communities

(Ruiz, 1991). In Guatemala, communities that have been marginalized historically, and into the present, encompass its Indigenous peoples.

One of the areas of staggering marginalization is economic. Guatemala's economy is one of the strongest in Central America and its economic growth is reflected by a steadily rising gross national product. Yet the income gap has been increasing as well; among Guatemala's 13 million inhabitants, 7 million live in poverty and 2 million live in extreme poverty, and nearly three-quarters of those living in extreme poverty are Indigenous (CIA World Factbook, 2016). 'The Maya are the major contributors toward the gross national product and the creation of the nation's wealth, but they receive the fewest benefits for their work' (Cojtí Cuxil, 1996: 21). Governmental regimes in postcolonial Guatemala have swung back and forth between politically opposing liberal and conservative leadership, but they have been consistent in categorizing the language and culture of the Indigenous majority as a detriment to national economic development and progress, serving as a classic example of language-as-problem orientation (Ruiz, 1984). Liberal governments have taken an integrationist approach for purposes of modernizing the economy, largely carried out through the expansion of public schooling, while conservative governments have maintained more segregationist social and economic policies. However, both liberal and conservative approaches have embodied an Indigenous language-as-problem orientation that stems from the colonial and postcolonial eras. Only in recent history – following the decades of a brutal civil war and the signing of the 1996 Peace Accord on Identity and Rights of Indigenous Peoples – has language as right been demanded, and notions of language as resource been gradually evolving.

Language-as-Problem Policies

As Ruiz (1988) explains, minority and non-Western languages have historically been framed as problems in the context of national development; the speakers of non-dominant languages are associated with social problems and 'backwardness.'

A new nation-state and economic development

A language-as-problem orientation was evident in the establishment of the nation-state. As part of New Spain, Guatemala declared independence in 1821, was briefly incorporated into Mexico in 1822, and became an independent republic in 1823. The following year, the Guatemalan congress called for only one national language:

The Constituent Congress of Guatemala, considering that there be one national language (and while those [Mayan languages] still used by

Indians are *so diverse, incomplete, and imperfect,* and are not sufficient for enlightening the [Maya] people or perfecting the civilization in that appreciable portion of the State), does decree and declare that: The Parish priest, in agreement with the municipalities of the people, should, through the most expedient, prudent, and efficient means, *extinguish the language of the Indians.* (Cited in and translated by J.B. Richards & M. Richards, 1997: 195; italics added)

Indigenous language-as-problem orientations continued: President Gálvez (1831–1838) attempted to force the Indigenous population to surrender their language, culture and ethnic distinctions. President Barrios instituted secular education in 1871 in an attempt to reduce the church's influence, and at the same time ushered in forced labor mechanisms to drive coffee production and exports that had severely disruptive consequences for Maya communities (Carey, 2006). Throughout the 1870s and 1880s education laws declared primary schooling compulsory, free, secular and practical under the national development model that viewed formal education and mandatory instruction in Spanish as a crucible for creating national identity, productive citizenship and efficient labor. Education legislation was carried out in concert with large-scale land privatization to break down social structures built around communal property. Through these policies, Maya communities lost control over land that their families had cultivated for generations, and were subjected to 'forced-labor laws, whereby Indians were required to work for the state or for private landowners designated by the state' (Fischer, 2001: 69). The early 1900s brought an emphasis on centralized control over school curricula and activities, such as the establishment of biannual standardized exams, standardized construction of new schools and hiring of exclusively non-Indigenous Ladino teachers. Formal public schooling at that time had specific objectives of assimilation for labor described by Grandin (2000):

> The school day itself was structured to accustom children to an ordered workday, marked by clocks and bells. The school year, which in 1920 ran from February to October, was designed around the demands of coffee planters rather than the needs of subsistence producers and helped discipline Indians into the cycles of agro-industrial production. (Grandin, 2000: 172)

While schooling did serve to 'discipline' rural labor in some regions, powerful German and Ladino landowners resisted incurring the costs of schooling their workers, and they feared an educated populace that might be unwilling to work the farms (Carey, 2006). Education infrastructure was extremely sparse in many rural areas and especially in the highlands, so large segments of Guatemala's Indigenous population were essentially unaffected by education legislation (J.B. Richards & M. Richards, 1997). The national education policies did have some effect, however, in shaping the urban education system and facilitating university expansion, both of which contributed to increases in a (non-Indigenous) middle class in the 20th century.

1944 Revolution

The 1944 October Revolution ushered in a ten-year period of increased access to education on a much broader scale than had occurred previously. President Arévalo was committed to building and improving Guatemala's schools, especially in rural areas. During his administration, schools were constructed, teachers' salaries were increased, and Ladino teachers were trained and sent to teach in Mayan communities. These integrationist policies continued under his successor, President Arbenz, and led to an increase in school attendance in the rural areas. During this period, State spending on education increased by 800% (Carey, 2006). The National Literacy Law was enacted in 1947, declaring illiteracy a national emergency (J.B. Richards & M. Richards, 1997). The National Indigenist Institute was established that same year and its local chapters were used to teach Spanish, math and vocational skills to Indigenous children and adults (Grandin, 2000).

In 1949, the First National Indigenous Teachers' Conference was held as well as the First Congress of Linguists. It was not until the First Congress of Linguists that systematic alphabets were first proposed for the four majority Mayan languages of Guatemala. These four official alphabets, like all others subsequently approved during the following decades by the National Indigenous Institute, were developed by foreign linguists and missionaries. Most notable among these foreign groups was the evangelical missionary Wycliffe Bible Translators, later to become the Summer Institute of Linguistics (SIL). These alphabets imposed conventions of Spanish orthography in order to standardize Mayan orthography and facilitate the transfer of literacy skills to and from the vernacular Mayan languages and Spanish (J.B. Richards, 1993). Under its mission of evangelization, SIL succeeded in building a substantial collection of educational materials, including mother-tongue literacy primers as well as translations of the New Testament into many Mayan languages. Like its work all over the globe, the goal of SIL's project was the assimilation of Indigenous peoples as a religious mission.

Civic assimilation through nationalized schooling reflected the liberal sociopolitical orientations of Presidents Arévalo and Arbenz: 'a state based on the model of European nation-statehood, which involved integrating the Indians into Western society. An educated, yet homogenous, population was seen as key to political stability and economic prosperity' (Fischer, 1996: 68; also see de la Peña, 2005). This vision came to an abrupt end when

President Arbenz was overthrown in 1954 in a CIA-supported coup; shifts in educational policy were immediate.

A 36-year civil war

Counter-revolutionary policies under President Armas in 1954 suspended mother-tongue adult literacy programs as 'leaders in government increasingly singled out Indians as the primary hindrance to national economic development' (J.B. Richards & M. Richards, 1997: 197). The anti-communist campaign of President Armas was fully aligned with US interests at the time. Shortly after the Cuban Revolution, a nascent revolutionary movement by former disaffected Guatemalan military officers emerged in Guatemala's eastern region (Fischer, 2001).

As the guerrilla movement expanded, the military began to use death squads and forced disappearances as anti-guerilla tactics both in urban centers and in the more Indigenous regions of western and north-central Guatemala during the 1970s. Within the context of the escalation of anti-guerilla measures, the Ministry of Education instituted a new version of its *castellanización* program. The program had been instituted several decades earlier in rural Indigenous communities as an introductory year prior to first grade to introduce Spanish and prepare children for school. The new bilingual program included use of the local language to support the transition to Spanish. This program, taught by Indigenous bilingual *promotores*, was designed to accelerate the process of acculturation of the Indigenous peoples within its language-as-problem orientation. Linguistic and cultural assimilation was assumed to be the inevitable path both for the good of Mayan children and the Mayan people in general, and for the economic and social 'progress' of the nation as a whole (J.B. Richards & M. Richards, 1996).

Military actions against the entire population were escalated, with an especially violent focus on the Indigenous western and northern highlands, as General Romeo Lucas García took control of the government in 1978 (M. Richards, 1985). 'Ladino elites' anxiety about Marxist revolutionaries converged with their long-smoldering fears of an Indian uprising, creating the ideological justification for the ethnocidal campaigns directed by the military' (Fischer, 2001: 70). Presidents Lucas García and General Ríos Montt (1982–1983) ratcheted up a genocidal campaign against Maya peoples. It was during this period, 1978–1984, that student and labor activists in the capital were disappearing at the rate of between 50 and 200 people per month (Fischer, 2001), and international pressure was mounting for the national government to address the needs of the Mayan population. In response, a new education law drafted by the Minister of Education under President Mejía Victores (1983–1986) was 'heavily influenced by members of the national and international academic and development community on the merits of bilingual education' (J.B. Richards & M. Richards, 1997: 200).

The Bilingual Education Project

Bilingual education began in Guatemala amid a mounting violent struggle that pitted the armed guerrilla opposition, academics, trade unionists and a growing sector of a disenfranchised middle class against an increasingly brutal military establishment. Parallel to an ever-increasing scorched earth policy of massacred villages, mass disappearances and social chaos in much of the country, the four-year Bilingual Education Project (PEBI), with a lion's share of funding provided by the United States Agency for International Development (USAID), was initiated in 1980 as a mechanism to increase levels of literacy and education in the country. In those years, more than half of the population could not read or write, with an illiteracy rate among Indigenous communities ranging from 75% to 90%, and even up to 100% in many Mayan towns and villages (J.B. Richards, 1989). Up to this point, the official language policy – decreed in the 1965 Constitution and encoded in the National Education Law – was based on a fundamental concept: that the multiplicity of Indigenous languages and cultures were a problem that represented national 'underdevelopment' and a threat to national unity, progress and modernization. The solution to this 'problem' was providing one to three years of bilingual education designed to successfully kick-start Indigenous children's acquisition of foundational reading and math skills and ease the transition to Spanish as the sole medium of instruction.

The PEBI created curriculum and materials for the four most widely spoken Mayan languages and applied them in ten treatment schools in each of the four linguistic regions. Despite its transitional nature and language-as-problem orientation, the pilot program did demonstrate substantially lower repetition and dropout rates, as well as improved reading scores on Spanish language and math assessments. The project had formidable setbacks due to the violence of the war, 'the most notable being the Army perpetrated murders of three of its senior Mayan technicians as well as some of its teachers and bilingual promoters' (J.B. Richards & M. Richards, 1997: 199). Many teachers and other leaders had to flee to foreign countries or go into hiding.

National Bilingual Education Program

During the transition from military to civilian government, a new national constitution was enacted in 1985, marking the first time in the country's history that the pluricultural and multilingual nature of Guatemalan society was legally recognized (Martínez, 1997). Purportedly, the 1985 Constitution was to reverse the assimilationist and falsely nationalistic postures of former governments (Montejo, 2005). Leaning on the promising outcomes of the Bilingual Education pilot project and fueled with continued funding and technical support from USAID, the government created the National Bilingual Education Program (PRONEBI) that was charged with 'reinforcing Mayan identity and promoting the harmonious and integral development of the Mayan population within a plural linguistic and cultural context.' Under this program, bilingual education coverage jumped from the 40 pilot schools to 400 schools located across the four majority language areas. Concurrently, scores of bilingual education *promotores* – Mayas who had an elementary-level education and who had been teaching Bilingual Castellanización – were trained as pre-primary and primary bilingual teachers through an accelerated professionalization program. Although PRONEBI started under the administration of Vinicio Cerezo (1986–1990), with violence levels decreasing somewhat, extrajudicial killings, disappearances and killings of Indigenous leaders continued through the signing of the Peace Accords in 1996.

When PRONEBI began, under a declared mission to revitalize the Mayan languages and reaffirm Mayan identity, there were very few people inside or outside the Ministry of Education who could foresee the magnitude of the task of 'providing preprimary and primary bilingual and bicultural education for the Indigenous school population' as called for in the new policy. Among the multitude of challenges, Mayan language and language dialect boundaries were not clearly delineated and no variant was recognized as the de facto standard that could be used for materials production. The numbers of school-age speakers of each language were not known and there were no measures to determine levels of language dominance or bilingualism. There were numerous competing Mayan language alphabets. There were no prescriptive grammars and only a few dictionaries existed; those that did were written in English or another language foreign to Guatemala.

Legacies of discrimination

Exacerbating things further, many parents and teachers alike were opposed to the idea of bilingual education, as they felt that the school was the place where their children should learn Spanish, viewed as the language of power, opportunity, and the key to progress and employment (Ferguson, 2006; Johnson, 2010; J.B. Richards 1987; Valdiviezo, 2009). These parents and teachers grew up when Indigenous languages were recognized simply as 'dialects' (*dialectos*) or 'tongues' (*lenguas*) (Ajb'ee, 1997; Collins, 2005; Garzon, 1998a; Simón, 1998). Many experienced language shaming throughout their lives – being forbidden or punished for speaking the language of their homes (Cotacachi, 1997; Crawford, 1996; Dorian, 1999; Ferguson, 2006). As described by Nelson (1999), 'they are products of the colonial system. It's not their fault. When they went to school, there were signs up prohibiting them from speaking their languages; they were punished. Children remember this;

they keep these colonial ideas inside them and then they teach the same thing' (Nelson, 1999: 143). The mere existence of Guatemala's contemporary model of bilingual intercultural education is markedly distinct from the education recent cohorts of teachers experienced during their own schooling. It is a radical departure from the type of teaching that the more senior teachers experienced and often continue to use in their classrooms (Johnson, 2011).

At home, many parents resisted the inclusion of Indigenous languages in the school since they feared it would limit their children's exposure to Spanish. In order to 'get ahead,' many Mayan families raise their children by interacting with them exclusively in Spanish, which they themselves speak as a second language (Johnson, 2013). Throughout Guatemala's history, monolingual speakers of an Indigenous language with no opportunity for dominant language acquisition have found themselves as 'a group that does not speak the language of government and commerce [that] is disenfranchised, marginalized with respect to the economic and political mainstream' (Hinton, 2001: 3). Whereas some communities view schooling as a key safeguard against hegemony and manipulation, many families living in extreme poverty have to weigh the costs of schooling (and its imposition of often foreign values) against the loss of their children's labor (Garzon, 1998c; Provasnik et al., 2002; Simón, 1998). Given the high opportunity costs of schooling, learning to speak and read Spanish has historically been the primordial reason parents sacrifice to send their children to school (J.B. Richards, 1998).

Within this historical context of ongoing denial of language rights, Mayan languages were predominantly viewed by Indigenous and non-Indigenous Guatemalans as confined to the 'sentimental domains' of the home and the community. There were thus few technical, scientific or educational terms in everyday Mayan language lexicons that could be incorporated into PRONEBI textbooks and teacher manuals. Thousands of neologisms were created to 'modernize' the languages and avoid the usage of Spanish loanwords. Existing materials in Spanish needed to be translated and adapted and new Mayan language materials needed to be written and illustrated. For Indigenous rural inhabitants, access to university education was negligible due to structural and linguistic barriers, geographical distance, limited transportation and limited resources (Collins, 2005; Warren, 1998). Within these constraints, few Mayas were trained in linguistics, anthropology or sociology and few educators had experience in curriculum design, graphic design, teacher training and supervision. Concepts like 'additive and subtractive bilingualism,' 'language proficiency,' 'linguistic competence,' 'sociolinguistic profiles,' 'pedagogical mediation,' 'transitional and maintenance bilingual education,' 'constructivism,' 'worldview' and 'cosmology' were entirely new. Also, what made an already difficult situation even more problematic and complicated was the fact that there were no trained bilingual education teachers; there were very few Maya teachers and those Maya who were trained as teachers were not literate in the language they spoke, and knew little about how to apply first and second language instructional methodologies.

Corpus planning

Another tension illuminating a pervasive language-as-problem orientation within the first iterations of bilingual education was the utilization of the Spanish alphabet to write the Mayan languages. In a 1987 meeting of Mayan linguists, it was decided to abolish Spanish spelling conventions 'based on a clear but revolutionary principle: the purpose of writing Mayan languages was to be for the inherent value of literacy in Maya and for the promotion of writing as an extension of their domains of usage and not just as a means for teaching literacy in Spanish' (England, 1996: 183), reflecting a foundation for a language-as-right orientation. The unified transparent Mayan 'alphabets' served to help catalyze language and culturally based political activism as a rallying point for the formation of the pan-Maya movement (Warren, 1996), now made up of hundreds of organizations and NGOs (Bastos & Camus, 2003; Cojtí Cuxil, 1997; Fischer & Brown, 1996; Montejo, 2005; Warren, 1998). The unification of Maya alphabets and growth of a pan-Maya identity was openly opposed by SIL (Cojtí Cuxil, 1996; England, 1996; J.B. Richards & M. Richards, 1996), which had been the chief proponents of the Spanish-based orthographies. Since the 1940s, the SIL had produced a large body of descriptive linguistic data and trained many Maya para-linguists, but their refusal to support the unified Mayan alphabets actually helped to unify activists of the pan-Maya movement (Warren, 1996). The pan-Maya alphabet, officialized by law in 1987, was adopted immediately by the Ministry of Education/PRONEBI for the production of mother tongue teaching and learning materials.

Language-as-Right Policies

Rights-based orientations may focus on language, but actually reflect a much broader struggle for human rights; language is the medium through which individuals and communities navigate all social realms (Ruiz, 1988).

Indigenous rights

Throughout the late 1980s and early 1990s, a growing international Indigenous rights framework contributed to the institutionalization of language policies that recognize the rights of Indigenous peoples worldwide. In 1989 the International Labor Organization (ILO) passed the landmark Convention 169 on Indigenous rights (Bertely Busquets, 2010; Martínez, 1997). This was followed shortly by the Indigenous Alliance of the Americas

position statement in 1990 that 'bilingual, intercultural education be officially recognized in the constitutions of all countries of the Continent.' The
Universal Declaration of Linguistic Rights, adopted in 1996, affirmed that
the exercise of individual linguistic rights could be made effective only if
equal respect is granted to the collective rights of all language communities
and groups.

In Guatemala, various national policies are associated with a shift toward
an Indigenous language-as-right orientation: the [Adult] Literacy Law and
the founding of the Institute of Linguistics of the Rafael Landivar University
(URL) in 1986; legislation unifying the Maya alphabet in 1987; legalization
of the Academy of Mayan Languages of Guatemala and the Declaration of
the Specific Rights of the Maya People in 1990; institutionalization of the
General Directorate of Intercultural Bilingual Education in 1995; creation of
the Vice Ministry of Bilingual Intercultural Education in 2003 and the enactment of the Law on Languages, wherein 21 Mayan languages (plus Xinka,
Garífuna and Spanish) were named official languages by the government of
Guatemala (Montejo, 2005). The 'Specific Rights of the Maya People,' presented in 1990 by the Council of Mayan Organizations of Guatemala as part
of the National Dialogue for Peace, outlined nine language rights as the
framework for their demands. These include: the formalization of Mayan
languages at the level of language communities; learning and mandatory use
of Mayan languages by public service officials; the use of Mayan languages
in the legal system and educational programs; funding and autonomy of the
Academy of Mayan Languages (ALMG); and the restructuring of the
Ministry of Education to allow the Maya to make their own decisions with
respect to education for the Maya population. Space for such participation
meant that PRONEBI continued to expand in the late 1980s and early 1990s,
offering bilingual education to schools in wider geographic areas and in additional Mayan languages. Slowly, PRONEBI began working as the base of a
growing movement that placed Mayan languages as central to Mayan ethnic
identity (M. Richards & J.B. Richards, 2001). In the 1990s, two historical
events gave impetus to the Maya people. The first was the awarding of the
Nobel Peace Prize to Rigoberta Menchú in 1992. The international nature of
the award was momentous in that it helped to illuminate the historical dis-
possession of Mayas in Guatemala, and more broadly the historical tragedy
of the Indigenous peoples of the Americas.

Bilingual intercultural education

The second historical event was the signing of the Agreement on Identity
and Rights of Indigenous Peoples between the Guatemalan National
Revolutionary Unity and the Government of Guatemala in 1995. This agreement was the first time the existence of Maya, Xinka, Garífuna and Ladino
were recognized as peoples. Furthermore, both the concept and the term

'intercultural' were introduced into the political and educational arena of Guatemala. Under Cultural Rights, the Agreement states, 'an effort must be made to promote contributions and exchanges that can help to enrich Guatemalan society.' Subsequently, under Education Reform, appears 'Expand and promote bilingual *intercultural education* and place emphasis on the study and knowledge of indigenous languages at all educational levels' (MINUGUA, 1995; italics added).

Soon after the signing of the 1995 Agreement, bilingual intercultural education was institutionalized by the State through the creation of the Ministry of Education's General Directorate of Bilingual Intercultural Education (DIGEBI), and the installation of bilingual intercultural education units in 15 of Guatemala's departments (states). In 1998, with funding from USAID, URL implemented a regional program to train Maya teachers in the areas of School Management, Curriculum and Linguistics. This expanded into a large scholarship program managed by URL and funded by USAID known as Edumaya that was specifically earmarked for training a cadre of Maya professionals in areas critical for the implementation of the Peace Accords. Through Edumaya, over 1000 Mayas obtained higher education degrees, including *profesorado, licenciatura* and master's degrees in bilingual intercultural education (Martins & Grimm, 2003). Several other programs funded by the international community (including the European Union, Finland, Germany, the United States, UNESCO and UNICEF) focused on improving access to and the quality of intercultural bilingual education at local levels. To better pinpoint the numbers of Indigenous language speakers and language boundaries, the Secretariat for Peace (SEPAZ) commissioned a language mapping study that involved universities, the Mayan Language Academy of Guatemala (ALMG), the Ministry of Education and other entities, resulting in the production of an official language map and linguistic atlas (M. Richards, 2003). Energized by the signing of the Peace Accords and a growing movement of Maya identity affirmation, numerous Maya-led foundations and NGOs (such as Fundación Rigoberta Menchú, Fundación Kaqchikel, Centro de Educación e Investigación Maya, Consejo Nacional de Educación Maya, Academia de las Lenguas Mayas de Guatemala, Oxlajuj Kej, and Cholsamaj) built grassroots initiatives focused on Mayan language corpus and status planning, cultural revitalization, materials production and publication, and the creation of Mayan Schools (J.B. Richards & M. Richards, 1996).

Policy versus practice

From a bottom-up perspective, the bilingual intercultural education model was intended as a move away from subtractive bilingual education and in support of Indigenous language maintenance, seen as 'having the potential to strengthen indigenous cultural and linguistic practices as well as to facilitate indigenous participation in mainstream society' (Aikman, 1997: 465). Because Guatemalan public schools have historically socialized Indigenous schoolchildren to deny or shed their identity and language (Cojtí Cuxil, 1996; Garzon, 1998a; Montejo, 2005), the inclusion of Guatemala's Indigenous languages in the Peace Accords (as well as other milestones noted above) had a substantial psychological impact for many Mayas (Ajb'ee, 1997); the institutionalization of Mayan language usage implies that language is a right.

However, some critics signal the fact that because the 1996 Peace Accords lack any real means of implementation, they equate to 'peace without justice' (Montejo, 2005: 4) without the power to actually change Guatemala's dominant language-as-problem orientation. Are these post-Peace Accord language policies simply a means of placating the Maya majority to avoid a mass political uprising, or are they simply give-away legislations bowing to international pressures (Ajb'ee, 1997)? Are they policies of containment rather than of transformation (May, 1998)? State and community motivation in supporting bilingual intercultural education must be examined, since 'bilingual education is almost everywhere inimical to language preservation' (Bernard, 1997: 140). A consortium of Guatemalan university activists points out that, despite the gains made, oppressive and discriminatory conditions are still present today in an education system that 'combines the concepts of social conformity and citizenship: it is designed to maintain the relations of power, exclusion and marginalization, particularly over the indigenous population' (Junta Cargadora, 2003: 149). And, poignantly, aversion to Mayan language and identity remains common in everyday discourse (Brown, 1998a; Garzon, 1998d; Montejo, 2005).

The discord between policy and practice is often evidenced at the classroom level. Johnson (2011) describes the limited and add-on nature of Indigenous language and culture in officially sanctioned bilingual intercultural classrooms in many regions of Guatemala. Although the existence of these classrooms is often viewed as progress, bilingual education models that simply expose children to songs and vocabulary do not contribute to language maintenance or reinforce students' cultural identity (Wilson, 1998) or promote improved learning outcomes. Luykx (1999) problematizes how many 'concrete gains in the area of Indigenous language maintenance fall into the category of "good things" – poetry contests, dictionaries, Indigenous language websites, heritage language classes, bilingual education – but none of them address the fundamental problem of intergenerational mother-tongue transmission' (Luykx, 1999: 3). While there are many 'good things' happening in Guatemalan classrooms, it is necessary to 'transform the institutional structures of schools themselves. In addition to the development of Native curricula … indigenous educators need pedagogies that work to disrupt the structures of inequality' (Grande, 2004: 6). A language-as-resource orientation is a promising avenue for disrupting the marginalizing practices that continue to be reproduced within a language-as-right legal framework.

Language as Resource?

As an alternative to the language-as-problem and language-as-right orientations, Ruiz (1988: 15) describes the potential benefits of utilizing a language-as-resource orientation, with a 'direct impact on enhancing the language status of subordinate languages; it can help ease tensions between majority and minority communities ... and it highlights the importance of cooperative language planning'. This is a promising avenue for reshaping language attitudes across the social spectrum.

Limited progress

During the initial three decades of bilingual-bicultural/multicultural/intercultural education in Guatemala, remarkable advances have been made in the codification, standardization and normalization of Mayan languages. These included: the development of texts, workbooks, manuals, readers, pedagogical grammars, dictionaries, posters, banners, calendars and interactive DVDs; the systematization of elements of Mayan cultures; the preparation of a cadre of bilingual teachers; the academic training of thousands of Maya professionals; and definitions and legalization of policies and standards for the education of Mayan children. Progress over the past 30 years in language policy and corpus planning has been significant, and 'Maya identity and culture remain strong ... but we cannot ignore the enormous weight of five centuries of continuous assimilationist and integrationist policies that we have suffered' (Raxche', 1996: 87).

Five hundred years of an educational system defined by the dominant Spanish language and its attendant Ladino cultures are not easily changed, especially when bilingual education has never received close to an adequate budget. Bilingual education, now managed within DIGEBI and highlighted under the country's official education policy, receives minimum funding within the national budget for education. Although the bilingual intercultural education system has consistently offered solid evidence of the increased educational success of Indigenous children, and greater cost-benefit than any other educational approach that Guatemala has utilized over the past 30 years (Patrinos & Velez, 2009), it has yet to be prioritized in the ministerial budget (ICEFI, 2011). The 1996 Peace Accords called for an expansion of bilingual intercultural education but, ostensibly due to the lack of funding, the percentage of pre-primary and primary schoolchildren with access to bilingual education increased only from 5% in 1996 to 18% in the period 2003–2009 (ICEFI, 2011: 14). In 2005, of the 7832 primary schools located in communities with significant Indigenous populations, only 1869 provided bilingual education (23.9%) (GHRC, 2010).

In Guatemala, many Maya and non-Maya educators and academics posit that the current bilingual education model has stagnated. Many argue that because bilingual intercultural education continues to be positioned on a traditionalist-integrationist educational platform, its objectives cannot be achieved. This may help to explain why there has not been an opportunity for its effective and comprehensive implementation in schools and class-rooms. Over the past decades, Indigenous language-as-resource planning has been piecemeal at best (Cojtí Cuxil *et al.*, 2007; Garzon, 1998c; J.B. Richards, 1998). Policies must recognize that vital Indigenous language use is linked to a community's history, status, demographics and degree of self-determina-tion (Crawford, 1996; Garzon, 1998b; Hornberger, 1998; May, 2001; Simón, 1998). The support and use of the language by the school can increase its legitimacy among community members (Berlin, 2000), but positive encour-agement for students' Indigenous identities must be explicit, ideally through curriculum, materials, language of instruction and pedagogy, among other structural reforms.

The challenges of bilingual intercultural education have been many: to serve as an instrument to preserve, rescue and revitalize Mayan languages; to strengthen and promote Maya worldview and values; to foster the unfold-ing of material, intellectual and spiritual vocation; and to promote dynamic, creative and reflexive participation. But, while bilingual intercultural educa-tion has opened access to schooling for Maya children and has served as an instrument to revitalize Mayan languages and cultures, it has not been ade-quately shaped as a vehicle to improve Maya children's learning outcomes within a community language maintenance context. If bilingual intercul-tural education is to truly serve as a vehicle for access to equitable and qual-ity education, greater focus needs to be placed on educational reform in schools and classrooms. The challenge is to ensure that children have quality educational opportunities not only in the early grades but throughout their school years within a language-as-resource orientation. Concrete actions that have been successful in other sites – some of which have been applied in Guatemala – include support for language nests for young children and the creation of Indigenous language publishing houses (Bernard, 1997), lob-bying for national level reforms and beginning locally run schools (King, 1997), and master-apprentice language programs (McCarty & Zepeda, 1999).

Maya *cosmovisión*

Building upon a foundation established by language-as-right policies, Maya activists have critiqued the purpose and outcomes of official bilingual education. The National Council of Mayan Education's (CNEM) vision of the intercultural nation-state describes the fundamental axes of 'education for life and work, education for a culture of peace in democracy and development, education for valorization of human beings in the life of the community, education in the context of integral, harmonious, balanced development with respect for nature' (CNEM, 1996: 11). CNEM scholars recommend that pedagogy should parallel the written Mayan spiritual guide *PopWuj*, which is based on observation, study, exemplification, repetition, correction, harmony and balance, representing a holistic form of learning that occurs through the family and the community, respect for oral language heritage, and recognition of the dualistic philosophy known as *kab'awil*. The CNEM text also recognizes the need to 'promote the transformation of decolonized teachers in the national system of education' (CNEM, 1996: 14). These recommendations are gradually filtering into the implementation of the base national curriculum (CNB) at the community level (Johnson, 2011).

Another source of language-as-resource activism is the ALMG. The ALMG is a coalition of Mayan language organizations representing each of Guatemala's languages and largely funded by the national government, yet able to act semi-autonomously. Organizations under the ALMG umbrella collaborate officially with the Ministry of Education at both national and departmental levels. In certain linguistic communities these organizations influence the curriculum and materials that are used in the schools, and they interact directly with schools, carrying out assessments of students' first and second languages and undertaking classroom observations (Johnson, 2010). The organizations conduct some teacher training directly and inform the regional teacher training agenda. The ALMG advances a language-as-resource orientation with its focus on the representation, codification and systematization of Maya mathematics and Maya worldview, values and principles. Maya values are generally acknowledged as including: hard work; community cooperation and support; a holistic and balanced respect for nature, elders and a supreme being; and the awareness of one's role in the community (Heckt, 1999; Raxche', 1996). This construction of Maya worldview, or *cosmovisión*, reflects a language-as-resource orientation, 'emphasizing self-determination, cultural pride, and pan-Mayan unity in the belief that a rejuvenated Mayan culture can peacefully lead Guatemala into a truly culturally pluralist future' (Brown, 1998b: 156).

Final thoughts

Language-as-resource planning is far more complex than creating a bilingual education system and addressing the technical aspects of its implementation. Bilingual intercultural education with a language-as-resource orientation builds on students' community-based identity. Although many debates on bilingual education focus on pedagogy or politics, the language-as-resource orientation fundamentally represents local-level empowerment 'which cannot necessarily be measured in number of words or phrases learned' (Craig, 1992: 23). Education that empowers communities requires Indigenous and local leadership of action research, teacher recruitment and placement, teacher training, continuous professional development, and production of quality teaching and learning materials, as well as greater organization and collaboration between educational agencies. Ruiz (1984) outlines some of the benefits of a language-as-resource orientation:

> It can have a direct impact on enhancing the language status of subordinate languages; it can help to ease tensions between majority and minority communities; it can serve as a more consistent way of viewing the role of [non-dominant languages] in society; and it highlights the importance of cooperative language planning. (Ruiz, 1984: 25–26)

We believe that it is time for Maya communities to make extraordinary efforts to shed 'imposed educational models' (Gegeo & Watson-Gegeo, 2002: 311) and reinvent multilingual education through language-as-resource orientation policies, building quality education that is focused on learning, embedded within the richness of language, culture, identity and diversity. These are integral resources that support the Guatemalan mosaic and need to be cultivated, fortified and treasured. While great strides have been made over the last 30 years, there is much more ground to cover before community languages are framed and incorporated as transformative resources (Hornberger, 1998; Ruiz, 1991).

We call for ongoing critical assessment: Is bilingual education in Guatemala associated with equitable enrichment opportunities for learning? Or is it associated with weak educational outcomes, deficit models, and piecemeal programming for poor and underserved children? Indigenous language-as-resource planning in Guatemala depends on the critical awareness of communities 'to understand more deeply possible connections between technocratic pedagogy and the political, social, and economic forces, and how their own culture can be accentuated or marginalized by the mass media, economic institutions, [and] educational institutions of the dominant society' (Manu'atu & Kepa, 2001: 3). It must be accompanied by sustainable, autonomous development that addresses community members' real cultural, linguistic and economic needs (Ferguson, 2006). Communities served by bilingual intercultural education themselves have to scrutinize the existing model to assess whether it is meeting real community needs and adequately preparing children to function successfully in a changing world, heeding communities' calls for access to the global economy. 'Consultation is not a substitute for representation' (Cojtí Cuxil, 1996: 33). The results must also be local, demonstrated when 'real development begins in each family in an atmosphere of emotional and material security' (Simón, 1998: 172). This type of language planning truly embodies a language-as-resource orientation as adroitly conceptualized by Richard Ruiz.

Although communities have been and continue to be justifiably wary of the government's motivations, the official educational use of Mayan languages (as well as the jobs that have been created for Mayan speakers as teachers and educators) has raised the status of Mayan languages in the eyes of its speakers and the nation at large. This increasing status has opened spaces for transformation at the local level and for critique of national language policies through questions such as those Richard Ruiz so often posed. (1) Who decides language and educational policies at the national and local levels? (2) How and by whom are language and educational policies implemented? (3) What are the interrelationships between top-down and bottom-up language and cultural revitalization efforts? And, (4) how are these relationships, policies and implementation strategies influenced by social, cultural, political and economic factors? Teachers and communities need to have greater input in the curriculum which, according to Maya activists, would ideally include cultural history, stories, ceremonies, epistemology, critical thinking, problem solving, traditions, customs and natural studies (Montejo, 2005; Ngai, 2006), in effect 'mayanizing the form and content of school teaching' (Cojtí Cuxil, 1996: 39).

Perhaps, as Ruiz (1991: 319) suggests, promoting a language-as-resource orientation 'can be an important factor in ethnic communities shedding their minority status', as communities, local authorities, parents and families, the local private sector, teachers, children and youth work together in the formulation and implementation of their *own* bilingual intercultural education.

References

Aikman, S. (1997) Interculturality and intercultural education: A challenge for democracy. *International Review of Education* 43 (5–6), 463–479.

Ajb'ee, O.J. (1997) Tensión entre idiomas: Situación actual de los idiomas mayas y el español en Guatemala. Paper presented at Latin American Studies Association Conference, Guadalajara, Mexico.

Bastos, S. and Camus, M. (2003) *Entre el Mecapal y el Cielo, Desarrollo del Movimiento Maya en Guatemala*. Guatemala: FLACSO/Guatemala.

Berlin, L. (2000) The benefits of second language acquisition and teaching for indigenous language educators. *Journal of American Indian Education* 39 (3), 19–35.

Bernard, H.R. (1997) Language preservation and publishing. In N. Hornberger (ed.) *Indigenous Literacies in the Americas: Language Planning from the Bottom Up* (pp. 139–156). Berlin: Mouton de Gruyter.

Bertely Busquets, M. (2010) Views from the hemisphere of resistance. In L. Meyer and B. Maldonado (eds) *Noam Chomsky and Voices from North, South, and Central America* (pp. 141–160). San Francisco, CA: City Lights.

Brown, R.M. (1998a) A brief cultural history of the Guatemalan highlands. In S. Garzon, R. McKenna Brown, J. Becker Richards and Wuqu' Ajpub' (eds) *The Life of our Language: Kaqchikel Maya Maintenance, Shift, and Revitalization* (pp. 44–61). Austin, TX: University of Texas Press.

Brown, R.M. (1998b) Mayan language revitalization in Guatemala. In S. Garzon, R. McKenna Brown, J. Becker Richards and Wuqu' Ajpub' (eds) *The Life of our Language:*

Kaqchikel Maya Maintenance, Shift, and Revitalization (pp. 155–170). Austin, TX: University of Texas Press.

Carey, D. (2006) *Engendering Mayan History: Kaqchikel Women as Agents and Conduits of the Past, 1875–1970.* London: Taylor & Francis.

CIA World Factbook (2016) The Economy of Guatemala. *The World Factbook* (accessed online 6 January 2016).

CNEM (Consejo Nacional de Educación Maya) (1996) Propuesta Maya de reforma educativa. Seminario Nacional de Educación Maya por la Paz. Xelju', Quetzaltenango.

Cojtí Cuxil, D. (1996) The politics of Maya revindication. In E. Fischer and R.M. Brown (eds) *Maya Cultural Activism in Guatemala.* Austin, TX: University of Texas Press.

Cojtí Cuxil, D. (1997) *El Movimiento Maya en Guatemala.* Guatemala: Cholsamaj.

Cojtí Cuxil, D., Son Chonay, E. and Rodriguez, D. (2007) *Nuevas Perspectivas para la Construcción del Estado Multinacional.* Guatemala: Cholsamaj.

Collins, W. (2005) Codeswitching avoidance as a strategy for Mam (Maya) linguistic revitalization. *International Journal of American Linguistics* 71 (3), 239–276.

Cotacachi, M. (1997) Attitudes of teachers, children and parents towards bilingual intercultural education. In N. Hornberger (ed.) *Indigenous Literacies in the Americas: Language Planning from the Bottom Up* (pp. 285–298). Berlin: Mouton de Gruyter.

Craig, C. (1992) A constitutional response to language endangerment: The case of Nicaragua. *Language* 68 (1), 17–24.

Crawford, J. (1996) Seven hypotheses on language loss causes and cures. Paper presented at Stabilizing Indigenous Language Conference, Flagstaff, Northern Arizona University.

Cummins, J. (2000) *Language, Power and Pedagogy: Bilingual Children in the Crossfire.* Clevedon: Multilingual Matters.

de la Peña, G. (2005) Social and cultural policies toward Indigenous peoples: Perspectives from Latin America. *Annual Review of Anthropology* 34, 717–739.

Dorian, N. (1999) Linguistic and ethnographic fieldwork. In J. Fishman (ed.) *Handbook of Language and Ethnic Identity* (pp. 25–42). New York: Oxford University Press.

England, N.C. (1996) The role of language standardization in revitalization. In E.F. Fischer and R.M. Brown (eds) *Maya Cultural Activism in Guatemala* (pp. 178–194). Austin, TX: University of Texas Press.

Fanon, F. (1967) *Black Skin, White Masks* (trans. C.L. Markmann). New York: Grove Press.

Ferguson, G. (2006) *Language Planning and Education.* Edinburgh: Edinburgh University Press.

Fischer, E.F. (1996) Induced culture change as a strategy for socioeconomic development: The Pan-Maya movement in Guatemala. In E.F. Fischer and R. McKenna Brown (eds) *Maya Cultural Activism in Guatemala* (pp. 51–73). Austin, TX: University of Texas Press.

Fischer, E.F. (2001) *Cultural Logics and Global Economies: Maya Identity in Thought and Practice.* Austin, TX: University of Texas Press.

Fischer, E. and Brown, R.M. (1996) Introduction: Maya cultural activism in Guatemala. In E. Fischer and R.M. Brown (eds) *Maya Cultural Activism in Guatemala* (pp. 1–18). Austin, TX: University of Texas Press.

Garzon, S. (1998a) Introduction. In S. Garzon, R. McKenna Brown, J. Becker Richards and Wuqu' Ajpub' (eds) *The Life of our Language: Kaqchikel Maya Maintenance, Shift, and Revitalization* (pp. 1–8). Austin, TX: University of Texas Press.

Garzon, S. (1998b) Indigenous groups and their language contact relations. In S. Garzon, R. McKenna Brown, J. Becker Richards and Wuqu' Ajpub' (eds) *The Life of our Language: Kaqchikel Maya Maintenance, Shift, and Revitalization* (pp. 9–43). Austin, TX: University of Texas Press.

Garzon, S. (1998c) Case study three: San Juan Comalapa. In S. Garzon, R. McKenna Brown, J. Becker Richards and Wuqu' Ajpub' (eds) *The Life of our Language: Kaqchikel*

Maya Maintenance, Shift, and Revitalization (pp. 129–154). Austin, TX: University of Texas Press.

Garzon, S. (1998d) Conclusions. In S. Garzon, R. McKenna Brown, J. Becker Richards and Wuqu' Ajpub' (eds) *The Life of our Language: Kaqchikel Maya Maintenance, Shift, and Revitalization* (pp. 188–200). Austin, TX: University of Texas Press.

Gegeo, D.W. and Watson-Gegeo, K.A. (2002) Whose knowledge? Epistemological collisions in Solomon Islands community development. *The Contemporary Pacific* 14 (2), 377–409.

GHRC (Guatemala Human Rights Commission) (2010) Education in Guatemala. Fact Sheet. Washington, DC: GHRC/USA.

Grande, S. (2004) *Red Pedagogy: Native American Social and Political Thought*. Lanham, MD: Rowman & Littlefield.

Grandin, G. (2000) *The Blood of Guatemala: A History of Race and Nation*. Durham, NC: Duke University Press.

Heckt, M. (1999) Mayan education in Guatemala: A pedagogical model and its political context. *International Review of Education* 45 (3/4), 321–337.

Hinton, L. (2001) Language revitalization: An overview. In L. Hinton and K. Hale (eds) *The Green Book of Language Revitalization in Practice* (pp. 3–18). Leiden: Brill Academic.

Hornberger, N.H. (1998) Language policy, language education, language rights: Indigenous, immigrant, and international perspectives. *Language in Society* 27 (4), 439–458.

ICEFI (Instituto Centroamericana de Estudios Fiscales), Save the Children (2011) *Educación Bilingüe en Guatemala, Logros, Desafíos y Oportunidades*. Guatemala: ICEFI and Save the Children.

Johnson, J. (2010) Cross-cultural professional development for teachers within global imbalances of power. *Journal of International & Global Studies* 2 (1), 118–133.

Johnson, J. (2011) Mapping a new field: Cross-border professional development for teachers. Doctoral dissertation, Teaching, Learning, and Sociocultural Studies, College of Education, University of Arizona.

Johnson, J. (2013) Teachers as agents of change within Indigenous education programs in Guatemala and Mexico: Examining some outcomes of cross-border professional development. Invited chapter in C. Benson and K. Kosonen (eds) *Language Issues in Comparative Education: Inclusive Teaching and Learning in Non-Dominant Languages and Cultures*. Rotterdam: Sense Publishers/Comparative and International Education Society.

Junta Cargadora Pro Creación de la Universidad Maya de Guatemala (2003) In *La Educación Superior Indígena en América Latina* (pp. 149–158). Caracas: Instituto Internacional de la UNESCO para la Educación Superior en América Latina y el Caribe, Entre Diseños.

King, K. (1997) Indigenous politics and native language literacies: Recent shifts in bilingual education policy and practice in Ecuador. In N. Hornberger (ed.) *Indigenous Literacies in the Americas: Language Planning from the Bottom Up* (pp. 267–284). Berlin: Mouton de Gruyter.

Luykx, A. (1999) *The Citizen Factory: Schooling and Cultural Production in Bolivia*. Albany, NY: SUNY Press.

Manu'atu, L. and Kepa, M. (2001) A critical theory to teaching English to speakers of other languages (TESOL): The promising focus for indigenous perspectives. Paper presented at the *PacSLRF Conference, University of Hawaii, Manoa*.

Martínez, E.B.C. (1997) La nueva educación indígena en Iberoamérica. *Revista Iberoamericana de educación* 13, 13–34.

Martins, L. and Grimm, N. (2003) *Edumaya Program and Impact on its Graduates*. Cleveland, OH: K'inal Winik Cultural Center, Cleveland State University.

May, S. (1998) Language and education rights for indigenous peoples. *Language, Culture & Curriculum* 11 (3), 272–296.

May, S. (2001) *Language and Minority Rights: Ethnicity, Nationalism and the Politics of Language*. Harlow: Pearson Education.

McCarty, T. and Zepeda, O. (1999) Amerindians. In J. Fishman (ed.) *Handbook of Language and Ethnic Identity* (pp. 197–210). New York: Oxford University Press.

MINUGUA (1995) United Nations Mission for the Verification of Human Rights in Guatemala. See http://www.guatemalaun.org/paz.cfm.

Montejo, V. (2005) *Maya Intellectual Renaissance: Identity, Representation, and Leadership*. Austin, TX: University of Texas Press.

Nelson, D. (1999) *A Finger in the Wound: Body Politics in Quincentennial Guatemala*. Berkeley, CA: University of California Press.

Ngai, P.B.Y. (2006) Grassroots suggestions for linking Native-language learning, Native American studies, and mainstream education in reservation schools with mixed Indian and White student populations. *Language, Culture and Curriculum* 19 (2), 220–236.

Patrinos, H. and Velez, E. (2009) Cost and benefit of bilingual education in Guatemala, a partial analysis. *International Journal of Education Development* 29 (6), 594–598.

Provasnik, S., Brush, L., Heyman, C., Fanning, M., Lent, D. and De Wilde, J. (2002) Changing girls' education in Guatemala. Paper presented at the *46th Annual Meeting of the Comparative International Education Society (CIES) Orlando, FL*.

Raxche' (Demetrio Rodríguez Guaján) (1996) Maya culture and the politics of development. In E. Fischer and R.M. Brown (eds) *Maya Cultural Activism in Guatemala*. Austin, TX: University of Texas Press.

Richards, J.B. (1987) Learning Spanish and classroom dynamics: School failure in a Guatemalan Maya community. In H.T. Trueba (ed.) *Success or Failure? Learning and the Language Minority Student*. New York: Newbury House Publishers.

Richards, J.B. (1989) Mayan language planning for bilingual education in Guatemala. *International Journal of the Sociology of Language* 77, 93–115.

Richards, J.B. (1993) The First Congress of Mayan Languages of Guatemala (1949). In J. Fishman (ed.) *The Earliest Stage of Language Planning: The 'First Congress' Phenomenon*. Berlin: Mouton de Gruyter.

Richards, J.B. (1998) Case study one: San Marcos La Laguna. In S. Garzon, R. McKenna Brown, J. Becker Richards and Wuqu' Ajpub' (eds) *The Life of our Language: Kaqchikel Maya Maintenance, Shift, and Revitalization* (pp. 62–100). Austin, TX: University of Texas Press.

Richards, J.B. and Richards, M. (1996) Maya education: An historical and contemporary analysis of Mayan language education policy. In E. Fischer and R.M. Brown (eds) *Maya Cultural Activism in Guatemala*. Austin, TX: University of Texas Press.

Richards, J.B. and Richards, M. (1997) Mayan language literacy in Guatemala: A sociohistorical overview. In N. Hornberger (ed.) *Indigenous Literacies in the Americas: Language Planning from the Bottom Up* (pp. 189–212). Berlin: Mouton de Gruyter.

Richards, M. (1985) Cosmopolitan world view and counterinsurgency in Guatemala. *Anthropological Quarterly* 58 (3), July.

Richards, M. (2003) *Atlas Lingüístico de Guatemala*. Guatemala: Universidad Rafael Landívar/Serviprensa.

Richards, M. and Richards, J.B. (2001) Linguistic diversity, interculturalism, and democracy. In C. Chase-Dunn, N. Amaro and S. Jones (eds) *Globalization on the Ground: Postbellum Guatemalan Democracy and Development*. Lanham, MA: Rowman & Littlefield.

Ruiz, R. (1984) Orientations in language planning. *NABE Journal* 8 (2), 15–34.

Ruiz, R. (1988) Orientations in language planning. In S.L. McKay and S.C. Wong (eds) *Language Diversity: Problem or Resource?* Boston, MA: Heinle & Heinle.

Ruiz, R. (1991) The empowerment of language-minority students. In C. Sleeter (ed.) *Empowerment Through Multicultural Education* (pp. 217–227). Albany, NY: State University of New York Press.

Simón, A. (Wuqu' Ajpub') (1998) Language contact experiences of a Mayan speaker. In S. Garzon, R. McKenna Brown, J. Becker Richards and Wuqu' Ajpub' (eds) *The Life of our Language: Kaqchikel Maya Maintenance, Shift, and Revitalization* (pp. 171–187). Austin, TX: University of Texas Press.

Warren, K.B. (1996) Reading history as resistance: Maya public intellectuals in Guatemala. In E.F. Fischer and R.M. Brown (eds.) *Maya Cultural Activism in Guatemala* (pp. 89–106). Austin: University of Texas Press.

Warren, K. (1998) *Indigenous Movements and their Critics: Pan-Maya Activism in Guatemala*. Princeton, NJ: Princeton University Press.

Wilson, W.H. (1998) The sociopolitical context of establishing Hawaiian-medium education. *Language, Culture, and Curriculum* 11, 325–338.

World Learning Report for USAID/Guatemala (2005) *Access to Intercultural and Bilingual Education Project in Guatemala, April 13, 1999–March 15, 2005*.

Valdiviezo, L. (2009) Bilingual intercultural education in Indigenous schools: An ethnography of teacher interpretations of government policy. *International Journal of Bilingual Education and Bilingualism* 12 (1), 61–79.

'Language as Catalyst': Exploring the Role of Linguistic Landscapes in the Framework of Richard Ruiz's 'Orientations in Language Planning'

Olga Bever

To my teacher …

Numerous actors, agencies, forces and factors continuously mediate and reproduce discourses of 'language as problem,' 'language as right' and 'language as resource.' Ruiz (1984) suggested these three concepts of language as, 'orientations in language planning,' delineating *a complex of dispositions toward language and its role, and toward languages and their role in society'* (Ruiz, 1988: 4). Ruiz's 'orientations in language planning' situate languages and speakers in relation to other languages, communities and individuals, stressing the complexity of linguistic and cultural diversities. These orientations facilitate the analysis of languages, language use and linguistic resources in settings where the objects of study are intrinsically embedded in larger sociopolitical, sociocultural and sociohistorical contexts. The orientations offer a multifaceted approach to study language education, language use and language contact, especially in multilingual communities. They highlight language status and language use as critical factors in constructing and negotiating group and individual identities. They articulate how language policies and practices intersect, collide and compete with the ideologies and interests of different groups, authorities and individuals (see Bever, 2010, 2015; Hornberger, 2003a). Thus, language policy concerning national, official, community and immigrant languages can benefit from Ruiz's approaches by looking at how and why particular languages are used in particular communities and sociocultural contexts. Ruiz's 'orientations in language planning' enable formulating strategies of how to position multilingual discourses and ideologies as a challenge to nationalistically oriented ideologies. Ruiz's approach enhances study of the relationship between languages and nation-states by determining the basis for critical positions on language policy and language planning including *diversity and multilingualism* versus *'one state – one language'* ideologies.

This essay explores how and why Ruiz's foundational three-part 'orientations in language planning' can be applied, further explored and evolved into a *'language-as-catalyst'* orientation: the particular case study is what linguistic landscapes reveal about the recent geopolitical conflict in post-Soviet Ukraine. The Ukrainian example speaks to many other multilingual countries, where language policy and linguistic practices negotiate local, national and global ideologies and discourses. Applying a basic definition of 'catalyst,' I show through this case study how we can examine the escalation of social and political tension through the lenses of linguistic landscape in the framework of Ruiz's orientations in language planning.

Language Policy and Linguistic Landscapes

In recent years, linguistic landscapes (LLs) have become an object of study and an important tool in the study of languages, communities and individuals. The classic definition of linguistic landscapes comes from Landry and Bourhis (1997):

> The language of public road signs, advertising billboards, street names, place names, commercial shop signs, and public signs on government buildings combines to form the linguistic landscape of a given territory, region, or urban agglomeration. (Landry & Bourhis, 1997: 25)

LLs have brought attention to the visual domain of languages use to multilingual multimodal signs in everyday environments in localities around the globe, revealing how languages are situated in the material world (Scollon & Scollon, 2003), and exploring the negotiation of language policies, linguistic diversities and sociocultural practices (Blommaert, 2010; Gorter, 2006; Laitinen & Zabrodskaja, 2015; Shohamy & Gorter, 2009).

As Shohamy and Gorter (2009: 1) argue, 'LL items … offer rich and stimulating texts on multiple levels – single words …, colorful images, sounds and moving objects and infinite creative representations.' Bever (2010, 2015) noted further that multimodality and the interconnection of linguistic and non-linguistic semiotic resources allow studying LLs as part of a broader sociocultural and sociopolitical context. The textual analyses of signs show the interplay of languages, scripts and non-linguistic semiotic devices, and uncover socially charged messages, resonating with particular ideologies and identities.

Multilingual multimodal signs have become a tool for examining the complexities and dynamics of multilingual societies and power relations. As

LLs respond to our ever-changing world, affected by digital communication, mobility, migration and globalization, they reveal the dynamic interplay of the sociolinguistic environment with social and linguistic practices. LLs refine the notion of linguistic minorities and minority languages, stimulating discussions not only from a numerical or language status perspective, but from the perspective of language dominance in a particular locality as a pre-ferred community language (Gorter *et al.*, 2012). LLs engage the creators and the readers of the signs in negotiation of sociolinguistic and sociocultural spaces, unveiling how and why language practices may comply with or con-tradict official language policy.

Earlier studies have outlined LL patterns in terms of the distribution of languages in LLs in various parts of the world (Israel, Japan, Thailand, Basque Country), identifying the differences between private and public signs, and distinguishing between 'top-down' signs (official signs placed by the govern-ment and other authorities) and 'bottom-up' signs (non-official signs placed by commercial enterprises and private entities) (Gorter, 2006). Later scholarship addresses the LL phenomena as 'semiotic landscape' (Jaworski & Thurlow, 2010), 'multimodal and multilingual phenomena' (Bever, 2015), and 'sociolin-guistic landscapes' (Laitinen & Zabrodskaja, 2015), highlighting qualitative research, critical ethnography and discourse analysis. This broader conceptual perspective of the field suggests a multidimensional multilayered approach to LLs to capture dynamic multilayered sociolinguistic and sociocultural pro-cesses and practices, globalization, multimodality, and contact between lan-guages, scripts and cultures (Bever, 2010, 2012, 2015; Blommaert, 2010, 2013).

The growing presence of English, as the language of globalization, com-mercialization and economic mobility (Blommaert, 2010; Crystal, 2003), further exhibits Landry and Bourhis's (1997) notion of the symbolic and information power of LLs. English proficiency in the local population varies across various localities (Huebner, 2006). In some places English and Roman script messages mainly target tourists or serve as a marketing tool (Martin, 2007; Piller, 2003). The local population may have very limited knowledge of English, while continuously using English language and Roman script in the linguistic landscape, thus addressing the global market and 'globalized envi-ronments' (Backhaus, 2006; Blommaert, 2010; Gorter, 2006).

LL studies have revealed that the dominance of a particular language in the LL may reflect the relative power and social status of a group within a particular community (Huebner, 2006). Further LL research has demon-strated that the official language policy in many places involves regulations and constraints on languages used in signs (Backhaus, 2006; Bever, 2010; Pavlenko, 2012). These regulations involve political decisions of local and national governments, supporting the status and prestige of particular lan-guages. Thus, languages and scripts in signs may conflict with official lan-guage policy, reflecting the complexities of local, national and global identities and ideologies. Local language practices ('bottom-up') may oppose official language policies ('top-down'), thus challenging the official language and assigning higher prestige to the local languages. In this way, the juxtaposition of languages and scripts in LLs reflects dynamics of social, cultural and political domains, and reveals a multiplicity of macro–micro interactions between languages, communities and individuals. In a broader sense, official and non-official ideologies can be extrapolated from the properties of the signs, negotiating the meanings of the text in particular social, cultural and political contexts and addressing particular audiences.

In this context, Ruiz's three orientations in language planning provide a critical framework and invite further development of the framework, which I undertake here through its application to LLs in relation to ethnographically, sociopolitically and socioculturally informed contexts. This is particularly relevant for sensitive areas of geo- and sociopolitical conflicts, where language policy ('top-down') and language use ('bottom-up') do not support each other, but coexist in an implicit negotiation of complex, multidimensional, local, national and global ideologies: it is this complexity embracing all three of Ruiz's orientations that suggests for me an overarching orientation of 'language as catalyst,' here understood as 'an agent that provokes or speeds significant change or action' (http://www.merriam-webster.com/dictionary/catalyst). Language conflicts in LLs demonstrate how the use of a non-official language is a *'resource'* for its speakers/users who are exercising their language *'right,'* while it is a language *'problem'* for both national policy makers and those who are denied use of and education in *their* languages. In such cases, local language use expresses opposition to the official language policy. The extension of this opposition to nationalistically oriented ideologies can symbolize the basis for a broader sociopolitical polarization and ultimately civil conflict. Such polarization became a critical point in the Ukrainian crisis of 2013–2014, turning the European integration and anticorruption 'Maidan' ('Euromaidan') revolution into deadly armed conflict in eastern Ukraine. The following discussion reveals how a language-as-catalyst orientation evolved as expressed in the LLs of post-Soviet Ukraine.

The Ukrainian Context: How Language Conflict Sparked a Geopolitical Crisis

Language policy, linguistic practices, and sociolinguistic and sociocultural contexts have become critical in examining and understanding the Ukrainian continuous crisis of 2013–2016. The conflict over language policy and language use has a long history in Ukraine, reflecting centuries of multilingualism and regional distribution of languages. Ukraine is geographically situated between Russia and European countries, with the eastern, western and southern regions becoming parts of Ukraine in different historical times (Kuzio, 2000; Magocsi, 1996; Mazenko, 2009). Historically and today,

Ukraine is a multilingual state with two dominant genetically close languages, Ukrainian and Russian, widespread balanced and unbalanced bilingualism and a mixed Ukrainian-Russian dialect, *surzhyk*. The main sociolinguistic characteristic of the country is Ukrainian regionalism with an asymmetrical distribution of languages along geographical lines: Russian has long been the preferred language in the east and south of Ukraine. The regional division and the sociohistorical and sociolinguistic makeup of the country have stimulated an ongoing debate in the literature about the role and status of the Ukrainian and Russian languages and Ukrainian-Russian bilingualism. This ongoing debate involves policies of russification and derussification in Ukraine during the Soviet and post-Soviet periods, the role of the Russian language as the lingua franca of the Soviet Union and the preferred language of numerous communities and individuals, and the relative status, prestige, cultural dominance and political power of the Ukrainian and Russian languages (Besters-Dilger, 2009; Bilaniuk & Melnyk, 2008; Kulyk, 2006, 2010, 2011; Mazenko, 2009; Sovik, 2007, 2010; Pavlenko, 2008, 2009, 2011, 2012; Taranenko, 2007).

Spolsky (2004: 116–117), referring to Martin (2002), points to various language policies involving ethnic and linguistic minorities and their implementation associated with turbulent historical periods in Czarist Russia and the Soviet Union: 'Czarist russification activities,' Lenin's 'indigenization (*korenizatsiia*),' and Stalin's 'sovietization ... expressed in Russian as lingua franca.' Grosjean (1982: 23), referring to Lewis (1972), states that while Russian became a lingua franca in the context of Soviet multilingualism, regional languages were supported: 'Some languages, such as Ukrainian, are widely used; they have a written tradition and literature, an extensive technological and scientific vocabulary, and they play an important role in regional life'. Mazenko (2009: 102) argues that 'objective sociolinguistic studies in Ukraine only become possible since the end of the 1980s,' and that during the Soviet time and up to the dissolution of the USSR in 1991, the status of the Russian language was elevated and it was favored over the Ukrainian language. Another critical factor is that, as part of conflicting post-Soviet discourses, Russian or Ukrainian language choice and language use have been often interpreted as pro-Russian or pro-Western political and cultural allegiance, highlighting the link between linguistic, ethnic and national identities and ideologies (Bilaniuk & Melnyk, 2008; Pirie, 1996). In sum, the turbulent history, asymmetrical distribution of languages, Soviet and post-Soviet policies and practices, and post-Soviet economic and political transformations continuously reconstruct and reshape complex, multilayered and multidimensional conflicting discourses and ideologies that underlie language policy and language use in Ukraine.

After the breakup of the Soviet Union in 1991, Ukraine became an independent state. As part of post-Soviet transformations, nation building and national identity formation, the Ukrainian government enforced a 1989 language policy with Ukrainian as the sole national and official language, thus threatening Ukrainian-Russian bilingualism, Russian language status, Russian language education and Russian language use (Pavlenko, 2006, 2008). According to this language policy, Russian received a status of 'minority' language, not in a numerical sense, but through the legal limitations of Russian language use in government, education, the public sphere, media and advertising (Bever, 2010; Pavlenko, 2006, 2008, 2009, 2011, 2012; Sovik, 2007). As Pavlenko (2012: 42) noted, the 'distinction between majority and minority groups "is not based on numerical size, but on clearly observable differences among groups in relation to power, status and entitlement" (May, 2006, p. 255).' Proclaiming Russian a minority language suggests that its speakers are denied equal rights and entitlements when compared to speakers of Ukrainian (Pavlenko, 2011, 2012).

However, despite this law, Russian remained the preferred language in many domains of language use in eastern and southern Ukraine, thus reinforcing competing and coexisting local and national ideologies (Bever, 2010, 2015; Bilaniuk, 2005, 2010; Pavlenko, 2006, 2008, 2009, 2012; Sovik, 2010). The unambiguous intent to promote Ukrainian identity formation and nation-building through 'Ukrainization' and 'de-Russification' has served to disengage the nation from the Soviet past associated with the Russian language and culture. Today, Ukrainian regionalism exhibits an asymmetrical distribution of languages: Ukrainian is dominant in the west and Russian is dominant in the east and south, while the central parts are more balanced. In addition, Russian is dominant in many urban centers across the country, while Ukrainian dominates in the rural areas (Khmelko & Wilson, 1998; Kuzio, 2000; Magocsi, 1996; Sovik, 2007). The struggle over language policy with equal rights for the Ukrainian and Russian languages has persisted in official, educational and other domains of language use. In 2012 the Ukrainian government passed the *Law on the Principles of the State Language Policy*. This law allowed the use of 18 regional languages as official regional languages when spoken by at least 10% of the people in a particular territory. According to this law, Russian received the status of a regional language in the eastern and southeastern regions of Ukraine, including the research site of this paper.

The Ukraine political crisis emerged in the fall of 2013 with the movement toward European integration. This crisis sparked 'Maidan'[1] (also called the 'Euromaidan') revolution in Kyiv, the Ukrainian capital, and led to subsequent geopolitical and economic crises and the bloody war in eastern Ukraine. The political turmoil and armed conflict in eastern Ukraine resulted in geopolitical changes, destroyed the peaceful lives of many cities and towns, displaced over 2 million people, and created thousands of deaths (widely reported in international media). To understand the background of the Ukrainian crises, it is critical to examine the Ukrainian state from sociolinguistic, sociohistorical and language policy perspectives. The prevailing media reports presented the Ukrainian crises in broad geopolitical and global terms, ignoring sociocultural and sociolinguistic forces. Most importantly, the reports put aside the fact that, after throwing out the pro-Russian identified president Yanukovich, the first vote of the Ukrainian Parliament after the 'Maidan' revolution in February 2014 was to repeal the 2012 *Law on the Principles of the State Language Policy*, thus removing Russian as an official regional language.

Linguistic Landscape as a Social Reality

In today's era of globalization, geopolitical tensions and mobility, linguistic and semiotic resources are powerful tools that reflect and construct social worlds. As a dynamic construct, LLs are a product and a process of the social realities and multilingual practices of the community. Various media (e.g. street names, shop signs, advertising posters, billboards, other media forms) constitute the semiotic and sociolinguistic landscape of a particular space (e.g. geographical, social, private, public). There are layers of ambiguities, hierarchies, combinations of various modes of representation, contact varieties of languages and scripts, and non-linguistic semiotic resources presented in advertising posters, billboards, shop signs, business signs, personal ads, etc. In this essay, LLs in an urban center of southeastern Ukraine provide data on the interaction of language policy and actual language use. The juxtaposition of Ukrainian, Russian and English, and of Cyrillic and Roman scripts, reflect negotiation of local, national and global ideologies and discourses, expressing the local language and culture, compliances with official language policy, and associations with the global market and modernity (Bever, 2010, 2011, 2015; Bilaniuk, 2005; Hornberger, 2003b; Pavlenko, 2008, 2009).

Below are LL signs selected from a larger set of photographs taken in 2009 in an urban center in southeastern Ukraine (Bever, 2010). The photographs were taken in the central part of a city known for its commercial and cultural activities and high density of signs of various categories: official and private notices, banks and financial institutions, entertainment establishments, restaurants and stores. These examples provide evidence for claims about language use in the community. LLs provide a broad spectrum of linguistic and non-linguistic elements, allowing analysis to shift from micro to macro and enabling examination of multilingual multimodal texts on different structural levels (from the phonemes and individual characters to the discourse level) (Bever, 2015; Kress & Van Leeuwen, 2001, 2006; Scollon & Scollon, 2003). Multilingual multimodal signs reveal ongoing negotiation of local, national and global ideologies by employing corresponding linguistic and semiotic practices. Analyses on various discourse levels allow differentiation of texts by symbolic and informational functions, thus resonating with particular political, cultural and linguistic groups. Use of the English language and Roman script conveys modernity, prestige and connection to the global market; the Ukrainian language signals officially regulated signs and compliance with the official language policy; Russian appears on various discourse levels addressing the intended personal message to the local population and conveying that Russian is a preferred language. In analyzing commercial signs by establishments (e.g. various stores, entertainment, restaurants, banks), it was noted that texts addressing the reader on a personal level (e.g. 'help wanted') are usually in Russian (Bever, 2010; Pavlenko, 2012). Thus, the signage of the city reveals that local language practices undermine official regulations, favoring multilingual practices on both individual and community levels.

Figures 1 and 2 belong to the same entertainment business. Figure 1 involves a multimodal interplay of colors, shapes, fonts, line orders, scripts and languages in contact. The primary colors of the sign are yellow and red, and are attractive to the viewer. The name of the business, a foreign looking/sounding *IGRO*, is in Roman capital letters, located in a central position. IGRO is a lexical invention related to the Ukrainian /gra/ and Russian /igra/ (the meaning in each language is 'game'). The informational line in Ukrainian describes the nature of the entertainment business (/*gral'ni avtomaty*/ '*slot machines*'). The logo 'IGRO service' on the top of the sign is a combination of English and English-sounding/looking words, framed in artistic looking costume feathers.

Figure 2 is a private sign on the front door of the same business. This is a job ad: 'administrator needed (a woman of 25–45 years old),' communicating the message in the language of the local community, namely Russian.

Figure 3 shows a local store door with two signs. The upper right sign is an official security alert in Ukrainian, complying with official language requirements. A lower sign in Russian is locally produced and gives information about local video surveillance.

Figure 1 Multimodal multilingual interplay in the sign of the entertainment business, IGRO

Figure 2 Business job ad

Figure 4 is a sign for financial services. On the top, there is an international name in English, while the rest of the sign is in Russian, stating that it is open every day, and announcing the currency exchange. The sign is a standing billboard with yellow and blue colors, resembling the Ukrainian flag.

It has been noted that restaurant menus and restaurant ads are in Russian (Bever, 2010). Figure 5 is a restaurant door poster naming chef's specials: while the poster is in Russian, it has VIP in English and Roman script.

Figure 3 A business door with Ukrainian and Russian security alert signs

Figure 4 Bilingual English-Russian financial services sign

The examples show consistent code-mixing: Ukrainian, Russian and English, and Cyrillic and Roman script appear on different discourse levels, favoring Russian for personal signage, and creatively using English to attract the viewer, while Ukrainian is used for official business signs (for detailed analyses see Bever, 2010). The main point of this discussion is that, despite the official language policy that was aimed at the reduction of the Russian language in various domains, Russian persists in the LL on a personal level, conforming to local linguistic practices. The messages in English and Roman script appear as business names, brand names, and international product and services names. English here is a symbol of

Figure 5 Restaurant door poster

modernity, mobility globalization and the world market. Ukrainian appears as a national and an official language in commercial signage to comply with the official language policy. As Landry and Bourhis (1997: 29) stated, the way languages and script appear in different signs demonstrates that 'the linguistic landscape may act as the most observable and immediate index of the relative power and status of the linguistic community inhabiting a given territory.' The LLs show that Russian persists, remaining a preferred language of community and confirming an ongoing negotiation of local, national and global ideologies.

This negotiation between Ukrainian and Russian has remained politicized during more than two decades of Ukrainian independence. Each post-Soviet president of Ukraine has been associated with pro-Ukrainian or pro-Russian language policy, and gained voter support based on the corresponding regional language distributions. The language policy and conflicting discourses around language status and language use served as a background for electing Yanukovich as a supporter of the Russian language and then served as a backlash against both him and the connection to Russia. Passing the Law on Regional Languages was an attempt to give an official status to 18 regional languages including Russian: vetoing this law, as a victorious act of the 'Maidan' revolution, created a context for an open confrontation. There is no direct causal relation between the Ukrainian war and the language policy, but language policy and language itself have served as catalysts in symbolizing and escalating the conflict.

As the Ukrainian conflict shows, LLs reveal that in geopolitically sensitive areas multilingual signs may bear the latent conflict over language use. However, the language policy conflict can 'catalyze' the situation, speeding up a latent linguistic conflict into an overt one, both in politics and in armed confrontation. The open but sometimes subtle ways that signs in Ukraine express the competition between Russian and Ukrainian remind the local population daily of the deeper social and political conflict, resonating with particular identities and ideologies. LLs continuously invoke the aspects of language *resource, problem, right*: each aspect expresses the underlying conflict. The combined effect of these daily reminders surrounds the population through the visual world. This constant exposure is a critical influence that heats up the underlying sociopolitical tension and serves as a catalyst to overt expressions of it.

Conclusion

This paper shows how and why local language use intersects with local, national and global ideologies and discourses and how Ruiz's (1984) three 'orientations in language planning' provide a fundamental framework for broader exploration and expansion of the field. The comprehensive analyses of LLs of a southeastern city of post-Soviet Ukraine (Bever 2010, 2012, 2015) show how and why local language practices negotiate local, national and global ideologies and map onto larger sociohistorical and sociopolitical contexts. The Ukrainian situation reveals how LLs define the status, role and value of particular languages, how multilingual practices comply or conflict with the official language policies, and how the juxtaposition of linguistic and non-linguistic resources in LLs negotiates identities, ideologies and discourses. This is in line with Ruiz's view on how to do research within and beyond his three *orientations*: 'One way ... is to discover them in policies and proposals that already exist; another is to propose or advocate new ones' (Ruiz, 1984, in McKay & Wong, 1988: 4). Thus, Ruiz's orientations in language planning should be argued from the critical perspective, within particular contexts, discourses, ideologies and identities. The discussion presented here supports a critical perspective on multilingualism and a critical view of how and why linguistic resources are used, represented and constructed through and within particular social discourses (Bever, 2010; Blackledge & Creese, 2010; Heller, 1999).

As this essay reminds us, social cohesion and political stability in Ukraine are defined in many ways by Ukrainian regionalism, language use and language policy itself. Since 1991 there has been an ongoing effort by the Ukrainian government to implement the shift toward Ukrainian in official and educational domains on both the policy and practice level. Although debates about the Ukrainian and Russian languages, language policy and language use have become a critical point of nation building and political stability in Ukraine, the southeastern Ukrainian urban center maintains Russian as the dominant language. Similarly to other cities of this region (e.g. Kharkiv), Russian is viewed locally as a 'legitimate' (Sovik, 2007) language of the community. This legitimacy is conditioned by the historical presence of a Russian-speaking population and historical use of Russian as a mother tongue, the language of education, politics, economics and everyday interaction. In analyzing the language situation in Kyiv, the capital of Ukraine, Pavlenko (2010: 149) argues that 'the new Ukrainian government ... has failed to create a homogeneous monolingual population.' While Ukrainian serves as an official language, Russian remains the preferred language of everyday interaction, business, cultural events and various media and commerce and consumption in many areas of Ukraine.

Following Fishman (2000: 89), domains of language use and language policy should be in line with the question: 'Who speaks what language to whom and when?' This is a critical point in exploring, applying and expanding Ruiz's (1984) orientations in language planning. While official bilingualism would have served as an indicator and a resource to maintain social cohesion, the official monolingual language policy in Ukraine provided conditions for language as problem in opposition to language as right, thus unveiling power relations, and making language use versus language policy a catalyst for open conflict.

The visibility of languages in LLs is informative when examining the Ukrainian sociolinguistic context and Ukrainian bi/multilingualism, both individual and territorial. The actual examples I presented above demonstrate how language is manipulated in LLs, so that public signs appear to comply with official language policy, but actually address the local population in their preferred language and respond to international developments. This is relevant to both Ukrainian and Russian languages, since privileging one language over another, or creating official limitations and reducing the prestige of either language, may complicate sociopolitical domains.

LLs in the Ukrainian context show how linguistic and ideological boundaries are contested and magnified through private and public manifestation of language use, revealing the link between languages, social practices, and political and ideological debates. As Hornberger points out, 'the centripetal globalizing tendency associated with English and the centrifugal, fragmenting tendency associated with local and minority languages and identities, exert pressure on the one language – one nation ideology of language policy and national identity' (Hornberger, 2003b: 2). Thus, the juxtaposition of Ukrainian, Russian and English in public spaces places Ukraine in a unique situation, with competing and coexisting ideologies of globalization, local fragmentation, nationalistic tendencies and national unity (Bever, 2010, 2011, 2015; Hornberger, 2003b; Pavlenko, 2008, 2009). The fragility of the Ukrainian situation was compromised in 2013–2014 by the conflict between language policy and language ideologies, which served as 'catalysts' in escalating this tension. Thus, the Ukrainian case illustrates how language served as a catalyst in providing conditions for the escalation of polarization between the pro-nationalistic power and pro-Russian forces in the eastern Ukraine, deepening historically defined regional and linguistic affiliations, and highlighting the vector of the geopolitical conflict.

The struggles over language policy and language use keep triggering ongoing debates and confrontations on various levels of the Ukrainian, Russian and global communities. In February 2014, the new 'Maidan' Ukrainian government voted to reverse the 2012 Law on Regional Languages that had allowed Russian as a regional language: this empowered Ukrainian as the only official language, thereby encouraging nationalistically oriented discourses. It reinitiated the struggle over the status and use of the two dominant languages, Ukrainian and Russian, reigniting the opposition between nationalistically oriented pro-Ukrainian and pro-Russian forces. This reinforced the pro-Russian movement in the Eastern regions of Ukraine, threatening the social cohesion and the unity of the country and resulting in deadly armed conflict in the eastern regions. Although the vote to repeal the 2012 law was later vetoed by the interim president, this only served further as an indicator and a catalyst of the open confrontation between nationalistic and multilingual forces and ideologies.

The ongoing Ukrainian crisis of 2013–2016 has demonstrated how language issues have served as a catalyst for the clash between local and national identities and triggered the escalation of open conflicts of contested and competing ideologies. It provoked social disintegration and deeper political and regional divisions, bringing language rights and language use to the front line of local, national and global politics and policies (Bever, 2015).

Afterword

This essay is dedicated to Dr Richard Ruiz, my graduate advisor, mentor, and one of the most influential figures in my academic and intellectual life. My first class with Dr Ruiz on language policy and language planning was a true discovery, a crusade against the unknown, and crystallization of my initial ideas about language in society and individuals. Later, Richard became my PhD Dissertation Director. He was a wonderful teacher and mentor, enthusiastic about students' independent thinking. Our research and friendship grew up out of our mutual passion for the world's linguistic and cultural diversities and multilingualism. Every meeting with Richard Ruiz brought enlightenment and encouragement. In his classes, he inspired and empowered students, giving us enough time and space to learn and grow. Richard was passionate about his research, teaching and his students' success and creativity. He became excited about LLs, and conducted his own research on LLs in Aruba. We shared our views and findings, trying to expand both language policy and LLs research. My academic life could have made a different turn if I had not taken his class on language policy and language planning. Now, my life has made a different turn because Richard Ruiz passed on to us, his students and colleagues, his legacy to build a responsible and passionate world.

Acknowledgments

My very special thanks to Dr Luis Moll and Dr Thomas Bever for their encouragement and support in helping me continue my academic and intellectual journey without Dr Richard Ruiz. I also thank Dr Nancy Hornberger and an anonymous reviewer for very helpful comments on this paper.

Note

(1) 'Maidan' in Ukrainian means 'an open square.'

References

Backhaus, P. (2006) Multilingualism in Tokyo: A look into the linguistic landscape. In D. Gorter (ed.) *Linguistic Landscape: A New Approach to Multilingualism* (pp. 52–66). Clevedon: Multilingual Matters.
Besters-Dilger, J. (2009) *Language Policy and Language Situation in Ukraine: Analysis and Recommendations*. Frankfurt am Main: Peter Lang.

Bever, O. (2010) Linguistic landscapes of post-Soviet Ukraine: Multilingualism and language policy in outdoor media and advertising. PhD thesis, University of Arizona.

Bever, O. (2011) Multilingualism and language policy in post-Soviet Ukraine: English, Ukrainian and Russian in linguistic landscapes. IREX Research Report. See https://www.irex.org/sites/default/files/pdf/multilingualism-language-policy-postsoviet-ukraine.pdf

Bever, O. (2012) Linguistic landscapes and environmental print as a resource for languages and literacy development in multilingual contexts. In M. Sanz and J.M. Igoa (eds) *Applying Language Science to Language Pedagogy* (pp. 321–342). Cambridge: Cambridge Scholars.

Bever, O. (2015) Linguistic landscapes as multimodal and multilingual phenomena. In M. Laitinen and A. Zabrodskaja (eds) *Dimensions of Sociolinguistic Landscapes in Europe*: *Materials and Methodological Solutions* (pp. 233–262). Sprachkönnen und Sprachbewusstheit in Europa/Language Competence and Language Awareness in Europe. Frankfurt: Peter Lang.

Bilaniuk, L. (2005) *Contested Tongues: Language Politics and Cultural Correction in Ukraine.* Ithaca, NY and London: Cornell University Press.

Bilaniuk, L. (2010) Language in the balance: The politics of non-accommodation on bilingual Ukrainian-Russian television shows. *International Journal of the Sociology of Language* 201, 105–133.

Bilaniuk, L. and Melnyk, S. (2008) A tense and shifting balance: Bilingualism and education in Ukraine. *International Journal of Bilingual Education and Bilingualism* 11 (3 & 4), 340–372.

Blackledge, A. and Creese, A. (2010) *Multilingualism: A Critical Perspective.* London: Continuum.

Blommaert, J. (2010) *The Sociolinguistics of Globalization.* Cambridge: Cambridge University Press.

Blommaert, J. (2013) *Ethnography, Superdiversity and Linguistic Landscapes.* Bristol: Multilingual Matters.

Crystal, D. (2003) *English as a Global Language* (2nd edn). Cambridge: Cambridge University Press.

Fishman, J. (2000) Who speaks what language to whom and when? In L. Wei (ed.) *The Bilingual Reader* (pp. 89–106). London and New York: Routledge, Taylor & Francis.

Gorter, D. (ed.) (2006) *Linguistic Landscape: A New Approach to Multilingualism.* Clevedon: Multilingual Matters.

Gorter, D., Marten, H. and Van Mensel, L. (eds) (2012) *Minority Languages in the Linguistic Landscapes.* Basingstoke: Palgrave Macmillan.

Grosjean, F. (1982) *Life with Two Languages: An Introduction to Bilingualism.* Cambridge, MA, and London, England: Harvard University Press.

Heller, M. (1999) *Linguistic Minorities and Modernity: A Sociolinguistic Ethnography.* London & New York: Longman.

Hornberger, N. (ed.) (2003a) *Continua of Biliteracy: An Ecological Framework for Educational Policy, Research, and Practice in Multilingual Settings.* Clevedon: Multilingual Matters.

Hornberger, N. (2003b) English in the global ecology of languages: The value of multilingualism. *BESIG Business Issues* 2, 2–6.

Huebner, T. (2006) Bangkok's linguistic landscapes: Environmental print, codemixing and language change. In D. Gorter (ed.) *Linguistic Landscape: A New Approach to Multilingualism* (pp. 31–51). Clevedon: Multilingual Matters.

Jaworski, A. and Thurlow, C. (eds) (2010) *Semiotic Landscape: Language, Image, Space.* London: Continuum.

Khmelko, V. and Wilson, A. (1998) Regionalism and ethnic and linguistic cleavages in Ukraine. In T. Kuzio (ed.) *Contemporary Ukraine: Dynamics of Post-Soviet Transformation* (pp. 60–80). Armonk, NY and London: M.E. Sharpe, Inc.

Kress, G. and Van Leeuwen, T. (2001) *Multimodal Discourse: The Modes and Media of Contemporary Communication*. London: Hodder Arnold.

Kress, G. and Van Leeuwen, T. (2006) *Reading Images: The Grammar of Visual Design* (2nd edn). London & New York: Routledge Taylor & Francis.

Kulyk, V. (2006) Constructing common sense: Language and ethnicity in Ukrainian public discourse. *Ethnic and Racial Studies* 29 (2), 281–314.

Kulyk, V. (2010) Ideologies of language use in post-Soviet Ukrainian media. *International Journal of the Sociology of Language* 201, 79–104.

Kulyk, V. (2011) Beliefs about language status and corpus in focus group discussions on the Ukrainian language policy. *International Journal of the Sociology of Language* 212, 69–89.

Kuzio, T. (2000) *Ukraine: Perestroika to Independence* (2nd edn). London, UK: Macmillan Press LTD.

Laitinen, M. and Zabrodskaja, A. (eds) (2015) *Dimensions of Sociolinguistic Landscapes in Europe: Materials and Methodological Solutions*. Sprachkönnen und Sprachbewusstheit in Europa/Language Competence and Language Awareness in Europe. Frankfurt: Peter Lang.

Landry, R. and Bourhis, R. (1997) Linguistic landscape and ethnolinguistic vitality: An empirical study. *Journal of Language and Social Psychology* 16 (1), 23–49.

Lewis, E.G. (1972) *Multilingualism in the Soviet Union*. The Hague: Mouton.

Magocsi, P.R. (1996) *A History of Ukraine*. Seattle: University of Washington Press.

Martin, T. (2002) *The Affirmative Action Empire: Nations and Nationalism in the Soviet Union 1923–1939*. Ithaca, NY: Cornell University Press.

Martin, E. (2007) 'Frenglish' for sale: Multilingual discourses for addressing today's global consumer. *World Englishes* 26 (2), 177–188.

May, S. (2006) Language policy and minority rights. In T. Ricento (ed.) *An Introduction to Language Policy: Theory and Method*. Oxford: Blackwell.

Mazenko, L. (2009) Language situation in Ukraine: Sociolinguistic analysis. In J. Besters-Dilger (ed.) *Language Policy and Language Situation in Ukraine: Analysis and Recommendations* (pp. 101–138). Frankfurt am Main: Peter Lang.

Merriam-Webster Online Dictionary (n.d.) Catalyst. See http://www.merriam-webster.com/dictionary/catalyst

Pavlenko, A. (2006) Russian as a lingua franca. *Annual Review of Applied Linguistics* 26, 78–99.

Pavlenko, A. (2008) Multilingualism in post-Soviet countries: Language revival, language removal, and sociolinguistic theory. *International Journal of Bilingual Education and Bilingualism* 11 (3 & 4), 275–314.

Pavlenko, A. (2009) Language conflict in post-Soviet Linguistic Landscapes. *Journal of Slavic Linguistics* 17 (1–2), 247–274.

Pavlenko, A. (2011) Language rights versus speakers' rights: On the applicability of Western language rights approaches in Eastern European contexts. *Language Policy* 10, 37–58.

Pavlenko, A. (2012) Transgression as the norm: Russian in linguistic landscape of Kyiv, Ukraine: A diachronic study. In D. Gorter, H.F. Marten and L. Van Mensel (eds) *Minority Languages in the Linguistic Landscape* (pp. 36–56). Basingstoke: Palgrave Macmillan.

Piller, I. (2003) Advertising as a site of language contact. *Annual Review of Applied Linguistics* 23, 170–183.

Pirie, P. (1996) National identity and politics in Southern and Eastern Ukraine. *Europe-Asia Studies* 48 (7), 1079–1104.

Ruiz, R. (1984) Orientations in language planning. *NABE Journal* 8 (2), 15–34.

Ruiz, R. (1988) Orientations in language planning. In S.L. McKay and S.C. Wong (eds) *Language Diversity: Problem or Resource?* (pp. 3–25). Boston, MA: Heinle & Heinle.

Scollon, R. and Scollon, S. (2003) *Discourses in Place: Languages in the Material World.* London: Routledge.

Shohamy, E. and Gorter, D. (eds) (2009) *Linguistic Landscapes: Expanding the Scenery.* New York and London: Routledge, Taylor & Francis.

Sovik, M. (2007) *Support, Resistance and Pragmatism: An Examination of Motivation in Language Policy in Kharkiv, Ukraine.* Stockholm: Acta Universitatis Stockholmiensis.

Sovik, M. (2010) Language practices and the language situation in Kharkiv: Examining the concept of legitimate language in relation to identification and utility. *International Journal of the Sociology of Language* 201, 5–28.

Spolsky, B. (2004) *Language Policy.* Cambridge: Cambridge University Press.

Taranenko, O. (2007) Ukrainian and Russian in contact: Attraction and estrangement. *International Journal of the Sociology of Language* 183, 119–140.

Threat Inversion and Language Maintenance in Puerto Rico and Aruba

Kevin S. Carroll and Joyce L. Pereira

This chapter uses Ruiz's threat inversion typology to frame the discussion of language threat and maintenance on the islands of Puerto Rico and Aruba. Using a case study approach, the authors present a description of how the linguistic context of the islands exemplifies two categories described in Ruiz's threat inversion typology. Through the use of document analysis and interviews with key players in language planning and policy, this chapter documents language maintenance on Puerto Rico and Aruba, with the goal of providing an accurate portrayal of how percep- tions of threat have facilitated language maintenance on the two islands. Ultimately, the chapter demonstrates the need for Ruiz's more nuanced typology of threatened languages.

Introduction

Richard Ruiz's impact on the field of language planning and policy (LPP) is immeasurable in that his theoretical contributions outlined in his (1984) paper have become part of the everyday discourse of those working in LPP around the world. Throughout his career at the University of Arizona, Dr Ruiz was particularly interested in the role that language maintenance has on language users, their identity and their access to education. With this chapter we pay tribute to the work of Dr Ruiz as we present the language contexts of Puerto Rico and Aruba within his newly published typology of threatened languages, known as 'threat inversion' (see Part 1 of this volume).

As a former graduate student and research assistant to Dr Ruiz, it was early on in Kevin's doctoral studies when we started creating the threat inversion typology, which Ruiz presented at the Georgetown University Round Table on Language and Linguistics (GURT) in 2006. His involvement in working with language scholars (particularly Joyce Pereira and Lydia

Emerencia) on the island of Aruba provided the impetus for his early conceptualization of the threat inversion typology. Dr Ruiz was often frustrated with how the term 'threat' was thrown around within academic and social discourses, which worked to trivialize language contexts where language shift had indeed commenced. The state of Arizona, where Dr Ruiz spent most of his career, has had a history of positioning English as a threatened language due to the consistent influx of Spanish-speaking immigrants to the state. In recent years, political discourse in Arizona has used 'threat' and 'endangered' to describe English while there has been no evidence of language shift. Meanwhile, within Arizona's borders, there are a variety of local Indigenous groups, Hopi, Navajo and Apache to name a few, whose languages have witnessed a significant shift toward English and are indeed endangered. Such a blatant misrepresentation of the linguistic reality did not sit well with Dr Ruiz and was the focus of much of his later work. As he argues in his 2006 unpublished paper included in Part 1 of this volume, the use of language-threat discourses when language shift is not ongoing is often targeted at linguistic minorities whose physical presence exemplifies a changing social context of which the linguistic majority are likely not in favor.

Kevin Carroll, Richard, Adam Schwartz, at University of Arizona Commencement, Tucson, AZ, May 2009.
Courtesy of Kevin S. Carroll.

While most of this paper builds off Carroll's dissertation research published in 2009, in which Pereira was a key participant, here we have written a collaborative piece using these earlier data and interspersing them with our more recent observations, since the original data were collected in the summer of 2008. Thus, the purpose of this chapter is twofold: we seek first to honor the life work of our esteemed mentor, colleague and friend; and secondly, to provide empirical evidence that there is value in Ruiz's threat inversion typology and that the contexts of Puerto Rico and Aruba are emblematic of two of his eight categories.

Richard, Patricia Azuara and Joyce Pereira, Aruba Language Institute, 2011. *Courtesy of Kevin S. Carroll.*

Review of the literature

In his discussion of threat inversion, Ruiz examines the ambiguity associated with language threat. On one end of the spectrum, language professionals have dedicated their careers to documenting language shift among the majority of the world's languages (Krauss, 1992, 2000). At the other end, there are powerful language communities that perceive their language to be threatened despite little to no evidence of language shift toward a less dominant language (Ager, 2001). Historically, influential countries such as the United States and France have passed language policies that restrict the use of minority languages to different extents. In these two cases, the media and other institutions work to augment fear and paranoia toward recent increases of immigrants who speak non-dominant languages (Santa Ana, 2002). The mere presence of these language users and how the media covers them impacts the way they are viewed within the dominant society. With that said, traditional methods of measuring language threat in the field have centered on intergenerational transmission and have often ignored the historical conditions that facilitate language shift. In the case study portion of this paper we will focus on how the historical contexts of Puerto Rico and Aruba have influenced language maintenance on the respective islands.

Assessing Language Threat

Language change is inevitable, and throughout the history of the world many languages have fluctuated in their influence and prestige. Such was the subject of Ostler (2005), who discussed the rise and fall of many of the world's former and current language empires. While language change and loss is part of the human experience, recent global trends have expedited language endangerment to the extent that Dalby (2003) estimates that half of the approximately 5000 languages used today will be lost within the next century. The 21st century has witnessed increased globalization and technology which has linked people throughout the world, making common languages necessary for communication among groups that in the past would have never have been in contact (Crystal, 2004). Now languages clash as they compete for space on the internet, in classrooms and in official legislation.

Undoubtedly, colonization resulted in the loss of many languages, but it has been only within recent memory that concentrated efforts to maintain and revitalize languages has started. Thus, the concept of 'language threat' ranges in its contextually based definition. We will now briefly explain four typologies used within the field of LPP to describe threatened languages.

Fishman's (1991) Graded Intergenerational Disruption Scale (GIDS; Table 1) is the most well-known and widely used typology to measure

Table 1 Fishman's GIDS

Stage 1	Some use Xish in higher level educational, occupational, governmental and media efforts (but without the additional safety provided by political independence).
Stage 2	Xish in lower governmental services and mass media but not in the higher spheres of either.
Stage 3	Use of Xish in the lower work sphere (outside of the Xish neighborhood/community) involving interactions between Xmen and Ymen.
Stage 4	Xish is used in lower education that meets the requirements of compulsory education.
Stage 5	Xish literacy is used in the home, school and community but without taking on extracommunal reinforcement of such literacy.
Stage 6	Marked by the attainment of intergenerational informal oralcy. In this stage Xish is used in informal domains and passed on to younger generations.
Stage 7	Most users of Xish are socially integrated and ethnolinguistically active but beyond childbearing age.
Stage 8	Users of Xish are beyond childbearing age, their role in society is minimal, and there is often a push toward saving the last remains of language in culture. The language is in the most advanced stages of attrition.

Source: Adapted from Fishman (1991).

language threat. Fishman argued that the key to successful language maintenance and revitalization is contingent on the success of the cross-generational transfer of language. He broke the language revitalization process into eight stages, ranging from Stage 8 on the bottom, where all speakers are beyond childbearing age and language death is imminent, to Stage 1, where the minority language is used in higher levels of education, government and possibly the media (Fishman, 1991). In other words, stability hinges on older members of the society passing their language to younger generations who in turn use the language.

Fishman's GIDS has been criticized because of the author's insistence on the importance of the vertical step-by-step manner in which, he argues, languages must climb in order to reverse language shift (Fishman, 1991). Scholars such as Hornberger and King (2001) have argued that the GIDS may work for some languages, but it does not work for larger languages such as Quechua, which has numerous varieties, and communities that are at different stages of language shift. Romaine (2006) voices similar criticisms toward Fishman's GIDS in that it does not necessarily account for 60% of the world's languages that have fewer than 10,000 speakers.

In response to a variety of critiques of the GIDS, Fishman's more recent work has articulated some of the misconceptions regarding his typology. Fishman's concluding chapter in *Can Threatened Languages Be Saved?* argued that reversing language shift (RLS) does not necessitate a 'lock-step stage-by-stage progression' of the GIDS (Fishman, 2001: 467). While Fishman answered many of his critics, he consistently argued for working one stage at a time toward RLS. He understood that such progression would simultaneously require work in other stages, but he warned of the dangers of working too hard in other stages and losing track of the needs of lower stages.

More recently, Fishman's GIDS has been elaborated by Lewis and Simons (2010) in what they call the Expanded GIDS (EGIDS). The purpose of EGIDS is more for classification purposes and less as a blueprint of how to reverse language shift. The EGIDS has 13 levels and has created different categories for internationally used languages and for national and regional languages (Levels 0, 1 and 2, respectively) and also makes other distinctions, such as whether the language has been codified (Stage 5), whether it is vulnerable for language shift (6b), or whether language shift has commenced (Stage 7). With the primary purpose being to identify the current state of language vitality, the EGIDS is the current typology used by Ethnologue, an organization that maps and works to describe languages used throughout the world.

A third method or typology for identifying threatened languages comes from Krauss (2000). Krauss's four-class category distinction of threatened languages is a quick and efficient way to obtain a general idea of how endangered a language is. Krauss's four classes range from Class A, where the language is still spoken by all generations, to Class D, where the

Table 2 Krauss's typology for threatened languages

Class A	Still spoken by all generations including children
Class B	Spoken only by parental generation and up
Class C	Spoken only by grandparental generation and up
Class D	Spoken only by the oldest, over 70, usually < 10 speakers—nearly extinct

Source: Adapted from Krauss (2000).

language is spoken only by the very oldest people in a community, usually fewer than 10 people (Table 2). Krauss's class system is also based on inter-generational transmission but, unlike Fishman's GIDS, this system allows for quick assessment of a large number of languages because it is based on smaller and generally more accessible data than would be required for a GIDS assessment.

The fourth typology, which was developed by Ruiz, describes the differences between language threat, language endangerment and threat inversion. As Ruiz argues, language threat is concerned with the perceptions of language users about their language, whereas language endangerment is associated with 'some objective grounding' that exemplifies how and why language shift is imminent or ongoing. The term *threat inversion*, on the other hand, is used to describe contexts where, in his words:

> a community of powerful, sometimes very powerful, language speakers claims that smaller, sometimes extremely small, languages and their users threaten them. The threat is not articulated as one against the life of the language, but rather against their way of life.

Ruiz's typology (as seen in Table 3) looks to conceptualize language threat by teasing out the differences between language endangerment (Category A) and language threat (Categories B–G) while fully understanding that threat inversion (Category H) comes into play when users of dominant languages feel threatened despite the unlikely prospect of future language shift.

With the publication of Ruiz's typology, language contexts that have undergone some language shift or that are in relatively stable positions have a typology that accounts for the threat associated with their particular context. For instance, different varieties of a LWC, such as Spanish in the US or French in Algeria (Category H), now have their own category, as do Indigenous languages like Xhosa in South Africa (Category D), where recent legislation has provided corpus, status and acquisition planning, but its low prestige has curbed its widespread use in domains of power. Ruiz's Category D would also encompass a language context like Quechua in Peru, which is threatened but not currently endangered (Hornberger & King, 2001). In addition to

Table 3 Ruiz's typology for threatened languages

Category	Description	Evidence	Danger
A	Unicentric minority/ Indigenous Ls in significant contact with an aggressive majority Language/Language of Wider Communication (LWC)	Significant L1[1] → L2[2]; disappearance of L1 (GIDS regression)	Language death
B	Stigmatized or minoritized varieties of pluricentric LWCs in large multilingual states (e.g. US Spanish varieties) where the LWCs are not in danger of extinction	Significant L1 → L2; diminished vitality (cf. Krauss)	Displaced and diminished L1 functions; cultural disruption
C	Majority minoritized languages in stable states in contact with LWCs but not in danger of either extinction or significant shift (Spanish in PR)	Anti-L2 LP[3]: legislation, rules, sanctions, etc.	Isolation, political polarization
D	Indigenous Ls in multilingual states (Xhosa in South Africa) not in imminent danger of language death	Pro-L1 LP: status, corpus and acquisition planning	Limited use of L1 in P[4] domains
E	Majority Indigenous languages in small states in contact with LWCs (Netherlands Antilles Papiamento)	L1/L2 functional differentiation	L1 confined to non-P domains; devaluing of L1
F	LWCs in small states that are threatened by LWCs in adjacent states (French in Quebec)	Political separation; endoglossic LP	Political antagonisms and isolation; gradual L1 → L2
G	Non-LWC majority languages that perceive threats from LWCs in adjacent states (Catalan in Spain)	Endoglossic LP	Political antagonisms and isolation
H	LWCs in large states that perceive threats from multilingualism consisting of 'smaller' languages (French Creole, Vietnamese) or other LWCs (Spanish in the USA, English in France)	Anti-L1 LP	Oppression of minority Ls and their speakers or co-optation of L1 community via certain forms of subtractive schooling

Note: [1]L1 = first language; [2]L2 = second language; [3]LP = language policy; [4]P = primary.

recognizing legitimately threatened languages, Ruiz's typology allows language planners to identify different aspects of languages that are perceived to be 'at risk.' Thus, the subject of this particular paper is the context of Spanish in Puerto Rico (Category C) and Papiamento in Aruba (Category E), where colonial history and immigration have played an influential role on perceptions of threat and consequently in language maintenance.

Methods

The two case studies presented in this paper were originally part of the author Carroll's dissertation, in which co-author Pereira played an influential role in the case on Aruba. The purpose of the research was to document and understand language maintenance in Puerto Rico and Aruba, with the goal of providing an accurate portrayal of how perceptions of threat have facilitated or hindered language maintenance on the two islands. Original data collection was divided into three areas: document analysis, interviews and observation field notes. Some seven years after the original data collection, we have revisited the data and incorporated our own lived experiences and observations on the two islands as we co-write this piece. For the reader, original interviews and personal communications are cited with a date for clarity.

Of particular focus in our data collection and analysis were the various historical documents related to language and education policy on both islands. This meant using primary sources collected from key participants. In addition to the analysis of historical documents and contemporary publications, Carroll interviewed key players in LPP efforts on both islands. In total, 11 interviews were conducted with 16 different participants: ten in Aruba (of which Pereira was one) and six in Puerto Rico. In Aruba, participants ranged in occupation and in their opinions regarding the importance of Papiamento, but because the major point of contention in Aruba has been around the use of Papiamento in the school system, the majority of the participants had ties to the field of education. In Puerto Rico, the language debate has been more political in nature, and therefore the six participants were all political leaders or academics who had specialized knowledge of LPP on the island. The third prong of the data collection was the field notes that were collected throughout Carroll's various stays on both of the islands. These field notes are now complemented with the lived experiences of the co-authors, who have both held various positions related to language and language policy on the islands on which they have lived and worked (Carroll in Puerto Rico and Pereira in Aruba). It should be noted that the field notes and our observations are not the primary dataset but worked to confirm statements in the interviews and document analysis through visual corroboration.

Language Maintenance in Puerto Rico

In Ruiz's typology, Category C represents the linguistic context of Puerto Rico, where Spanish is the language of the majority but minoritized when viewed through the island's colonial relationship with the United States. Similarly to the categories that lie between A and H in Ruiz's typology, Spanish in Puerto Rico has experienced little language shift toward English despite over 100 years of American colonization. Nevertheless, given Puerto Rico's colonial relationship and the fact that Spanish is a stigmatized minority language in the United States, there is some cause for concern. Puerto Rico's ambiguous commonwealth status provides local autonomy but does not allow the same fiscal or legal flexibility of being an incorporated state or an independent entity. Such political status has put major decisions in the hands of Washington politicians and New York investors. In this section we will provide a brief historical overview of language threat on the island nation, with specific attention paid to the immigration and emigration patterns and the school system.

Language and colonization

Puerto Rico is the easternmost island in the Greater Antilles, and it is one of the three Spanish-speaking nations in the Caribbean (Dominican Republic and Cuba are the other two). The island, originally colonized by Spain for some 400 years, was one of the jewels of Spain's conquest in the Americas. Within a short time after the arrival of the Spanish, a majority of the Taino population had perished because of disease and mistreatment. At the same time, many of the Spanish men took Taino women as their wives and started a new race that would become one of the pillars of modern-day Puerto Rican identity – *mestizaje*. Adding to the mixture of race and languages were countless African slaves brought in to work on the numerous sugar plantations on the island. The eventual mix between Spanish, African and Indigenous blood is often recognized as an integral part of understanding what it means to be Puerto Rican (J.L. Vega, personal communication, 13 June 2008). In addition to the racial influence resulting from the intermarrying of Tainos and Spaniards, the Spanish conquistadores borrowed many of the names that the Tainos used for places in Puerto Rico, such as Humacao, Caguas, Mayagüez and El Yunque, as well as names of plants and fruit like *guayaba* and *cacao* (Vaquero de Ramírez, 1991). Within a few generations, however, the Taino language had been replaced entirely by Spanish[1] (Vaquero de Ramírez, 1991).

In the late 19th century, when many of the Spanish colonies fought for their independence, Puerto Rico remained satisfied with its political association with Spain. In fact, because of relatively positive trade agreements with European nations, much of the political elite felt an affinity to Spain and wished to prove their loyalty. Nonetheless, during this time, Puerto Rico sought local autonomy, albeit with the understanding that it would continue to be protected under the powerful Spanish flag. Local autonomy was finally granted on 9 November 1897 (Morales Carrión, 1983: 120). However, later that year Spain ceded Puerto Rico, along with the Philippines and Guam, to the United States in concessions from the Spanish-American War (Morales Carrión, 1983).

The United States' success in the Spanish-American War made them an instant global power, and the island of Puerto Rico would eventually become a place where American companies could expand their sales and manufacturing. Unlike the scarcely populated western territories of California, New Mexico and Arizona, which were all eventually incorporated as states, Puerto Rico was one of the most densely populated places in the Americas. Census data from 1900 reported that the 'Total population was 953,243 with a population density seven times that of Cuba, twice that of Pennsylvania, and almost equal to the industrial state of New Jersey' (Morales Carrión, 1983: 137). Puerto Rico's population density was so high that it severely inhibited the influx of English-speaking migrants seen in California and other states in the west. The lack of space for English-speaking Americans to settle differentiated the linguistic development of Puerto Rico from that of Hawaii and other states that joined the union later in US history. The fact that there has been no sizeable English-speaking population to move to Puerto Rico is one of the reasons Spanish has been successfully maintained (S. Clampitt-Dunlap, personal communication, 10 June 2008).

Despite the change in colonial power, which consequently positioned English and Spanish as co-official languages, Puerto Ricans remained Spanish at heart and continued to use Spanish as a symbol of their loyalty and local identity. Since 1898, Spanish and English have held joint official language status, with the only exception coming in 1991, when Governor Hernández Colón briefly made Spanish the sole official language. This designation lasted only until 1992, when Pedro Rosselló was elected governor and quickly repealed the symbolic action (F. Martin, personal communication, 11 June 2008).

Since 1898, the political elite in Puerto Rico have struggled with the US government to regain the local autonomy they had been granted by the Spanish. It was the opinion of many in the United States, however, that Puerto Ricans were uncivilized heathens who were in dire need of colonization. The mixed blood of the majority of the population only served to fuel that belief and conjured up racist ideas when discussions regarding autonomy were raised. Those discriminatory attitudes are exemplified in a statement by a judge appointed by President Wilson to the US District Court, who wrote, 'The Puerto Ricans have the Latin-American excitability, and I think America should go slow in granting them anything like autonomy. Their civilization is not at all like ours yet.' In subsequent months Judge Hamilton added, 'the mixture of black and white in Porto Rico threatens to create a

race of mongrels of no use to anyone, a race of Spanish American talkers'
(quoted in Morales Carrión, 1983: 188).

Contesting the language of instruction

The United States' attempt at colonization came primarily through the
public education system. The public school system has always been a
symbol and a tool by which the United States and Puerto Rican governments have worked to instill a sense of culture and identity among Puerto
Ricans. Algren de Gutiérrez (1987) provides a detailed account of the various
attempts on the part of US-appointed governors to implement English-only
education in the public school system. Algren de Gutiérrez explains that
these policies to 'Americanize' Puerto Ricans were met with strong opposition on the part of both teachers and the political elite. After a half century
of failed policies to try to Americanize Puerto Ricans, in 1949 the US
granted Puerto Rico local autonomy and the right to elect their own governor. Throughout the period in which the island was governed by outside
forces, the political elite was successful in creating an idealized perception
of what it meant to be Puerto Rican. This imagined identity has centered
on the image of a *campesino* or poor man from the countryside, despite the
fact that most islanders lived in coastal and urban areas. Part of this image
hinged on the use of Spanish, and since this period, not being able to use
Spanish has been a marker of those who do not belong or are outsiders to
the island (Morris, 1996).

Throughout Puerto Rico's association with the United States, English
has been perceived as a threat to Puerto Rican identity and a symbol of US
colonization. While language policy in the original colonization era (1898–
1952) ranged from a full attempt to shift Spanish-speaking Puerto Ricans to
monolingual English, to the recognition of the importance of Spanish in
primary education, the intent to change Puerto Ricans' sense of identity
consistently marked the period (Schmidt, 2014).

According to Vélez (2000: 6), throughout 'the first 50 years of American
rule, colonial administrators implemented an educational language policy
whose goal was to Americanize the population and make English the
dominant language.' Thus, from 1898 to 1949 English was largely the language of instruction in the public school system, but the amount of English
instruction varied greatly because there were various policy changes
regarding the language of instruction (see Algren de Gutiérrez, 1987 for a
detailed account of different policies regarding the teaching of English). As
Puerto Rico got closer to being granted its own local autonomy, more
emphasis was given to Spanish in the primary grades. English, however,
was always used as the medium of instruction at the secondary level. In
fact, until 1949 all high school studies throughout the island were conducted in English.

At that point in the island's history, the few students who made it to high school tended to be from the elite families on the island. As Schweers and Hudders (2000: 66) stated, 'The small elite that continued in high school, however, became fully bilingual, thus exacerbating the difference between the classes.' The 1949 shift to Spanish-medium instruction throughout primary and secondary schools resulted in unprecedented access to public education for the poor. The policy change along with an improved economy resulted in a resounding shift in student demographics which motivated the elite to pull their children out of the public schools and put them in fee-paying private schools where English played a more integral part of the curriculum. To this day islanders view private schools as superior to their public school counterparts largely because it is assumed that students will be better prepared in English (Ladd & Rivera-Batiz, 2006). Access to English plays an ever-important role, since the colonial relationship with the US makes purchasing college textbooks published in English much more affordable than imported books in Spanish. Therefore, it is common that post-secondary courses at universities require students to purchase textbooks in English despite the fact that the lectures and exams are often in Spanish (Carroll et al., 2015).

The political history of Puerto Rico has had a major impact on the language(s) used on the island. The early Spanish colonization of the island forcibly worked to eradicate native Taino speakers and Spanish quickly became used as the lingua franca among islanders. However, since being annexed by the United States in 1898, English has threatened the role of Spanish on the island through its joint official status. As the 20th century evolved, English continued to grow in local prestige despite nationalist movements that link Puerto Rican identity to being able to speak Spanish. Spanish in Puerto Rico is indeed stable; however, given the island's unique political relationship with the United States resulting in a lack of sovereignty and an economy and education system which is largely dependent on their colonizer, there is a legitimate, albeit minimal, threat posed to Spanish in Puerto Rico.

Language in Aruba

The language context in Aruba is exemplified in Ruiz's Category E: Papiamento is the Indigenous language in contact with languages of wider communication (LWCs), namely Dutch, English and Spanish. The 'contact' between Papiamento and the other languages on Aruba is peaceful in the sense that societal multilingualism is the norm. This type of contact differs greatly from 'full contact,' which is covered in Category A, where the goal of policy makers is not multilingualism but monolingualism. Therefore, a language designated to be in 'full contact' is one that is fighting the encroachment of the dominant language(s). What is not known is the extent, if at all, that Papiamento is 'devalued' because of its lack of use in formal instruction.

Language and colonization

The island of Aruba is located in the Caribbean Sea, approximately 18 miles north of the country of Venezuela. This small island is 19 miles long and six miles across at its widest part. Aruba, together with Bonaire and Curaçao, form the ABC islands, more formally known as the Dutch Leeward Islands. Aruba is also commonly referred to as part of the Netherlands Antilles, which it was until 1986 when it received *Status Aparte* from the Kingdom of the Netherlands, granting the island its own local autonomy. Currently, Aruba has two official languages, Dutch and Papiamento, but many of the island's 101,000 residents are also fluent in English and Spanish.

In 1499 the Spanish discovered the island of Aruba, which was sparsely populated by Caquetio Indians (Razak, 1995). Shortly after the Spanish arrived, the island was declared the *isla inutile* or useless island and was largely abandoned as a Spanish holding. The 17th century saw the emergence of the Dutch as colonizers, and the islands of Aruba, Curaçao and Bonaire were claimed under the Dutch flag between 1634 and 1636 (Fouse, 2002). The Leeward Islands served as a strategic trading point for the West Indian Company (WIC), which ran the islands administratively until they were formally handed over to the Dutch government in 1792 (Fouse, 2002: 57). The island of Curaçao, with its natural port, was the focal point of the Dutch expansion into the Americas and was the scene of the majority of the slave trade involving the Dutch. Despite its close proximity to Curaçao, Aruba did not have as much exposure to the slave trade because the island was not colonized until much later than both Curaçao and Bonaire. It was not until the late 18th century that any significant population moved to Aruba.

The first large settlements in Aruba were transplants from Curaçao who largely used Dutch for official business and Papiamento as the lingua franca. Papiamento is said to have originated through filling the need for a lingua franca on the island of Curaçao before large swaths of people moved to Aruba. In Curaçao, the population comprised Dutch merchants and their African slaves along with small groups from other European nations and a large Portuguese-speaking Sephardic Jewish population. These groups brought a collection of diverse languages, cultures and histories, creating a scenario where a common language was necessary to communicate between the masses. While the exact language or languages used among the people throughout the 18th century is highly contested among scholars on the ABC islands, most agree that the 18th century was an important period in the creation and formation of the language of Papiamento (Fouse, 2002; Martinus, 1996; Rupert, 2012).

The formation of Papiamento, as well as its subsequent survival, had a lot to do with its role as a lingua franca among the diverse inhabitants of the Leeward Islands. As is customary when people of different language groups come together, a compromise must be struck in order to communicate. The social context of the Leeward Islands was a little different from traditional colonies in the New World because there were essentially three different groups of people (Dutch merchants, Portuguese-speaking Sephardic Jews and slaves from West Africa) confined to a relatively small space, each using its own language. Such linguistic diversity resulted in the urgent need for a common language that would enable islanders to communicate among one another.

Over time, Papiamento emerged as a viable Creole language that was spoken and embraced as the lingua franca by all three groups living in Curaçao. Papiamento then traveled with its speakers to the islands of Aruba and Bonaire. On all three islands, Dutch has always been viewed among the elite as superior and the language that should be used for formal education.

Despite official language policies demanding the use of Dutch in formal domains, the general populations of Aruba, Bonaire and Curaçao continued to use Papiamento as the language of the masses:

> Indeed, many observers came to the conclusion that Dutch had little worth in the islands despite its official status in government and the schools, and that the second generation of Dutch children were growing up limited in their Dutch language ability, while learning Papiamentu instead. (Fouse, 2002: 139)

As a result, Dutch's high political status did not translate into an abandonment of Papiamento. This was partly because of an insular upper-class system on the islands, which rarely resulted in non-Dutch gaining access to high government positions. Thus, with little access to power, users of Papiamento had little motivation to learn Dutch.

Toward the beginning of the 20th century, the Dutch government had to start competing with American influence, which was introduced upon the opening of the Lago Oil and Transplant Company, a subsidiary of Standard Oil of New Jersey. Arubans point to 1929, when the construction for the large refinery started, as a turning point in Aruban history. In contrast to their cousins in Curaçao, whose refinery was run by Royal Dutch Shell, the Lago Company and its English-speaking owners attracted English speakers from all over the West Indies. Many of these English speakers came from St Eustatius (an English-speaking island in the Netherlands Antilles) as well as other islands such as Barbados and Trinidad. The new group of English-speaking immigrants started their own community in San Nicolas, which is located on the southern end of the island, close to the refinery.

The presence of the English speakers and a major US business changed the linguistic complexion of the island in a matter of years. While Dutch was still the official language, Arubans now had more incentive to learn another language other than Papiamento. After the arrival of the Lago Company, Dutch continued to symbolize a culture and authority that seemed very distant to many Arubans.

The eventual closing of the Lago refinery in 1985 sent the economy into a downward spiral (Boekhoudt-Croes, 1996). The closing resulted in the island's unemployment skyrocketing from 5% to 27% (Emerencia, 1996), prompting the government to respond with incentives to bolster the tourism sector. Shortly thereafter, the economy improved and made Aruba a prime destination for immigrants seeking work in the newly created sector (Emerencia, 1996).

The new industry created the need for immigrants, many of which came from Spanish-speaking countries such as the Dominican Republic, Colombia and Venezuela, among others. As with past immigration trends, Arubans felt that immigrants who did not speak their language or know the common cultural practices threatened their local way of life. According to Luciano Milliard, a law professor at the University of Aruba, every time there has been a wave of immigrants, there has also been a countermovement to define and redefine what it means to be Aruban (Milliard, 2008).

Along with increased immigration, Aruba's movement to break away from the Netherlands Antilles through *Status Aparte* played a major role in the development of Aruban identity. Led by Betico Croes, one of Aruba's most beloved leaders, there was a powerful initiative to define what it meant to be Aruban. Croes and his followers rallied around Aruba's *'dushi* Papiamento' (sweet Papiamento) and culture. The masses who followed and believed in Betico's rhetoric were often descendants of other Arubans. According to Milliard, many immigrants and descendants of immigrants felt that the

> Aruba promoted by Betico [Croes] was an idealized variety, which, as immigrants, they did not fit into ... [nevertheless] Aruba gained *Status Aparte* in 1986, and Croes's influence and leadership in the formation of the *Movimiento Electoral di Pueblo* (People's Electoral Movement) were instrumental in the garnering of Aruba's current political status and in the formation of a conscious national identity among Arubans. (L. Milliard, personal communication, 5 May 2008)

Status Aparte was awarded to Aruba in 1986, providing the island with separate and complete autonomy within the Kingdom of the Netherlands but under the Dutch crown. Such distinction allowed Aruban politicians to concentrate on their own local affairs instead of having to pass through political channels in Curaçao, which had been the practice when they were part of the Netherlands Antilles. Along with *Status Aparte*, Aruba adopted a spelling system that was based on the etymology of words, which differs from the phonemic-based spelling system used in Curaçao and Bonaire.

While this change worked to provide a clear distinction between the Papiamento used on the three islands, it has also made it more difficult for literature to be shared between the small island nations.

Contesting the language of instruction

Language threat in Aruba has centered specifically on the use of Papiamento, or lack thereof, in the education system. While many multilingual postcolonial countries have adopted mother-tongue instruction for the majority of the population, Aruba has not. Thus, with its roots in Dutch colonization, Papiamento has struggled to garner a sense of legitimacy as the medium of formal education. As a result, those who are able to ascend to the highest positions in the country do so largely because of their knowledge of and education in Dutch. Therefore, the relationship between the languages and the people representing said languages results in a context where there is an unequal struggle for power. This is very much the case in the Aruban education system, where the language of the majority, Papiamento, is still treated by many as a minority language, creating major consequences for efficient and effective development.

As Table 4 suggests, Dutch is the first language of only 6.2% of Aruban students; however, because of the island's political relationship with the Netherlands, its publically funded curriculum is extremely similar to the Dutch system, where Dutch is the sole language of instruction. Although advocacy for the use of Papiamento in education has a long history, it was only in the 1980s that the government of Aruba started considering changes in the educational policy and the integration of the language school curricula. Thankfully, since the late 1960s Aruba has developed education and language professionals who are currently working in the Department of Education and at the teacher preparation college Instituto Pedagogico Arubano (IPA). These professionals, who are native users of Papiamento and

Table 4 First-language profile of Aruban students

	Relative percentages	Absolute numbers
Papiamento	71.4%	15,227
Spanish	12.1%	2,575
Dutch	6.2%	1,313
English	5.5%	1,181
Unknown	2.6%	561
Other	2.2%	451
Total	100%	21,308

Source: Departamento di Enseñansa (2014).

who have been educated in Dutch, bring to the classroom what non-islanders who speak only Dutch found difficult to do: empathy, passion and first hand cultural and linguistic understanding (Dijkhoff & Pereira, 2010).

Since the national movement started in the 1960s, Papiamento has been associated with Aruban identity, and its position in society and different domains has grown. Below is a summary of some of the major gains for Papiamento over the past half-century.

- Since the 1950s, Aruba's parliament and central government use Papiamento in all their meetings and communication with the public.
- In 1976 an official orthography was created for Papiamento.
- Established in 1990 as a teacher's college, the IPA now offers a bachelor's degree for teachers teaching Papiamento as a subject.
- Papiamento has been the co-official language with Dutch since 2003.
- Since 2004, Papiamento has been a compulsory subject in secondary schools, and since 2015 an optional exam subject.
- Since 2009 an innovative pilot project, 'Proyecto Scol Multilingual' (SML), has been trialed in two primary schools in which Papiamento is being used as medium of instruction up to the fourth grade.
- In 2015, Aruba was able to welcome its first teachers with a master's degree in Papiamento as the result of a collaborative program between IPA and the University of Curaçao.
- Among Arubans, Papiamento is the predominant language of the local media.
- Papiamento is used in kindergarten, special education, and some levels of the lower vocational school as the medium of instruction.
- Currently, IPA is working to update all Aruban teachers through in-service training with professional development in Papiamento grammar, orthography, literature and communication.
- Written works, like Papiamento textbooks, reading books, and mathematics in Papiamento, continue to be published for use in formal education.

The result of almost 200 years of Dutch-only education, which positioned Papiamento as an inferior language, has led islanders who use the language for their daily activities to be skeptical and distrustful about the qualities of their language. Today, despite research and an official decision to introduce Papiamento into the Aruban education system, many Arubans still do not believe that such a move should happen, so much so that many do not believe that their language can function as the main language of instruction in education.

While Aruba is heading toward a multilingual primary school model where Papiamento will play an important role, the prognosis for its use in secondary education is moving in the opposite direction. As recently as 2012,

Aruban officials signed an agreement with the Dutch Ministry of Education that, by 2016, the Aruban secondary education system (HAVO/VWO) will be reorganized in accordance with Dutch regulations (Commissie AVO, 2014). The direct consequence of these actions will be an increased emphasis on Dutch in the secondary schools.

The shift toward a Dutch-based curriculum comes on the heels of Peterson's important study (2015) showing that the favorite and most active language between Aruban youth is still Papiamento, with a score of 60%. English held second place with 28%, Spanish had third place with 8% and Dutch had only 4%. These results clearly suggest that Dutch is not an active language among the youth and, considering these results, one must question its effectiveness and use in formal education.

While the political relationship with the Netherlands has positioned Dutch as the go-to language of government-funded education, a relatively new threat to Papiamento is the popularity of English. English is not only popular among the island's youth, but using English borrowings through code switching and code mixing of Papiamento and English has become a trend. Furthermore, English has started to make an impression on the linguistic landscape, since advertisements on the radio and television and in newspapers are increasingly in the language. While Papiamento has yet to be implemented as the medium of instruction in schools, Dutch remains a very difficult and unpopular medium of instruction. Given the global influence of English, some have advocated for its use instead of Dutch in secondary schools. However, given the linguistic insecurities of Arubans, English poses an additional threat to Papiamento which would seriously increase should it become the medium of instruction in secondary education.

Discussion

The continued colonial history of Puerto Rico and Aruba has directly impacted the potential threat that islanders perceive toward their respective mother tongues. Throughout this section we will focus on how perceptions of threat have impacted the languages used in formal education from primary through post-secondary levels. Ultimately, we will argue that the perception of threat is an important part of language maintenance of Spanish and Papiamento on the two islands.

As mentioned earlier, the most commonly used typologies for identifying language threat were created to identify language shift (Krauss, 2000) and provide language planners a detailed account of how to reverse language shift (Fishman, 1991). However, these typologies, along with others, provide little insight into the complexity of environments where languages are only perceived as threatened. Ruiz's threat inversion typology (published in this volume) accounts for language contexts that do not fit cleanly into previously published typologies. The use of this typology within the field of LPP will facilitate categorizing different language contexts that exhibit a complex mixture of social, political and psychological factors that have led to the perception of threat.

In the cases considered here, the use of the threat inversion typology proved fruitful in delineating differences between language contexts that are generally grouped together. Category C (perceived threat to a majority minoritized language), into which Puerto Rico fell, was evidenced by the policies that have worked to limit the teaching of English on the island and which consequently have supported the maintenance of Spanish. Given the unique status of Puerto Rico in the US colonial experience, it still remains unclear to what extent the United States would go to ensure that English plays an official role on the island.

The case of Papiamento in Aruba also falls relatively cleanly into Category E (perceived threat to a majority Indigenous language), as Spanish in Puerto Rico did within its respective category. The context represented in the case of Papiamento on Aruba is undoubtedly deserving of its own category. Historical evidence along with the continued political associations with the Netherlands continue to create the potential for Papiamento (L1) to be relegated to non-power domains, as has been the case in Aruba's past. Thus, Ruiz's 'danger' column is relevant to the case of Aruba. Despite Papiamento's fit in Category E, we suggest that more needs to be made of what exactly constitutes Ruiz's L2 distinction. Within a multilingual context such as Aruba, L2 could mean a number of different languages, all with varying status and prestige. While Ruiz was undoubtedly referring to the second official language, Dutch in this case, both English and Spanish currently present a more realistic threat. Thus, limiting the discussion of threat to the official L2 can be deceiving in that other languages involved in the context can present an equal or even greater threat than the official language. Nevertheless, given the complexity of developing a new typology of threatened languages, this is a minor critique. Continued research, exploring cases representing the other categories in Ruiz's typology, is necessary in order to gain a more nuanced understanding of the new typology.

Further analysis of the complexity of the perception of threat lends itself to a better understanding of how ideas and perceptions are amplified throughout society. The case studies of Aruba and Puerto Rico have highlighted how one's experiences with the difficulty of learning a colonizer's language and restrictive colonial policies, coupled with the rhetoric that accompanies nationalist agendas, can work to create a perception that one's language and nationalism are threatened.

The perception of threat and discussions of language threat have worked to unite different groups on both islands. In both Aruba and Puerto Rico, the perception of threat has been just that: a perception of something that could potentially result in language shift. Other language contexts where language shift has already occurred fall into a different category because the language is not simply perceived to be threatened but is indeed threatened as evidenced by language shift.

The detailed case studies of Aruba and Puerto Rico shed light on the complexity of language threat as well as how perceptions of threat have grown and manifested themselves throughout history. Unfortunately, these are only two of the literally thousands of language contexts that need to be documented. The case studies presented here provide examples of different ways in which languages can be successfully maintained despite an adverse political climate. It is important for the LPP field to document endangered languages and describe language contexts that are currently undergoing language shift, but it is also important to understand language contexts where language has been maintained. Understanding the success of programs tied to the maintenance of particular languages can potentially result in the application of similar programs in other language contexts.

Thus, one of the central arguments of this research is that those who are influencing and creating language policies must be attuned to the historical relevance of past policies and efforts. As time passes, different language groups are perceived as threats, yet the knowledge that is gained from past experiences can serve as a guiding factor in dictating the appropriate measures for future action. Past policies should not be the sole impetus for new policies, but they do indeed need to be understood so that the same or similar mistakes are not made more than once. Hence, the findings and maintenance efforts from the cases of Aruba and Puerto Rico are in no way generalizable, but certain aspects of their success might be applicable to other environments that have not witnessed language shift but where there is the perception of language threat from an outside language or languages.

One of the specific areas of LPP that needs to be examined in more detail is prestige planning (Haarmann, 1990). The maintenance of Papiamento in Aruba and Spanish in Puerto Rico is clearly related to islanders' ability to maintain the prestige of the local language. The frequency of local festivals in Puerto Rico, which work to maintain and strengthen local identity, also work to maintain the language. Likewise, the use of Papiamento as the language in which children learn valuable literacy skills works to build the prestige of Papiamento. Prestige-planning efforts undoubtedly are being utilized in a variety of language environments, yet most of these ventures have yet to be recognized or studied.

Conclusion

The case studies of both Aruba and Puerto Rico reflect two categories within Ruiz's threat inversion typology and highlight why both contexts have been successful in maintaining their local language. History and immigration patterns always play a key role in the maintenance or loss of any language, but conscious efforts on the part of both Arubans and Puerto Ricans have also worked toward preserving and maintaining the status and prestige of Papiamento and Spanish, respectively. Despite successful language maintenance, both islands still have plenty of work to do regarding language. The use of Dutch-medium instruction still works to handicap Aruban students, whose first language is not Dutch. On the island of Puerto Rico, the colonial relationship with the United States has politicized English education to the point where many Puerto Ricans do not receive the education necessary to make them bilingual.

Throughout the years of colonization, both Papiamento and Spanish have continued as symbols of the strength and tradition of Arubans and Puerto Ricans, respectively. Although it is important for locals to be cognizant of the significance of their local languages, it is also important that islanders use language as a means to be inclusive instead of exclusive. Perceived threat can lead to actions being taken against speakers of languages who are perceived to pose a threat on the local language. Thus, it is important that, in both contexts, systems are adopted to allow immigrants and/or return migrants viable opportunities to learn the majority language of Papiamento and Spanish, respectively.

In an ever-globalizing world, it is important that nations such as Aruba and Puerto Rico maintain their native languages, which they have been able to do with great success over the past 200 years or more. However, given that both island nations are politically affiliated with large, respected world powers and their economies are largely dependent on tourism and outside investment, the linguistic contexts of the island are not as stable as language contexts in larger autonomous nation-states identified in Ruiz's Category H.

Despite successful language maintenance on Aruba and Puerto Rico, both islands could benefit from improved language-in-education planning. Doing so would require the creation of a comprehensive and holistic approach that actively mobilizes all sectors of the community to weigh the benefits of mother-tongue instruction in the case of Aruba and societal bilingualism in the case of Puerto Rico. Creating public awareness to combat the position that Papiamento is inadequate for formal schooling and English is a threat to Puerto Rican identity could potentially have a positive impact not only on language maintenance but on access to more meaningful education among the youth on both islands.

Note

(1) While many historians have reported that the Taino language was completely wiped out, more recent moves to revitalize the language have occurred in other Caribbean countries where the Taino people lived (Taliman, 2001).

References

Ager, D.E. (2001) *Motivation in Language Planning and Language Policy*. Clevedon: Multilingual Matters.

Algren de Gutiérrez, E. (1987) *The Movement Against Teaching English in the Schools of Puerto Rico*. Lanham, MD: University Press of America.

Boekhoudt-Croes, R. (1996) *Multilingualismo i enseñansa: Language needs in Aruban education*. Unpublished Master's thesis, Catholic University of Nijmegen.

Carroll, K.S., Rivera, R. and Santiago, K. (2015) Questioning linguistic imperialism: Language negotiation in an agriculture classroom. In A. Fabricius and B. Preisler (eds) *Transcultural Interaction and Linguistic Diversity in Higher Education* (pp. 164–187). New York: Palgrave Macmillan.

Commissie AVO (2014) *Bijlage – Beleidsvoorstel inzake aanpassingen exameneisen en aantal vakken in havo en vwo*. Oranjestad, Aruba: Directie Onderwijs.

Crystal, D. (2004) *The Language Revolution*. Malden, MA: Polity Press.

Dalby, A. (2003) *Language in Danger: The Loss of Linguistic Diversity and the Threat to Our Future*. New York: Columbia University Press.

Departamento di Enseñansa (2014) Relato anual 2013–2014. See http://www.ea.aw/documento-a-publicacion/relato-anual.

Dijkhoff, M. and Pereira, J. (2010) Language and education in Aruba, Bonaire and Curaçao. In B. Migge, I. Léglise and A. Bartens (eds) *Creoles in Education: An Appraisal of Current Programs and Projects* (pp. 237–272). Philadelphia, PA: John Benjamins.

Emerencia, L. (1996) Changing challenges for Aruban schools. *21st Century Policy Review* 3 (1–2), 150–176.

Fishman, J.A. (1991) How threatened is 'threatened'?: A typology of disadvantaged languages and ameliorative priorities. In J.A. Fishman (ed.) *Reversing Language Shift: Theoretical and Empirical Foundations of Assistance to Threatened Languages* (pp. 81–121). Clevedon: Multilingual Matters.

Fishman, J.A. (2001) *Can Threatened Languages Be Saved? Reversing Language Shift, Revisited: A 21st Century Perspective*. Clevedon: Multilingual Matters.

Fouse, G.C. (2002) *The Story of Papiamentu: A Study in Slavery and Language*. Lanham, MD: University Press of America.

Haarmann, H. (1990) Language planning in the light of a general theory of language: A methodological framework. *International Journal of the Sociology of Language* 86, 103–126.

Hornberger, N.H. and King, K.A. (2001) Reversing Quechua language shift in South America. In J.A. Fishman (ed.) *Can Threatened Languages Be Saved?* (pp. 166–194). Clevedon: Multilingual Matters.

Krauss, M. (1992) The world's languages in crisis. *Language* 68 (1), 4–10.

Krauss, M. (2000) Native American languages act amendments act of 2000: Hearing on S.2688, 20 July.

Ladd, H.F. and Rivera-Batiz, F.L. (2006) Education and economic development. In S. Collins, B. Bosworth and M. Soto-Class (eds) *The Economy of Puerto Rico: Restoring Growth* (pp. 189–238). Washington, DC: Brookings Institution Press.

Lewis, M.P. and Simons, G.F. (2010) Assessing endangerment: Expanding Fishman's GIDS. *Revue roumaine de linguistique* 2, 103–119.

Martinus, E.F. (1996) *The Kiss of a Slave: Papiamento's West-African Connections*. PhD Dissertation, University of Amsterdam.

Milliard, L. (2008) Defining and redefining identity. *Nos Florin* 9, 68–69.

Morales Carrión, A. (1983) *Puerto Rico: A Political and Cultural History*. New York: Norton.

Morris, N. (1996) Language and identity in twentieth century Puerto Rico. *Journal of Multilingual and Multicultural Development* 17 (1), 17–32.

Ostler, N. (2005) *Empires of the World: A Language History of the World.* New York: Harper Collins.

Peterson, R.R. (2015) *Youth Engaged in Sustainability – National Youth Study Aruba.* Oranestad, Aruba: University of Aruba.

Razak, V. (1995) Culture under construction the future of native Arubian identity. *Futures* 27 (4), 447–459.

Romaine, S. (2006) Planning for the survival of linguistic diversity. *Language Policy* 5 (4), 443–475.

Ruiz, R. (1984) Orientations in language planning. *NABE Journal* 8, 15–34.

Ruiz, R. (2006) Language threat and endangerment. Paper presented at the Georgetown University Round Table on Language and Linguistics, Washington, DC, 5 March.

Rupert, L.M. (2012) *Creolization and Contraband – Curaçao in the Early Modern Atlantic World.* Athens, GA: University of Georgia Press.

Santa Ana, O. (2002) *Brown Tide Rising: Metaphors of Latinos in Contemporary American Public Discourse.* Austin, TX: University of Texas Press.

Schmidt, J. (2014) *The Politics of English in Puerto Rico's Public Schools.* Boulder, CO: First Forum Press.

Schweers, C.W., Jr. and Hudders, M. (2000) The reformation and democratization of English education in Puerto Rico. *International Journal of the Sociology of Language* 142, 63–87.

Taliman, V. (2001) Taino Nation alive and strong. *Indian Country Today Media Network. com*, 24 January. See http://indiancountrytodaymedianetwork.com/2001/01/24/taino-nation-alive-and-strong-85125.

Vaquero de Ramírez, M. (1991) Español de América y lenguas indígenas. *Estudios de Lingüística* 7, 9–26.

Vélez, J.A. (2000) Understanding Spanish-language maintenance in Puerto Rico: Political will meets the demographic imperative. *International Journal of the Sociology of Language* 142, 5–24.

Part 6

Communities as Linguistic Resources Across the Americas: A Symposium of Essays

Language, Voice and Empowerment Frameworks
Mary Carol Combs and Sheilah E. Nicholas

Indigenous Youth Language Resources, Educational Sovereignty and Praxis: Connecting a New Body of Language Planning Research to the Work of Richard Ruiz
Leisy Wyman, Candace Kaleimamoowahinekapu Galla and Luz Jiménez-Quispe

The Missing Voices in Colombia Bilingüe: The Case of Ĕbĕra Children's Schooling in Bogotá, Colombia
Amparo Clavijo Olarte and Ángela Pamela González

Learning about Linguistic Resources Through Home Engagements: Opportunities for Latina Preservice Teachers to Shape Their Language Orientations
Iliana Reyes and Ana Christina Da Silva Iddings

Richard and Mary Carol Combs in Rabat, Morocco, June 2013
Courtesy of Yvonne Gonzalez/Teresa L. McCarty.

Richard, Norma, Leisy and Sheilah, April 2011, University of Arizona, Tucson
Courtesy of Janelle Johnson.

Richard and Candace, University of Arizona, Tucson 2010
Courtesy of Candace Kaleimamoowahinekapu Galla.

Richard, Luz and Cathy Amanti at University of Arizona Commencement, Tuscon, AZ, December 2013
Courtesy of Luz Jiménez.

Richard and Amparo, Heredia, Costa Rica, 2007
Courtesy of Kevin S. Carroll.

Language, Voice and Empowerment Frameworks

Mary Carol Combs and Sheilah E. Nicholas

Introduction

The chapters in this volume attest to the important work that Richard Ruiz has contributed to the field of language planning, an eclectic discipline that draws from sociolinguistics, anthropology, political science, social psychology, economics and education. Historically, language planning was defined as an activity pursued on a national or governmental level to solve a language 'problem' (Fishman, 1968), as well as deliberate decision making and change in spoken or written language codes (Rubin & Jernudd, 1971). Richard was influenced by these ideas, but he was also deeply interested in how the language planning attitudes – or orientations – of nations, governments and groups affected the development and implementation of language and education models 'on the ground' (see, for example, Ruiz, 1984, 1990, 1993/1994, 1995). Like his academic predecessors, Richard engaged in 'corpus' or 'status' planning projects in multilingual settings (most recently, in Aruba, Puerto Rico, Bolivia and the United States). However, his scholarly work attempted primarily to unearth *why* people established particular language policies and how those policies connected to deeply held though often unconscious ideologies.

Richard Ruiz: Critical Theorist and Gentle Pedagogue

Perhaps less known about Richard Ruiz was that he was also influenced by critical pedagogy as an intellectual subject and instructional practice. He had an intense admiration for Brazilian educator Paulo Freire, whose seminal text *Pedagogy of the Oppressed* influenced so many people. In fact, Richard was an expert interpreter of Freire's work, and one of the first scholars to remind us that Freire's notion of 'empowerment' – which some in our field have advocated for the 'disempowered' – is not a gift from the powerful to the powerless. What he meant is that teachers and schools do not empower or disempower their students; rather, they create the conditions under which students can empower themselves – or not.

Richard's analysis of Paulo Freire's theory of emancipatory education reminds us that nothing is emancipatory if it is imposed from above. True liberation comes from the organic development of a critical consciousness and students are front and center in this process. Through the process of meaningful dialogue, questioning and problem posing, students come to understand the nature and source of their oppression. They come to know the world and their place within it in order to transform the world. Like Freire, Richard also believed that a child's language, culture and lived experience should not merely be included in the curriculum – it should *be* the curriculum. Yet Richard did not presume to understand the historical and political oppression of his students of color as a 'co-participant' in their experience. Rather, he acknowledged what Ellsworth (1989) has called a 'pedagogy of the unknowable,' in which differences are seen as strengths and in which students educate their teachers.

This chapter focuses on this lesser known aspect of Richard's work. We have four goals: first, to revisit the article in which these ideas are discussed (in Christine Sleeter's 1991 edited volume, *Empowerment Through Multicultural Education*; Ruiz, 1991); secondly, to problematize the concept of empowerment as Freire originally presented it; and thirdly, to foreground from that same article Richard's analysis of the concept of the importance of *voice* and how it differs from *language*. Finally, we offer a contemporary example of Freirean empowerment that led directly to the development of *conscientização* (critical consciousness). Perhaps more importantly, this example illustrates the importance of voice, as Richard theorized it, in relationship to language. Our example is the small but resilient American Indian Language Development Institute (AILDI) that takes place every summer in Tucson at the University of Arizona where we live and work. For more than 30 years, AILDI has created an intellectual and practical context for Indigenous language revitalization. In this intimate and empowering space, Indigenous practitioners and elders, sometimes the last living speakers of their tribal or community languages, collaborate with university instructors, visiting researchers and each other to consider why languages decline and to practice pedagogical strategies to revalidate and revitalize them.

Academic [Mis]Interpretations of the Empowerment Process

In his graduate seminars on critical pedagogy, Richard was fond of pointing out that the word 'empower' was a transitive verb, meaning that in an English sentence it takes a direct object. For example, the phrase *we empower them* implies that we endow or authorize people with some kind of power or ability that they presumably do not already have. 'If I empower you,' Richard used to ask, 'am I giving you a gift? Is it something that I do to or for you? Do you have a role to play in your own empowerment?' Richard used this philosophical conundrum to make the point that the grammatical transitivity of 'empower' masked the more collaborative process involved in 'empowerment' as theorized by Paulo Freire.

Richard was particularly concerned about scholarly work which claimed an ideological anchor in Paulo Freire's notion of *emancipatory education*, but yet appeared to fundamentally misunderstand the dialectical relationship between teachers and students and the reciprocal exchange of knowledge inherent in this notion. For example, Richard was critical of Jim Cummins' influential 1986 article in the *Harvard Educational Review*, 'Empowering minority students: A framework for intervention.' In this article he drew in part from Paulo Freire's analysis of the relationships of power between teachers and minority students and between schools and communities. Cummins proposed a 'framework for intervention' which sought to equalize these power differentials in order to improve academic outcomes for minority students.

The central tenet of the framework was the idea that 'students from "dominated" societal groups were "empowered" or "disabled" as a direct result of their interactions with educators in the schools' (Cummins, 1986: 4). Cummins was troubled that the national push for English-only instruction and high-stakes testing for language minority students would devalue their linguistic and cultural identities and reduce their prospects for academic success. He theorized that language minority students were disabled by policy makers and teachers who created and maintained unequal power and status relations with students that attributed academic failure to the students themselves, rather than seeing school failure as a manifestation of intergroup inequality in the wider society. More importantly, minority students were disempowered in much the same way that their families and communities were disempowered by interactions and practices within majority societal institutions (Cummins, 1986: 6). Consequently, Cummins proposed the reorganization of school structures to: (1) incorporate students' languages and cultures into the school curriculum; (2) encourage family and community participation as an integral part of the students' education; (3) promote the active use of students' home languages; and (4) assess language minority students authentically. The implication of Cummins' empowerment framework was that progressive teachers can and should empower their linguistically diverse students for academic success. A framework for empowerment also would yield multiple benefits:

> Students who are empowered by their school experiences develop the ability, confidence, and motivation to succeed academically. They

participate competently in instruction as a result of having developed a confident cultural identity as well as appropriate school-based knowledge and interactional structures. … Students who are disempowered or 'disabled' by their school experiences do not develop this type of cognitive/ academic and social/emotional foundation. Thus, student empowerment is regarded as both a mediating construct influencing academic performance and as an outcome variable itself. (Cummins, 1986: 6)

Cummins' analysis of the disempowering effects of unequal power relationships between language minority students and their teachers resonated with many in the field, including publishing companies. Since the publication of Cummins' article, numerous textbooks have incorporated (and still incorporate) the word 'empowering' in their titles.[1]

Empowerment is Not a Gift

Richard Ruiz did not dispute the need for teachers and policy makers to develop an awareness of unequal power relations in schools or to address them squarely in classroom interactions and beyond. Rather, he criticized the presumed passivity of the 'empowered' groups in the interrogation and disruption of their disempowered status. In Cummins' empowerment framework, disempowered students appeared to play no direct role in their own empowerment, and this represented a serious misinterpretation of Freire's work. Richard argued that empowerment was not an action or outcome that one does to or makes happen for another. Nor was it a gift from the powerful to the powerless. If radical pedagogues treat empowerment as a gift, he wrote, 'they are not yet radical' (Ruiz, 1991: 223).

In *Pedagogy of the Oppressed* (1970b), Freire exposed the dehumanizing effect of 'banking education,' an ideology that reduced education to a mechanical act of 'depositing knowledge.' In this model of education, students are seen as empty receptacles into which the teacher deposits the prescribed content of the curriculum, to be withdrawn and used at a later time (on a test, for example). Banking education discourages students' creativity, power and agency because it views them as marginal and adaptable, thus forestalling the development of critical consciousness and the ability to 'read the world' in order to transform it. Freire also argued that banking education views knowledge as 'a gift bestowed by those who considered themselves knowledgeable upon those whom they consider to know nothing' (Freire, 1970b: 58).

That only teachers possess knowledge and power and, conversely, that students have no knowledge, power or agency, are fundamental assumptions of the banking approach. The belief that only those in power were capable of providing knowledge and experience to the powerless mirrored Freire's objection to the views of literacy educators in Latin America who described rural and impoverished illiterate adults as 'starving for letters' or 'hungry for words.' If rural or impoverished communities were hungry, literacy educators were charged with bringing words to the people in order to save them from starvation:

> As understood in this concept, man [and woman] is a passive being, the object of the process of learning to read and write, and not its subject. As object his [or her] task is to 'study' the so-called reading lessons which in fact are almost completely alienating and alienated, having so little, if anything, to do with the student's socio-cultural reality. (Freire, 1970a: 8)

The disruption of this idea, of course, constitutes the heart of Freire's pedagogy of the oppressed, a radical pedagogy which is 'forged *with*, not *for*, the oppressed (whether individuals or peoples) in the incessant struggle to regain their humanity' (Freire, 1970b: 33, emphasis in the original).

Richard's critique of Cummins' empowerment framework was collegial. He praised the influence that Cummins' ideas have had on the field of language minority education and bilingual education in particular: 'Cummins is one of only a handful of academics whose work consistently determines the direction of the literature in this area' (Ruiz, 1991: 222). We agree. But like Richard, we also agree that empowerment pedagogy, as Paulo Freire initially problematized the approach, is not something that one person does to or for another. Empowerment is a reciprocal process in which students empower themselves through the development of a critical consciousness. This process nominally may be aided by the teacher, who works to create the conditions under which students begin to empower themselves.

Language and Voice

We now move to the question of *voice*, which Richard distinguished from language. Much of the literature on language planning and policy recognized the relationship between language and power, but less frequently analyzed 'voice' as a separate aspect of language. He provided two examples of policies that included a people's language but not their voice. The first example surfaced a paradox – the inclusion and validation of the Spanish language in maintenance or dual language bilingual education programs in the United States as a way to preserve the language of the students. Yet the Spanish of the classroom more often than not did not represent the Spanish of the community because bilingual teachers in these programs 'rarely speak the language of the child; either they have learned a textbook language that no one actually uses in everyday conversation, or they confine their speech to standard forms because of their sense of what is proper or acceptable classroom behavior' (Ruiz, 1991: 219). In addition, bilingual teachers may have internalized deficit ideologies about the social dialects of Spanish or the translanguaging practices common in their students' homes and communities (e.g. *lonche* instead of *almuerzo*, or *carro* instead of *automóvil*). Because these practices were 'nonstandard,' reasoned some bilingual teachers, they were therefore improper. If improper, they could not be encouraged in the classroom.

The second example of the bestowal of language without voice is one that Richard has addressed elsewhere in his published work. This concerned the elevation to official status in 1975 of the Quechua language in Peru. Quechua was declared a co-official language of the country, together with Spanish, but the decision was largely symbolic; Quechua communities played almost no role in the declaration. Both examples illustrate a circumstance in which people were provided with language but not necessarily voice. According to Richard, this situation was perhaps the most evil form of colonialism because everyone, including the colonizers, recognized the false generosity of allowing people to use their language, while simultaneously ensuring that they were not heard.

Over the years, we had numerous lively and philosophical conversations with Richard. These happened in his office, at department meetings, and during the department's Wednesday afternoon *cafecitos* with students and faculty. Because all three of us had been faculty members in AILDI, our conversations occasionally focused on the history of the institute and how effective it had been in revitalizing Indigenous languages. We shared the concern that, in both large and small Native American communities, the shift from an Indigenous language to English appeared as robust as ever. Additionally, unabated was intense pressure on schools and communities from top-down federal mandates like No Child Left Behind and, in Arizona, Proposition 203 and the rigid interpretations of this English-only law by the state legislature and department of education. Nevertheless, one of the clear successes of AILDI, it seemed to us, was the developing agency and determination of the participants to [re]learn and use their languages at home. Participants gradually understood that no-one had the legal or administrative authority to prohibit the use of an Indigenous language in any context. Indeed, AILDI participants came to understand that they did not have to ask permission to use their languages or to revitalize them. What they had to do instead, as Blackfeet educator Darrell Kipp reminds us, was to 'teach the children to speak the language. There are no other rules' (Kipp, 2000: 3).

In our discussions about how we might honor Richard's theoretical contribution to critical pedagogy and notions of empowerment, we decided to highlight the linguistic journey of one of us (Sheilah Nicholas), who through AILDI began to reclaim Hopi, the language she was born into but stopped speaking when she entered public school in Winslow, Arizona. The institute provided Sheilah with the pedagogical tools and, opportunities for self-reflection and the confidence to re-appropriate the Hopi language and, through Hopi, her voice.

Sheilah's Narrative

I claim a long history with AILDI that began in 1991, first as a student, co-instructor, research-apprentice and program coordinator. As we noted earlier, AILDI is an exemplary model for providing the *conditions* to assist and support institute participants in an empowering process. As such, AILDI played a pivotal role in propelling me toward developing a personal *voice* that has significantly shaped my cultural, professional and intellectual trajectory and identity. Currently, I am an AILDI faculty instructor from the Department of Teacher, Learning and Sociocultural Studies' (TLSS) Program in Language, Reading and Culture (LRC). For me, AILDI exemplifies the reciprocal relationship of knowledge exchange and 'giving back' inherent in Freire's notion of emancipatory pedagogy/education. For the 2016 summer program, along with faculty and graduate student colleagues from the University of Arizona's Native American Linguistics program, Tohono O'odham Community College, and tribal community programs, I was the instructor for two courses, 'Language as Voice, Culture as Lived in Education' and 'Introduction to Immersion Instruction.' In addition, I led supplementary workshop with Mary Carol Combs entitled 'Claim Your Sovereignty – Make a Language Plan.'

In this narrative, I illuminate the notion of 'voice' as Richard articulated it, or *empowerment* as embodied in the process of *conscientização* (critical consciousness) in my progression from student to scholar to language educator. I highlight key events that I view as moments of conscious awareness brought about by individuals – instructors, mentors, peers and family – who worked to create the conditions that both surfaced and cultivated my capacity to understand the cultural cognitive schema (Newhouse, 2014), the cultural map that was the embodiment of my identity, as my colleagues Norma González and Luis Moll have called my 'Funds of Knowledge' (González *et al.*, 2005).

During my graduate student AILDI experience, instructor and linguist Akira Yamamoto played a pivotal role in initiating the empowering process I was to experience. His use of poetry as a genre to explore the linguistic structure and rhythms as well as surfacing the linguistic and cultural expressions of our community languages was the catalyst to a critical consciousness regarding my heritage language. My attempts to recall Hopi words to describe images of 'home' became a moment I still refer to as a 'rude' awakening to language shift in my personal life; although I retained a receptive ability, I struggled to articulate my thoughts and memories in the Hopi language. Astonished by this revelation, I asked Akira, 'What happened to my language?' His response was an assurance that my language, internalized in childhood (Hopi was my first language and language of use until entering school), remained within. I needed only to pull it from the inner recesses of body and memory.

AILDI provided a critical opportunity – I met and embarked on a long-term tutelage and apprenticeship with Hopi scholar and instructor Emory Sekaquaptewa, a relationship during which I would reclaim my speaking ability, develop Hopi literacy, investigate the underlying circumstances of community-wide Hopi language shift and become a language educator of my tribal language. This relationship cultivated, within spaces established by AILDI, a clan-kinship reconnection. Emory was my clan uncle and, in this cultural sense, his role in my empowering process was a responsibility he quietly assumed: to assist and guide me in acquiring the inherent wisdom of the cultural knowledge conveyed through what I have come to refer to as 'language as cultural practice' (Nicholas, 2008) or an understanding of the transmission mechanism of the Hopi oral tradition. Onondaga scholar David Newhouse (2014) describes wisdom as 'a heightened mental capacity that enables one to see beneath the surface of things, to see things and the forces that affect them … acquired through conscientious and conscious application of knowledge and deliberate cultivation of the conditions necessary to acquire knowledge' (Newhouse, 2014: 76).

It was also in the context of AILDI that I *heard* the voice of Hualapai educator and AILDI founder Lucille Watahomigie and that of her community about their concerns with high dropout rates, dismal numbers of Hualapais pursuing higher education, and a persistent negative attitude toward school and schooling among community youth. Her community asked, 'Why have the schools failed to educate our people? Why have the schools failed to nurture the intellectual and social-affective development of our children?' (Watahomigie, 1995: 190). This was eye-opening. Moreover, Lucille candidly asserted that part of the answer to these questions lay in the need for Indigenous communities and community educators to engage in 'reverse brainwashing,' that is, to acknowledge and confront the fact that Indigenous peoples have been brainwashed with the notion that language and culture are barriers to academic success and should be forgotten. This privileging of community voice compelled me to reflect on my own teacher practices acquired through Western pedagogical frameworks and to engage in reversing the brainwashing that was a part of my own academic and professional trajectory.

A significant aspect of AILDI is the *professionalization* context it provides, an ideological and implementational space (Hornberger, 2002, 2006) in which participants – Indigenous and non-Indigenous scholars, linguists, educators, practitioners – collaborate through dialogue and together create, interpret and appropriate language education policy. This describes global/local language planning from the bottom up (Hornberger, 2012) in practice, with

AILDI providing the context and space as well as the conditions in which Indigenous perspectives are voiced and *heard*. In their work with Andean Indigenous educators, Hornberger and Swinehart (2012) assert that such experiences enter 'into a dynamic' with individuals' personal language policies and practices, 'marking their adult lives with stronger identification with Indigenous language and culture' (Hornberger & Swinehart, 2012: 35). My professionalization experiences and professional formation confirm this. As well, the reference to 'adult lives' resonated strongly for me in that my empowering process began well into adulthood and largely in the context of AILDI.

Interestingly, AILDI provided experiences that were both characteristically academic and rigorous (participants were required to enroll in two three-unit university courses) but quite unique in conditions and outcomes. The condition of encounters and engagement with other Indigenous peoples in co-convened classes of undergraduate and graduate as well as traditional and non-traditional students created a context in which the potential challenges of academic status, formal training as well as levels of cultural and linguistic expertise and proficiency to the individual and collective outcomes merged and blurred; we were all learners and teachers. In fact, the focus of this context became one of necessitating linguistic flexibility in using Indigenous languages and collaborative deliberation in conceptualizing and articulating new concepts and realities through Indigenous epistemological perspectives and experiences. In this process of co-construction of linguistic expertise and pedagogical epistemologies, AILDI participants became members of a community of practice intimately bonded daily and into the evenings, immersed in activities over four weeks in this work of language reclamation and revitalization. The institute environment and atmosphere was one of establishing *community* and a community Indigenous languages oral event. AILDI's culminating 'micro-teaching' activity positioned each institute participant as both a teacher of an Indigenous language and a learner of other Indigenous languages. Further, the micro-teaching activity privileged 'local [Indigenous] semiotic systems' (Hornberger & Swinehart, 2012: 41) and, in doing so, undoubtedly revitalized a collective sense of our Indigeneity. As such, privileging our local semiotic systems worked as a heuristic tool to fundamentally impact our educational philosophies in challenging existing pedagogies (Hornberger & Swinehart, 2012).

Many AILDI participants returned year after year to relive this empowering experience. In my case, these experiences *re*directed my attention and *re*commitment to Hopi epistemology: the Hopi cultural and linguistic framework, has for millennia guided the Hopi people along life's continuum and informed the response to contemporary situations of change throughout the Hopi experience; it has been the enduring resource and reliable frame of reference toward an unknown future (Hall, 1976; Nicholas in McCarty *et al.*, forthcoming). These experiences further propelled me to engage actively in support of heritage language revitalization in general and specifically in my heritage community of Hopi. From 2004 to 2010, the opportunity to replicate a similar professionalization space in my home community empowered me further.

Hopilavayi Summer Institute, 2004–2010

From 2004 to 2010, the Hopi Tribe's Culture Preservation Office (HCPO) through the Hopilavayi Program[2] directed focused attention on assisting reservation school-based Hopi language and culture programs outlined in tribal resolutions (H-129-94, H-022-98) mandating 'the infusion of the Hopilavayi and culture in the school system to meet the needs of Hopi children' (Hopi Tribal Council, 2005: para. 3). The goal of these efforts was to provide professional development for individuals who had the responsibility or professional and personal interest in teaching the Hopi language in the formal spaces of schools[3] or community programs – paraeducators employed in the schools as teacher assistants, Head Start teachers and certified classroom teachers, as well as community members. The venue for providing tribal assistance was the conception, design and implementation of the Hopilavayi Summer Institute, a four-week intensive summer program of academic coursework, professional development and practicum experience in heritage language teaching with the goal of producing speakers of Hopi among the youth population in school and community-based language and culture programs.

The institute offered a rigorous program of courses: an introduction to language revitalization, oral immersion approach methodology, curriculum development, classroom management, action research and basic Hopi language literacy development, which I developed and delivered as the primary institute instructor. The significant programmatic outcomes included the development of the *Tsaamiwisqam-Kyeekelt*, Mentor–Apprentice Model for language teaching, a community-wide oral immersion event model, *Naatuwpi* (Self-*Re*discovery through the language), and a culture-based language teaching teacher manual (see Nicholas, forthcoming). The institute also achieved a significant capacity-building outcome. From the overall number of participants, a cohort of four individuals advanced to become mentor-instructors (2010 Institute); two subsequently earned a master's degree specializing in Indigenous [Hopi] heritage language teaching (2010).

In effect, the Hopilavayi Summer Institute as a tribal initiative provided the venue for creating the *conditions* for the institute participants to *(re)* empower themselves and *(re)*assert their *voice* (Ruiz, 1991) in reclaiming their inherent role and responsibility as the first teachers of the community youth expressed in the Hopi language as *itaatumala*, our life work. In the extended kin-/clanship network, this life work was assumed in the roles of these individuals as parents, grandparents, aunts, uncles, brothers and sisters. Over seven years of summer language education, a cohort of language educators who returned each summer attained a critical understanding of contemporary Hopi linguistic and cultural ecology and the language teaching skills to help carry out tribal mandates for language revitalization in schools amid and within the context of high-stakes accountability or, more aptly, within 'a geography of struggle and resistance' (Feld & Basso, 1996: 4).

In reflection, I view this undertaking as a collaborative, dynamic and organically evolving process of empowerment occurring for and between the Institute participants as language teachers and myself in assuming the role of language instructor-educator. We were all 'cultural insiders' (Rogers & Jaime, 2010: 196), personally impacted by the phenomenon of Hopi to English language shift in our lives, in the lives of our family members and community. We had come together in the Institute space to embark on this journey together; this in itself was an empowering beginning. In a forthcoming article, I wrote:

> The 2004–2010 trajectory of Hopilavayi Summer Institute documented here exemplifies the *possibilities of sustainability* of a fully tribally and community supported Hopi language education professionalization program. Within this ideological and implementation space – 'a place to regroup, take on new ideas, share new understandings with like-minded people who care about these issues' (Blair *et al.*, 2003: 101) – important work had been realized that included Hopi specific models of linguistic and cultural pedagogy as well as leadership potential untapped but now identified.

It is the adult community of traditional and contemporary educational practitioner-educators who are positioned as critical to the work on this language issue by creating and cultivating the conditions to listen to and hear their own voice.

Conclusion

Richard Ruiz exemplified Freirean pedagogy by gently but persistently posing intellectually engaging questions to students and colleagues alike. He rarely provided direct answers but waited for us to make sense of the questions on our own terms and through our own experiences. Although Richard occasionally offered alternative perspectives, he was never overtly didactic. He preferred a dialogical approach that viewed participants as equals: 'That is an interesting comment and, what do you think about this?' or 'Here is another idea too' and 'How would the situation look if …'.

We would like to conclude this chapter with a passage from Paulo Freire's hopeful and affirming text *Pedagogy of Hope* (1992: 23). Richard Ruiz was a humble, deeply thoughtful and erudite scholar. But he was also a hopeful man. This passage reminds us of our beloved friend, colleague and mentor, who if he were watching us today would urge us to read the world by reading the word:

No one leaves his or her world without being transfixed by its roots, or with a vacuum for a soul. We carry with us the memory of many fabrics, a self soaked in our history, our culture; a memory, sometimes scattered, sometimes sharp and clear, of the streets of our childhood, of our adolescence; the reminiscence of something distant that suddenly stands out before us, in us, a shy gesture, an open hand, a smile lost in time and misunderstanding, a sentence, a simple sentence ...

Notes

(1) A cursory internet search of publishing companies yielded the following results: *Empowering Students with Technology*; *Empowering Students to Thrive in a Changing World*; *Empowering Students in the Performing Arts*; *Empowering Students to Manage Behavior*; *Empowering Teachers: What Successful Principals do*; *Empowering Beginning Educators*; *Empowering Family–Teacher Partnerships*; *Empowering the Mentor*, and many others.
(2) The Hopilavayi Program was established in response to the 1998 Hopi Language and Education Plan (HELP) and is housed in the Hopi Tribe's Culture and Preservation Office (HCPO).
(3) Each of the seven elementary and K-8 schools provided a Hopi language and culture program operating as grant, federal or private (one) schools including two public junior high/high schools. This information was collected from participant applications.

References

Blair, H., Paskemin, D. and Laderoute, B. (2003) Preparing Indigenous language advocates, teachers, and researchers in western Canada. In J. Reyhner, O. Trujillo, R.L. Carrasco and L. Lockard (eds) *Nurturing Native Languages* (pp. 93–104). Flagstaff, AZ: Northern Arizona University.

Cummins, J. (1986) Empowering minority students: A framework for intervention. *Harvard Educational Review* 56 (1), 18–36.

Ellsworth, E. (1989) Why doesn't this feel empowering? Working through the repressive myths of critical pedagogy. *Harvard Educational Review* 59 (3), 297–324.

Feld, S. and Basso, K.H. (1996) *Senses of Place*. Santa Fe, NM: School of American Research Press.

Fishman, J. (1968) Sociolinguistics and the language problems of developing countries. In J.A. Fishman, C.A. Ferguson and J. Das Gupta (eds) *Language Problems of Developing Nations* (pp. 3–16). New York: John Wiley & Sons.

Freire, P. (1970a) The adult literacy process as cultural action for freedom. *Harvard Educational Review* 40 (2), 205–225.

Freire, P. (1970b) *Pedagogy of the Oppressed*. New York: Seabury Press.

Freire, P. (1992) *Pedagogy of Hope: Reliving Pedagogy of the Oppressed*. Continuum: New York.

González, N., Moll, L.C. and Amanti, C. (2005) *Funds of Knowledge: Theorizing Practices in Households, Communities, and Classrooms*. Mahwah, NJ: Lawrence Erlbaum.

Hall, E.T. (1976) *Beyond Culture*. New York: Doubleday.

Hopi Tribal Council (2005, December 7) Hopi Tribal Council Resolution H-010-2006. Hopi Tribe, AZ: Author.

Hornberger, N.H. (2002) Multilingual language policies and the continua of biliteracy: An ecological approach. *Language Policy* 1 (1), 27–51.

Hornberger, N.H. (2006) Nichols to NCLB: Local and global perspectives on U.S. language education policy. In O. García, T. Skutnabb-Kangas and M. Torres-Guzmán (eds) *Imagining Multilingual Schools: Languages in Education and Glocalization* (pp. 223–237). Clevedon: Multilingual Matters.

Hornberger, N.H. and McCarty, T.L. (2012) Globalization from the bottom up: Indigenous language planning and policy across time, space, and place. *International Multilingual Research Journal* 6 (1), 1–7.

Hornberger, N.H. and Swinehart, K.F. (2012) Not just situaciones de la vida: Professionalization and Indigenous language revitalization in the Andes. *International Multilingual Research Journal* 6 (1), 35–49.

Kipp, D.R. (2000) *Encouragement, Guidance, Insights, and Lessons Learned for Native Language Activists Developing Their Own Tribal Language Programs*. Browning, MT: Piegan Institute.

McCarty, T.L., Nicholas, S.E. and Wyman, L.T. (2012) Re-emplacing place in the 'global here and now' – critical ethnographic studies of Native American language planning and policy. *International Multilingual Research Journal* 6 (1), 50–63.

Newhouse, D. (2014) On reading Basso. In N. McLeod (ed.) *Indigenous Poetics in Canada* (pp. 73–81). Waterloo, ON: Wilfrid Laurier University Press.

Nicholas, S. (2008) Becoming 'fully' Hopi: The Hopi language in the contemporary lives of Hopi youth – a Hopi case study of language shift and vitality. Unpublished doctoral dissertation, University of Arizona.

Nicholas, S.E. (forthcoming) The Hopilavayi Summer Institute: A tribal model of assistance for heritage language teacher preparation. In C.K. Galla and M.E. Romero-Little (eds) *He Wa'a Ke Kula; Na Ka 'Ōlelo E Uli (Schools Are Canoes; Language Steers Them)*. Stabilizing Indigenous Languages Symposium Anthology, SILS 2014, Hawai'i.

Rogers, C.A. and Jaime, A.M. (2010) Listening to the community: Guidance from Native community members for emerging culturally responsive educators. *Equity & Excellence in Education* 43 (2), 188–201. doi:10.1080/10665681003719657.

Rubin, J. and Jernudd, B.H. (1971) (eds) *Can Language Be Planned?* Honolulu: University of Hawaii Press.

Ruiz, R. (1984) Orientations in language planning. *NABE Journal* 8 (2), 15–34.

Ruiz, R. (1990) Official languages and language planning. In K.L. Adams and D.T. Brink (eds) *Perspectives of Official English* (pp. 11–24). Berlin: Mouton de Gruyter.

Ruiz, R. (1991) The empowerment of language-minority students. In C.E. Sleeter (ed.) *Empowerment Through Multicultural Education* (pp. 217–227). Albany, NY: State University of New York Press.

Ruiz, R. (1993/1994) Language policy and planning in the United States. *Annual Review of Applied Linguistics* 14, 111–125.

Ruiz, R. (1995) Language planning considerations in Indigenous communities. *Bilingual Research Journal* 19 (1), 71–81.

Watahomigie, L. (1995) The power of American Indian parents and communities. *Bilingual Research Journal* 19 (1), 189–193.

Indigenous Youth Language Resources, Educational Sovereignty and Praxis: Connecting a New Body of Language Planning Research to the Work of Richard Ruiz

Leisy Wyman, Candace Kaleimamoowahinekapu Galla and Luz Jiménez-Quispe

In this chapter, co-authors draw upon Richard Ruiz's scholarly legacy to discuss growing trends within Indigenous youth multilingualism research in diverse contexts in Canada, the US, Australia, the Circumpolar North, Asia and Latin America. Recent ethnographic studies offer insight into the ways that Indigenous young people's language ideologies, multilingual voices, forms of cultural production and political engagement emerge within dynamic, (trans)local educational ecologies and institutions. In the chapter, we analyze key themes and examples from this work in light of Ruiz's influential scholarship on language orientations (1984, 1988, 2010), language planning in Indigenous communities (1995), voice and empowerment (1991), and his writings with Luis Moll on educational sovereignty and related, promising research directions for language minority students (Moll & Ruiz, 2002, 2005). We also identify new directions for praxis-oriented research (Brayboy, 2005; Lather, 1986; McCarty & Wyman, 2009) that recognizes and engages Indigenous youth as resources in intergenerational language reclamation movements, and language planning and policy.

Introduction

Current language planning and policy research highlights the ways in which complex, contradictory policy movements toward multilingualism and English dominance are converging in diverse contexts around the world. Studies also show how Indigenous community members are negotiating these movements by sharing and reclaiming Indigenous linguistic and cultural resources through dynamic practices and policy-making efforts in particular (trans)local educational ecologies and institutions. In the last two decades, a growing number of scholars have used ethnographic approaches to study Indigenous youth multilingualism, seeking to understand: (1) youth language ideologies; (2) youth experiences with Indigenous language learning opportunities (or relative lack thereof) in educational settings; (3) youth efforts to maintain and reclaim Indigenous language resources; and (4) youth assertions of language rights within broader Indigenous movements. While initial studies on Indigenous youth and multilingualism were largely focused in North America (McCarty & Wyman, 2009; Wyman *et al.*, 2014) and Australia (Kral, 2012; Simpson & Wigglesworth, 2008), studies in a widening range of global contexts including areas of the Global South have begun to illuminate trends and important differences in Indigenous youth experiences, educational opportunities and responses to globalization. The growing global literature on Indigenous youth multilingualism and participation in grassroots language planning and policy making exposes 'complex ideological contestations of neoliberal and nationalistic agendas,' and provides important insight into the ways Indigenous, as well as other minority youth 'interpret, resist, transform and negotiate policies that fail to recognize their language and sociocultural identities' (Phyak & Bui, 2014: 101). Importantly, this literature also highlights ways that youth and others are shaping efforts to maintain, promote, reclaim and extend the use of Indigenous languages as key resources for Indigenous peoples. The majority of scholars in this area have demonstrated long-term commitment to Indigenous language planning and policy; many self-identify as Indigenous community members, fill multiple roles as Indigenous language scholars, learners and speakers, and activists, and are committed to the ethical guidelines of Indigenous research (Smith, 2012). As such, their work is often developed with and for Indigenous community members, and focuses on praxis – the 'deep and explicit' connection of theory and practice that enables researchers 'to make an active change' in the situations they are examining (Brayboy, 2005: 440; Brayboy *et al.*, 2012; see also Lather, 1986; McCarty & Wyman, 2009).

In this chapter, we identify ways in which Richard Ruiz's scholarly work provides key insights for policy makers who are working through the choices, dilemmas and contradictions accompanying relatively new policy and research stances toward Indigenous languages in endangered language contexts (cf. Hornberger, 2006). In addition, we synthesize recent examples of ethnographic research focused on understanding and supporting Indigenous youth multilingualism in diverse contexts in Canada, the US, Australia, the Circumpolar North, Asia and Latin America, discussing key themes in light of Ruiz's influential writings on language orientations (1984, 2010c), language planning in Indigenous communities (1995), voice (1991), and Ruiz's work with his close colleague Luis Moll on educational sovereignty and promising directions for related research (Moll & Ruiz, 2002, 2005). We also speak to Ruiz's legacy from our varying relationships to Ruiz as scholars with longstanding connections to Indigenous language planning. Wyman, a non-Indigenous scholar who has conducted research in southwestern Alaska with a focus on Indigenous youth multilingualism and language planning since the 1990s (Fredson *et al.*, 1998; Wyman, 2012, 2013; Wyman *et al.*, 2010a, 2010b), first read Ruiz's influential language planning research as a graduate student. She was then privileged to work alongside Ruiz for almost a decade as a young faculty member in the Language Reading and Culture department at the University of Arizona. Galla, a Native Hawaiian scholar, studied language planning with Ruiz as a graduate student at the University of Arizona. Since that time, she has brought her long-term interest in the use of digital technologies in Indigenous language planning to work in the American Indian Language Development Institute, Ka Haka 'Ula O Kéelikōlani College of Hawaiian Language at the University of Hawai'i Hilo, and her current work as a faculty member in the department of Language and Literacy Education at the University of British Columbia. Jiménez-Quispe, an Aymaran scholar with a strong background in language policy, also studied language planning with Ruiz as a graduate student at the University of Arizona, after working with Indigenous teachers and peoples to write a new educational law in Bolivia. Jiménez-Quispe now works as the first woman university president in the Pedagogical University of Bolivia, where she has the responsibility for improving professional development for Indigenous and all teachers across the country. Below we reflect from our varied positions and work with youth, adults and language planning efforts in different national and international contexts.

Using Ruiz's work, we identify major trends across recent Indigenous youth multilingualism studies, discussing tensions and possibilities for framing Indigenous youth as resources within multilayered contemporary policy environments and (trans)local Indigenous movements.

Resource Orientations to Language and Youth in Complex Policy Environments

In the field of language planning, Ruiz was most often cited for his work in distinguishing language orientations, in which he argued for a language-as-resource orientation as a productive and respectful framework for recognizing community strengths and forging political alliances. Ruiz's influential discussions of the ways that orientations to language frame what is seen as 'natural' and 'unthinkable' about language formed important, early thinking on the ways that language ideologies – power-laden assumptions about language that are shaped at conscious and subconscious levels (Woolard, 1998) – move across educational systems and society in ways that marginalize and/or empower language minority youth and communities. Over the course of his career, Ruiz also underscored the importance of recognizing the connections between language, identity and emotion, arguing that bi/multilingualism should be viewed as a good in and of itself.

Revising some of his early statements about potential tensions surrounding struggles for language rights (Ruiz, 1984), Ruiz also highly praised the way that many of his former students and close colleagues used language rights orientations to advocate for multilingual policies, programs and the empowerment of language minority communities around the world. In his later work, Ruiz argued that a language-as-resource orientation serves a precursor to language rights (Ruiz, 2010b). Writing with Moll, Ruiz additionally stressed the urgent need for research on the possibilities for reorganizing learning environments including schools to support the maintenance of marginalized communities' languages and Funds of Knowledge (González et al., 2005; Moll, 1992), and support communities' language rights (Moll & Ruiz, 2002, 2005).

Ruiz, and later many others, argued that within a language as resource (Ruiz, 1984, 2010b) framework, the value of language must be seen as multifaceted, and cannot be reduced to a narrowly framed, instrumentalist question of what languages can be used to do in the world. Ruiz was also a strong critic of the ways in which exoglossic language policies focus primarily outwards from Indigenous communities, and give primacy to dominant, often colonial languages, in schools (Ruiz, 1995). As Ruiz noted, such policies commonly operate upon faulty views originating in early Western social science that certain languages are languages of modernity, rationality, and economic and social mobility, while other languages like Indigenous languages are tied to traditional views and authentic practices, and bolster simplistic, binary assumptions that 'modern' and 'traditional' orientations and practices cannot co-exist with contemporary society (Ruiz, 1995, discussing Fishman, 1990; see also Lee, 2009; Wyman, 2012). Arguing that all languages have value based on links to identity and emotion, as well as instrumental functions, Ruiz further critiqued the ways in which exoglossic policies send strong messages about the 'hierarchical stratification of languages in society where some are better because they are more useful, some are small and invalid because there is little return for the investment of learning and using them' (Ruiz, 2010a: 8), undermining minority languages in the eyes of community members and contributing to language shift. Ruiz contrasted these policies with endoglossic – community oriented – policies that 'give primacy to and promote an (I)ndigenous language' (Ruiz, 1995: 75), arguing that Indigenous communities must use endoglossic policies to foster Indigenous language maintenance and reverse language shift, and be wary of mixed bilingual policies that easily fall short of achieving real parity between Indigenous languages and language(s) of wider communication (Ruiz, 1995: 78).

Acknowledging that education scholars must accommodate economic instrumentalist concerns, Ruiz (2010b) urged language planning and multi-lingual education scholars to keep in perspective how many endangered languages 'have lived for many generations without the esteem of outside communities in large part because their speakers give them value' irrespective of social mobility concerns, and work to 'create opportunities for the rest of us to gain some of that appreciation' (Ruiz, 2010b: 162). Asserting that 'a call for instrumentalism may include, but goes beyond, economics' (Ruiz, 2010b: 164), Ruiz also called on language planners to give 'guidance on how to promote the use of minority languages' (Ruiz, 2010b: 164) in multiple domains of everyday life and school curricula, to raise understanding of the ways that minority languages can serve as 'media of instruction' and 'as vehicles for social and cultural integration' (Ruiz, 2010b: 167).

Multiple trends in education and language policy have made Ruiz's arguments, and call to action, more important than ever in our current, global moment. International, federal and tribal policies have responded to growing international Indigenous movements and increasing worldwide trends toward increasing language endangerment by codifying the rights of Indigenous peoples to teach their ancestral languages in schools (McCarty *et al.*, 2015). In many countries around the world, as well, 'grass roots Indigenous movements have wrested educational control from the state, reclaiming local Indigenous authority over the content and medium of instruction in schools serving Indigenous students' (McCarty & Nicholas, 2012: 1). Broad political mobilization and the work of the United Nations Educational, Scientific and Cultural Organization (UNESCO) and others have increased the global use of mother tongue based and mother language education (MTB-MLE) and recognition of linguistic human rights (Tupas, 2014; see also Hornberger, 2006; López, 2009). In many countries in Latin America and elsewhere, laws offering explicit and broad support for Indigenous language education have increased, and Indigenous mobilization has extended related educational reform into teacher training colleges and universities (López, 2009). Studies show that 'the use of otherwise marginalized mother tongues in the classroom helps arrest the decline in their use in the broader social and public spaces of the community, elevate its status and prestige in the community and, in some cases, validate their viability as potential academic languages through the process of intellectualization' (Tupas, 2014: 114). Research also shows how multilingual education 'activates voices for reclaiming the local,' offering youth and their communities opportunities to reclaim, among other things, 'local knowledges, local identities, local languages, local practices, local voices, local literacies, local standards, local demands, local experiences, folk wisdom and native representations' (Hornberger, 2009: 206–207).

At the same time, mother tongue-based multilingual education 'continues to face structural and ideological challenges to its successful implementation' (Tupas, 2014: 113). In some countries 'vast gaps exist between apparent desire and implementation' of ambitious laws supporting Indigenous languages (López, 2009). In his work, Ruiz discussed how previous histories of language and power and continuing instrumentalist concerns have led many nations to adopt former colonial languages for official and public purposes, given the ways 'colonial power and its institutions have pervaded the life of the colony' (Ruiz, 1995: 175). Ruiz also wrote extensively on the ways that ideologies privileging English are deeply engrained in the US political psyche and power structures, noting how multiple policies such as anti-immigrant backlashes against bilingual education, commonplace schooling practices such as the tracking of English language learners in schools, and the high-stakes testing movement have worked against ongoing efforts to value and support minority community linguistic resources (Moll & Ruiz, 2002, 2005).

In recent decades, neoliberal policies have flowed across more centralized and decentralized educational systems around the world, further challenging multilingual policies in schools in diverse contexts. A growing array of actors have additionally become involved in constructing 'youth' as a sociocultural category, including, among others, economic analysts, leaders of powerful NGOs, global marketers of style-related products from music to clothing, and politicians who view youth as primary national security and international policy targets, given youth engagement in militarization and radicalism, and grassroots political movements around the world (Sukarieh & Tannock, 2015). As globalization creates uncertainty and worry about shifting market, job and societal conditions, educational policies have framed youth in secondary and higher educational settings, in particular, as needing skills for success in global markets; governments and NGOs have also promoted and grafted related ideologies and practices related to accountability, at-riskness and larger conceptions of teaching and learning onto educational institutions around the world (paraphrasing Hull *et al.*, 2009: 132, discussing Sukarieh & Tannock, 2008).

In many places, related policy agendas have centered around high-stakes assessment in school systems, and the promotion of English as a language of global power. In some contexts, high-stakes testing in English has worked as a de facto language policy (Menken, 2008), placing direct pressures on Indigenous school-based language programs, counteracting historic gains in Indigenous language planning (for example, see Wyman *et al.*, 2010a, 2010b). In some countries, dramatic changes in global markets have also reshaped local language ideologies, secondary and postsecondary educational systems, and the promotion of English as a new necessary language of international social mobility and migration, adding layers of language hierarchies into school systems that previously promoted other colonial languages such as Spanish (Reynolds, 2009; Messing, 2013). An expanding group of countries are 'exuberantly embracing English as an economic asset', while some regional polities have designated English as a language of future economic integration, further entrenching and reshaping 'inequalities of multilingualism' at the structural and ideological level (Tupas, 2014: 118, 114). Private schools in many countries have also started 'marketing English as a commodity representing an abstract indication of "quality education"' (Phyak & Bui, 2014: 109), as economic anxieties have fed an 'ever-expanding post-secondary education sector' (Sukarieh & Tannock, 2015).

Broad groups of policy makers are working to address the complexities and possibilities of multilingual education against this backdrop of historical and recent policy trends, seeking transformative opportunities in wide-ranging contexts, spaces and levels of schooling and society (Hornberger, 2006). A growing number of Indigenous and other language minority communities have also renewed their efforts to take more direct control and ownership over school systems and assessment practices (Housman et al., 2011), seeking systemic change that will firmly orient educational systems toward maintaining, reclaiming and augmenting, rather than undermining, community Funds of Knowledge and multilingualism as key community resources. Growing groups of transnationally connected actors in pro-Indigenous movements are also exchanging ideas of new ways to reform educational systems to embrace Indigenous knowledge and empower Indigenous communities (López, 2009; McCarty & Nicholas, 2014).

Scholars focusing on youth and globalization (Hull et al., 2009; Maira & Soep, 2005), English language pedagogy (Sarigianides et al., 2015) critical youth literacy (Jocson, 2015; Johnson & Rosario-Ramos, 2012), youth style and cultural practice (Bucholtz, 2002; Paris, 2012), youth and new media (Akom et al., 2008; Rymes, 2011), hip-hop studies (Alim et al., 2009) and youth activism and action research (Davis, 2009; Ginwright et al., 2006; Middaugh & Kirshner, 2015; Paris & Winn, 2013) have strongly critiqued the kinds of deficit assumptions about young people and their language practices that commonly bolster movements toward educational standardization. Many also argue for research that supports and strengthens young people's connections to marginalized, heritage communities and multilingual competencies as a source of empowerment, exploring the use of culturally sustaining pedagogies (McCarty & Lee, 2014; Paris & Alim, 2014) and calling for social and sociolinguistic justice (Bucholtz et al., 2014). Indigenous youth and multilingualism scholars with longstanding connections to Indigenous language planning efforts (McCarty & Wyman, 2009; Wyman, 2012; Wyman et al., 2014), have taken a similarly active stance, conducting research on the ways in which Indigenous youth and their communities are negotiating the trends above.

In the following sections, we share research on the ways youth are negotiating language asymmetries, ideologies and transformational possibilities in diverse contexts.

Indigenous Youth Language Ideologies

Until the late 1990s, the few language planning studies that focused on Indigenous youth in endangered language communities framed youth as 'problems to be fixed' en route to school achievement, bilingualism and/or reversing Indigenous language shift, 'beings in need of cultural re-programming' (Reynolds, 2009: 234) and/or as gullible imbibers of the 'cultural nerve gas' of new media (Krauss, 1998), (discussed in Wyman *et al.*, 2014). In the past two decades, many studies have illuminated a much more complex picture of the ways in which youth are actively interpreting and negotiating dominant and Indigenous language ideologies in the educational and social worlds around them.

In his early work, Ruiz (1995: 77) noted how language asymmetries are 'easily perceived by the children, whose motivation for learning the languages is affected by the perceived status associated with them'. Later, Moll and Ruiz (2002, 2005) discussed how language ideologies are also mediated in the processes that shape who students become. Noting how even children develop language ideologies that influence strong feelings about heritage languages and English, Moll and Ruiz discussed how these feelings are not simply transmitted in linear ways from adults, or language programs, policies and teacher practices in schools, to children, but also involve the ways in which children themselves observe language inequalities in society, and the language uses of peers around them, and shape their language uses accordingly (Moll & Ruiz, 2005).

To this day, many Indigenous youth negotiate dominant language ideologies and related discourses that stigmatize Indigenous languages as belonging to the past, and frame dominant languages as the route to social mobility (cf. May, 2015; Ruiz, 1995). In some settings, youth face punishment including suspension or expulsion for mere use of Indigenous languages to peers; recent related cases have occurred in US schools that have no overt language policy (Kroupa, 2014) and schools where Indigenous languages are taught at the primary level, but students are forbidden to speak vernacular languages at the secondary level, as in three recent cases in the Philippines (Tupas, 2015). In many more settings, Indigenous youth do not face overt discrimination against their languages in schools, yet read clear signs of structural racism in patterns of programming, staffing, everyday practices and overt and covert messages that send strong messages about which languages are valued, and which are ignored or treated as unvaluable. Damaging discourses about Indigenous language speakers as rural and backward also shape the structures and language ideologies that students encounter in some schools, in spite of favorable bilingual policies at the national level (Huaman, 2014). A dominant 'ideology of disfluency' further frames Indigenous language reclamation movements, youth and whole communities as 'unsuccessful' language learners when they do not reach the high bar of fluency for all (Meek, 2011).

Indigenous language ideologies, as well, can be 'complex, heterogeneous, contradictory, and even contentious' (Field & Kroskrity, 2009: 6) and emergent in ways that can be difficult for youth to navigate. As language shift progresses in endangered language communities, speakers and learners understandably value community members with high levels of Indigenous language competency; most commonly these are elders who are viewed as bearers of Indigenous knowledge and history. Related ideas about speaker-hood outside and within Indigenous communities can disenfranchise youth who might otherwise claim 'speakerhood in some form' (Hill, 2002), leading to denigration and/or misrecognition of youth's often hybrid and complex heteroglossic linguistic repertoires (McCarty et al., 2009). Discourses of pride and shame can also produce powerful 'ideological crosscurrents' for youth in endangered language settings (McCarty et al., 2006; see also Lee, 2007, 2009; Messing, 2013).

'(Y)outh language is generally monitored by laypeople and professionals alike as a harbinger of societal language maintenance or shift' (Woolard, 2011: 619), and language ideologies may proliferate quickly when community members and/or outsiders try to make sense of language endangerment, or maintain or document an endangered language (Hill, 2006; see also Field, 2009; Wyman, 2009). Adults sometimes mistakenly assume that Indigenous youth are turning away from their Indigenous identities by speaking dominant languages (Wyman, 2012), positioning youth as 'subjects of blame for cultural and linguistic loss in their communities' (Huaman, 2014: 72), 'shaming the shift generation' (Reynolds, 2009), and/or stigmatizing the language practices of youth (Anderson, 2009; Field & Kroskrity, 2009). Indigenous adults may also underestimate the remaining Indigenous language competencies of youth in shifting communities (McCarty et al., 2006) and respond to changing youth practices by lowering their expectations for endangered language learning and use, further naturalizing vicious cycles of ideological change and linguistic accommodation in everyday interactions (Wyman, 2012; see also Rymes, 2006). Some youth express frustration at being blamed for not speaking endangered languages when circumstances out of their control including historically oppressive language policies, dominant language schooling, parental choices to protect children from linguistic discrimination, neoliberal policies with drastic consequences on local economies, and/or family migration have reduced their language learning opportunities (Lee, 2007; Reynolds, 2009; Wyman, 2012, 2013). Other youth may express resentment when state policies that ostensibly support Indigenous languages, and/or prioritize Indigenous language speakers for particular jobs, are not accompanied by concrete opportunities for Indigenous language learning in schools (Muehlman, 2008).

At the same time, it would be a mistake to assume that orientations toward English as a language of global opportunity and/or intergenerational disconnect and miscommunication are primary forces of language shift and endangerment. A major theme coming out of the Indigenous youth multilingualism literature is how complex ideological mixes produce linguistic insecurities and/or related feelings of discomfort, embarrassment and/or shame among Indigenous youth who feel like they can't speak their ancestral languages, or speak them well. Young people's linguistic insecurities and feelings about Indigenous language use also stem from the ways in which many youth are growing up in educational ecologies marked by lack of access to key Indigenous language learning resources and opportunities (Lee, 2007, 2009, 2014; McCarty *et al.*, 2013; Wyman, 2012; Wyman *et al.*, 2014). Studies show how commonly youth in shifting communities continue to voice Indigenous language ideologies and related discourses that value elders as knowledge keepers, community practices and Indigenous languages as important to maintain and/or reclaim a unique worldview, knowledge system and identity. Almost all Indigenous youth multilingualism studies to date have also uncovered individuals and groups of youth who express strong desires to speak their Indigenous languages to strengthen their connections to elders, Indigenous knowledge systems and community practices, even when they do not see themselves as speakers. Many youth in diverse settings around the world further declare it is their responsibility to bring their languages into the future, seeing Indigenous languages as important cultural resources (Wyman *et al.*, 2014). Youth report and have been observed encouraging one another to speak their languages (Cru, 2015a; Wyman, 2012). Critical consciousness-raising efforts can also help youth move from 'emphasizing a discourse of speaker-centered shame to society-centered injustice' when youth discuss how their language uses and complex identities related to larger structural inequalities shape socio-economic status, rural–urban dynamics and migration (Huaman, 2014: 78).

Emerging ideologies related to language and identity 'are symbiotic with language revitalization efforts and are crucial to their success,' since they hold the potential to 'reinforce the high level of commitment needed to make grassroots language programs work' (Field & Kroskrity, 2009: 24). As we show below, a growing number of studies are highlighting concrete ways that Indigenous youth are working through the complexities of language ideologies and situations around them to become engaged in language reclamation and *language activism* – 'energetic action focused on language use' (Combs & Penfield, 2012: 462) in order to assert language rights and promote the wellbeing of their communities. The combined scholarly literature also shows how Indigenous youth in many contexts are (re)valuing Indigenous languages as important cultural resources in ways that cut across national borders, regions of the world, rural and urban divides, speaker/non-speaker binaries, and on- and offline behaviors, offering promising possibilities for Indigenous language planning and policy.

Youth, Educational Ecologies and Educational Sovereignty

Throughout his career, Ruiz asserted that recognition of minority languages as resources in schools could have a dramatic effect on the social, emotional and academic wellbeing of language minority students and their communities. In his later work with Moll, Ruiz also powerfully argued that scholars who wish to support language minority youth and their communities must vigilantly seek to disrupt the structural forces that rob minority communities of language resources. Moll and Ruiz (2005: 310, discussing van Dijk, 1996) noted that 'a key dimension of ideologies is their cross-situational potential as socially-shared resources for thinking, for both groups and individuals, that can be drawn upon (or not) and applied in different contexts.' They also sought new ways to conceptualize minority group rights to additive forms of education that would honor and build upon students' cultural and linguistic resources.

In his work with Moll, Ruiz was inspired by the work of Lomawaima, McCarty and others to develop the term *educational sovereignty* and expand this concept to envision new directions for the schooling of minority youth in general, and Latino/a youth, in particular. As Moll and Ruiz (2005: 296) wrote, 'We use the term educational sovereignty to capture the need to challenge the arbitrary authority of the white power structure to determine the essence of education for Latino/a (and other minority) students.' To promote educational sovereignty, Moll and Ruiz placed strong emphasis on the importance of 'challenging the ideological and structural constraints that are so dominant' in the schooling of language minority youth through research that situates 'teaching and learning within a broader educational ecology', and research that strategically and vigorously builds on 'the culturally-grounded resources of children, families and communities' (Moll & Ruiz, 2002: 368) to create additive forms of schooling. Seeing educational sovereignty as 'a term of both resistance and affirmation, signaling the recognition of a negative history to be challenged, and the hope of a positive future to be grasped', (Moll & Ruiz, 2005: 296), Moll and Ruiz further laid out promising directions for research to improve the educational conditions of Latino/a and other language minority youth, which we will discuss below.

Today, leading scholars in Indigenous education argue that the concept of educational sovereignty offers a vision of 'a pedagogic positioning firmly rooted in its own self-determined linguistic and cultural identifications, yet expansive enough to respect and reciprocate the linguistic and cultural traditions of others' (McCarty & Lee, 2015: 357). Noting how '(e)ducational sovereignty is an act of community building and change to reflect community needs, resources, and goals' (McCarty & Lee, 2015: 344), they also underscore Moll and Ruiz's argument that, '(a)n essential dimension of educational sovereignty is the extent to which communities feel themselves to be in control of their language behaviors' (Moll & Ruiz, 2005: 299, discussed in McCarty & Lee, 2014).

Ruiz (1995: 78) noted that the implementation of endoglossic policies and related efforts to reshape education 'must work to strengthen both instrumental and sentimental functions for the (I)ndigenous language in the community. They also must be comprehensive in scope,' commenting:

> (G)enerally, the more formal the contexts in which language policy is implemented, the less effect it will have on language maintenance. This means that the electronic and print media, social activities, social service providers, and other everyday centers of community life must be included in the implementation strategies by which language policies are promoted. In this way, our language policies have more of a chance to become more closely associated with our language behavior. (Ruiz, 1995: 78)

Throughout his career, Ruiz urged language planning scholars to attend to the affective value and usefulness of languages for often-unrecognized instrumental functions, seeking to understand community members' uses, and potential uses, of language in activities, spaces, services and forms of media that are commonly erased in school contexts. Moll and Ruiz (2005) underscored, for instance, the importance of looking at non-school settings as essential spaces for extending the educational ecology of children, noting how such spaces depend 'crucially on the network of support it can generate' (Moll & Ruiz, 2005: 313–314) and how involved community members can help mediate constraints to sustain learning in community-based settings.

Multiple studies now highlight ways that Indigenous youth may connect to Indigenous knowledge by intently observing and learning side by side with adults, take up increasing responsibilities as they 'pitch in' with family and community work, and/or participate in ritual activities (Rogoff, 2014; Urrieta, 2013). Even as Indigenous language resources are eroding and communities actively worry about language shift and endangerment, youth may have continuing opportunities to develop language competencies and strong attachments to Indigenous languages and Indigenous knowledge systems as they participate in ceremonial activities, historically rooted family and community land-use practices, and/or more recently adopted cultural practices. Some Pueblo youth in the southwestern United States and many youth from rural Indigenous communities in Latin America, for instance, develop Indigenous language competencies as they work in fields alongside relatives in family- and community-scale farming in rural and/or agricultural regions (Huaman, 2014).

Many Indigenous language programs in endangered language communities seek to reclaim Indigenous language learning by involving youth in ceremonial and/or land-use practices. Youth from the Cochiti Pueblo in the southwestern United States, for instance, have reconnected to ancestral farming practices through a community-based language revitalization program (Huaman, 2014). A recent study in Ottawa, Canada, also shows how family literacy programs in community centers can provide the context for urban Inuit to 'mak(e) spatial and material connections to cultural and linguistic knowledge and to the practices associated with Inuit homelands' (Patrick et al., 2013), by engaging youth and adults in storytelling activities around objects related to land-use practices like hunting and fishing.

Reflecting on work with youth in the Hawaiian language revitalization movement, Wilson and Kamanā (2014) note the importance of connecting language revitalization movements to place, deep understanding of Indigenous knowledge systems, and related ancestral language and land-use practices. At the same time, in seeking linguistic and educational sovereignty, Indigenous language advocates must counter 'two world', colonizing stereotypes that reinforce faulty ideas that Indigenous languages and forms of knowledge are solely connected to traditional land-use practices, and/or face-to-face local activities, and are therefore unfit for use in schools (Wilson & Kamanā, 2014). Nicholas's recent research underscores how many Hopi youth growing up in ancestral villages have participated from birth in activities associated with Hopi cultural institutions – baby namings, weddings, traditions – planting corn by hand, social dances and religious rites of passage and ceremonies. Among Nicholas' research participants, such experiences fostered a shared 'sense of belonging and responsibility,' aesthetic connection to a collective Hopi way of life, and 'emotional commitments to the ideals of a communal society' (Nicholas, 2008: 338). Participation in community-based activities ranging from a men's sacred society to a Miss Indian Arizona competition also helped individuals expand their knowledge of dynamic cultural practices, deepen their commitment to Hopi as an endangered ancestral language, and take up additional Indigenous language learning (Nicholas, 2014) as youth took particular gendered and individualized pathways into community life in a rapidly shifting context.

Wyman's (2009, 2012, 2013) longitudinal study of Yup'ik youth in a rural Alaskan village undergoing language shift also showed how youth develop language ideologies and competencies in relation to both collective and individualized experiences with historically rooted and more recently adopted cultural practices. Almost all of the youth in Wyman's study used Yup'ik and translanguaged as they participated in valued hunting, fishing and gathering practices with adults and one another, and shared stories with peers about their experiences in taking up increasing responsibilities and related gender roles in a contemporary subsistence society. At the same time, young people's language ideologies, communicative repertoires and confidence levels using Yup'ik beyond token words, phrases and predictable statements also varied according to young people's individualized trajectories, as youth navigated particular family language policy-making situations (King *et al.*, 2008), and experiences with schooling, community institutions, peer groups, new media, migration and post-secondary opportunities. As a whole, the longitudinal study highlighted the power of collective opportunities for Indigenous language learning through connection to culturally significant land-use practices and related forms of Indigenous knowledge. It also underscored the importance of attending to young people's learning opportunities, practices and emerging language ideologies as youth accumulate specific experiences within dynamic families, communities-of-practice, institutions and (trans) local spaces over time.

Praxis-oriented research that explores Indigenous young people's uptake and use of technology and new media further expands our awareness of the ways in which Indigenous young people's learning opportunities and educational ecologies extend across digital, as well as face-to-face networks.

Digital Technologies and Networked Publics

In their work on educational sovereignty, Moll and Ruiz (2005) critiqued digital divides, and the discrepancies between the kinds of intellectual work done with technology in schools serving wealthier and more marginalized and lower class communities. They also encouraged researchers to consider how to 'use technology to create fundamentally new circumstances' for young people's schooling (Moll & Ruiz, 2005: 316). Many Indigenous communities are on the wrong side of digital divides, even as Indigenous youth become increasingly connected to the internet around the world and take up mobile communication devices. While some countries including Mexico and Peru have adopted ambitious one-to-one laptop programs in schools, recent research in these and other contexts underscores how 'simple access to technology has not provided much benefit, and often worsens classic educational divides' (Warschauer, 2012: 134), and the importance of the 'social envelope' that technology comes in, in terms of the 'technical and social support provided to children as they learn' (Warschauer, 2012: 131; Waschauer & Matuchniak, 2010).

Many Indigenous scholars and others have now explored the potential of digital technologies for Indigenous language revitalization and reclamation efforts. Galla (2009, 2010, 2012) discusses how technology can preserve aspects of Indigenous languages, provide opportunities for materials to be developed and disseminated across geographical boundaries, create new domains for language use, raise the visibility of Indigenous languages and bring youth who are primary users of technology together with elders who are language and culture experts. The incorporation of digital technologies in language revitalization efforts supports what Ruiz continuously advocated for: spaces that create the conditions for empowering the voice(s) of minority language speakers and learners (Ruiz, 1991). Youth are now involved in intergenerational digital efforts ranging from projects documenting elders' Indigenous oratory to projects creating language learning materials including books, films and talking dictionaries (examples in McCarty *et al.*, 2014). Indigenous youth and young adults in many communities are also developing language apps to support the learning of endangered languages (examples in Petersen, 2013). Wide-ranging educational spaces support this work, including technology courses in Indigenous language institutes (McCarty *et al.*, 2014), youth-focused Indigenous language planning efforts in transnational NGOs (Tulloch, 2014), and community-based critical media production programs that target youth from diverse backgrounds, such as the Youth Radio program's Mobile Action Lab (Soep, 2015). Many young Indigenous language activists are also exploring new possibilities for integrating media- and placed-based forms of education in particular language reclamation efforts. Kroupa and his Arikara colleagues, for instance, have sought new means of engaging youth in technology-enhanced language learning through texting and an Arikara language learning app, even as they have worked to rebuild physical ceremonial spaces to support the renewal of community life and Indigenous language learning among youth on the Arikara reservation (Kroupa, 2014, 2015). As youth and young leaders seek to integrate Indigenous language and culture reclamation across spaces and networks, their work disrupts common assumptions about Indigenous language learning, and binary assumptions about face-to-face and digital learning environments.

Intergenerational digital storytelling is another strong thread within a broader movement to indigenize media 'as the appropriation and transformation of technologies to meet the cultural and political needs of indigenous peoples' (Iseke & Moore, 2011: 32, discussing Prins, 2004). Intergenerational sensitivity, Indigenous language ideologies and ethical issues related to the control, framing and distribution of Indigenous knowledge must all be carefully considered within efforts to use Indigenous languages and Indigenous Funds of Knowledge in new media. Iseke and Moore (2011) share processes they have used to foster collaborative relationships of respect and reciprocity in various stages of community-based digital storytelling projects involving Indigenous elders and youth from their Métis and Mik'maw communities, respectively, while offering youth opportunities to reaffirm storytelling traditions, challenge stereotypical representations, and take control of self-representation through video production.

Indigenous youth are also fostering critical language awareness by connecting to community knowledge and recreating ways of being Indigenous within new *networked publics* – 'publics that are restructured by networked technologies' that simultaneously serve as '(1) the space constructed through networked technologies and (2) the imagined collective that emerges as a result of the intersection of people, technology, and practice' (boyd, 2010: 1). Multiple studies, for instance, are exploring Indigenous young people's language use on social networking sites such as Facebook. Recent research with Yucatec Mayan youth in Mexico shows how youth may experiment with Indigenous language use in social media spaces, using features that are commonly stigmatized in school spaces, such as inconsistent spelling of Indigenous languages, and features common to online environment print such as the vague division of spoken and written word, and combinations of borrowed terms from dominant languages and slang. As youth support language experimentation and linguistic flexibility in moment-to-moment positioning with peers online, this may help minimize young peoples' feelings of linguistic insecurity toward Indigenous language use (Cru, 2015a).

Multiple studies additionally show how work with digital media can provide key learning opportunities and generate networks in contexts where formal educational institutions fall short of providing culturally responsive (Brayboy & Castagno, 2009) and/or culturally sustaining and revitalizing pedagogy (McCarty & Lee, 2014, building on Paris & Alim, 2014). Kral's long-term, engaged research with Indigenous youth in Australia shows how government investment in media design spaces within youth centers, libraries and arts centers in some remote Indigenous communities has created affordances for Indigenous youth to acquire technological expertise, engage in digital multimedia and music production, and work on cultural heritage and entrepreneurial projects with elders. In these centers, youth developed innovative community-centered multimodal projects and took up new local professional and leadership roles in ways that were particularly striking given very high secondary-school leaving rates (Kral, 2012). Kral has also showed how some youth demonstrated high motivation to write Indigenous languages and develop hybrid language practices in social media spaces, as they simultaneously negotiated nonexistent opportunities to develop Indigenous language literacy in schools (Kral, 2015).

Social media spaces dedicated to particular Indigenous languages may create ways for community members to share and increase linguistic competences in endangered languages, as youth and adults work through the complexities of language shift, endangerment and reclamation across 'sociolinguistic borderlands' (McCarty, 2014) and 'repertoires of difference' (Rymes, 2011), within communities that stretch across rural and urban spaces, and/or national borders. On a public social media site devoted to the Yup'ik language in Alaska, for instance, youth and adults share stories, as well as questions and insights concerning the complex, sociolinguistic and emotional dynamics of Indigenous language endangerment, shift and reclamation, often crowdsourcing specific questions about Yup'ik terms, use, spelling and/or translation (Gilmore & Wyman, 2013).

In their discussions of educational sovereignty, Moll and Ruiz highlighted research on the ways that '(I)ndigenous communities on both sides of the Mexico-US border use electronic media to convey information on health, political reform, education, and language to each other' (Moll & Ruiz, 2005: 298, discussing Bixler-Marquez, 1998). Moll and Ruiz argued that, 'The control (these communities) have over the dissemination of essential information is an exercise in educational sovereignty' since 'it affords them the opportunity to decide how and to what degree they will interact with the communities around them' (Moll & Ruiz, 2005: 298). In the US, Canada and elsewhere, one way that Indigenous community members are currently sharing information on issues of concern is the use of hashtag activism across new media platforms, as in the recent 'Dear Native youth' Twitter campaign where Indigenous adults offered youth strength, encouragement and advice for negotiating the challenges of damaging school systems, the #MMIW (Missing and Murdered Indigenous women) campaign, and the Idle No More campaigns originating in Canada (Recollet, 2015). Native Hawaiian youth and young adult teachers from immersion schools have played prominent, leading roles in the #WeAreMaunakea movement that began in Hawai'i to protect sacred sites.

Together, these trends and related studies highlight how Indigenous youth can become agents who use media to create educational opportunities and societal change as they respond to inequities and the potential loss of Indigenous knowledge alongside adults. While not all of the media-related efforts above are focused on Indigenous language per se, together these offer insights into new possibilities for Indigenous educational sovereignty. In the following sections, we share additional examples of Indigenous youth media and language activism.

Indigenous Youth Cultural Production in New Transnational Linguistic Markets: Indigenous Hip-hop

In a world of continuing and new flows of people, resources and ideologies, Moll and Ruiz (2005) wrote of the potential for new transnational dynamics to create new 'linguistic marketplaces,' reshaping ideas about language proficiencies and capital in the global economy. They also noted how multiple dynamics 'may help establish the desirability of bilingualism and biliteracy for all populations' (Moll & Ruiz, 2005: 316), by repositioning language minority youth in new ways as part of peoples who form part of larger and international communities.

Leading scholars of critical language pedagogies are seeking new ways to extend previous research to consider how youth may simultaneously see themselves as part of specific heritage communities, and also (trans)local communities that form around particular forms of youth cultural production (Paris & Alim, 2014). Indigenous hip-hop serves as a particularly strong example of the ways Indigenous youth are challenging damaging assumptions about Indigenous languages within (trans)national flows of youth culture, taking advantage of new linguistic marketplaces, and using both heritage and youth-related language practices as members of particular Indigenous communities, pan-Indigenous communities and hip-hop communities. 'Indigenous hip-hop artists throughout the Americas are currently challenging cultural genocide and contemporary post-racial discourse by utilizing ancestral languages in hip-hop cultural production' (Navarro, 2015: 1), drawing inspiration from a transnational cultural movement that places value on finding authentic means of 'keeping in real' in ways that seek to disrupt racism and other forms of marginalization (Alim *et al.*, 2009). Many Indigenous hip-hop artists 'utilize hip-hop as a medium to engage the process of decolonization by: (1) disseminating a conscious pan-Indigeneity through their lyricism and calls to alliance building; (2) retaining and teaching Indigenous languages through their songs, and (3) implementing a radical orality in their verses that revitalizes both Indigenous oral traditions/storytelling and the early politicized "message rap" of the 1970s and 1980s,' aiding decolonization work by reinforcing 'collective pan-Indigenous consciousness' and connecting with transnational Indigenous movements across the Americas 'that all fight for greater Indigenous cultural and political rights in the Americas' (Navarro, 2015: 2–3).

Young Indigenous rappers and artists may shape their music in relation to multiple community-based Indigenous institutions that reflect longer-running Indigenous movements. A quickly-growing Indigenous language hip-hop movement in the Yucatan peninsula, for example, attracts youth to language revitalization work through 'the central place that orality, verbal fluency and creativity play in its lyrics'; and also the way that youth value rap as a music genre that they associate with modernity (Cru, 2015b: 4). In the region, Mayan cultural agencies' ideologies of linguistic purism exist in tension with youth and community members' hybrid language practices. Nevertheless, young rappers work with an adult language activist from their community to post transcripts of lyrics on YouTube in a standardized orthography. Youth also participate in Mayan cultural institute song contests, and use regional Indigenous radio stations to distribute their music to Mayan speakers in Yucatan. By separating Mayan and Spanish language stanzas in their music and actively using multiple platforms, youth use strategic essentialism to claim space in varying linguistic markets, while they make their work accessible to non-Mayan speaking community members abroad (Cru, 2015b).

Jiménez-Quispe (2013) and others show how hip-hop has been taken up as a central form of Indigenous youth expression, transnational connection and political commentary in Bolivia, as well. The epicenter of the hip-hop revolution in Bolivia is El Alto, a large, predominantly Indigenous city near La Paz that grew rapidly after a drought, neoliberal economic policies and the privatization of public and industries caused massive urban migration across the country (Tarifa, 2013: 399). Since that time, El Alto has become a central site of youth protest in the country's dramatic transformation toward a pro-Indigena government and the first Indigenous president, and a vibrant and powerful group of Indigenous youth have embraced hip-hop as a way to express new cosmopolitan and Indigenous identities through hybrid music in Spanish, Quechua, Aymaran and English. Multiple studies have documented how the Indigenous youth of El Alto have played an important role in the social transformation of Bolivia, and how the hip-hop artists of El Alto have played active roles promoting critically conscious transnational Indigenous identities within the hip-hop networks of Latin America and beyond (Hornberger & Swinehart, 2012; Jiménez-Quispe, 2013; Tarifa, 2013).

There are many complexities as Indigenous young people engage with media, education and activism through new cultural forms. While some Indigenous hip-hop artists express new visions of Indigenous feminist, anti-colonial work (Jiménez-Quispe, 2013; Navarro, 2014; Tarifa, 2013), for instance, others may take up 'defiant Indigeneity' and sovereignty in ways that simultaneously imagine and forward heteronormative and patriarchal visions of Indigenous power (Teves, 2011: 93; cf. Paris & Alim, 2014). Indigenous hip-hop artists may tap into flows of youth cultural trends promoted by large corporate industries such as MTV who sell youth cultural production, youth critique and visions of youth activism to large audiences around the world, while they simultaneously shape 'forms of knowledge transfer and social mobilization' that proceed somewhat 'independently of the actions of corporate capital and the nation-state system' in grassroots globalization (Appadurai, 2000: 3). Artists' varying communicative repertoires and (non-)access to Indigenous language learning opportunities additionally shape whether, when, how and how much artists use Indigenous languages as they support and promote Indigenous collective identities and critical Indigenous perspectives in their work.

Nevertheless, studies show how many Indigenous youth and adults are working through these complexities in ways that revalue Indigenous languages in transnational linguistic marketplaces through hip-hop, using processes that can be fruitfully compared to other forms of Indigenous knowledge exchange, organizing and empowerment in globalization. Hornberger and Swinehart (2012), for instance, compare the transnational linguistic revaluing and connection taking place in Wayna Rap in El Alto to that of the well-known PROEIB-Andes master's program in bilingual intercultural education in Cochabamba, Bolivia, which serves Indigenous students from across Latin America. In their analysis, the researchers show how, in both Wayna Rap and PROEIB, 'speakers' fluency in Indigenous languages and Spanish affords them added symbolic capital in the social marketplace (Bourdieu, 1991) of both Bolivian and globalized, transnational networks, disrupting language ideologies of Indigeneity in the Andes' (Hornberger & Swinehart, 2012: 499). Indigenous members in both sites are also empowered to draw on their full communicative repertoires, using 'multilingual, multimodal, and mixed-code communicative practices' (Hornberger & Swinehart, 2012: 500) and voices.

Our final examples focus on arrangements that support youth taking up new identities and empowering themselves within educational systems and engaged, intergenerational policy-making efforts.

Transforming Indigenous Youth Academic and Policy-making Pathways

In their work on educational sovereignty, Moll and Ruiz (2002) argued for the importance of research that explored 'the reorganization of the schooling experience itself to mediate ingrained structural constraints,' and help youth 'reenvision their opportunities and identities as academics' in ways that allow them to remain connected to their heritages. They also argued for research that promotes 'forms of schooling that deliberately attempt to build upon the resources of the students and their communities in doing academic work' (Moll & Ruiz, 2002). Moll and Ruiz asserted that educational sovereignty signals 'the strength and power a social setting like a school can garner by developing strategic social networks to create '"cultural spaces" that will enhance its autonomy, mediate ideological and programmatic constraints, and provide additive forms of schooling for its students' (Moll & Ruiz, 2005: 300). They also noted that 'perhaps the best examples of the type of educational sovereignty we are proposing can be found in the literature on (I)ndigenous schooling' (Moll & Ruiz, 2005: 298).

Multiple ethnographic case studies now highlight how particular Indigenous communities have built individual schools that stand as shining examples of school-based language reclamation, and culturally sustaining and revitalizing pedagogy (McCarty & Lee, 2014; see also McCarty & Nicholas, 2014). The Māori movement in New Zealand and the Hawaiian movement in the US have further demonstrated how relatively small but energetic efforts to foster school–community connections around language reclamation can grow over time to positively affect entire K-12 school systems, higher educational settings, and wider and wider swaths of community members (Hermes & Kawai'ae'a, 2014; Wilson & Kamanā, 2011).

Indigenous youth multilingualism research could benefit tremendously from additional research on youth language ideologies, learning experiences, and young people's trajectories within these schools and movements.

A recent study of Indigenous students' interactions in one school in Paraguay demonstrates how processes of change emerging over multiple timescales in educational systems may help Indigenous youth mediate damaging, historically rooted ideological assumptions about language and academic identities. In the study, Mortimer and Wortham analyzed how the implementation of multilingual policies over the course of decades, the practices developed in one classroom over the course of months, and specific short-term classroom events all combined to help a group of young Guarani students ideologically value and affirm a Guarani classmate's identity as an Indigenous language-speaking, rural, low-income student who also achieved high academic performance. Through their interpretations of their classmate's Indigenous language proficiency and academic achievement, youth showed how they were in the process of moving beyond damaging language ideologies and stereotypes born of 'centuries-long histories of colonialism and language contact,' that associated Indigenous language speaking, ruralness and poverty with ignorance and rudeness (Mortimer & Wortham, 2015: 169).

Multiple recent studies have also shown the potential for Indigenous youth to reclaim endangered languages once they leave constrained secondary school environments and enter higher educational spaces that encourage Indigenous language learning, planning and policy. In one study of 'former youth' in Tlaxcala, Mexico, for instance, participants recalled how they took up a new dedication to Mexicano language and culture after they encountered a pro-Indigena discourse and even single related assignments in university classes (Messing, 2013). Lee (2014) has used activities in undergraduate classes to raise Navajo and Pueblo young people's critical Indigenous consciousness about language issues, engaging youth in deep reflection on their language learning pathways, community situations and possibilities for language reclamation. In their collaborative autoethnography, Chew *et al.* (2015) detail the ways that they themselves have used higher education spaces to reclaim their ancestral languages of Chickasaw, Wampanoag and Southern Washoe, respectively, creating new discourses, spaces and uses for Indigenous languages while empowering themselves as young adult language activists and graduate students.

Studies are also beginning to show how the collective empowerment of young adults within higher educational spaces may lead to increased language learning opportunities for younger groups of students in Indigenous communities. Kroupa, for instance, describes how he and a small group of young men from the critically endangered Arikara language community formed a passionate community of practice dedicated to Indigenous language reclamation, transforming their lives by working with a linguistic anthropologist, reclaiming resources from ethnographic archives and organizing peer-focused immersion efforts at the University of Indiana. Over time, the young leaders have expanded their efforts to develop online and community-based language learning opportunities for elementary and secondary school youth (Kroupa, 2014, 2015).

Access to language in higher educational spaces 'must be complemented by space which privileges Indigenous knowledge and languages, and allows Indigenous students to develop as scholars and professionals committed to language reclamation work' (Chew *et al.*, 2015: 85); such campus spaces for the expression and sharing of student feelings and ideas coupled with intellectualization and critical thinking on language issues remain scarce (Huaman & Stokes, 2011). To help diverse Indigenous university students who did not have access to 'courses on Indigenous languages, revitalization, policy development and advocacy, and program administration' pursue goals ranging from learning their own languages to learning about language policy, Huaman and Stokes developed a face-to-face language group and an Indigenous language and policy-focused blog at the Santa Fe Indian School, which they modeled on a 'Reclaiming Mothertongues' blog set up at another university. The 'confluent physical and virtual spaces' offered students opportunities to 'cultivate not only a sense of fellowship, but also consider solution-oriented language work, whether at home, in their communities, or thousands of miles away at school' (Huaman & Stokes, 2011: 9). The website created by Huaman, Stokes and their students also allowed contributors 'to rapidly connect with the activities and experiences of others to gain exposure to a variety of language possibilities within revitalization, protection, preservation and maintenance – including specific ideas around leadership, policy development and advocacy, fellowship and acknowledgement and celebration of successes' and served as 'a controlled and centralized repository of digital and multi-media resources, from journal articles on language policy to Inupiaq rap' (Huaman & Stokes, 2011: 10).

Galla, Wyman and Jiménez-Quispe have participated in a set of annual, hybrid videoconference courses that have used digital spaces and tools to bring a 'critical mass of prominent Indigenous and non-Indigenous scholars together with emerging Indigenous faculty and students in an international space for Indigenous collaboration' for almost a decade (Galla *et al.*, 2014: 194). The videoconference courses, which focus on Indigenous knowledge and Indigenous wellbeing, were originally developed by leading scholars of Indigenous education, including leaders of the Hawaiian language immersion schools, to 'affirm subaltern knowledge, create "free spaces" for identity affirmation and reconstruction, and provide access to academic power in higher education' (Gilmore, 2010: 2). The courses are now run primarily by Indigenous faculty who work together with students across post-secondary institutions in Hawaii, Arizona, Alaska, New Zealand and Canada (Galla *et al.*, 2014). Among other important outcomes, the courses have helped young adult Hawaiian immersion school graduates and other second language learners of Hawaiian develop awareness of Indigenous education efforts and issues in diverse contexts, and join a global network of Indigenous scholar-activists as they have taken up new identities as immersion teachers, and worked on developing curricula centered on Indigenous knowledge for new generations of students.

Indigenous students in higher education may very actively engage language policy and practice (Davis, 2014; Davis & Phyak, 2015; Phyak & Bui, 2014), by working across academic and community spaces, and participating in direct efforts to change formal policies alongside Indigenous adults. At Tribhuvan university in Nepal, for instance, Phyak has encouraged Indigenous youth to take up 'important roles toward ensuring that indigenous linguistic, cultural, and educational rights are upheld' in a new Nepali constitution that has been the focus of intense negotiation and ratification in a dynamic and contested national policy context (Pyhak & Bui, 2014: 102). Phyak also facilitates a *Language Policy and Youth* project, 'join(ing) (I)ndigenous young people in ELP activities such as marching in mass street rallies for linguistic, political, and cultural rights; exploring linguistic, educational, and political inequalities; participating in critical dialogue about how ideologies shape language policies; holding awareness-raising workshops; and supporting development of plans for creating schools as multilingual spaces.' Importantly, Phyak works with both Indigenous youth and village leaders to observe language practices in and out of school, organizing 'village meetings to discuss issues concerning language, education, and development' and strategize ways to create 'space for indigenous languages and cultures in school and other public spheres' (Davis & Phyak, 2015: 149).

In a transnational policy-making effort, Inuit young people have increasingly claimed 'voice, choice and agency' (Tulloch, 2014, discussing Hornberger, 2006; McCarty, 2006) in their work alongside adults as intergenerational language planners and policy makers in the Inuit Circumpolar Council. As members of the Inuit Circumpolar Youth Council, Inuit university students and others come together from across Alaska, Canada, Russia and Greenland to generate strategies for addressing language endangerment within and across their home communities and countries. Early in the work, youth council members had to negotiate challenges like a council-wide policy requiring everyone to make formal representations solely in Inuit languages, which showed a lack of understanding of young people's situations growing up with varying competencies in communities undergoing language shift without access to strong immersion programs. Working through these and other challenges with community members in sustained engagement over time, youth and adults in the council developed a powerful intergenerational discourse of care and shared commitment to language policy making in and out of the council (Tulloch, 2014).

The work of Jaqi Aru, a group of urban Indigenous linguistics students at the University of El Alto in Bolivia, serves as one of the most dramatic examples of a sustained youth language planning effort involving activities that are simultaneously located within academic institutions, online, and across local and transnational communities. Additionally, the group shows how Indigenous academics can play a key role in making space for Indigenous students to take advantage of online affordances provided by transnational digital activist groups to empower themselves and create new resources for their communities. In a long-term effort with Ruben Hillari, Victoria Tinta and the organization Global Voices, a group of Aymaran students who migrated to the city from rural villages as older youth and students who grew up in El Alto have created a massive online space featuring news and cultural items in Aymaran. The Jaqi Aru group has published thousands of articles together, and framed their work as creating online content both for Aymaran community members in Bolivia, Peru, Chile, Spain and elsewhere who have access to the internet, and rural Aymaran community members who will access the internet in the future. The group spreads word of their activities through Twitter, Facebook, YouTube and Flickr; in recent years, the group has also worked on creating a Facebook interface and Wikipedia site in Aymaran (Jiménez-Quispe, 2013).

Together, these examples show how higher educational spaces are key resources for Indigenous youth and communities. They also evidence some of the ways in which sustained intergenerational collaborations can draw upon and/or reconfigure higher educational spaces to promote Indigenous knowledge creation within broader language planning and policy movements.

Discussion

As we have demonstrated above, Indigenous youth multilingualism research is illuminating a wide variety of contexts, cultural flows, educational spaces and configurations within which 'young people are given the opportunity to learn alongside and about previous generations,' and interact 'with members of older generations who not only are willing to share the lessons learned through the communities' histories of struggle, but also allow young people to actively contribute to and shape the direction of new efforts for social change' (Johnson & Rosario-Ramos, 2012: 53; cf. Torre & Fine, 2006; Ginwright & Cammarota, 2006; Wyman et al., 2014). Around the world, Indigenous youth are engaging the central power of self-definition and self-determination through Indigenous language activism, finding and creating dynamic venues of Indigenous multilingual, multiliterate and intergenerational voice and empowerment (cf. Ruiz, 1991). In many Indigenous communities, young people's negotiations and multilingual practices are also part of ongoing, intergenerational efforts to assert educational sovereignty 'by tapping into existing cultural resources in both local and distant communities to situate and redefine teaching and learning within a broader educational ecology' (Moll & Ruiz, 2005: 306; 2002). Recognizing the educational ecologies of Indigenous students in and out of formal educational spaces, the expression of Indigenous voices on and offline and new forms of Indigenous language activism expand our understanding of the instrumental and sentimental functions for Indigenous languages, thereby countering damaging and powerful assumptions that languages associated with modernity and traditional heritage practices are inherently separate, and cannot co-exist (Ruiz, 1995). Examples like the ones above also powerfully show how 'advocacy of the retention of Indigenous languages, does not presuppose an essentialized understanding of the language-identity link, nor a retreat into the equivalent of a bucolic, antediluvian, rural (Indigenous) romanticism epitomized in the traditional rural–urban divide' (May, 2014: 232). One need not be an essentialist to resist the loss of Indigenous languages that 'carry cultural knowledge and ways of being – a certain habitus if you will – that are threatened right along with them' (Lyons, 2010: 139).

Many studies above additionally disrupt commonplace assumptions about which languages do and do not support the development of academic identities by showing how young people may choose to learn and expand their uses of heritage and endangered languages as they move into young adulthood (cf. He, 2010; Woolard, 2011), and how university spaces might be restructured to support related opportunities for additive learning in a global, interconnected world. Such studies are timely and relevant for policy makers seeking to reform post-secondary educational institutions to redress past linguistic oppressions, create new pathways for Indigenous students and Indigenous language learning, and become more responsive to Indigenous communities. As part of the broad vision of the recent Truth and Reconciliation Commission (TRC) in Canada, for instance, policy makers are urging post-secondary institutions to respond to the urgent needs for Aboriginal language revitalization by creating university and college degree and diploma programming to support the development of learners' proficiency and competency in Aboriginal languages (TRC, 2015). In Latin America, as well, Indigenous multilingual education efforts in multiple countries are now focusing on university-level reform to support Indigenous young people's languages and identities, provide better professional development for young Indigenous teachers, and create spaces for powerful learning that will serve as the basis for continued societal transformation (López, 2009).

The studies we have discussed above further expand our knowledge of the ways in which youth who self-identify as Indigenous language learners may become invested in community language issues, and commit energetic action toward reclaiming Indigenous language resources as they engage with

Indigenous scholar-activists through work in academic, as well as community-based, online and transnational efforts and organizations. Above we have shown how Indigenous youth multilingualism studies fit within comparative and international Indigenous education research that 'is interested in multiple definitions and practices of education – formal, nonformal and informal – and multiple epistemologies linked with educational processes' (Huaman, 2014: 71). Such research encourages 'collaborative, transparent, participatory, and transnational' research that 'serves the purpose of furthering Indigenous goals for educational development where Indigenous peoples can themselves identify issues and priorities, learn from other Indigenous sites, anticipate problems, predict outcomes, envision desirable futures, and share solutions' (Huaman, 2014: 71).

There remains much work ahead to understand how Indigenous youth multilingualism research might be leveraged to disrupt dominant language ideologies, transform the structures of schooling, address language policy and practice, and inform broad, intergenerational efforts to assert educational sovereignty. Scholars must also be careful of the ways that research that is too narrowly focused on youth might inadvertently downplay the importance of engaging a much wider array of actors in engaged language policy and planning, including adult Indigenous community members and activists, family members and educators in schools as key policy makers. Even critical youth scholarship can sometimes lean toward valuing youthful innovation, and fleeting forms of cultural production and activism over long-term community engagement, responsibility, accountability and transformation. '(M)any young people and students [also] occupy material, social and symbolic positions that make it relatively easy for them to quickly form visible protest movements, yet simultaneously difficult for them to sustain these movements' (Sukarieh & Tannock, 2015: 109–110). Nevertheless, Indigenous youth research can help us 'consider what educational approaches, pedagogies, programs, and theories can best constitute equitable and powerful contexts for learning and identity formation in a global world and ... do our best to help create them' (Hull et al., 2009: 150).

Looking globally, 'One of the most important lessons learned from the implementation of educational programs and projects in (I)ndigenous contexts is that the direct involvement and participation of (I)ndigenous communities, representatives and intellectuals is essential to ensure improved educational quality' (López, 2009: 49). Former students of Ruiz who are Indigenous scholar-activists and others are now demonstrating ways that the work above and Ruiz's scholarship can be used to forge new pathways for Indigenous learners, and extend support for Indigenous languages as key resources in diverse global contexts. In her current position as president of the Universidad Pedagógica Bolivia, for instance, Jiménez-Quispe is working to create an institutional network for supporting Indigenous language maintenance and reclamation in her home country, taking up a national research project with others to develop a research database to support Indigenous language instruction in elementary and secondary schools. With colleagues, Jiménez-Quispe is creating centers for developing future Indigenous teachers, and working on systemic means of developing, collecting and distributing publications, texts and materials to support Indigenous language instruction nationwide. As part of this work, Jiménez-Quispe and her colleagues are also envisioning new ways to create academic programs to involve community members, Indigenous teachers who speak their languages, and Indigenous students in engaged language planning and policy.

In her current position at the University of British Columbia, Galla now teaches courses on applied linguistics and Indigenous language education to diverse Indigenous, immigrant, international and mainstream students. In her classes, Galla uses Ruiz's work on language as resource and language rights and the United Nations Declarations on the Rights of Indigenous Peoples to raise students' critical awareness of the historical impact of language policies on Indigenous languages in North America, and to honor and make space for diverse languages in her classroom. Galla also uses activities to position her students as language knowers and users with the power to teach their languages to others. Indigenous students often enter Galla's courses stating, 'I don't know my language,' and later express surprise as they come to recognize how much they really know about their Indigenous languages and Indigenous Funds of Knowledge.

In her work, Galla has also developed introductory course modules for instructors working for UBC's well-known NITEP program in urban and rural UBC campuses to raise Indigenous students' awareness of Indigenous languages as key educational resources through exploration of Indigenous histories, contemporary practices and educational possibilities. In a related module that focuses on exploring how youth contribute to language revitalization and reclamation in artistic and performative ways, students read research that frames Aboriginal hip-hop artists as Indigenous cosmopolitans (Proulx, 2010), and learn about hip-hop artists who use the Musqueam language (Dobbin & Walters, 2011). Indigenous students also produce and share creative artifacts that include their Indigenous languages in songs, spoken word, poetry, paintings and/or videos, and learn to use immersion methods to design supportive learning environments for others.

Along with the examples highlighted throughout this chapter, Jiménez-Quispe and Galla's work illuminates how researchers and others might inform, extend and strengthen wide-ranging, intergenerational and international efforts to transform educational environments for Indigenous youth and their communities. Throughout our chapter, using the lens of Indigenous youth multilingualism and reflections on our collective work, we have also shown how Ruiz's ideas about language as resource, language rights, language ideologies, the educational ecologies of language minority students, voice and empowerment, and Ruiz' work with Moll on educational sovereignty and related research directions may continue to provide key insights for those in the field of language planning and policy making around the world today.

Acknowledgments

The authors are grateful to the Indigenous youth and communities with whom we work for inspiring and contributing to the efforts described within. We also thank Iliana Reyes and Amparo Clavijo for inviting an early draft of this paper to be part of a session honoring the work of Richard Ruiz at the BiLatAm: International Symposium on Bilingualism and Bilingual Education in Latin America. Many thanks go to Nancy Hornberger for inviting us to develop the paper into a chapter for this special volume, and for her enthusiasm, guidance and patience as editor. Additionally, we thank Luis Moll, our anonymous reviewer and Kristian Putra for their helpful feedback on earlier chapter drafts.

References

Akom, A.A., Cammarota, J. and Ginwright, S.A. (2008) Youthtopias: Towards a new paradigm of critical youth studies. *Youth Media Reporter* 2 (4), 1–30.

Alim, H.S., Ibrahim, A. and Pennycook, A. (2009) *Global Linguistic Flows: Hip Hop Cultures, Youth Identities, and the Politics of Language*. New York: Routledge.

Anderson, J. (2009) Contradictions across space-time and language ideologies in Northern Arapaho language shift. In P. Kroskrity and M. Field (eds) *Native American Language Ideologies* (pp. 48–76). Tucson, AZ: University of Arizona Press.

Appadurai, A. (2000) Grassroots globalization and the research imagination. *Public Culture* 12 (1), 1–19.

Bixler-Márquez, D. (1998) Multilingual, long-distance community education in Mexico's Sierra Tarahumara. *La Educación, Año XLII* 129–131 (I–III), 121–139.

Bourdieu, P. (1991) *Language and Symbolic Power*. Cambridge, MA: Harvard University Press.

boyd, d. (2010) Social network sites as networked publics: Affordances, dynamics, and implications. In Z. Papacharissi (ed.) *Networked Self: Identity, Community, and Culture on Social Network Sites* (pp. 39–58). London: Routledge.

Brayboy, B. (2005) Toward a tribal critical race theory in education. *Urban Review* 37 (5), 425–446.

Brayboy, B. and Castagno, A. (2009) Self-determination through self-education: Culturally-responsive schooling for Indigenous students in the USA. *Teaching Education* 20 (1), 31–52.

Brayboy, B.M.J., Goug, H.R., Leonard, B., Roehl, R.F., II and Solyom, J.A. (2012) Reclaiming scholarship: Critical Indigenous research methodologies. In S.D. Lapan, M.T. Quartaroli and F.J. Reimer (eds) *Qualitative Research: An Introduction to Methods and Design* (pp. 423–450). San Francisco, CA: John Wiley.

Bucholtz, M. (2002) Youth and cultural practice. *Annual Review of Anthropology* 31, 525–552.

Bucholtz, M., Lopez, A., Mojarro, A., Skapoulli, E., VanderStouwe, C. and Warner-Garcia, S. (2014) Sociolinguistic justice in the schools: Student researchers as linguistic experts. *Language and Linguistics Compass* 8 (4), 144–157.

Chew, K.A.B., Greendeer, N.H. and Keliiaa, C. (2015) Claiming space: An autoethno-graphic study of Indigenous graduate students engaged in language reclamation. *International Journal of Multicultural Education* 17 (2), 73–91.

Combs, M.C. and Penfield, S. (2012) Language activism and language policy. In B. Spolsky (ed.) *The Cambridge Handbook of Language Policy* (pp. 471–474). Cambridge: Cambridge University Press.

Cru, J. (2015a) Language revitalization from the ground up: Promoting Yucatec Maya on Facebook. *Journal of Multilingual and Multicultural Development* 36 (3), 284–296.

Cru, J. (2015b) Bilingual rapping in Yucatan, Mexico: Strategic choices for Maya language legitimation and revitalization. *International Journal of Bilingual Education and Bilingualism*; doi:10.1080/13670050.2015.1051945.

Davis, K.A. (2009) Agentive youth research: Towards individual, collective, and policy transformations. In T.G. Wiley, J.S. Lee and R. Rumberger (eds) *The Education of Language Minority Immigrants in the USA* (pp. 202–239). Bristol: Multilingual Matters.

Davis, K.A. (2014) Engaged language policy and practices. *Language Policy* 13 (2), entire issue.

Davis, K. and Phyak, P. (2015) In the face of neoliberal adversity: Engaging language education policy and practices. *L2 Journal* 7 (3), 146–166.

Dobbin, N. and Walters, K. (2011) *Ancient Musqueam Language Revived Through Hip Hop*. See http://thethunderbird.ca/2011/04/05/ancient-musqueam-language-revived-through-hip-hop/

Field, M. (2009) Changing Navajo language ideologies and changing language use. In P. Kroskrity and M. Field (eds) *Native American Language Ideologies* (pp. 48–76). Tucson, AZ: University of Arizona Press.

Field, M.C. and Kroskrity, P.V. (2009) *Native American Language Ideologies: Beliefs, Practices, and Struggles in Indian Country*. Tucson, AZ: University of Arizona Press.

Fishman, J.A. (1990) What is reversing language shift and how can it succeed? *Journal of Multilingual and Multicultural Development* 11, 5–36.

Fredson, A., Mann, M., Dock, E. and Wyman, L. (1998) *Kipnirmiut Tiganrita Igmirtitlrit: Qipnermiut Tegganrita Egmirtellrit: The Legacy of the Kipnuk Elders*. Fairbanks, AK: Alaska Native Language Center.

Galla, C.K. (2009) Indigenous language revitalization and technology: From traditional to contemporary domains. In J. Reyhner and L. Lockard (eds) *Indigenous Language Revitalization: Encouragement, Guidance & Lessons Learned* (pp. 167–182). Flagstaff, AZ: Northern Arizona University.

Galla, C.K. (2010) Multimedia technology and Indigenous language revitalization: Practical educational tools and applications used within Native communities. Unpublished dissertation, University of Arizona.

Galla, C.K. (2012) Sustaining generations of Indigenous voices: Reclaiming language and integrating multimedia technology. *World Indigenous Nations Higher Education Consortium Journal* 2012, 59–67. http://static1.squarespace.com/static/566c802b69492e9db2afb48e/t/57039e872fe1312243fea9e6/1459854987962/2012+WINHEC+Journal+reduced+file.pdf (accessed 14 July 2016).

Galla, C.K., Kawai'ae'a, K. and Nicholas, S.E. (2014) Carrying the torch forward: Indigenous academics building capacity through an international collaborative model. *Canadian Journal of Native Education* 37 (1), 193–217.

Gilmore, P. (2010) Cross-institutional collaborations in Indigenous education: The Arizona experience. Paper presented at the annual meeting of the American Educational Research Association, Denver, CO.

Gilmore, P. and Wyman, L. (2013) An ethnographic long look: Language and literacy over time in Alaska Native communities. In K. Hall, T. Cremin, B. Comber and L. Moll (eds) *International Handbook of Research on Children's Literacy, Learning and Culture* (pp. 121–138). Malden, MA: Wiley-Blackwell.

Ginwright, S. and Cammarota, J. (2006) Introduction. In S. Ginwright, P. Noguero and J. Cammarota (eds) *Beyond Resistance! Youth Activism and Community Change: New Democratic Possibilities for Practice and Policy for America's Youth*. New York: Routledge.

Ginwright, S., Noguero, P. and J. Cammarota (eds) (2006) *Beyond Resistance: Youth Activism and Community Change: New Democratic Possibilities for Practice and Policy for America's Youth*. New York: Routledge.

González, N., Moll, L. and Amanti, C. (eds) (2005) *Funds of Knowledge: Theorizing Practices in Households, Communities and Classrooms*. New York: Routledge.

He, A. (2010) The heart of heritage: Sociocultural dimensions of heritage language learning. *Annual Review of Applied Linguistics* 30, 66–82.

Hermes, M. and Kawai'ae'a, K. (2014) Revitalizing Indigenous languages through Indigenous immersion education. *Journal of Immersion and Content-Based Language Education* 2 (2), 303–322.

Hill, J. (2002) 'Expert rhetorics' in advocacy for endangered languages: Who is listening and what do they hear? *Journal of Linguistic Anthropology* 12 (2), 119–133.

Hill, J. (2006) The ethnography of language and language documentation. In J. Gippert, N. Himmelmann and U. Mosel (eds) *Essentials of Language Documentation* (pp. 113–128). Berlin: Mouton de Gruyter.

Hornberger, N.H. (2006) Voice and biliteracy in Indigenous language revitalization: Contentious educational practices in Quechua, Guarani and Māori contexts. *Journal of Language, Identity & Education* 5 (4), 277–292.

Hornberger, N. (2009) Multilingual education policy and practice: Ten certainties (grounded in Indigenous experience). *Language Teaching* 42 (2), 197–211.

Hornberger, N. and Swinehart, K. (2012) Bilingual intercultural education and Andean hip hop: Transnational sites for Indigenous identity. *Language in Society* 41, 499–525.

Housman, A., Dameg, K., Kobashigawa, M. and Brown, J. (2011) Report on the Hawaiian oral language assessment (H-OLA) development project. *Second Language Studies* 29, 1–59.

Huaman, E. (2014) 'You're trying hard, but it's still going to die': Indigenous youth and language tensions in Peru and the United States. *Anthropology & Education Quarterly* 45 (1), 71–86.

Huaman, E. and Stokes, P. (2011) Indigenous language revitalization and new media: Postsecondary students as innovators. *Global Media Journal* 11 (18), 1–15.

Hull, G., Zacher, J. and Hibbert, L. (2009) Youth, risk and equity in a global world. *Review of Research in Education* 33, 117–159.

Iseke, J. and Moore, S. (2011) Community-based Indigenous digital storytelling with elders and youth. *American Indian Culture and Research Journal* 35 (4), 19–38.

Jiménez-Quispe, L. (2013) Indians weaving in cyberspace: Indigenous urban youth cultures, identities and politics of language. Unpublished dissertation, University of Arizona.

Jocson, K. (2015) New media literacies as social action: The centrality of pedagogy in the politics of knowledge production. *Curriculum Inquiry* 45 (1), 30–51.

Johnson, L. and Rosario-Ramos, E. (2012) The role of educational institutions in the development of critical literacy and transformative action. *Theory Into Practice* 51 (1), 49–56.

King, K.A., Fogle, L. and Logan-Terry, A. (2008) Family language policy. *Language and Linguistics Compass* 2008, 2.

Kral, I. (2012) *Talk, Text and Technology: Literacy and Social Practice in a Remote Indigenous Community*. Bristol: Multilingual Matters.

Kral, I. (2015) Pedagogy or practice? Indigenous youth and language maintenance in out of school settings. 4th *International Conference on Language Documentation and*

Conservation (ICLDC). See http://scholarspace.manoa.hawaii.edu/handle/10125/25386 (accessed 24 January 2016).

Krauss, M. (1998) The condition of Native North American languages: The need for realistic assessment and action. *International Journal of the Sociology of Language* 132, 9–21.

Kroupa, K.T. (2014) Efforts of the Ree-volution: Revitalizing Arikara language in an endangered language context. In L.T. Wyman, T.L. McCarty and S.E. Nicholas (eds) *Indigenous Youth and Bi/multilingualism: Language Identity, Ideology, and Practice in Dynamic Cultural Worlds* (pp. 168–186). New York: Routledge.

Kroupa, B. (2015) Efforts of the Ree-volution: Revitalizing Arikara language in an endangered language context. Paper presented at the *Second International Conference on Heritage/Community Languages*. March, 8, University of California, Los Angeles.

Lather, P. (1986) Research as praxis. *Harvard Educational Review* 56 (3), 257–277.

Lee, T.S. (2007) 'If they want Navajo to be learned, then they should require it in all schools': Navajo teenagers' experiences, choices, and demands regarding Navajo language. *Wicazo Sa Review* Spring, 7–33.

Lee, T.S. (2009) Language, identity, and power: Navajo and Pueblo young adults' perspectives and experiences with competing language ideologies. *Journal of Language, Identity & Education* 8, 307–320.

Lee, T.S. (2014) Critical language awareness among Native youth in New Mexico. In L.T. Wyman, T.L. McCarty and S.E. Nicholas (eds) *Indigenous Youth and Bi/multilingualism: Language Identity, Ideology, and Practice in Dynamic Cultural Worlds* (pp. 130–148). New York: Routledge.

López L.E. (2009) Reaching the marginalized: Intercultural education in Latin America. Paper commissioned for Reaching the Marginalized. EFA Global monitoring report 2010. See http://unesdoc.unesco.org/images/0018/001866/186620e.pdf (accessed 24 January 2016).

Lyons, S. (2010) There's no translation for it: The rhetorical sovereignty of Indigenous languages. In B. Horner, M. Lu and P. Matsuda (eds) *Cross-language Relations in Composition* (pp. 127–141). Carbondale and Edwardsville, IL: Southern Illinois University Press.

Maira, S. and Soep, E. (eds) (2005) *Youthscapes: The Popular, the National and the Global*. Philadelphia, PA: University of Pennsylvania Press.

May, S. (2005) Language rights: Moving the debate forward. *Journal of Sociolinguistics* 9 (3), 319–347.

May, S. (2014) Contesting metronormativity: Exploring Indigenous language dynamism across the urban-rural divide. *Journal of Language, Identity & Education* 13 (4), 229–235.

McCarty, T.L. (2006) Voice and choice in Indigenous language revitalization. *Journal of Language, Identity & Education* 5 (4), 309–315.

McCarty, T.L. (2014) Negotiating sociolinguistic borderlands – native youth language practices in spaces, time and place. *Journal of Language, Identity & Education* 13 (4), 254–267.

McCarty, T.L. and Lee, T.S. (2014) Critical culturally sustaining/revitalizing pedagogy and Indigenous education sovereignty. *Harvard Educational Review* 84 (1), 101–124.

McCarty, T.L. and Lee, T.S. (2015) The role of schools in Native American language and culture revitalization: A vision of linguistic and educational sovereignty. In W.J. Jacob, S.Y. Cheng and M.K. Porter (eds) *Indigenous Education: Language, Culture and Identity* (pp. 341–360). Dordrecht: Springer.

McCarty, T. and Nicholas, S. (2012) Indigenous education: Local and global perspectives. In M. Martin-Jones, A. Blackledge and A. Creese (eds) *The Routledge Handbook of Multilingualism* (pp. 145–166). London: Routledge.

McCarty, T.L. & Nicholas, S. (2014) Reclaiming indigenous languages: A reconsideration of the roles and responsibilities of schools. *Review of Research in Education* 38, 106–136.

McCarty, T.L. and Wyman, L.T. (2009) Indigenous youth and bilingualism – theory, research, praxis. *Journal of Language, Identity & Education* 8 (5), 279–290.

McCarty, T.L., Romero-Little, M.E. and Zepeda, O. (2006) Native American youth discourses on language shift and retention: Ideological cross-currents and their implications for language planning. *International Journal of Bilingual Education and Bilingualism* 9 (5), 659–677.

McCarty, T., Romero-Little, M., Warhol, L. and Zepeda, O. (2009) Indigenous youth as language-policy makers. *Journal of Language, Identity & Education* 8 (5), 306–319.

McCarty, T.L., Wyman, L. and Nicholas, S. (2013) Activist ethnography with Indigenous youth – lessons from humanizing research on language and education. In D. Paris and M. Winn (eds) *Humanizing Research: Decolonizing Qualitative Inquiry with Youth and their Communities* (pp. 81–104). Malden, MA: Wiley-Blackwell.

McCarty, T.L., Romero-Little, M.E., Warhol, L. and Zepeda, O. (2014) Genealogies of language loss and recovery: Native youth language practices and cultural continuance. In L. Wyman, T. McCarty and Nicholas, S. (eds) *Indigenous Youth and Multilingualism: Language Identity, Ideology, and Practice in Dynamic Cultural Worlds* (pp. 26–47). New York: Routledge.

McCarty, T.L., Nicholas, S.E. and Wyman, L.T. (2015) 50 (0) years out and counting: Native American language education and the four Rs. *International Multilingual Research Journal* 9 (4), 227–252.

Meek, B. (2011) Failing American Indian languages. *American Indian Culture and Research Journal* 35 (2), 43–60.

Menken, K. (2008) *English Language Learners Left Behind: Standardized Testing as Language Policy*. Clevedon: Multilingual Matters.

Messing, J. (2013) 'I didn't know you knew Mexicano!': Shifting ideologies, identities and ambivalence among former youth in Tlaxcala, Mexico. In L. Wyman, T.L. McCarty and S. Nicholas (eds) *Indigenous Youth and Multilingualism: Language Identity, Ideology, and Practice in Dynamic Cultural Worlds* (pp. 111–129). New York: Routledge.

Middaugh, E. and Kirshner, B. (2015) *#youthaction: Becoming Political in the Digital Age*. Charlotte, NC: Information Age.

Moll, L. (1992) Bilingual classroom studies and community analysis: Some recent trends. *Educational Researcher* 21 (2), 20–24.

Moll, L.C. and Ruiz, R. (2002) The schooling of Latino students. In M. Suárez-Orozco and M. Páez (eds) *Latinos: Remaking America* (pp. 362–374). Berkeley, CA: University of California Press.

Moll, L.C. and Ruiz, R. (2005) The educational sovereignty of Latino students in the US. In P. Pedraza and M. Rivera (eds) *Latino Education: An Agenda for Community Action Research* (pp. 295–320). Mahwah, NJ: Lawrence Erlbaum.

Mortimer, K. and Wortham, S. (2015) Analyzing language policy and social identification across heterogeneous timescales. *Annual Review of Applied Linguistics* 35, 160–172.

Muehlman, S. (2008) 'Spread your ass cheeks': And other things that should not be said in Indigenous languages. *American Ethnologist* 35 (1), 34–48.

Navarro, J. (2014) Solarize-ing Native hip-hop: Native feminist land ethics and cultural resistance. *Decolonization: Indigeneity, Education & Society* 3 (1), 101–118.

Navarro, J. (2015) WORD: Hip Hop, language and indigeneity in the American. *Critical Sociology* 1–15. doi:10.1177/0896920515569916.

Nicholas, S.E. (2008) Becoming 'fully' Hopi: The role of the Hopi language in the contemporary lives of Hopi youth – a Hopi case study of language shift and vitality. Unpublished doctoral dissertation, American Indian Studies Program, University of Arizona.

Nicholas, S. (2014) "Being" Hopi by "Living" Hopi: Redefining and reasserting cultural and linguistic identity: Emergent Hopi youth ideologies. In L. Wyman, T. McCarty and S. Nicholas (eds) *Indigenous Youth and Multilingualism: Language Identity, Ideology, and Practice in Dynamic Cultural Worlds* (pp. 70–89). New York: Routledge.

Paris, D. (2012) Culturally sustaining pedagogy: A needed change in stance, terminology, and practice. *Educational Researcher* 41 (3), 93–97.

Paris, D. and Winn, M. (eds) (2013) *Humanizing Research: Decolonizing Qualitative Inquiry with Youth and their Communities.* Malden, MA: Wiley-Blackwell.

Paris, D. and Alim, S. (2014) What are we seeking to sustain through culturally sustaining pedagogy? A loving critique forward. *Harvard Educational Review* 84 (1), 85–100.

Patrick, D., Budach, G. and Muckpaloo, I. (2013) Multiliteracies and family language policy in an urban Inuit community. *Language Policy* 12, 47–62.

Peterson, R. (2013) *iDecolonize: A review of Indigenous Language-Learning Apps,* blog. See https://rising.globalvoices.org/blog/2013/06/21/idecolonize-a-review-of-indigenous-language-learning-apps/ (accessed 30 January 2015).

Phyak, P. and Bui, T. (2014) Youth engaging language policy and planning: Ideologies and transformations from within. *Language Policy* 13, 101–119.

Prins, H. (2004) Visual anthropology. In T. Biolsi (ed.) *A Companion to the Anthropology of American Indians* (pp. 506–525). Malden, MA: Blackwell Press.

Proulx, C. (2010) Aboriginal hip hoppers: Representin' Aboriginality in cosmopolitan worlds. In M.C. Forte (ed.) *Indigenous Cosmopolitans: Transnational and Transcultural Indigeneity in the Twenty-first Century.* New York: Peter Lang.

Recollet, K. (2015) Glyphing decolonial love through urban flashmobbing and Walking with our Sisters. *Curriculum Inquiry* 45 (1), 129–145.

Reynolds, J. (2009) Shaming the shift generation: Intersecting ideologies of family and linguistic revitalization in Guatemala. In P. Kroskrity and M. Field (eds) *Native American Language Ideologies* (pp. 213–237). Tucson, AZ: University of Arizona Press.

Rogoff, B. (2014) Learning by observing and pitching in. *Human Development* 4 (57), 69–81.

Ruiz, R. (1984) Orientations in language planning. *National Association of Bilingual Education Journal* 8 (2), 15–34.

Ruiz, R. (1988) Orientations in language planning. In S.L. McKay and S.C. Wong (eds) *Language Diversity Problem or Resource: A Social and Educational Perspective on Language Minorities in the United States* (pp. 1–25). New York: Newbury House.

Ruiz, R. (1991) The empowerment of language minority students. In C.E. Sleeter (ed.) *Empowerment Through Multicultural Education* (pp. 217–227). Albany, NY: State University of New York Press.

Ruiz, R. (1995) Language planning considerations in Indigenous communities. *Bilingual Research Journal* 19 (1), 71–81.

Ruiz, R. (2010a) *English Language Planning and Transethnification in the USA.* See http://www.telescope.enap.ca/Telescope/docs/English%20papers/volume16/vol-16-3_richard_ruiz.pdf (accessed 24 January 2016).

Ruiz, R. (2010b) Reorienting language-as-resource. In J.E. Petrovic (ed.) *International Perspectives on Bilingual Education* (pp. 155–172). Charlotte, NC: Information Age.

Ruiz, R. (2010c) Reorienting language-as-resource. In J. Petrovic (ed.) *International Perspectives on Bilingual Education: Policy, Practice, and Controversy* (pp. 155–172). Charlotte, NC: Information Age Publishing.

Rymes, B. (2006) Relating word to world: Indexicality during literacy events. In S. Wortham and B. Rymes (eds) *Linguistic Anthropology of Education* (pp. 121–150). Westport, CT: Praeger.

Rymes, B. (2011) Deference, denial and beyond: A repertoire approach to mass media and schooling. *Review of Research in Education* 35, 208–238.

Sarigianides, S., Lewis, M. and Petrone, R. (2015) How re-thinking adolescence helps re-imagine the teaching of English. *English Journal* 104 (3), 13–18.

Simpson, J.H. and Wigglesworth, G. (eds) (2008) *Children's Language and Multilingualism: Indigenous Language Use at Home and School.* London: Continuum.

Smith, L.T. (2012) *Decolonizing Methodologies: Research and Indigenous Peoples* (2nd ed.): Zed.

Soep, L. (2015) Phones aren't smart until you tell them what to do. In E. Middaugh and B. Kirshner (eds) *#youthaction: Becoming Political in the Digital Age* (pp. 25–41). Charlotte, NC: Information Age.

Sukarieh, M. and Tannock, S. (2008) In the best interests of youth neoliberalism? The World Bank and the New Global Youth Empowerment Project. *Journal of Youth Studies* 11 (3), 301–312.

Sukarieh, M. and Tannock, S. (2015) Youth rising? *The Politics of Youth in the Global Economy.* London: Routledge.

Tarifa, A. (2013) Hip Hop as empowerment: Voices in El Alto, Bolivia. *International Journal of Qualitative Studies in Education* 25 (4), 397–415.

Teves, S. (2011) 'Bloodline is all I need': Defiant indigeneity and Hawaiian Hip Hop. *American Indian Culture and Research Journal* 35 (4), 73–101.

Torre, M.E. and Fine, M. (2006) Participatory action research (PAR) by youth. In L. Sherrod (ed.), *Youth Activism: An International Encyclopedia* (pp. 456-462). Westport, CT: Greenwood.

TRC (Truth and Reconciliation Commission of Canada) (2015) *Truth and Reconciliation Commission of Canada: Calls to Action.* Winnipeg, MB: TRC. See http://www.trc.ca/websites/trcinstitution/File/2015/Findings/Calls_to_Action_English2.pdf (accessed 25 January 2016).

Tulloch, S. (2014) Igniting a youth language movement: Inuit youth as circumpolar agents of language planning. In L. Wyman, T. McCarty and S. Nicholas (eds) *Indigenous Youth and Multilingualism: Language Identity, Ideology and Practice in Dynamic Cultural Worlds* (pp. 149–167). New York: Routledge.

Tupas, R. (2014) Inequalities of multilingualism: Challenges to mother tongue-based multilingual education. *Language and Education* 29 (2), 112–124.

Tupas, R. (2015) Inequalities of multilingualism: Challenges to mother tongue-based multilingual education. *Language and Education* 29 (2), 112–124.

Urrieta, L. (2013) Familia and Communidad-based saberes: Learning in an Indigenous heritage community. *Anthropology & Education Quarterly* 44 (3), 320–335.

van Dijk, T. (1996) *Discourse, Racism and Ideology.* Islas Canarias, Spain: RCEI Ediciones, Universidad de La Laguna.

Warschauer, M. (2012) The digital divide and social inclusion. *Americas Quarterly* Spring, 130–136.

Warschauer, M. and Matuchniak, T. (2010) New technology and digital worlds: Analyzing evidence of equity in access, use, and outcomes. *Review of Research in Education* 34, 179–225.

Wilson, W.H. and Kamanā, K. (2011) Insights from Indigenous language immersion in Hawai'i: The case of Nāwahī school. In D. Tedick, T. Fortune and D. Christian (eds) *Immersion Education: Practices, Policies, Possibilities* (pp. 36–57). Bristol: Multilingual Matters.

Wilson, W.H. and Kamanā, K. (2014) Commentary: A Hawaiian revitalization perspective on Indigenous youth and bilingualism. In L. Wyman, T. McCarty and S. Nicholas (eds) *Indigenous Youth and Multilingualism: Language Identity, Ideology and Practice in Dynamic Cultural Worlds* (pp. 187–200). New York: Routledge.

Woolard, K.A. (1998) Language ideology as a field of inquiry. In B. Schieffelin, K. Woolard and P. Kroskrity (eds) *Language Ideologies: Practice and Theory* (pp. 3–47). New York: Oxford University Press.

Woolard, K. (2011) Is there linguistic life after high school? Longitudinal changes in the bilingual repertoire in metropolitan Barcelona. *Language in Society* 40, 617–648.

Wyman, L. (2009) Youth, linguistic ecology, and language endangerment: A Yup'ik example. *Journal of Language, Identity & Education* 8 (5), 335–349.

Wyman, L. (2012) *Youth Culture, Language Endangerment and Linguistic Survivance*. Bristol: Multilingual Matters.

Wyman, L. (2013) Indigenous youth migration and language contact: A Yup'ik example. *International Multilingual Research Journal* 7 (1), 66–82.

Wyman, L., Marlow, P., Andrew, C.F., Miller, G., Nicholai, C.R. and Reardon, Y.N. (2010) High stakes testing, bilingual education and language endangerment: A Yup'ik example. *International Journal of Bilingual Education and Bilingualism* 13 (6), 701–721.

Wyman, L., McCarty, T. and Nicholas, S. (eds) (2014) *Indigenous Youth and Multilingualism: Language Identity, Ideology, and Practice in Dynamic Cultural Worlds*. New York: Routledge.

The Missing Voices in Colombia Bilingue: The Case of Ĕbĕra Children's Schooling in Bogotá, Colombia

Amparo Clavijo Olarte and Ángela Pamela González

As language educators, we are concerned with the role of English as a foreign language among Indigenous minority groups that arrive in Bogotá's public schools because of forced displacement. Our concern is shared by other Colombian scholars who have discussed the linguistic national policies with regard to their limited conception of bilingualism as only Spanish and English (De Mejía, 2005, 2006; De Mejía & Fonseca, 2007; Guerrero, 2010; Usma, 2009). Using Ruiz's (1984) language orientations to policy and planning, McCarty (2011, 2013) and Hornberger's (1996, 1998, 2008) contributions to the study of Indigenous rights to their own language and culture, this paper presents a community-based pedagogy (CBP) as an active critical pedagogy to construct relevant content through children's narratives and literacies. The community-based participatory research (CBPR) approach proposed by Ferreira and Gendron (2011) was used to analyze the educational implementation that made Indigenous children's language and culture visible through their stories. It emphasizes participatory appraisal and design development, participatory implementation, and action. Individual stories of displacement written in Ĕbĕra and Spanish, interviews with Ĕbĕra parents and teachers, and the language teacher's notes represented the data in the study. Findings evidenced that CBP curriculum enhanced students' language rights and evolving identity, that their Ĕbĕra-Spanish biliteracy developed gradually leaving the role of English as a possibility to be the third language in the future, and the school educational project introduced multiculturalism as a local and national reality.

Introduction

This chapter is written to honor the professional contributions to language planning and policy education in Latin America by Richard Ruiz (1984). His influential framework that informed linguistic policies and pedagogies in the Americas is relevant to discuss the local and national situation of displaced Indigenous groups in Bogotá, Colombia. We are particularly concerned with the fact that public schools in Bogotá are not prepared to welcome Indigenous children in their schools and classrooms, as there is lack of information about their schooling and the languages they speak, and their culture and ethnicity are seen from a deficit perspective. Thus, the lack of knowledge about Colombia as a plurilingual country presented social, linguistic and cultural challenges to Indigenous Emberá children arriving to the *Liceo* in Bogotá. Colombian scholars like Guerrero (2010) and De Mejía (2007) question the Bilingualism National Plan that privileges a limited form of bilingualism (English-Spanish) thought only for the elite. Guerrero cites Ruiz (1994) to defend that 'Colombia has a variety of languages that should be seen as resources and not as problems' (Guerrero, 2009: 11).

For this study, Ruiz's views of language as right and language as resource are central concepts to address the linguistic and social needs in the schooling process of Ěběra children whose families arrived in Bogotá because of forced displacement due to violence in their home territories. Ruiz (1984, 1995) defends the right of Indigenous minority speakers to speak their own language in a Spanish-dominant school culture. In turn, he proposes a view of language as resource that helps learners to access knowledge from their own and other languages. Thus, the use of both Ěběra and Spanish in the literacy activities of Ěběra children at school helped them use their mother language as a resource to learn Spanish.

Moreover, this chapter is framed within a community-oriented pedagogy that provides backing for the Indigenous children's community-oriented ways of learning in schools in their *territorio* that differ profoundly from the established teacher-centered pedagogy that predominates in mainstream classrooms of Bogotá. In this study, a community-based participatory pedagogy (CBP) that focuses on constructing community-relevant content was implemented and children's narratives of learning experiences before displacement were reconstructed. Parents' narratives of life in their territory and the experience of coming to Bogotá were also part of the curricular activities within a CBP.

From the language orientations previously mentioned, we focus on Indigenous language as right and as resource to build upon in Ěběra-Spanish bilingual education for Ěběra children. We do it through the implementation of new linguistic policies in school- and community-based education. According to Corson (1998), community-based education starts with people and their historical and social reality, permitting them to become actively involved in developing their own futures through the school and the community. It is indeed a social action in which all the activities, learning environments and frameworks are created by the participants for their interests.

We start the chapter by addressing Indigenous schooling issues globally and describe the Latin American and Colombian contexts as a way to understand the local educational situation regarding Ĕbĕra language and culture at the *Liceo* in Bogotá. We use studies carried out by McCarty with Indigenous populations from Alaska and Canada, Hornberger's studies with Indigenous people in South America, and Philips' study about the Warm Springs Indian Reservation in Oregon, USA to frame our study of Ĕbĕra children's schooling process in Bogotá. We then describe the research methodology used in the study carried out at the *Liceo*, its physical location, the participants, instruments for data collection and the curricular planning implemented to include this group of Indigenous children's language and culture in the school. The curricular activities carried out with children included: providing home–school direct relations and dialogues mediated by a speaker of the native language; bringing the activities of the school and the community closer together; and organizing bilingual exchange opportunities for the students in which they present aspects of their own culture. The findings of the study are presented through two categories: Life Stories and the construction of Ĕbĕra children's social and linguistic identities; and Shifting Languages in their storytelling. Lastly, we draw conclusions from the research experience.

Indigenous schooling

Champagne (2009) considers that, in most scenarios, educational systems across the globe have been inadequate for Indigenous students with regard to recognizing their ethnic rights and providing academic success. As a result, Indigenous students from around the world have demonstrated a lack of enthusiasm for schooling in its traditional dominant-culture form. Although Indigenous groups consider education as a relevant element to empower their social and cultural conditions, some curricular and educational contexts lack knowledge about Indigenous people's ways of learning, causing a mismatch between the community interests and schools.

However, Somali and Kincheloe (1999) assert that there is a shift toward recognizing Indigenous models of education and this is conducive to a legitimization of their human rights and an empowerment of their cultural particularities. In this regard, Deyhle and Swisher (1997) propose eliminating the differentiation between the classroom and the community, and basing the learning in cooperative tasks among students and teachers, both being learners who avoid praise, criticism or recitation. Such initiatives look for reconciliations between the intrinsic culture of the students and their learning process, seeking to base teaching methodology on students' past learning experiences and to build curricula on the interests of the specific ethnic group. Within a context of education of Indigenous minority groups, communities are able to claim and make their traditions and languages visible and relevant, and at the same time they offer students successful and fairer learning experiences that secure the continuity of their societies (May & Aikman, 2003).

Philips' (1983) ethnography about the Warm Springs Indian Reservation is a unique example of a geographically and culturally isolated group that maintain different ways of communicating from that of the Anglo culture. Philips highlights the fact that different groups in Warm Springs spoke different languages but the use of English as a lingua franca contributed to the disappearance of group identities. Warm Springs' children's schooling experiences were maintained in interactional isolation from the Anglo world into which they were supposed to become assimilated. Philips asserts that 'because the interactional network of Warm Springs is largely Indian, their network of interaction is a culturally distinctive social milieu that has been maintained and has facilitated culturally different ways of communicating' (Philips, 1983: 38).

In the broadest sense, the education of Indigenous groups has been a powerful tool for the rise of community awareness and the performance of collective actions for language and cultural awakening. Thanks to this awareness and collective action, some schools have reconsidered and analyzed new ways of schooling. McCarty and Watahomigie (1998: 132) believe that these programs have created new contexts for native language literacy, facilitated the credentialing of Indigenous teachers, and raised the value of Indigenous languages in communities and schools.

Although these first steps demonstrate the potential shared within committed Indigenous groups, there are still significant pragmatic challenges to the implementation of education for Indigenous groups. Altman and Fogarty (2010) recognize that, to be able to close the educational breach, nations need to recognize cultural and structural difference and diversity. Educational systems also have to take into account singular, local necessities and concerns in language education and pertinent practical skills acquisition.

The Latin American context

According to López (2009), Latin America is one of the most linguistically and culturally diverse areas of the world; it holds over 650 Indigenous groups who speak approximately 550 different languages and sustain invaluable cultural resources. Most Indigenous peoples live in biologically diverse territories, but they are no longer found only in remote rural areas. Due to social, economic and political issues, Indigenous communities and individuals have moved into cities and towns in all countries of the region

(Champagne, 2009). Although their presence in the region represents a significant part of the population and sustains some of the main cultural backgrounds, Indigenous people continue to suffer discrimination, marginalization, poverty and conflict. In Latin America, some groups and individuals are being dispossessed of their traditional lands and their belief systems, cultures and languages, and their ways of life are continuously threatened (Champagne, 2009).

Within the context of education, López (2009) states that schooling initially excludes Indigenous students due to pedagogies based on the Western language of power, resulting in many Indigenous children repeating or failing in school. He also asserts that the few who are able to achieve the school standards move to the main cities. Among many factors, the rejection of Indigenous languages in the classroom has negatively affected the educational situation of Indigenous students. López asserts that Indigenous educational deficits range from exclusion to limited access, especially in higher education.

Another concern about the education of Indigenous as speakers of minority languages in Colombia is related to the bilingual programs for majority language speakers that privilege English as the second main instructional language and position it as an academic target before any native tongue. In this regard, De Mejía (2006: 154) argues that the rights of minority Amerindian or Creole languages have been generally undervalued and associated with an 'invisible' form of bilingualism.

There have also been diverse strategies in order to keep Indigenous children in schools. In rural areas, some schools have involved not only the Indigenous students themselves but also the communities to which they belonged. In examples where the Indigenous language is taught as a second language alongside Spanish and English in Peru and México, López (2009) shows that there has been a relevant recent positive impact on new ways of schooling and in the vision of students.

The Indigenous organizations have also worked together to adopt an educational system that allows them to take the most convenient pedagogic paths for every community: most national teacher unions in Latin America including ANDE Costa Rica,[1] UNE Ecuador, CONMERB Bolivia, UNE Paraguay, CTERA Argentina, CEA Argentina, CPC Chile, SUTEP Peru, CNTE Brazil and CONTCEPI Colombia are building a contextualized educative profile that recognizes the needs of their particular communities, including aspects such as language, conception of authority, political structure, family, *territorio*, spirituality, and their version of their own history (CONTCEPI, 2012).

The Colombian context

Colombia is a multicultural country; besides Spanish, more than 65 Indigenous languages are spoken (Landaburu, 1999). Ethnic and linguistic diversity is present all across the land and it is made more visible due to internal conflicts such as violence and poverty which are causes for the displacement and movement of communities. Bogotá as the capital city became the first option to take refuge in for many Indigenous groups suffering from displacement conditions. In addition, other groups like Ěbĕra Katios from Bagadó, Chocó who do not have violent groups acting in their territories are also moving to the main cities due to poverty and starvation. Education, housing and employment are basic needs that must be fulfilled for the populations migrating to Bogotá. Consequently, public schools in Bogotá are required to provide quality education for Indigenous children as Colombian citizens.

Although policies proclaim a positive legal environment for the Indigenous population and their education, the statistics portray a different reality. In 2005, the Administrative Statistics Department (DANE) conducted the national census in Colombia. One of the variables analyzed was the schooling level of students across the country. The DANE states that the educational differences between the Indigenous population and other ethnic groups need to be visible, taking into account that most of Indigenous groups live in natural rural Indigenous reserves where there are few educational institutions and where only primary school is offered. Few ethno-education programs allow the integration of their oral traditions with the general knowledge of the common-stream society (Romero, 2005).

Even though most educational systems function apart from the Indigenous peoples with minor elements of interculturalism, there are also some initiatives that look for the collective and pertinent construction of pedagogies that deal with the cultural particularities of each group. One of these efforts, the Makú Jogúki-OEK or Educative System for the Indigenous Kankuamo from Santa Marta, Colombia has been constructed based on the concerns and perspectives of the community with the goal of making sure that every member of the group is a participant. They also adhered to their philosophical tradition *Ley de Origen*,[2] or Law on Origins, and built up the proposal following several particular stages. In the first place, they consulted the *Zhatukwa*, or the most knowledgeable chief, through the elderly to determine the spiritual orientation of the proposal. Secondly, they organized collectively the components, dimensions and variables of the educative system, and thirdly, they attended local meetings where every member of the community could discuss and analyze the educational units and generalities of the proposal. Finally, there was open discussion in the general assembly or general meeting where decisions were made (Arias *et al.*, 2008).

In February 2012 the CONTCEPI (the entity in charge of the collective construction of the Indigenous educational system in Colombia) presented to the SEIP[3] an initiative of several Indigenous organizations to formalize a proposal for 'their own education for Indigenous populations' across the Colombian territory as a whole. The bases for this proposal are fourfold: Indigenous people's philosophy of origins; Indigenous worldview; Indigenous people's cosmovision; and Indigenous people's own law in every community. The SEIP aims at maintaining unity among Indigenous populations regarding natural relationships with the context and the prevailing society. This educative system intends to focus on the learning of the native language, cultural values, all the original forms of art, the production processes, traditional medicine, rituality, the management of the soil, their own history and orality, and community work (CONTCEPI, 2012).[4]

Again, some of the principal challenges for these proposals are their scope and the diverse political and social conditions needed to make them effective for a larger number of the Indigenous population. Moreover, there is a growing number of new urban Indigenous students who attend non-intercultural and monolingual schools where the curriculum and pedagogy need to be revised.

Ĕbĕra language pedagogy

The Constitutional Colombian Court recognized in the Document of 2009 that there are 34 endangered Indigenous groups whose culture, language and living conditions are at risk due to the violence and the violation of their fundamental individual and collective rights. Among these groups are the Ĕbĕra Katío, the Ĕbĕra Dobidá and the Ĕbĕra Chamí.

Some new generations of Ĕbĕra Indigenous children grow up listening to Spanish and they do not know the native Ĕbĕra language. Some of them stop speaking the language when the acculturation process takes place; the language and culture are lost in schools where the children are the minority and have to adapt to the new context as they are asked to read and write in Spanish while their native culture and languages are neglected (Aguirre et al., 2013).

Framed on the collective work by the Indigenous organizations in Colombia, and bearing in mind the generalized concern about the rescue of their traditions and language, the Chamí communities are advancing the elaboration of a 'pedagogical model.' The process is an ongoing effort that has been initiated with analysis and understanding of Ĕbĕra language as they develop the first manual for the pronunciation and writing of Ĕbĕra Chamí.

Although in 2002 the community Ĕbĕra Chamí from Purembará, Chocó (Colombia) worked for the elaboration of a writing system in the Ĕbĕra language (Romero, 2002), it was not until 2013 that the community presented a methodological path to write Ĕbĕra, alongside a pedagogical project in which 43 teachers worked to tutor 1500 Indigenous children in the native language. This proposal was elaborated under the advice of grandparents and *nokos* (Indigenous governors) and aims at the defense of the Ĕbĕra identity and culture wherever new Ĕbĕra generations can be found. Furthermore, it presents a phonological and orthographic description of the language from the community perspective (Aguirre *et al.*, 2013). Ěběra Katios or Dobida have been in the same struggle for the past 10 years; however, according to their leaders, there have been several setbacks regarding the absence of governmental support and lack of communication among members of the community.

In conclusion, there are several concerns about the education of Indigenous populations in local, national and international contexts; however, in recent years, a collective shift toward the integration of the native culture and language in educational systems has brought evidence of an enhancement of Indigenous identity in particular communities. Although these advances are not massive and still present a set of practical challenges for their development, the community and collective work are presented here as a positive starting point. In the following section, we present a theoretical review of CBP and its influences in Indigenous contexts.

Theoretical Framework for Community-based Pedagogy

In the global context, educational researchers like May (1994), McCarty and Watahomigie (1998), Corson (1998) and Hornberger (2008) have studied ways in which to integrate the Indigenous people in the educational context without neglecting their linguistic and cultural backgrounds. Moved by collective reasons, they have informed their research with CBP theory. May (1994), for instance, argues that community-based education is a response to the historical domination of Indigenous groups in educational contexts where the languages and cultures have been devitalized, forcing the Indigenous peoples to merge with the dominant culture and making uneven the success levels between Indigenous and non-Indigenous students. May (1994) also states that CBP answers the need for *self-determination*, a currently growing principle, that seeks to reclaim and revalue their educational and linguistic rights.

In The United States, McCarty (1998) presents the case of Hawaiian and Alaskan native communities' cultural disruption and language loss due to language education policies that failed to incorporate their linguistic backgrounds and obliged them to learn English. In her work, McCarty argues that, when the inclusion of Indigenous community-based initiatives took place, the languages and the promotion of Indigenous rights were enhanced. In an Australian multicultural school holding an Indigenous population, May (1994) used community negotiation and professional education to reform the education system completely, providing a critical approach to policy making and integrating an empowering approach to education in which diversity was seen as a pedagogic opportunity rather than a deficiency, and cultural respect was essential to give students more life opportunities while preserving their own identities.

Hornberger's (2000) research was located in three Andean countries in which the inclusion of CBPs has fostered in Quechua communities:

[a] growing recognition that interculturality must be self-consciously defined and that a strengthened (intercultural) national identity is based on respect among all groups and discrimination against none. To the degree that language practices at both macrolevels (policy) and microlevels (practitioner) reflect these evolving conceptions of culture and interculturality, they challenge existing power inequities and the ideological paradox underlying them. (Hornberger, 2000: 194)

In the initiatives mentioned above, Indigenous CBPs implied a way of reorganizing school settings and curricula as well as the perception of the self and the ways the members see the world and relate to it, encouraging Indigenous values including respect and humility, and inviting the community to be close observers and creators of their own future.

In the present study, the vision of CBP is informed by the work of authors committed to both Indigenous and non-Indigenous contexts, whose main interests are the advancement of the knowledge, concerns and potentials of the community in educational institutions (Corson, 1998; May & Aikman, 2003; McCarty, 1998; Moll et al., 1992; Sharkey & Clavijo, 2012).

According to Corson (1998), community-based education starts with people and their historical and social reality. It permits them to become actively involved in the development of their own futures through the school and the community. It is indeed a social action in which all activities, learning environments and frameworks are created by the participants and for their interests.

Sharkey and Clavijo (2012) argue that the curriculum of CBPs recognizes 'the realities of curriculum standards that teachers must address' (Sharkey & Clavijo, 2012: 131), but gives priority to the reproduction of local knowledge and acquaintances in the students' context and families – in other words, the inclusion of what Moll et al. (1992) have termed Funds of Knowledge 'to refer to the historically accumulated and culturally developed bodies of knowledge and skills essential for household or individual functioning and well-being' (Moll et al., 1992: 133).

Another theoretical issue related to CBP is its influence on language rights and language policies. May and Aikman (2003) refer to CBPs as a 'bottom-up language planning process' (cf. Hornberger, 1996), where it is not the dominant group who makes the decision or exercises control over the language or its use in the school context, but it is the community who determines the linguistic necessities in classrooms and complementary outside scenarios. Although these efforts still face several challenges, they have proven effective toward the preservation of minority languages and cultures. May and Aikman argue that there is also a need for a 'top-down recognition of this process' in which educators, planners and policy makers value these types of initiatives and set new relations with the communities they work with (May & Aikman, 2003: 145).

The Study

Through the lens of a study carried out by the second author as a bilingual public school teacher in her classroom (Gonzalez-Ariza, 2014), we discuss teacher agency for curricular and ideological transformations that occurred within the school, the classroom and the community. Critical aspects such as Indigenous language rights, national policies and bilingualism lead to a shared ground where changes can obtain the local nature that make them relevant for a specific community. This common ground is the curriculum – the base of what should be included in the teaching-learning process, to whom and by whom, and how this should be taught.

In this classroom, the framework used to address our concern about the schooling process for the Ẽbẽra Indigenous children at the *Liceo* in Bogotá was community-based participatory research (CBPR). This research orientation allows integrating the Indigenous populations' own perspectives, recognizing that 'the Indigenous philosophies, epistemologies, histories, art and other modes of knowledge, can all be potential sources of social science theories and concepts' (Alatas, 2006: 86).

Methodology

CBPR is a framework in which the research questions are addressed collectively in order to respond to specific necessities of the community, with members and translators participating in the research process as active collaborators. Ferreira and Gendron (2011) explain that the cultural and linguistic information gathered from the community is used to inform the research process; an educational component is designed and implemented to serve the needs of the community; and the results of the research have a reciprocal impact in the reality of the participants. They propose six research stages to CBPR: (1) preparatory partnering; (2) participatory appraisal and design development; (3) participatory implementation; (4) action; (5) participatory monitoring and evaluation; and (6) education.

- *Preparatory partnering* is the first stage of CBPR, in which a relationship between the members of the Indigenous community and the academic institution is established. In our study with Ẽbẽra Indigenous children, for example, the invitation came from the teacher researcher interested in helping to better the educational conditions for Indigenous children and families. Thus, special attention was given to networking, cooperation, collaboration and partnership (Amuwo & Jenkins, 2001).

- *Participatory appraisal and design development* deals with the way research that incorporates the knowledge and the experience of the people can be valued as having methodological rigor, scientific objectivity and appreciation for the value of CBPR model by all stakeholders including the communities themselves, academia and funding foundations/agencies.
- *Participatory implementation* implies the community participating at multiple levels of the implementation of the research project.
- *Action* in CBPR refers to the recognition that people in a community engage in their world and gain knowledge, which informs their subsequent engagement with the world, which in turn produces knowledge.
- *Participatory monitoring and evaluation* assume the self-reflexive capacity of participatory research that enables its continued assessment of the relative utility and transformative aspects of the research as related to the community.
- Lastly, *Education*, as a synonym of action within a Freirean view to CBPR aims at empowering marginalized and oppressed peoples through a democratic process of creating knowledge.

The implementation of CBPR with the Indigenous community of Ĕbĕra children included having parents, interpreters and school staff collaborate to establish a relationship of trust and respect. Equally important was the active participation of both the Indigenous community and the school to transform the oppressing realities of a monolingual, monocultural school and a fixed curriculum to include the experiences of Ĕbĕra children as critical resources for learning.

The *Liceo*

The *Liceo*, a public school located in downtown Bogotá, holds approximately 600 students from preschool to 11th grade whose families belong to socio-economic strata 0–3. (There are seven socio-economic levels that determine the income of Colombians: extremely poor belong to Strata 0 and 1, middle class to Strata 2, 3 and 4, and the wealthier class in Strata 5 and 6). Among students, there are children from different parts of Colombia and Ecuador including two Indigenous communities – Ĕbĕra and Quechua. The school also includes children in extreme poverty conditions, in some cases children suffering ill-treatment and battering, sexual abuse, and lack of social and nurturing conditions. These aspects produce a high range of school withdrawal, low academic performance, hunger, feelings of injustice, drug and alcohol abuse and youth violence, according to information provided by the school coordinator.

The school curriculum at the *Liceo* in 2009 when the group of Indigenous children arrived focused on business management. However, due to the multicultural and multilingual concerns that emerged with the group of Indigenous students, the emphasis changed the language curriculum to focus on literacy practices of Spanish as L1 and English as L2. Indigenous children interacted with their peers in their native languages but performed classroom tasks exclusively in Spanish. Most of Indigenous parents only speak their native language.

Ěběra language in the schooling of Indigenous children was supported by the presence of interpreters who mediated children's learning. Spanish as the language of instruction was also introduced and the role of English as their third language was not emphasized since Indigenous children were bilingual Ěběra-Spanish speakers.

Participants

Eighteen immigrant Ěběra children from Risaralda (Chamín) and from Chocó (Katio) aged 8–12 participated in the study. These children are native Ěběra speakers living with their families in the Bogotá city center since 2009. As soon as they arrived at school, they were placed in a classroom called *Primeras letras (initial letters)*, and *Aceleración (acceleration)*, created by the National Ministry of Education (MEN) where the curriculum focused on Spanish literacy goals while Ěběra was only used in oral interactions among children. The families lived in two shelters and made a living from the aid received from the government. Many of the mothers' main occupation was handcrafting and, in some cases, they had to beg in the streets to increase their earnings; the fathers worked in informal sales or as leaders in Indigenous organizations.

The interpreters and research co-participants were an Ěběra Dobida woman married to a Katio, mother of two students in the school, who speaks fluent Spanish, Ěběra Dobida and Ěběra Katio. Her role in the research was as icebreaker with the school and the community, and as a voice in the interest of the families regarding the schooling process. She also translated the questions to the interviewees and helped in the design of the bilingual material for the pedagogical component. An Ěběra Katio leader was in charge of bringing the children from the shelters to the school every day and he was the Ěběra spokesperson for the community decisions in the school. He also worked as an interpreter between the full-time teacher and the students. By 2011, interpreters were officially working at the school since the teachers and the Ěběra community identified the necessity for a mediator to communicate between the school and teachers. Thus, the school academic council and the Secretary of Education of Bogotá (SED) agreed to hire them as interpreters.

Other participants include the Ěběra students' full-time teacher who was an Afro-American woman who had worked with the Ěběra population years before. She was in charge of administering the school curriculum in Spanish to the Indigenous children. The school coordinator was also interviewed on several occasions in order to analyze the schooling process of the Indigenous communities from an administrative perspective.

Instruments

Interviews were the main source of data – semi-structured interviews accompanied by conversations with participants and translators. Riessman's perspective of the interview, in which participants 'negotiate how they want to be known by the stories they develop collaboratively with audiences,' was used (Riessman, 2002: 707).

Secondly, children's artifacts described and collected during the planning and implementation of the pedagogical component gave an account of literary practices that were analyzed under the scope of the research question. Finally, sources such as students' school files and records of their attendance at school, grade reports in the *Acceleration* groups, informal community knowledge collected from relatives at the shelters, ministry or secretary of education, documents in the schools and documents related to minority learners in Bogota/Colombia were analyzed as well.

During the pedagogical implementation, Ēbĕra language did not have a written system established yet and students used Spanish phonemes to represent Ēbĕra orality. Consequently, both Ēbĕra and Spanish written material was used for the pedagogical intervention.

Validation process

Taking into account the fact that Indigenous people do not often see themselves represented in the results of research or, if they do see themselves, they often do not recognize their representation (Smith, 1999), this study adopted a serious and rigorous validation process of the interpretation of data collected. The present research recognized and placed Indigenous people at the center of the story, bearing in mind the particularity of the context and participants and never seeing their experiences as universal 'truths' that can be generalized or transferred to other communities. Therefore, we used member validation and check. Specifically, we used participatory monitoring and evaluation (Ferreira & Gendron, 2011) where the data are presented to the Ēbĕra community (interpreters, leaders and children) to provide feedback about the cultural acceptability and effectiveness of the process of collection.

The role of the researcher

The role of the researcher was based on a Freirian perspective that the researchers are community members or academicians who consider themselves students and learners of the community (Freire, 1993). Due to the delicate nature of the interpretation of data collected from the Ěběra community, some relevant aspects were considered when planning and conducting the present study. In the first place, the teacher-researcher in the school was considered a 'culture outsider' since she did not belong to the Ěběra community. In such manner, she constantly needed to reflect on, and be critical of, her own culture, values, assumptions and beliefs and to recognize that these are not the 'norm.' She also needed to become aware of, and open to, different worldviews and ways of knowing. Finally, the participation of Ěběra co-researchers is addressed as a remarkable source of contextualized information from the insider perspective.

Ethical considerations

Since this study deals with a sensitive and vulnerable community, we paid special attention to cultural diversity and the ethical issues inherent in conducting research with Indigenous students. This study fully complies with the International Society of Ethnobiology's (ISE, 2006) Code of Ethics for research with Indigenous populations, taking into account aspects such as self-determination, reciprocity, respect and participation. Advocating the right of ownership of the information in the study, we do not mention the real names of children, parents or interpreters. All participants signed a consent form (Appendices 1 and 2).

The Curriculum at *Liceo*

At this stage, Ruiz's idea of language as resource for learning is relevant to illustrate the way Ěběra children used their native language to tell their stories and to learn Spanish. Curricular activities were designed to integrate writing opportunities in Spanish and Ěběra for the development of biliteracy and to collect students' life stories in order to inform the school community about previous learning experiences and specific cultural aspects of the Ěběra culture.

The curriculum proposed to the *Liceo* by the bilingual teacher had three main goals, of which the first two were: to use the mother tongue in the development of Spanish as a second language and a curricular shift from monolingual, monocultural ideologies that claimed Spanish as the first dominant language to inclusive multicultural plurilingual ideologies that recognize Ěběra children's voices. This approach was consistent with Ruiz's (1984) right and resource orientations in language policy and planning that permanently seek spaces for multiple languages in society to create possibilities to voice the language of all members of plurilingual societies, here the minority Indigenous groups that form our Colombian society.

The curricular activities focused on including community assets in the school curriculum, using Ĕbĕra language to write texts and students' narratives, and developing Ĕbĕra literacy skills through the construction of life stories. The final goal included integrating Ĕbĕra parents, as well as musical, agricultural and artistic traditions in the classroom.

In order to accomplish the main pedagogical goals, the pedagogical intervention was co-constructed with the schoolteachers and interpreters based on Fishman's (1991) strategies to promote minority language interest. These included: providing home–school direct relations and dialogues mediated by a speaker of the native language; bringing the activities of the school and the community closer together; and organizing bilingual exchange opportunities for the students in which they presented aspects of their own culture.

Mubabia ze burata: Life story book

The main pedagogical goals for this literacy activity were to have Indigenous children tell their life stories. In each session, children talked about specific moments in their lives to develop their personal narratives. In the first session, children designed the cover of the book in which they pasted a photo of themselves and wrote personal information including name, native community, age, gender, date of birth and other relevant dates that were important in their lives. They were asked to interview their parents about the *Ambachaquera* 'family', specifically about the story of their family conformation and the early stages of their lives (Figure 1).

In the second session, the main topic was life back in the *territorio* or *Injua*. Children worked in groups based on their place of origin. They were asked to describe through drawings the daily life when they were living in the territory, including literacy practices and the main activities they used to have at home and at school. Then they were asked to describe in the book these activities plus their motives for leaving the territory.

In drawings children vividly described their native land and the way of living before coming to the city. In Figures 2 and 3 the child portrays himself and his family as central characters. The river and the plantain trees are also important sources for food and survival for the Indigenous families. When describing places, children were also presenting the way they learned traditional activities and their own role in the community.

In the third session, children were asked to talk about Bogotá, their first impressions, their main activities, the adaptation process and their life in Bogotá. In the last session, children described their life in the school, the use of language, the daily routine and their preferences between staying at home and going to school. Some of them were interviewed about the stories written in the book.

The writing of this book was accompanied by pedagogical support from parents, interpreters and the teacher. The parents aided in recalling the

Figure 1 Description of family

Text translation: Family. Hi. I want to tell you the story of my mother and father. My mother loves me very much and she helps me a lot to study but sometimes I do not pay attention to her. I can help her when I story more. The story of my father. My father wanted me to go to work if I do not want to study.

My brothers and I. Hello, I am the oldest brother and I have two sisters. I like to play with my friends and I also like to watch television, also I like when I am with my sisters. They like to play with their friends and they ask me to help them with their homework, and [illegible word] likes doing homework more than playing.

Figure 2 Drawing of Ĕbĕra territory depicted by children

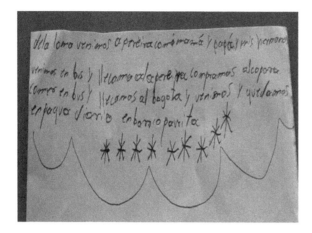

Figure 3 Text describing their trip to Bogotá

Text translation: We come from the mountains to Pereira with my mother, my father and my siblings. We came by bus and we arrived in Pereira. We bought something to eat on the bus, we arrived in Bogota, and we stayed at barrio Parrita where we pay fees to stay all in a room daily.

stories while the children were writing, and the interpreters supported their process of writing in Ěběra or Spanish.

Social and cultural activities with Ěběra families

There were social and cultural activities to recognize diversity at school. The members of the Ěběra community were invited to the school to present specific assets of their culture to the whole school community; they were allocated physical space to display their presentations while students from all grades visited the exhibitions. Among the presenters was the mother of a Chamí girl who exhibited the art of Ěběra jewelry while explaining the symbolic meaning of the colors, sizes and shapes and their connection with gender and race. A group of Ěběra Katio musicians presented their work on traditional Indigenous music using native instruments; a group of Ěběra parents introduced some native techniques to cultivate medicinal plants, and started crops that were nurtured by the Ěběra children during the school year.

Chamí members formed a cultural group that represented the traditional dances of the Indigenous Ěběra. These group practices and presentations were exclusive to the shelter or Indigenous meetings. In September 2012, they accepted the invitation by a group of teachers (social science, Spanish and English language) to present in the classroom and to teach the dances within the school community. After much practice, in November 2013 they presented traditional dances at the district contest to represent the *Liceo* (Figure 4). The pedagogical objective for the activity was to foster multicultural understanding by the integration of Ěběra artistic traditions in the

Figure 4 Ěběra children representing the Liceo in a district cultural event

classroom and to provide opportunities for the representation and recognition of the school's multicultural assets.

Findings

In this section, we present two categories that emerged from the interpretation of students' narratives. *Life stories and the construction of Ěběra children's social and linguistic identity* and *Shifting languages in telling their story*. In the first category, we identify key themes in children's stories and turning points in children's ethnic and linguistic identities. The second category deals with the combined use of Ěběra and Spanish languages in the schooling processes of Ěběra children. The institutional decision to accept and support the inclusion of a native language different from Spanish at school represents an improvement toward the recognition of Indigenous populations' rights to their own language and culture. We briefly describe the categories and illustrate them with examples from the data collected.

Life stories and the construction of Ěběra children's social and linguistic identities

The key themes in Ěběra children's stories were *territory, family, displacement, Bogotá as a new culture, and the school*. Through the development of their stories, Indigenous children described specific situations and turning points in their lives but mainly they introduced themselves to the school community.

The presentation of the life stories in the school community produced a turn in the design and implementation of educational initiatives. Children's cultural particularities informed teachers and school administrators about the acculturation process that every Ěběra child was experiencing, and issues of gender, race and multicultural communication were then taken into account. The shift is reflected in teacher comments that moved away from earlier harsh declarations where the ideal scenario did not contemplate the presence of Indigenous population at schools, such as the following:

> We do not have the appropriate pedagogical tools for them to preserve their culture, now they are tattooing their bodies and dyeing their hair. The best thing is that they returned to their territory. (Biology middle school teacher statement in the academic council meeting, March 2011)

Instead, a completely different view emerged of the identity construction and self-image of students as potential pedagogical tools for the development of multicultural competence, as in this comment:

> Many ideas occur to me to work on cultural integration between the non-Indigenous children and the Ëbĕra children. For example, we can have cultural circuits. They can teach other children about particular cultural aspects and games and share with their peers part of their life to find things in common. At school, we can all use Ëbĕra words that can make them feel as an important part of the institution and we can recognize the cultural richness that we have. (Social science teacher interview, May, 2013)

This change recognized Indigenous people's own inherent perspectives, experiences, language and customs, and the right that they have to transform their realities according to what is relevant in their lives and contesting the marginalized ideal Western perspective of how an Indigenous student should be like.

Life stories and identity

Ëbĕra children's life stories were collected in order to look for reconciliations between the intrinsic culture of the students and their learning process in a multicultural context and also to recognize past learning experiences that influence their self-vision in the present. In their stories, Ëbĕra children play with identifications, images, descriptions, feelings, struggles and rationalizations in order to offer their own interpretation of their roots, a justification for their current life story and the resolution to position themselves as particular persons in their particular social contexts. Murray (1995) points out that one of the basic functions of self-narratives is to relate the stories we live and tell our identities, since those stories actually shape who we are. In Figure 1 above, the sample of an Ëbĕra narrative where the child describes and positions himself as a main actor in his family relations, the description is constructed using Spanish as L2. In this sense, he learns the language and now he is using it to develop awareness of who he is.

The collection of the children's stories followed themes such as *territorio Ĕbĕra* 'Ĕbĕra land', displacement, Bogotá and the school; in Figure 2 there is a graphic description of the native land and way of living before coming to the city. When describing places, children were also presenting the way they learned traditional activities and their own role in the community. They also explored the changes they faced when coming to Bogotá and contrasted their identity when living in their land compared to when living in the city.

These past experiences are social representations of the community identity and draw a historic narrative that can serve as a portrayal of the ways Ĕbĕras respond to new challenges. They also expose personal experiences and the reconfiguration of social and personal identities based on the correlation between their past and present. Besides, the acknowledgment of children's life stories changed what was said and thought about the Ĕbĕras and contested racial and discriminatory discourses.

McCarty (2011: 124) states that in narratives we can also find 'counter-themes of pride in identity, use of the home language, and respect for community values, rituals, and knowledge.' All of these are present in Indigenous children's stories and the selection and use of these themes contest the 'narratives of shame, stigma, humiliation, and a deficit discourse surrounding languages and identities' (McCarty, 2011: 123). According to Pavlenko (2002), narratives serve second language learners as a powerful tool to make teachers and students' voices heard: she states that ' the telling of life stories in a new language may be a means of empowerment that makes it possible to express new selves and desires previously considered untellable' (Pavlenko, 2002: 214). In this sense, we observed that Spanish allowed Ĕbĕra children to tell different lived-experiences, where sometimes the command or non-command of the language serves as a boundary of learning or as a site of struggle. Finally, we consider the work on narratives as a key aspect in the study since it made visible the intergenerational impact of school and language learning on Ĕbĕra Indigenous youth. In terms of textual advances, storytelling encouraged students to compose descriptions of past and present experiences using bilingual strategies and developing literacy skills.

Shifting languages in their storytelling

The language integration was framed on the community-based activity of collecting life stories of the children using Ĕbĕra or Spanish according to the individual proficiency of the child. An Ĕbĕra Chamí boy telling the story of the trip from their native land to Bogotá, for example, decided to write in Ĕbĕra. After collecting the assignment, the boy was interviewed and asked about his writing style and the use of the native language. In his answer, he explained some of his literacy practices when writing in L1:

I can write in Spanish and I know how to write in Ěběra using the sounds of Spanish; when I do not have the word in Ěběra, I write it in Spanish. (Semi-structured interview, May 2012)

The boy uses phonetic equivalences of Spanish to write in Ěběra and when he cannot find an equivalent word, he writes it directly in Spanish. The inventions used in his text evidence biliteracy practices that emerge from the use of both languages to make connections and to create meaning (cf. Hornberger, 2003). Other children opted for using Spanish instead of Ěběra to complete the assignment.

When another boy was interviewed, he had an opinion about the difficulty level of orality versus writing in both languages:

It is easier to speak Ebera but it is easy to write in Spanish because Margarita, the teacher, teaches us how to write and understand Spanish. (Semi-structured interview, May 2012)

In this second example, the child acknowledges a difference between oral and written linguistic scenarios; he also develops preferences for a language in every specific communicative situation, apparently favoring Spanish in writing since this has been the main language of reading and writing instruction in the school.

The importance of the use of both languages is constantly revealed in students' literacy practices. Ěběra as well as Spanish seem to shape the linguistic environment in children's daily lives, particularly since they have become permanent residents in the urban context and need the command of each language in specific communicative situations. This study supports the idea that the most effective and efficient approach for attaining relevance and educational aspirations in the language classroom is the inclusion of literacy practices in both languages without favoring Spanish but recognizing that, by boosting Indigenous students' Spanish language abilities and literacy, their opportunities for employment and their chances to access higher education increase significantly.

In conclusion, the integration of the native language in literacy assignments provides students with literacy options in the fulfillment of tasks and it presents a set of pedagogical opportunities that reveal students' linguistic particularities and preferences. Using the native language to promote literacy confirms the positive impact also observed in Indigenous communities in Peruvian and Mexican contexts (López, 2009). López concluded that the integration of native languages in the diverse classroom fostered literacy development, but also positions students as Spanish speakers who need to develop literacy abilities in the dominant language in order to achieve personal aspirations. In this respect, Ruiz asserts, 'Since languages live in communities, the common life activities of the community must be the targets of language policies. This means that the electronic and print media, social activities, social service providers, and other everyday centers of community life must be included in the implementation strategies by which language policies are promoted' (Ruiz, 1995: 78).

Conclusion

The study presented addressed key principles of the education of Indigenous groups related to language rights, educative policy making, literacy development and the importance of CBPR. It evokes the work of Latin-American educators and sociologists such as Freire, Ruiz and Fals Borda.

Ruiz's contributions in defense of minority language rights through his leading work on language planning with governments from countries in Central and South America left us a legacy that entail a strong conviction on our part as educators to continue seeking for equalizing opportunities for minority groups that have been traditionally marginalized. His political view on the rights of Indigenous communities to their language and culture through his concepts of language as right and as resource urge us to continue working toward supporting the maintenance of linguistic diversity in the Americas.

Freire's contributions to the education of marginalized populations through his rural adult literacy programs combined social theories to address the political dimensions of education (particularly the relationship between education and social change) and to connect these theoretical discussions to concrete pedagogical strategies.

Ruiz's work also echoes the work of Colombian sociologist Orlando Fals Borda (1987) on social pedagogy and participatory action research in Latin America. His theory, action and participation (PAR) methodology to social research was committed to furthering the interests of exploited groups and classes in many third world countries since the 1970s. The main purpose of PAR is to help communities to understand and transform the world through collective inquiry about their own reality.

Similarly to PAR, in this study, CBP performed with Ĕbĕra children turned a narrow vision of monolingual education into a more inclusive school environment by promoting the integration of Ĕbĕra adult members in the pedagogical process. This inclusive teaching material helped improve the position of the Ĕbĕra language as a minority language in the school context. It also exposed the need for local policies that revitalize the native languages and contest dominant educative language policies that promote the loss of endangered languages.

Although this is a minor advance in intercultural understanding for policy making in Colombia, it indicates that the particularities of minority children need to be considered in the school contexts. Adopting pedagogies that consider new ways to look at education in terms of its relevance, reciprocity, time management, acculturation processes, ethnic versus urban identity construction, and marginalization can be beneficial to the education of Indigenous minority groups. This also confirms what Champagne (2009) states regarding the globalized lack of enthusiasm of Indigenous people for schooling in its traditional dominant culture form. Although the Ēbĕra community considers education as a relevant element to empower their social and cultural conditions, their motivations are not reflected in the traditional curriculum of the school.

Finally, this pedagogical intervention using Ēbĕra language in the stories of displacement and Ēbĕra culture through their arts and crafts demonstrates the richness of Ēbĕra language and culture as community and regional resources. It reinforces Hornberger's (2000) statement about the growing recognition that interculturality must be self-consciously defined and born from local actions aimed at social change, innovation, and acknowledgment of autonomy and community values.

Notes

(1) Costa Rican National Association of Educators (ANDE Costa Rica): http://www. ande.cr; Ecuadorian Educators National Union (UNE Ecuador): http://www.une.org. ec/; Bolivian National Teacher Confederation (CONMERB BOLIVIA): http://conmerb.org/; Paraguay National Teacher Union (UNE PARAGUAY): http://www.unesn. org.py/; Argentina Educators National Union (CTERA Argentina): http://www.ctera. org.ar/; Chile: http://www.colegiodeprofesores.cl/; Peru National Teacher Union (SUTEP): http://www.iadb.org/res/publications/pubfiles/pubR-474.pdf Brazil National Confederation of Education Professional Workers: http://www.cnte.org.br/; Colombia. National Commission for Work and Education of Indigenous Populations (CONTCEPI): http://www.territorioindigenaygobernanza.com/col_09.html; https:// en.wikipedia.org/wiki/National_Indigenous_Organization_of_Colombia
(2) See http://www.crihu.org/2012/09/la-ley-origen.html.
(3) SEIP Indigenous Educational System: http://www.mineducacion.gov.co/1621/article-214913.html; Colombian Indigenous Peoples' Worldview: https://www.culturalsurvival.org/publications/cultural-survival-quarterly/colombia/intercultural-health-processes-colombian-amazon
(4) Education viewed from the Indigenous cosmovision and ways of knowing: http://www.scoop.it/t/educacion-desde-la-cosmovision-y-pensamiento-ind-genas.

References

Aguirre, D., González, R. and Panchi, M. (2013) *Karta Ēbĕra beďea ɓu kawabiy ita. Manual de enseñanza y escritura ĕbĕra-chamí.* See http://antioquia.gov.co/PDF2/MANUAL_EMBERA.pdf (accessed April 2014).
Alatas, F. (2006) *Alternative Discourses in Asian Social Science: Responses to Eurocentrism.* New Delhi: Sage Publications.
Altman, J. and Fogarty, L. (2010) Indigenous Australians as 'no gaps' subjects: Education and development in remote Australia. In I. Snyder and J. Nieuwenhuysen (eds) *Closing the Gap in Education: Improving Outcomes in Southern World Societies* (pp. 109–128). Clayton, Vic.: Monash University Publishing.

Amuwo, S.A. and Jenkins, E. (2001) True partnership evolves over time. In M. Sullivan and J.G. Kelly (eds) *Collaborative Research: University and Community Partnership* (pp. 25–44). Washington, DC: American Public Health Association.

Arias, J., Amador, B. and Toro, C. (2008) *Makú jogúki: Ordenamiento educativo del puebloindígena kankuamo.* Sierra Nevada de Santa Marta: Resguardo Indígena Kankuamo. See http://www.colombiaaprende.edu.co/html/home/1592/articles-213863_archivo1.pdf (accessed April 2014).

Champagne, D. (2009) *United Nations: State of the World's Indigenous Peoples.* New York: Contemporary Education.

CONTCEPI (2012) Perfil del sistema educativo indígena propio, Bogotá: S.E.I.P. CONTCEPI.

Corson, D. (1998) Community-based education for Indigenous cultures. *Language, Culture and Curriculum* 11 (3), 238–249.

De Mejía, A.M. (2005) Bilingual education in Colombia: Towards an integrated perspective. In A.M. De Mejia (ed.) *Bilingual Education in South America* (pp. 48–64). Clevedon: Multilingual Matters.

De Mejía, A. (2006) Bilingual education in Colombia: Towards recognition of languages, cultures and identities. *Colombian Applied Linguistics Journal* 8, 152–168.

De Mejía, A. and Fonseca, L. (2007) *Orientaciones para políticas bilingües y multilingües en lenguas extranjeras en Colombia.* Bogotá: Centro de Investigación y Formación en Educación Universidad de los Andes.

Deyhle, D. and Swisher, K. (1997) Research in American Indian and Alaska native education: From assimilation to self-determination. *Review of Research in Education* 22, 113–194.

Fals Borda, O. (ed.) (1987) *The Challenge of Social Change.* International Sociology Series. London: Sage Publications.

Ferreira, M.P. and Gendron, F. (2011) Community-based participatory research with traditional and Indigenous communities of the Americas: Historical context and future directions. *International Journal of Critical Pedagogy* 3, 153–168.

Fishman, J. (1991) *Reversing Language Shift: Theory and Practice of Assistance to Threatened Languages.* Clevedon: Multilingual Matters.

Freire, P. (1993) *Pedagogy of the Oppressed.* New York: Continuum.

Gonzalez-Ariza, A. (2014) Ěběra immigrant children schooling process in Bogotá. Unpublished master's thesis, Universidad Distrital, Bogotá.

Guerrero, C.H. and Quintero, A. (2009) English as a neutral language in the Colombian national standards: A constituent of dominance in English language education. *Profile* 11 (2), 135–150.

Guerrero, C. (2010) Language policies in Colombia: The inherited disdain for our native languages. *HOW* 16, 11–24.

Hornberger, N.H. (ed.) (1996) *Indigenous Literacies in the Americas: Language Planning from the Bottom Up.* Berlin: Mouton.

Hornberger, N. (1998) Language policy, language education, language rights: Indigenous, immigrant, and international perspectives. *Language in Society* 27, 439–458.

Hornberger, N.H. (2000) Bilingual education policy and practice in the Andes: Ideological paradox and intercultural possibility. *Anthropology and Education Quarterly* 31 (2), 173–201.

Hornberger, N.H. (ed.) (2003) *Continua of Biliteracy: An Ecological Framework for Educational Policy, Research and Practice in Multilingual Settings.* Clevedon: Multilingual Matters.

Hornberger, N. (2008) *Can Schools Save Indigenous Languages? Policy and Practice on Four Continents.* London: Palgrave Macmillan.

ISE (International Society of Ethnobiology) (2006) International Society of Ethnobiology Code of Ethics (with 2008 additions). See http://ethnobiology.net/code-of-ethics/.

Landaburu, J. (1999) Clasificación de las lenguas indígenas de Colombia. See http://www.banrepcultural.org/blaavirtual/antropologia/lengua/clas00.htm (accessed April 2014).

López, L. (2009) *Reaching the Unreached: Indigenous Intercultural Bilingual Education in Latin America. Background Paper Prepared for the Education for All Global Monitoring Report 2010*. Paris: UNESCO.

May, S. (1994) *Making Multicultural Education Work*. Clevedon: Multilingual Matters.

May, S. and Aikman, S. (2003) Indigenous education: Addressing current issues and developments. *Comparative Education* 39 (2), 139–145.

McCarty, T.L. (1998) Schooling, resistance, and American Indian languages. *International Journal of the Sociology of Language* 132, 27–41.

McCarty, T. (2011) *Ethnography and Language Policy*. New York: Routledge.

McCarty, T. (2013) *Language Planning and Policy in Native America: History, Theory, Praxis*. Bristol: Multilingual Matters.

McCarty, T. and Watahomigie, L.J. (1998) Indigenous community-based language education in the USA. *Language, Culture and Curriculum* 11 (3), 315–325.

Moll, L., Amanti, C., Neff, D. and Gonzalez, N. (1992) Funds of knowledge for teaching: Using a qualitative approach to connect homes and classrooms. *Theory into Practice* 31 (2), 132–141.

Murray, K. (1995) Narrative partitioning: The ins and outs of identity construction. See http://home.mira.net/~kmurray/psych/in&out.html (accessed April 2014).

Pavlenko, A. (2002) Narrative study: Whose story is it anyway? *TESOL Quarterly* 36 (2), 213–218.

Philips, S.U. (1983) *The Invisible Culture: Communication in Classroom and Community on the Warm Springs Reservation*. New York: Longman.

Riessman, C.K. (2002) Doing justice: Positioning the interpreter in narrative work. In W. Patterson (ed.) *Strategic Narrative: New Perspectives on the Power of Personal and Cultural Storytelling* (pp. 195–216). Lanham, MA and Oxford: Lexington Books.

Romero, A. (2005) *Documento DANE: La visibilización estadística de los grupos étnicos colombianos censo 2005*. Bogotá: Imprenta Nacional.

Romero, F. (2002) La oralidad y la escritura entre los Embera-Chamí: Aspectos educativos. Universidad Tecnológica de Pereira. See http://www.naya.org.ar/congreso2002/ponencias/fernando_romero_loaiza3.htm (accessed April 2014).

Ruiz, R. (1984) Language orientations. *NABE Journal* 8 (2), 15–34.

Ruiz, R. (1995) Language planning considerations in Indigenous communities. *Bilingual Research Journal* 19 (1), 71–81.

Sharkey, J. and Clavijo, A. (2012) Community-based pedagogies projects and possibilities in Colombia and the United States. In A. Honigsfeld and A. Cohan (eds) *Breaking the Mold of Education for Culturally and Linguistically Diverse Students* (pp. 129–137). Lanham, MD: R & L Education.

Smith, L.T. (1999) *Decolonizing Methodologies: Research and Indigenous Peoples*. London: Zed.

Somali, L.M. and Kincheloe, J.L. (1999) *What Is Indigenous Knowledge?* New York: Flamer Press.

Usma, J. (2009) Education and language policy in Colombia: Exploring processes of inclusion, exclusion, and stratification in times of global reform. *PROFILE* 11, 123–141.

Appendix 1: Consentimiento Informado

Apreciado(a) Padre de Familia:

Durante el desarrollo de Entrevistas se pretende recopilar valiosa información que se empleara en la sistematización y publicación de la investigación 'Ĕbĕra Immigrant Children Schooling Process in Bogotá', 'El proceso de escolarización de los niños Ĕbĕra en Bogotá'.

En todos los casos, se tratará la información que provenga de su hijo de manera confidencial, para lo cual se usarán nombres ficticios, a menos que usted indique lo contrario. Atentamente, solicito su autorización para emplear la información, para lo cual le agradezco completar el formato que encuentra a continuación y entregarlo a la mayor brevedad.

Agradezco su gentil atención.

APG

Autorización

Por la presente manifiesto mi autorización para que se emplee la siguiente información recolectada (favor marcar con un visto bueno o una equis):

Trabajos en clase _____ Videos durante las clases _____ Fotografías durante las clases _____

Reportes orales _____ Trabajos escritos _____ Conclusiones de grupos de discusión _____

conversaciones _____

Manifiesto que conozco y comprendo el uso que se dará a la información por mí suministrada, con base en los principios éticos propios de las Ciencias Sociales.

Aclaro que tengo la libertad de retractarme, si así lo deseo, y que se me ha dado la oportunidad de preguntar acerca de los propósitos para los cuales se espera utilizar la información. Para ello cuento con la voluntad expresa del equipo investigador, quienes estarán dispuestos a responder mis interrogantes.

Manifiesto que he leído y comprendido perfectamente lo anterior y que todos los espacios en blanco han sido completados antes de mi firma y me encuentro en capacidad de expresar mi consentimiento.

Nombre del (la) padre (madre)   (a):_____

Firma del (la) padre (madre)   (a): _____

CC. No _____   Expedida en _____

Nombre que sugiero se emplee, cuando se use información por mí suministrada _____

Fecha: _____   Teléfono:_____

Correo electrónico

Appendix 2: Consentimiento Informado

Apreciado(a) Docente:

Durante el desarrollo de Entrevistas se pretende recopilar valiosa información que se empleara en la sistematización y publicación de la investigación 'Ěběra Immigrant Children Schooling Process in Bogotá', 'El proceso de escolarización de los niños Ěběra en Bogotá'.

En todos los casos, se tratará la información que provenga de usted de manera confidencial, para lo cual se usarán nombres ficticios, a menos que usted indique lo contrario.

Atentamente, solicito su autorización para emplear la información, para lo cual le agradezco completar el formato que encuentra a continuación y entregarlo a la mayor brevedad.

Agradezco su gentil atención.

APG

Autorización

Por la presente manifiesto mi autorización para que se emplee la siguiente información recolectada en

Entrevistas _____-Trabajos en clase _____ Videos durante las clases ____Fotografías durante las clases _____ Reportes orales _____ Trabajos escritos _____ Conclusiones de grupos de discusión _____ conversaciones ____

Manifiesto que conozco y comprendo el uso que se dará a la información por mí suministrada, con base en los principios éticos propios de las Ciencias Sociales.

Aclaro que tengo la libertad de retractarme, si así lo deseo, y que se me ha dado la oportunidad de preguntar acerca de los propósitos para los cuales se espera utilizar la información. Para ello cuento con la voluntad expresa del equipo investigador, quienes estarán dispuestos a responder mis interrogantes.

Manifiesto que he leído y comprendido perfectamente lo anterior y que todos los espacios en blanco han sido completados antes de mi firma y me encuentro en capacidad de expresar mi consentimiento.

Nombre del (la) docente: _____ Firma _____

CC. No _____   Expedida en _____

Nombre que sugiero se emplee, cuando se use información por mí suministrada _____

Fecha: _____

Learning About Linguistic Resources Through Home Engagements: Opportunities for Latina Preservice Teachers to Shape Their Language Orientations

Iliana Reyes and Ana Christina Da Silva Iddings

This chapter is written and inspired in loving memory of Richard Ruiz – a kind and generous human being, colleague, and Maestro *of* Maestros.

In this chapter we focus on a longitudinal study in which we sought to create and document multiple opportunities for early childhood educators, community and family members to enter into dialogue and explore together ways to learn and attend to diverse linguistic, social, cultural and community backgrounds of linguistically diverse and bilingual children from a *language-as-resource* perspective. In particular, we share findings about Latina preservice teachers' experiences during home engagements that allowed them to build relationships with students' families beyond the walls of the classroom and to develop close understandings about their own perspective on *linguistic orientations and attitudes* (Ruiz, 1984) as well as those of their bilingual students (Reyes & Da Silva Iddings, 2012). These new understandings were then leveraged as resources for learning in order to enhance the literacy development of their emergent bilingual students (Reyes, 2006).

We embrace Richard Ruiz's definition of *language orientations* to refer to a 'complex of dispositions toward language and its role, and toward languages and their role in society' (Ruiz, 1984: 16). Our study with preservice teachers focuses on their own reflection at the level of family and school language use; their reflections, framed within the language *orientations* that Ruiz proposed and shared in his framework for language planning, provide an opportunity for a better understanding of how one's own linguistic resources can be used as a catalyst to appreciate and tap into children's and families' bilingual knowledge. Moreover, these orientations help us see, through the lenses of young preservice teachers, how they relate and expand their language attitudes and notions toward bilingualism and multiliteracies through their field experiences at home and community with diverse children.

About Latina Preservice Teachers' Bilingualism and Home Literacies: Resources or Barriers?

Our primary purpose in designing *home and family* engagements as a key part of our program was to counter a still-prevalent ideology that emergent bilingual children and their immigrant families are somehow literacy deficient or that they lack resources (i.e. a deficit-oriented perspective). Through this work we argue for a shift in what is defined or counted as 'legitimate' literacies and we also argue for the need to emphasize teacher education practices where scaffolding is provided for *all* teachers to have the opportunity to reflect on and rethink important and pressing issues regarding teaching in diverse communities (Da Silva Iddings & Reyes, forthcoming). In this chapter we share examples of our research from working with three Latina preservice teachers who were part of a larger study in our early childhood program focusing on family and community literacies. As these students identify their own language and literacy experiences as resources, they are able to rethink what literacy means, taking in consideration bilingualism – theirs and those of the young children they work with, breaking stereotypes and negotiating shifts in language orientation.

About Families and Communities as Linguistic Resources for Teacher Education

Teachers face the challenge of getting to know the local communities where they will end up teaching as part of their fieldwork experiences and beyond. We know that the increased diversity in classrooms in the US and abroad is a reality as part of a constant flow and adjustment of communities; therefore, teachers must feel confident and develop competencies that enable them to integrate academic knowledge along with tools that support learning for diverse young learners (Nieto, 2002). Through a recent early childhood teacher education reform we named CREATE,[1] we aim to provide our preservice teachers with the opportunity to benefit from experiencing and working with children and families in diverse contexts and not only from one context. This in turn helps them expand and rethink their definition of literacy, and to become more conscious of the significance of working with and including families from diverse contexts and other community members in their everyday pedagogical practices.

The home engagements that are part of the early childhood CREATE program, along with course requirements, were designed to get to know a child beyond the walls of the classroom and as a departure from the traditional home visit model that other programs have implemented (e.g. Head Start) with working-class and diverse families (Kirkland, 2013), which emphasize an assistive perspective. Through the program's course requirements in the early childhood major, we support and guide preservice teachers in interacting with a family and their young child (4–6 year olds) to learn about their day-to-day family literacy practices. While the preservice teachers learn about significant language and literacy milestones for young children in the classroom, in practice they also experience learning with the child at school, classroom and at home. In CREATE, we designed this feature of the early childhood program as a main objective to transform the experiences of preservice teachers as well as those of children and their families. By supporting and guiding them in learning about the linguistic Funds of Knowledge (González et al., 2005) and bilingual and bicultural experiences they share with their young students, we create a space for them to problematize and rethink their own language attitudes in relation to language as problem/right/resource orientations.

Through a series of redesigned courses, preservice teachers are assigned as partners with a family and a young child (preschool to first grade level) who is developing early literacy and bilingualism. Actively participating and learning from the family and community literacy practices grants preservice teachers opportunities to better understand the relationship between language and literacy development (Ortiz & Ordóñez-Jasis, 2005). Therefore, in our program courses we asked preservice teachers to be involved in family and community interactions related to getting to know the children's literacies, getting to know the families and getting to know the communities through a series of projects that had as its objective for them to reflect on what they have experienced and learned in relation to family and community literacies and local resources. The purpose of these activities was to broaden their understanding of language and literacy developing in the home, and beyond commonly accepted forms of language and literacy in the classroom, because literacy can be found in various domains and through different expressive means (Morrell, 2004).

Through class assignments, we emphasized the importance of reflection and documentation (Gandini & Kaminski, 2004) as part of the process for these preservice teachers to document their own learning processes about the many language and literacy practices already existing within the diverse families and local communities but which often go unacknowledged by those in powerful roles (Lee, 2001; Moll & González, 1994).

The preservice teachers were required to participate in a series of about 12 home engagements throughout the two-year program. During their first year, they were placed in preschool classrooms. Therefore, they (with help from our Community Liaison) would select a case study child whose family's home language was other than English, and contact the family for consent and to arrange for the engagements to take place on a consistent basis throughout the year. During their second year in the program, the students were placed in K-2 public school classrooms, and the same procedures would apply. Families were selected strictly on a volunteer basis. The purpose of working with one family each year was for the students to engage in a sustained relationship with the families and to examine and hopefully disrupt any preconceived assumptions they may have had about culturally and linguistically diverse families. Modes of documentation and reflection the teachers engaged in included detailed field notes about their observations and interactions in the homes, debriefing notes and reflection journals for each home engagement. These reflections were especially focused on how language and literacy played an important role in the families' interactions. The researchers analyzed all of these documents, looking for instances of shifts in language orientation.

The teachers' reflections, such as the one shared in the quote below by one of our participants, Luisa, allowed the preservice teachers to share their insights about the home engagements and to give us (faculty) in-depth perspectives as to how their own notions of language and literacy broadened as they engaged in literacy events and conversation with their assigned case study:

> When I was told about the home visits last semester I was thrilled to work with a family because I love meeting new people and also learning about different cultures. ... What was required from my part was to go in the home and create a *safe and trusting* relationship with the family because that was the only way I was going to learn about important things and their interests in life. ... The reason why it's important to share our own personal experiences with the families is to create a *strong* rapport.

Luisa, who identified as Latina and grew up fluently bilingual in Spanish and English in the Southwest, reflects on the importance of building *strong* rapport and *confianza* (trust) with her case study child and the family (Valdés, 1996). She reported on the ways she related with the case study family by going beyond focusing only on basic information to share her own personal experiences in order to make connections with the case study child's language and literacy development and *Funds of Knowledge* (González et al., 2005). Being bilingual herself, she searches for different avenues into building rapport and also for learning about literacy and language Funds of Knowledge.

However, that is not always the case, for preservice teachers who come from a monolingual background may have very differing views on the educational conditions of culturally and linguistically diverse children because of their own experiences, which have not provided opportunities to challenge the status quo in their day-to-day context (Brochin Ceballos, 2012; Nieto, 2003; Reyes *et al.*, 2016).

The analyses presented in this chapter focus on providing a closer look at preservice teachers' reflections, done as part of their class presentations and written assignments. Reyes *et al.* (2016) describe the ways by which the preservice teachers were guided through a series of community literacy events and experiences that allowed them to get a closer understanding about the significance of community life and what is there for the children and families to experience as part of their daily local literacies, while dispelling notions of what *is not* there for these children. During these field experiences the preservice teachers are guided toward paying close attention to the diversity of languages and literacies available to children but not always recognized by teachers (Gutiérrez & Rogoff, 2003).

The vignettes we share here include reflections from three Latina preservice teachers on their family interactions as they observed and engaged in conversation with the case study children and their families to understand some of the family bilingual literacy practices. We particularly look for ways in which these preservice teachers and the children's parents describe young children's literacy practices and their ways of using their native language to leverage their early literacy development, including reading and writing. The reflections were part of their written class assignments and end of year interviews from their junior year. All the sources, written reflections and transcript material were reread and analyzed by the researchers to construct the various domains in which language and literacy orientations were evident. Here we highlight three themes that emerged in our analyses of their reflections and documentation: connecting their personal stories with bilingualism and bilingual practices; family knowledge as valuable – language and literacy as resources; and expanding understandings of literacy – from 'no literacy' to 'transnational biliteracy.'

Connecting personal stories with bilingualism and bilingual practices

A powerful way for the preservice teachers to begin their reflection on language use and bilingual practices was to share and present their own literacy stories and histories through narratives about the *ways* they themselves experienced learning to read, write and how they traveled along the continua of biliteracy for those that considered themselves bilinguals (Hornberger, 2003). These three Latina teachers, Gisela, Luisa and Teresa,[2] identified their own bilingualism, in Spanish and English, as a resource in growing up in

Mexican immigrant families and then as a resource to use as a learning tool and strategy with their students. Teresa, for example, reports:

> I guess that, me being bilingual, it's actually a plus technique, because I'm able to reach more to the families because of that second language. Because I do speak Spanish, enough to understand it and teach kindergarten in Spanish, I was able to use a lot of their native language. Again, that was really nice that I had done the home visits and communicated with parents, because I understood that their other language was Spanish. Whereas before, I was just making those assumptions.

Gisela also identifies the native language as an asset in order to engage with her case study family, particularly the dad who had a preference for speaking in Spanish:

> During the entire visit we spoke mainly Spanish; the father seemed to be more comfortable with it. I was more comfortable with it too. The parents told me that Emma has recently been speaking more Spanish than usual. I wonder if I was an influence for her decision of language, since we talked to her during the last visit about the importance of knowing Spanish (or another language). I told her about my experience as a bilingual adult, I told her I was able to get a lot of jobs because I knew Spanish. I learned in this visit that the brother prefers Spanish because the *abuelita* raised him for almost 9 years (he is 12 now) and the grandmother would only speak Spanish to him. (Gisela, Field note reflection)

Gisela, like Teresa, has knowledge of bilingualism and second language (L2) development because of her own experiences growing up bilingual in the Southwest with her family (González, 2001). She was able to make direct assessments about the impact of understanding language and literacy development and the impact of the native language development of her case study child to her early literacy competencies. These examples and teachers' own bilingualism contributed to composing an *additive* and language-as-resource perspective as part of their orientations toward bilingualism and multilingual literacies.

Family knowledge as valuable: *Language and literacy as resources*

The preservice teachers engaged with children and their families on an average of three times during the semester. Through a dialogue around Funds of Knowledge with the parents and families at the beginning of the semester, they learned about the home cultural and linguistic background. Luisa, for example, identified her case study family as being from the Tijuana,

Mexico–San Diego, California border region. The family shared with her about their *transnational* practices where Victor (case study boy) and his cousins had the opportunity to learn English and use their bilingualism across border experiences because of work and schooling opportunities (Lam & Warriner, 2012; Reyes, 2012). She was also able to identify the family's current but dynamic language practices by describing that the family 'speaks and uses Spanish for family interactions.' However, Luisa also explains in her field notes how, over time, Victor responds more and mostly in English. She notes during her last visits in the fall semester that 'he responds only in English' to his parents. Furthermore, she is able to reflect on the fact that the 'family's first language is a resource and the parents in particular use it as an asset.' She goes on further to explain that almost in a parallel manner, there is a *language shift* occurring because of Victor's preference for speaking and responding in English to his parents and at school. This is an important shift, documented in the literature, in terms of bilingualism, which may occur and become prevalent in potential bilingual children's daily literacy practices when the preference shifts toward the dominant language (Moll & Ruiz, 2002; Zentella, 2002). Although the parents might be aware of this shift and continue to reinforce the first language use at home, there is a subtle priority and pressure on immigrants at the societal level in the US context toward mastering the dominant language (Suárez-Orozco & Suárez-Orozco, 2001).

Despite this pressure for children to develop English, often at the expense of Spanish, Gisela states how the native language is part of the child's linguistic Funds of Knowledge which she sees as much connected to the child's culture:

> Another one (linguistic fund of knowledge) is their native language is Spanish so I just feel like you incorporate culture in their life. Culture shouldn't end at home when they leave, but it should also be welcome at school and also for parents to come into class. (Gisela, Interview, 2012)

Being bilingual herself, Gisela is able to document and highlight these important language practices and the significance of culture for her family case study; during the interview she highlights how she sees bilingualism as a linguistic resource for the family and how Emma's (case study child) culture should not 'end at home'; instead she has begun to implement a bilingual and dual language perspective into her curriculum and classroom activities.

Expanding understandings of literacy: *From no literacy to transnational biliteracy*

During an interview, Luisa reflects on her growing-up experiences at home:

> When I was a child, I really didn't have *any* exposure to literacy at home, so just like go watching now how parents are with literacy and books at

> home, makes me really happy to see because I didn't have that at home.
> I come from a Spanish speaking family, and I don't know if it is the cul-
> ture we have, that is not really focused on books. ... But just like family
> literacy is the focus, the family has literacy at home like at school.

In this quote, Luisa focuses on traditional definitions of literacy to include only reading competencies, and emphasizes the 'lack of exposure' to liter-acy because of the lack of opportunities for her parents to buy books; how-ever, she struggles to connect her other cultural literacies, such as oral histories, documented as significant in other immigrant communities, as part of her repertoire of literacies (Lam & Warriner, 2012). This challenge of emphasizing only narrow forms of literacy as *the* way to be literate is prevalent in current discourse and literacy programs (Delpit & Kilgour Dowdy, 2003; Heath, 1983; Reyes *et al.*, 2016). It is this same belief and approach to literacy that reinforces stereotypes and creates challenges for teachers as they reflect on language orientations toward minoritized com-munities and their young bilingual students. Moreover, it is not an auto-matic process for Luisa to identify and translate other literacies that are not valued as strongly as those more 'formal' literacies are valued in the class-room context.

Gisela, on the other hand, uses her own background knowledge of how she learned in her childhood to expand definitions of literacy. She goes beyond a conceptual approach to use her personal experience and her own linguistic Funds of Knowledge. For her example, in her documentation she uses the concept of oral stories, such as the *cri-cri* song, that connects oral literacy and a local popular children's Mexican singer and his songs to chil-dren's Spanish early literacy development. In addition, she also explores her understanding of non-traditional meanings of literacy based on what she sees in her case study home:

> I noticed some things in the home as sources of literacy that I did not
> notice before. The first thing I noticed was a large portrait of the *Lady*
> *of Guadalupe* on the wall near the entrance. This shows me that religion
> is key in the household, and could be a source of literacy for the kids,
> especially if it is practiced in both languages. I also saw many photos
> of different family members on the wall. During my first visit there,
> Alicia loved to tell me different stories about the photographs. These
> types of photos are so important when it comes to developing story-
> telling skills. They help her to recall events and express the events
> orally to me.

Finally, we learned of Teresa's bilingual and *transnational* experiences growing up in Mexico as a child and how these experiences expand her defi-nition of literacies to include stories, reading and writing fluently in Spanish.

She also goes on to share how these experiences helped her especially as she began working with preschool emergent bilingual children in the US:

> I started practicing my teaching skills with preschool students by ... leyéndoles y contándoles acerca de mi <u>cultura</u>, así como mis fiestas de cumpleaños. [by ... reading to them and telling them stories about my <u>culture</u>. Like my birthday parties.]

She was able to engage children by using Spanish to tell stories about her favorite activities and holidays, as she explains: 'I shared with them stories about my culture, like celebrations, including my birthday parties.' As part of her documentation and reflection, she uses images and bilingual text to share in class, as shown in her documentation and presentation material:

Connecting Personal Stories with Pedagogy

" I guess that, me being bilingual, it's actually a plus technique, because I'm able to reach more to the families because of that second language".

Inicie practicando mis cualidades como maestra en prescolar...

reading to them and telling them stories about my <u>culture</u>. Like my birthday parties.

I started practicing my teaching skills with preschool students by...

leyéndoles y contándoles acerca de mi <u>Cultura</u>, así como mis fiestas de cumpleaños.

Final Thoughts

The preservice teachers' experiences shared in this chapter demonstrate how their native home language, Spanish, and their bilingualism supports and furthers their understanding of their students' family literacy practices. In addition, through the home and family engagements they were able to observe, identify and describe various cultural ways of utilizing oral and written language in Spanish and English which families and children draw upon in their daily lives (Barton & Hamilton, 2000; Heath, 1983; Reyes, 2006).

Through the scaffolding they had in their coursework, many of them were able to start moving beyond a traditional perspective of literacy and language development to one that included the local literacies in one or two languages, and multiple ways of being able to view a child's language and literacy learning. Gisela uses her bilingual and cultural knowledge, along with academic strategies in the classroom, to describe how she sees the child's learning across subjects and contexts:

> Although I have learned many new things this semester the one thing that has stayed with me and will be carried on through my career as a teacher is the importance of documentation. The idea of being 'participant-observers' is relevant to all aspects of teaching; whether it is math, science, reading or helping English Language Learner students make progress in learning a second language. In doing so we take snapshots of where a child is, how they are progressing, what areas they are excelling in and what areas of development need more attention. Sometimes as teachers we can get caught up with the routine of the day and we don't devote a day to really observe. With photos, hard copies of their work, video and voice recordings we can look and reflect on things that were missed at the time. Throughout the semester we have documented the work and development of our preschool and elementary child in many different ways.

Gisela, Teresa and Luisa, the three participants presented here, who were bilingual themselves and had knowledge of second language learning, were able to make direct assessments and connections about the impact of understanding language and literacy development by observing the child they each worked with during their field experience and engaging in what literacy means for each of these children and their families. Their own knowledge of a second language and their own bilingualism supported the composing of an *additive* view of bilingualism as part of their language orientation and attitudes toward children and families' multiple literacies (King & Fogle, 2006).

Moreover the vignettes shared here deepened our understandings of Latina preservice teachers' experiences and their process of reflecting on language orientations to identify their own Funds of Knowledge along with those of their students. Specifically, opportunities such as the home engagements designed and integrated explicitly as part of their early childhood teaching and learning experiences provided the way to best support these preservice teachers, who were bilingual themselves, to develop attitudes reflective of language-as-resource orientations. Through their interactions with the families and children at home, they were able to describe students' cultural knowledge and literacy competencies beyond the classroom context to include local literacies in the families' native language (Perry *et al.*, 2008). The opportunity to participate on family home engagements and community literacy events afforded preservice teachers space to expand their definitions of literacy to include bilingualism and multiliteracies as resources in their day-to-day experiences.

Over time, through these program experiences, the preservice teachers were able to identify literacy practices within families, switching from learning *about* the family and the child to learning *with* the child about his family linguistic resources. In the case of these Latina, first-generation teachers, they focused on the native language (Spanish) and bilingual learning experiences during home engagements to connect to their own linguistic resources and those of their case study families. The official practicum experiences provided and required by our early childhood program acknowledged and validated bilingualism as a linguistic resource for them and for young students. Other preservice teachers with a similar program experience were able to recognize the family's home language and bilingual background as well (see DaSilva Iddings & Reyes, forthcoming; Reyes *et al.*, 2016); however, they focused mainly on the child's English language development as part of their assignment description – providing only a partial view of what the child and family experiences were like and how these contributed to the child's early literacy development and potential to develop bilingualism.

The language orientations reflected in the attitudes of these three Latina preservice teachers varied from more conventional views and definitions of language and literacy to perspectives consistent with a language-as-resource orientation in terms of how native language use and bilingualism can support children's critical literacy thinking and cultural experiences. And although they struggled, as other teachers who work in *English only* classroom environments, to translate some of their language attitudes and theoretical explanations into action as part of their classroom activities, they strived to continue translating bilingualism as a resource orientation into their everyday practice. Ruiz's language orientation framework is reflected here as part of young Latina preservice teachers' attitudes toward their own continuum of bilingualism and biliteracy. For them, growing up bilingual themselves has been an asset; however, this has often gone unrecognized by the educational system and their own schooling experiences where English hegemony has been upheld and a 'language-as-problem' orientation has led many educational program efforts. Notwithstanding, the preservice teachers' language attitudes toward the families with whom they entered into relationships, and their own language experiences, were also shaped by the home engagements provided as part of the ECE program and curriculum. Consequently, a language-as-resource orientation received some important validation at the program level in a higher education institution and as future teachers of young children growing up in our multilingual communities. We suggest starting now on the development and implementation of early language and literacy programs that invite and engage preservice teachers to identify, explore and validate their own and also the children's bilingualism and multiliteracies for all, especially in diverse communities. It is our hope that such programs will continue reshaping preservice teachers' attitudes in ways reflective of an orientation toward language as resource, at a personal, community and institutional level.

Notes

(1) CREATE – Communities as Resources in Early Childhood Teacher Education is our redesigned early childhood program at the University of Arizona College of Education. For additional information about project objectives see www.createarizona.org.
(2) All names are pseudonyms.

References

Barton, D. and Hamilton, M. (2000) Literacy practices. In D. Barton, M. Hamilton and R. Ivanič (eds) *Situated Literacies: Reading and Writing in Context* (pp. 7–15). London: Routledge.

Brochin Ceballos, C. (2012) Literacies at the border: Transnationalism and the biliteracy practices of teachers across the US-Mexico border. *International Journal of Bilingual Education and Bilingualism* 15 (6), 687–703.

Da Silva Iddings, A.C. and Reyes, I. (forthcoming) Community literacy engagements as opportunities for pre-service teachers to learn about funds of knowledge. In A.C. DaSilva Iddings (ed.) *Re-designing Teacher Education for Culturally and Linguistically Diverse Young Students: Towards a Critical-Ecological Approach.* New York: Routledge.

Delpit, L. and Kilgour Dowdy, J. (eds) (2003) *The Skin That We Speak: Thoughts on Language and Culture in the Classroom.* New York: New Press.

Gandini, L. and Kaminsky, J.A. (2004) Reflections on the relationship between documentation and assessment in the American context: An interview with Brenda Fyfe. *Innovations in Early Education: The International Reggio Exchange* 11 (1), 5–17.

González, N. (2001) *I Am My Language: Discourses of Women and Children in the Borderlands.* Tucson, AZ: University of Arizona Press.

González, N., Moll, L. and Amanti, C. (eds) (2005) *Funds of Knowledge: Theorizing Practices in Households, Communities, and Classrooms.* New York: Routledge.

Gutiérrez, K.D. and Rogoff, B. (2003) Cultural ways of learning: Individual traits or repertoires of practice. *Educational Researcher* 32 (5), 19–25.

Heath, S.B. (1983) *Ways With Words: Language, Life, and Work in Communities and Classrooms.* Cambridge: Cambridge University Press.

Hornberger, N. (ed.) (2003) *Continua of Biliteracy: An Ecological Framework for Educational Policy, Research, and Practice in Multilingual Settings.* Clevedon: Multilingual Matters.

King, K. and Fogle, L. (2006) Bilingual parenting as good parenting: Parents' perspectives on family language policy for additive bilingualism. *International Journal of Bilingual Education and Bilingualism* 9 (6), 695–712.

Kirkland, K. (2013) Effectiveness of home visiting as a strategy for promoting children's adjustment to school. *Zero to Three Journal* 33 (3), 31–38.

Lam, W.S.E. and Warriner, D. (2012) Transnationalism and literacy: Investigating the mobility of people, languages, texts, and practices in contexts of migration. *Reading Research Quarterly* 47 (2), 191–215.

Lee, C.D. (2001) Is October brown Chinese? A cultural modeling activity system for underachieving students. *American Educational Research Journal* 38 (1), 97–142.

Moll, L.C. and González, N. (1994) Lessons from research with language-minority children. *Journal of Reading Behavior* 26 (4), 439–456.

Moll, L.C. and Ruiz, R. (2002) The schooling of Latino children. In M.M. Suarez-Orozco and M.M. Paez (eds) *Latinos Remaking America* (pp. 362–374). Cambridge: Cambridge University Press.

Morrell, E. (2004) *Linking Literacy and Popular Culture: Finding Connections for Lifelong Learning*. Norwood, MA: Christopher-Gordon.

Nieto, S. (2002) *Language, Culture, and Teaching: Critical Perspectives for a New Century*. Mahwah, NJ: Lawrence Erlbaum.

Nieto, S. (2003) Challenging current notions of 'highly qualified teachers' through work in a teachers' inquiry group. *Journal of Teacher Education* 54 (5), 386–398.

Ortiz, R.W. and Ordóñez-Jasis, R. (2005) Leyendo juntos (reading together): New directions for Latino parents' early literacy involvement. *Reading Teacher* 59, 110–121.

Perry, N.J., Kay, S.M. and Brown, A. (2008) Continuity and change in home literacy practices of Hispanic families with preschool children. *Early Child Development and Care* 178 (1), 99–113.

Reyes, I. (2006) Exploring connections between emergent biliteracy and bilingualism. *Journal of Early Childhood Literacy* 6 (3), 267–292.

Reyes, I. (2012) Biliteracy among children and youths. *Research Reading Quarterly* 47 (3) 307–327.

Reyes, I. and Da Silva Iddings, A.C. (2012) Family, community and school literacy connections. *International Qualitative Research Conference, Guanajuato, Mexico*.

Reyes, I., Da Silva Iddings, A.C. and Feller, N. (2016) Building relationships with diverse students and families: A funds of knowledge perspective. *Journal of Early Childhood Literacy* 16 (1), 8–33.

Ruiz, R. (1984) Orientations in language planning. *Bilingual Research Journal* 8 (2), 15–34.

Suárez-Orozco, C. and Suárez-Orozco, M. (2001) *Children of Immigration*. Cambridge, MA: Harvard University Press.

Valdés, G. (1996) *Con Respeto. Bridging the Distances Between Culturally Diverse Families and Schools: An Ethnographic Portrait*. New York: College Teachers Press.

Zentella, A.C. (2002) Latin@ Languages and Identities. Latinos! An Agenda for the 21st Century. In M. Suárez-Orozco and M. Páez (eds) *Latinos: Remaking America*. Berkeley, CA: University of California Press.

Afterword: Richard Ruiz

Colin Baker

Introduction

When Richard Ruiz died on 6 February 2015, it was a wretched day. We lost his love and commitment to family and friends, his generous and perceptive contribution to his university students and university colleagues, his calm presence and quiet influence for the greater good of all, and his wise and influential contribution to international scholarship and academia.

While there cannot be happiness about his early passing, there can be joy in celebrating his life and love, his influence and impact. This collection of writings is such a joyful celebration. It creates a lasting memory and tribute to an outstanding scholar, a generous colleague, and a person who was a force for good in all he did and said.

The Collection of Papers

This collection reveals Richard's width of scholarship, depth of thinking and breadth of reading. He wrote with great insight and understanding not only about language planning and policy but also about bilingual education. There is a typology of language endangerment, a history of languages in the US, discussions of language legislation and language learning, language and the law, language and empowerment, a humorous exposition of burritos, Israel in the time of Jesus, the distinction between syntagmatic and paradigmatic conceptions, and even a parable of the pigs.

There are some phrases in his writings that are remarkable, even unforgettable. For example, 'There is still no adequate explanation as to why the United States should... disrupt a 200 year history of relatively successful language tolerance' (Ruiz, 1990: 24). Then with the English language probably in mind: 'language groups [with] their social, economic, political and technological predominance in the world, are in no obvious danger of any resource loss; yet, they engage in aggressive defensive activities characteristic of languages in danger of imminent demise' (Ruiz, 2006: 7).

With some humor: 'Phoenix has been for a long time a "suburb" of Los Angeles, and California is the tail that wags the dog called Arizona' (Ruiz, 2008c: 645). Then, writing amusingly about burritos: 'Sticks and stones will break my bones, but words will change my taste buds' (Ruiz, 2008b: 6). And if that is not enough fun, Richard teases us with his 'Parable of the Pigs'. Almost every sentence is astute and mocking (Ruiz, 1992/1996).

Apart from the fun and humor, there is a social concern and anxiety that disturbs, even frightens: 'The world will end one day, and the overriding cause is more likely to be a shortage of such human resources as language and culture, which could aid in promoting international understanding, than a shortage of such physical resources as coal and oil' (Ruiz, 1983: 65). There is also a powerful contrast: 'Majority groups talk about law. Minority groups talk about justice' (Ruiz, 2000: 6).

In a book review (Ruiz, 2008a: 1) Richard efficiently sums up in the fewest of words what most of us need a whole book to say: 'The best conditions for the promotion of language development in classrooms are those that (a) provide many and varied opportunities to use the language for significant purposes; (b) emphasize communication over form; (c) are not rigidly organized; (d) are based on student interests; and (e) are challenging without producing anxiety in students.'

A most memorable quote is when writing about Jesus as a bi/multilingual. Richard provides a profound message for all people, irrespective of language and culture, current or future time, realm or residence: 'He did not insist on a language requirement for entrance into the citizenship of heaven' (Ruiz 2003: 5). Amen.

The Editor: Nancy Hornberger

We are grateful to Nancy Hornberger for having the vision to create this celebration, for working tirelessly to accumulate this collection, and creating Richard's library of ideas and innovation that will be influential for years to come.

When this collection was first suggested to Richard not too long before he died, he was only slowly interested because of his modesty. Thank you, Nancy, for persuading Richard that it was essential to publish internationally a collection of his outstanding writings, some of which had been hidden due to his unpretentiousness and humility.

There follow two personal and contrasting additional comments to this collection to portray his international academic stature, but also to express that he was much loved for his 'persona'.

Language as Problem, Right and Resource

Richard's ideas and writings on language policy and planning, on bilingual and language minority education, are important in Arizona, in the US, but also to every continent and country where bilingualism and multilingualism are present. He not only helped shape those topics but also influenced worldwide scholars and students across three decades. Passionate about social justice and educational equity, he championed what was right and just, important and impactive. His influence has been global, and that will continue.

The trinity of *'language as a problem, right and resource'* is a memorable, neat and rhythmical categorization that trips beautifully off both the tongue and page. Using a writing and speaking device called the Rule (or Power) of Three, as in 'liberté, égalité, fraternité,' and much loved in Martin Luther King's oratory (e.g. 'insult, injustice, exploitation'), Richard created an effective, catchy and powerful 'trium perfectum.'

As an academic who also worked directly for government for a decade on national language planning, it is possible for me to assert that Richard Ruiz's tripartite language planning conceptualization is influential, inspiring and ingenious. Published in 1984, he was a prophet of the evolution of language planning in Europe and elsewhere. His influence has been (and still is) international. To explain.

In the decades of the 20th century up to approximately the 1980s, the dominant view had been 'language as problem.' That view has not yet disappeared. Bilingualism was thought to bequeath cognitive, personality and social problems. A lowered IQ, split personality and cultural dislocation were considered the individual problems of dual language ownership. Education and societal problems were seen to result from bilingual education such as lowered achievement and less cohesiveness and integration in a nation.

'Language as right' (in the face of language minority discrimination throughout the world) became a crusade to counteract these widespread perceptions of language as problem. The promotion of democracy, greater self-determination and individual liberties helped herald in an era where the rights of individuals, language groups and countries were contested in courtrooms and constitutions, surrounded by pressure and protests. This led to evolution and change. Language rights, at a local, national and international level, began to expand in the 1970s and 1990s, and continue to develop in this decade.

For some, obtaining language rights became an endpoint. It was a victory in itself. Conviction about the crucial nature of rights occasionally translated into the desire for orthodoxy. This is where Richard Ruiz was, and still is so important. Rights are much needed but not enough. Rights can lead to conformity rather than conviction. Hearts and minds are more likely to be won when bilingualism and bilingual education are understood as an individual and societal resource. The doubting public and politicians need persuading that bilingualism and bilingual education can result in so many advantages for the child and adult in such crucial areas as communication, culture, cognition, character and cash. Improved citizenship, social cohesion and integration, plus increased international trade can also derive from effective and well specified bilingual education. 'Languages as a resource' have to be advertised and marketed to persuade, influence and encourage.

Richard Ruiz was thus a prophet of the evolution of ideas about the value of language at individual and societal levels. From perceptions of problems and the realization of rights, the next level is to regard languages as a resource. Recent decades show some progress toward achieving Richard's vision of 'language as resource' as quintessential to matured and progressive language planning and policy.

Richard overlooking the public square in Marrakech, Morocco, June 2013
Courtesy of Yvonne Gonzalez/Teresa L. McCarty.

The Footprints of Richard Ruiz

Richard was a man of fun and humor. So it was a fitting celebration of his witty humanity that staff and students at the University of Arizona remembered him with a 'Peanut Butter Jelly Time,' and a special College of Education 'Café' event (which Richard had started for students and staff to meet and become friends). Also, his life was celebrated by a ceremonial community run from the El Rio Neighborhood Center to the Chávez Building on the University of Arizona Campus. As the organizers poetically and poignantly requested:

> *It is not a race, competition or athletic event and the slowest runner sets the pace. It is a prayer and ceremony in motion. The footprints we leave behind leave our prayers for him, his family and to the universe.*

This book expresses great gratitude to a Harvard French graduate for his considerable contribution to liberté, égalité, fraternité. Loved and loving, quietly spoken but loudly influential, small in size but enormously inspiring, Richard was devoted to people and to his passionate academic and Christian vision of an enriched, enhanced and more equitable world.

References

Ruiz, R. (1983) Ethnic group interests and the social good: Law and language in education. In W.A. Van Horne (ed.) *Ethnicity, Law and the Social Good* (Vol. 2, pp. 49–73). Milwaukee, WI: University of Wisconsin System American Ethnic Studies Coordinating Committee/Urban Corridor Consortium.

Ruiz, R. (1990) Official languages and language planning. In K. Adams and D. Brink (eds) *Perspectives on Official English: The Campaign for English as the Official Language of the USA* (pp. 11–24). Berlin: Mouton.

Ruiz, R. (1992/1996) The parable of the pigs. Unpublished.

Ruiz, R. (2000) Asymmetrical worlds: The representation of the ethnic in public discourse. Unpublished.

Ruiz, R. (2003) Jesus was bilingual. Unpublished.

Ruiz, R. (2006) Threat inversion and language policy in the United States. Unpublished.

Ruiz, R. (2008a) The knowledge base of bilingual education. Review of: *The Encyclopedia of Bilingual Education* (J. González, ed.). Boulder, CO: Education Review, National Education Policy Center.

Ruiz, R. (2008b) The ontological status of burritos. Unpublished.

Ruiz, R. (2008c) Paradox of bilingual education. In J. González (ed.) *Encyclopedia of Bilingual Education* (pp. 646–651). Thousand Oaks, CA: Sage.

Contributors

Colin Baker was Pro Vice Chancellor at Bangor University, Wales, UK (2007–2012) and Full Professor of Education (1994–2012). He is the author of 17 books and over 60 articles on bilingualism, with specific interests in language planning and bilingual education. His book *Foundations of Bilingual Education and Bilingualism* (Multilingual Matters, 1993, 1996, 2001, 2006, 2011) has been translated into Japanese, Korean, Spanish, Latvian, Georgian, Greek, Vietnamese and Mandarin Chinese. He was Editor of the *International Journal of Bilingualism and Bilingual Education* for 15 years and Co-Director of a US$10 million Bilingualism Research Centre based at Bangor University.

Olga Bever is Assistant Research Professor in the College of Social and Behavioral Sciences at the University of Arizona. Dr Richard Ruiz was her PhD Dissertation Director, and later they became colleagues and collaborators. Dr Bever's research examines multilingual and multimodal practices in linguistic landscapes and various media. Her research shows how diverse linguistic and non-linguistic semiotic devices contribute to the development of linguistic and cultural awareness, and reveal the intersection of language policy, language education and language use.

Kevin S. Carroll is an Associate Professor in the Department of Graduate Studies in the College of Education at the University of Puerto Rico – Río Piedras. A former graduate student of Richard Ruiz at the University of Arizona, Dr Carroll's research examines language practices inside bilingual educational contexts. He is particularly interested in how language policy facilitates the use of translanguaging in formal instruction.

Amparo Clavijo Olarte, PhD, is a professor of literacy at Universidad Distrital in Bogotá, Colombia. She is a former graduate student of Richard Ruiz at the University of Arizona. She is the Editor of the *Colombian Applied Linguistics Journal*, a peer-reviewed journal. Her research interests include literacy and biliteracy, bilingualism and community-based research in language teacher education. She has received a Fulbright scholarship as guest

Colombian researcher in the US in 2016 for her project 'Local Literacies as Critical Resources for Teacher Education: Local and Global Impacts'.

Mary Carol Combs is an Associate Professor in the Department of Teaching, Learning and Sociocultural Studies at the University of Arizona. She teaches courses in bilingual education, English as a second language methods, Indigenous language revitalization, and language policy and planning. Her research interests include education policy and law, sociocultural theory, immigration and education, second language acquisition, sheltered instruction and ELL teacher preparation. She met Richard Ruiz in late 1988 in Washington, DC; he recruited her into the doctoral program in Language, Reading and Culture in the University of Arizona. Ruiz served as a mentor and friend for the next 27 years.

Candace Kaleimamoowahinekapu Galla (Native Hawaiian) is an Assistant Professor in the Department of Language and Literacy Education at the University of British Columbia, whose interest intersects the areas of Indigenous language revitalization, teaching, learning and digital technology. As a doctoral student of Richard Ruiz in the Department of Language, Reading and Culture at the University of Arizona, her research and teaching has been greatly influenced by his earlier work on language as a right and a resource. His mentorship, guidance, support, wisdom, humor, and 'walking the hallway' will always be cherished and valued.

Perry Gilmore, PhD, a sociolinguist and educational anthropologist, is Professor of Language, Reading and Culture (LRC), and Second Language Acquisition and Teaching (SLAT) faculty at the University of Arizona. She is also Professor Emerita and affiliate faculty of the Alaska Native Language Center at the University of Alaska Fairbanks. Gilmore is the author of numerous ethnographic studies and co-editor of several major ethnography collections, including *Children In and Out of School: Ethnography and Education, The Acquisition of Literacy: Ethnographic Perspectives* and *Indigenous Epistemologies and Education: Self-Determination, Anthropology and Human Rights.* Her most recent book, *Kisisi (Our Language): The Story of Colin and Sadiki,* documents the creative invention of a private Swahili pidgin language by two five-year-old friends in postcolonial Kenya. Gilmore is the past President of the Council on Anthropology and Education.

Ángela Pamela González is a language teacher and researcher of Indigenous minority students' literacy in Bogotá. She is a former graduate student of Dr Amparo Clavijo at Universidad Distrital in Bogotá. Her master's thesis entitled 'Ěběra immigrant children schooling process in Bogotá' received a meritorious recognition in 2004. She is currently a visiting international faculty member in a public school in North Carolina.

Norma González is Professor Emerita in the Department of Teaching, Learning and Sociocultural Studies at the University of Arizona. She is an anthropologist of education whose work has focused on language practices and ideologies, language socialization, community–school linkages, bilingual education and Funds of Knowledge. She is past president of the Council of Anthropology and Education and author of *I Am My Language: Discourses of Women and Children in the Borderlands* and co-editor, with Luis Moll and Cathy Amanti of *Funds of Knowledge: Theorizing Practices in Households, Communities and Classrooms.*

Nancy H. Hornberger is Professor of Education and Chair of Educational Linguistics at the University of Pennsylvania, USA. Her research interests include the linguistic anthropology of education, bilingualism and biliteracy, language planning and policy and Indigenous language revitalization. Author/editor of more than 150 articles, chapters and books, she has researched, taught, lectured and advised on multilingual language policy and education for Indigenous and minoritized populations in the US and throughout the world. She counts herself lucky to have been Richard's first PhD student.

Ana Christina da Silva Iddings is a Professor of Language, Literacy and Culture at the University of Arizona. Her research centers on the learning ecologies of linguistically/culturally diverse students; family and community resources in diverse urban in- and out-of-school contexts; and partnerships between family-community-school-university that support the literacy learning of linguistically diverse learners and emphasize educational opportunity and equity.

Luz Jiménez-Quispe is an Aymara woman from Bolivia. She was Richard Ruiz's student at the University of Arizona, where she was also an instructor for SEED, an international Indigenous teacher preparation program headed by Dr Ruiz and Dr Norma González. Currently, she is president of the Universidad Pedagogica in Bolivia, where she is working on postgraduate programs for all teachers in her country. In this work, she uses Richard Ruiz's work for researching Indigenous language vitality, and promoting intercultural, intracultural and plurilingual programs for Indigenous teachers and leaders. She is also working on language planning with the Plurinational institute of Languages and Cultures.

Eric J. Johnson is an Associate Professor of Bilingual/ESL Education at Washington State University Tri-Cities. His research interests include language policy and planning in K-12 schooling contexts, immigrant communities, parent and community engagement, funds of knowledge, bilingual education, language and social justice, and Hispanic Serving Institutions.

Richard's openness to informal mentorship (and swift replies to email) greatly informed Eric's growth as a graduate student in anthropology at the cross-state institution, Arizona State University – as well as through the tenure process at Washington State University.

Janelle M. Johnson is an Assistant Professor of STEM Education in the Department of Secondary Teacher Education at Metropolitan State University of Denver. Dr Johnson's work centers on inclusive STEM pedagogies in formal and informal teaching and learning contexts. As a PhD student she worked closely with Richard Ruiz in the Department of Language, Reading and Culture, in the Scholarships for Education and Economic Development program for teachers from Mexico, and on the soccer field. She met Richard through Mike and Julia Richards when she was teaching in Guatemala.

Erin Mackinney is Assistant Professor of Bilingual/ESL Education at Roosevelt University in Chicago, Illinois. A former graduate student of Richard Ruiz at the University of Arizona, her research interests include dual-language program development and language maintenance within bilingual programs. She recently co-edited *Critical Views on Teaching and Learning English Around the Globe: Qualitative Research Approaches* (Information Age Publishing, 2016).

Teresa L. McCarty is the G.F. Kneller Chair in Education and Anthropology at the University of California, Los Angeles. Her research, teaching and outreach focus on Indigenous education, language revitalization and language education policy and practice. She began her academic career as a colleague of Richard Ruiz at the University of Arizona, where she also codirected the American Indian Language Development Institute, a program that Richard helped institutionalize there. She credits Richard with mentoring her into the field of language planning and policy. Her recent publications include *Ethnography and Language Policy* (2011), *Language Planning and Policy in Native America* (2013), and *Indigenous Youth and Multilingualism* (with L.T. Wyman and S.E. Nicholas, 2014).

Luis C. Moll is Professor Emeritus in the Department of Teaching, Learning and Sociocultural Studies, College of Education, University of Arizona. His main research interest is the connection among culture, psychology and education, especially as it relates to the education of Latino children in the US. Among his honors, he was elected to membership in the National Academy of Education (1998), named Fellow of the American Educational Research Association (2009), and was awarded the Medal for Distinguished Service by Teachers College, Columbia University (2015). His most recent book is *L.S. Vygotsky and Education* (Routledge, 2014).

Sheilah E. Nicholas is a member of the Hopi Tribe in northeastern Arizona. She is Associate Professor in the Department of Teaching, Learning and Sociocultural Studies at the University of Arizona, Tucson. The focus of her scholarly work includes: Indigenous/Hopi language maintenance and reclamation; Hopi language teacher education; Indigenous language ideologies and epistemologies; and cultural and linguistic issues in American Indian education. Her current publications draw on her dissertation, a case study of the vitality and contemporary role of the Hopi language in the context of language shift, and from her work with the Hopi Tribe's Hopilavayi Summer Institute (2004–2010). Richard Ruiz played an instrumental role in the department's recognition of her outreach work to the Hopi community.

Brendan H. O'Connor is Assistant Professor in the School of Transborder Studies at Arizona State University. He studied with Richard Ruiz as a PhD student in Language, Reading and Culture at the University of Arizona. Dr O'Connor is a linguistic anthropologist of education whose research and teaching focus broadly on language, identity and the cultural context of schooling in the US-Mexico borderlands. Dr O'Connor's recent work appears or is forthcoming in *Anthropology & Education Quarterly, Journal of Language, Identity & Education, Latino Studies, Linguistic Landscape* and *Linguistics and Education.*

Joyce L. Pereira has a Masters in Dutch Language and Literature, with a specialization in Papiamento and Applied Linguistics. From 2009 to 2014 she worked with Richard Ruiz, who directed the Institute for Language Planning at the University of Aruba and the Instituto Pedagogico Arubano. She is currently working on her doctoral thesis at the University of the Netherlands Antilles. Her thesis deals with the position of Papiamento in the education system of Aruba.

Iliana Reyes, PhD, is a Research Scientist at CINVESTAV, Mexico City, and associated faculty in Language, Reading and Culture at the University of Arizona. Her areas of expertise include early literacy, bilingualism and biliteracy, and language socialization in immigrant and Indigenous communities. Reyes' current research in México explores issues of multilingual education in an Indigenous, Náhuatl-Spanish community where family, children and teachers collaborate to revitalize the Indigenous language. She met Ruiz in 2001 as a new Assistant Professor at the University of Arizona, and he became her Academic *Padrino*, working together on language issues including a project in Guatemala on adult bilingual education.

Julia B. Richards is a Foreign Service Officer with the United States Agency for International Development (USAID), where she leads education policy dialogue, and designs, manages and evaluates educational programs for underserved, ethnolinguistic populations. Julia earned her PhD from the University of Wisconsin-Madison where she studied under Richard Ruiz in the Department of Educational Policy Studies. Richard introduced her to the fields of sociolinguistics and language education policy and planning which she has pursued throughout her professional career, including over 25 years in Guatemala teaching and working on language, identity and education issues and her more recent work to improve education quality in Liberia and Mozambique.

D. Lane Santa Cruz is second generation Chicanx and a doctoral candidate in the Department of Teaching, Learning and Sociocultural Studies at the University of Arizona. Her family migrated over the last 100 years from Tarahumara and Eudeve/Opata pueblos in Chihuahua and Sonora to Tohono O'otham territory Chuk-Shon. Through auto-historia, she has developed critical consciousness of the historical process of deculturalization/deIndigenization experienced by the Chicanx people. Richard Ruiz was her long-time mentor whose teachings she will continue to draw understanding from and use as a guide. Her work focuses on non-compulsory democratic educational spaces and the possibilities for economic and democratic collectivism.

Leisy Wyman is an Associate Professor in the Language, Reading and Culture (LRC) Program of the Department of Teaching, Learning and Sociocultural Studies at the University of Arizona. Her work focuses on youth learning and development, Indigenous education, language socialization, bi/multilingualism, and language policy and planning. She is author of the book *Youth Culture, Language Endangerment and Linguistic Survivance*, and co-editor, with Teresa McCarty and Sheilah Nicholas, of the book *Indigenous Youth and Multilingualism: Language Identity, Ideology, and Practice in Dynamic Cultural Worlds*. She remains grateful for Richard Ruiz's generosity towards colleagues, students and others throughout the years she worked with him in LRC.

Lauren Zentz is Assistant Professor of Applied Linguistics at the University of Houston. She was a student of Richard's at UA and was also one of many proud to be his teammate on Real LRC, the department's winningest intramural soccer team in modern history. Her forthcoming book explores identity and motivation among undergraduate English majors in Central Java, emphasizing the impacts of global language policy trends and state language policies on Indonesia's public education system. The book, to be published in the Encounters series at Multilingual Matters, is dedicated to Richard, and strongly influenced by his mentorship.

Ruiz CV 2005

RICHARD RUIZ
Professor
Department of Teaching, Learning and Sociocultural Studies
Program in Language, Reading and Culture
Head of the Department of Mexican American Studies
University of Arizona
Tucson, Arizona 85721
Office: (520) 621-1311
FAX: (520) 621-1853
e-mail: ruizr@email.arizona.edu
Home: (520) 795-3319
01.01.15

Education

AB	Harvard College, 1970
	Area of Concentration: Romance Languages and Literatures
	Field of Concentration: French Literature
MA	Stanford University, 1976
	Major: Anthropology
	Minor: Philosophy
PhD	Stanford University, 1980
	Major: Philosophy of Education
	Supporting Fields: Bilingual Education and Anthropology

Employment

2012–	Department Head, Mexican American Studies, University of Arizona
2003–2007	Interim Department Head, Department of Teaching & Teacher Education, University of Arizona

2001–2004	Director of Social Justice, American Educational Research Association
1996–	Professor of Language, Reading and Culture, University of Arizona
1993–1999	Department Head, Department of Language, Reading and Culture, University of Arizona
1989–1996	Associate Professor of Language, Reading and Culture, University of Arizona
1987–1989	Assistant Professor of Language, Reading and Culture, University of Arizona
1986–1987	Assistant Professor of Educational Foundations and Administration, University of Arizona
1980–1985	Assistant Professor of Educational Policy Studies, University of Wisconsin–Madison
1976–1980	Instructor, Department of Educational Policy Studies, University of Wisconsin–Madison

Honors and Awards

1966–1970	Harvard University Scholarship
1970	AB *cum laude*, Harvard College
1971–1976	Doctoral Fellowship, Ford Foundation
1982–1983	Research Fellowship in the Social Sciences, Rockefeller Foundation
1988	Selection to National Panel of Judges, Annual Dissertation Award (National Association for Bilingual Education)
1992	Selection to Carnegie Working Group on the Reauthorization of the Elementary and Secondary Education Act
1992	Selection to Clinton-Gore Transition Team on Education
1993	Selection to National Board for Professional Teaching Standards (English as a New Language Standards Committee)
1997	Visiting Scholar, University of Wisconsin Center for Education Research
1997	Working Group Member, Spencer Foundation Task Force on Immigration
1999	Outstanding Faculty Award, University of Arizona Office of Hispanic Affairs
2000	Graduate Student Advocate of the Year, selected by the University of Arizona Graduate and Professional Student Council

2000	Distinguished Visiting Professor, Mexican Academy of Sciences
2001–	Faculty Fellow (Retention), University of Arizona
2004	Maria Urquidez Laureate Award for outstanding service to bilingual children
2005	Faculty Fellow (Recruitment), University of Arizona College of Education Award for Outstanding Service
2005	College of Education Outstanding Service Award, University of Arizona
2009	Lifetime Achievement Award, Hispanic Alumni Association, University of Arizona
2009	Likins Inclusive Education Award, University of Arizona
2011	Appointed University of Arizona Honors Professor

Editorial Boards

1991–1999	Member of Editorial Board, *Urban Education*
1992–1997	Member of Editorial Board, *Teaching Education*
1994	Special Issue Editor, *Urban Education* (Hispanics and Education)
1994–1999	Editor, *Bilingual Research Journal*
1996–1998	Member of Editorial Board, *Review of Educational Research* (AERA)
1997–	Editorial Board, *El Imparcial* (Sonora-Arizona Spanish language weekly newspaper)
2000–2006	Board of Editorial Advisors, *Journal of Teacher Education* (AACTE)
2003–2006	Chair, Publications Committee, American Association of Colleges for Teacher Education
2006–	Scientific Advisory Board, *Matices en Lenguas Extranjeras* (Universidad Nacional de Colombia)
2008–2014	Associate Editor, *Anthropology and Education Quarterly*
2012–	Member, Editorial Board, *Critical Multilingualism Studies*

Special Committees and Task Forces

1995–1997	Presidential Task Force on the Role and Future of Minorities in the American Educational Research Association (by Linda Darling-Hammond, President)
1995–1991	Independent Review Panel for the National Assessment of Title I and Other Federal Education Programs (by M. Smith, Undersecretary of Education)

1997–1991	Social Justice Advisory Committee of AERA (Gwen Baker, Director of Social Justice)
1998–1991	Multicultural Education Committee, American Association of Colleges of Teacher Education (by David Emig, President)
1997–1999	Presidential Task Force on Governance in AERA (by Alan Schoenfeld, President)
2004–2006	Presidential Task Force on the role of Special Interest Groups in AERA
2007–2008	Member, Search Committee for the Provost, University of Arizona
2008–	Member, Selection Committee, University of Arizona, Regents Professors
2010–	Member, Selection Committee, University of Arizona Reads
2014–	Member, Working Group on Academic Freedom (University of Arizona)

University Service

1997–1993	Member, Graduate College Graduate Studies Committee
1997–	Member, affiliated faculty of Mexican American Studies
1997–	Member, affiliated faculty of Latin American Studies
1998–	Member, affiliated faculty of Interdisciplinary Committee of the Second Language Acquisition and Teaching Program (Executive Committee 1998–01, 2002–5)
1998–2000	Member, Executive Committee, Interdisciplinary Program in Comparative Cultures and Literary Studies
1997–1999	Member, Coordinating Committee, Heads-Up (University-wide Department Heads group)
1999–1990	Member, SLAT Academic Program Review Self Study Committee
1999–1990	Chair, Promotion and Tenure Review Committee for Teresa McCarty
2002–2003	Member, Search Committee for the Dean of the College of Education
2003–2006	Member, Diversity Coalition, University of Arizona
2003–	Member, Cultural, Ethnic, Gender and Area Studies Team, University of Arizona
2004–2006	Member, General Education Review Committee, University of Arizona
2006–2007	Chair, 5th-Year Review Committee for Director of Mexican American Studies

2007– 2007	Chair, 3rd-Year Review Committee for the Department Head of Women's Studies
2007–2008	Member, Search Committee for the Provost, University of Arizona
2010–	Member, UA Reads Book Selection Committee
2010–	Member, University of Arizona College of Humanities Promotion and Tenure Committee
2012–2013	Chair, Search Committee for Head of English Department
2013–	Member, Coordinating Committee for UA HEADS-UP
2014–	Member, Diversity Coalition, University of Arizona
2014–	Chair, Search Committee for the Executive Director of the Southwest Institute for Research on Women
2014–	Member, Working Group on Academic Freedom, University of Arizona
2014–	Co-Chair, Strategic Priorities Faculty Initiative (SPFI), University of Arizona
2014–	Member, Academic Program Review (Department of Spanish & Portuguese)
2015–	Member, Executive Committee, Second Language Acquisition and Teaching Interdisciplinary Program

Professional Service

1997–1998	Member, AERA Presidential Task Force on the Role and Future of Minorities
1998–1999	Member, AERA Presidential Task Force on Governance
1998–2000	Member, AERA Social Justice Advisory Committee
2000–2001	Chair, AERA Standing Committee on Social Justice
1998–	Editorial Boards (see above)
1997–	Member, National Board of Professional Teaching Standards, (English as a New Language Committee
1998–2001	Member, Multicultural Education Committee (AACTE) American Association of Colleges of Teacher Education
1995–	Member, Independent Review Panel on the Assessment of Title I
1999–2000	Outside evaluator for Promotion and Tenure (Hunter College, Boston College, Boston University, University of Colorado, University of San Francisco, Texas A&M University, Columbia University)
2001–2004	Director of Social Justice, American Educational Research Association

2004–2006	External evaluator for the Master's Program, Division of Bicultural-Bilingual Education, University of Texas, San Antonio
2005–2007	Principal Investigator, West Regional Equity Network (Region IX Federal Equity Assistance Center)
2008–	Co-Principal Investigator, Project SEED (Professional Development for Mexican Educators)
2010–2013	Program Chair, Division G (Social Context of Education), American Educational Research Association
2014–	Chair, External Review Committee, Graduate Programs, University of California-Davis

Consultantships

1997–1998	Technical Consultant on the *Prospects* Study, ABT Associates, Chicago
1997–	Consultant on language planning and education, Instituto Pedagogico Arubano, Aruba
1997–1999	Consultant to the Teacher Education Program, University of Sonora
1999	Consultant on bilingual education to Arizona Senator Elaine Richardson
2000–	Consultant on adult literacy programs, Government of Guatemala
2000–	Consultant on multicultural teacher education, UNESCO & Government of Bolivia
2000–	Advisory Board for the Master's Degree in Indo-American Linguistics, Centro de Investigación y Estudios Superiores en Antropología Social, Mexico City
2001–	Consultant on Curriculum, Colegio Teresiano, Ciudad Obregon, Mexico
2007	Consultant to 4 Colombian public universities (Distrital, Tecnologica, Nacional, Antioquia) on curriculum and program development in language education
2009–	Director, Language Planning Institute, Aruba

Published Research (Selected)

1983	Ethnic group interest and the social good: Law and language in education. In W.A. Van Horne (ed.) *Ethnicity, Law, and the Social Good*. Milwaukee, WI: American Ethnic Studies Coordinating Committee

1983   Quechua language planning in Peru (with Nancy
            Hornberger). In J. Cobarrubias (ed.) *Language Planning and
            Education*. Berlin: Mouton
1984   Orientations in language planning. *NABE Journal* 8, 15–34
1985   La crise des langues aux Etats-Unis. In J. Maurais (ed.) *La
            crise des langues*. Quebec: Conseil de la langue francaise/
            Paris: Le Robert
1987   Language, ethnicity, and polity. Introduction to W.A. Van
            Horne (ed.) *Ethnicity and Language*. Milwaukee, WI: Institute
            on Race and Ethnicity
1987   Criticisms of English language behavior in the United
            States. *Journal of Intensive English Studies* 1, 65–85
1988   Bilingualism and bilingual education in the United States.
            In C.B. Paulston (ed.) *International Handbook of Bilingualism
            and Bilingual Education*. New York: Greenwood Press
1988   Considerations in the education of gifted Hispanics. In C.J.
            Maker and S. Schiever (eds) *Critical Issues in Gifted Education*.
            Austin, TX: Pro-Ed
1988   Orientations in language planning. In S.C. Wong and S.
            McKay (eds) *Language Diversity: Problem or Resource?* New
            York: Harper and Row
1989   Official languages and language planning. In K. Adams
            and D. Brink (eds) *Perspectives on Official English*. The Hague:
            Mouton
1990   *Allocation of Resources and Minority Access to Graduate
            Education*. Norman, OK: Center for Research on Minority
            Education Occasional Paper
1991   The empowerment of language minority students. In C.
            Sleeter (ed.) *Empowerment Through Multicultural Education*.
            Albany, NY: SUNY Press
1992   ASL and language planning in Deaf education (with Steve
            Nover). In B. Motley (ed.) *A World of Change: One Hundred
            Years of Teacher Preparation at Gallaudet University*.
            Washington, DC: Gallaudet University
1993   Language and curriculum development in Deaf education
            (with Steve Nover). In B. Schick and M.P. Moeller (eds)
            Models of Deaf Education. Omaha, NE: Boy's Town National
            Research Hospital
1993   Critical research issues in bilingual secondary education. In
            C. Simidge-Dudgeon (ed.) *Proceedings of the Third National
            Research Symposium on Limited-English Proficient Students*.
            Washington, DC: Department of Education

1994   Language planning and policy in the US. *Annual Review of Applied Linguistics*, 14 (Winter)

1995   *Hispanics and Urban Education*. Editor of Special Issue of *Urban Education* (Winter)

1995   Considerations in language planning for Indigenous communities. *Bilingual Research Journal* 19, 119–130

1995   The role of first language development in education. In L. Emerencia and A.-M. Halley-Groot (eds) *Ervaringen en nieuwe denkbleeden in taalonderwijs en taalplanning* (pp. 28–34). Aruba: Instituto Pedagogico Arubano

1995   Language and cognitive development. In L. Emerencia and A.-M. Halley-Groot (eds) *Ervaringen en nieuwe denkbleeden in taalonderwijs en taalplanning* (pp. 107–121). Aruba: Instituto Pedagogico Arubano

1995   Language planning in indigenous communities. In L. Emerencia and A.-M. Halley-Groot (eds) *Ervaringen en nieuwe denkbleeden in taalonderwijs en taalplanning* (pp. 141–145). Aruba: Instituto Pedagogico Arubano

1995   Creating a multicultural orientation through children's literature (with C. Klassen). In C. Sleeter and J. Larkin (eds) *Developing Multicultural Teacher Education Curriculum* (pp. 129–145). Albany, NY: SUNY Press

1996   Bilingual education. In C. Grant and G. Ladsen-Billings (eds) *The Dictionary of Multicultural Education*. Phoenix, AZ: Oryx Press

2000   Comment in Agora: The impact of high stakes testing. *Journal of Teacher Education* 51 (4), 289–290.

2000   The schooling of Latino students (with L. Moll). In M. Suárez-Orozco and M. Páez (eds) *Latinos in the 21st Century: Mapping the Research Agenda*. Berkeley, CA: University of California Press

2000   *TACAL: Proyecto piloto en alfabetización en Guatemala*. 68-page report on literacy in Guatemala prepared for the Ministry of Education and the Interamerican Development Bank. Guatemala: MINEDUC

2002   'Sounding American': The consequences of new reforms on English language learners (with several others). *Reading Research Quarterly* 37 (3), 328–343

2003   The concept of educational sovereignty (with Luis Moll). In P. Pedraza (ed.) *The National Latino Education Research Agenda*. Hillsdale, NJ: Erlbaum

2006   *Rethinking the language-as-resource orientation*. Forthcoming in *Language Policy*

2006	Threat inversion and language in the US. Forthcoming in *GURT 2006*
2007	The education of English language learners in the middle grades (with M. Jimenez-Silva). In *Education in the Middle Years*. Tampa, FL: Helios Education Foundation,
2007	The paradox of bilingualism. In J. Gonzalez (ed.) *Encyclopedia of Bilingualism and Bilingual Education*. Thousand Oaks, CA: Sage
2008	The knowledge base of bilingual education. *The Education Review* November
2009	Re-orienting language as resource. In J. Petrovic (ed.) *International Perspectives on Bilingual Education: Policy, Practice, Controversy*. Charlotte, NC: Information Age Publishing
2010	L'aménagement linguistique de l'anglais et transethnification aux États-Unis. *Télescope: Revue d'Analyse Comparée en Administration Publique* 16 (3), 96–112
2011	Afterword (Cooking with Nancy). In F. Hult and K. King (eds) *Educational Linguistics in Practice: Applying the Local Globally and the Global Locally* (pp. 173–178). Bristol: Multilingual Matters
2013	La política lingüística en los EEUU. *Colombian Journal of Applied Linguistics* (in press)
2013	*Collected Writings on Language Planning and Education.* Philadelphia, PA: Multilingual Matters (in press)
2015	Culturally-sustaining pedagogy and education (with Norma Gonzalez). In D. Paris and H.S. Alim (eds) *Culturally Sustaining Pedagogy in Theory and Practice*. New York: Teachers College Press (in preparation)
2015	Thirty Years After 'Orientations in Language Planning' (in preparation). *Bilingual Research Journal*

Unpublished Work

1982	*Anticipations of Modern Cognitive Style Theories.* Madison, WI: Technical Report for the Wisconsin Center for Education Research
1983	*World View Studies: A Review and Appraisal.* Madison, WI: Technical Report for the Wisconsin Center for Education Research
1985	*Language Teaching in American Education.* Washington, DC: Report for the National Institute of Education, Washington.
1992	*Report of the K-12 Task Force* (a chapter in the Clinton-Gore Education Transition Team Briefing Book, with seven co-authors). Washington, DC: US Department of Education

1993   *Report and Recommendations of the Carnegie Working Group on Hawkins-Stafford Reauthorization* (with 15 co-authors). Stanford, CA: Carnegie Working Group
1995   *Brandeis Brief on Article 28 (Official English) of the Arizona State Constitution* (with 20 co-authors). Tucson, AZ: National Center for Court Interpretation
1999   *Measured Progress: The Report of the Independent Review Panel on the Evaluation of Federal Education Legislation* (as a member of the Panel). Washington, DC: US Department of Education
2006   The education of English language learners in the middle years. Report to the Helios Foundation

Paper Presentations (Selected)

1981   *Law and language in education.* Invited presentation at the Second Colloquium on Ethnicity and Public Policy, Green Bay, WI (May)
1981   *Orientations in language planning.* Paper presented at the International Conference on Language Problems and Language Policy, Cancun, Mexico (December)
1982   *Eidos: Its usefulness in cross-cultural cognitive studies.* Paper presented at the 6th International Congress of the Association for Cross-cultural Psychology, Aberdeen, Scotland (July)
1982   *Cognitive style and ethnic diversity: A view from anthropology.* Paper presented at the annual meeting of the American Psychological Association, Washington, DC (August)
1983   *Nonformal bilingual education.* Paper presented at the International Conference on Language Planning and Social Problems, Curacao, Netherlands Antilles (December)
1984   *Spanish as a sacred language.* Paper presented at El Espanol en los Estados Unidos V, Chicago, IL (October)
1985   *Internationalization of bilingual education.* Seminar presented at the Bilingual Bicultural Center, Arizona State University, Tempe, AZ (November)
1986   *Language planning developments in the United States.* Symposium presented at the annual meeting of the National Association for Bilingual Education, Chicago, IL (April)
1986   *International case studies in language policy and bilingualism.* Symposium presented at the annual meeting of the American Educational Research Association, San Francisco, CA (April)
1987   *Language officialization as an aspect of language planning.* Invited paper for the Conference on Official English in the Border States, Arizona State University, Tempe, AZ (March)

1987	*Bilingual education and foreign language education in the United States*. Paper presented at the annual meeting of the American Educational Research Association, Washington, DC (April)
1987	*The politics of language officialization*. Paper presented at the annual meeting of the Teachers of English to Speakers of Other languages, Miami, FL (April)
1987	*The politics of English language amendments*. Keynote address to the first annual meeting of the Oregon Bilingual Association, LaGrande, OR (May)
1987	*The politics of English language amendments II*. Keynote address to the second annual meeting of the Oregon Bilingual Association, Monmouth, OR (November)
1987	*English language amendments and education*. Invited paper to the annual meeting of the National Council of Teachers of English, Los Angeles, CA (November)
1988	*Twenty years after the Bilingual Education Act*. Invited presentation to the Research in Bilingual Education SIG at the annual meeting of the American Educational Research Association, New Orleans, LA (April)
1988	*Cultural literacy and cultural pluralism*. Invited presentation to the Symposium on the Opening of the American Mind, St Mark's Presbyterian Church, Tucson, AZ (October)
1988	*The effects of Proposition 106 on education in Arizona*. Invited presentation to the Language Rights Symposium of the Tucson, AZ Association for Bilingual Education (October)
1988	*Proposition 106 and the teaching of English*. Invited presentation to the Arizona English Teachers Association annual meeting, Tucson, AZ (October)
1989	*Communicative competence in the multicultural classroom*. Invited major session for the Arizona Teachers of English to Speakers of Other Languages annual meeting, Yuma, AZ (February)
1989	*Official English in Arizona: Lessons for the nation*. Keynote address to the annual meeting of the Arizona Association for Bilingual Education, Flagstaff, AZ (April)
1989	*Multicultural perspectives on literacy*. Invited presentation to the National Reading Conference annual meeting, Austin, TX (November)
1989	*Multicultural education in teacher education*. Invited presentation to the Teacher Education Faculty, University of Wisconsin-Parkside (November)

1989	*Multiculturalism in higher education.* Invited presentation to the Harvard Graduate School of Education (November)
1989	*English yes, official no.* Invited panelist at the annual meeting of the National Council of Teachers of English, Baltimore, MA (November)
1990	*Empowerment, voice and language.* Paper presentation at the annual meeting of the American Educational Research Association, Boston, MA (April)
1990	*The theta factor in education.* Paper presentation at the annual meeting of the American Education Research Association, Boston, MA (April)
1990	*Language and education in the Hispanic Southwest.* Invited keynote address at the 250th anniversary celebration of the University of Pennsylvania, Philadelphia, PA (May)
1990	*Allocation of resources and minority access to graduate education.* Invited paper to the Symposium on Minority Graduate Education, Desegregation and Cultural Diversity sponsored by the Center for Research on Minority Education in celebration of the Centennial of the University of Oklahoma, Norman, OK (September)
1990	*Explaining minority group school failure.* Invited address to the Arizona Minority Child Network annual meeting, Mesa, AZ (October)
1990	*What is multicultural about teacher education?* An invited presentation to the Michigan Association of Colleges for Teacher Education, East Lansing, MI (November)
1991	*A theoretical framework for multicultural education in the university.* Paper presentation at the annual meeting of the National Association for Bilingual Education, Washington, DC (January)
1991	*International and comparative perspectives on language and language education.* Organizer and Chair of symposium at the annual meeting of the American Educational Research Association, Chicago, IL (April)
1991	*Interdisciplinary multicultural teacher education.* Invited presentation to the Teacher Education faculty of Michigan State University, East Lansing, MI (April)
1991	*English language amendments and public policy.* Invited panelist at the Conference on Linguistic Pluralism, Michigan State University, East Lansing, MI (April)
1991	*Education as a service delivery system.* Invited workshop at the 5th International Native Education Conference, Winnipeg (April)

1991	*'Normal' language programming for bilingual children.* Invited address to the Arizona Speech-Language-Hearing Association annual meeting, Tucson, AZ (March)
1991	*Forming a coalition of interest between bilingual education and ESL.* Keynote address to the annual meeting of the Arizona Teachers of English to Speakers of Other Languages, Tucson, AZ (March)
1991	*Cooperation and competition between ESL and bilingual education organizations.* Keynote address to the annual meeting of the Arizona Teachers of English to Speakers of Other Languages Association, Tucson, AZ (March)
1991	*Ethnicity and education policy.* Panel presentation at the annual meeting of the American Educational Research Association, Chicago, IL (April)
1991	*Multiculturalization of teacher education.* Address to the Teacher Education Faculty, Michigan State University, East Lansing, MI (April)
1991	*Hispanic responses to the English Language Amendment.* Invited address to the Symposium on Language Pluralism, Michigan State University, East Lansing, MI (April)
1992	*The Southwestern demolinguistics project.* Paper presented at the annual meeting of the National Association for Bilingual Education, Albuquerque, NM (January)
1992	*Federal language planning in the United States.* Seminar presented to the National Languages and Literacy Institute of Australia, Melbourne (March)
1992	*Language policy development in the Federated States of Micronesia.* Five-day workshop presented to the Ministry of Education of the FSM, Pohnpei (March)
1992	*Weaving affirmative action into AERA* (invited panelist), annual meeting of the American Educational Research Association (April)
1992	*Language planning for native communities.* Two-day workshop presented at the Annual Conference on Native Education, Winnipeg (May)
1992	*ASL and language planning in Deaf education* (with Steve Nover). Conference celebrating 100 years of Teacher Education at Gallaudet University (June)
1992	*Critical issues in secondary bilingual education.* Paper presented at the Third National Research Symposium on the Education of Limited-English Proficient Students, Washington, DC (August)

1992	*Multicultural education in the programs of the Rockefeller Foundation*. Invited presentation to a meeting of Rockefeller Foundation program directors, Chicago, IL (September)
1992	*The role of ASL in the education of Deaf children* (with Steve Nover). Presentation at the Sixth Annual Conference on Deaf Children, Omaha, NE (October)
1992	*The bilingual-bicultural approach in Deaf education for Hispanic students*. Keynote address to the Conference on the Deaf Hispanic Experience, San Antonio, TX (November)
1993	*La imagen de las dos manos en la educación de los hispanos*. Keynote address (in Spanish) to the Annual Conference for Spanish-speaking parents at the California School for the Deaf, Riverside, CA (February)
1993	*The shape of the new Title VII*. Presentation to the meeting on Language Policy at the University of Texas, San Antonio, TX (February)
1993	*Reshaping Title VII: Update on legislative proposals*. Paper presented at the annual meeting of the American Educational Research Association, Atlanta, GA (April)
1993	*Literacy and language policy in native communities*. Paper presented at the annual meeting of the American Association of Applied Linguistics, Atlanta, GA (April)
1993	*The new Bilingual Education Act* (Response to Eugene Garcia). Invited presentation at the Conference on 'Making a Difference for Students At Risk,' Princeton, NJ (October)
1994	*Indigenous languages in education*. Invited presentations to the First Congress on Indigenous Languages and Education in Aruba (March)
1994	*Bilingual bicultural education and the Deaf*. Invited presentation to the Indiana School for the Deaf, Indianapolis, IN (September)
1995	*Bilingualism and Deaf education*. Invited presentation to the New Mexico School for the Deaf, Santa Fe, NM (February)
1995	*Principles of Indigenous language instruction*. Presentation at the Segundo Encuentro Multicultural de Educacion Especial, Tlaxcala, Mexico (October)
1995	*Infusing multiculturalism into literacy curriculum*. Invited presentation to the National Reading Conference, New Orleans, LA (December)
1996	*A research agenda for bilingual education*. Research Institute of the National Association for Bilingual Education, Orlando, FL (March)

1996	*English officialization and transethnification in the USA.* Paper presented at the annual meeting of the American Anthropological Association, San Francisco, CA (November)
1997	*The role of the school in preventing language death.* Invited symposium to the Wisconsin Center for Education Research, Madison, NY (January)
1997	*El multiculturalismo en la formación de maestros.* A series of four lectures given in Mazatlán, Culiacán, and Los Mochis, Sinaloa, Mexico, sponsored by the Sinaloa State Department of Teacher Education
1997	*A typology of language death.* Paper presented at the annual meeting of the American Educational Research Association, Chicago, IL (March)
1997	*The role of research in policy considerations in bilingual education.* Paper presented at the annual meeting of the American Educational Research Association, Chicago, IL (March)
1997	*Speaking Chicano in the bilingual classroom.* Paper presented at the annual meeting of the National Council of Teachers of English, Detroit, MI (November)
1997	*Children's language as resource in a time of English-only.* Paper presented at the annual meeting of the National Council of Teachers of English, Detroit, MI (November)
1998	*Transethnification and the politics of language in the US.* Keynote address to the Arizona Teachers of English to Speakers of Others Languages, Tucson, AZ (October)
1999	*The paradox of bilingual education in the USA.* Lecture in the Faculty-Community Lecture Series of the University of Arizona, Tucson, AZ (February)
1999	*Language politics and English officialization in the USA.* Invited lecture to the Facultad de Lenguas at the 4to Congreso de las Americas, University of the Americas, Puebla, Mexico (September)
1999	*Bilingual-multicultural education at the crossroads.* Invited presentation at the annual meeting of the National Association for Multicultural Education, San Diego, CA (November)
1999	*The politics of language.* Chair and presenter at the Second Language Policy Symposium, Bar-Ilan University, Ramat Gan, Israel (November)
2000	*Asymmetrical universes: The representation of the ethnic in public discourse.* Presentation to the Invitational Symposium on the Public Representation of Youth Violence, annual meeting of the American Educational Research Association, New Orleans, LA (25 April)

2000	*Language planning and indigenous communities.* Three lectures in Spanish at the Centro de Investigaciones y Estudios Superiores en Antropología Social in Mexico City (August)
2001	*Jesus was bilingual: International perspectives on heritage language development.* Keynote address to the California Association for Bilingual Education, Los Angeles, CA (February)
2001	*El proyecto TACAL y la alfabetización en Guatemala.* Invited presentation to the Latin American Reading Conference (IRA), Guatemala City (February)
2001	*Seminario en Planificación Lingüística.* Lectures in language planning and applied linguistics to the Master's class in Indoamerican Linguistics, Centro de Estudios y Investigaciones Superiores en Antropología Social, Mexico City (July)
2002	*La bi-alfabetización en Guatemala.* Presented at the Congreso de Latinoamericanistas Europeos, Amsterdam (June)
2002	*The teacher as language artist.* Keynote address to the Micronesian Education Conference, Guam (November)
2003	*The education of teachers for Latino students in the USA.* Keynote address to the Cultural Competence Symposium, Tucson, AZ (April)
2003	*Dialogs in Black and Brown.* Symposium at the annual meeting of the American Educational Research Association, Chicago, IL (April)
2004	*Indigenous literacy and identity in Guatemala.* Presented at the conference on Education, Social Development and Empowerment Among Indigenous Peoples and Minorities: An International Perspective, Beer-Sheva, Israel (June)
2004	*Language rights and language interests.* Keynote address to the Southern Africa Applied Linguistics Conference, Limpopo, South Africa (July)
2004	*The role of the school in preserving endangered languages.* Presented at the University of Pretoria, South Africa (July)
2004	*The relation of research to language policy development.* Presented at the Rand Afrikaans University, Johannesburg, South Africa (July)
2004	*The preparation of bilingual teachers.* Presented to the University of the Western Cape, Cape Town, South Africa (July)
2004	*Preparing teachers for language minority students.* Presented at the University of Cape Town, South Africa (July)
2004	*Curriculum development in teacher education.* Presented to the workshop Trainers of Teachers in Southern Africa, PRAESA, University of Cape Town, South Africa (July)

2004   *Policy developments in language minority education.* Seminar for the Language Policy Group, University of the Free State, Bloemfontein, South Africa (July)

2004   *The problem of language rights.* Seminar for the Department of Philosophy, Stellenbosch University, Cape Town, South Africa (August)

2004   *The legacy of Brown.* Presented at the Conference on Education and the Law, Tucson, AZ (September)

2004   *Literacy models for Indigenous Latin America.* Presented at the Conference on Imagining Schools, Columbia University, New York (September)

2005   *Future directions for policy in the education of English language learners.* Keynote address, National Research Conference on English Language Learners Struggling to Learn, Scottsdale, AZ (November)

2006   *Language planning for Deaf education.* Keynote address to the CAEBER Conference, Gallaudet University, Washington, DC (March)

2006   *Linguistic planning.* Keynote address to the Round Table on Applied Linguistics, Universidad Distrital, Bogota, Colombia (October)

2006   *Planificacion Linguistica y la linguistica aplicada.* Keynote address to the 2nd International Symposium on Bilingualism and Bilingual Education in Latin America (October)

2006   *The dangerous intersection of individual and culture.* Presented at the annual meeting of the American Anthropological Association, San Jose, CA (November)

2007   *Language threat and endangerment.* Presented at the Georgetown University Round Table, Washington, DC (March)

2007   *English and language endangerment.* Keynote address to the International Conference on Language Policy, Nairobi, Kenya (May)

2007   *Literacy and social justice in adolescent education.* Presented at the annual meeting of the American Educational Research Association, Chicago, IL (April)

2007   *Amenaza invertida y la política de la lengua en EEUU.* Invited presentation to the International Congress of Applied Linguistics, San José, Costa Rica (October)

2008   *The power of English.* Keynote address to the International Conference on Applied Linguistics, Normal University of Taiwan, Kaoshiung (April)

2008	*Chinese heritage language education in the US.* Presented to the English Department, Taiwan Normal University, Kaoshiung (April)
2008	*Bilingual education in the United States.* Presented to the Department of English, Taiwan National University, Taipei (April)
2009	*Seminars in language planning and curriculum development.* Presented to the faculty of the University of Aruba, Oranjestad (June)
2009	Seminars in language planning, presented to the Universidad Nacional de Costa Rica, Chorotega (October)
2009	*La transetnificación y la política de la lengua.* Keynote address to the 2nd Congreso Internacional de Lingüística Aplicada, Universidad Nacional de Costa Rica, Heredia (October)
2009	*Some questions on language planning.* Presented to the 2nd Congreso Internacional de Lingüística Aplicada, Universidad Nacional de Costa Rica, Heredia (October)
2010	*Introducing Papiamento into Aruba's schools.* Presented at the First International Heritage Languages Conference, Los Angeles, CA (February)
2011	*The many faces of English.* Keynote address to the Arizona Teachers of English to Speakers of Other Languages, Tucson, AZ (April)
2011	*Language and social justice on the border.* Presentation to the 13th Annual International Conference on Education, Athens, Greece (May)
2011	*Education in the United States.* Presentation to the Transnational Institute, Amsterdam (June)
2011	Language planning seminars, University of Aruba (October)
2011	*Countering the deficit orientations about linguistically diverse students: Teachers using students' heritage ways of speaking as valuable resources.* Invited presentation to the National Council of Teachers of English, Chicago, IL (November)
2012	*Complicating ethnicity, race, and multilingualism in literacy research, teaching, and teacher education* (discussant). Annual meeting of the Literacy Research Association, San Diego, CA (November–December)
2013	*¿Why should language be planned?* Presentation to the Faculty of Letters Ben M'Sik, Casablanca, Morocco (June)
2013	*The school's role in language maintenance and shift.* Presentation to the Faculty of the École Normale Supérieure, Rabat, Morocco (June)

2013	*Language rights and language interests.* Presentation to the Department of English, Faculté des Lettres et Humanités, Mohammed V University, Rabat, Morocco (June)
2013	*Language as resource in teacher education.* Presentation to the Vivir Mexico/Special Education Group, Guanajuato, Mexico (July)
2013	*The school and the community.* Presentation to the Azusa Unified School District Leadership Seminar, Azusa, CA (August)
2014	*POEM on words and whether they make a difference.* Keynote address to the SLAT RoundTable, University of Arizona (March)
2014	*Language and social justice on the border.* Presentation to the Faculty of Anthropology and Social Justice Education, University of Massachusetts, Amherst, MA (November)
2014	*Bilingualism in schools and communities.* Presentation in the School of Education, Boston College, Chestnut Hill, MA (November)

Index